Y0-DCW-327

DYING FOR FRANCE

McGILL-QUEEN'S STUDIES IN THE HISTORY OF IDEAS
Series Editor: Philip J. Cercone

Dying for France

Experiencing and Representing the Soldier's Death, 1500–2000

Ian Germani

McGill-Queen's University Press
Montreal & Kingston • London • Chicago

© McGill-Queen's University Press 2023

ISBN 978-0-2280-1635-9 (cloth)
ISBN 978-0-2280-1636-6 (ePDF)

Legal deposit first quarter 2023
Bibliothèque nationale du Québec

Printed in Canada on acid-free paper that is 100% ancient forest free
(100% post-consumer recycled), processed chlorine free

This book has been published with the help of a grant from the Federation for
the Humanities and Social Sciences, through the Awards to Scholarly Publications
Program, using funds provided by the Social Sciences and Humanities Research
Council of Canada.

| Funded by the Government of Canada | Financé par le gouvernement du Canada | Canada | Canada Council for the Arts | Conseil des arts du Canada |

We acknowledge the support of the Canada Council for the Arts.

Nous remercions le Conseil des arts du Canada de son soutien.

Library and Archives Canada Cataloguing in Publication

Title: Dying for France : experiencing and representing the soldier's death,
1500-2000 / Ian Germani.

Names: Germani, Ian, 1957- author.

Series: McGill-Queen's studies in the history of ideas; 87.

Description: Series statement: McGill-Queen's studies in the history of ideas;
87 | Includes bibliographical references and index.

Identifiers: Canadiana (print) 20220438935 | Canadiana (ebook) 20220438994 |
ISBN 9780228016359 (cloth) | ISBN 9780228016366 (ePDF)

Subjects: LCSH: Soldiers—France—Death—History. | LCSH: France—
History, Military.

Classification: LCC DC45.7 .G47 2023 | DDC 944—dc23

This book was typeset by Marquis Interscript in 10/12 New Baskerville.

Contents

Illustrations

Acknowledgments

There are many individuals and organizations without whom this book would never have been written and for whom I would like to express my deep appreciation. At the University of Regina, the Humanities Research Institute provided generous financial support that facilitated research in France. The Inter-Library Loan Department at the Dr John Archer Library did an outstanding job of helping to find and supply the diverse research materials I required. My friends and colleagues in the Department of History were also generous with their support, inspiration, and constructive criticism. I owe special thanks to Philip Charrier and Thomas Bredohl, who read and commented on substantial sections of the manuscript, as well as to Raymond Blake. History student Hannah Jeffery provided valuable and capable assistance in compiling the bibliography.

In France, the staff of various libraries, museums, and archives provided support and assistance. My thanks go, individually, to Fanny Lefaure at the Musée de l'Armée, Aldo Battaglia at the Musée de la Contemporaine, and Olivier Racine at the Établissement de Communication et de Production Audiovisuelle de la Défense for facilitating my visits and explorations of their collections. More generally, I am grateful for the assistance I received at the Bibliothèque nationale de France in Paris, the Archives nationales at St Denis, and the Archives de Guerre at Vincennes.

The ideas in this book were first tried out at a variety of international conferences and gatherings of scholars. I am grateful especially to colleagues in Australia for opportunities to present them at sessions of the George Rudé Conference. Also, thank you to the Center for the Study of War and Memory at the University of South Alabama and to the Group for War and Culture Studies in the United Kingdom for providing similar opportunities. Concerning publications flowing from those conferences, the editors of *The Journal of War and Culture Studies, Lingua Romana,* and *French History and Civilization* have graciously allowed me to use material from the following articles:

"Dying for Liberty in the French Revolutionary Wars," in *French History and Civilization: Papers from the George Rudé Seminar* 9 (2020): 97–108.

"The Great War: A Turning Point in the History of Death?," in *Lingua Romana: A Journal of French, Italian, and Romanian Culture* 13, no. 1 (2020): 45–56 Available at http://linguaromana.byu.edu/current-issue/.

"The Soldier's Death in French Culture: A Napoleonic Case Study," in *Journal of War and Culture Studies* 9, no. 3 (August 2016): 1–15. Reprinted by permission of the publisher (Taylor and Francis Ltd, http://www.tandfonline.com).

"The Soldier's Death: From Valmy to Verdun," in *French History and Civilization: Papers from the George Rudé Seminar* 6 (2015): 133–8.

At McGill-Queen's University Press, my thanks go to Kyla Madden, who provided kind and helpful advice at many stages in the preparation of the manuscript. I am very grateful, too, for the thoughtful comments and suggestions from the anonymous readers who graciously accepted the invitation to review the manuscript. Thanks are owed also to James Leahy, for careful copy-editing, as well as to Stephen Ullstrom, for his diligence in preparing the index. Finally, thank you to two individuals who have sustained this book and its author over many years, in many ways. Whatever merit the book's translations from the French texts possess is owed to hours of careful proofreading and patient tutelage on the part of Brian Rainey, who has over more than three decades inspired in me a boundless respect for the translator's art. Any remaining infelicities or inaccuracies are, of course, my own responsibility. To Karen Klassen, who has unconditionally put up with its author and the demands it has made on him, this book is dedicated.

DYING FOR FRANCE

For Karen

Introduction

Adjutant Gaëtan Evrard was not anticipating trouble as he struggled up the steep hillside outside the village of Sper Kunday in the Uzbin valley on the afternoon of 18 August 2008. Evrard and the thirty men under his command from the eighth regiment of the marine parachute infantry (*8ᵉ régiment parachutiste d'infantrie de marine* – 8ᵉ RPIMa) were on a reconnaissance mission, their third since they had arrived in Afghanistan on 5 August. Supporting Evrard's section (Crimson 2) were a section of the Chad Regiment of Foot (*régiment de marche de Tchad* – RMT) (Red 4), two sections of the Afghan National Army (ANA), a dozen American "specialists" in air support, and four Afghan interpreters: a total of three hundred men. Evrard's section advanced painfully up the slope, each man sweltering beneath the burden of a flak jacket, helmet, Famas assault rifle, and six magazines of ammunition. Some also carried first-aid kits, radios, or snipers' rifles. The difficult terrain meant they had to leave their four armoured vehicles behind with Red 4. Suddenly, at 3:45 p.m., as they neared the summit, the French paratroops came under sustained fire. Scrambling for cover and returning fire as best they could, Evrard's men found themselves caught in a crossfire between two enemy detachments, while Red 4 was prevented by a third from coming to their aid. The machine guns of the armoured vehicles were at the limit of their range. Evrard radioed to the Forward Observation Base at Tora, pleading for help: "Hurry, Captain," he urged, "Nobody is able to support me … I am pinned down by steady fire. It is like Bazeilles here, Captain, like Bazeilles!"[1]

Help was forthcoming. The Quick Reaction Force from Surobi was first on the scene, with eighty men, including paratroops and an 81-mm mortar unit. Air support, provided primarily by American A10 and AC-130

---

1 Merchet, *Mourir pour l'Afghanistan*, 34–5.

gunships, enabled the survivors of Evrard's force first to break contact with the enemy and then, as they were joined by further reinforcements from Kabul, to turn the tables on their assailants. By 4:30 a.m. the next morning, the French had retaken control of the hill. In the meantime, Evrard's section had suffered heavy casualties. One man after another was felled by enemy fire and then their comrades were hit as they sought to lend assistance. A paratrooper who had tried unsuccessfully to resuscitate a wounded colleague was struck by several bullets as he brought Evrard a radio set. "He put himself in front of me," recalled Evrard, "as if to protect me."[2] Of the thirty-one men from Evrard's section, ten were killed and seventeen wounded. Eight of the ten were killed by enemy fire, one by an edged weapon. The remaining death was caused when one of the French armoured vehicles rolled over, crushing the occupant of its turret and severely wounding two other men.

Adjutant Evrard's representation of his situation at the time of the Uzbin ambush is remarkable. Under extreme duress and without reflection, he instantly equated his situation with an event from the Franco-Prussian War of 1870 immortalized by a painting of Alphonse de Neuville entitled *The Last Cartridge* (fig. 0.1). That event was the defence of Bazeilles by the men of the Blue Division, who fought on without hope of victory until their ammunition was exhausted. Memory of this heroic defeat became a founding myth for the French marines, as well as an important means to salvage national pride in the wake of defeat. By recalling that battle, as men died around him, Evrard gave a meaning to his experience and to the deaths of his comrades: like the soldiers of Bazeilles before them, they were dying for France. That understanding was echoed in the official discourse during the days that followed, as the dead were honoured and as their compatriots sought to make sense of their deaths. The immediate response of President Nicolas Sarkozy was to fly to Kabul to meet with soldiers of the French contingent. Back in Paris, on 20 August the president paid his respects to the dead in the courtyard of the Invalides – "in this shrine of military memory" – before ten tricolour draped coffins, each bearing a newly awarded medal of the Legion of Honour. His speech recognized the soldiers' service to the nation, affirming that the "price of blood" they had paid was the cost of France fulfilling its international obligations as a great power: "They gave their lives far from their homeland for the sake of their duty, for the freedom of the Rights of Man, for the universal values that are at the heart of our Republic." Their deaths, said Sarkozy, were honourable: "I know very well that the word honour may

2   Ibid., 37.

0.1. Alphonse de Neuville, *The Last Cartridge.* 1873.

sound contemptible in front of the body of a twenty-year-old man. And yet to give one's life with honour, is to fulfill that life."[3] The president's words were calculated both to explain the French army's mission in Afghanistan and to give meaning to the deaths of the ten French soldiers who had been killed in the ambush.

The official discourse that emerged after the ambush at Uzbin, embodied in symbol, ritual, and word, was redolent of references to the nation, to history, to political ideals and even to values – duty and honour – that had a longer lineage than the nation itself. From 2008 on, French soldiers who died in Afghanistan were accorded dignities that had been denied to those killed on similar missions overseas, in Indochina, Algeria, Chad, Lebanon, the Ivory Coast. Previously, the public had greeted soldiers' deaths with relative indifference. Bodies had typically been quietly repatriated without ceremony.[4] Not everybody was convinced the change was a good thing. What better way to persuade the enemy that his strategy was working than to respond to an attack by immediately sending the president to the battle front or by insisting upon the emotional impact of the hurt

3 Speech of Nicolas Sarkozy, 20 August 2008, https://www.vie-publique.fr/discours/ 171909-declaration-de-m-nicolas-sarkozy-president-de-la-republique-en-hommag.

4 Marchal, *L'hommage politique*, 33–40.

inflicted? The political instinct to intensify the emotions engendered by such occasions ran the risk of creating the impression of a lack of resilience.[5] Nor did the official discourse necessarily prevail. The press was generally sympathetic in its references to soldiers who died in Afghanistan, but it tended to represent them as victims rather than as heroes. The circumstances surrounding their deaths were referred to as tragedies comparable to air or road accidents, rather than as an essential and unavoidable aspect of waging war, however repugnant. Not even the official discourse was immune to this tendency. Prime Minister François Fillon referred to "tragic events," in a speech of 2011, President Sarkozy to "victims of the most cowardly crimes" in another of 2012.[6] Furthermore, the focus on the bereaved families – the families of the soldiers who died at Uzbin were flown to Afghanistan less than a month afterwards to learn more about the circumstances in which their loved ones had died – contributed to a "privatization" of the soldiers' deaths, to the detriment of narratives emphasizing national or collective interests. The logical outcome of this tendency has been for the soldier's death to be perceived as a tragedy to be avoided at all costs and to hold those in authority to the same standard of responsibility as in civilian life. Thus, in a process that has been described as the "judiciarization" of warfare, the families of two of the soldiers killed at Uzbin, Julien Le Pahun and Rodolphe Penon, filed a legal challenge in 2009 claiming that the soldiers' lives had been deliberately placed in danger by their commanders, who were therefore criminally liable.[7] The legal claim was dismissed, but it was a sign that in the early twenty-first century the soldier's death had become unacceptable.[8]

The responses of government, media, and public opinion to the deaths of the eighty-nine French soldiers who died in Afghanistan between 2001 and 2012 demonstrate the extreme unease attached to the idea of the soldier's death in contemporary French culture. In recent years, not only has there been manifest a tension between the official discourse and public attitudes concerning the soldier's death, but public opinion itself has been conflicted. At the same time as it has come to view the soldier's death as an unacceptable tragedy, the public has also viewed it with growing

5   Ibid., 113; Merchet, *Mourir pour l'Afghanistan*, 153–4.

6   Marchal, *L'hommage politique*, 112.

7   "Peut-on juger un soldat?" *Le Petit Journal*, 3 Nov., 2009; Samuel Duval, "Soldats français tombés en Afghanistan: Rendez-nous nos héros!," *Le Monde*, 11 March 2010; Barthélemy, *La "judiciarisation" des opérations militaires*.

8   For an insightful analysis of the "schizophrenic" attitude of contemporary opinion concerning the soldier's death, see Gauthier Dupire, "Il faut achever le 'zéro mort'!," *Le Monde*, 13 April 2012.

indifference, as if battlefield death were nothing more than a workplace accident, an occupational hazard for those who choose the soldier's trade.[9] By privatizing the soldier's death, by treating it primarily as an individual and familial tragedy, French society has detached it from the narratives – above all the narrative of citizens dying for the nation – that gave it a collective meaning.[10]

This loss of meaning attached to the soldier's death is striking in a country where the narrative enshrined in the phrase *mourir pour la patrie*[11] has been extraordinarily potent for many centuries. This narrative reached its apogee during the First World War and is physically represented in 30,000 French communes by the monuments to the dead erected in the aftermath of that conflict. The unease generated by the ten deaths in a single day at Uzbin, of eighty-nine over an eleven-year period in Afghanistan, contrasts with the collective response to the experience of 27,000 deaths in a single day on 22 August 1914, 1.4 million over a four-year period from 1914 to 1918. Collective commitment to the cause of national defence enabled French society to endure the unprecedented loss of the Great War. The soldier's death was terrible to bear and doubts grew, particularly after the war, but the narrative of sacrifice for the sake of the nation made it meaningful for most French people. Clearly, public perceptions and attitudes have undergone a sea change in the hundred years since the First World War. This book seeks to understand that change by considering the history of the soldier's death in France over the long term, from the Renaissance to the present.

The subject of the soldier's death in French history is vast, with as many different dimensions as there are varieties of history. It is connected obviously to military history, but also to the histories of mentalities, emotions and culture, gender and masculinity, art and literature, economies and populations. Its parameters were first explored in a seminal article by André Corvisier, published in 1975. This identified three fundamental problems to be considered in relation to the soldier's death: "In the first place, the problem is one of sensibility and ethics: the attitude of the soldier confronting death. Nor can one escape the quantitative problem of the weight of military death in relation to general mortality. From these two problems

9 Dupire is particularly insightful on this "schizophrenic" public attitude. See ibid.; see also Marchal, *L'hommage politique*, 113–15.

10 For an important commentary on this theme see the interview between Jean-Dominique Merchet and Danièle Hervieu-Léger, in Merchet, *Mourir pour l'Afghanistan*, 155–8.

11 "To die for the homeland."

derives a third, that of the representation of the soldier's death and its place in the life of a society."[12]

Since these words were written, many historians have taken up the gauntlet thrown down by Corvisier to examine these problems relating to the soldier's death in specific periods of French history. Although there has been no survey of the problem as broad as Corvisier's, which extended its scope from the Middle Ages to the twentieth century, several innovative works by cultural and military historians, although not necessarily focusing either on the soldier's death or on French history, have helped to broaden our understanding of the three problems defined by Corvisier. The present work seeks to build upon the work of these historians as well as upon the insights of scholars working in the many different fields identified above to provide an understanding of some of the changes and continuities in the way the soldier's death has been experienced and represented in modern France.

Of fundamental importance to this investigation is the work of John Keegan, the British military historian whose book, *The Face of Battle*, brilliantly deconstructed conventional battle narratives as a prelude to his own, far more convincing reconstructions of the battlefield experiences at Agincourt, Waterloo, and the Somme.[13] By reflecting on weapons technology and tactics, battlefield topography, and on the evidence provided by soldiers and surgeons, Keegan gave new insight into how soldiers gave and received death in battle. Keegan's study showed that the incidence and the experience of death in battle have varied considerably over time, as weapons systems, forms of combat, and methods of medical evacuation and care have evolved. His work has inspired a plethora of studies focused on battlefield experience and "the sharp end" of war, which are admirably synthesized by Michael Stephenson in *The Last Full Measure: How Soldiers Die in Battle*.[14] In France, Hervé Drévillon, Yann Lagadec, and Stéphane Perréon are among those who have applied Keegan's approach to the study of battles from the French past.[15] Like the work of these historians, this study emphasizes the central importance of death in battle, but it also places emphasis upon the striking fact that until the First World War the proportion of soldiers who died of illness while on campaign far exceeded the numbers who died of wounds received in combat. One of the arguments of this book is that soldiers themselves helped to propagate a positive

12 Corvisier, "La mort du soldat," in Corvisier, *Les hommes, la guerre et la mort*, 368.
13 Keegan, *The Face of Battle*.
14 Stephenson, *The Last Full Measure*.
15 Drévillon, *Batailles*; Lagadec and Perréon, *La bataille de Saint-Cast*.

view of battlefield death because they lived perpetually in the shadow of other deaths that, from their perspective, were even less appealing.

The "battle studies" of Keegan and his successors depended heavily upon the evidence provided by soldiers themselves, in their letters, diaries, and memoirs. Historians have understandably been wary of these sources. Memoirs, sometimes written long after the events to which they refer, are far from the unadulterated vectors of "truth" their authors often claimed them to be. Matilda Greig writes that we should be "deeply wary of treating memoirs as the straightforward testimony of eyewitnesses."[16] In addition to depending upon their own, ever more unreliable, memories of the past, writers sometimes incorporated "memories" that were not theirs, but which derived either from stories they had heard or from other books or histories they had read.[17] Their writings sometimes echoed propagandistic representations and sometimes resisted them. Memoirists often had ulterior motives in writing, whether it was to set the record straight, to honour former comrades, or simply to make money. Often, relatives and editors were heavily involved in curating veterans' memoirs, pruning them of anything that might be perceived as disreputable.[18] War memoirs tell us at least as much about the times in which they were written or published as they do about the times they describe. Writers sought to portray themselves in a sympathetic light according to contemporary standards. They were therefore selective in their choice and interpretation of events. According to French war memoirists who campaigned in Italy, from the sixteenth century to the twentieth, they were unfailingly both chivalrous and irresistible to Italian women! Nor are more immediate sources, such as personal correspondence, necessarily more reliable. Letters to wives and parents commonly sought to provide reassurance; they therefore made light of or ignored altogether war's horrors and dangers. Despite these shortcomings, soldiers' stories, whenever and in whatever form they were communicated, are invaluable for the insights they provide, sometimes unwittingly, into how their authors came to feel about past events. This book relies heavily upon them, as well as upon the stories of nurses, doctors, chaplains, and other witnesses to French soldiers' experiences of death and dying in war.[19]

Soldiers' stories, particularly war memoirs, are the source material for Yuval Harari's study of *The Ultimate Experience*, which considers how soldiers

16 Greig, *Dead Men Telling Tales*, 141.

17 Dwyer, "Public Remembering, Private Reminiscing," 248.

18 Greig, *Dead Men Telling Tales*, 172–3.

19 Philip Dwyer convincingly makes this argument with respect to the Revolutionary and Napoleonic Wars in "War Stories," 561–85.

made sense of the battlefield experience over more than five hundred years, from 1450 to 2000. Harari argues that the period from 1740 to 1865 marked a fundamental cultural transition in the understanding of the battlefield experience, as that experience came to be perceived as a revelatory one. Prior to the mid-eighteenth century, soldiers' memoirs were laconic and indifferent in their references to battlefield encounters with death, whether these involved the killing of others, their own near escapes, or the deaths of comrades. "Most memoirists, if they bother to narrate the death of close friends and cherished commanders, do so matter-of-factly, without consecrating it to any high ideals, without redeeming it by patriotic and heroic slogans [...] without lamenting war's cruelty, and apparently without learning anything from it."[20] With the rise of the eighteenth-century cult of sensibility, however, says Harari, "bodies begin to think,"[21] and "the extreme bodily experiences of war [...] [become] a sublime gateway to otherwise inaccessible truths and realities, which *change* the warrior instead of merely testing him."[22] Inflicting or witnessing death became key experiences, prompting memoirists to describe in detail the emotions they inspired.

For all its brilliance, Harari's interpretation has been challenged. Brian Sandberg, in a study of seventeenth-century French military memoirs, shows not only that they had substantial emotional content but that their authors were also deeply affected by their experiences.[23] Louis de Pontis, rushing to the bedside of his mortally wounded friend, Jean Zamet, said that he "could not utter a word because my heart had ceased beating."[24] He also commented vividly upon his own near-death experience, buried alive by an explosion: "I found myself so unwell at having been crumpled and buried beneath the earth [...] that I remained shaken for a month, which left me inconsolable."[25] While Harari is undoubtedly correct that we should not expect early modern warriors to view their experience through the disenchanted eyes of the twentieth and twenty-first centuries, they were clearly often more affected by those experiences than they sometimes cared to admit, even to themselves. Similarly, while it is also true that greater significance was assigned to it by its participants as warfare became more clearly defined as an extraordinary or distinct realm of human activity, many soldiers continued to relate their experiences in a way that was

20 Harari, *The Ultimate Experience*, 71.
21 Ibid., 129.
22 Ibid., 197.
23 Sandberg, "His Courage," 133–4.
24 Ibid., 141.
25 Ibid., 139–40.

matter-of-fact, even indifferent. As this study will demonstrate, in all periods of modern warfare the soldier's death has been perceived as both transcendent and as utterly banal.

Harari's study also addresses the third of the problems defined by Corvisier, relating to the cultural representations of the soldier's death. In this respect, the visual arts provide an important body of evidence. Considering that evidence, Harari argues that just as soldiers began to describe in detail the extreme physical and emotional sensations that came from the encounter with death, artists too bore witness to the importance of that experience as a moment of revelation. Their paintings of dying generals did not fail to include the stares of other soldiers as witness to that moment: "Their stares register the experience of combat; and the message to the viewers is that the soldiers are undergoing a deep experience, that the soldiers know they are undergoing a deep experience, and that we viewers are in an inferior position to understand and know what they experience. Death in battle is no longer just heroism. It has also become 'an experience.'"[26] Battlefield pietas such as Benjamin West's commemorating the death of Wolfe (1770) and John Singleton Copley's representing *The Death of Major Peirson* (1783), in Harari's view, were prime exemplars of this changed representation of death in battle, focusing on "the knowing stare" of the soldier-witnesses.[27] The present study considers some French counterparts to these eighteenth-century British images. It was during that century when images celebrating the heroic deaths of common soldiers first began to proliferate, a trend that culminated during the French Revolution, when the crisis of foreign invasion prompted an unprecedented effort to mobilize the nation for war. Images of youth heroes like Bara and Viala who died fighting to defend the revolution proliferated alongside those of political martyrs of liberty. Images representing the deaths of ordinary soldiers did not disappear once the revolution had passed its most radical phase, although increasingly they were replaced by images of generals who also died fighting for the republic. Even under Napoleon, prints and paintings depicted the deaths of ordinary soldiers or junior officers, such as Latour d'Auvergne and Captain Auzouy. Art critics were uneasy about paintings that depicted the violence and bloodshed of war. Painters of Napoleonic battles had to respect contemporary taste by refraining from too realistically representing the soldier's death.

In the nineteenth century, important changes occurred in printing technology and in media production that greatly increased not only the speed at which images of war were reproduced but also the extent of

26 Harari, *The Ultimate Experience*, 225.
27 Ibid., 224.

their diffusion. First, the technique of lithography, whereby chemical processes were used to make prints from limestone templates, represented a significant advance on traditional techniques of copperplate and wood-block engraving: good quality prints could be produced relatively quickly, cheaply, and in large numbers. Even more important was the advent around mid-century of the illustrated press. This depended upon a new technique for producing engraved images whereby they were first drawn and then carved in relief on boxwood ends. These rivalled metal engraving plates for detail and durability and they facilitated the simultaneous printing of images and text. Cheap illustrated newspapers such as *L'Illustration* or *La Guerre Illustrée* brought images of war from the battle fronts to a mass audience in a matter of days. Accompanied by detailed reports from war correspondents, these images helped to create a new awareness of war's realities. Images of the dead, especially, were shocking to contemporary sensibilities.[28]

Although the Franco-Prussian War inspired a trend toward greater realism in military painting, most artists continued to shy away from the wounded body. This trend was accentuated during the First World War. The advent of front-line photography led to a steep decline in the production of *images d'Épinal*, the naive, idealized representations of war that had been produced since the seventeenth century. It also undermined the authority of war art more generally. To represent the soldier's death in an age of industrialized warfare was problematic for both traditional and modernist painters. All the same, several did so in memorable ways.

Harari's book says little about the second of Corvisier's problems, concerning the relationship between military death and the general mortality within society. A book that does address this issue is Hervé Drévillon's *L'individu et la guerre: Du Chevalier Bayard au Soldat inconnu*. In this masterly survey of the changing demands placed on the individual as modern warfare has evolved, Drévillon reflects upon the social and psychological impacts of military death. Comparing the military deaths sustained by France in the War of the Spanish Succession (310,000), the wars of the French Revolution (458,000) and the Napoleonic wars (900,000), Drévillon calculates that the Napoleonic wars, particularly in their final years, were characterized by a significant escalation in military mortality by comparison with the two earlier conflicts.[29] He argues that because the War of the Spanish Succession occurred at a time when society was still afflicted by great demographic crises, such as those of 1693 and 1709, the overall demographic and psychological impact of military losses was less significant

28 Brown, *Mass Violence and the Self*, 177–9.
29 Drévillon, *L'individu et la guerre*, 182–3.

than during the revolutionary and Napoleonic periods.[30] The implication is that battlefield death was perceived to be less terrible at a time when the ravages of death from epidemic disease, famine, or the endemic violence of civil society were essential facts of life. Building upon these insights, and taking into account demographic and cultural trends in modern France, particularly attitudes toward death, the present work argues that as death has been pushed to the margins of modern life, the deaths of young men on the battlefield have come to seem increasingly anomalous and unnatural.[31] The massive and enduring psychological impact of the First World War is to be explained both by the enormous scale and intensity of the slaughter – a similar number of Frenchmen lost their lives in the four years from 1914 to 1918 as throughout the entire twenty-three years of the revolutionary and Napoleonic wars – as well as by the fact that in the years surrounding the war the Western experience of death was profoundly transformed. The war itself came at the end of a half-century of medical advances that brought about a massive decline in infant mortality. This helped to set in stark relief the terrible fate of the generation of 1914. During the war itself, the established conventions surrounding death were sorely tested, their impracticality amid so much death contributing to their progressive abandonment following the war. It was in the postwar period that the most disenchanted images of the soldier's death appeared, in both art and literature.

Although there have been important changes and turning points in the representations of the soldier's death, most notably those associated with the First World War, the continuities in those representations are also striking. The values of "honour," and "homeland" have been universal referents in the discourses surrounding the soldier's death from the Renaissance to the present. They were as central to the funeral eulogies given by Archbishop Bossuet at the court of Louis XIV as those given in the courtyard of the Invalides by President Sarkozy. Yet the meaning of those words is fluid, their relationship to one another uncertain. They have meant different things to different people in different times and places. The chapters that follow show how understandings of honour and patriotism as well as their significance in motivating soldiers to risk their lives in battle have evolved over time. Most chapters begin, like this introduction, by providing an account of one or more soldiers' deaths. This is used as a vehicle to embark upon a broad analysis of the experiences and representations of the soldier's death during specific periods of French history.

30 Ibid., 184.
31 On the Western denial of death, see especially Ariès, *The Hour of Our Death*, 559–601.

Broadly speaking, the book divides the history of the soldier's death into three periods. During the first period (chapters 1–3), extending from the Renaissance to the French Revolution, the aristocratic ideal of an honourable death was challenged by both the changing realities of warfare and the rise of the modern state. Honour as the prime justification for military death was first adapted to the needs of the absolute monarchy and then rejected altogether during the most radical phase of the French Revolution, which elevated devotion to the homeland in its place as inspiration to the citizen-soldiers of the new, revolutionary armies. Honour enjoyed a revival under the Directory, however, providing an essential element of the Napoleonic synthesis of old regime and revolutionary values. Patriotism remained in the ascendant throughout the second period (chapters 4–6), extending from Napoleon's rule to the First World War. During the long nineteenth century, war became progressively more destructive at the same time as soldiers' lives became more valuable. Explaining and justifying the destruction of those lives required elevating the cause of the homeland to new heights as well as insisting upon both the necessity and the rewards of sacrifice on its behalf. This logic was evident in representations of the soldier's death inspired by the Franco-Prussian War and the First World War. The tremendous slaughter of the First World War was a shock to this system of representations. That shock conditioned the third period (chapters 7–9), following the end of the First World War, which was characterized by growing uncertainty about the values of patriotism. While those values were upheld in the culture of commemoration that emerged after the First World War and was renewed under the leadership of Charles de Gaulle after the Second, disenchanted representations also manifested themselves. These representations are considered here in relation to art and literature of the interwar period, to the changing attitudes concerning the fates of colonized soldiers in the Second World War, and in the conflicted responses of French soldiers to the war in Algeria.

Chapter 1 recounts the death of the Prince of Talmont at the Battle of Marignano in 1515. It focuses upon the primacy of honour as a motivating force for the military aristocracy at the time of the Renaissance and the Italian wars, considering the "fine death" that was the aspiration of knights such as the Chevalier Bayard. It also shows how contemporary chronicles representing the death of Bayard evolved to insist increasingly upon the association of the warrior's honour with the values of service to God, king, and country. Chapter 2 jumps ahead to the eighteenth century, following the lead of André Corvisier in considering the death of the Chevalier d'Assas at the Battle of Clostercamp in 1760. This chapter demonstrates not only the tremendous changes that occurred in warfare and society as the experiment of monarchical absolutism evolved under the Bourbon dynasty, but also the increasing emphasis placed upon service to the state and upon the utility of the soldier's death. The eighteenth century also witnessed a democratization of the soldier's death, as "subaltern heroes" were celebrated in images and verse. Chapter 3 begins by considering the death in the Nancy mutiny of 1791 of Lieutenant Desilles and examines the unprecedented ideological mobilization of France during the French Revolution, which elevated the sacrifice of heroes like Desilles as the duty of every citizen. During the radical phase of the Terror, the revolutionaries contrasted the civic devotion of ordinary citizens with what they perceived to be the corrupt notion of aristocratic honour. Honour retained a powerful allure, however, and it made a comeback during the later years of the revolution, when eulogies of revolutionary generals reprised those of Louis XIV's marshals. The harsh conditions of revolutionary warfare, amply revealed in soldiers' writings, gave the lie to propagandistic images of battlefield death.

Chapter 4 begins with the death of Marshal Lannes following one of the deadliest of Napoleon's battles, the Battle of Aspern-Essling in 1809. It shows how Napoleonic propaganda synthesized old regime and revolutionary models of military heroism and how, in the bulletins of the Grande Armée, it was increasingly the emperor rather than the nation that justified the soldier's sacrifice. This chapter considers the social and psychological impacts of the increase in the scale and intensity of warfare and of the concomitant rise in military mortality. The battlefields of Napoleonic Europe temporarily reversed the trend toward the physical separation of the living and the dead as well as the increasingly sentimental attitude of society toward the dead. Napoleonic propaganda celebrated military triumph rather than commemorating the dead, and its ultimate legacy was a cult of military glory that laid its burden upon subsequent generations.

Glory is difficult to reconcile with defeat and French armies have not always been victorious. The Franco-Prussian War of 1870–71 shocked contemporaries by the suddenness and completeness of Prussia's victory. In its aftermath, images of French soldiers sacrificing their lives without hope of victory became a means to salvage national pride as well as to model the attitudes required to achieve *revanche* in the future. Under the old regime soldiers' deaths were only considered meritorious if they were useful; under the Third Republic the more futile they were, the more they were admired. Chapter 5 considers the death of Henri Regnault at the Battle of Buzenval in January 1871 in this context. The war generated a new awareness of war's horrors and an unprecedented determination to provide sepulchres for all soldiers who had died. The tendency toward a more realistic representation of the soldier's death was limited in both degree and duration, however, giving way to increasingly propagandistic images.

The First World War inevitably occupies a central place in this study. It was the costliest of all France's modern wars in terms of human life, and the great majority of the lives lost were those of soldiers. The war generated a vast amount of contemporary testimony that continues to expand as collections of letters and other writings come to light. Historians of the First World War have taken the lead in exploring war cultures, and there are fine studies not only of soldiers' and civilians' attitudes toward death and dying but also of the commemorative culture that grew out of the war. Chapter 6 begins with the death of Eugène-Emmanuel Lemercier at Les Éparges in the spring of 1915 before considering the tensions between idealized representations of the soldier's death and the harsh realities that began to emerge in the writings of soldiers, surgeons, nurses, and chaplains during the war. Chapter 7 considers the aftermath of the war and the disenchanted view of the soldier's death that emerged in art and literature within the broader context of the commemorative culture that was beginning to take shape.

The ideal of patriotic self-sacrifice did not die with the First World War, although it was seriously called into question. Chapter 8 considers its revival during and after the Second World War as a means for recovering national self-respect in the wake of the defeat of 1940. This chapter begins by considering the death of Charles N'Tchoréré, one of many colonized Black troops murdered after surrendering to German forces in 1940.[32] This acknowledges the importance of these troops in the French army and underlines the radicalization of warfare during the Second World War, a trend that France did not escape. While patriotic representations insisted upon the willing sacrifice of colonial subjects grateful for the benefits of French civilization, the reality was that many fought because they had little choice. In their homelands and in France itself they have increasingly been represented as victims of an ungrateful *mère patrie*. The ninth and final chapter considers the soldier's death in the context of the Algerian war of independence of 1954–62. This was the last war France has fought in which young conscripts fulfilling their obligatory national service were compelled to serve. Their attitudes and feelings toward the prospects of dying in this unacknowledged war reflected the contradictions of a society that was experiencing significant social and cultural change. The Algerian war was also fought by professional soldiers, however, such as Marcel Bigeard and the

---

32 I have generally followed the lead of Claire Miot in using the adjective "colonized" rather than "colonial" to refer to soldiers from the French overseas empire, since it describes the status of those soldiers in a colonial system that subjected people as well as territories. Occasionally, depending upon context, I have retained the more traditional adjective. Miot, *La première armée française*, 21.

"paras" who were idealized in the novels of Jean Lartéguy. These men, some of whom became implicated in the rebellion of the OAS,[33] insisted upon their obedience to a concept of honour that was at odds with their obligations to the authority of the established government. They also sought to preserve and revitalize traditional notions of the soldier's sacrifice. Aided by his photographer, Marc Flament, Bigeard idealized the soldier's death as a transcendent experience.

The Algerian war, which pitted Algerian against Algerian and Frenchman against Frenchman, was in many respects a civil war. Certainly, it was fought with the bitterness and cruelty on both sides that are commonly perceived to be intrinsic to civil wars. It is one of four major civil wars experienced by France that are touched upon in this study. The others are the French Wars of Religion of the sixteenth century, the war in the Vendée at the end of the eighteenth century, and the war ending in the defeat of the Paris Commune in the nineteenth century. In these conflicts soldiers were sometimes perpetrators and sometimes victims of acts of extreme violence. Historians and theorists have reflected at length on the reasons for the exceptional brutality of civil wars. Stathis N. Kalyvas identifies four categories of explanation, emphasizing respectively: 1) political breakdown; 2) ideological polarization; 3) transgression of established norms of behaviour; and 4) security dilemmas arising from disparities in warfare technology.[34] It is beyond the scope of this study to choose between these arguments, all of which have some merit in relation to France's civil wars. In all four cases considered here, however, acts of extreme cruelty were facilitated by both circumstance and ideology. The circumstances attending siege warfare, as well as rural and urban insurgency, broke down the distinction between combatants and non-combatants at the same time as they fostered the anxieties and frustrations that spilled over into violence. Ideologically, in all four cases it was the perceived "otherness" of the enemy, who was both dehumanized and denied legitimacy as a combatant, that fed the fear and contempt that in turn led to torture and massacre. What is also notable in all four cases is the impulse not just to kill but also to desecrate the bodies of defeated adversaries. This desecration, the very opposite of the sanctification of soldiers whose deaths occurred in other contexts, served to demoralize enemy soldiers by denying them even the consolation of an honourable death. Profaning the body of the enemy was not exclusive to civil wars, as we shall see, but occurred in any context where the perceived illegitimacy or alterity of the victims was seen to justify such treatment. In

33 "Organisation armée sécrète."
34 Kalyvas, *The Logic of Violence*, 3.

such situations, the last resort of the defeated was to affirm their dignity as soldiers and as human beings by dying bravely.

The episodes considered in this study reveal some important changes and continuities in the realities and representations of military death since the Renaissance. The discourse surrounding the soldier's death, with its referents of "honour," "glory," and "homeland," has preserved a remarkable continuity over time, despite significant changes to both the content and contexts of those words. In recent years, however, that discourse has struggled to maintain its hold. A variety of factors have contributed to this, including a relatively more peaceful international situation since the unification of Europe and the ending of the Cold War, a declining sense of belonging to the nation, the professionalization of the armed forces, and changing attitudes toward youth and individual self-realization. Most importantly, death has beat a retreat from everyday life: medicalized, marginalized, denied. The soldier's death has become as unacceptable as any other. Yet for as long as modern states require armed forces to defend their interests, they will need to find ways to digest the fact of the soldier's death. As Pierre Chaine wrote in his classic 1917 work, *Mémoires d'un rat*, "War for the historian is just a synchronicity of movements and dates; for the leaders it represents a formidable labour and for the observer an interesting spectacle. But for the soldier who fights in the ranks, war is only a long encounter with death."[35]

35 Chaine, *Les mémoires d'un rat*, 82.

Dying for Honour:
The Renaissance

THE DEATH OF THE PRINCE OF TALMONT

Charles de la Trémoille, Prince of Talmont, received sixty-two wounds, according to contemporary sources, during the Battle of Marignano, which was fought on 13–14 September 1515, and died three days later.[1] We do not know the nature of his wounds, although five of them were described as mortal and we can presume, since the prince had been in the thick of the fight between the French advance guard and the Swiss heavy infantry, that they were mostly cuts and penetrations caused by edged weapons, principally swords, pikes, and halberds. The number of wounds was important to contemporaries as a measure of valour and for that reason may have been exaggerated. Nevertheless, they may reasonably be taken as an indication of the battle's ferocity. Martin du Bellay described how the two sides had fought themselves to exhaustion by the end of the first day's fighting: "and such was the confusion, in the darkness of night, that in many places French and Swiss slept beside one another, ours in their camp and theirs in ours; and the king slept all night in his armour (except for his helmet), on a gun carriage [...] Recognizing one another at the break of day, each returned to his own flag; and the battle recommenced more furiously than the evening before."[2] Du Bellay estimated that of the 35,000 Swiss soldiers who fought in the battle, 14–15,000 were killed, including many of the most experienced leaders.[3] While not enumerating French

1 Bouchet, *Panégyrique*, 178.

2 Bellay, *Mémoires*, 265.

3 Ibid., 267. Jean Bouchet estimated 15–16,000 Swiss casualties. Bouchet, *Panégyrique*, 178. Didier Le Fur, in a recent study, states that of 21,000 Swiss soldiers who left Milan before the battle only 13,000 returned, of whom 1,500 were seriously wounded (many of these were later massacred following the surrender of Milan to the French). Le Fur estimates that the French army suffered 8,000 dead and over 1,000 wounded. Le Fur, *Marignan*, 116–17.

casualties, he acknowledged that these were far from negligible. Like other chroniclers, du Bellay listed some of the principal Italian and French nobles who were killed in the battle, including the son of Count Petilano, "a young man who had long wanted to find himself fighting for the king," who led a charge against the retreating Swiss, "in which he was killed, and many others with him."[4] Jean Bouchet, a chronicler to whom we owe most of what we know about the death of Charles de la Trémoille, stated, "This meant the loss of many worthy men of France, and even the majority of a band of young French princes and lords who were in the advance guard."[5] The French may have lost as many as twenty prominent captains at Marignano.[6]

Charles de la Trémoille was therefore one among many who died at Marignano. We know virtually nothing about most of those who were killed. The deaths of common soldiers – as opposed to noblemen – were unrecorded and uncommemorated, their bodies unceremoniously piled into mass graves. We can safely presume many of them suffered extremely unpleasant ends. We know that the French artillery – "seventy-four large pieces" – was used to deadly effect against the close formations of Swiss infantry, causing them "a marvelous discomfort."[7] The musketry of French and German infantry fighting in French employ also caused the Swiss "great harm."[8] Pressing forward to the attack, the Swiss pikemen exacted a heavy price in return. The pike, several metres in length and deployed in dense thickets, was an effective weapon against the famed French heavy cavalry. Meanwhile, Swiss halberdiers slipped between the ranks of pikemen to disembowel horses and hack at the French infantry and dismounted men-at-arms; swords and daggers sought the unprotected joints and visors of protective coats of armour. Not all the victims were killed by firearms and edged weapons. Such was the press of battle that many must have been trampled or crushed to death. This is at least suggested by the experience of a young squire, who was praised by the chroniclers for using his body as a shield to protect his master and who was pulled from the fray, an action "of which he had great need, as much because of the blows he had taken, as for the number of men who had passed over him, so that he barely had the strength to breathe."[9] Some soldiers were even burned to death. The Lord of Florange claimed responsibility for the deaths of eight hundred

4 Bellay, *Mémoires*, 266–7.
5 Bouchet, *Panégyrique*, 178.
6 Potter, *Renaissance France at War*, 209.
7 Florange, *Mémoires*, 193.
8 Ibid., 196.
9 Bellay, *Mémoires*, 266.

1.1. Urs Graf, *Schlachtfeld*. 1521.

Swiss soldiers after he set fire to the house in which they had sought refuge.[10] The violence of the battle inspired one of the few early modern artworks to dwell on the atrocities of war. This was *Schlachtfeld*, engraved by the Swiss artist Urs Graf in 1521 (fig. 1.1). Graf was a Swiss mercenary who was in all likelihood present at Marignano; his famous engraving showing the battlefield strewn with dismembered corpses may have been his way of exorcising the traumatic memories of the first great defeat suffered by the Swiss in the Italian wars.[11] Another contemporary work of art that conveyed a sense of bodies crushed in the melee was a bas-relief sculpted in 1551 by Pierre Bontemps for the funerary monument of Francis I in the basilica at Saint Denis (fig. 1.2).

Amid all the anonymous deaths that occurred at Marignano, Charles de la Trémoille was relatively well favoured. The circumstances surrounding his death were amply documented by Jean Bouchet in the panegyric he

10 Florange, *Mémoires*, 231–2.
11 On this topic see Roeck, "The Atrocities of War," 129–40. On Graf's engraving see Bächtiger, "Marignano: Zum 'Schlachtfeld' von Urs Graf."

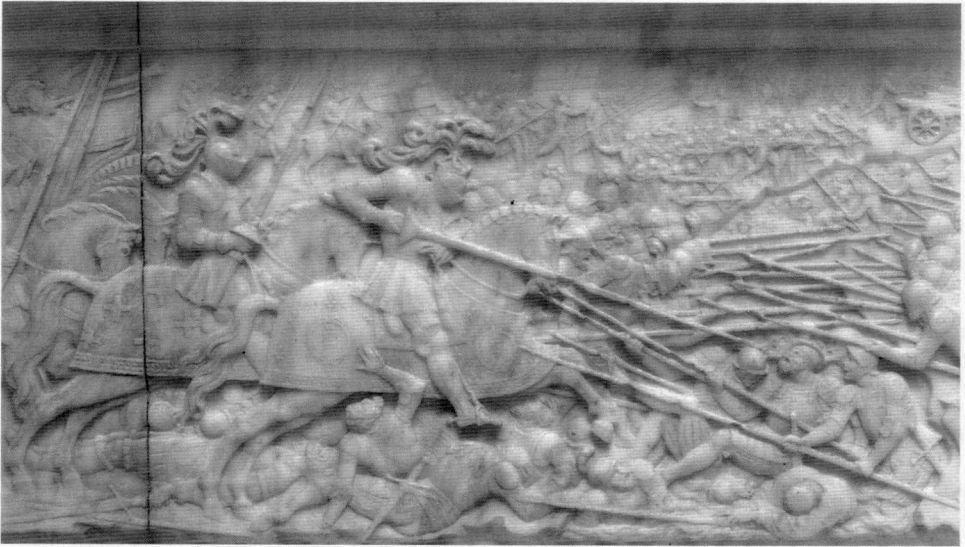

1.2. Battle of Marignano in 1515. Relief on the base of the funerary monument of Francis I (1494–1547), by Pierre Bontemps. 1550.

wrote in honour of Louis de la Trémoille, Charles's father, who also fought at Marignano, but who survived his son for a further ten years before meeting his own end at the Battle of Pavia in 1525. Carried wounded from the battlefield by his childhood mentor, the knight Regnault de Moussy, the younger La Trémoille was tended by physicians in his tent, who at first gave the father hope of his son's survival. These hopes were not at first dispelled by King Francis, who was made aware by the surgeons of Charles's impending death but who sought to soften the blow by evoking examples from ancient Rome of fathers who had been happy for their sons to die in battle. For his part, the dying youth declared a stoic acceptance of his fate. "I die in the prime of my life, but I have no regrets, since it so pleases God, and He has granted me grace to die in the service of the king and of the public interest."[12] The father was no less stoical. "I knew my son could die young in war or elsewhere," he said. "And did not hope he would live forever; but, seeing him drawn to the place of danger where men of good heart put themselves for the public good, I looked upon him as already dead." Louis de la Trémoille expressed satisfaction at the manner of his

12 Bouchet, *Panégyrique*, 178.

son's death, "after receiving sixty-two wounds, for the maintenance of the public good and in a just war."[13]

Such satisfaction was not shared by all. Charles de la Trémoille's embalmed body – save for the heart and entrails which, along with those of other French nobles killed in the battle, were to be interred in a memorial chapel to be built on the battle site – was returned to the family home at Thouars, in France, for burial. There it was received by the young man's mother, Gabrielle de Bourbon, who was inconsolable, despite the best efforts of those around her to raise her spirits. The Bishop of Poitiers delivered a funeral oration in which he directly addressed the mother, reminding her of death's ubiquitous, unpredictable, and arbitrary nature and insisting that, of the many deaths her son might have had, that which he experienced was one to envy.

Consider, Madam, that my late cousin and your son did not die of any of these terrible accidents, but as a man of virtue, alongside people of merit; not among the beasts, but with humans; not among brigands and pirates, but in a just war; not from the bites of wild animals, but by a martial blade; not by cannon, but by blows of the lance; not in a cowardly way, but bravely; not alone, but accompanied by his father; not in the service of tyrants, but in that of his king; not shamefully, but honestly, covered with honour, wrapped in renown and in the love and grace of God.[14]

After all, concluded the Bishop, it was better for Charles to have died in the prime of his youth, bestowing upon his family a legacy of "perpetual glory," rather than living another thirty years, "and then to die in his bed or elsewhere of a horrible illness."[15] The bishop's words were unavailing, however, and despite a pious exchange of letters with her husband, the mother went into a decline from which she did not recover. Louis de la Trémoille was left to rail against death, which had deprived him of a wife and son, both of whom should naturally have outlived him: "I have lost one to the sword, the other to sorrow, and I will lose myself to anguish."[16]

Jean Bouchet's account of the death of the Prince of Talmont no doubt contains a fair amount of invention in its idealized representation of the noble and pious sentiments expressed by all concerned. It is nonetheless revealing of contemporary attitudes toward the soldier's death at a

13 Ibid., 181–2.
14 Ibid., 189.
15 Ibid., 190.
16 Ibid., 203.

particularly important time of historical change. Talmont's death at the
Battle of Marignano occurred at the time of the Italian Wars, during which
the institutions and conventions of medieval warfare were transformed by
new weapons and new methods. During the years from 1494 to 1559, Italy
became a crucible into which were poured the disparate military traditions
that had been developing in various parts of Renaissance Europe. German
and Swiss mercenaries brought the discipline and tactics that made them
the most feared and sought-after heavy infantry. Invading French armies
brought the artillery that had blasted the English from their castles in the
Hundred Years War, as well as a heavy cavalry, organized in *compagnies
d'ordonnance*, that was the preserve of the French nobility.[17] The Spanish
brought infantry armed with the new firearms, principally the arquebus,
and were the first to develop an effective combination of heavy and light
infantry, mixing pikemen with arquebusiers.[18] Light cavalry, equipped
with bows or firearms, came principally from the Balkans. Italy itself
provided a tradition of professional generalship represented by the
condottiori, or mercenary captains. The merger of these traditions marked
both the "twilight of chivalry" and the birth of modern warfare.[19] These
changes, which rendered warfare more lethal and undermined the battlefield dominance of the armoured knight, profoundly affected the culture
of the military nobility to which the Prince of Talmont belonged. The
representations of the soldier's death from this epoch were shaped by
the need to adapt medieval traditions to modern conditions. Those representations have haunted subsequent representations down to the present
day. The heroic model of a "fine death" – such as that of the Prince of
Talmont – had tremendous purchase in a society where the military nobility
enjoyed social and political pre-eminence, where the basic facts of life were

17 The French cavalry was organized into "lances." At the time of the Italian wars,
each lance comprised one man-at-arms, a *coutilier*, two archers (occasionally still equipped
with bows, but increasingly armed in similar fashion, although more lightly, than men-at-
arms: a sort of medium cavalry), and a couple of pages. The fighting strength of a lance was
therefore three or four men. See Potter, *Renaissance France at War*, 70–85.

18 The arquebus, developed in the 1420s and 1430s, was the first effective hand-held
firearm. Fired by means of a slow-burning match, the arquebus was the antecedent of the
heavier matchlock musket developed in the 1520s, which required a fork rest because of
its weight. See Black, *European Warfare, 1494–1660*, 70, 87.

19 Nicolas Le Roux, *Le crépuscule*; Mallett and Shaw, *The Italian Wars*, 177–97. The
army commanded by Francis I at Marignano comprised approximately 2,500 lances
(15,000 men), plus about 30,000 infantry, approximately half of whom were *landsknechts*,
including the "Black Band," a unit that fought in the black clothes of mourning. In addition to seventy–two heavy guns, mounted on wheeled carriages, the army possessed
approximately 3,000 "light artillery" weapons, including the principal infantry firearm, the
arquebus. Le Fur, *Marignan*, 70–3.

harsh and death – often violent – a familiar presence. As those circumstances changed – as the military nobility declined in importance; as lives became more comfortable and society safer; as individual identities took on greater importance than collective ones; as death was banished from everyday experience; and as war itself came to be perceived as an extraordinary rather than a normal state of affairs – so that model has lost its traction. Many of these changes were either slow or late in coming, however, with the result that variations of the heroic model, adapted according to regime and circumstance, have had remarkable staying power. Already, as early as the sixteenth century, we can see evidence of this adaptability and durability as the aristocratic ideal of a beautiful death was subtly altered in the interests of the French monarchy. During the second half of the century, however, the authority of the crown reached its nadir as the kingdom was torn by civil war. Religious hatreds threatened to undermine combatants' respect for the rules of war defined by the chivalric code and heroic images of the noble warrior were displaced by unheroic representations of soldiers as agents in the massacre of innocent civilians.

BEAUTIFUL DEATHS – AND UGLY ONES

The Bishop of Poitiers's funeral oration for the Prince of Talmont provides us with a good sense of what French nobles of the sixteenth century imagined constituted a fitting death: one that was the result of a fair fight in a just cause in the service of one's legitimate monarch. Given that noble identity was still pre-eminently associated with military service, it was taken for granted that the most appropriate end for a noble was to die in combat. Indeed, so determined was one ailing noble to die such a death that, learning from his doctor that he had only hours left to live, he insisted upon being caparisoned, "from head to toe," in his finest armour to take leave of his retainers. Brantôme wrote approvingly of this next best thing to a *belle mort*, that it was "the finest death one has ever heard spoken of since kings wore crowns."[20] Death in combat, by exhibiting his courage, enhanced the warrior noble's personal reputation as well as the honour of his lineage. Honour was a complex commodity, incorporating notions of virtue, dignity, and reputation, but not exactly synonymous with any of these. In a society where transactions of all kinds depended upon trust, honour was paramount, to be preserved at any price, even at the cost of one's life. Pertaining to all layers of society, honour was a collective possession that might belong to a corporation, an institution, or a family. An individual

20 Brantôme, *Oeuvres complètes*, vol. 1, 314–15.

could add to the honour of his relatives and descendants by behaving in ways that were deemed appropriate to his or her place in society. Alternatively, he or she might lose honour by behaving inappropriately. For the military aristocracy, appropriate behaviour meant adhering to the values of chivalry, encapsulated in the notions of virtue, courage, piety, courtesy, and loyalty, which were modelled by the heroes of *chansons de geste* and chivalric romances.[21] Courage was foremost among these values. Honour depended upon acting fearlessly on the field of battle. Hence, the most famous knights, including Pierre Terrail de Bayard and Louis de la Trémoille, were given the title "without fear" by their admiring contemporaries.[22] It was considered far better to die on the battlefield than to endure the shame and dishonour incurred by behaving in a cowardly way. In the words of Boyvin de Villars, "It is better to lose one's life gloriously than to live in infamy and misery."[23] Blaise de Monluc advised that soldiers should never be afraid when going into battle: "If you die there, you will dishonour neither yourself nor your posterity, and so you will be buried with an immortal reputation, which is all that men who bear arms should desire."[24] Louis d'Ars, motivating his men before an attack on an Italian town in 1503, declared: "Better to die here honourably under the shield of virtue, than to live shamefully, under the shadow of cowardice."[25]

The military memoirs and chronicles of the sixteenth century were therefore filled with accounts of soldiers' deaths that exemplified this readiness to die for honour and reputation. Brantôme, writing during the reign of Henri IV, cited the example of Charles III, Constable of Bourbon, who supposedly declared his willingness to die as he exhorted his men before leading the imperial attack on Rome in 1527. Referring to an astrologer's prediction that he would die in the capture of a town, Bourbon declared "I swear to you that this is the least of my worries, and it bothers me little to die, if, in dying, my body remains with everlasting glory, renowned by all!"[26] According to Brantôme's account, the constable proceeded to match his words with deeds, leading the assault in a distinctive white tunic and suffering a mortal wound as he mounted a scaling

---

21 For a useful summary of the discourse on chivalry, see Lynn, *Battle*, 78–85. For a helpful definition of honour, distinguishing it from associated concepts such as "renown" and "dignity," see Nassiet, *La violence*, 178–206; see also Le Roux, *Le crépuscule*, 19–55.

22 "Sans peur et sans reproche" – "without fear and without reproach" – was the formula famously applied both to Bayard and to La Trémoille. Germa-Romann, *Du "bel mourir,"* 29.

23 Cited in ibid., 70. For the criteria that defined a *belle mort* for contemporaries, see ibid., 136–7.

24 Monluc, *Commentaire et lettres*, vol. 2, 119.

25 Auton, *Chroniques de Louis XII*, vol. 3, 6.

26 Brantôme, *Oeuvres complètes*, vol. 1, 266.

ladder. As he lay dying, his final request was that his body be covered and quietly removed, to avoid any discouragement to the attacking force. "And just as he uttered these words with a brave heart," wrote Brantôme, "as if he had suffered no harm, he came to the end of his final days as a mortal."[27] Brantôme made clear that the constable's fearless words and deeds were an inspiration to his men, who, once they heard of his fate, "fought even more fiercely to avenge his death." A Spanish standard bearer, struck fatally by a bullet as he entered the breach, passed his flag to his superior, declaring, "Captain, I give my honour to your safekeeping, for I am dead." Finally, the captain himself performed his own feats of courage. Knocked senseless in a struggle with French soldiers, he lost the flag with which he had been entrusted. Returning to the fray, however, he recovered another "and going forward fighting like a lion, was so successful that he led the chant, *Victoria, victoria! Imperio, Imperio!* [...] with the result that the city was taken."[28]

Brantôme's account of the attack on Rome is reminiscent of Jean d'Auton's earlier description, from the reign of Louis XII, of the attack by German and Burgundian forces on the French defenders of Novara in 1500. On this occasion, it was the courage of a mortally wounded French nobleman, the "Bastard of Amezay," that received praise. Engaged in hand-to-hand combat with a Burgundian standard-bearer, Amezay was wounded by numerous gunshots:

But, for all that, he did not release his grip [on the enemy flag] and by sheer force tore it from the Burgundian's fist, wrapping it around his arm in spite of his enemies [...] Like another Epaminondas, the Duke of Thebes, who, joyously, while dying, kissed the shield with which he had so vigorously defended the public interest, so did the Frenchman, notwithstanding the extreme sobs that racked his body [...] similarly, without showing any sorrow at his impending death, carry the standard to his lodging, knowing that happy Fame embellished by virtue after temporal death, bears the triumph of eternal praise.[29]

D'Auton, like Brantôme, insisted upon the complete absence of fear – the joyfulness, even – of the soldier as he went to his death.

Even from these few examples of representations of the soldier's death from the Italian Wars, we can see that reality had to be forced to fit the

27 Ibid., 268.
28 Ibid., 269–70.
29 Auton, *Chroniques de Louis XII*, vol. 1, 210.

chivalric mould. This is apparent in the simplest of terms. If we return to the Bishop of Poitiers's funeral oration, one of the oppositions the bishop emphasized in his definition of a good death was that between a death caused by gunfire (cannon) and one caused by edged weapons (blows of a lance). Firearms were widely perceived to be associated with cowardice, undermining the essential chivalric principle of a fair fight and denying their victims a truly honourable death. "Would to God that this unhappy instrument had never been invented," wrote Blaise de Monluc of the arquebus, condemning it as a weapon used by "the most cowardly and villainous, who would not dare to look in the face those they bring down from afar with their miserable bullets."[30] Yet, of the deaths we have so far considered in this chapter, only that of the Prince of Talmont was caused by a "martial blade." The others, from the Constable of Bourbon to the Bastard of Amezay, were all caused by gunshots. The accounts do not dwell on this, as both Brantôme and d'Auton contrive to emphasize the element of hand-to-hand combat in the struggle for control of standards on the ramparts of besieged cities. The fact remains, however, that even these exemplary deaths fell short of the ideal standard in a significant way. Indeed, what was arguably the most exemplary death of all, that of the Chevalier Bayard, also fell short given that Bayard was himself the victim of a gunshot wound, received during the retreat from Robecco in 1524. This is apparent from the account of the Loyal Serviteur: "The good knight, as confidently as if he had been in his own house, got the men-at-arms marching, withdrawing at a good pace, his face always toward the enemy and, sword in hand, inspired more fear in them than a hundred others; but by the will of God, a gunshot was fired, the bullet from which struck him in the vitals, and severed his spine. When he felt the blow, he cried: 'Jesus!' and then said: 'Alas! My God, I am dead.'"[31] Once again, the inconvenient fact that Bayard was killed by a firearm is relatively unimportant in a narrative that emphasizes the formulas of chivalry. Nothing must be allowed to spoil the image of a noble death. Hence the insistence upon Bayard's constantly facing the enemy, sword in hand, even though this cannot have been literally true given that he was managing a retreat.

Although it is easy for us to see in accounts such as this evidence that the age of chivalry was passing, the military and social dominance of the military aristocracy undermined by the democratizing effects of the infantry and firearms revolutions, that is not how contemporaries like Brantôme, d'Auton, and the *Loyal Serviteur* saw things. Rather, they sought to assimilate to the discourse of chivalry the realities of the new warfare that emerged

30 Monluc, *Commentaires et lettres*, 52.
31 Mailles, *Très joyeuse, plaisante et récréative histoire*, 413.

from the Italian Wars. Their purpose was to insist that despite the new, ever more deadly environment of the modern battlefield, heroic exploits and beautiful deaths were still possible. Their best efforts, however, could not mask the reality that death now came to the soldier not in an equal, face-to-face test of his skill and strength, but from afar, unperceived, as a matter of chance. The memoirs of Robert de la Marck III, Lord of Florange, recounting his campaigns in Italy, provide a litany of noble lives suddenly ended by artillery or arquebus fire. From 1511, he recalled accompanying a commissar of artillery to survey the ground prior to laying siege to the town of Concordia. The commissar was hit in the head by a shot fired from an arquebus and died eight days later.[32] Florange wrote with rather greater relish of the death shortly thereafter of a Spanish captain, Gabriel de Peralta, decapitated by a French cannonball as the two armies shadowed one another before Bologna. Peralta was known to wear a gold chain around his neck, "and afterwards, a French adventurer went to look for both the chain and the head."[33] Florange's description of the Battle of Ravenna (1512) included an anecdote concerning two French infantry captains who, after enduring three hours of artillery bombardment, sat down together to refresh themselves, "and while drinking, a cannon shot carried them both off, which was a great shame."[34] In describing the siege of Novara (1513), he wrote that "the artillery of the castle and town wrought great murder upon the landsknechts[35] and foot soldiers and killed many of them, and there was one landsknecht close by the Young Adventurer [La Marck habitually referred to himself this way, in the third person], who had both legs carried away, and many others were badly wounded."[36] In describing the siege of Milan in 1522, Florange noted the death of Antoine Colonna, whose leg was torn off by a cannon shot fired from the city and who died six hours later. This death was particularly poignant because the city was defended by the victim's brother, Prosper Colonna, "who was extraordinarily sorrowful and had his [Antoine's] body carried to Rome in the greatest triumph possible, and his burial was fine and honourable."[37] At the siege of Pavia in 1525, Florange again witnessed a young companion, Claude de Longueville, Duke of Orléans, killed by an arquebus shot as they surveyed the town together. The shot, wrote Florange, "went right through his heart." Longueville "said only three words: 'I am, I am dead!'; and was carried off

32 Florange, *Mémoires*, vol. 1, 67.
33 Ibid., 74.
34 Ibid., 90.
35 *Landsknechts* were mercenary soldiers from Germany.
36 Florange, *Mémoires*, vol. 1, 127.
37 Ibid., vol. 2, 59.

quite dead."[38] The account of Longueville's death is one of relatively few passages where Florange emphasizes the tragedy of a young life prematurely cut short. "Never were people so afflicted," he wrote, describing the feelings of the noble entourage who gathered around the young man's body, "and, upon my faith, they were right, because he was the most courageous prince, and the finest person in a thousand, aged eighteen years, well loved by the king and by everyone."[39]

Throughout this narrative of lives ended by firearms, Florange expresses a sort of amazed incomprehension at the way in which combat and death in battle had been transformed by the new weaponry. In describing the failure of an assault on a breach in Pavia's defences, he emphasized the effect of the enemy's artillery: "And in the attack a standard-bearer who entered the breach [...] and fully three hundred men were killed and as many wounded, the majority of whom died of artillery strikes, without a single blow by hand. And Monsieur Bussy lost seven captains in the attack; and eight hundred men were killed there, from the king's side and from the Swiss, [including] those who were wounded and died later, without a single blow by hand."[40] The repetition of the phrase "without a single blow by hand," underlines Florange's sense of awe that such a combat, almost entirely dominated by firearms, was possible. For other writers, such incomprehension amounted to denial. Witness Jean Bouchet's account of the French defeat at Pavia, during which his hero, Louis de la Trémoille, was killed by a shot from an arquebus:

The French certainly had the worst of it, more by misfortune than because of the prowess and skill of our enemies; because, as they themselves have written and confessed, their army was less well ordered than ours; also, the arquebuses carried by their cavalry (whom the French feared not) did more harm to the French than their prowess and valour: and if the whole French army had acquitted themselves as well as the king and the princes, captains and gentlemen surrounding him, it would have won, because in the first charge involving the king and the said Lord de la Trémoille, who was wounded in the face, above and below the eye, were accomplished many great and fine feats of arms that, by the strength of blows and without artillery, killed two or three hundred enemy men-at-arms.[41]

38 Ibid., vol. 2, 175.
39 Ibid., vol. 2, 176.
40 Ibid., vol. 2, 188.
41 Bouchet, *Panégyrique*, 231.

Bouchet's ill-concealed scorn not just for the enemy's tactics but also for the failure of the bulk of the French army to live up to the example set by Francis I and the flower of French chivalry constituted a refusal to admit that the age of chivalry was coming to an end.

There were many other ways in which the facts of the noble deaths reported by the writers of memoirs and panegyrics were at odds with the discourse of chivalry that contained them. It is true that the discourse of chivalry influenced the conduct of war, inspiring celebrated occasions when knights challenged one another to single combat. On such occasions, the reality of warfare was made to conform to an ideal. The legend of the Chevalier Bayard was celebrated precisely because of his participation in these chivalrous interludes. In 1503, during the French campaign in Naples, Bayard had reportedly overcome illness and the strength of the Spanish knight, Sotomayor, killing the latter in single combat and thereby cleansing his honour of Sotomayor's insults. He also supposedly fought in a contest between thirteen (some say eleven) French knights and an equal number of Spanish ones, in which the combatants were eliminated from the field as soon as they were unhorsed. On this occasion, the Spanish had the advantage, but Bayard and one other French knight manoeuvred behind a rampart composed of the bodies of dead horses until a draw was declared and honour deemed to have been satisfied.[42] Generally, however, the ideals of chivalry characterized less the reality of warfare than the alternative reality of jousts and tournaments.[43] The celebration of Bayard's chivalrous exploits masked a much harsher reality. Contemporary descriptions of sixteenth-century battles, despite the way they are framed within the discourse of chivalry, are often more evocative of the slaughterhouse and of grim, frenzied massacres than they are of the tournament or joust.

Once again, the memoir of Florange is instructive on this point. The Prince of Talmont may have held the unenviable record for the number of wounds received in a battle, but Florange must have run him a close second. After the Battle of Novara (1513), he wrote, his father had searched the battlefield for his two sons. He found Florange among the dead. The "Young Adventurer" was unrecognizable, "because he had forty-six really bad wounds, the least severe of which took six weeks to heal."[44] Multiple wounds were worthy of note as a badge of honour. Of course, it was

---

42 For analysis of the various versions of these events, see the biography by Jacquart, *Bayard*, 132–3; see also Potter, *Renaissance France at War*, 92.

43 As John Lynn explains, the tournament or joust had developed because even during the Middle Ages the reality of warfare had failed to live up to the ideals of chivalry. See Lynn, *Battle*, 73–109.

44 Florange, *Mémoires*, vol. 1, 128.

important those wounds should be on the front of the body, indicating the recipient had not dishonourably turned away from the fight. Gaston de Foix, the French commander killed at the Battle of Ravenna (1512), "was wounded by so many blows," wrote Brantôme, "that, from chin to forehead, he had fourteen."[45] But we might also take multiple wounds as evidence that combat was sometimes fuelled by irrational passions, by the urge to wound and re-wound long after the enemy's capacity to resist had been overcome. Certainly, many of Florange's battle accounts suggest that mercy was rarely shown, even to a defeated foe. His description of Agnadello, where the Venetian army was defeated by the French in 1509, stated that thousands of dead bodies were piled in a heap that reached two pikes' lengths (over ten metres) in height. Many of the victims had been asphyxiated, he said, and afterwards, "more than thirty thousand were buried in five ditches."[46] Most historians agree that Guiccardini's estimate of 8,000 casualties for the battle is a more plausible calculation than that of Florange, but there is no disputing that the French refused to take prisoners or that the Venetian army was traumatized by the defeat.[47] As for Novara, the battle in which Florange was so severely wounded, his claim that there was only a handful of survivors from the three or four hundred men in the front rank of the landsknecht formation that bore the brunt of the battle with the Swiss is entirely plausible. A recent study estimates that the French army suffered 40–50 per cent casualties in the battle (5,000 to 6,000 dead) and that two-thirds of the landsknechts, abandoned to their fate by the French cavalry, were killed by their implacable Swiss foes.[48] The slaughter may have been as great at the Battle of Ceresole (1544), where the Swiss soldiers, this time fighting on the French side, were once again determined to take no prisoners. On this occasion, Monluc demonstrated that he had no compunction about exploiting to the full the deadly effectiveness of the arquebus he so deplored. In his account of the battle, Monluc took credit for putting arquebusiers in the second rank of the French infantry formation, with the object of killing the captains in the enemy's front line. The tactic, which depended upon the arquebusiers holding their fire until within a pike's length of the enemy, worked to perfection. "There took place a great killing," wrote Monluc. "Not a shot missed."[49]

45 Brantôme, *Oeuvres complètes*, vol. 3, 14. The Loyal Serviteur estimated fourteen or fifteen: Mailles, *Très joyeuse, plaisante et récréative histoire*, 327.

46 Florange, *Mémoires*, vol. 1, 130–2.

47 Le Roux, *Le crépuscule*, 152; Mallett and Shaw, *The Italian Wars*, 89–90.

48 Florange, *Mémoires*, vol. 1, 128; Le Roux, *Le crépuscule*, 154; Olivier Bangerter, *Novare (1513)*, 100.

49 Monluc, *Commentaires et lettres*, vol. 1, 278.

Although firearms were clearly a great leveller on the battlefield, the chances of surviving such massacres were at least slightly better for men of rank than they were for ordinary soldiers. Indeed, it is important to note that most battle narratives, written by noblemen for other noblemen to read, expressed scant interest in common soldiers; the latter were there merely to make up the numbers. Bartolomeo d'Alviano, the commander of the Venetian army at Agnadello, was one individual who, because of his rank, was given quarter by the French and therefore escaped the slaughter that was the fate of the men under his command. In Florange's account, Alviano exchanged courtesies with King Louis XII, apparently more conscious of honour gained than of lives lost. "Notwithstanding that he had lost," said d'Alviano, "there was still sufficient honour to be won from a battle in which a French king had fought against him in person."[50] An anecdote recounted by Brantôme concerning the Battle of Pavia (1525) provides an unwitting insight into the ways social inequalities were reflected on the battlefield, sometimes making the difference between life and death. François de Bourbon, the Count of Saint-Paul, wrote Brantôme, "fought so valiantly that he was found among the dead hovering on the brink of death. And, feeling the pain as a soldier was beginning to cut off a finger to remove a valuable ring, he cried out and identified himself; hence the soldier picked him up and took him to Pavia, where he was so well cared for that he escaped death."[51] Furthermore, once recovered, the fortunate Count evaded his captors and returned home without paying any ransom. Clearly, Saint-Paul owed his survival entirely to his social status and to the perception of a battlefield scavenger that he was of more value alive than dead. That men of high rank might be ransomed undoubtedly was an important factor in saving them from the fate of so many common soldiers who lay wounded on the battlefield, to be stripped and left to die, or perhaps mercifully dispatched. Thus, Alisprand Madruzzo, discovered lying naked among the dead after the Battle of Ceresole, "having seven or eight wounds," was recognized and rescued by a light horseman.[52] Not that there were any guarantees. Another anecdote from Brantôme about the Battle of Pavia told the story of Jacques de Chabannes, Lord of la Palice, who was taken prisoner by the Spanish Captain Castaldo. Another Spaniard, "the cruel Buzarto," envious of the "prize and honour" of such a capture, simply fired an arquebus into the French knight's cuirass, killing him outright. Despite such a shocking end, contrary to all the principles of chivalry, Brantôme did his best to provide a positive conclusion: "So died

50 Florange, *Mémoires*, vol. 1, 32.
51 Brantôme, *Oeuvres complètes*, vol. 3, 203.
52 Monluc, *Commentaires et lettres*, vol. 1, 278–9.

this good captain and honourable lord, who could not have died differently: because whoever begins well has a good ending."[53]

At times, the refusal to take prisoners for ransom was deliberate policy. Florange notes that when Peschiera fell to French troops after the Battle of Agnadello (1509), the garrison was massacred, save for the captain and two other officers. On this occasion, not even their rank and wealth were a protection for the three captives. Despite the offer of a ransom of 100,000 ducats, and despite the entreaties of his own officers, Louis XII ordered the prisoners to be hanged. The point of the executions, according to Florange, was to terrorize the citizens of other Venetian cities, which were thereby cowed into delivering their keys to the French.[54] A similar motive prompted the French to hang from the battlements all two hundred soldiers from the garrison at Garigliano following their surrender, which they had delayed until after the French army was forced to bring up its siege artillery. According to Jean d'Auton, the only ones to escape were the Captain, whose wife – "marvelously beautiful" – pleaded successfully for his life, and one soldier from whose neck the noose slipped, with the result that he fell into the moat, breaking a leg but preserving his life.[55] Otherwise, the capture of besieged cities provided the most notorious instances of massacre, where various motives, including greed, lust, and desire for revenge might lead to the slaughter not just of the garrison, but also of civilians, including women and children. Following the capture of Brescia in 1512, wrote Florange, "Forty thousand men were killed and the whole town pillaged and put to sack." On this occasion, greed appears to have been a motivator: "And there were some men-at-arms who did so well out of it that they and their children felt it for the rest of their lives."[56] Another combatant from the Italian wars, Blaise de Monluc, attributed the slaughter of the inhabitants of Ascoli in 1529 to the desire of his soldiers to avenge him after he had been wounded in the siege: "Note that I was so liked by the soldiers of all the companies, that they all agreed to kill and not to take any prisoners, for which reason they killed all the men, women and children, even those in the crib, and then set fire to the town."[57]

Monluc proved himself to be a pitiless combatant on occasion, particularly during the French Wars of Religion. Waging war against the Huguenots in the southwest of France, he described how his men hunted them through the vineyards, "like when one shoots at game." In a civil war, he said, one

53 Brantôme, *Oeuvres complètes*, vol. 1, 379.
54 Florange, *Mémoires*, vol. 1, 34.
55 Jean d'Auton, *Chroniques de Louis XII*, vol. 2, 44.
56 Ibid., 82.
57 Monluc, *Commentaires et lettres*, vol. 1, 82.

should not take prisoners. "It is not like in foreign wars, where one fights for love and honour [...] in civil wars one must be master or valet, given that we live under the same roof; and so it is necessary to resort to rigour and cruelty."[58] Capturing sixty or eighty Huguenots at Gironde, he had them all hanged, "on the pillars of the market, without any ceremony." He left the signs of his passage, he wrote, hanging from the trees that lined the roads.[59]

These accounts demonstrate that the soldier's death was often ignominious, sometimes deliberately so. The account of his voyages by the renowned French military surgeon, Ambroise Paré, provides abundant testimony to the grim circumstances in which many soldiers died. In describing the capture of Turin in 1536, Paré stated that, having defeated the enemy, the French trampled on the bodies of the dying as they rode into the city, "which caused me great compassion in my heart."[60] Although Paré's prejudice against Spanish soldiers requires that his accusations of cruel behaviour on their part be treated with some skepticism, it is worth noting his claim that Spanish troops assigned to collecting the wounded following the siege of Metz simply tossed the dying out of their carts, "and buried them in the mud and the mire, saying they had no orders to bring back the dead."[61]

At times, the death meted out was deliberately calculated to deprive its victims of honour by subjecting them to an undignified form of execution. Noblemen, normally accorded the privilege of execution by decapitation, might instead be subjected to the indignity of hanging. Paré provided an example of this from the aftermath of the defeat of a Spanish garrison by French forces at Villane. The attacking force had endured heavy losses as the result of an accidental explosion that had revealed the position of its guns to the defenders during a night-time attack. They were therefore disinclined to show mercy once they had created a breach. The town's defenders were slaughtered, except for "an extremely beautiful, young and strapping Piedmontese woman, whom a great lord wanted to keep him company at night, for fear of the Bogeyman." Finally, the captain and ensign commanding the garrison were "hanged and strangled" from the battlements over the town gates as a warning to all enemy troops not to be "so bold and so foolish" as to defend such places "against such a great army."[62] Equally callous was the slaughter of twenty or thirty enemy soldiers who were taken prisoner following the siege of Château le Comte in 1552.

58 Ibid., vol. 2, 425.
59 Ibid., vol. 2, 442.
60 Paré, *Oeuvres complètes*, vol. 3, 689–90.
61 Ibid., 708.
62 Ibid., vol. 3, 690.

According to Paré, the Army Council ordered all soldiers who had taken prisoners in the hope of exchanging them for ransom, to kill them immediately upon pain of death, "which was done in cold blood."[63] Among the cruelties of which Paré accused the Spanish following the surrender of the French garrison at Hesdin was that of pulling on a rope tied around their victims' genitals, "as if they had wanted to ring a bell," causing them "to die cruelly at their hands," or at the very least to lose their genitals. "There you have their great cruelty and perfidy," he concluded. "Believe it if you will."[64]

Paré's memoir bears witness to acts of extreme cruelty, but also to at least one that, although he described it also as a "great cruelty," was in fact a mercy killing. Following the capture of Turin in 1536, Paré came across four dying enemy soldiers. An old soldier, realizing that nothing could be done for them, proceeded to cut their throats, "gently and without anger," saying only that he hoped someone would do as much for him should he find himself in such a plight.[65]

It was not only enemy soldiers who were subjected to harsh, degrading treatment. Military executions were common and an accepted means for keeping order in unruly armies.[66] The biographer of François de Vieilleville, recounting the latter's actions as Governor of Metz, detailed the exemplary executions whereby he sought to impose discipline on the city's garrison. A soldier who had killed a comrade in a quarrel was condemned to decapitate the body of his victim before suffering the same fate himself. "This brave example of justice," affirmed the writer, "humiliated the soldiers marvelously."[67] Similarly, he praised de Vieilleville's "great justice" in ordering three soldiers to be broken on the wheel and seven others hanged for stealing from local merchants, stating that it caused "a marvelous tremor in the garrison."[68] Particularly significant was the deliberate stripping of a corrupt sergeant-major of the trappings of nobility before his execution, as well as the subsequent display of his body in the public square, dressed in the clothes of a common peasant. This was described as "a spectacle worthy of great pity, to see such a man, dead and stiff, stretched on a table, with a faded, tattered old hat [...], old gaiters and clogs, who for twenty years wore nothing but silk stockings and velour slippers, and was always

63   Ibid., vol. 3, 700.
64   Ibid, vol. 3, 712.
65   Ibid., vol. 3, 690.
66   Potter, *Renaissance France at War*, 197–9.
67   Carloix, *Mémoires de la vie de François de Scépeaux*, 194.
68   Ibid.

covered in gold chains."[69] Strangled to death in his prison, the disgraced nobleman was deliberately refused the noble death of decapitation.

DEATH FROM ILLNESS AND WOUNDS

Some deaths were therefore rendered deliberately ignoble. Indeed, a key component of a "fine death" was "courtesy," involving expressions of respect from both friends and foes.[70] To withhold such respect or to express its opposite was to diminish the worth of the person concerned. But deaths could also be perceived as ignoble without a deliberate intent to make them so. If death on the battlefield itself seems a far cry from the chivalric ideal, how much further away from that ideal were deaths that occurred away from it. For certainly that was the fate of the great majority of soldiers throughout the early modern period. Although precise figures do not exist before the eighteenth century, certainly far more soldiers died of disease than of wounds. One calculation is that for every soldier who was killed in battle, three died of accidents or wounds and six died of illness. To calculate the overall mortality of early modern wars, it is therefore necessary to multiply battle deaths by a factor of ten![71] Plague, typhus, yellow fever, malaria, pleurisy, smallpox, even apoplexy and gout, all took their toll on soldiers on campaign.[72] Florange recounted that his uncle died in Italy after falling into a river and contracting a fever. On this occasion, insult was added to injury, since the victim's troubles began when he was struck on the nose by a snowball containing a stone: a doubly undignified way to die![73] At times, whole armies melted away from disease. Such was the fate of Lautrec's army that laid siege to Naples in 1528, ravaged by typhus. Brantôme wrote that nine-tenths of that army perished. Lautrec was one of those who died, although Brantôme sympathetically attributed his death less to illness than to the bitterness and despair he felt because of his army's plight.[74] Blaise de Monluc returned home from that campaign badly wounded, having refused to allow surgeons to amputate his arm, but also "wishing for death a thousand times more than for life; because I had lost

---

69 Ibid., 215.

70 Germa-Romann, *Du "bel mourir,"* 136.

71 Jacques Dupâquier, "Guerres classiques et démographie," *in La guerre à l'époque moderne*, Bulletin de l'association des historiens modernistes, no. 3, 1979. Cited in Cornette, *Le roi de guerre*, 290. André Corvisier notes that during the Napoleonic wars, for every soldier who died of wounds there were three or four who died of illness. He argues that the imbalance was probably even greater during earlier centuries. See Corvisier, *Les hommes*, 380.

72 Hélène Germa-Romann, *Du "bel mourir,"* 256–7.

73 Florange, *Mémoires*, vol. 1, 63–5.

74 Brantôme, *Oeuvres complètes*, vol. 3, 30–2.

all the lords and friends who knew me, who were all dead."[75] Eight years later, Monluc helped to inflict similar suffering on an imperial army that had invaded Provence by destroying the mills it needed to grind grain. The hardship that resulted, he wrote, "put their camp into such a disorder of maladies and funerals, particularly among the Germans, that I doubt a thousand of them returned to their homeland."[76] Another imperial army, this time laying siege to Metz in 1552, was estimated by Ambroise Paré to have lost twenty thousand men principally to "hunger, plague and cold."[77] Paré painted a grim picture of soldiers covered in snow and up to their knees in mud, lacking either boots or shoes. François de Vieilleville's memoirs recorded that the frostbitten imperial soldiers begged the French to put them out of their misery.[78]

While nobles may have enjoyed an advantage over commoners because of their easier access to adequate nutrition and medical care, illness nonetheless took a high toll of noble casualties. For all his expertise at treating wounds, Paré's ministrations did nothing to prevent Marshal de Montejan from dying of a "hepatic flux."[79] To the military aristocracy deaths from illness were deplorable. Du Bellay and Brantôme both wrote regretfully of the death of Bartolomeo D'Alviano, "surprised by a flux of the bowels [...] which was a great shame, since he was in his time a great warrior and a good captain."[80] In describing the death of François de Daillon, killed at Ravenna, Brantôme explicitly condemned death caused by illness as "hideous" and "unworthy." Explaining that Daillon had nearly died of illness while serving as governor of Legnano, he wrote, "But the God of arms did not wish that the hideous and frightful death from illness in bed should overcome him, a death certainly unworthy of his [Daillon's] valour, led him to recover, rise from his bed and die more gloriously at the Battle of Ravenna, fighting very valiantly."[81] Bayard himself, stricken by a fever while between campaigns at Grenoble, was not too pious to address "the most piteous complaints" to God, asking why the latter had not allowed him to be killed alongside the Duke of Nemours at the Battle of Ravenna (1512), rather than leaving him to die "in my bed like a flea."[82]

75   Monluc, *Commentaires et lettres*, vol. 1, 104.
76   Ibid., 124–5.
77   Paré, *Oeuvres complètes*, vol. 3, 707.
78   Carloix, *Mémoires de la vie de François de Scépeaux*, 184.
79   Paré, *Oeuvres complètes*, vol. 3, 692.
80   Bellay, *Mémoires*, vol. 1, 79. See Germa-Romann, *Du "bel mourir,"* 257.
81   Brantôme, *Oeuvres complètes*, vol. 2, 417–18.
82   Mailles, *Très joyeuse, plaisante et récréative histoire*, 336–7. See also Germa-Romann, *Du "bel mourir,"* 144–5.

To his relief, Bayard recovered and, as we have seen, achieved the death he desired on the field of battle.

Death caused by wounds was certainly perceived to be preferable to death from illness, but all the same it was not the equal of a death that took place on the field of battle. A good example of this is provided by the case of Jean de Medici, a nobleman whose leg was shattered during the siege of Pavia in 1525. Although he endured the subsequent amputation with great courage, holding the candle as the surgeon operated, he died all the same, uttering the complaint, "And why must I die here in plasters? This is a cruel disappointment for me."[83] Brantôme also noted the disappointment of two French nobles who were fatally wounded on the eve of the Battle of Pavia: "But it is said that they were both so disappointed to be absent from this battle that was taking place under their noses, and two days after their wounds, that they both died from regret."[84]

The two French nobles did not die of disappointment, of course, but of the effects of gunshot wounds. One had his thigh shattered and the other lost his arm to the surgeon's knife. In all likelihood, they died in agony as gangrene set in, despite the Duchess of Ferrara providing them with the best of care. Indeed, as Ambroise Paré frankly admitted, the medical arts of the day were often powerless to deal with gunshot wounds. Although he was not reticent about claiming success for his treatments, Paré confessed that "those who are wounded by arquebuses, often die, or are forever crippled or mutilated."[85] Paré discovered that sometimes less treatment was better than more. During the 1536 campaign in Italy, having exhausted his stock of boiling oil for cauterizing wounds, he realized that soldiers who had not had their wounds treated in this way did better than those who had.[86] Often, the surgeon's ministrations came too late. After the Battle of Saint Quentin in 1557, Paré wielded his knife on wounds that were "stinking greatly, and full of worms, with gangrene and rot." "In spite of all my efforts," he admitted, "many of them died."[87] In such circumstances, it is not hard to understand the preference for a death that came quickly, on the field of battle. The irony is that so few, relative to the numbers who perished from wounds or disease, were granted one.

83 Brantôme, *Oeuvres complètes*, vol. 2, 9–10.
84 Ibid., vol. 2, 422–3.
85 Paré, *Oeuvres complètes*, vol. 2, 163.
86 Ibid., vol. 3, 691.
87 Ibid., vol. 3, 721.

MUTATIONS

Although it may have been shaken by the heavy losses sustained in the Italian Wars, particularly in the Battle of Pavia, many factors helped to sustain the sixteenth-century French military aristocracy's commitment to the ideals of chivalry and of an honourable death. This ideal made perfect sense to a class whose social pre-eminence derived first and foremost from its function of providing military service. In theory, the *impôt du sang* was the price paid by the aristocracy for the honours and privileges it received from a grateful king. By celebrating the heroes who showed their willingness to serve and to die in the king's service, the nobility justified its privileges. No matter that only a minority of nobles chose the profession of arms.[88] The ideal of an honourable death in battle also made sense given that life was short and precarious anyway. Although infant mortality was particularly high, with only half of all children born likely to reach their tenth birthdays, bubonic plague and other epidemic diseases were no respecters of age.[89] Ambroise Paré's statement that the abandoned imperial camp after the siege of Metz, covered with unburied corpses, was like the Holy Innocents cemetery in Paris "during some great mortality" is a reminder that epidemics regularly visited mass death upon the civilian population of sixteenth-century France.[90] As Laurence Brockliss and Colin Jones write, "Deaths in battle in early modern Europe were a haystack in comparison to the Alpine heights reached by plague- and epidemic-related mortality."[91] Prior to 1670, there was not a single year that the plague – spread by a bacillus carried by fleas inhabiting the black rat – did not bring sudden death to some part of France, with surges of mortality reaching pandemic proportions every eleven years on average until 1536, every fifteen years thereafter. Towns experiencing a visitation might expect to lose between a quarter and a half of their populations to this dreaded killer. Angers lost a third of its population of 25–30,000 during the

---

88 Cornette, *Le roi de guerre*, 293–6. Cornette estimates that the number of nobles who gave military service in the seventeenth century was between 6 per cent and 30 per cent, depending upon period and region. Jean-Marie Constant states that a quarter of noble families fought in the wars of Renaissance France, a third in the subsequent wars of religion, and 40 per cent in the wars of Louis XIII and Louis XIV. Constant, *La noblesse française*, 12. Nicolas Le Roux concedes that most nobles did not go to war. Le Roux, *Le crépuscule*, 23. David Potter notes that, despite the renaissance of chivalry in the sixteenth century, "there were many more nobles than places in the King's army." Potter, *Renaissance France at War*, 67.

89 Dupâquier, *Histoire de la population française*, vol. 2, *De la Renaissance à 1789*, 224.

90 Paré, *Oeuvres complètes*, vol. 3, 707.

91 Brockliss and Jones, *The Medical World of Early Modern France*, 55.

epidemic of 1583–84.[92] At such times, normal social relations and public services might break down entirely as the wealthy fled, streets were deserted, and the dead left unburied.[93] Plague was not the only invisible killer. Typhus and typhoid fever, smallpox, and lung diseases, including pneumonia, pleurisy, and tuberculosis, all took a significant toll, as did syphilis, the first epidemic of which was spread by soldiers accompanying Charles VIII's army invading Italy.[94] Nor were elites spared these harsh facts of life. The diary of a Paris bourgeois, which reported diligently on births, deaths, and marriages in the royal family, as well as military victories and defeats, recorded that in 1515, the same year as the Battle of Marignano, the queen gave birth to a daughter, "who has since passed from life to death at the age of four or five years."[95] The nobleman's unflinching readiness to go to his death in battle was merely the counterpart of the "tame death" of the commoner who lay on his deathbed undemonstratively orchestrating his departure from this world.[96] Both confronted death with the same resignation. In the popular genre of *Danses macabres*, which emphasized the theme of equality before death, the soldier's death was represented down to the sixteenth century as essentially the same as that of everybody else.[97]

The general readiness of Renaissance society to idealize the "fine death" of the noble warrior can also be understood as a function of that society's high tolerance for violence in social relations. Familiarity with violent death was scarcely limited to times of foreign or even civil wars. Public executions were a normal feature of daily life, as our Parisian's diary makes clear. Again referring to the year 1515, it recorded that on 22 June a man was decapitated for having strangled his wife.[98] The year following, there was a report of the hanging of "a young boy, not yet sixteen years old," who had been convicted of stealing from his master, a jeweller.[99] Typically, the macabre spectacle of such executions also involved the display of the victim's remains, left to hang for several days from a gibbet.[100] In addition to state-sponsored violence were very high levels of interpersonal violence, particularly among the young and the nobility.[101] The nobleman had to

92 Lebrun, *Les hommes et la mort*, 307.
93 Ibid., 430–5.
94 Brockliss and Jones, *The Medical World*, 38–53.
95 Lalanne, ed., *Journal d'un bourgeois*, 18.
96 Ariès, *The Hour of Our Death*, 5–28.
97 Corvisier, *Les hommes*, 382–3. See also Harari, *The Ultimate Experience*, 78–86.
98 Lalanne, ed., *Journal d'un bourgeois*, 14.
99 Ibid., 37.
100 Lebrun, *Les hommes et la mort*, 416–22.
101 Muchembled, *Une histoire de la violence*, 75–128, 247–300.

be ready to defend – and if necessary die for – his honour at all times. Indeed, single combat between nobles – in the form of the duel – became a feature of civil society at the very moment when it was becoming anachronistic on the battlefield.[102]

Over time, all these factors changed. By the time of the Renaissance, careers in administration, finance, or the law were already beginning to displace the profession of arms as avenues of social advancement. There is evidence that by the eighteenth century respect for human life had increased relative to the value placed upon personal and family honour. Society's tolerance for the violent settling of scores had also diminished.[103] A "good" Christian death in bed gained in esteem in relation to the "fine" warrior's death in combat.[104] The latter continued to have its place, but within a military sphere increasingly dominated by the absolutist state and distinct in its values and culture from those of civil society.

Clearly, the model of what was considered a fine death was flexible enough to change with the times. As the French monarchy increased in power and pretensions, the medieval ideal of holy war, which promised salvation to soldiers who gave their lives crusading against the infidel, became secularized; or, rather, it was co-opted by the monarchy. By the early fifteenth century, at the height of the Hundred Years War, it was the sacred cause of the homeland, incarnate in the person of the king, which was presumed to require the soldier's sacrifice. And it was that sacrifice that was held to justify him in the eyes of God. In the words of Robert Blondel, "No-one need fear death, in fighting for his country."[105] By the sixteenth century, the cause of the king had itself become sacred, religion and politics inextricably intertwined. The victory of Francis I at Marignano was widely interpreted by royal publicists as the culmination of a religious crusade. Since the battle was fought on a religious holiday celebrating the Cross, it was sometimes named "the day of the Holy Cross."[106] Francis I became the model of a Christian warrior-prince.[107] Bayard, his most loyal servant, became the exemplar of the Christian warrior.[108]

---

102 Nassiet, *La Violence*, 114–20; Carroll, *Blood and Violence*, 130–80.
103 See Nassiet, *La violence*, 289–316.
104 Germa-Romann, *Du "bel mourir,"* 271–308.
105 Cited in Cornette, *Le roi de guerre*, 307.
106 Le Fur, *Marignan*, 238.
107 Writing in 1624, Nicolas Caussin memorably described Francis as "the first gentleman of Christianity [...] He has sealed his honour by the blood of the lamb, he has allied valour to piety, the monarchy to humility, the wisdom of the crucifix to the government of the world, the nails and thorns of the passion to the diadems of kings and to the pleasures of the court." Cited by Cornette, *Le roi de guerre*, 442.
108 Cornette, *Le roi de guerre*, 299.

From the appearance of the first biography of Bayard, by Symphorien Champier, (1525), Bayard was represented as a Christ-like figure, humbly giving himself up to the will of God. Several of his exploits, accomplished against the odds or despite physical illness, implied divine intervention. Champier's description of the thigh wound Bayard received in an attack on Brescia and of his subsequent suffering, much more fulsome than was usual for the time, also prefigured his final sacrifice.[109] The parallels with Christ's passion were insisted upon in the account of Bayard's last campaign as, suffering from illness, he protected the French rearguard, sacrificing himself so that the army could be saved. Finally, laid beneath a tree, symbol of the cross, Bayard, "in the jaws of death," piously sought God's mercy, invoking in his last prayer the passion of Jesus as the necessary means for his own unmerited salvation.[110] So universally was Bayard recognized as an exemplar of Christian virtue, claimed Champier, that the soldier who had fired the fatal shot that killed him not only cursed the inventor of the "diabolical engine" by which had been killed "the most noble and valorous of all knights," but also abandoned the military life for one of religious mourning.[111] Later writers embellished Champier's account of Bayard's death, adding even more obvious religious signs. Brantôme claimed that at the moment he was struck, Bayard grasped the hilt of his sword, "and kissed its intersection [with the blade] as a sign of the cross of Our Lord."[112]

To his biographers, Bayard was much more than just an exemplar of Christian piety. He was also unfailing in his determination to serve his king. The whole point was to insist that devotion to God and devotion to one's prince were one and the same thing. Champier was responsible for inventing a dialogue between the dying Bayard and the Constable of Bourbon that became for later generations the best-known aspect of the Bayard legend. In Champier's version, the constable offered medical aid to Bayard, who responded by saying:

Sir, this is not the time for me to seek doctors of the body, but those of the soul[.] I know that I am mortally wounded and beyond saving, but I praise God for giving me the grace to know him at the end of my life and final days,

109 Champier, *Histoire des gestes*, 67–70.

110 Ibid., 149.

111 Ibid., 116. See also Le Roux, *Le crépuscule*, 157, 236–7, 318–20; and Crouzet, "Un chevalier," 285–94. Bayard's life and death, says Crouzet, resonated with the religious aspirations of the French nobility at the time of the Italian wars: "Must we not deduce, from the rediscovered obsession of a whole society for chivalrous adventures, pushed perhaps to new limits, a religious longing, is this not the only way to explain the frenzy for war and deeds of the French warriors who traversed the mountains?," 294.

112 Brantôme, *Oeuvres complètes*, vol. 2, 383.

and to recognize my sins, because I have followed war all my life and done many harmful and sinful deeds: and know well that God has given me an incomparable and far greater grace than I deserve; and accept death as his will, my only displeasure in dying that I can give no future service to my sovereign king [...] I pray to God that after my death the sovereign has such servants as I would wish to be.[113]

The Constable of Bourbon was supposed to have reflected as he left Bayard, "It is pitiful to see this noble knight die thus who always so nobly, and loyally served his princes kings of France [...] Does France know what she has lost today in this noble knight Bayard[?]"[114] The dialogue became an important part of the Bayard myth because of its juxtaposition of the loyal servant (Bayard) who served his king to his dying breath and the disloyal one (the constable) who betrayed his king and even fought against him to serve his own interests. This opposition also helps to make sense of an earlier episode from Bayard's life, also invented by Champier, according to which Francis I was knighted by Bayard on the field of battle at Marignano.[115] The essential point of this anecdote was to bolster the chivalrous reputation of Francis I following the latter's capture at Pavia, by linking him, not to the treasonous constable, who had given him his spurs in his coronation ceremony at Reims, but to the impeccable figure of Bayard, now transformed into a paragon of chivalrous virtue.[116] In the 1540s, Martin du Bellay embellished the dialogue imagined by Champier. Du Bellay had Bayard directly admonish the Constable: "Do not pity me, sir. I am not to be pitied, because I die a worthy man; but I pity you, seeing you serve against your prince, your motherland, and your oath."[117] Brantôme faithfully reproduced the same words a generation later, adding that "I believe this speech stung Monsieur de Bourbon, but he and everyone else were so determined to give chase and follow up the victory, that Monsieur de Bourbon thought no more of it, and besides he saw well enough that it was true."[118] Between them, Bayard's biographers insisted that among the virtues making up the perfect knight, loyalty to

113 Champier, *Histoire des gestes*, 114–15.
114 Ibid., 115.
115 Ibid., 98–9.
116 On this theme, see Le Fur, *Marignan*, 260–1.
117 Martin et Guillaume du Bellay, *Mémoires*, 451. Bayard's modern biographers judge the conversation to be apocryphal. See Jacquart, *Bayard*, 310. Jean Giono, in his book on the Battle of Pavia, writes of the encounter: Giono, *The Battle of Pavia*, 75.
118 Brantôme, *Oeuvres complètes*, vol. 2, 386.

king and country had pride of place. This aspect of Bayard's image only received greater emphasis as royal absolutism took shape under the Bourbons in the seventeenth century.[119]

Du Bellay was far from being the only writer in the sixteenth century to establish such a close connection between service to king and country and the warrior's honour. Jean Bouchet, in his panegyric devoted to Louis de la Trémoille, has his hero utter the following speech prior to a battle against Breton rebels: "And if we remain victors, consider, Gentlemen, the benefit and usefulness we will have provided to the king and to the entire kingdom, and the honour, glory, profit and renown that we will acquire; and on the other hand, if, by our cowardice, we are overcome, we will see the destruction of our country, of our houses, women, children, and the consumption of our property, to our perpetual shame."[120] In Bouchet's imagination, as much as in du Bellay's, essential components of a warrior's honour were obedience to his king and defence of his homeland. This emphasis took on increasing significance after the Italian Wars, particularly as the unity of Christian Europe was fractured by the religious reformations and the medieval idea of holy war or crusade in defence of Christendom lost its allure.[121] The increased importance placed upon the utility of a soldier's service even prompted criticism of soldiers who sought glory by exposing themselves needlessly to danger. Thus, Bernard de Nogaret, Marquis de la Valette, was criticized by his secretary for his "temerity" in exposing himself to enemy fire, without even the protection of armour, while placing his artillery for the siege of Roquebrune. The marquis was killed by a bullet to the head. Similarly, in the seventeenth century, historians looking back at the death of Claude de Longueville added to the praises of earlier writers, such as Florange, the reproach that he "imprudently reconnoitred the fortifications."[122]

All the same, it is notable that in spite of Bayard's supposed rebuke to the Constable of Bourbon Brantôme nonetheless described the constable, fighting against his king in the service of Emperor Charles V, as a great and honourable captain. Although of ever-growing importance, service to king and country was but one aspect of the honour for which soldiers of the sixteenth century were willing to lay down their lives. Although their images were modified over time to reflect changing values, the figures of

119 On the evolution of Bayard's image over the course of subsequent regime changes, see Jacquart, *Bayard*, 341–66; and Le Roux, *Le crépuscule*, 345–60.

120 Bouchet, *Panégyrique*, 86.

121 Contamine, "Mourir pour la patrie," 11–44.

122 Cited in Germa-Romann, *Du "bel mourir*," 288–9.

warrior heroes like Bayard continued to be evoked down through the centuries as the embodiment of a notion of military honour that, while inextricably linked to ideals of patriotism and of Christian sacrifice, remained a powerful motive force in its own right.

DYING FOR FAITH: THE FRENCH WARS OF RELIGION

Both the chivalric code of honour and the image of the soldier as a model of service and self-sacrifice were sorely tested by the French Wars of Religion. French military history in the sixteenth century is commonly represented as a story in two parts. During approximately the first half of the century, ending with the Treaty of Cateau-Cambrésis of 1559, the wars that involved French soldiers were generally foreign ones. Fought mostly along the Rhine and in Italy, these wars were sustained by the dynastic rivalry of the Valois kings of France and the Habsburg rulers of Spain and the Holy Roman Empire. Valois pretensions were dealt a severe blow, however, by the death in 1559 of Henri II (notoriously, as the result of a jousting accident) and by a succession of very young or incapable monarchs. During the second half of the century, from 1562 to 1598, France's wars were mostly internal as no fewer than eight civil wars – the French Wars of Religion – racked the kingdom. French society was profoundly shaken by these wars, which weakened the crown's authority and intensified the effects of coincidental economic and demographic crises. Characterized by extreme violence and by a breakdown of the distinction between combatants and non-combatants – traits commonly associated with civil wars – the French Wars of Religion had implications both for how death was experienced by soldiers and for how it was represented. As religious differences caused violence to spill over conventional limits, the warrior's code of honour was a significant factor in preserving the social cohesion of the military nobility and in regulating violence. The accumulation of hatred and mistrust was such, however, that not even great nobles – let alone ordinary soldiers – could count upon the courtesy that was owed in principle to an honourable foe, especially at the delicate moment of surrender. It was not the deaths of soldiers, though, that caught the imagination of contemporaries. Instead, the wars generated an iconography that graphically depicted massacres of civilians, especially women, children, and clerics. Soldiers were more likely to be represented as tormentors rather than defenders of civilians, the perpetrators of violent death instead of its victims. For a more positive image of them to prevail would require a change in civil-military relations that was unimaginable in France in the second half of the sixteenth century.

French society was thoroughly militarized by the Wars of Religion. The regular armies raised by the French crown and by the French Protestant leaders were not dissimilar in size and composition to those that had been engaged in the Italian Wars, although the royal army raised for the second war (1567–68) was, at 72,210, larger by about a third. Thirty-six per cent of that force was composed of foreign mercenary contingents, most notably heavy infantry from Switzerland and light cavalry from Germany.[123] Both sides depended upon foreign troops, although their numbers diminished as the money to pay them became harder to find. But the wars were fought not just by regular armies in the field. As the confessional divide deepened and communities began to take up arms many towns organized civic militias. In Paris, some members of the bourgeois militia, whose function was nominally to keep order, became significant perpetrators of religious violence. Indeed, it was not uncommon for professional troops to become helpless bystanders to or even the targets of such violence. Believing themselves to be engaged in a holy war, militant militiamen played a prominent role in the popular violence that erupted in the capital in 1567 and, more notoriously, in the Saint Bartholomew's Day massacres of 1572.[124] More extreme yet in their crusading zeal were the confraternities that developed in some parts of the kingdom. A model for these was provided by the plan for a confederation signed by leading clerics and nobles at Toulouse on 2 March 1563, which called for nothing less than a complete militarization of society in the service of God and an absolute determination to destroy all heretics.[125] In Dijon in 1567 the brotherhood of the Holy Spirit aspired to raise two hundred horsemen and 250 infantry "for the maintenance of our said faith and religion, and of the said crown." The brothers swore a solemn oath to support one another to the death, "without regard to any friendship, relation or alliance that we might have with those who undertake the opposite."[126] It was this type of single-minded assertion of religious loyalties over those of friendship and family that fuelled the violence of civil war. There were other manifestations of this crusading spirit. In 1562, Durant de Pontèves, sieur de Flassans, a self-styled *chevalier de la foi*, raised an armed band in Provence. Each soldier wore a rosary around his neck and had a white woolen cross sewn to his hat. Singing canticles, these holy warriors marched behind a Cordelier monk, Guillaume Taxil, who carried a wooden crucifix bearing the figure of a bleeding Christ. Taxil

123 Wood, *The King's Army*, 63–5.
124 Diefendorf, *Beneath the Cross*, 160–71.
125 Crouzet, *Les guerriers de dieu*, vol. 1, 380–1.
126 Ibid.

and six hundred of Flassans's followers perished in the stronghold of Barjols when it was stormed by Protestant troops on 6 March.[127]

The character of military operations during these civil wars, in which there were relatively few pitched battles and many sieges, further militarized society, breaking down the distinction between combatants and non-combatants. Civilians of a city under siege were pressed into service to build or repair fortifications, to ferry food and ammunition to the soldiers, or to take care of the wounded; not uncommonly, they took up arms as well. The successful defence of Chartres from attack by the Protestant army in 1568 depended not just on the 4,000 troops sent by the king to man the ramparts, but also upon six hundred men from the civic militia who joined them, over a thousand citizens who stuffed their beds into breaches in the city walls, and hundreds of others, from bakers to blacksmiths, who supplied the needs of the garrison.[128] Jacques de Thou, in describing the defence of Rouen in October 1762, declared that "Even the women, to inspire the men, walked about amidst fire and shot without fearing death, and with a surprising intrepidity provided all the services that could be expected of their sex."[129] Civilians also shared the hardships and dangers of the soldiers, particularly in a city taken by storm. Perhaps a thousand people were killed in Rouen when it fell to royal troops after a sustained attack lasting five days. "To judge the situation in which Rouen then found itself," wrote de Thou, "one has to imagine that the most cruel and horrible spectacle is that of a town taken by assault and abandoned to the inhumanity and avarice of the soldier, who seeks to satisfy his passions."[130] In 1591–92, the city endured a second siege, lasting five months. Rouen was not sacked this time, but its people suffered all the same. Although relieved by the arrival of Spanish troops in the nick of time, hunger and disease caused by the circumstances of the siege resulted in a severe mortality crisis that endured for many months after the armies had departed. There were three times as many burials in Rouen in 1592 as in a normal year.[131]

Much of the violence of the French Wars of Religion did not involve soldiers directly but stemmed from escalating tensions between rival faith communities that, stimulated by incendiary preaching and mutual provocation, gave rise to a "war in the streets."[132] Military and civil violence

127 Ibid., 392.
128 Wood, *The King's Army*, 215–19.
129 Thou, *Histoire universelle*, vol. 4, 429.
130 Ibid., 433.
131 Benedict, *Rouen during the Wars of Religion*, 102, 222.
132 Diefendorf, *Beneath the Cross*, 159. The classic study of the anatomy of the crowd in the religious riot is Natalie Zemon Davis's study of "The Rites of Violence," in Davis, *Society and Culture*, 152–87.

were discrete phenomena; high levels of civil violence did not necessarily correspond to high levels of military violence.[133] Soldiers were participants in the broader culture, however, and in states of mind that manifested themselves in what contemporaries themselves recognized to be extreme acts of violence and cruelty. Historian Denis Crouzet argues that the mutilation and desecration of bodies, both living and dead, derived on the Catholic side from impulses to expose the heretic's carnal, bestial nature, and to provide a foretaste of the torments of hell. For Protestants, who targeted priests, it was an exercise in retributive justice and terror calculated to punish their enemies' past crimes and to prevent future ones by impressing upon them the evidence for the inevitable triumph of God's righteousness.[134] The violence of soldiers also answered to more immediate, military considerations, including the impulses to avenge their own losses, to avoid the inconvenience of feeding and managing prisoners of war, as well as to deter the resistance of other garrisons by making harsh examples. In 1562, as a wave of massacres and counter-massacres swept across the south and the southwest of France, the merciless treatment of the enemy was a function both of religious animosities and of military circumstance.

This mixture of religious and military imperatives played out in Provence in the summer of 1562, as the Baron d'Adrets made it his mission to avenge the atrocities committed by Italian mercenaries at Orange. The Italians had subjected the townspeople to a wide range of cruelties, including burning, impaling, and hanging: "the women were hanged from doors and windows; children were torn from their breasts and dashed against walls; girls were raped."[135] In response, d'Adrets embarked on his own reign of terror, refusing all quarter to the garrisons of Montélimar, Pierrelate, and Montbrison. According to Agrippa d'Aubigné, d'Adrets later represented his actions as a just punishment of his Catholic enemies, claiming "that he had repaid them in kind to a much lesser extent, having regard to the past and the future." With respect to the future, it was only by making harsh examples, he said, that one might "change a merciless war into a courteous one." Furthermore, his cruelty toward the enemy was also calculated to affect the motivation of his own men: "he did not want to see his troops flee from the rear if they had the chance; but by removing from them all hope of pardon, they should see no other shelter than the shadow of the flag, no life but in victory."[136]

133 See Wood, "The Impact of the Wars of Religion," 153.
134 Crouzet, *Les guerriers de dieu*, vol. 1, 240–300, 607–26.
135 Agrippa d'Aubigné, *Histoire universelle*, vol. 2, 52.
136 Ibid., 73–4.

Not all the violence was premeditated. One of the riskiest moments in combat is that of surrender, when soldiers put down their arms in the hope or expectation that their lives will be spared. The Wars of Religion present many instances in which terms of surrender were negotiated but not respected. This was the case in December 1562, when a hundred Protestants defending the Château de Graves, near Villefranche, surrendered to a Captain Vesin. The terms of surrender were, according to a Protestant contemporary, agreed and written down. When the Protestant soldiers, led by Captain Savignac, emerged from the castle, however, they were set upon by Vesin's men. All but thirteen were killed. "There was no mercy shown whatsoever, for great cruelty was exercised on that day; notwithstanding that the aforesaid Vesin was first cousin to the aforesaid Savignac, he did not refrain from exercising his cruelty or inhumanity: because once murdered, their private parts were cut off and put in their mouths, which is hard to relate. But so as not to break the thread of history, it is necessary to preserve the memory to make known the pitilessness of men, such cruelties as not even the Turks and Saracens would employ."[137] To this commentator, the massacre at Graves was a premeditated betrayal orchestrated by Captain Vesin. In Catholic chronicler Jacques-Auguste de Thou's account, however, which makes no mention of the mutilations, it was the Protestant soldiers who first violated the terms of the surrender. These specified that only officers might retain their weapons. According to de Thou, several of the Protestant soldiers were discovered to have concealed their arms: "Either because they wanted to take precautions against the peasants, whose fury they feared, or because they were given bad advice, they decided to hide some weapons in their packs and baggage."[138] Discovery of this deceit, says de Thou, precipitated the massacre. In his narrative, which contains the plausible detail of the soldiers' fear of peasants, the massacre is represented as a surrender that failed not because of deliberate perfidy but simply because of the difficulties men had in the aftermath of battle to put aside their anger, fear, and distrust of one another. Similarly, de Thou explains the massacre of the garrison of Taraube by Catholic soldiers under the command of Monluc as the consequence of a failed surrender. Although terms were agreed and hostages exchanged as a guarantee, several shots were fired by the defeated Protestants and one of the Catholic hostages was killed. The Protestant commander had one of the culprits hanged from the battlements, but this failed to appease Monluc, who ordered the massacre of the entire garrison. "This order was carried out with as much precision as barbarity. These wretches were brought, one

137 Rigal, ed., *Mémoires d'un Calviniste*, 82.
138 De Thou, *Histoire universelle*, vol. 4, 413.

after the other, out of the monastery where they had been put; they were tied together in fours, and they were killed by sword, dagger, or pike; the soldiers added insult to cruelty, setting fire beforehand to their private parts. After this horrible carnage, they were thrown down a deep well."[139] Religious hatred clearly intensified the perennial problem of negotiating the difficult moment when combat ends and of guaranteeing respect for the lives and bodies of the defeated. Also, atrocity begat atrocity. When word reached the Protestant commander Duras of Monluc's cruelties in Guyenne, Duras carried out reprisals at Caylus, in the Roüergue. In the words of de Thou, "Once the town and castle had been taken, sixty priests were massacred there with all the barbarity that religious hatred inspired in the two parties."[140]

The noble code of honour was a bulwark, though a fragile one, against the hatreds and fears generated by religious division and civil war. To be sure, as Benjamin Deruelle has demonstrated, that code was far from an anachronism. It remained essential to the maintenance of the social cohesion and the moral authority of the military aristocracy throughout the sixteenth century.[141] In the wars' aftermath, both Catholic and Protestant chroniclers could claim that the rules of a "good war" had generally been observed by the military aristocracy. Acknowledging that civil wars were reputed to be "the cruelest of all," Brantôme nonetheless entertained the suggestion that those in France had witnessed more chivalrous deeds even than in foreign wars.[142] Yet such claims covered comportments that were widely divergent. The Duke of Guise won praise for his generous treatment of Louis de Bourbon, Prince of Condé, the Protestant leader who was taken prisoner at the Battle of Dreux (19 December 1562), with whom he went so far as to share his bed on the night following the battle. But there was little criticism of Jean Perdriel de Bobigny for his deliberate killing of Marshal Jacques d'Albon Saint-André, who was also captured (by the opposing side) at the same battle. According to the rules of chivalry, the fate of a knight who had surrendered was entirely at the discretion of his captor. Furthermore, it was legitimate to kill a captive who was not a knight, who had failed to observe the rules of war, or who was a heretic or infidel. Bobigny's motive for the killing was generally presumed to have been personal, arising from his ill treatment in Saint-André's service. It could be justified, however, by Saint-André's violation of the rules in giving his surrender first to Bobigny and then offering it to the Prince de Porcien,

139 Ibid., 422.
140 Ibid., 416.
141 Deruelle, *De papier, de fer et de sang*, 559–66.
142 Brantôme, *Oeuvres complètes*, vol. 5, 384.

thus breaking his word to Bobigny.[143] De Thou, despite his Catholic sym-
pathies, reproached Saint-André rather than his killer. "This great captain,
having enjoyed under Henri II the most brilliant fortune, and spent his
life amid delights and luxury, at the cost of the State and of individuals [...]
finally received from the hand of God the just punishment for so many
crimes, and was killed by the man from whom it seemed he had the least
to fear; this should teach great men not to abuse their fortune, and never
give any insult or injury to their inferiors."[144] The killing of Saint-André
shows that the rules of chivalry left plenty of room for nobles to pursue
personal vendettas in the context of civil war. The conventions of a "good
war" were sufficiently flexible, when interest and opportunity coincided,
not to get in the way of a good murder. All the same, as Benjamin Deruelle
has argued, the fact that the code of chivalry could be diversely interpreted
or that it could justify very different behaviours was perhaps less important
than its function in providing a common cultural code to nobles on both
sides. In this sense, by reducing their "otherness," it might be presumed
to have served the common interest of the military nobility and to have
regulated, if not diminished, the violence of war.

A sign that the chivalric code was outmatched by the rising tide of
violence was the death of the Prince of Condé at the Battle of Jarnac
(13 March 1569). If the generous treatment the prince had received at
the Battle of Dreux was a model of honourable conduct, that which he
experienced at the Battle of Jarnac was anything but. Having been unhorsed
and wounded in the melee, Condé offered his surrender to two gentlemen,
who promised to spare his life. Subsequently, however, the guards of the
Duke of Anjou (the future King Henri III) rode up, Jean-François de
Montesquiou among them. Montesquiou promptly fired a pistol shot into
the head of the prince, killing him instantly.[145] Historian Denis Crouzet is
blunt in his judgment that the killing of the Prince of Condé was an affront
to the rules of chivalry and tantamount to an extrajudicial execution. In
his view, it marked a turning away from the chivalrous conventions that
had been respected in the early battles of the civil wars and a radicalization
of violence that prefigured the Saint Bartholomew's Day massacre
of 1572.[146] At the time, Catholic propagandists paid little attention to how
Condé died or who was responsible, instead insisting upon the significance

143 This incident is explored in depth in Deruelle, "Faire bonne guerre," 109–22. See
also Deruelle, *De papier, de fer et de sang*, 559–66, 513–57.

144 De Thou, *Histoire universelle*, vol. 4, 482–3.

145 This is the generally accepted version of Condé's death, but far from the only one.
See Boltanski, "Dans cette bataille," 123–9.

146 Crouzet, *Les guerriers de dieu*, vol. 2, 47.

DE TRISTIBVS FRANCIAE.

Liber Secundus.

1.3. *De Tristibus franciae.* The body of the Prince of Condé paraded on a donkey after the Battle of Jarnac.

of his death in eliminating the leader of the Protestant forces. A pamphlet celebrating the battle written by the Jesuit Emond Auger declared: "In this battle the head of the serpent fell and was crushed, Louis de Condé and thirty of the principal rebel chiefs and an uncertain number of common men." If only a few more heads had fallen, it continued, "France would have become peaceful once more, instead of being exhausted and reduced to extreme misery."[147] Condé's death was also exploited symbolically. The

---

147 Cited in Boltanski, "Dans cette bataille," 132.

body of the prince, stripped of its armour and any signs of noble status, was paraded on the back of a donkey, its arms and legs hanging down on either side (fig. 1.3). This posthumous degradation represented Condé as a false messiah who was guilty of usurping divinely ordained royal authority and consequently unworthy of the privileges enjoyed by loyal nobles. The bullet he received from Montesquiou's pistol was thus no more than he deserved.[148] Condé's fate demonstrated that not even the blood of a prince was adequate protection from the radicalized politics of civil war.

Although the military memoirists and chroniclers of the sixteenth century focused their writings on the fates of noblemen like the Prince of Condé, the number of nobles who died in the wars of religion, though unsustainably large, was a tiny fraction of the number of ordinary soldiers who were killed. Nicolas Froumenteau, an official who in 1581 published a remarkable accounting of the war's human and material costs, calculated that thus far the wars had cost 32,950 noble lives, but that 656,000 French and 32,600 foreign soldiers had also been killed.[149] James B. Wood has closely analyzed Froumenteau's data, showing that an average French diocese suffered eighteen more noble deaths than was normal every year of the war compared with 612 additional deaths of ordinary soldiers.[150] Military operations took an appalling toll in lives. Wood's study of the royal army indicates that at the Battle of Dreux, where 30,000 men fought, one soldier in three became a casualty and one in five was killed.[151] Sieges could be even more costly than battles in the field. The army that unsuccessfully laid siege to La Rochelle in 1573 lost two-thirds of its strength, dwindling from 22,000 men to 7,400 over six months. Eight major assaults on the citadel cost the attackers ten casualties to every one for the defenders. Officer casualties were particularly high; 73 per cent of the officer corps was killed or wounded. Wood estimates six thousand combat casualties and a similar number lost to disease and desertion.[152] Such figures suggest that the high rate of military mortality claimed by Froumenteau may not be far off the mark.

In addition to his calculation of military deaths, Froumentau provided figures for the numbers of clerics who had been killed (8,760) and of the civilians who had been massacred (26,300). He also calculated how many women and girls had been "massacred, strangled or drowned" (1,235),

148   For analysis of the multiple levels of meaning in this ritual and the ways its memory was perpetuated, see ibid., 138–9. See also Crouzet, *Les guerriers de dieu*, vol. 2, 47–8.

149   Barnaud, *Le secret des finances*, vol. 3, 378.

150   Wood, "The Impact of the Wars of Religion," 140.

151   Wood, *The King's Army*, 201.

152   Ibid., 269–71.

1.4. Jean Perrissin and Jacques Tortorel, *The Battle of Saint Denis*. 1569–70.

adding those who had been raped (12,300).[153] Although it seems likely these figures were an under-estimate, it is striking that his calculation of military deaths so greatly exceeded that of civilian deaths. For what caught the attention of people at the time and has held that of historians ever since was the massacre of civilians. This is especially apparent from the iconography of the period. Of the forty prints produced by Jean Perrissin and Jacques Tortorel "touching the Wars, Massacres and troubles occurring in France in these last years"[154] there are twenty-one scenes of battles and sieges, including six devoted to the Battle of Dreux. Yet most of these scenes, presenting distant views of dense military formations, lack the emotional impact of the five prints depicting scenes of massacres. An example of the former is the print showing the Battle of Saint-Denis (10 November 1567),

153 Barnaud, *Le secret des finances*, vol. 3, 378–9.

154 Franklin, *Les grandes scènes historiques du XVIᵉ siècle*, title page. Cited in Benedict et al., "Graphic History," 175.

in which Constable Anne de Montmorency was mortally wounded (fig. 1.4).
One struggles to identify the figure of the constable as he falls from his
horse, even though this combat was placed in the very centre of an otherwise
largely bloodless representation of the battle. In contrast, the print of the
massacre at Tours (July 1562) provides a shocking close-up of the atrocities
committed by Catholic troops who recaptured the town from Protestant
forces. Soldiers are shown in gruesome detail hanging, clubbing, shooting,
impaling, and drowning their victims. The judge of the Presidial court
hangs from a tree as he is disemboweled. Corpses litter the riverbank,
carrion to be devoured by dogs and crows (fig. 1.5).[155]

In contemporary iconography, therefore, soldiers were represented
much more memorably as the agents of death rather than as its victims.
This is not to say that the battle deaths of prominent figures were not
represented or celebrated. Montmorency was accorded a state funeral after
dying at the age of seventy-four of wounds received at the Battle of Saint-
Denis, as was Anne de Joyeuse, a favourite of Henri III who was killed at
the Battle of Coutras (20 October 1787). At Montmorency's funeral a royal
emissary spoke of the constable's death in battle as the crowning achievement of a life of service to the monarchy.[156] Yet the most compelling image
of the soldier at the time of the Wars of Religion was diabolical rather than
saintly, associated not with the ideals of self-sacrifice and service, but rather
with the crimes of murder, rape, and pillage. Images of massacres like those
produced by Perrissin and Tortorel resonated because they were entirely
believable to a public that during the Wars of Religion became only too
familiar with the depredations of soldiers. Wherever soldiers passed, crops
were ruined, livestock stolen, women violated, and men held to ransom,
tortured, and killed. In the autumn of 1587, German mercenaries left a
trail of destruction as they marched across Lorraine. Writing to the king
on 13 September, Gaspard de Schomberg informed him that the Duke of
Lorraine had the previous day counted eighteen villages that were burning.[157]
A petition sent to the king on behalf of the common people of the Vivarais
in 1579 described the "torments and cruelties" they had suffered at the
hands of "gentlemen, captains and soldiers":

Some had thick ropes and chains around their heads and were so squeezed
and tightened that their eyes [...] came out. Others were entirely buried in
manure, where they were left to rot in an unbearable stench [...] Others

155 See the discussion of this print in ibid., 193–200. On its influence, particularly on
Agrippa d'Aubigné, see Benedict, *Graphic History*, 182–3.
156 Deruelle, *De papier, de fer et de sang*, 296.
157 Moriceau, *La mémoire des croquants*, 317.

Le maffacre fait à Tours au mois de Iuillet, 1562.

La premiere de Tours s'esleue contre ceux de la Reli-   Se fait demeurer fans boyre n'y manger deux ou trois
gion, & en maffacre iufqu'au nombre de deux cens ou   iours: Puis les tue & noye. Mefmes noint attaché le
cinq cens, lesquels premierement d'vne Eglise, où on   Prefident Prony goys à vn arbre, luy arrache le cœur
les auoit mis prisonniers, au fauxbourg de la Riche.   & les entrailles.

1.5. Jean Perrissin and Jacques Tortorel, *The Massacre at Tours*. 1569–70.

were thrown alive into wells and ditches, and left there like dogs, shouting, and screaming miserably [...] Others, both men and women, were enclosed in belfries, towers, and other places, with the doors blocked up, to test, by the longest and cruelest death there is, how many days they could live without eating. Others were tied and garotted to benches and at the foot of their beds or to trees [...] And others had their feet fricasseed in grease from which some died and others were rendered impotent. Women and girls endured every sort of violence.[158]

Soldiers did not have things entirely their own way. In 1576, the foraging of German *reiters*[159] near Dijon prompted an angry response from villagers whose livestock had been stolen, "and the rising of the populace was such

---

158 Mazon, *Notes historiques*, 55–6.
159 Light cavalry, less heavily armoured than the traditional men-at-arms and relying on firepower (pistols) rather than shock (the lance).

that it fell upon some of the said *reiters* [who had] strayed, and many were killed, robbed and their horses brought into the town."[160] Peasant discontent in southeastern France erupted into rebellion in 1578–80. More widespread revolts occurred in the 1590s as resistance to the garrisons of the Catholic League expressed a nationwide revulsion against civil war.[161]

Given that soldiers were such a manifest threat to the safety and freedom of ordinary people, it is a wonder that their image as self-sacrificing servants of God, king, and country had as much currency as it did. Clearly, that image had valuable uses to the elite groups that collaborated in the governance of the country and in providing leadership to its armies. For it to mean very much beyond those elites, however, would require a complete transformation of the civil-military relations that prevailed during the wars of religion. Only the enhancement of the authority of central government, internal pacification, and the displacement of armies and warfare from the interior to the frontiers of France could bring this about. These changes, intrinsic to the emergence of the system of government known as monarchical absolutism, took place over the course of the seventeenth and eighteenth centuries. They helped to make possible the emergence of a new understanding of the soldier's death, one that was increasingly utilitarian and democratic, under the old regime.

160   Gabriel Breunot, *Journal*, ed. by Joseph Garnier (1864–1866). Cited in Moriceau, *La mémoire des croquants*, 286.
161   Heller, *Iron and Blood*, 120–3.

2

Dying for King and Country:
The Old Regime

THE DEATH OF THE CHEVALIER D'ASSAS

The death of the Chevalier d'Assas at the Battle of Clostercamp on 15 October 1760 would have remained as unknown and uncelebrated as those of the thousands of other French soldiers who died in the Seven Years War had it not been for Voltaire; or rather, had it not been for a letter the great *philosophe* received from the Chevalier de Lorri. Like d'Assas, Lorri was an officer in the Auvergne regiment, one of those that bore the brunt of the fighting at Clostercamp, a fierce battle fought in the woods and marshes of the Rhineland between an Anglo-German army commanded by the Hereditary Prince of Brunswick and a French army commanded by the Duke de Castries. "I believe it would be difficult to name a livelier and more stubborn infantry battle than that of Clostercamp," wrote the Baron de Besenval. "The battlefield was heaped with dead, without a single enemy uniform to be seen on our ground, or a single French uniform on that of the enemy."[1] In his reply to Lorri, written from Ferney on 26 October 1768, Voltaire wrote that he was so touched by the story of d'Assas that he was determined to make an addition to his history of the reign of Louis XV. "I do not wish to die," said Voltaire, "without doing justice to a man who so gallantly died for his homeland."[2] The subsequently amended passage began by declaring that although brave deeds performed by soldiers in wartime were numberless, some were "so singular, so unique in character, that it would be letting down the homeland to allow them to be forgotten."[3] Voltaire then recounted how the Chevalier d'Assas, sent during the night by the French commander to investigate gunshots that might indicate a

---

1   Besenval, *Mémoires*, vol. 1, 153.
2   Voltaire, *Oeuvres complètes*, vol. 42, *Correspondance*, 177.
3   Voltaire, *Oeuvres complètes*, vol. 15.2, 353.

surprise enemy attack, fell into the hands of enemy grenadiers. "Raising
their bayonets, they threatened to kill him if he made a sound. D'Assas,
gathering himself to strengthen his voice, shouted: 'Come to me, Auvergne!
Here are the enemy!' He fell instantly, pierced by bayonets."[4] In Roman
times, concluded Voltaire, such heroes had statues erected to honour them.
In modern times, however, they were forgotten.

Voltaire's account of the death of the Chevalier d'Assas is not the only
one. Several narratives record the recollections of soldiers who were present at the Battle of Clostercamp. Jean-Baptiste Donatien de Vimeur, Count
Rochambeau, the colonel commanding the Auvergne regiment, was himself
wounded in the battle. Rochambeau's memoirs, published in 1811, essentially confirmed Voltaire's version. According to Rochambeau, it was a
Corporal Richelieu who first raised the alarm. The Auvergne Regiment,
on the left of the French line, bore the brunt of the attack and the *chasseurs*
under Captain d'Assas were in the thick of the fighting. Warned by an
officer that he was firing on his own side, d'Assas advanced alone to confirm
that it was indeed the enemy before him. His last words before dying, said
Rochambeau, were "Fire *chasseurs*, they are the enemy!"[5] Less reliable,
perhaps, were the 1823 memoirs of Lombard de Langres, who, on the
strength of his father's testimony, attributed the heroic defiance of d'Assas
to a Sergeant Dubois. According to de Langres *père*, d'Assas himself survived
long enough to be carried back to camp where he supposedly proclaimed,
"Brothers! it was not me, it was Dubois who cried out."[6]

Rochambeau's account largely agrees with one provided in 1790 by a
chasseur named Lelarge, who accompanied Corporal Richelieu in making
a reconnaissance of the situation. According to Lelarge, it was he who first
alerted Corporal Richelieu to the presence of the enemy. He fired a musket
shot to illuminate the scene, allowing him to see the enemy grenadiers
"arrayed like a wall," their bayonets wrapped in handkerchiefs. It was the
commotion thus created by Lelarge that prompted d'Assas to investigate,
leading to his encounter with the Hanoverian pickets "posted four paces
from us." Lelarge overheard not only the exchange of words (in German)
between d'Assas and the enemy soldiers but also "the rustle of the bayonets
against his bones" as d'Assas was stabbed to death.[7] He then fired a second

4 Ibid., 354.
5 Rochambeau, *Mémoires militaires*, vol. 1, 163.
6 Lombard de Langres, *Mémoires*, 230–3.
7 [A]rchives [N]ationales, AA 62, pl. 1550, no. 47, 3–4. The testimony of Lelarge was
recorded in a letter written to the National Assembly on 26 February 1791, by a constitutional cleric named Bricoteaux. This evidence came to light in the National Archives at the
time of an exhibition on the Chevalier d'Assas to commemorate the bicentenary of his
death. See Babelon, ed., *Chevalier d'Assas*, 15–16, 18.

shot to raise the alarm. Lelarge's account was brought to the attention of the French National Assembly in 1791 by a constitutional clergyman anxious that the *chasseur* should not be denied the recognition he deserved because of his lowly status. "Thus France owes its salvation, its victory to his two shots. It is also indebted to him for the four flags that he was miraculously able to preserve on the edge of the marshes. Lelarge marked himself out according to his ability by exploits of major importance. Should he alone be without compensation because of his commonality, his modesty, his understated greatness of spirit?"[8] Interestingly, the clergyman noted only in passing the detail in Lelarge's account which revealed that the first indication of the enemy presence at Clostercamp was given by none of the military men for whom the credit has been claimed, but by a woman. It was a female camp follower from a company of German soldiers attached to the French army and that had been surprised by the enemy, said Lelarge, who first raised the alarm. This woman arrived at the French headquarters at 2 a.m., mounted on a horse galloping "with its belly to the ground," and shouting a warning in German "with all her strength."[9] Lelarge translated this for the benefit of Rochambeau, who then deployed detachments to reconnoitre, including those to which Lelarge and d'Assas belonged.

Notwithstanding these later accounts, which spread the glory to common soldiers if not as far as female camp followers, it was the aristocratic Chevalier d'Assas who was hailed as the hero of Clostercamp. In 1777, his family was awarded an official pension. He was celebrated in prose and in verse as a model of patriotic devotion and his image was reproduced in popular prints as well as on ceramic tableware. Identified as a "French Curtius," d'Assas was compared to the mythical Roman warrior, Marcus Curtius, who in 362 BC had supposedly appeased the gods and saved Rome by sacrificially hurling himself and his mount into a pit opened by an earthquake in the Roman forum (fig. 2.1). In the early stages of the French Revolution, Desilles, an officer killed seeking to prevent violence during the mutiny at Nancy in 1790, was represented as "a new d'Assas."[10] The following year a play representing the death of the Chevalier d'Assas was performed on the stage at Lyons. In the climactic scene, d'Assas took as long to die as a nineteenth-century operatic diva, repeatedly declaring, as he witnessed the battle won and the French flag raised aloft, his satisfaction that his death was the instrument of his nation's triumph: "I take to the grave your sorrow, the esteem of my country ... My death is the finest moment of my life."[11]

8 AN, AA 62, pl. 155C, no. 47, 3.
9 AN, AA 62, pl. 155C, no. 47, 3.
10 See, for example, Berton, *Le nouveau d'Assas*.
11 Dubois, *La mort du Chevalier d'Assas*, 48.

LE CURTIUS FRANÇAIS,ou LA MORT DU CH.ᴱ.ᴿ D'ASSAS.

À l'honneur français.

A Paris chez le Noir, Mᵈ Fourniſleur du Cabinet des Eſtampes du Roi, demeurant au Louvre & rue du Coq S.Honoré.

2.1. J.B. Simonet, *The French Curtius, or the Death of the Chevalier d'Assas.* 1781.

Historians have acknowledged the importance of the posthumous cult celebrating the Chevalier d'Assas. Most importantly, André Corvisier emphasized its role in elaborating a new model of military death: one which by its emphasis upon the anonymous, unheralded self-sacrifice of the ordinary soldier contrasted with the traditional model of medieval chivalry, wherein the noble warrior's death on the battlefield represented the apogee of a glorious career. Corvisier contrasted the heroism of the Chevalier d'Assas (and possibly of Sergeant Dubois) with that of the Chevalier Bayard, which had occurred over two centuries earlier: "The hero is no longer one who has accomplished deeds of prowess, but one who has given his life, with or without fame, to defend his homeland […] It is no longer a question of death as the culmination of a brilliant career, but death as an exemplary sacrifice."[12] More recent historians have endorsed Corvisier's argument. Arnaud Guinier, writing of the eighteenth-century French army, emphasizes that the death of the Chevalier d'Assas, representing "the incarnation of the passage from an heroic model to a sacrificial ideal of death in battle," embodied the principle, increasingly important in the second half of the eighteenth century, that both life and personal glory should be given up for the sake not only of the regiment, but also of the nation.[13] Hervé Drévillon, considering the French officer corps of the seventeenth century, writes that "the evolution underlined by André Corvisier is essential. The ethic of sacrifice constituted a fundamental vector for the adaptation of the nobility to the culture of service."[14] Both Guinier and Drévillon support the view, therefore, that the representations of the death of the Chevalier d'Assas reflected important transformations in the military culture of old-regime France. Indeed, the contrasting representations of the death of the Chevalier d'Assas and of the Chevalier Bayard reflect important changes in war, society, and military culture in early modern France. Above all, they demonstrate how the ideal of aristocratic honour was adapted to the needs of the absolutist state, to the disciplined armed forces of the military revolution, and to the ever more lethal battlefields of the old regime. Nevertheless, even before the French Revolution helped to bring into the light "subaltern heroes" such as Lelarge or Corporal Richelieu, the idea was beginning to gain currency that neither honour nor sacrifice were the preserves of the aristocracy.

CHANGES IN WARFARE

Between the sixteenth and eighteenth centuries, momentous changes occurred in war and society that exposed the tensions in the discourse of honour and ultimately shifted its emphasis from glory to sacrifice. The elaboration of the absolutist state was fundamental to this change, as was the military revolution that accompanied it, as both cause and effect. In the seventeenth century, the French army was transformed from an aggregate of temporary, privately raised companies into a permanent, disciplined, hierarchical, state-commissioned force. Modern firearms made battle progressively more lethal, enhancing the role of the infantry and shifting the officer's role away from the impulsive display of heroism toward rational command and control. The abandonment of the pike and the adoption of the flintlock musket and socket bayonet at the beginning of the

12 Corvisier, "La mort du soldat," 387.
13 Guinier, *L'honneur du soldat*, 322.
14 Drévillon, *L'impôt du sang*, 338.

eighteenth century were particularly important in making battles more deadly and in placing a premium on discipline and drill. An important sign of these changes, noted by Arnaud Guinier, is that between the War of the Austrian Succession and the Seven Years War French officers ceased to take their place on the battlefield in front of their men, but instead stood behind them, performing surveillance rather than setting an example.[15] The Baron de Besenval recorded that at Clostercamp the resolve of the inexperienced Normandy regiment had to be bolstered by staff officers, aides-de-camp, and volunteers – "in a word, everybody who was on horseback" – forming a barrier to prevent them from retreating.[16] This is not to say that officers ceased to pay the "blood tax." Besenval had his horse killed under him at Clostercamp and Rochambeau noted that *all* the officers of *chasseurs* and grenadiers from the Auvergne regiment were either killed or wounded. The Chevalier d'Assas had plenty of company. Total casualties from the regiment were 58 officers and over 800 men.[17] Besenval, who took leadership of several battalions of Auvergne infantry after losing his horse, said he was "horrified by how few men were still with the colours." He paid tribute to the regiment "which, without question, is one of the bravest regiments in the king's service."[18] Overall, the French army sustained losses of 14 per cent in the battle, making it one of the harder-fought engagements involving that army in the Seven Years War.[19]

The French army in which the Chevalier d'Assas served at Clostercamp was very different from those in which the Chevalier Bayard had fought during the wars for Italy. The most important changes were organizational and took place over the course of the seventeenth century, during the reigns of Louis XIII and Louis XIV. The fundamental change was a transition from the "aggregate contract" to the "state commission" army. The "aggregate contract" army was a function of the system of military entrepreneurship that had developed during the Renaissance and culminated during the Thirty Years War. It provided rulers with the convenience of ready-made military forces through the means of independent mercenary captains and powerful nobles who contracted to raise, equip, supply, and

15 Guinier, *L'honneur du soldat*, 78.
16 Besenval, *Mémoires*, vol. 1, 148.
17 Rochambeau, *Mémoires militaires*, 162.
18 Besenval, *Mémoires*, vol. 1, 149.
19 Bodart, *Losses of Life*, 101. Bodart interpreted the relatively low casualty figures for the French army in the battles it fought in the Seven Years War as a function of the poor quality of that army: "with rare exceptions, the troops, under poor leaders, fought badly, both courage and fighting spirit as well as discipline leaving much to be desired; the small relative losses in the few victories and more frequent defeats bear witness to the weak resistance of the French soldiery."

manage those forces, many of whom were foreign in origin (hence the large numbers of Swiss and German heavy infantry fighting with or against the French armies during the Italian Wars of the sixteenth century). Such forces were typically employed only for specific campaigns and could therefore be disbanded in peacetime. During the war with Spain from 1635 to 1659, however, Louis XIII began the transition toward the "state commission" army, whereby French officers were commissioned to raise semi-permanent forces that were equipped, uniformed, and disciplined in accordance with government directives and, most importantly, whose loyalty was to the king rather than to a mercenary captain. Although the cost was great and although it relied, through the purchase system, upon the willingness of French officers to contribute to the upkeep of their regiments from their own pockets, the state commission army provided the basis for a politically reliable standing army that significantly enhanced state power both at home and abroad.[20]

The change in army structure facilitated the extension and strengthening of royal administrative control. Under the direction of the Secretaries of State for War, Michel le Tellier and his son, Louvois, who between them continuously occupied the position from 1643 to 1691, intendants were empowered to oversee the conduct of officers and *commissaires de guerre*, imposing central authority and sanctioning abuses. Royal authority over the appointment of officers was asserted, particularly through the creation of non-venal ranks, such as lieutenant-colonel and major. The High Command was brought into line as aristocratic officers were compelled to accept a hierarchical chain of command based increasingly on professional merit and seniority rather than on social rank or status. Most famously, in 1672 Louis XIV made an example of three marshals who challenged their subordination in the table of ranks to Marshal-General Turenne, compelling them each to serve for fifteen days as lieutenants-general directly under Turenne's command.[21] The enhancement of the army's administration resulted in the adoption of a common uniform in 1670, the establishment of a veteran's hospital in 1674 – the famous Hôtel des Invalides – and development of a system of *étapes*, or network of magazines, to bring order to the army's supply.[22]

Organizational and administrative change was accompanied by a significant growth in the army's size. From a maximum size of 50–60,000 men in the sixteenth century, the French army progressively grew to a theoretical strength of 420,000 (actual numbers were probably closer to 340,000)

20 Lynn, *Giant of the Grand Siècle*, 6–9.
21 Martin, "The Army of Louis XIV," 118. See also Rowlands, *The Dynastic State*, 298–9.
22 Martin, "The Army of Louis XIV," 116 and 119.

by the end of the seventeenth. This wartime strength fell back to 140,000–145,000 following the end of the Nine Years War (1688–97). The army's numbers rose again during the War of the Spanish Succession (1701–14) to reach a theoretical peak of 380,000 men. Peacetime and wartime strengths in the eighteenth century generally remained on a par with those achieved at the height of the reign of Louis XIV.[23]

Changes in the size and structure of armies were accompanied by equally significant changes in military technology and in the conduct of war. Two changes that were of particular importance were the development of modern military fortifications based on the angled bastion – the *trace italienne* – and the refinement of early modern firearms, culminating in the weapon that would be standard for infantry throughout the eighteenth century: the flintlock musket with socket bayonet. More accurately referred to as a *fusil*, the flintlock musket was distinguished from its predecessor, the matchlock, by its firing mechanism. Instead of using a lighted match to ignite the powder in the priming pan, the flintlock depended upon sparks from a flint striking against a metal plate. The significance of this change was that it made operation of the weapon safer and simpler, facilitating a faster rate of fire, perhaps double that of the matchlock. The introduction of iron ramrods and paper cartridges in the eighteenth century were additional improvements that enabled a trained infantryman, in ideal conditions, to fire as many as five shots a minute.[24] The invention of the socket bayonet in the late 1680s by Vauban also accelerated the decline of the pike, so that ultimately most infantrymen were uniformly equipped with firearms. Despite these technological changes, smoothbore muskets remained notoriously inaccurate. Eighteenth-century experiments, confirmed by more recent tests, indicated that at a range of 75 metres only 60 per cent of shots might be expected to hit a target the size of an enemy battalion; at 300 metres, the proportion dropped to 20 per cent.[25] Nevertheless, concentrated platoon fire at short range could have a devastating effect, as was demonstrated at the Battle of Fontenoy (1745). The incident from the battle celebrated by Voltaire, when the Count d'Auteroches doffed his hat and invited the English Guards to fire first, is often cited as an example of the civility that restrained warfare in the eighteenth century. As Hervé Drévillon points out, however, the officer's gesture was a death sentence for the men in the front rank of the French line. According to Voltaire, 263 men died and 674 were wounded in the

23 Lynn, *Giant of the Grand Siècle*, 55.
24 Ibid., 458–64. See also: Hall, *Weapons and Warfare*, 149; Black, *European Warfare, 1660–1815*, 39.
25 Hall, *Weapons and Warfare*, 139–40.

ensuing fusillade, delivered in rolling volleys by successive platoons in ranks of four from a range of only thirty paces.[26] The increased effectiveness of infantry firepower and the commensurately more lethal battlefield may paradoxically have limited wars by making at least some generals more concerned to preserve their armies through a cautious strategy than to risk their destruction in battlefield encounters. The frequency of battles was further limited by the proliferation of fortresses based on the *trace italienne*. Strategically placed fortifications impeded the mobility of armies and compelled them to undertake lengthy siege operations. There were bloody and decisive battles in the eighteenth century, but campaigns tended to be dominated by sieges as well as by inconclusive marches and counter-marches.[27] All the same, it should not be assumed that sieges were necessarily a softer option than field battles. The English force that captured Lille in 1708 did so only at the cost of 14,000 casualties.[28] Charles-Étienne Bernos was a soldier in the French army that besieged Berg-Op-Zoom in 1747. He later wrote that the French army sustained 15,000 casualties in capturing the town, 544 of them belonging to his own regiment.[29] Bernos himself had a narrow escape when he was excused duty in a detail that was blown up by an enemy counter-mine. Only a sergeant and a drummer were not buried alive by the explosion. "We dug out all those who perished in the mine," wrote Bernos. "They were unrecognizable, burned and black like negroes."[30]

Given the enhanced firepower of eighteenth-century armies, most battlefield wounds were caused by firearms. André Corvisier's analysis of two surveys from the Invalides indicates that in 1715–16, 71.4 per cent of wounds were caused by gunshots, 10 per cent by artillery, 15.8 per cent by swords, 1.5 per cent by bayonets. In 1762, 68.8 per cent were caused by gunshots, 13.4 per cent by artillery, 14.7 per cent by swords, and 13.4 per cent by bayonets. In addition to revealing that most wounds were caused by firearms, the figures also show small increases over time in

26 Drévillon, *L'individu et la guerre*, 131–2; Voltaire, *Précis du siècle de Louis XV*, in *Oeuvres complètes*, vol. 15.2, 240. The figures are provided by Drévillon. My calculation (244 dead and 737 wounded), based on Voltaire's rather confusing figures, is slightly at odds with that of Drévillon. Jean-Pierre Bois cites a contemporary source from the Archives de Guerre that indicates the regiment suffered ninety-eight dead (two of whom were officers) and 313 wounded. Jean-Pierre Bois, *Fontenoy 1745*, 89, 105. Whatever the exact numbers, they are, as Drévillon says, "terrifying."

27 For contrasting perspectives concerning the decisiveness of eighteenth-century warfare, see Black, *European Warfare, 1660–1815*, 67–86, and Weigley, *The Age of Battles*, xi–xiii.

28 Black, *European Warfare, 1660–1815*, 112.

29 Bernos, "Souvenirs de campagne," 757.

30 Ibid., 754.

wounds caused by artillery and bayonets. The figures also reveal a decline in the kinds of wounds resulting from siege warfare: only 8 soldiers admitted to the Invalides in 1762 had been wounded or buried by mines, as opposed to 34 in 1715–16. A further point of interest is that analysis of the locations on the body where the wounds were received indicates that although they were more or less equally distributed between the left and right sides of the body in 1715–16, by 1762 they were significantly more concentrated on the left side. The change would seem to reflect the increased importance of close-order tactics, whereby the infantryman turned his right side away from the enemy to aim and fire his musket, leaving his left side exposed to enemy fire.[31]

Although changes in technology and tactics significantly increased the potential lethality of battles in the eighteenth century, soldiers were still far more likely to die of disease than of wounds sustained in combat. Of the 600,000 casualties sustained by the French army in the eighteenth century, 54 per cent succumbed to illness, 32 per cent were wounded, and 14 per cent were killed in action or died from wounds received in battle.[32] A study of mortality in the French infantry from 1716 to 1748 indicates that average mortality was 19.13 per 1,000 over seventeen years of peace and 31.79 per 1,000 over sixteen years of war. In other words, for every hundred soldiers who served, nearly two a year might be expected to die in time of peace, rising to three in time of war.[33] Furthermore, the wartime increase in mortality was not necessarily a result of combat. It is notable that during years of war mortality doubled or tripled in the winter months of December and January, when armies generally went into winter quarters. Normally, in time of war May was the month of peak mortality, reflecting the coincidence of the arrival of springtime epidemics and the opening of the campaigning season. The increase of winter mortality in wartime is likely explained by uncomfortable winter quarters on enemy soil and the attendant privations.[34] Charles-Étienne Bernos described the epidemic that ravaged the French garrison besieged at Egra (now Cheb) in Bohemia in 1742. He did not precisely identify the disease, saying only that it turned the victims' tongues and gums black and that only the strongest constitutions recovered. Two-thirds of those admitted to hospital died within three days, said Bernos, who attributed his own survival to the ministrations of

31 Corvisier, *L'armée française*, vol. 2, 673–81.
32 Lucenet, *Médecine, chirugie et armée*, 99.
33 Lucenet, "La mortalité dans l'infanterie," 399.
34 Ibid., 403.

a surgeon's aide who recognized and took pity on him.[35] The vulnerability of soldiers to disease was magnified in colonial theatres of war. In the American Revolutionary War, eight soldiers died of disease for every one who died of wounds.[36]

Military deaths need to be considered in relation to those of civilians. The eighteenth century was relatively benign for the French population, which enjoyed a period of steady growth after the crisis years that marked the final decades of the reign of Louis XIV. The famine years of 1693–94 had resulted in 2.8 million deaths in a population of only twenty million, a mortality comparable to that experienced by France during the Great War, when the population was twice as large![37] The harsh winter of 1709 brought another demographic disaster in its wake. But with the Sun King's passing things began to improve. Effective administrative measures ensured that the plague's visitation to Marseille, which killed 40,000–50,000 of the city's residents in 1720, was its last great incursion on French territory. The following decades were important epidemiological and demographic turning points. Infectious diseases became less prevalent, while chronic illnesses came to the fore. Mortality and fertility rates went from high to low.[38] Life expectancy steadily improved, from 23.8 years at birth for men in 1740–49 to 27.5 years in 1780–89.[39] The population of France grew by a third over the course of the eighteenth century, from 21.5 million in 1700 to 28.6 million in 1790.[40] Nevertheless, despite the retreat of the plague, the century still experienced significant outbreaks of epidemic disease, especially typhoid, which afflicted civilians and soldiers alike. In 1748, the final year of the War of the Austrian Succession, mortality in the French infantry rose to 45.88 per 1,000, a figure "almost identical" to the mortality rate for the civilian population. The 4,097 infantrymen who were listed on the troop registers as having died in that year were a tiny percentage of the total of 925,000 people who are estimated to have died in the kingdom as a whole.[41] Undoubtedly, the convergence in the patterns of military and civilian mortality, as well as the relatively small

35 Bernos, "Souvenirs de campagne," 672. The disease was probably typhus, which ravaged the French army in central Europe from 1741–43. At the end of January 1743, a quarter of the army of Marshal de Belle-Isle was seriously ill. See Lucenet, *Médecine, chirugie et armée*, 114.

36 Pichichero, *The Military Enlightenment*, 122.

37 Brockliss and Jones, *The Medical World*, 358.

38 Ibid., 356–9.

39 Dupâquier, *Histoire de la population française*, vol. 2: *De la Renaissance à 1789*, 236. The corresponding age expectancies for women were 25.7 and 28 1.

40 Ibid., 64–5.

41 Lucenet, "La mortalité dans l'infanterie," 400.

proportion of military deaths, meant that the psychological impact of the soldier's death was relatively minor in comparison with later periods, when those patterns and proportions underwent major transformations.

WAR AND SOCIETY

The changes to the organization, management, and discipline of armies over the course of the seventeenth century significantly changed the relationship between soldiers and civilians. The initial expansion of the army in the seventeenth century was experienced by French society as an extremely painful process. The tripling of the burden of taxes to meet the needs of the expanding army during the war with Spain (1635–59) caused hardship especially to the peasantry, prompting a wave of peasant uprisings. Peasant discontent was exacerbated by the physical presence of soldiers. Poorly paid and inadequately supplied by the emergent absolutist state, soldiers lived at the expense of local populations. They took what they wanted, whether it was food, wood, livestock, or women, with scant regard for local sensibilities. Villagers saw little difference between the behaviour of invading Spanish soldiers and that of French soldiers who were just passing through. The passage of troops in the king's service, wrote an official from the Auvergne in 1636, was "the plague and the poison that will invade and destroy this state if it is not promptly stopped." The disorder was so frightful, he continued, "that all the pirates and the scum of the seas from all the corners of the earth could hardly commit such excesses, no company either on horse or on foot passing without taking a heavy payment and inflicting all sorts of violence, sackings, and ransoms."[42] At times, the violence of soldiers toward civilians was systematic, rather than incidental, as troops were billeted on recalcitrant taxpayers to enforce payment or, as in the case of the infamous *dragonnades* after 1685, to enforce religious conformity. They were also employed, of course, to suppress the major uprisings such as those of the Croquants in the west and southwest of France in 1636–37 and 1643–45. The Duke de la Valette, reporting in 1630 to Cardinal Richelieu on the defeat of Croquant rebels in the town of Eymet, in Périgord, claimed that his men had killed 14,000 rebels.[43] Although rebels sometimes benefited from the support and leadership of former soldiers, they were generally no match for regular forces. The cream of the royal army, including six hundred musketeers under the command of d'Artagnan, was sent to the Vivarais in 1670 to suppress the rising known

42 Porchnev, *Les soulèvements populaires*, 59.
43 Ibid., 88.

2.2. Jacques Callot, *Peasants Take Revenge on Soldiers*. 1633. From the series The Miseries of War.

as Roure's Revolt. At the "Battle" of Villedieu, 112 rebels were killed and 120 taken prisoner; the king's army suffered only two casualties. "We killed as many as we wanted," recalled the Count d'Aligny.[44] The soldiers were not always so dominant. In Périgord, Pierre Greleti waged a successful partisan war against royal troops for several years until in 1641 he negotiated an amnesty for himself and his two hundred followers in return for their promise to serve in the royal army.[45] The fury of peasants who acquired the opportunity to take their revenge on soldiers is reflected in one of Jacques Callot's series of prints, dating from 1633, depicting *The Miseries and Misfortunes of War*. The print depicts peasants in the process of slaughtering a detachment of soldiers whom they have ambushed. As its caption makes clear, the peasants were not content with simply killing the soldiers, which they accomplished using various weapons, including agricultural implements (a raised flail is prominent in the centre of the image). They also stripped the clothes from the soldiers' bodies to compensate for their stolen property (fig. 2.2).

By the eighteenth century, the vexed relationship between soldiers and civilians had significantly improved. The expansion of the military bureaucracy under Louis XIV was largely responsible for this. The establishment of the Hôtel des Invalides and the eventual inscription of 30,000 veterans

44   Cited in Ribon, *D'Artagnan en Ardèche*, 210.
45   Porchnev, *Les soulèvements populaires*, 94–6.

on its rosters was a measure calculated to eliminate the threat to public order that former soldiers represented. The setting up of hospitals for wounded and veteran soldiers was the military counterpart of the "great enclosure" of the late seventeenth century whereby carceral institutions were established to clear the streets of beggars, the insane, and other perceived threats to good order.[46] Furthermore, beginning in the 1690s, soldiers themselves were increasingly confined to barracks instead of billeted on local populations. Barracks provided a means to help prevent desertion and to discipline the troops as well as to protect civilian populations. By the middle of the eighteenth century, barracks existed in over three hundred towns.[47] After 1653, the great era of civil conflict and peasant rebellions came to an end. Domestic peace reduced the friction between soldiers and civilians, as did the fact that most of the wars in which France was subsequently involved in the eighteenth century were fought on foreign soil. As their relationship became less antagonistic and as civil conflict diminished, civilians began to see soldiers in a more sympathetic light. For the first time, it became plausible to see the soldier as a defender or protector rather than as a menace.[48] The grim imagery of civil–military relations represented by Callot's prints gave way to the benign imagery of Watteau. In prints like *The Company's Escort* Watteau represented bucolic scenes of soldiers and their female camp-followers peacefully enjoying the countryside (fig. 2.3).[49] In the theatre, too, as Christy Pichichero has shown, in the eighteenth century soldiers began to be depicted as sympathetic characters possessed of domestic as well as of military virtues, ready not just to defend their homeland but also to help their civilian hosts sort out their everyday troubles. The unwarlike images of soldiers presented in popular plays such as Louis Anseaume's *The Militiaman* (1762), in which a sergeant cleverly defends the love interest of his superior officer against third-party machinations, seem far removed from images of the soldier's

---

46 A royal decree of 1708 established military hospitals in fifty-one French cities, providing care to soldiers that, in the eighteenth century, was superior to that provided in hospitals for the general population. Vess, *Medical Revolution in France*, 24. On this theme see Michel Foucault, *Discipline and Punish*.

47 Colin Jones, "The Military Revolution," 161–2. On the development of a more positive image for soldiers in the eighteenth century, see also Jean-Paul Bertaud, "Military Virility," 306; and Corvisier, "Les héros subalternes."

48 Ibid., 162.

49 On Watteau's images of soldiers see Wile, *Watteau's Soldiers*. See also Pichichero, "Le soldat sensible."

2.3. Jean-Antoine Watteau, *The Company's Escort.*

death, but they helped to make it possible to imagine that death in a new way.[50] So long as it was civilian lives and property that were sacrificed to the needs of the army and so long as soldiers were perceived to be rapacious brigands, there could be little place for representations exalting the soldier's sacrifice. Typically, this was not a theme of official art under the old regime. Battle paintings, such as those produced by Adam Frans van der Meulen for Louis XIV, focused on the king and his senior officers in the foreground, with the men they commanded arrayed in static lines in the distance and no obvious spilling of blood.[51] A typical example is a painting in Apsley House depicting Louis XIV at a siege (fig. 2.4). Shifting the emphasis in artistic representations of battle to the sacrifice of the ordinary soldier depended upon a re-evaluation of that soldier's worth to society and even upon a new appreciation of him as a thinking, feeling human being.

50 On eighteenth-century theatrical representations of soldiers, see Pichichero, *The Military Enlightenment*, 167–72.

51 Mainz, "Deflecting the Fire," 239.

2.4. *Louis XIV at a Siege.* Painting in Apsley House, London.

HONOUR REDEFINED

As warfare and civil–military relations changed, heroic deeds, especially heroic deaths, lost a little of their lustre. A new ethic was needed to match the professionalism, discipline, and self-control that were required of the modern soldier. Some historians argue that this ethic was provided by the growing vogue for neo-stoicism. Joël Cornette notes a revival of interest in the works of Seneca and Epictetus as well as the influence of these neo-stoic philosophers on modern authors such as Justus Lipsius and Pierre Charron. In his treatise on wisdom, first published in 1601, Charron built upon the ideas of Justus Lipsius to provide a neo-stoic definition of the ideal soldier: one who was master of his emotions and impulses, considered in his actions, resolute in combat, controlled in victory, philosophical in defeat.[52] The ideal general was "provident, well advised, calm, cool, and

52 Charron, *De la sagesse*, 538–44. See also Cornette, *Le roi de guerre*, 61–3. On neo-stoicism, see, Oestreich, *Neostoicism*.

collected, far from all temerity and precipitation."[53] Battle was to be risked only in the most favourable circumstances, victory never pushed to the point where it inspired desperation in the enemy. As for soldiers, they must fear their officers more than the enemy. Their valour was to be cultivated through military exercises, the hard work of digging trenches, building barricades, and carrying heavy loads, as well as by maintaining good order whether in camp or on the march. Good discipline also required soldiers to possess the virtues of continence, modesty, and abstinence, which were to be encouraged through recognition and honours for the good, "severe punishment" for the bad. Above all, they were to be obedient, so that the general's orders were followed without question.[54] Hervé Drévillon qualifies this emphasis on neo-stoicism, arguing that early modern military thinkers were eclectic in their reading of the ancients and were as likely to draw their inspiration from Polybius, Caesar, Plutarch, or Livy as from Seneca or Epictetus. Whatever the inspiration, the results were a "civic militarism" that emphasized, in addition to courage, the virtues of wisdom, moderation, discipline, and magnanimity.[55]

Increasingly, the "fine death" that was the culminating glory of the warrior began to draw criticism. Charron may have concluded his description of the ideal soldier by writing "it is never forbidden to die on the bed of honour, which is better than to live in dishonour,"[56] but a growing number of writers were inclined to view the eagerness of young men needlessly to expose their lives as foolhardy. We have already noted the beginning of this trend by the end of the sixteenth century. In 1592 Bernard de Nogaret, Marquis de la Valette, was criticized for recklessly exposing himself to enemy fire while siting his artillery.[57] Two years later, it was Henri IV himself who deplored the death at the siege of Laon of d'Anne d'Anglure, seigneur of Givry, declaring that "his death was not at all necessary for the task I had given him."[58] In the seventeenth century, the memoirs of Montglat and de Pontis cast further discredit on the idea of "a fine death."[59] De Pontis, for example, recounted an incident from the siege of Montauban in 1621, when he had entrusted a soldier by the name of Montably with a perilous mission to hurl barrels packed with gunpowder and other flammable materials at an enemy position. De Pontis's final injunction was that

---

53 Charron, *De la sagesse*, 538.
54 Ibid., 535–7.
55 Drévillon, *L'impôt du sang*, 324–6.
56 Charron, *De la sagesse*, 544. See also Cornette, *Le roi de guerre*, 63.
57 Germa-Romann, *Du "bel mourir,"* 288–9.
58 Ibid., 289.
59 Ibid., 290–1.

Montably was to retire immediately after executing his mission, leaving the final assault to others. "If he had believed me I would have been entirely satisfied by this affair," wrote de Pontis, "but this young man, more generous than obedient, could not help himself, after the successful execution of his orders, from charging the enemy sword in hand. He received a musket shot which killed him on the spot, which caused me significant displeasure amidst the joy that we felt to have succeeded so completely in our enterprise."[60]

During the reign of Louis XIV royal disapproval intensified for officers who unnecessarily put their lives at risk. In his guide for the conduct of officers, *La conduite de Mars*, Courtilz de Sandras wrote approvingly of the king's insistence that cavalry officers wear cuirasses: "because everyone knows, valour is an effect of wisdom, and temerity an effect of brutishness; hence one would have to be more brutish than all the beasts put together, to want to expose oneself to a certain death and which is of no use to anyone when one has the means to avert it."[61] The royal campaign against recklessness seems to have had an effect. Guy Rowlands notes that the last time nobles collectively put their personal glory ahead of their duty to the king was at the crossing of the Rhine in 1672, when several of them, including the young Duke de Longueville, provoked Louis's displeasure by getting themselves killed.[62] All the same, the official *Gazette de France* gave no hint of that displeasure in its report of the engagement, insisting instead that "the bellicose comportment" of Longueville had hastened the enemy defeat by the inspiration it gave to the officers and men of the French army, with the effect that "none withheld from paying in his person, and from completely fulfilling his duty, after such a powerful example."[63] The problem of noble temerity persisted, therefore, as Vauban's condemnation of the unnecessary casualties suffered during the siege of Maestricht in 1673 indicates. "I don't know whether to refer to the aptitude we have for clumsily showing ourselves, and needlessly placing ourselves uncovered outside the trenches, as ostentation, vanity, or sloth. But I know that this negligence or this vanity (however you want to call it) cost over a hundred men during

60 Pontis, *Mémoires*, 298.
61 Courtilz de Sandras, *La conduite de Mars*, 202.
62 Rowlands, *The Dynastic State*, 9. Voltaire wrote disparagingly of this incident in his *Siècle de Louis XIV*. "Nobody would have been killed on that day," he wrote, "without the imprudence of the young Duke de Longueville." The enemy had been ready to surrender, claimed Voltaire, until the duke, "his head filled with wine fumes," killed an officer with a pistol shot, thereby prompting the Dutch infantry to take up their arms. Longueville was killed by the subsequent volley of fire. Voltaire, *Siècle de Louis XIV*, vol. 1, 208. See also Quarré d'Aligny, *Mémoire*, 27–8.
63 *Gazette de France*, 22 June 1672.

the siege, who carelessly got themselves killed or wounded for no reason. This is an original sin the French will never correct in themselves, unless God, who is all powerful, reforms the whole species."[64] After the siege of Maestricht changes were made to the composition of the elite troops of the Royal Household – which included the famous companies of musketeers – that were calculated to economize on the spilling of noble blood. In 1676 a new company of horse grenadiers was formed. Unlike the King's musketeers, which filled their ranks with nobles, the new formation was recruited by selecting commoners from the grenadier companies of the regular army. Specialists in siege warfare with a reputation for not taking prisoners, the horse grenadiers took on the role of assault troops to prepare the way for the musketeers.[65] At the siege of Namur in 1692, where the attack was led by the horse grenadiers, the officer commanding the First Company of Musketeers sought to cool the ardour of his men by threatening summary execution for any who advanced beyond him on the field of battle. According to a contemporary account, the horse grenadiers attacked "with such impetuosity and such great ardour that nothing could resist them, killing all who fell beneath their hands," and leaving very few alive to receive quarter from the musketeers.[66]

The most famous of the French soldiers who fell at Maestricht in 1673 was Charles de Batz-Castelmore, Count d'Artagnan, the musketeer whose exploits later inspired the romances of Alexandre Dumas. D'Artagnan was killed in fierce fighting for control of an outlying fortification (a *demi-lune*) covering the Porte de Tongres, the location of the decisive, and ultimately successful, French attack. D'Artagnan's death was certainly represented as glorious by his contemporaries, one of whom famously declared that "D'Artagnan and Glory have the same coffin,"[67] and it did at least have the merit of helping to prepare the French victory. "Our advantage would have been one of the happiest, as well as the most glorious," reported the *Gazette de France*, "if Monsieur d'Artagnan, who played such an important part, had not been killed there by a musket shot to the throat."[68] But even d'Artagnan's admirers admitted he lacked prudence. "Few people would have taken a decision as hazardous as the one he took," commented Count Quarré d'Aligny, an officer of musketeers who was himself severely wounded

64 Vauban, *Journal du siège de Maëstricht*, cited in Drévillon, *Batailles*, 162; see also Pujo, *Vauban*, 68.

65 Masson, *Les Mousquetaires*, 84–92.

66 Lamoral, *Abrégé chronologique*, vol. 2, 303.

67 Saint-Blaise, *Journal du siège et de la prise de Maestricht*. Cited in Courtilz de Sandras, *Mémoires de Charles de Batz-Castelmore Comte d'Artagnan*, 24.

68 *Gazette de France*, 1 July 1673.

in the attack and who said of d'Artagnan's death, "if one died of sorrow, I would in truth be dead." While acknowledging that many courtiers saw d'Artagnan's action as manifesting "the recklessness of a young man," d'Aligny declared that the saving grace of d'Artagnan's suicidal attack – in which 120 officers, eighty musketeers and seven hundred other soldiers were also killed or wounded – was that "the great valour of M. d'Artagnan and of the brave musketeers won Maestricht for the king."[69] Hervé Drévillon aptly comments on how this ambivalent response to the death of d'Artagnan reflected changing values: "The sacrifice of d'Artagnan thus abandoned the register of the 'fine death' where military deeds existed within a self-referential system of values, whereby an heroic action was sufficient unto itself, whatever the outcome of the battle or war. To be appreciated, acts of bravery had henceforth to be useful."[70] True honour might, according to this new system of values, require a form of self-denial that was alien to the traditions of chivalry: the sacrifice of glory for the sake of service. To be truly honourable, wrote Charron, an action had to satisfy three require-ments: it had to overcome danger, difficulty, or suffering; it had to be useful to the public; and it had to be accomplished voluntarily, without obligation. The greatest honour, he said, was attached to those actions that brought the least personal profit or recognition. "It is much more honorable," he wrote, citing Cato, "for people to ask why a statue has not been raised to me, than for them to ask why one has."[71] In the eighteenth century, this emphasis upon selfless devotion to the public cause was underlined by distinguishing between the "hero" and the "great man," the former "moti-vated by personal ambition," the latter by only the purest devotion to "the glory of his master and the wellbeing of the *patrie.*"[72] Writing in 1762, Louis Basset de la Marelle explicitly distinguished between the "warrior hero" and the "patriot hero."[73] Although Saint-Lambert, who wrote the *Encyclopédie*'s entry on Honour, believed that Glory and Honour were closely connected – "wherever glory is prized, there is honour" – he also insisted

. 69 Quarré d'Aligny, *Mémoire*, 56–7. Cited in Petitfils, *Le véritable d'Artagnan*, 263; Drévillon, *Batailles*, 157–63.

70 Drévillon, *Batailles*, 163–4.

71 Charron, *De la sagesse*, 300.

72 Turpin de Crissé, *Amusements philosophiques et littéraires de deux amis* (Paris: Prault, 1754). Cited in Pichichero, *The Military Enlightenment*, 161. Pichichero shows that the pro-ponents of the eighteenth-century military enlightenmnent articulated a model of heroism that, combining the traits of the "hero" and the "great man," "united warrior virtues with moral and political virtues." Ibid., 162.

73 Louis Basset de la Marelle, *La différence du patriotisme national chez les François et les Anglais* (Lyon: Chez Aimé Delaroche, 1762). Cited in ibid., 162.

that it was up to rulers to ensure that "the idea of honour and virtue is connected to the observation of all the laws; that the warrior who lacks discipline is as dishonoured as one who flees from the enemy."[74]

The military heroes from the reign of Louis XIV were increasingly celebrated as models of service. Praise was given even to officers whose careers were unmarked by any of the demonstrations of impetuosity and courage that were the traditional mark of the warrior. Marshals Fabert and Catinat were praised instead for their constancy in the king's service, for their self-restraint, and for their moderation.[75] They were hailed not for spilling blood but for economizing on it. Nicolas Rémond des Cours described Catinat's victories in the War of the League of Augsburg as "a new kind of triumph" in which "he sapped the strength of those whose blood he disdained," allowing the enemy to retreat unmolested to their winter quarters.[76] Heroes of the traditional type, whose courage was deemed to know no limits, continued to receive praise. That praise was, however, increasingly qualified. Jean de Gassion, whose leadership of the French cavalry at the Battle of Rocroi helped to achieve victory at the very outset of the Sun King's reign, was an archetypal warrior hero, nicknamed *La Guerre* by Cardinal Richelieu because of his uncompromising dedication to combat.[77] Théophraste Renaudout, who wrote an obituary in 1647 for the official newspaper, the *Gazette de France*, praised Gassion for his prompt obedience to orders, as well as for "his valour and his prudence, neither of which ever abandoned the other, save that the former always came first."[78] While citing with approval Gassion's equanimity in the face of death – he quoted him as saying "It profits me either to live or die, provided it is in the service of God and the king" – Renaudot nonetheless connected it to the "vice" of Gassion's Protestant upbringing and his belief in predestination.[79] He also indicated that Gassion unnecessarily put himself in harm's way while directing the siege of Lens in 1647, effectively inviting the shot that killed him. Initially, it was hoped that Gassion would survive the musket shot that struck him in the head, as he

74 Diderot, *Encyclopédie*, vol. 17, 708–10. See also Starkey, *War in the Age of Enlightenment*, 71.

75 Drévillon, *L'impôt du sang*, 344–51.

76 Nicolas-Rémond des Cours, *Les véritables devoirs de l'homme d'épée. Particulièrement d'un homme qui veut réussir dans les armées* (Amsterdam: Adrian Braakman, 1697), 94. Cited in Drévillon, *L'impôt du sang*, 345.

77 Drévillon, *L'impôt du sang*, 409.

78 Renaudot, *Récit véritable*, 5.

79 Ibid., 6.

had received a similar wound five years earlier, but he died after four days of suffering, at the age of thirty-eight.[80] There were no such reservations about imprudent behaviour eighteen years on for another marshal with Protestant origins who was also killed while directing siege operations. The great Marshal Turenne, decapitated by a cannonball at the siege of Salzbach (27 July 1675), was praised by Cardinal Fléchier in his funeral oration for putting his talents as a general totally at the disposal of his monarch, contributing to Louis's glory without any concern for his own. Fléchier represented Turenne as a model of discipline and restraint. Paying tribute to Turenne's valour, Fléchier cautioned his listeners: "Do not understand by that word, gentlemen, a bravery that is vain, indiscreet, intemperate, that seeks danger for its own sake, which exposes itself without purpose, and the only goal of which is reputation and the vain applause of men. I speak of a bravery that is wise and controlled [...] which, in the midst of danger, prepares for every eventuality and takes every advantage, but which calculates its strengths; which undertakes the difficult, and does not try the impossible [...] and is ready to die in victory, or to survive defeat, in the accomplishment of its duties."[81] Similarly, the rebellious behaviour of the Prince of Condé during the Frondes (1648–53) was forgotten by later biographers, who instead insisted upon his exploits at the Battle of Rocroi (1643), where he was held to have put his duty to the general good ahead of his personal interests.[82]

The cost to the aristocracy of this culture of service and sacrifice was significant. The expansion of the royal army in the seventeenth century encouraged a remilitarization of the nobility. It is estimated by Michel Nassiet that at the height of Louis XIV's reign between 19,500 and 21,700 nobles pursued a military career. They represented 32–45 per cent of the heads of noble families at the time, approximately twice the proportion of nobles who had served under Charles VIII or Francis I.[83] Some noble families were careful to ensure their continued survival by choosing non-military occupations for their menfolk. In Champagne, for example, Gabriel de Saint-Belin may have been dissuaded from becoming a soldier because both his uncles were killed in the service of Louis XIII. Similarly, neither Lévy nor Pierre de Salse followed their father into the army; all five of their uncles had been "killed arms in hand in the service" and dynastic survival depended upon the preservation of their own lives.[84]

80 Ibid., 15–16.
81 Fléchier, *Oraison funèbre de Turenne*, 12–13.
82 See Cornette, *Le roi de guerre*, 370–3.
83 Nassiet, "La noblesse à l'époque moderne," 97.
84 Bourquin, "Les carrières militaires," 282.

Other families were not so careful. All seven brothers from the de Noüe family became officers in the army of Louis XIV.[85] That such profligacy was not a strategy for preserving noble lineages is evident from the history of an illustrious Angevin family. Lieutenant-General Jacques de Rougé, the first Marquis of Plessis-Bellière, was mortally wounded at the Battle of Castellamare on 16 November 1654. Of his three sons, Pierre de Rougé, the eldest, was killed at the age of twenty at the Battle of Saint Gotthard in 1664. The second died young and the third, François-Henri de Rougé, Marquis of Plessis-Bellière, died in the king's service at Suse in 1692. François-Henri had two sons who survived infancy. The eldest, Jean-Gilles, was killed serving as an infantry colonel at the siege of Saragossa in 1707, at the age of twenty-five. The other, Henri-François, was killed in a duel when he was only seventeen years old. Jean-Gilles left one male heir, Louis, who became the fourth and last Marquis of Plessis-Bellière. Louis was killed accidentally in Champagne in 1733 "at the head of his regiment." Since both of Louis's children died in infancy, his death marked the end of an aristocratic family for which a military career and a soldier's death were all that life promised for its male members.[86] One understands the brutal stoicism of the Marquise d'Autichamp in upbraiding her daughter-in-law for grieving the death of her son, killed in battle at the age of sixteen: "Madam, it's what you should have expected in marrying a d'Autichamp The king pays them for that. I had the sad experience of it in losing my husband, as do you in losing your son."[87] Madame de Sévigné, whose correspondence amply documented the grief of French courtiers whose sons were killed in Louis XIV's wars – "Everyone is crying, or is afraid of crying,"[88] she wrote after news arrived in Paris of the nobles who died with Longueville in the crossing of the Rhine in 1672 – adopted a similar tone of fatalism. Writing to the Countess de Guitaut after the Battle of Neerwinden in 1693, she advised her to "Take as much care of your two little sons as you are able; because when they get the taste for the hunt, you will be able to restrain them no more than little lions. You will remember then that the ball has a commission, that no-one goes who is not sent by order of Providence, and that the bravest and the most exposed die in their beds *when it pleases God.*"[89]

---

85 Ibid., 283.
86 Lebrun, *Les hommes et la mort*, 309.
87 Ibid., 308–9.
88 Sévigné, *Lettres*, vol. 2, 113.
89 Ibid., vol. 10, 119.

HEROIC SUBALTERNS

Turenne and Condé were France's greatest generals of the seventeenth century, so it is unsurprising that they were celebrated as glorious paragons of all the military virtues. What was different about the eighteenth-century tributes to the Chevalier d'Assas was that they celebrated a figure who, although noble, was otherwise quite ordinary, an officer of junior rank with no long list of exploits or victories to his name. Increasingly, eighteenth-century writers considered that ordinary soldiers, as well as their nobly born officers, could be moved by the impulses of honour and patriotism. Indeed, the reform-minded officers who promoted the military enlightenment of the eighteenth century rejected the Frederician model of military organization, which appeared to reduce the soldier to the role of unthinking automaton, ruled by fear of his officers and the lash. Instead, they promoted the idea that the French soldier was an autonomous, moral being motivated more by fear of dishonour than by fear of punishment. He simply needed to be presented with models to emulate.[90]

Those models were provided by works such as Laurent Bérenger's *École historique et morale du soldat et de l'officier*, which recounted dozens of anecdotes of military heroism. Bérenger affirmed that soldiers required "a spirit capable of braving every danger, and which is affected only by honour and glory." Praising them for their courage in combat and their indifference in the face of death, Bérenger promised those who died in battle a sort of immortality, in the enduring memory of their unit. "When it [death] is received gloriously, life has been long enough. Will you not live eternally in the memory of the unit you distinguished by your valour, which will be held up as an example to your successors?"[91] Models of such self-sacrifice were duly provided, such as the "generous devotion" of a sergeant who ordered the men he commanded in a completed mine to withdraw so that he could blow the mine, the enemy above and himself sky high: "Directly he struck the lighter, fired the powder and perished for his homeland."[92] Nevertheless, conceding that anonymous self-sacrifice on behalf of regiment or nation was too austere an ethic for most soldiers, Bérenger devoted many more of his anecdotes to heroic actions

---

90 On this topic, see Guinier, *L'honneur du soldat*, 291–323. See also Pichichero, *The Military Enlightenment*. Pichichero identifies Maurice de Saxe as a prominent pioneer of the military enlightenment who inspired subsequent thinkers such as Jean Colombier to insist upon the need to treat soldiers with respect for their physical and emotional well-being and, ultimately, for their rights as human beings. Pichichero, *The Military Enlightenment*, 110–50.

91 Bérenger, *École historique*, vol. 1, 36.

92 Ibid., 49.

in which the heroes survived their exploits, often to be rewarded by a sum of money (to be generously distributed among their comrades) or by promotion.[93]

There were early signs of this new emphasis upon the sacrifice of the ordinary soldier during the War of the Austrian Succession (1740–48). *The Military Academy or the Subaltern Heroes* was the title of a work of fiction by Claude Godard d'Aucourt that narrated the exploits of a group of Parisian friends who fought at the Battle of Fontenoy. D'Aucourt parodied Voltaire's famous poem on the battle, providing his own verses celebrating the "heroic subalterns" whose fictional biographies were included in the footnotes. Supposedly, the poem was read in the hospital at Lille after the battle, "where death triumphed and paraded its furies," and where surgeons "ran from bed to bed; blood flows, this sad place entirely echoes with a thousand frightful cries; death follows the barbarians, applauds them, and beneath its feet, in place of flowers, are thrown arms, legs and bloody corpses, English and French combined."[94] D'Aucourt thus expressed his contempt both for military medicine and for Voltaire's bloodless paean that celebrated the glory won by Louis XV at Fontenoy but ignored the price paid by ordinary soldiers.[95]

The Seven Years War (1756–63) marked a more important turning point in the development of the cult of patriotic sacrifice. For the first time, war was represented not as a conflict between kings or dynasties, but between entire nations.[96] Printed propaganda celebrated the heroism of ordinary French soldiers and their willingness to sacrifice themselves on behalf of

93 See, for example, ibid., 30–1.

94 Godard d'Aucourt, *L'académie militaire*, 292–302. See also Corvisier, "Les héros subalternes," 833; and Drévillon, *L'individu et la guerre*, 133–4.

95 Despite their unsavoury reputation, which persisted into the revolutionary and Napoleonic era, French military hospitals made impressive advances in the eighteenth century in caring for wounded and sick soldiers. A comprehensive code governing military hospitals was established in 1718 to regulate personnel, hygiene, and treatment. Innovative surgeons developed new surgical techniques, and in 1772 the first mobile ambulances were attached to armies in the field. In the last years of the old regime, when one in three patients at the Hôtel-Dieu in Paris died, the death rate at the Hôtel des Invalides was only one in forty. Heroic efforts were made to care for the wounded who flooded into Lille after the Battle of Fontenoy, with "exceptional" results: a mortality rate of only 16 per cent. See Lucenet, *Médecine, chirugie et armée*, 67. All the same, the practice persisted of prioritizing treatment by military rank rather than by medical urgency. Ordinary soldiers were last in line for treatment, regardless of the severity of their wounds. See Pichichero, *The Military Enlightenment*, 124–5. Pichichero also comments insightfully on the subversion by d'Aucourt's work of official narratives, which were silent on the role of ordinary soldiers. Ibid., 151–9. See also Vess, *Medical Revolution in France*, 23–31.

96 On this theme, see especially Bell, *The Cult of the Nation*, 78–106.

the nation. An account of the French capture of Port Mahon, on the island of Minorca, declared that every soldier and every officer behaved as if victory depended upon him alone: "even the wounded and dying thought only of the success of the attack."[97] Poems celebrated this victory by affirming the willingness of French soldiers to sacrifice their lives in assaulting the enemy ramparts:

> While detesting the savage instinct
> Of this inhumane *Suicide*,
> To which, by either weakness or rage
> The fateful hand is driven,
> Let us celebrate the infinite glory
> Of him who knows the value of life;
> But who knows he owes it to his kings,
> To his honour, to his homeland,
> And fearlessly sacrifices it
> Once they make their voices heard.[98]

French soldiers who were killed in the conflict became, in this war propaganda, emblematic of the nation itself. One of the most famous of these patriotic heroes was Joseph Coulon de Jumonville, infamously massacred with eight of his soldiers in the Ohio Valley in 1754, while the two countries were still nominally at peace, by British troops under the command of a twenty-two-year-old George Washington. In a preface to his widely read poem *Jumonville*, Antoine-Léonard Thomas emphasized the representative character of Jumonville. "He is no longer an ordinary person," wrote Thomas, but one who, "in his role as envoy, represents the august body of his nation."[99] In this respect, Jumonville's identity as "an ordinary French officer," unknown prior to the events surrounding his death, was an advantage. Thomas himself cited the precedent of antiquity to justify the celebration of a lowly born hero: "What! Are titles and grandiosity always necessary to be worthy of our attention [...] With us funeral eulogies are reserved only for those who bore pompous titles during their lives. But in Athens and Rome, all those who had served the homeland, or who died for it, had a right to the praises of their co-citizens."[100] In his poem, Jumonville became the embodiment of French virtue:

97 Anon., *Recueil général des pièces*, 78.
98 Anon., "Ode," in ibid., 17.
99 Thomas, *Poésies diverses*, 17.
100 Ibid., 18.

Such is the character of the virtuous Frenchman.

Deeply devoted to honour and to the laws.

Ignorant of the frightful art of committing crimes,

Terrible in war, amiable in peace,

A just and sincere friend, a generous enemy,

The Frenchman is too great to suspect a crime.[101]

Jumonville thus became the victim of his own virtue as much as of English perfidy. In describing his death, Thomas made it clear that Jumonville died for France:

Unworthily pierced by deadly lead;

He falls at the feet of his executioners.

Three times he lifts his heavy eyelids,

Three times his dying eyes close to the light.

In dying, the tender memory of France

Comes to comfort his great spirit and his final breath.

He dies: trampled by the feet of an inhumane band,

His torn limbs quiver upon the ground.[102]

Thomas's poem, by emphasizing the bloodthirsty cruelty of the English and a barbarity that was shocking even to the native allies of the French, justified French vengeance, deliberately departing from historical truth to provide a satisfyingly bloodthirsty fate for the English, who are made by the poet to suffer French wrath at the hands of Jumonville's brother, de Villiers. In this way, the discourse of war propaganda moved beyond the mild antagonism of dynastic rivalry toward the irreconcilable enmity between nations.

The emphasis upon the willingness of ordinary soldiers to sacrifice themselves on behalf of the nation only intensified in the last years of the old regime.[103] A history of the Auvergne regiment published by a veteran

101 Ibid., 34.

102 Ibid., 37. See also Bell, *The Cult of the Nation*, 78–87.

103 Indeed, as Christy Pichichero argues, popular plays such as Buirette de Belloy's *Le siège de Calais* (1765), which celebrated both civilian and feminine heroism, "fostered a national culture of militarism." This extended the ideal of patriotic self-sacrifice beyond the military sphere and prefigured the revolutionary and Napoleonic culture of "total war." As Pichichero notes, there were limits to official and public acceptance of this expansion of military heroism beyond traditional categories. Although there were female military heroes in the seventeenth and eighteenth centuries who received somewhat grudging royal recognition and even the reward of pensions for their service, they are notably absent from works

soldier in 1783 and which was prefaced by a poem to the memory of the
Chevalier d'Assas, made it clear that at Clostercamp the willingness of
d'Assas to sacrifice himself was matched by that of heroic subalterns. The
author cited the example of a Corporal Colleville, who had belatedly
rejoined the regiment on the eve of battle and who, about to die of his
wounds, declared to his comrades, "My God, how happy I am to have arrived
yesterday evening!" Another corporal, Claude-Antoine Jacob, his leg broken
by a bullet, "dragged himself to a neighbouring house, leaned against the
wall, and recommenced firing for as long as he still had cartridges and
strength." A sergeant entrusted with the job of burying the dead drew the
appropriate lesson for soldiers affected by the loss of their comrades: "Why
do you mourn them? They defeated the king's enemies [and] died arms
in hand: are they not happy?"[104]

The extent to which common soldiers were in fact motivated by the
patriotic devotion and spirit of self-sacrifice celebrated by such authors was
controversial at the time and has since been debated by historians. Voltaire,
paying tribute to officers who had died in the War of the Austrian Succession,
pointedly excluded common soldiers from his praise. These he defined as
"murderous mercenaries, whom the spirit of debauchery, libertinage, and
rapine caused to leave their fields [...] Considered all together, marching
in order under a great captain, they create the proudest and most imposing spectacle in the universe; taken individually, in the drunkenness of
their brutal frenzies (with a few exceptions), they are the dregs of nations."[105]
Increasingly, however, military thinkers rejected such negative appraisals,
with their implication that soldiers could be controlled and motivated to
fight only by a rigid discipline and fear of draconian punishment. Douazac,
writing in 1753, argued that the best way to persuade French soldiers to
fight was not by coercing them but by appealing to their sense of honour:
"I now ask if the subordinate nature of the Prussians and Germans suits
the French; and if it is not better, on the contrary, to make use of the
Frenchman's vivacity, thoughtlessness, and vanity? He wants to have honour,
he must be led by honour; honour alone makes him act."[106] While German
soldiers could be motivated only by fear of punishment or by drink, said
Douazac, the French soldier fought willingly, "because he is assured that

such as Bérenger's. A play about the siege of Calais that was more radically feminist than
Belloy's, Barnabé Farmin de Rozoi's *Décius français*, was rejected by the *Comédie française*
and never performed. Pichichero, *The Military Enlightenment*, 151–91, 157.

    104 Anon., *Précis historique*, 47–8.
    105 Voltaire, *Oeuvres complètes*, vol. 23.2, 231.
    106 Douazac, *Dissertation sur la subordination*, 33. See also Guinier, *L'honneur du soldat*,
217–18.

by obeying, he will come out of it with honour: and every one of them fights and acts as if he were engaged in a personal affair of honour."[107] Joseph Servan, in his widely read *The Soldier Citizen*, provided a model for the ideal soldier as the embodiment of civic virtue, motivated by honour and patriotism: "Don't be afraid of making him cowardly. Start by making him humane. If you have succeeded in inspiring in him a love of country, nothing will be able to diminish his courage."[108] This re-evaluation of the common soldier had important implications for the army's disciplinary regime. Although the military penal code preserved the draconian punishments that were supposed to terrify soldiers into obedience, the practice of military discipline became less arbitrary, less extreme, and increasingly sought alternative punishments calculated to encourage and exploit the soldier's sense of honour. The penal code was modified in 1775 so that only in rare cases was the death penalty incurred for desertion. Compelling wayward soldiers to run the gauntlet remained a common punishment and occasionally resulted in soldiers dying from the beating they thereby received at the hands of their comrades. Corporal punishment was, however, increasingly viewed as an affront to the dignity of both the officer who administered it and to the soldier who received it, even when applied in the form of blows from the flat of a sword. The penchant for sanctions that appealed to the soldier's honour is illustrated by the measure taken by the Marshal de Richelieu in 1756 to control drunkenness in his army during the siege of Port-Mahon: soldiers who were guilty of this infraction were denied the honour of participating in the next day's attack. The effectiveness of the measure in an army with an otherwise well-deserved reputation for drunkenness is indicative that this appeal to the soldier's honour was not in vain.[109]

The few military memoirs written by rank-and-file French soldiers provide further evidence that their officers' faith in their sense of honour was not misplaced. They lend support to the contention of historian Ilya Berkovich that soldiers of the old regime (not just French ones) internalized the concepts of military honour that were given definition by their social and military superiors. Old-regime soldiers fostered an identity for themselves as courageous, tough, and resilient, men who did not shirk their duty and were loyal to their comrades.[110] The memoir of

107 Douazac, *Dissertation sur la subordination*, 35.

108 Servan, *Le soldat citoyen, ou Vues patriotiques sur la manière la plus avantageuse de pourvoir à la défense du royaume, 1741–1780* (Neufchâtel, 1780), 233. Cited in Bertaud, "Military Virility," 309.

109 Guinier, *L'honneur du soldat*, 250–90.

110 Berkovich, *Motivation in War*, 182.

Charles-Étienne Bernos, recording his service in the Limousin Regiment during the 1740s, provides evidence for the culture of military masculinity that characterized the eighteenth-century French army. Offered the post of regimental secretary, normally held by a sergeant, and the exemption from service this implied, Bernos at first declined. "With respect to the exemption from service," wrote Bernos, "I saw this as an advantage that would in time of war suit only a coward who would accept that one of his comrades should risk his life for him."[111] Regimental rivalries were expressed in terms of this discourse of masculine honour. While on leave in Paris, Bernos passed the time with his comrades "agreeably enough," save for "a few quarrels" with a regiment of guards whom they rudely disparaged as "ducks of the Mein" for having swum to safety during the Battle of Dettingen.[112] Bernos's memoir demonstrates that French enlisted men, like their officers, were ready to defend their honour at the point of a sword, or, in the event that as prisoners of war they were denied swords, of a sharpened stick![113] Duelling, an essential feature of noble culture in the sixteenth and seventeenth centuries, taking an annual holocaust of victims, had been effectively repressed under Louis XIV but remained a feature of military culture down to the French Revolution.[114] One writer even claimed that it was a standard rite of passage "to take the pulse" of new recruits by testing their courage in a duel. The latter found themselves confronted by "the disagreeable choice either to fight or to be dishonoured."[115] Such confrontations were viewed by the authorities with indulgence. Jean Rossignol escaped punishment after wounding a comrade in a duel in 1776 by explaining to his sergeant-major that "a soldier who had been affronted would be dishonoured if he did not fight, and that I preferred, despite my inexperience, to be killed or wounded rather than to be taken for a coward."[116]

111 Bernos, "Souvenirs de campagne," 748.
112 Ibid., 745.
113 Ibid., 738. The two soldiers who settled their differences in this way, while prisoners of war with Bernos in Austria, were sentenced to fifteen days in prison by their commanding officer, which is an indication of the indulgence with which duelling was viewed in the army.
114 Nassiet, *La violence*, 290–4.
115 Mauvillon, *Le soldat parvenu*, 29–31.
116 Rossignol, *La vie véritable*, 16–17.

CONCLUSION

Glory and sacrifice were inseparable components of the military discourse of honour throughout the early modern period. Bérenger was as convinced in the eighteenth century as Monluc had been in the sixteenth that to die in the breach was an appropriate end for a military man.

He is animated by all the feelings of glory; he views the breach as a fine theatre for his valour, or as an honourable sepulchre. He resolves to save his motherland or to die on its ruins; he defends and inspires his comrades; he makes of his body a living rampart, and you might say he is a living shield for his co-citizens. Covered by a noble dust, weakened by a hundred glorious wounds, stained by his own blood, he slays another thousand; he attacks even when he can no longer defend himself; he defies the arrows that pierce him; he closes the breach with his dying body, and after a thousand fine deeds, exhausted by so many victories, he falls once more proudly upon the rubble of the motherland with which he seems, dead though he is, still to threaten the enemy. These are the heroes who must be crowned after their deaths. It is for them that the art of statuary was invented. Every citizen should have their portraits and a hundred mausoleums should be raised to them.[117]

Nevertheless, even in Bérenger's paean to glory the repeated invocation of the motherland betrays the transition insisted upon by Corvisier, from the warrior's death as worthy on its own terms to the soldier's death as a sacrifice for the sake of his homeland. With the revolution, as France moved into a new and even more destructive period of warfare, its soldiers would continue to be inspired by a mixture of motives as patriotic self-sacrifice rivalled the ambition for glory and honours. During the first stages of the revolutionary wars, Sacrifice was in the ascendant. Then came Napoleon, and Glory would have its due.

117 Bérenger, *École historique et morale*, vol. 1, 319.

3

Dying for Liberty:
The French Revolution

THE DEATH OF DESILLES

The young lieutenant Antoine-Joseph-Marc Desilles was one of perhaps as many as five hundred French soldiers who died because of the fighting of 31 August 1790, in what came to be known as the Nancy Affair, but he alone among the victims achieved individual fame. In August 1790, Desilles was serving in the Régiment du Roi, garrisoned at Nancy in the frontier province of Lorraine. The regiment was one of three – the others were the Mestre-du-Camp cavalry and the Swiss Châteauvieux infantry – that in the second summer of the French Revolution, rebelled against the authority of their officers. Radicalized through their attendance at the meetings of Nancy's Jacobin club and tired of waiting for their arrears of pay, the soldiers finally took the law into their own hands. The men of the Régiment du Roi, who wore the tricoloured cockade as a sign of their sympathy for the revolution, blockaded their officers in their quarters and compelled the quartermaster-treasurer to give them 150,000 livres.[1] The other regiments soon took similar action. Their mutiny was short-lived, however, as the Marquis de Bouillé was dispatched by the French National Assembly at the head of 5,000 men to restore order. Arriving at the city gates on 31 August, Bouillé called upon the mutinous troops to return to discipline, release their hostages, and surrender four leaders from each regiment. Although those terms were accepted, mutual suspicion resulted in an outbreak of fighting at the Stainville gate, which Desilles sought in vain to prevent. The first report reaching the National Assembly to describe his action, from the Directory of the department of the Meurthe, stated that Desilles had placed himself across the mouth of a cannon that had been

---

1   Bertaud, *La révolution armée*, 47–8.

drawn up to defend the gate, declaring to the soldiers who aimed their muskets at him "that they could fire, but he would stay in this place."[2] Subsequently, this mundane expression became embellished. "Don't fire!" he cried, according to the words on a contemporary engraving, "They are your friends, they are your brothers, the National Assembly has sent them, will you dishonour the Régiment du Roi?"[3] The report from Nancy went on to say that Desilles was struck by four musket balls in the ensuing fusillade, concluding that his wounds, "happily, are not mortal."[4]

The final words of the report from Nancy proved to be premature. Desilles had received as many as fifteen wounds, and the surgeons were unsuccessful in their efforts to extract one of the bullets. For several weeks, he lay dying in the home of his comrade, Mulnier, in Nancy's Place Royale. His death was announced to the National Assembly on 22 October.[5] The assembly, which had earlier thanked Desilles for his "heroic devotion"[6] – and received in turn a letter of appreciation from the young officer's father[7] – was well aware that many other soldiers had also died in the bitter street fighting that had followed his heroic gesture.[8] Its decree of 3 September promised to provide for the wives and children of the national guardsmen under General Bouillé's command who had been killed. The general took his revenge on those mutineers who had survived the fighting. In the ensuing repression, one was broken on the wheel, twenty-two were hanged, and forty-one condemned to thirty years in the galleys.[9] Eventually, the mutineers who were not executed would be amnestied and achieve celebrity status as heroes of freedom in a Jacobin-inspired Festival of Liberty (15 April 1792). For the time being, however, their only defenders were radical journalists like Marat and Prudhomme. The National Assembly reserved its accolades for the victims who had died fighting for the

---

2 *Archives parlementaires*, vol. 18, 527. Desilles's words, as reported in the *Journal de Paris* on 4 September, were "vous me tuerez plutôt que de tirer," or, roughly translated, "you will have to kill me before firing." A detailed account published in October 1790, by Léonard, an officer of the Mestre-du-Camp regiment, attributed the following words to Desilles: "strike … let me not be witness to your shame." Léonard, *Relation exacte et impartiale*, 130–1.

3 Cited in Pupil, "Le dévouement du Chevalier Desilles," 79. See also Hould, ed., *L'image de la Révolution française*, 323.

4 *Archives parlementaires*, vol. 18, 527.

5 Ibid., vol. 19, 763.

6 Ibid., 530.

7 *Archives parlementaires*, vol. 19, 425.

8 General Bouillé's report to the Assembly estimated that there were three hundred dead. *Journal de Paris*, 4 September 1790. Léonard's detailed summary indicated seventy-eight dead and 124 wounded from Bouillé's army; 110 dead and 154 wounded from the side of the "rebels." Léonard, *Relation exacte et impartiale*, 150–3.

9 Bertaud, *La révolution armée*, 47.

forces of order, holding a funeral ceremony in their honour on
20 September 1790, on the same Champ de Mars where only a few months
earlier, on the 14 July anniversary of the storming of the Bastille, units of
National Guard from every part of the country had sworn to defend
the Nation, the Law, and the King.[10] The funeral ceremony deliberately
evoked that earlier Festival of Federation, representing the deaths of the
soldiers who died at Nancy as the fulfillment of the oaths they had taken.
Inscriptions on the altar of the fatherland affirmed that these soldiers had
died "for the defence of the law" and that "their glory is eternal like the
empire of liberty." A deputy reported to his colleagues in the National
Assembly that the young soldiers of the National Guard who surrounded
the mausoleum atop the altar of the fatherland "seemed, around this
venerable tomb, to take their first lesson in dying for the homeland."[11]

Desilles was honoured, like these anonymous victims of the fighting at
Nancy, for his sacrifice in defence of the law. Even before succumbing to
his wounds, he was celebrated on the Parisian stage. *Le nouveau d'Assas*, a
one-act play, with music and verse, was performed at the Théâtre de la
Nation in early October 1790.[12] The Desilles of the play, determined to
prevent the spilling of blood at any cost, was represented baring his breast
to the mutinous Swiss soldiers and declaring, "Well then, cruel ones! Fire
on me! Let me be the first victim of your fury! In losing my life, I will be
spared the pain of seeing my comrades and brothers massacred." Of his
own wounds he said, "They are nothing" and, apparently ignoring the
futility of his sacrifice, thanked heaven "that only my blood has flowed."
The wounded hero was then embraced by the commander of the Metz
National Guard, who declared "You are another d'Assas, you are worthy
of a civic crown. This action immortalizes you!"[13] Finally, Desilles was
crowned by the women of Nancy, who called upon their sons to emulate
his example: "may they one day imitate your courage and serve their homeland by such acts of devotion."[14] A similar coronation later took place
within the National Assembly itself. A ceremony was held there on
29 January 1791 in which a National Guard battalion from Montmartre
bestowed upon the assembly a bust of Desilles sculpted by the same Mulnier

10 The National Guard was a bourgeois militia created at the time of the uprising of
14 July 1789, with the dual purpose of safeguarding the changes accomplished by the
revolution and controlling any further upheavals on the part of the lower classes. See
Dupuy, *La Garde nationale*, 37–87.

11 *Archives parlementaires*, vol. 19, 108.

12 Dejaure, *Le nouveau d'Assas*; Berton, *Le nouveau d'Assas*. See the description in the
Journal de Paris, 19 October 1790.

13 Berton, *Le nouveau d'Assas*, 78.

14 Ibid., 81–2.

who had "daily bathed his honourable wounds with tears of patriotism and friendship." The deputy Gouy d'Arsy justified the celebration of Desilles's apotheosis, declaring that the consecration of his image by the assembly would inspire new defenders of the constitution, eager to emulate Desilles in becoming "demi-Gods." The bestowal of a civic crown upon Desilles would, he said, inflame the hearts of 500,000 Frenchmen who would answer the assembly's call to arms. The president of the National Assembly, the Abbé Grégoire, responded by declaring that because of his "glorious deeds" this "new d'Assas" belonged to the nation: "Adopted by the nation, he is henceforth the friend, the relative of all those who are determined to sacrifice their lives in defence of the constitution; and the brave soldiers who surround this bust, perform at this moment a familial duty." To reinforce the point, as the artist Jean-Jacques-François Le Barbier placed a civic crown upon the bust of Desilles, musicians performed the air, "Where better to be than in the bosom of one's family?"[15] The National Assembly concluded its apotheosis of Desilles by approving the commission of a painting by Le Barbier of Desilles's sacrifice, based on a drawing already sketched on site, to serve as a pendant to the painting of the Tennis Court Oath that had been commissioned from Jacques-Louis David.[16]

Unlike David, who never finished his famous sketch of the Tennis Court Oath as a painting, Le Barbier did complete a full-size painting of Desilles's heroic action at Nancy, but not until June 1794 (fig. 3.1). By then, the constitutional monarchy of 1790 had been replaced by the republican Terror and the reputations of Desilles and the mutineers whom he had confronted had undergone a complete reversal. The Swiss soldiers who were the victims of Bouillé's repression were amnestied in December 1791 and their newly recovered freedom was celebrated in a Festival of Liberty orchestrated by David on 15 April 1792.[17] Desilles, now perceived as "a traitor in the service of counter-revolutionaries," had fallen from grace.[18] Exhibited at the biennial Salon of 1795, Le Barbier's painting no longer suited the political moment. Although the story of its representations underlines the ephemerality of the fame surrounding the death of Desilles, it also illustrates several important developments in the representation of

15　*Archives parlementaires*, vol. 22, 564–5.

16　It is likely that Le Barbier had been soliciting this commission for some time, perhaps as early as 28 September, when the suggestion was first made in the Assembly by Barère, without mentioning Le Barbier by name. In December, Le Barbier presented the Assembly with drawings as models both for an engraving and for the painting that was commissioned on 29 January 1791. See Pupil, "Le dévouement du Chevalier Desilles," 81.

17　Ironically, an engraving of Le Barbier's drawing of Desilles's action was presented to the Legislative Assembly only two days after the Festival of Liberty. Ibid., 83.

18　Cited in ibid., 90.

3.1. Jean-Jacques le Barbier, *The Heroic Courage of the Young Desilles,
August 31 1790, in the Nancy Affair.* 1794.

the soldier's death that became characteristic of the entire revolutionary
period. Firstly, the efforts by Le Barbier to acquire an official state commission for his various depictions of the event, as well as to disseminate
them to a wide public, were a significant initiative to enhance the status of
images representing the sacrifice of contemporary soldiers, placing them
on the same level as the history paintings that dominated the Salons and
celebrated the heroes of ancient Greece and Rome. Secondly, artists, playwrights, and politicians alike, while emphasizing the pathos surrounding
the death of Desilles – the devotion of his friend Mulnier, who cared for the
dying soldier and then sculpted his bust from an impression of his death
mask; the tears shed by Desilles's father at the sight of that bust – also
insisted that it was a sacrifice willingly accepted not only by Desilles but by
those closest to him. Grégoire's assertion that heroes like Desilles properly
belonged to the family of the nation is revealing. At a time when death was
becoming a more intimate, family occasion, it normalized the soldier's
death by defining for him a new family, consisting of his brothers-in-arms.

It also, while acknowledging the power of filial affection, did so only to insist more forcefully upon the transcendent imperative of patriotism, modelling examples of self-sacrifice that were incumbent upon men, women, and children alike. While the heroes whose deaths were celebrated varied according to the political vagaries of the revolution, these aspects of patriotic martyrdom remained constant. The proliferation of images of the soldier's death in a wide range of media was a measure of the intensification of international conflict during the wars of the French Revolution as well as of the heightened engagement of the French people in a culture of total war.

DEATH'S NEW REGIME

It was the outbreak of war between revolutionary France and its neighbours in April 1792 that made models of patriotic self-sacrifice like Desilles immediately relevant to the lives of millions of ordinary French men and women. The French revolutionary wars witnessed a significant intensification of warfare and an unprecedented mobilization of human populations. They also involved mass killing on a new scale at the very time when mass mortalities from other causes – epidemic disease or famine – were, in France at least, becoming less common. The deluge of military deaths sustained by the French population between 1792 and 1815 – 458,000 for the wars of the French Revolution, 900,000 for those of Napoleon – was no longer the drop in the bucket of overall mortality that soldiers' deaths had been at the time of the War of the Austrian Succession.[19] It would seem likely that the unprecedented prominence of military deaths among the causes of mortality intensified their psychological impact, particularly given the increasingly sentimental attitudes of contemporaries toward death. The proliferation of representations of the soldier's death during the revolutionary wars is evidence of this heightened impact. Those representations were both cause and effect of the intensification of warfare, at once a means to mobilize society for war and a way to digest its consequences.

Among contemporaries, it was the German poet Goethe who, having witnessed the Battle of Valmy on 20 September 1792, most memorably expressed the sense of the revolutionary wars as a historical turning point. "From this place and from this day," he wrote, "begins a new era in the history of the world."[20] Many historians have commented on the contrast between the portentous words of the poet and the inconsequential reality

19 Houdaille, "Les armées de la Révolution," 845; Houdaille, "Pertes de l'armée de terre," 50.

20 Cited in Bertaud, *Valmy*, 251.

of the "cannonade" at Valmy, a skirmish that resulted in only three hundred French and two hundred Prussian casualties.[21] Nevertheless, most would agree that the following years witnessed major changes in European warfare. In principle, at least, the declaration of the *levée en masse* on 23 August 1793, with its stirring preamble announcing the mobilization of the entire French population for war, regardless of age or gender, marked the advent of total war. The repudiation of conventional restraints on warfare, such as those requiring acceptance of the surrender of prisoners of war or respect for the non-combatant status of women and children, were further manifestations of this impulse toward the radicalization of warfare. Historians have seen the repression of counter-revolution in the Vendée, where as many as half a million men, women, and children may have died, as the realization of total war, aimed at the complete annihilation of the enemy and recognizing no distinction between combatants and non-combatants.[22] David Bell aptly cites a letter from the republican General Westermann as evidence for the total nature of the war in the Vendée. "I have crushed children under the hooves of horses, and massacred women who, these at least, will give birth to no more brigands," Westermann wrote to the Convention. "I do not have a single prisoner with which to reproach myself. I have exterminated everyone."[23]

Critics of the idea that the French revolutionary wars marked the advent of total war point out that the reality rarely matched the rhetoric. Conscription, introduced in February 1793, did produce huge armies – as many as 750,000 men were in the French armies in 1794 – but these dwindled in size in subsequent years.[24] A calculation of the average army size during the revolutionary wars (45,000) indicates little change from the War of the Austrian Succession and the Seven Years War (47,000). Battles increased in frequency during the French Revolution, but the number of battles involving over 100,000 men on both sides was the same (twelve) for both periods of conflict.[25] Despite the dehumanizing rhetoric employed to justify a no-holds-barred approach to warfare, casualty rates were generally lower than those of the Seven Years War, on average only 8 per cent of total effectives and, according to Bodart, rarely

21 Smith, *The Greenhill Napoleonic Wars Data Book*, 26–7.

22 Notoriously, the National Convention decreed on 26 May 1794, that no British or Hanoverian soldiers would be taken prisoner. Robespierre, in his final speech to the Convention on 9 Thermidor (27 July 1794), complained that republican troops ignored the decree. Guiomar, *L'invention de la guerre totale*, 118. On the Vendée, see ibid., 104 and 151; Bell, *The First Total War*, 154–85.

23 Cited in ibid., 173.

24 Forrest, *Napoleon's Men*, 8.

25 Palmer, "Frederick the Great," 100.

exceeding 15 per cent. Although Bodart notes the exception of the viciously fought war in the Vendée, where Vendéan battle casualties numbered as high as 86 per cent, he concludes of revolutionary warfare that "War began to be conducted much more humanely than formerly."[26]

Certainly, as Hervé Drévillon points out, the transition from revolutionary to Napoleonic warfare marked a sharper escalation in the scale and intensity of warfare than did that from the old regime to the revolution. Drévillon estimates the average number of deaths suffered by the French armies during the revolutionary wars to be 38,000 per year, a figure that, although significantly larger than the 24,000 per year during the War of the Spanish Succession (1702–13), pales in comparison with the 75,000 deaths sustained on average during the Napoleonic wars.[27] The three-day Battle of Leipzig fought in October 1813 far exceeded in scale, intensity, and mortality any of the battles fought during the revolutionary wars. Of the 203,133 men in the Grande Armée who fought at Leipzig, 46,343 (22.8 per cent) were killed or wounded.[28] Nevertheless, it is important not to underestimate the impact of the loss of life in the earlier period, nor the emotional and cultural challenges of coming to terms with that loss. The analysis of Jacques Houdaille shows that during the years from 1793 to 1795, French military deaths were on average 95,000 per year, exceeding by a considerable margin (20,000) the average for the Napoleonic wars. The generation born between 1770 and 1774 bore an unequal share of this burden, accounting for 268,000 out of an estimated total of 534,000 deaths. Houdaille calculates that this represented 23 per cent of the young men from this generation who reached the age of twenty.[29] This percentage exceeded that which Houdaille calculated for the generation born between 1790 and 1795 and who experienced the disastrous campaigns of 1812–13 (20.5 per cent). It also came remarkably close to the scale of loss suffered by the classes born between 1891 and 1895, who bore the brunt of French losses in the First World War (24.5 per cent).[30]

26 Bodart, *Losses of Life*, 105–7.

27 Drévillon calculates that these figures represented 1.12 per cent, 1.35 per cent, and 2.5 per cent of the French population at the time of the War of the Spanish Succession, the French revolutionary wars, and the Napoleonic wars, respectively. Drévillon, *L'individu et la guerre*, 183.

28 Smith, *The Greenhill Napoleonic Wars Data Book*, 466.

29 Houdaille, "Les armées de la Révolution," 845. For the purposes of this analysis, Houdaille relies upon a calculation of total losses for the revolutionary period that varies from his own calculation of 458,000.

30 Houdaille, "Pertes de l'armée de terre," 50.

Assessing the impact of these losses on French society depends upon an assessment of their significance in relation to the general patterns of mortality at the time of the French Revolution as well as to contemporary attitudes toward death. Historians have identified the late eighteenth and early nineteenth centuries as an important turning point in Western attitudes and practices in relation to death and dying. There were changes in outlook, as death was resisted, dechristianized, and sentimentalized. A new regime of death began to be defined, as "your" death supplanted "my" death as a focus of emotion. There were also changes in burial and memorial practices: the dead were exiled from communal graves in churchyards to individualized plots in suburban cemeteries, where they served the purposes of a new commemorative culture.[31] Underlying these changes was the gradual increase in life expectancy stemming from small but cumulative changes in medicine and obstetrics, as well as in public hygiene and administration, which contributed to a significant decline in mortality, particularly that of infants. For women, life expectancy at birth rose from 32.1 during the decade of the revolution to 39.3 in the decade from 1820–29. For men, life expectancy at birth rose by 39 per cent (10.8 years) between the last years of the old regime and 1830.[32] Changing demographic realities accompanied the emergence of a more secular outlook, focused more on this world than on the one to come. Historians point to the evidence of such a change occurring over the course of the eighteenth century in the reduction of religious bequests in wills and in the diminishing concern expressed by testators concerning the funeral rites and religious services to be observed on their behalf.[33] Increasingly, wills called for simplicity in funeral rites, as their authors asked to be buried "without show or worldly pride."[34] At about the same time, concern for both the moral and physical well-being of society prompted the clearing out of human remains from urban churchyards and the opening of more salubrious and orderly suburban cemeteries.[35] Most importantly, the change in attitudes toward death was manifest in a "revolution in feeling," which, according to Philippe Ariès, occurred "within one or two generations" at

---

31 On changing attitudes toward death see Vovelle, *La mort et l'occident*; Ariès, *The Hour of Our Death*; Favre, *La mort dans la littérature*; McManners, *Death and the Enlightenment*. On the emergence of a new culture of commemoration at the time of the revolution see especially Legacey, *Making Space for the Dead*; Thomas Laqueur, *The Work of the Dead*; and Joseph Clarke, *Commemorating the Dead*.

32 Dupâquier, ed., *Histoire de la population française*, vol. 3: *De 1789 à 1914*, 282.

33 Vovelle, *Piété baroque et déchristianisation*, 75–107.

34 Vovelle, *La mort et l'occident*, 418.

35 On the emergence of a new burial culture in Paris, see Legacey, *Making Space for the Dead*, 17–98.

the beginning of the nineteenth century. Preoccupation with "my death," focused upon making the necessary provisions for one's own death, gave way to a preoccupation with "your death" – the death of one's closest friends or relations. To Ariès, this change was the manifestation of an affective revolution that, at the same time as it made family relationships more intimate and more emotionally intense, also made the death of the "other" intolerable, justifying both outpourings of grief and unprecedented efforts to compensate for the loss through memorialization.[36]

Revolutionary representations of the soldier's death require consideration in the context of the sharp escalation in military mortality during the revolutionary and Napoleonic wars and of the affective revolution that was at the same time transforming attitudes toward death. The soldier's sacrifice was valorized in word, image, and song not only to mobilize society for the war effort, but also to provide it with consolation and compensation. Public representations insisted upon the rewards obtained in return for the sacrifice endured, both for society in terms of its present and future security and for the soldier himself, with respect to his reputation and memory. They frequently acknowledged and even emphasized the emotional price to be paid by family members who bore the burden of the sacrifice of husbands, fathers, and sons. Nevertheless, recognition of the right to tears was always followed by the injunction to dry one's eyes; to look beyond the loss of a loved one and see instead the homeland's benefit. Civilians and soldiers alike echoed this ideology of willing self-sacrifice in their own testimony. There is evidence, however, that for most soldiers enduring the revolutionary wars was not primarily a matter of exalted patriotism trumping personal or familial affection; rather, it was above all about the acquisition of a numbed indifference to suffering. For civilians, too, and particularly women, it was a matter of making do, waiting for news, and wondering whether their menfolk would ever return.

WILLING SACRIFICE

From the moment battle was joined with the foreign enemy in the spring of 1792, French politicians and publicists celebrated the willingness of citizens to lay down their lives for liberty. The first encounters with Austrian troops were ignominious, as troops advancing on Mons under the command of General Dillon fled back to Lille at the first sight of the enemy and, to the subsequent delight of the royalist press, massacred their

36 Ariès, *The Hour of Our Death*, 442, 471–2.

general.[37] Heroes were needed to prevent the public from becoming discouraged by reports of these events. They were quickly found. The patriotic press exploited the story recounted by General Alexandre Beauharnais concerning Grenadier Pie, who was wounded in an encounter with the enemy near Quiévrain and who had supposedly begged his commander to end his suffering – "so that I do not see the shame of this day" – as he lay dying beside his musket.[38] Pie, who did not in fact die, was quickly the recipient of tributes such as that of the Jacobin club of Douai, which promised to award him a sword of honour. "What man could be worthier of it," asked one journalist, "than one who would rather die than bear the sorrow of a sad day; whose dying gaze turns toward the weapon he cannot use, at the very moment when he feels most bound to it in the service of his homeland?"[39] In Paris, two infantry battalions, one from the line army, the other from the National Guard, also presented a sword to the Legislative Assembly, to be passed on to "their brave comrade, Grenadier Pie," whom they likened to "Marius expiring on the ruins of Carthage." Their gesture was greeted by warm applause from the assembly.[40] A couple of weeks later, a letter from Beauharnais was read to the assembly that described the "touching ceremony" in which Pie was awarded his sword by Generals Rochambeau and Luckner.[41] The recovering grenadier was inundated with gifts, including a gold medal from the Jacobin club of Perpignan, a gold-handled cane from a Parisian volunteer, as well as a pair of gloves and a tricoloured sash from a citizen of Lille. The gloves were embroidered with a sword surmounted by a liberty bonnet and the sash with the pertinent slogan, "Live free or die."[42]

Other heroes who also expressed their willingness to die for liberty soon took their place beside Grenadier Pie in the war reporting of the revolutionary press. On 15 May, Gorsas recounted in the *Courrier des Départemens* the exploit of Citizen Thénard, who led a party of fifteen French soldiers in an unequal struggle against sixty Austrian hussars. Called upon to surrender, Thénard responded by crying "Live free or die!" with "all the exaltation of his spirit and his voice" and proceeded to blow out the brains of the nearest hussar. Finally, recounted Gorsas, Thénard "put down his weapon, proudly regarded his enemies, waited for death and fell pierced

---

37 See *L'ami du roye* (by Montjoye), 4 May 1792; and *La Gazette Universelle*, 4 May 1792.

38 *L'Ami Jacques, Argus du Département du Nord*, 4 May 1792.

39 Ibid., 10 May 1792.

40 *Archives parlementaires*, vol. 43, 311.

41 Ibid., vol. 44, 129.

42 Ibid., vol. 44, 703; vol. 45, 351–2; *L'Ami Jacques, Argus du Département du Nord*, 15 May 1792.

by a thousand shots, still crying 'Live free or die!'"[43] Challenged by rival journalists concerning the authenticity of the anecdote, Gorsas reiterated his praise of "this worthy soldier, who can be called the d'Assas of the revolution." He invited his critics to examine the letter he had received from an officer serving at the front which he claimed to have cited "word for word."[44] The day after recounting the story of Thénard, Gorsas reported the defiant words of a Sergeant Denis Rousselot, who inspired the recruits under his command with the words, "If I fall back, kill me, just as if one of you falls back, I will kill him."[45] On 6 June, Gorsas cited another letter received from the front, this time telling the story of a seventeen-year-old serving in a battalion of Parisian volunteers, "who ended his life in the most glorious manner." Shot through both cheeks, "this poor child" had bound his own wounds and attempted to fight on from the cart where he had been placed by his comrades, until he succumbed to overwhelming odds: "Exhausted [...] he fell upon the cart and waited for death, even demanded it. He was hacked into a thousand pieces by those brigands who should have respected his courage. Such are the actions that do honour to civic spiritedness, yet they are allowed to perish!"[46]

The pattern of responding to military setbacks by publicizing the heroic resistance of citizens prepared to sacrifice their lives for the sake of freedom was well established, therefore, before the military crisis of early September 1792, when the fortresses of Longwy and Verdun fell to the invading Prussians commanded by the Duke of Brunswick. By this time, the monarchy had been overthrown by the uprising of 10 August, itself a manifestation of popular anger at the notorious "Brunswick manifesto," which had threatened the people of Paris with death and destruction in the event the royal family were harmed. News of the surrender of Verdun, leaving the way open for an enemy invasion, contributed to the febrile atmosphere in the French capital that resulted in the September massacres. In these circumstances, to allay panic and fear, stories of revolutionary heroism were desperately needed. They were found in the resistance of Lille and Thionville, frontier towns that declined to emulate the examples of Longwy and Verdun, instead mocking the forces that lay siege to them. In Lille, the citizens were reported to have crowned enemy cannonballs with liberty bonnets, while at Thionville a wooden horse was paraded on the ramparts bearing a feedbag and a sign saying that Thionville would

43 *Le Courrier des Départemens*, 15 May 1792.
44 Ibid., 6 June 1792.
45 Ibid., 16 May 1792.
46 Ibid., 6 June 1792.

not surrender until the horse had eaten its hay.[47] But even Verdun provided
a model of revolutionary heroism, in the person of its commander, Nicolas-
Joseph Beaurepaire, who preferred to commit suicide by blowing his own
brains out rather than accept the decision of the municipality to surrender.
According to Delaporte, who reported on the surrender to the Legislative
Assembly on 6 September, Beaurepaire had committed this act in the midst
of the municipal council.[48] This claim was repeated six days later by another
deputy, Delaunay, who denied that Beaurepaire's gesture had been an
expression of weakness or despair, but rather stemmed from the judgment
that his death, by providing an example to friends and enemies alike, would
be more useful than his life. Delaunay went on to argue that Beaurepaire's
remains should be transferred to the Pantheon, the former Church of
Saint Genviève that had been converted by the revolutionaries into a temple
to great men and that had already received the remains of Voltaire and
Mirabeau. "Will they say that the honours of the Pantheon must be reserved
for great talents?" Delaunay asked, before answering his own question:
"The finest talent is to serve one's country and to die for it."[49] He went on
to describe the galvanizing effect the sight of the hero's remains would
have on the battalions of French soldiers that were already advancing
toward the front: "Imagine how profound an impression will be made on
our warriors by the sight of a funeral carriage bearing the remains of a
man who died for freedom: this sight will raise spirits, inspire courage, and
animate all hearts with the desire for vengeance."[50] In October, Beaurepaire
became the first military hero to be interred in the Pantheon.

Delaunay's account of Beaurepaire's suicide, reinforcing the idea that it
had taken place in full view of Verdun's city council, was subsequently proved
to be false. On 11 November 1792, a citizen of Verdun presented himself
at the bar of the National Convention and in a lengthy defence of the town's
population denounced as "absurd tales" the versions of Beaurepaire's death
that had been retailed in the capital.[51] Later studies have confirmed his
view. Writing in 1911, Xavier Pétigny presented evidence demonstrating
that Beaurepaire had not died in front of the municipal council, but alone
in his room. Whether he had died by his own hand or that of another was
a question on which the historian reserved judgment.[52] Pétigny judged that

47 See the reports in the *Révolutions de Paris*, 13–20 October 1792; *Le Patriote Français*,
29 September 1792.
48 *Archives parlementaires*, vol. 49, 419.
49 Ibid., vol. 49, 592.
50 Ibid.
51 *Archives parlementaires*, vol. 53, 361.
52 Ibid., 155.

Delaunay's speech was "full of errors and sophistries," but he also acknowledged its "prodigious effect" in establishing the myth of Beaurepaire.[53] Contemporary playwrights, poets, and artists were all inspired to produce tributes to Beaurepaire, who was depicted shooting himself in front of the Prussian envoy, surrounded by horrified councillors (fig. 3.2). Although the citizen from Verdun attacked a "foolish play [performed] at the [theatre of the] Varieties,"[54] for its inaccuracy, Beaurepaire's death and apotheosis continued to be represented on the stage. In one play, a female goddess of Liberty descended upon a cloud to place a crown of immortality on the hero's remains as they were carried to the Pantheon.[55] In another, it was a male figure of Destiny who arrived to promise victory. Beaurepaire's wife was also represented in this version, her anguish at her husband's death quickly giving way to a call for vengeance:

Frenchmen, avenge me, avenge yourselves
May the people, armed with your thunder,
Destroy and crush to powder
The murderers of my husband.[56]

There were even references to Beaurepaire in plays celebrating other contemporary acts of resistance to the foreign enemy. In a play about the siege of Thionville, first performed in June 1793, the son of Thionville's commander, General Wimpfen, expressed his desire to emulate Beaurepaire, "this French Brutus": "What destiny could be finer," he asked, "than to carry into the darkness of the tomb the regrets of my father and my homeland?"[57] At the climax of the play, the younger Wimpfen achieved his desire, deliberately impaling himself on a bayonet to prevent the enemy from using him as a hostage in seeking his father's surrender. The lesson of his sacrifice was left to be summed up by Wimpfen senior: "an exemplary Frenchman, he dies for his Motherland. / His oaths were sworn to Her, his duty is fulfilled."[58]

On 20 September 1792, the Prussian invasion was famously stopped at the Battle of Valmy, and a little over a month after that, on 6 November, the revolutionary armies won another victory, this time over the Austrians at Jemmapes. These battles did not fail to provide new examples of heroic

53 Pétigny, *Beaurepaire*, 183.
54 *Archives parlementaires*, vol. 53, 361.
55 Lesur, *L'apothéose de Beaurepaire*.
56 Leboeuf, *La patrie reconnaissante*.
57 Saulnier, *Le siège de Thionville*, 5.
58 Ibid., 29.

TRAIT SUBLIME DE COURAGE ET DE DÉVOUEMENT.

BEAUREPAIRE, Commandant du premier Bataillon de Mayenne et Loir, se donne la mort à Verdun en présence des Fonctionnaires publics, lâches et parjures, qui veulent livrer à l'ennemi le poste confié à son Courage. M. Delaunay, d'Angers au nom de la Commission extraordinaire, a fait un raport dont le resultat a été le projet de decret suivant (adopté à l'unanimité et applaudi de même)
L'Assemblée Nationale decrete que le corps de Beaurepaire Commandant du premier Bataillon de Mayenne et Loir, sera transporté de S.te Menehould, et déposé au Panthéon Français. L'inscription suivante sera placé sur sa tombe).
Il aima mieux mourir que de Capituler avec les tyrans.
A Paris chez Villeneuve, Graveur, Rue Zacharie, S.te Severin, Maison du Passage, N.º 72.

3.2. Villeneuve, "A sublime act of courage and devotion." The death of Beaurepaire at Verdun, 2 September 1792.

self-sacrifice that were celebrated by the patriotic press. On 19 October, the *Annales Patriotiques et Littéraires de la France* published a letter from General Kellermann's army that described three examples of patriotic devotion from the Battle of Valmy. The first concerned soldiers under Beurnonville's command who refused to obey his order to sit down to make themselves less vulnerable to enemy cannon fire. The second related the story of a young soldier who obtained permission to leave the ranks to embrace the body of his brother, who had been killed. Having paid "this fraternal tribute to nature," the young man returned to his post, crying "*vive la Nation!*" Finally, the letter cited the last words of the mortally wounded Lieutenant-Colonel Lornier to the comrades who surrounded him: "My friends, this intrepid warrior said to them, your attentions are useless to me, return to the enemy, I die happy, the cause of liberty triumphs."[59] Following the Battle of Jemmapes, attention focused on Lieutenant Bertèche, who was wounded by forty-one sabre cuts and a pistol shot after killing seven enemy soldiers.[60] Presented to the National Convention in March 1793 by General Beurnonville, whose life he had saved, Bertèche was crowned with a civic wreath and presented with a sword of honour. The blood he had shed was compared by the president of the Convention to that recently shed by Michel Lepeletier, a member of the Convention who had been assassinated for having voted for the death of Louis XVI and whose remains had gone to join those of Beaurepaire in the Pantheon. The president's words represented Bertèche as a living martyr of liberty: "Brave Bertèche, like Lepeletier, you spilled your blood to cement freedom; but thanks be to the spirit of France, it is not your ashes we will cover with flowers; it is your forehead." Bertèche responded appropriately, saying that he had only one regret in receiving this tribute from the Convention: "that is to have only one life to offer it for the salvation of the republic."[61]

The representation of the soldier's sacrifice as the epitome of devotion to the republic reached its apogee in 1793–94, Year Two of the republic and the most radical phase of the revolution. At a time when the National Convention and its ruling Committee of Public Safety were dominated by the radical Montagnards, who also held sway over a national network of Jacobin clubs and were supported by the Parisian popular movement of militant sans-culottes, the armies themselves were a principal target for propaganda celebrating the willingness of ordinary soldiers to lay down life and limb for the nation. There were many manifestations of the cult

59 *Annales patriotiques et littéraires*, 19 October 1792.
60 *Archives parlementaires*, vol. 53, 328; vol. 54, 715.
61 Ibid., 634.

of the common soldier in Jacobin propaganda. The Jacobins and their supporters contrasted the perfidy of the old caste of officers, many of whom remained attached to their uniforms of Bourbon white and resisted the switch to republican blue, with the patriotic idealism of the citizen soldier. The opposition between the corrupt value system of the old regime, with its emphasis on honour and glory, and the new values of the republic was articulated in typically blunt fashion by Jacques-René Hébert in *Le Père Duchesne*, a newspaper that was distributed to the armies in vast numbers. "Under the frightful reign of despotism," wrote Hébert, "our old tyrants were not content just to devour the substance of the sans-culottes, and to get fat off their sweat and their blood; they stole from them the very glory of their exploits. When ten to twelve thousand men had died for the fatherland, no more was said of it than Gascons say about their bad debts; all the honour went to the general who had stayed with the reserve during the battle; fellows who had not even smelled the powder passed for intrepid warriors."[62] "Glory" and "honour," for Hébert, were false attributes, achieved through usurpation. "The only reward for a fine action in the eyes of a true republican," he insisted, "is the respect of his fellow citizens."[63] Claiming that republican soldiers went to battle "as if they were going to a ball, singing and dancing," Hébert insisted that "the last cry of the dying is always a cry of joy, the last words they say are: *vive la liberté, vive la république*." He went on to cite examples of republican self-sacrifice from the Army of the Nord, describing how soldiers continued to affirm their devotion to the republic even as the surgeons removed their shattered limbs. One, Sergeant Denis Siboul, having lost both feet to a cannonball, continued to call out "*vive la liberté, vive la république*," as he endured the surgeon's knife. The only tears the wounded gunner shed were for the sake of the four children he would no longer be able to support. Assuring Siboul that the National Convention would take care of his loved ones, *Le Père Duchesne* represented him to its readers as the "model of republicans[:] his first thought is for his homeland, but since he is also a man and a father, that is one more virtue."[64]

The contrast between the selflessness of ordinary soldiers and the cupidity of the generals was also a theme of the *Anti-fédéraliste*, another newspaper that supported and was supported by the revolutionary government. "While the leaders and perfidious mandatories dishonour themselves by a cowardly apostasy, the citizens and soldiers manifest a heroism that once could only be found in history," claimed the paper on 29 September 1793. The same

62 *Le Père Duchesne*, no. 321.
63 Ibid.
64 Ibid.

issue contrasted the treasonous conduct of General Houchard, whom it denounced as a "vile conspirator," comparing it unfavourably to the heroism of a corporal who had fought under Houchard's command at the Battle of Hondschoote, François Maraton, who had single-handedly attacked twelve enemy soldiers, killing four of them and capturing the gun carriage they were pulling. When offered a reward by the representatives on mission to the army, the only reward Maraton would accept was "the post of honour."[65] Presenting such examples to the people, claimed the editors of the *Anti-fédéraliste*, would augment their energy and increase their hatred for "the scoundrels who would like to render useless so many sacrifices." It therefore approved the project of the Abbé Grégoire to distribute a civic manual to publicize acts of republican heroism. The newspaper evoked the "the delicious tears of admiration" that would be inspired by stories such as that of a gunner who, "covered with wounds," refused medical treatment to return to his post.[66] Grégoire himself insisted upon the need to celebrate the heroism of ordinary soldiers. "Feudal honour used insolently to reject the soldier from the temple of honour," Grégoire declared: "he must now enter in the same way as a general."[67] Grégoire went on to cite numerous examples of patriotic devotion, including that of David, a grenadier sergeant who used a corkscrew to dig an enemy bullet out of his own breast in order to charge his musket and to fire it back at the enemy; and that of another grenadier wounded at Mons, who, "at a moment when to reach the enemy we were filling in a ditch, even by rolling corpses into it, wanted to be thrown in himself, so that he could still be useful to the homeland after his death: his last breath was a homage to liberty."[68]

The National Convention's Committee of Public Instruction followed through on the promise to collect and distribute such stories of republican heroism. The *Recueil des actions héroïques et civiques des républicains français* was published in instalments and each printing of 150,000 copies distributed to the armies, popular societies, and schools. The *Recueil* celebrated both civic and military heroism, but it gave priority to expressions of the readiness of French men and women of all ages either to die themselves or to accept the deaths of their loved ones on behalf of the republic.[69] Typical was the story of Rose-Liberté Barrau, a woman who served as a

---

65 *L'Anti-fédéraliste*, 29 September 1793.

66 Ibid.

67 Grégoire, *Rapport*, 4.

68 Ibid.

69 On the significance of the *Recueil* in creating a radically new model of courage that was egalitarian, patriotic, and inclusive of women and civilians as well as soldiers, see Clarke, "'Valour Knows Neither Age nor Sex.'"

Leyrac et Barrau son épouse, tous deux Grenadiers. Lai.

Actuellement qu'ils mordent la poussiere, je te dois tous mes soins.

26 Thermidor An 2.

3.3. "Now that they have bitten the dust, I give all my attention to you." Victory achieved, Rose Barrau assists her wounded husband, Leyrac.

grenadier in the Army of the Pyrénées-Occidentales alongside her brother and her husband. During an attack on a Spanish position Barrau's brother was killed and her husband wounded. "Republican virtue triumphed over love just as it had triumphed over nature," however, and Liberté Barrau carried on the fight until the enemy had been defeated. Only then did she return to minister to her wounded husband (fig. 3.3).[70] The republic came before life and it came before family. Thus, Alexis Emonet was praised for volunteering to finish his brother's sentry duty on the banks of the Rhine

70 Bourdon, *Recueil des Actions Héroïques*, no. 1, 19. A later issue of the *Recueil* recounted the exploits of another cross-dressing female soldier, Rose Bouillou, in almost identical terms. Thibeaudeau, *Recueil des Actions Héroïques*, no. 5, 7.

after the latter's head had been taken off by a cannonball: "Despite the entreaties of his comrades, who wished to spare him this sad spectacle, he insisted on being taken to the place where his brother's blood had flowed, and where his bloody corpse would inflame the desire to avenge his death, or to perish as gloriously; and it was only after fulfilling his duty to his homeland, that he paid to nature the tribute of his sensibility."[71] In many cases, sometimes most improbably, soldiers themselves were supposed to have articulated their willingness to sacrifice their lives. In republican propaganda, even soldiers without mouths were made to speak. It seems hardly likely that the gunner who lost his lower jaw to a cannonball was still able to say, "Do I need a jaw to fight our enemies? I have my two arms, I have my good sight; that is enough to aim a cannon, and to knock off more than one enemy jaw."[72] More plausible, at least, was the story of Pierre Cornu, a twenty-year-old standard bearer who refused to abandon his flag in order to save himself and declared "I am content, I die for my homeland," as he succumbed to superior numbers. The youth's words were echoed by his father, who was reported to have "cried no tears on his son's grave": "I am content," he said, "since he died for the republic."[73] A captain, dying of gunshot wounds in hospital, declared "I am going to die, but the republic will live; I willingly sacrifice my life to it; if only I had a thousand lives to give."[74] His sentiments were supposedly shared by all the other wounded soldiers in the hospital: "Their eyes always fixed upon the motherland, they thought only, in the midst of the most painful operations, of the happy moment when they would be able to shed the rest of their blood for her."[75]

The stubborn refusal of republican soldiers to make any concession to the enemy was an essential feature of these heroic anecdotes. In some cases, as in that of the youth hero Joseph Bara, this took the form of soldiers refusing to utter disloyal words. Called upon to cry "Long live the king!" by Vendéan rebels, Bara shouted a defiant "Long live the republic!" at the cost of his life (fig. 3.4).[76] In other cases, this uncompromising spirit was expressed in a refusal to be taken prisoner, even if the alternative was to die, like Beaurepaire, by one's own hand. Citizen Duchemin, a battalion commander, was praised for his "sublime action" in shooting himself, "preferring death to surrendering the arms confided to him by the homeland

---

71 Thibaudeau, *Recueil des Actions Héroïques*, no. 5, 32.
72 Bourdon, *Recueil des Actions Héroïques*, no. 4, 19
73 Thibaudeau, *Recueil des Actions Héroïques*, no. 5, 12.
74 Ibid., 22.
75 Ibid.
76 Bourdon, *Recueil des Actions Héroïques*, no. 1, 18. On the cult of Bara, see Jaeglé, "Bara"; Monnier, "Le culte de Bara"; Vovelle, "L'enfance héroïque."

MORT HÉROIQUE DU JEUNE BARRA
à qui la Patrie reconnaissante a accordé les honneurs du Panthéon.
ses dernières paroles.
à toi F ... brigand, le cheval de mon colonel et le mien ah' bien oui.
à Paris, chez SERGENT, et C.ᵉ Quai de l'École, N.° 17.

3.4. "The heroic death of young Barra to whom the grateful Homeland has granted the honours of the Pantheon."

for its defence."[77] Martin Vinay, a volunteer from the Drôme, was celebrated for killing himself with his own sword rather than fall into enemy hands, declaring with his final words, "At least the enemy won't take me alive" (fig. 3.5).[78] Yet another soldier, wounded, was represented imploring a comrade to finish him off, saying, "My friend, take from me what life I have left. I prefer to die by your hand than by that of my country's enemies."[79] These accounts drove home the point that for republican soldiers their love of country was so powerful and their hatred of the foe so implacable

77 Bourdon, *Recueil des actions héroïques*, no. 3, 9.
78 Grasset Saint-Sauveur, *Les fastes du peuple français*, no. 45.
79 Ibid., no. 37.

Martin Vinay, Volontaire au 3me Bataillon de la Drôme.

L'Ennemi du moins ne m'aura pas vivant.

Le 20 Novembre 1793. V.S.

3.5. "At least the enemy won't take me alive." Martin Vinay, Volunteer of the Third Drôme Batallion.

they were able to rise above every instinct of self-preservation – not to mention society's taboos against self-immolation – and to resist the enemy even when the only possible form of resistance was to take their own lives.[80]

Artists quickly took the opportunity to depict the heroic acts recounted in the *Recueil.* The Commune des Arts, established in 1793 with the purpose of dedicating the arts to the service of the revolution, voted to begin each of its meetings by reading two stories from its pages.[81] When, the following year, the Committee of Public Instruction invited artists to submit designs for the artistic competition known as the *concours de l'an II,* about one-third of the 140 submissions were inspired by the heroic anecdotes recounted in the *Recueil,* making a strong case for the primacy of contemporary history over antiquity as a subject for artists.[82] By no means were all the subjects chosen military or male. Six artists, for example, depicted the heroism of a woman who kept a group of Vendéans from invading her home by threatening to ignite a barrel of gunpowder.[83] Artists were generally reticent about showing soldiers' wounds and there were still some who preferred allegorical representations to realistic ones. Anatole Devosge and Pierre Peyron, for example, who both received prizes for their drawings of wounded and dying soldiers, depicted them in ancient garb, surrounded by allegorical figures representing the Homeland, Virtue, Immortality, and Recognition.[84] Devosge was a student of Jacques-Louis David, whose paintings of the assassinated deputies Lepeletier and Marat were displayed in the National Convention. David did not enter the *concours de l'an II,* but his canvas depicting the dying boy soldier Bara did depict one of the *Recueil*'s subjects. David deliberately eschewed any historical specificity in his painting of Bara. Instead, inspired by Robespierre's idealization of Bara, he sought to elevate the dying youth hero to mythic status by representing his body as nude, unmarked, and of indeterminate sex, a universal symbol of republican virtue (fig. 3.6).[85] More realistically gruesome depictions of soldiers' bodies disfigured by wounds appeared later, beginning in 1796, when many of the anecdotes recounted in the *Recueil* were illustrated by the engraver L.F. Labrousse and published, again by instalments, under the title *Les fastes du peuple français.*[86] In contrast to the nude, unblemished

---

80 On the theme of heroic suicide, see Reynier, "Le héros militaire," 216.

81 Biard and Maingon, *La souffrance et la gloire,* 111.

82 Olander, "Pour transmettre à la postérité," 291; Jourdan, *Les monuments,* 348.

83 Ibid., 311.

84 Biard and Maingon, *La souffrance et la gloire,* 112; Réunion des Musées Nationaux, *La Révolution française,* vol. 3: *La révolution créatrice,* 860–4.

85 Olander, "Pour transmettre à la postérité," 293–302. See also *Joseph Bara*; and Musée Calvet, *La mort de Bara.*

86 Grasset Saint-Sauveur, *Les fastes du peuple français.*

3.6. Jacques-Louis David. *Death of Joseph Bara.*

body of David's Bara, François Lavigne, a seventeen-year-old volunteer, was shown standing in the uniform of the republic, blood pouring from the stumps of his arms, shouting, "Comrades! Avenge me, because I no longer have any arms" (fig. 3.7).[87]

TEARS DENIED

During the revolution, patriotic sentiment was expected to prevail over every other feeling, including the ties of affection linking defenders of the homeland to the families they left behind. This principle was established from the very beginning of the revolutionary wars. Reporting on the victory at Jemmapes, the *Courrier des Départemens* commented on the response of a father who learned of the death of his son, Citizen Boucher, who had reportedly died with the words "*Ça ira*" on his lips. "Boucher's father, learning of the death of his son, at first succumbed to the immediate impulses of feeling, but as fatherly love gave way to that of the homeland, 'I still have

87 Biard and Maingon, *La souffrance et la gloire*, 113.

François Lavigne agé de 17 ans Volontaire du Bon de la Somme

Camarades! vengez-moi, car je n'ai plus de bras!

31 Août 1793 V.S.

3.7. "Comrades! Avenge me, because I have no arms!" François Lavigne, aged 17, Volunteer of the Somme Batallion.

a son able to bear arms,' said this virtuous citizen. 'I will unhesitatingly make of him a painful sacrifice, for the success of my homeland, the happiness of men and the destruction of the tyrants.'"[88] Very similar in its description of paternal grief subsumed by patriotic emotion and renewed sacrifice is an anecdote reported to the Convention in September 1793 by the popular society of Épinal. The Society had received a letter from a Citizen Denis offering three hundred *livres* to a volunteer prepared to take the place of his seventeen-year-old son, one of three sons whom he had "offered ... to the homeland," all of whom had been killed in battle. Denis declared his conviction that this patriotic gesture would diminish his grief. The society expressed its recognition of the patriotism of both father and son, decreeing that its forthcoming festival dedicated to the assassinated revolutionary Jean-Paul Marat would also honour "the children of Epinal who died for liberty and equality" and whose names would be inscribed on the altar of the homeland.[89] The correct response of the model citizen to bereavement was therefore to double down on the sacrifice already made, effacing the anguish of loss through another act of patriotic generosity. The festival held at Épinal on 30 September in honour of the martyrs of liberty expressed sorrow for the loss of two illustrious representatives of the people, Jean-Paul Marat and Pierre Baille, as well as for the anonymous "children of the republic" who had been killed fighting in the republican armies. The spirit of sorrow was, however, accompanied by that of vengeance. At the parish church of Épinal, the secretary of the popular society intoned a prayer to the Supreme Being that began by invoking His mercy for those who had sacrificed their lives for freedom but which then became an appeal for Him to punish the enemies of the republic: "Appear, all powerful God, arm yourself with the sword of your justice, strike down, exterminate all the kings, these princes, these brigands who seek to sully France [...] place yourself at the head of our legions, lead them everywhere to victory." In dispatching his account of the festival to the National Convention, the secretary expressed his hope that the society's tribute would strengthen the public spirit and "encourage the zeal of the young to avenge the blood of its elders who died for the one and indivisible republic."[90]

Popular societies such as the one in Épinal played a significant role in channelling the grief experienced by communities as news filtered back of soldiers who were killed fighting on the frontiers. The sorrow of relatives was accorded respect and sympathy, but those relatives also were expected

88   *Le Courrier des Départemens*, 7 December 1792.
89   *Archives parlementaires*, vol. 75, 339.
90   Ibid., 332.

to affirm their undimmed patriotism as well as their acceptance of their loss for the sake of the homeland. The popular society of Valence, in the Department of the Drôme, recorded that news of the death of "brave Captain Deneyrol,"[91] who was killed fighting on the Spanish frontier, had "plunged the city into sorrow." Its report began with a description of how the captain had died in his soldiers' arms, crying "How happy I am to die for my homeland! Long live the republic!" It then went on to describe how, "after a moving homage to the patriotism and devotion of a father who, having only one son, had given him to France," the society had approved a motion to place Deneyrol's father and his property under the protection of the city. The following day, the father himself came to the meeting of the popular society. "Everybody was silent as he entered," continued the report, "so incapable did we feel of consoling such a great sorrow." Jean Deneyrol then spoke to the assembly, thanking it for its tribute to "my tender son … this dear son whom I offered to the homeland" and concluding with a reaffirmation of his patriotism: "I beg the assembly to be persuaded that the loss of my son has not at all changed the love I have for the republic. On the contrary, I could not better avenge his death than by remaining faithful to it, and I am always ready to sacrifice my life if the public happiness demands it!"[92] Once again, grief was channelled into an expression of readiness for further sacrifice.

Tributes to the defenders of the republic such as those at Épinal and Valence were clearly, as Joseph Clarke has demonstrated, genuine expressions of sorrow that sought to console local communities for the loss of their menfolk who had been killed or wounded in the war.[93] All the same, as was the case at Épinal, where the symbolic itinerary passed from sombre prayers in a church to patriotic singing in the open air and where women's sashes of black crepe gave way to tricoloured ones, festivals honouring the defenders of the fatherland usually provided an emotional script for their participants.[94] The prescribed succession of emotions was clearly summarized in a report of the ceremony held at Lisieux to honour the republican martyrs Marat, Lepeletier, and Beauvais. "The tears we shed on their funeral urns were soon ended," the report declared. "Our souls expanded, our hearts were electrified by seeing these three heroes living

91 Jean François Victor Deneyrol, born 25 June 1769, joined the Twelfth Batallion of volunteers from the Drôme in August 1792. He was killed in July 1794. [S]ervice [H]istorique de la [D]éfense, [A]rchives de [G]uerre: Armée de Terre, Xw 30: Volontaires nationaux: Doubs, Drôme, Eure.

92 SHD, AG, Armée de Terre, Xw 30: Volontaires nationaux: Doubs, Drôme, Eure, no. 110.

93 Joseph Clarke, *Commemorating the Dead*, 250–1.

94 *Archives parlementaires*, vol., 76, 332.

and dying for the cause of freedom. Amidst a thousand cries of *Vive la République*, to the sound of a warlike and harmonious music, we all swore to avenge their deaths, and not to lay down arms until the crowned scoundrels who carried off our best friends are buried beneath the ruins of their thrones."[95] At some festivals the denial of tears was made explicit: "Let us not shed useless tears; / let us imitate their devotion and celebrate their virtues," instructed a banner at a festival held in Toul to honour Marat, Lepeletier, and the "defenders of the homeland."[96]

The association of the sacrifice of humble soldiers with that of the illustrious martyrs of liberty exalted by the Convention in 1793–94 was a common feature of local festivals held during the Terror. At Saint-Aignan, in the Department of Loire-et-Cher, a festival held on 30 November 1793 to celebrate the destruction of feudal titles and the planting of a liberty tree surrounded a wounded veteran from the war in the Vendée with busts of Marat, Lepeletier, Voltaire, and Rousseau; this "living victim supported by crutches" was explicitly associated with the martyrs of liberty as a symbol of the price to be paid for freedom.[97] During the Terror the sacrifices of common soldiers were recognized by local Jacobin clubs and their bereaved families were offered public relief by the national government. In some cases at least, popular societies perpetuated the memory of the heroes of the Year Two beyond the end of the Terror. In Valence, a ceremony to celebrate the signature of the Peace of Leoben, on 28 May 1797, paid tribute to Martin Vinay, the volunteer who had killed himself in November 1793 with his own sabre rather than be taken prisoner by enemy troops. A print depicting Vinay's suicide (see figure 3.6) was fixed to the monumental pyramid erected in memory of the local soldiers who had been killed. The Vinay family were honoured participants in the festival, "since it was their blood and the feelings that they had inspired in him that produced this exemplary action." Vinay's mother and father were presented with a laurel wreath laced with cypress and tricoloured ribbons while a cannon fired a salute.[98] Popular societies also sought to preserve the reputations of soldiers who had been killed in action and thereby to spare the feelings of bereaved family members. The popular society of Foix, in the Ariège, received a letter from a Brigadier-General Lemoine in September 1794 expressing outrage that "cowardly calumniators sought to bring desolation into the bosom of families whose children died with arms in hand defending the liberty of their country." The general had

95 Ibid., vol. 78, 509.
96 Ibid., vol. 81, 72.
97 Ibid., vol. 81, 51.
98 SHD, AG: Xw 30: Volontaires nationaux: Doubs, Drôme, Eure, no. 119.

received a complaint from the father of a Captain Amardel, who had been killed fighting in the army of the East Pyrenees on 12 July. "His father let me hear his moans," wrote the general, "and I rushed to his aid to defend the memory of one of my brothers in arms."[99] The society approved the receipt of an attestation that defended Amardel against the charge of cowardice. The attestation condemned Amardel's calumniators – "That is how aristocrats seek to bring sorrow into the bosom of respectable families who should expect nothing but tender consolation from their co-citizens" – affirming that he had fought bravely to the end.[100] At the same time, the popular society approved a festival to inaugurate an obelisk on which the names of Amardel and all local soldiers who had been killed would be inscribed. The society affirmed the importance of such tributes as a guarantee of immortality for these martyrs of liberty: "Granite and marble will eventually crumble. Nothing resists the destructive blows of time: but the man who dies for the homeland never dies."[101]

Despite such local efforts to perpetuate and defend the memory of ordinary soldiers, the Directory (1795–99) generally provided little in the way of recognition or relief to them or their families.[102] The Festival of the Foundation of the Republic held to mark the beginning of Year Six of the republic (22 September 1797) was a rare instance when the Directory recognized the sacrifices of relatively low-ranking soldiers, paying tribute to three wounded veterans, one of whom had lost his legs, another his arms, and the third his eyes.[103] Otherwise, the Directory's recognition of the revolutionary armies focused almost exclusively upon the generals who commanded them. Solemn funeral ceremonies were held to honour generals who died serving the republic, most notably Hoche, Joubert,

99 SHD, AG, Xw 7: Volontaires nationaux: Ariège: Letter of 20 September 1794.

100 SHD, AG, Xw 7: Volontaires nationaux: Ariège: Société populaire de Foix, meeting of 4 Fructidor Year Two (12 July 1794): Copie de l'attestation du Conseil d'Administration du 1er bataillon des Grenadiers.

101 SHD, AG, Xw 7: Volontaires nationaux: Ariège: Société populaire de Foix, meeting of 4 Fructidor Year Two (12 July 1794).

102 See Clarke, *Commemorating the Dead*, 253–72.

103 *Messager du Soir*, 4 Vendémiaire, Year Six (25 September, 1797); *Journal des Hommes Libres*, 3 Vendémiaire Year 6 (24 September 1797). The three veterans were nonetheless officers, all holding the rank of captain. The *Courrier de l'Armée d'Italie* identified them specifically as: Captain Étienne Baron, twenty-three years old, who lost his arms to a cannonball at the siege of Huningue; Captain François Martin, aged twenty-four, who lost his legs in the naval battle of 1 June 1794 (known to the English as "the Glorious First of June"); and Captain J.B. Gauthier, thirty-six, who was severely wounded at the siege of Haguenau, "having lost both eyes and his cheek, and part of his upper jaw shattered." *Le Courrier de l'Armée d'Italie*, 5 October 1797.

Duphot, and Marceau.[104] These ceremonies often insisted upon the sorrow felt at the deaths of these military leaders, an emotion that the organizers themselves deliberately cultivated. A ceremony to honour General Hoche at Lyon featured a speech by Citizen Bérenger, a "Professor of Eloquence and Literature," whose eulogy, according to the publication that recounted it, swept his audience along on a tide of emotion: "Our spirits were suspended between sobs and admiration; we wept, we want to keep weeping; we want to weep again; we wish to be nourished, broken by sorrow."[105] Such sorrowful feelings were on occasion intensified by the presence of the bereaved relatives of the deceased. "Tears flowed," reported the *Messager du Soir*, at a funeral ceremony in Paris when the father of Lazare Hoche placed a laurel branch before the bust of his son on the Altar of the Fatherland: "One of the spectators cried, 'Let anyone say that virtue has no reward!' a simple and sublime expression that moved your heart, O unfortunate father, and which will leave profound memories of this sad ceremony in the spirit of the spectators who tenderly repeated it."[106] Eulogists of Joubert, some of whom addressed their words directly to Madame Joubert, made much of the pathos of the general's recent marriage and the call of duty that took him from the arms of his new bride to rejoin his army in Italy, where he found death and glory at the Battle of Novi: "The voice of the homeland tells him that he must not hesitate between a wife and brothers in arms who must be brought back to the path of victory."[107] The words addressed to Madame Joubert indicate that the point of this appeal to emotion was to demonstrate how powerful were the imperatives of patriotism, which prevailed even over the entirely legitimate but private imperatives of newlywed affection. Ironically, Joubert's marriage in fact delayed his departure to rejoin the Army of Italy by ten days and consequently resulted in the Battle of Novi taking place on terms less favourable to the French than if he had left when first ordered to do so. Joubert's biographer refers to this negligence of duty as an uncharacteristic but serious "professional error."[108] The eulogists also ignored the likelihood that the marriage was as much the result of a political intrigue as it was a love match.[109] Comparing her to the women of

104 On these funerals, see Gainot, "Le dernier voyage," 97–113.
105 Anon., *Procès-verbal de la cérémonie*, 12. In all probability, this was Laurent Bérenger, who had authored *L'école historique et morale du soldat et de l'officier* before the revolution. See chapter 2 in this volume.
106 *Le Messager du Soir*, 4 October 1797.
107 Anon., *Éloge funèbre du Général Joubert*, 17
108 Schmitt, *La vie brève de Barthélemy Joubert*, 350.
109 Ibid., 348–50; see also Buatois, "Un général du Directoire: Joubert," 72.

Sparta who instructed their menfolk to come back either with their shields or on them, one orator said to Madame Joubert: "Strong woman, you will weep more for the homeland's loss than for your own."[110] Another told her, "The pains you suffer and which will never end, still shape one of the finest destinies a woman can have on this earth!"[111] What Madame Joubert – the nineteen-year-old "Zéphyrine," Françoise Félicité de Montholon – really thought of her fine destiny we do not know. For the orators who so readily told her what she thought, the role of bereaved spouse was deemed to be as enviable as that of deceased hero. The speeches over, young girls sang of their sympathy and their envy for Madame Joubert, while men and boys sang of vengeance.[112]

Tears were generally deemed more appropriate for women than for men. An orator at a ceremony held to mourn Hoche at Pithiviers, in the Department of the Loiret, was carried away on a wave of sentimentality as he imagined the sorrow of a young Vendéan woman who attributed the survival of her family to Hoche's pacification of the Vendée. The tears of the woman whom he had conjured had poured into his own breast, the speaker declared. "Let your tears flow," he responded. "A free people applauds them and shares them."[113] The expectation that sorrow would be displaced by more virile emotions was, however, expressed in yet another tribute to Hoche: "The only tears worthy to honour a great man are those that spread the desire to emulate him. Repair then, as best you can, the loss you have suffered by a new devotion; rekindle in your hearts the love of the fatherland."[114] More bloodthirsty were the words spoken by General Moreau at a funeral ceremony for Joubert, which were directed specifically at the soldiers of the Army of Italy: "It is less by tears that his memory must be made eternal," Moreau assured them, "than by spilling the blood of Russians and Austrians [...] Let us fly to avenge his death by new battles."[115]

DYING FOR HONOUR AND GLORY

The shift from recognizing the exemplary sacrifices of common soldiers during the most radical phase of the revolution, to prioritizing those of generals during the reaction that followed was accompanied by a significant change in the representation of the values associated with the soldier's

---

110 Cornet, *Discours*, 10.
111 Anon., *Procès-verbal de la cérémonie*, 26–7; Garat, *Éloge funèbre de Joubert*, 24–5.
112 Collignon, "Ode funéraire," 4.
113 Anon., *Éloge funèbre de Lazare Hoche*, 10–11.
114 Rivière, *Discours*, 11.
115 Anon., *Pompe funèbre du général Joubert*, 2.

death. The emphasis upon the specific values of liberty and republicanism was replaced by a more generalized patriotism. The words "honour" and "glory" were restored to respectability. Dead heroes were as likely to be compared to warriors who had served the monarchs of the old regime as to the soldiers who had fought for Rome or Greece. This rehabilitation of past military heroes culminated after the Directory had been overthrown when the remains of Marshal Turenne were solemnly transferred from Saint Denis to the Temple of Mars (this was the Hôtel des Invalides, the home for veteran soldiers established by Louis XIV, renamed by the revolutionaries) on 21 September 1800.[116] By this time, death was no longer a fate chosen by republican soldiers as the logical outcome of a war to the finish between completely incompatible ideologies, because the only possibilities in such a conflict were victory or death. Rather it had been restored to its former status as a dignified end to a military career, achieved in combat with a respected enemy, and honoured by friend and foe alike.

This change in the representation of the soldier's death was particularly striking in published accounts describing the death and funeral honours of General Marceau. François-Séverin Marceau was killed near Altenkirchen by an Austrian sniper while serving with the Army of the Sambre-et-Meuse in 1796. His commander-in-chief, General Jourdan, recounted Marceau's death in a speech to the Council of Five Hundred on 21 August 1797:

A Tyrolean *chasseur*, hidden behind a tree, recognized him by the distinctive signs of his rank, took aim and fired a carbine shot through his body.

Marceau slowly withdrew, ordered his officers to conceal from the men he commanded the fatal shot that had struck him, sent word to me, gave some orders; finally, he continued to serve his homeland, although his face showed the palour of death.

Marceau was taken to Altenkirchen by some grenadiers. I rushed to his side, accompanied by my staff. We wept tears; Marceau alone remained calm. He said to us, "General, my friends, why do you weep? I am happy to die for my country. General, in the name of the friendship that unites us, I recommend to you the officers who have served beside me, and my family."[117]

Up to this point, Jourdan's narration of Marceau's death, complete with the dying soldier's injunction to his comrades to staunch their tears, was typical, resembling so many others recounted since the beginning of the

116 *Gazette National, ou le Moniteur Universel*, 23 and 25 September 1800.
117 Jourdan, *Discours*, 3–4; *Gazette National, ou le Moniteur Universel*, 25 August 1797.

revolutionary wars. Jourdan went on, however, to describe the respect shown to Marceau by the Austrians, in whose care he was compelled to pass his final hours. "It will be sweet for me to give justice to the fairness and humanity of the enemies I have so often fought," said Jourdan: "As soon as the enemy advance guard occupied Altenkirchen, General Hadick sent a security guard to General Marceau, and then came to offer his care and assistance. General Kray, that old warrior who had fought Marceau over two campaigns, came to his side; tears flowed from his eyes, and holding Marceau's hand in his for an hour, his deep silence and his pain paid tribute to the French general."[118] This tribute to the enemy's "fairness and humanity" was a striking contrast to the representations of an infamous and barbarous foe that had characterized republican propaganda during the Year Two. It harked back to an older tradition whereby the deepest mark of a soldier's reputation was the honour accorded him by his enemies. The tears of General Kray were reminiscent of those supposedly shed by General Montecuccoli in 1675 upon receiving news of the death of his old adversary, Marshal Turenne,[119] or those shed by his Spanish captors over the dying Chevalier Bayard in 1524.[120] The parallel between the deaths of Bayard and Marceau, both mortally wounded by snipers while covering a retreat on horseback and subsequently cared for by their enemies, did not escape contemporaries. Emira Sergent-Marceau, in presenting a portrait of Marceau to the Council of Five Hundred, called for the shield of Marceau to be suspended from the Pantheon alongside that of Bayard. "He lived *without fear* like that illustrious warrior; he died *without reproach* like him," she said. "Like him, he saw his death bed watered by the tears of the heroes he commanded, and by the enemies against whom he had fought."[121] Accounts of the funerary tributes accorded to Marceau made it clear that the enemy shared in those tributes. Two Austrian regiments apparently vied for the honour of escorting Marceau's remains as they were returned to the care of his comrades for burial. The transfer was treated with due ceremony. The general's remains, enclosed in a

118 Ibid.

119 Ramsay, *Histoire de Henri de la Tour d'Auvergne*, vol. 2, 364. Ramsay's poignant account of Turenne's death emphasized the sorrow of Montecuccoli: "The Count of Montecuccoli, with a greatness of spirit rare among rivals, seemed to feel only sorrow, and often repeated these words: *A man has died who was an honour and a credit to mankind.*" Ramsay's final tribute to Turenne, emphasizing his disinterested devotion to the fatherland, qualified only by his respect for the laws of justice and humanity, repeated Montecuccoli's epitaph as the last words of his book. Ibid., 382.

120 Mailles, *La très joyeuse*, 214.

121 Sergent-Marceau, *Présentation au Conseil des Cinq-Cents*, 1–2.

sky-blue casket, were placed on a carriage that was draped in black. The Austrian guard of honour led Marceau's riderless horse in the procession. As an additional mark of respect, General Kray insisted that the blindfolds be removed from the eyes of French officers who had been admitted through Austrian lines. "They are unworthy of such a ceremony," he said. "Anyway, what do we fear? Have they not lost the best part of their forces today?" The following day, as the body was escorted through Coblentz to Petersburg, where it was buried under a "grassy pyramid," artillery salutes were fired by both the French garrison, in Coblentz, as well as by the Austrian garrison in Ehrenbreitstein: "It seemed as if that redoubtable fortress belonged to the French."[122]

A year and a day later, the *Messager du Soir* published a remarkably similar account of the funeral of General Hoche, in virtually the same location. A letter describes the participation of the garrison of Ehrenbreitstein in the ceremony. The approach of the funeral convoy, which included the Austrian commander, marching alongside French officers, was saluted by troops drawn up on the glacis and by cannon fire from the fortress.[123] Such ceremonies, in which military identity took precedence over national allegiance, demonstrate the extent to which purely military values had come to the fore. The culmination of this trend was reached with the tributes to Latour d'Auvergne, who was killed at Neuburg on 27 June 1800. The death of "the first grenadier of the army" was commemorated by his comrades of the forty-sixth demi-brigade, who embalmed his heart and marched with this sacred object, enclosed within a gold and silver urn, suspended from their flag. At regimental roll calls, Latour d'Auvergne's name would continue to be called, the sergeant-major responding: "he died on the field of honour."[124] The site where he fell was to be marked by a monument "consecrated to the virtues and to courage [... and] placed in the safe-keeping of the brave men of all countries."[125] Nothing could state more clearly the idea that soldiers "of all countries" belonged to a fraternity that was set apart from civilian life and united by a distinct set of values that transcended political and national divisions.

The elevation of Latour d'Auvergne to heroic status represented the logical end point of this evolution that witnessed the revival of honour and glory as the pre-eminent military values. Latour d'Auvergne was not only *like* Turenne; the great marshal's blood actually flowed through

122 Anon., "Le dernier combat de Marceau," in *Carnet de la Sabretache* (1899), 272–87.
123 *Messager du soir*, 14 Vendémiaire year 6 (4 October 1797).
124 Buhot de Kersers, ed. *Correspondance de la Tour d'Auvergne*, 356–8.
125 Ibid., 344; Anon., *Vie politique et militaire de Latour-d'Auvergne*, 15.

the veins of the first grenadier of the army. In the words of one eulogist: "He recognized that the last drops of that formidable warrior's blood flowed through his veins, and he had barely reached the age of fourteen when he formed the inner resolve only to lose the rest of that precious blood in serving his fatherland."[126] Only after a lengthy military career, extending from the old regime to the new, did Latour d'Auvergne achieve this destiny, after nobly taking the place of the son of a friend who, the last of five brothers, had been conscripted. "I have little fear of danger at my age," he is supposed to have said; "the most desirable death is that of a grenadier on the field of battle."[127] The end, when it came, was appropriately glorious: "This hero so worthy of our deepest regrets, fell pierced by a lance thrust to the heart, but his dying eyes enjoyed the sight of the enemy's flight; he died content" (fig. 3.8).[128]

Latour d'Auvergne prepared the way for his eulogists in his own correspondence, which insisted upon his constant commitment to his homeland. A letter written in the aftermath of his imprisonment by the English in 1795 gives some sense of this:"My republican spirit being incapable of dissimulation or of bending to the circumstances, I always presented myself as I was, a Frenchman and a patriot. The revered symbol of my nation, the tricoloured cockade, was always on my cap and my costume in prison was the same as I wore in battle. It was this that provoked the hatred unleashed upon me and the persecutions I had to endure."[129] Self-righteous declarations like this did not prevent contemporaries from celebrating Latour d'Auvergne's "modesty" and self-abnegation. His reluctance to accept the honours that were offered to him was insisted upon. He accepted a decoration from the king of Spain, but not the pension that came with it. Compelled through poverty to request money from the revolutionary government, he took only a fraction of what was offered. Awarded promotion, he declined any senior office. He accepted only with the greatest reluctance the sword of honour offered him when he was named "First Grenadier of the Armies of the Republic." "The more he shunned honours, the more they were thrust upon him," wrote one eulogist. "He loved equality so much and believed himself so little superior to his comrades that he was truly afflicted by this distinction."[130]

126 Ibid., 7.
127 Ibid., 13.
128 Ibid., 14.
129 Buhot de Kersers, ed., *Correspondance de la Tour d'Auvergne*, 264.
130 Dorat-Cubières, *Les regrets d'un Français*, 14–15.

Mort de LA TOUR D'AUVERGNE, 1.er Grenadier de la Rép. fe

Tué le 9. Messidor. An 8. sur la hauteur d'Oberhausen en avant de Neubourg, d'un coup de lance porté au cœur par un
Hulan, pendant qu'il arrachoit une Enseigne des mains d'un autre.

La Tour d'Auvergne était le dernier exploit de Turenne.

A Paris chez Jean.t M.d d'Estampes et Fabriquant de papier; porté rue Jacques

3.8. "The death of Latour d'Auvergne, First Grenadier of the French Republic. Killed [...] by a lance thrust to the heart from one Hulan, while he was wresting a standard from the hands of another."

The celebration of Latour d'Auvergne was particularly important because it embodied a new model of military devotion. Latour d'Auvegne stood for "honour, glory, talent, and virtue,"[131] but he also stood for a patriotism that was completely divorced from politics. This was made explicit in a tribute by the poet Dorat-Cubières. Stating that there had been generals willing to serve the monarchy but not the republic, others who were republican but who only identified the republic with one party or another, Dorat-Cubières insisted that Latour d'Auvergne's loyalties were of a different order. "He had been a hero under the monarchy; he was one under the republic; he would perhaps have been one even under the reign of the *Grand-Seigneur*."[132]

A soldier did not need to know who ruled the state; all he needed to know was where the enemy was and how to fight. The same point was made about Turenne in a speech read by Lazare Carnot upon the occasion of the transfer of the marshal's remains to the Invalides, on 21 September 1800. This time, it was Turenne who was compared to Latour d'Auvergne, among other revolutionary soldiers. "It was not at all to the maintenance of the political system then dominant, that he dedicated his efforts, that he sacrificed his life, but to the defence of his country, independent of any system. The love of the homeland was his motive, as it was in our time that of Dampierre, Dugommier, Marceau, Joubert, Desaix, Latour-d'Auvergne."[133]

The recognition accorded to Latour d'Auvergne as the First Grenadier of the Armies of the Republic as well as the posthumous tributes to his memory took place in 1800, shortly after the coup that brought to power as First Consul another soldier – Napoleon Bonaparte – who also claimed to represent a patriotism above all spirit of party. The celebration of Latour d'Auvergne as a model soldier who fought and died both for the principles of the revolution as well as for glory and honour was consistent with the values the new government claimed to represent. The eclipse of Liberty as the ultimate inspiration for soldierly virtue had largely been accomplished by the time of the Consulate. Under Napoleon, as vast new armies of men were raised to fight far from France, it was above all for Glory and Honour that they would be called upon to die.

131 Anon., *Vie politique et militaire de Latour-d'Auvergne*, 8.

132 Dorat-Cubières, *Les regrets d'un Français*, 9–10.

133 *Gazette National ou Le Moniteur Universel*, 23 September, 1800. General Dampierre was killed at Valenciennes, 9 May 1793; General Desaix was killed at the Battle of Marengo, 14 June 1800. A funeral ceremony honouring Desaix and General Kléber, who was assassinated in Egypt, also on 14 June, was held in the Place des Victoires in Paris on 22 September 1800.

CIVIL WAR

The reaffirmation of the traditional code of military honour served to moderate the violence of war. Gestures of mutual respect between enemies, such as those attending the burials of Marceau and Hoche, were indicative of a broader intention on the part of the combatants to fight fairly and to accord humane treatment to enemy soldiers who were wounded or taken prisoner. During the French revolutionary wars such conventions were generally observed in the war with foreign powers, even during the most intense period of ideological conflict and in spite of a notorious decree by the National Convention instructing French troops not to take English or Hanoverian troops prisoner. Where the soldier's code of honour held no sway, however, was in the war against the internal enemy, against those French men and women who, at one time or another, took up arms against the revolution. Such rebels were not to be treated with the generosity reserved for an honourable foe, but instead with the rigour reserved for common criminals. A law of 29 March 1793 prescribed the death penalty for French citizens bearing arms against the republic. The revolution's implacability toward its internal enemies embittered the conflict between republican soldiers and the *émigré* nobles who fought alongside the forces of the enemy coalition. Sergeant Fricasse recalled an exchange of words between two brothers, one fighting for the republic, the other against it, at the siege of Maubeuge in 1793. "You are not worthy to live," shouted the republican. "You are not a human being, but a true barbarian." Few *émigrés* were taken prisoner according to Fricasse, since "they did not give themselves up willingly." [134] A French surgeon, Adrien-Jacques Renoult, confirmed this impression, recalling that fifty *émigré* prisoners of war whom he had treated were "horribly cut about, not having wanted to surrender," because of their expectation that they would be shot anyway. [135]

The grim logic of the revolution's hatred for its internal enemies fed the "dirty war" in the Vendée, the civil war in the west of France that cost perhaps as many as 250,000 lives between March 1793 and May 1795. [136] "This war is nothing like the one we are fighting against the coalition powers," reported A.-F. Momoro in October 1793. What made it different, in his eyes, was not only that the enemy was French, but that it consisted of the whole population of the region, including the women, whom he said served as spies and, when required, also as soldiers: "It is against an entire population that we must fight." Momoro, like most republicans,

134 Larchey, ed., *Journal de marche du Sergent Fricasse*, 16–17.
135 Renoult, *Souvenirs*, 11–12.
136 Martin, *La guerre de Vendée*, 299.

habitually referred to the enemy in the Vendée as "brigands."[137] This choice of words was significant since it denied the Vendéans the status of legitimate combatants. The revolutionaries used many other terms to describe their enemies in the Vendée: "horde," evoking the historic threat of nomadic tribes to European civilization, was common: "Catholic horde," "horde of brigands," "fugitive and fanatical horde," were descriptions that represented the Vendéans as beyond the pale not only of the law but also of reason and civilization.[138] The revolutionaries also favoured the use of hygienist metaphors, comparing the Vendéans to a contagion, such as the plague or rabies and thereby justifying a therapeutic "purge," which was a euphemism for extermination.[139] This dehumanizing rhetoric helped prepare the extremes of violence that characterized the war in the Vendée: the massacres of men, women, and children by republican "blues" and the counter-massacres of vulnerable detachments of soldiers by royalist "whites." As with the French Wars of Religion, the road to mass killing in a civil war was paved by the dehumanization of the enemy.

In the Vendée, there were individuals who were prepared to follow to the bitter end the logic of Momoro's view that the war had to be waged against an entire population. The representative on mission, J.-B. Carrier, writing to the Committee of Public Safety from Nantes in December 1793, reassured the Committee that his goal was "the prompt extermination of the brigands" and that to achieve it he would issue orders to put to death all people of both sexes and to burn everything, "because there is not one who has not borne arms against the republic, so we must absolutely and totally purge its soil."[140] The following month, General Turreau outlined to the committee his plan for mobile columns to traverse the Vendée: "My intention is to burn everything," he said, proposing to preserve only the infrastructure necessary to provide cantonments for the army. If his plan were properly supported, the general claimed, within a fortnight the Vendée would be cleared of houses, food supplies, and weapons. The only inhabitants left would be those in the backwoods who had escaped the soldiers' "most scrupulous perquisitions." Turreau made it clear that he had no compunction about killing women or children, although he requested a written order absolving him in advance of personal responsibility for such a policy.[141] Soon, his "infernal columns" were wreaking destruction

---

137 SHD AG B 5/7–13. Report by A.-F. Momoro, 13 October, 1793.

138 Rolland-Boulestreau, *Les colonnes infernales*, 42.

139 Ibid., 50–4.

140 SHD AG B 5/7–73. Carrier to the Committee of Public Safety, 11 December 1793.

141 SHD AG B 5/8–20 and b 5/8–27. Letters of Turreau to the Committee of Public Safety, 16 and 24 January 1794.

on a terrifying scale. In the village of Lucs-sur-Boulogne, the column commanded by General Cordelier slaughtered 459 people in a single day,
two hundred of them women and girls, and 110 of them infants under
seven years of age.[142] General Grignon, commanding one of the columns,
compared its work to a hunting expedition. "We have [...] beaten the
woods and brush," he wrote. "Those scoundrels are effectively spread
around the farmsteads, in twos and threes, and are going about their regular
work. I took a score of them and gave them hospital passes."[143] Grignon's
casual attempt at black humour leaves no doubt that he and his men were
on a killing spree. The objectives defined by Carrier and Turreau, explicitly
abandoning any distinction between combatants and non-combatants and
aiming at the complete annihilation of the enemy, have provided reasons
to see the civil war in the Vendée as a prototype for "total war."[144] In its
atavistic rituals of massacre and torture, as well as in the scope it provided
for individuals and groups to pursue through extreme violence their own
objectives and vendettas, it also harked back to the wars of religion.[145]

In this war of extermination, republican soldiers were both perpetrators
of atrocities and their victims. Étienne Joliclerc was frank in explaining to
his mother in a letter written in January 1794 the murderous intent of
the infernal columns as they (and he) were about to set out: "We will bring
steel and fire, rifle in one hand, torch in the other. Men and women, all
will be put to the sword. All must perish, except the little children."
Joliclerc's next letter, dated 27 April 1794, was written from a hospital
bed after he had been wounded following an ambush. His regiment had
lost fifty-two men, "whom we found on the road while returning after
dinner; all with their heads broken or their bodies pierced by bayonets."
Summing up his experience, Joliclerc wrote, "If I told you all the cruelties
that are committed in the Vendée, on both sides, it would make your hair
stand on end."[146]

Although soldiers like Joliclerc were loath to admit to it, fear was clearly
a significant part of their experience. It conditioned their cruelty as well
as their cowardice. Generals sometimes acknowledged the fears of their

142   Martin, *La guerre de Vendée*, 301.

143   SHD AG B 5/8–17. Letter of General Grignon to General Commaire, 14 January
1794.

144   Bell, *The First Total War*, 154–85; Jean-Yves Guiomar, *L'invention de la guerre
totale*, 101–4.

145   Rolland-Boulestreau, *Les colonnes infernales*, 264–5. Jean-Clément Martin also
notes the hybrid nature of the violence in the Vendée, which combined "archaic practices"
derived from the wars of religion with democratic ones inaugurated by the revolution. See
Martin, *Violence et révolution*, 162.

146   Joliclerc, *Joliclerc*, 155–62.

men in their correspondence. General Turreau reported that there were soldiers who, though perfectly good for service on other fronts, were terror-stricken in the Vendée by "the very name of the brigands." General Cordelier wrote that in combat his men were horrified by the "frightful howling" of the enemy.[147] Dubois-Crancé reported to the Committee of Public Safety that "this war is cruel and no prisoners are taken on either side. Our soldiers fear the brigands the way children fear rabid dogs."[148] It was fear that prompted twenty officers from the garrison at Mortagne to write to their general in February 1794, pointing out their vulnerability to "that horde of slaves who could in spite of every precaution easily come in and massacre the brave defenders."[149] It is likely the officers at Mortagne had in mind the fate of the garrison at Cholet, which fled in panic follow-ing an incursion by Vendéan forces. General Turreau did his best to put a good face on this defeat in his report to the Committee of Public Safety, blaming the garrison's flight on "the cowardly example of a few battalions" who had spread fear of the enemy. Rather than focus on these failings, Turreau emphasized the heroism of the garrison's commander, General Moulins, who, "indignant at the cowardice of his troops," vainly tried to rally them and to lead them into battle. Wounded, and about to fall into the enemy's hands, Moulins killed himself with his last shot. Another republican hero – "one of the bravest soldiers, most capable officers, and purest republicans" – was thus created to downplay the debacle result-ing from terror-stricken soldiers who had taken flight. Ironically, Turreau called for Cholet to be razed and for the army's base of operations to be moved to Mortagne, which, unlike the officers who were based there, he judged to be a more defensible location.[150]

MANY WAYS TO DIE

It was not the prospect of a hero's death that caused the republican soldiers at Cholet to take to their heels, but the fear of becoming victims of a mas-sacre. The reality of the soldier's death in the dirty war of the Vendée was a far cry from the revolutionary ideal. The ideal soldier's death, according to revolutionary publicists, was death received in the heat of battle, facing the enemy, in the instant of victory. This ideal was borrowed by the

147 Cited in Rolland-Boulestreau, *Les colonnes infernales*, 34.

148 SHD AG B 5/8-32. Letter from Dubois-Crancé, 2 February 1794.

149 . SHD AG B 5/8-56. Letter signed by twenty officers from the garrison at Mortagne, to General Huch, 21 February 1794.

150 SHD AG B 5/8-39. Letter of General Turreau to the Committee of Public Safety, 9 February 1794.

revolutionaries from the ancient Greeks and Romans and applied indiscriminately to contemporary heroes, often with scant regard for the truth.
In fact, whether in the Vendée or on other fronts of the revolutionary wars,
there was little prospect of soldiers dying such a hero's death. Most soldiers
did not die in battle or of wounds sustained in combat. Far more died of
illness. Although roughly one in three men who served in the revolutionary
armies from 1792 to 1803 died on active service, only one in twenty
(75,000 overall) was killed in battle. Even if we assume, like Jacques
Houdaille, that the majority of those who died in hospital (179,000) died
from their wounds, the total of all men who died as a result of enemy action
would not rise above one in five of those who served.[151] The remaining
deaths were of men who died in enemy captivity (20,000) or who went
missing and were presumed dead having failed to return home (180,000).
It is likely that most of the latter died of illness.[152] Lacking adequate food,
clothing, shelter, or pay (at times, they were paid in *assignats* whose value
had been ruined by inflation), soldiers were vulnerable to disease. Jacques
Fricasse wrote that, after enduring a winter with the Army of the Sambre-
et-Meuse on the Rhine when sentries had frozen to death and soldiers had
been reduced by hunger to digging up seed potatoes planted by local
peasants, only two men in his company of sixty did not come down with
fever in the summer of 1795. "The fever was bad, because many died
from it," he wrote, complaining that the flies were so thick you could cut
them with a sword and that there was no shortage of fleas and lice: "We
endured our purgatory in this place, tormented night and day."[153]

Most soldiers died, whether of wounds or disease, in hospital. French
military hospitals, poorly funded, understaffed, and swamped by soldiers
afflicted with fevers, dysentery, pulmonary illnesses, scabies, and venereal
disease, were "antechambers of death." Of 315 soldiers serving with the
Army of the Pyrénées Orientales who died in the Hospital of Equality at
Pézenas in 1795, only one died of wounds. In this case, yellow fever was
the biggest killer, with pulmonary and intestinal illnesses, infections, and
gangrene accounting for the remainder of the victims. A report on the

151 David Vess's analysis of the records of military hospitals in 1792–93 indicates that
on average, only 22 per cent of patients had been wounded. The number of soldiers
admitted suffering from fever outnumbered those with wounds by a factor of two or three
to one. Mortality rates of men suffering from fever ranged from one in ten to one in three.
Vess, *Medical Revolution*, 138–9.

152 These calculations are from Houdaille, "Les armées de la Révolution," 842–9.
Houdaille's assumption that most soldiers who died in hospital died of wounds is doubtful,
given both the unsavoury reputation of military hospitals as vectors for disease and the
records of those hospitals.

153 Larchey, *Journal de marche du Sergent Fricasse*, 69.

hospital from the municipal council stated that "most of our brothers in arms, far from recovering their health, find there an almost certain death, given the dampness of the soil, the insalubrity of the air and the ease with which they can procure fruits and other foods quite contrary to their illnesses."[154] It is revealing that in August and September 1793, when the fighting on the Spanish frontier was at its most intense, the number of deaths from disease recorded by the hospital at Béziers was still more than twice the number resulting from wounds.[155] Pierre-François Percy, a surgeon attached to the French army in Switzerland in 1799, described the military hospital in Zurich. "It is a very bad place and the costly repairs made to it, while making it bigger, did not make it any cleaner. We did not heal a single major wound, not one amputee; the wounded lived there for ten or twelve days; then they came down with hospital fever and expired."[156] Soldiers themselves saw hospital as a place from which to escape if they were to survive. "I will stay sick as long as I remain in hospital," a soldier from the Army of the Pyrénées Orientales wrote to his father from Toulouse, asking him to obtain a certificate from the municipality to allow him to recover at home.[157]

Not all the ailments speeding revolutionary soldiers to an early grave were physical. Nostalgia, or *mal de pays*, was held responsible for one in twenty deaths.[158] First identified by a Swiss physician, Johannes Hofer, in 1688, nostalgia afflicted soldiers in many armies, but especially those who served in the French armies of the revolutionary and Napoleonic wars. It manifested itself as an acute alienation from the constraints of the military life and a yearning for the familiar that was for many soldiers unbearable. This alienation may have been particularly intense in the French army because of the emphasis placed since the revolution upon the identity of the revolutionary soldier as a free man enjoying a dignity denied to the "slaves of tyrants." For some soldiers, reconciling this image with the experience of a strict and at times draconian military discipline was impossible. From their perspective, they had been given their freedom by the revolution only to be subjected to a new form of slavery.[159] To their credit, most physicians attached to the armies dealt with the affliction sensitively, recognizing that the best remedy was leave to return home, at least temporarily.

154 Alberge, "Vie et mort des soldats," 21.
155 In August, the hospital recorded 6,561 deaths from illness, 3,172 from wounds. In September, the numbers were 464 and 121, respectively. Ibid., 21.
156 Percy, *Journal des campagnes*, vol. 1, 45.
157 Bouscayrol, *Cent lettres de soldats*, 226–7.
158 Dodman, *What Nostalgia Was*, 68.
159 Ibid., 103.

Nevertheless, this was not always possible. Without relief, men afflicted by nostalgia languished in misery, fell ill, and died. The death certificates of the 30,000 French soldiers who died of yellow fever during the expedition to Saint Domingue in 1801 often cited nostalgia as a contributory factor.[160] *Canonnier* Bricard noted the fate of a group of replacements who joined his unit in 1794: "a large portion of the conscripts from Normandy fell ill; many became so sad that in four or five days they passed from life to death."[161]

Although the prospect of their dying miserably in hospital was greater than that of dying gloriously on the battlefield, soldiers expressed their preference for the latter. "Is there a finer sacrifice than to die for one's country?" Joliclerc asked his mother. "Would you prefer that I died on straw, in my bed, at Froidefontaine, or in some work activity, in the woods, at the quarry, or on some building?"[162] Although Joliclerc was less reticent than many in admitting to the perils of combat in his letters home, he was entirely typical in professing both an ardent patriotism and an appetite for battle. Pierre Girardon was also typical in his insistence that neither illness nor the privations he had suffered on campaign would prevent him taking his place on the battlefield. "It is necessary to march or die, there is nothing else to say. I have an illness that I would not have for a hundred louis; a fortnight of rest would sort me out, but I would not leave my post for all the treasures of the universe. I suffer like a wretch; I am to be pitied! A bullet or a cannonball would finish me off nicely; I have no regrets, I will have laboured as a true republican and I would die happily arms in hand."[163] This mixture of patriotism and pride, misery and self-pity was common to many letters written by soldiers of the revolution. Those letters implied that death on the battlefield was not to be feared; it would at least put an end to the miseries of life on campaign.

Another way in which soldiers endorsed the ideal of death in combat was in their frank admiration for comrades whose lives ended in that fashion. Sergeant Jacques Fricasse, recounting a battle fought on 24 May 1794, wrote: "I saw during this engagement brave republicans covered in wounds gather up all their remaining strength at the moment they were about to take their last breath, strive to kiss this [tricoloured] cockade, the sacred emblem of our conquered freedom; I heard them address to the heavens ardent vows for the triumph of the armies of the

160 Ibid., 78.
161 Bricard, *Journal du Canonnier Bricard*, 90. Also cited in Dodman, *What Nostalgia Was*, 97.
162 Joliclerc, *Joliclerc*, 169–70.
163 Maury, ed., *Lettres de volontaires républicains*, 27.

republic."[164] By unironically echoing the heroic anecdotes dispensed to them by republican propaganda, soldiers like Fricasse affirmed their commitment to patriotic self-sacrifice, ideally accomplished on the field of battle. Such stories might well inspire the skepticism of our disenchanted age, but that would be to underestimate the exaltation of individuals who felt they were living in extraordinary times and were therefore driven to actions that at times defy rational understanding.[165]

The exploits recounted in so many stories of soldiers fighting to the death both reflected and concealed the realities of battlefield death. Analysis of unit records shows, unsurprisingly, that most wounds were caused by firearms. The effects of artillery – firing round shot, case (a canister that discharged musket balls or shrapnel when fired), or explosive shells – were particularly destructive. Philippe-René Girault described the effects of cannon fire at the Battle of Valmy in 1792. He and his fellow musicians quickly abandoned their attempts to play their instruments when they came under fire and began to take casualties. "The same discharge of artillery which had frightened us, had carried off twenty-one men from the first rank in our fifth company," wrote Girault. "We were forced to lie on the ground to avoid the shell fragments."[166] To his relief, Girault was unharmed: "Happily, I got away with just having my uniform plastered by the brains of an officer who was killed a few paces in front of me."[167] Only 11 per cent of wounds were caused by edged weapons (swords, lances, and bayonets) with the percentage highest for wounds to the head (39 per cent) and arms (21 per cent), lowest to the belly (0 per cent) and legs (2 per cent). Overall, there were 4.5 times as many wounds to the extremities as to the head. The relatively small number of recorded head wounds, combined with the relatively high percentage of such wounds caused by edged weapons, suggests that a significant number of wounds to the head caused by firearms were immediately fatal and therefore went unrecorded.[168]

Firearms and edged weapons were not the only instruments of death. Battles in the open field may have been more frequent than under the old regime, but siege operations were still common, as was the practice of mining enemy positions and then blowing them up. Such explosions could cause terrible injuries. Dominique-Jean Larrey witnessed the explosion of

164 Larchey, ed., *Journal de marche du Sergent Fricasse*, 29.

165 For the revolutionaries' fascination with heroic death, see Martin, *Violence et révolution*, 174–6.

166 Girault, *Mes campagnes*, 17.

167 Ibid.

168 This analysis is taken from Bertaud, Reichel, and Bertrand, *Atlas de la Révolution française*, vol. 3: *L'armée et la guerre*, 44.

a mine under a French redoubt on the Spanish frontier in 1794. "One cannot imagine a more frightening and horrible picture than that explosion," he wrote, describing how guns, masonry, men, and pieces of men were thrown indiscriminately into the air. Larrey and his fellow surgeons treated seventy-six of the victims who were not immediately killed. "Some had lost one or more limbs, others were burned on the entire surface or large regions of their bodies; some, for whom the shock had been violent or who were burned through to the internal organs of the belly died within hours of entering the field hospital." In many cases, the surgeons performed multiple amputations. Although Larrey wrote with satisfaction that "All our operations were in general a complete success," it would seem likely that many of the wounded subsequently died of shock or gangrene.[169]

Not all soldiers who died at the enemy's hand did so in the heat of action. Although it is generally assumed the National Convention's decree ordering soldiers not to accept the surrender of British and Hanoverian troops was widely ignored, there were clearly occasions – and not just in the Vendée – when both sides killed defenceless enemy soldiers in cold blood. Philippe-René Girault confessed to killing an Austrian soldier who attempted to surrender, "but it was forbidden to take prisoners, and it was necessary for me, to my great regret, to run him through with my bayonet."[170] The Austrians themselves, as General Dellard recounted, were no less merciless. Of forty men with whom he was captured, twenty-seven were immediately killed. Dellard was stripped of all but his shirt and underwear and roughly handled by his captors. "It must be admitted that the conduct of the National Convention, in France, provoked harsh reprisals against us by the war of extermination it intended to wage against the English," he wrote.[171] The war within France was waged even more pitilessly.

Some soldiers did not die by the enemy's hand, but by that of their own comrades, victims of a military justice that oscillated between extremes of indulgence and severity, according to circumstance.[172] Commandant Virien witnessed the execution of twelve grenadiers, condemned for pillaging during the siege of Maastricht in October 1794. Virien's comments indicate that in his view the grenadiers were victims of bad luck: "similar cases presented themselves every day, and as long as the evidence did not pertain to some hard cases that one didn't object to sacrificing as an example corps commanders never allowed the full rigour of the penal code to weigh upon

169 Larrey, *Mémoires*, vol. 1, 91–7.

170 Girault, *Mes campagnes*, 47.

171 Général baron Dellard, *Mémoires militaires sur les guerres de la Révolution et de l'Empire* (Paris, n.d.). Cited in Bertaud, *La vie quotidienne*, 289.

172 Germani, "The most striking and the most terrible examples."

brave soldiers who were hungry."[173] Soldiers who confronted the firing squad unflinchingly earned the admiration of their comrades. Witnessing the execution of six grenadiers who had gone on a drunken rampage in 1795, Louis-Joseph Bricard wrote that the soldiers refused the blindfolds they were offered, saying that "they had seen death a thousand times and never had they been afraid." Linking arms, the condemned men themselves gave their executioners the order to fire. One remained standing after the first volley. "Well then! What about me, comrades?" he declared, inviting a second volley, which killed him. "Their courage and their steadfastness surprised all the spectators who melted in tears," wrote Bricard.[174]

In the face of so many evident perils, both on and away from the battlefield, soldiers rarely admitted to more than a momentary loss of courage. To judge by their own writings, revolutionary soldiers like Joliclerc, Fricasse, and Bricard were true to the models of patriotic devotion celebrated in revolutionary propaganda. Although at times they excoriated fellow soldiers whose selfishness or avarice betrayed the republic, they clearly distinguished between those "scoundrels" and "true soldiers" like themselves. "Brave soldiers resisted the enemy attacks," wrote Bricard in describing the French retreat from Germany in 1796, "while cowards occupied themselves with pillage to avoid the battle."[175] Understandably, soldiers did their best to conceal from their correspondents and even from themselves evidence that they were not always fearless in the face of the enemy. Concerned to allay the fears of anxious relatives, in their letters home soldiers only occasionally admitted their own. A volunteer from the Meuse wrote frankly – almost in stream of consciousness – to his parents of his impressions upon witnessing his comrades fall in battle: "I was a skirmisher; I saw the cannonball from very close; earth [thrown up by it] struck me hard in the face; I saw good men knocked down ... I will tell you that in seeing the first ones fall we were afraid; our sergeant gave us some brandy; he said to us, 'don't be afraid, have courage' but when I saw him fall I was not singing; I was waiting my turn, I saw bombs and bullets coming straight at us."[176] Few correspondents were so frank about their own feelings under

173 Virien, "Souvenirs," 245–6.

174 Bricard, *Journal du Canonnier Bricard*, 173. On another occasion, Bricard expressed his sympathy for two young drummer boys who were executed for pillage while four others were compelled to watch. "The older one died courageously enough, but the younger called with all his strength for his mother to save him. The other four little ones made the plain ring with their cries. None of the soldiers were able to witness that event without shedding tears." Ibid., 127.

175 Ibid., 231.

176 SHD, AG Xw 66: Volontaires nationaux: Meuse: letter of 24 August 1794.

fire. Others revealed their true feelings in their almost euphoric response to surviving close calls on the battlefield. Directly addressing the children for whom he wrote his memoir, François-René Cailloux described how, seconds after leaving his tent during the siege of Thionville in 1792, an enormous fragment from an Austrian shell had impaled his bed. "This was the prelude to many other dangers from which I was protected by that same Providence," wrote Cailloux, whose memoir recounts a litany of near misses.[177] He described how on one occasion he had flung himself to the ground in anticipation of a shell burst, only to be saved by a courageous veteran who snuffed out the shell's fuse with his bare fingers. "This little incident had attracted the attention of the whole regiment," he wrote, "which, the danger once past, was cheered up by it, as was I."[178] Étienne Joliclerc wrote to his uncle in the same spirit of cheerful relief to describe how he owed his survival to having a wide gait, since a cannonball had passed between his legs, only slightly bruising his thighs before killing the man behind him.[179]

Soldiers' letters for the most part made little reference to casualties and rarely revealed their sentiments concerning the deaths of comrades. They enumerated casualties matter-of-factly, usually to make the point that the enemy had suffered heavier losses than the French. A volunteer from the First Battalion of the Indre reported on 16 December 1793 that his unit had sustained two hundred casualties in an attack on a Prussian redoubt. He went on to express his satisfaction that the battalion "has acquired a great renown by its courage" and had been rewarded with a sword of honour and a prize of 1,200 livres presented by the representatives on mission.[180] Another soldier from the same battalion, however, wrote to his father a few weeks later that "it made me cry" when he witnessed "poor little Meslin" wounded by a gunshot and then "cut to pieces" by enemy soldiers. "No soldier in the battalion was mourned like him," wrote François Robin.[181] François Gaudrion, also from the First Battalion, wrote more pragmatically to his mother of the same events, saying that "since the day I was wounded, our battalion has mounted two more attacks where Meslin had the misfortune to be killed: an accident along with others that surely you have heard about [...] And then we pushed them back with stunning force all the way to Wissembourg where there were many of those

177 Cailloux, *Souvenirs de guerre*, 66.
178 Ibid., 132.
179 Joliclerc, *Joliclerc* 121.
180 SHD, AG: Xw 49 Volontaires nationaux: Indre: letter of 16 December 1793.
181 SHD, AG: Xw 49 Volontaires nationaux: Indre: letter of 4 January 1794.

scoundrels laid out on the ground."[182] Letters such as these reveal that the continuation of military operations left little time or energy for sentimentality toward fallen comrades.

Some soldiers, however, were clearly affected by the deaths of comrades, particularly if they were close friends or relatives. Tiry, a grenadier fighting to defend Mayence in 1793, wrote with affecting simplicity to his wife that "Citizen Marville, my lieutenant, was killed, on 15 April, by a bullet through his head. I will mourn him all my life."[183] Louis-Joseph Bricard, a gunner in an artillery regiment from Paris, provided a harrowing account of the torments he suffered when his brother was killed at the Battle of Neerwinden in 1793. Bricard lost sight of his brother, who was serving the same gun, when enemy cavalry attacked them, causing a "horrible butchery." Fearing his brother had been killed, Bricard wandered the battlefield desperately looking for him. "Filled by cruel uncertainty, I carried on my search on the battlefield, [which was] covered in dead and wounded. I learned that one of our friends, named Blerzy, had just been killed; the death of this brave and estimable comrade caused me to choke on my tears. I kept running from body to body. Many comrades came to me and tried to console me by persuading me that my brother was not dead. Then the rain came, with the night, to spread darkness over the battlefield."[184] Finally, Bricard was informed by a comrade that his brother had suffered "the kindest death a warrior can have." He had been cut in two by a shell and "died without having time to let out a breath."[185] It seems likely that the death of Bricard's brother was less gentle than his comrade's words. All the same, the news caused Bricard, who had not eaten or slept for three days, to lose consciousness. His emotional ordeal was far from over. Bricard feared to impart the news of his brother's death to their parents. "Knowing the very great sensibility of my father and mother," he wrote, "I was afraid for their lives."[186] Nearly three years later, by which time his father had also died, Bricard returned home on leave for a tearful reunion with his mother and sisters: "We stayed for at least a quarter of an hour, all together, without being able to say a word; enclosed in a small room, we wept for my father and my brother."[187] There were more tears when Bricard's leave ended; his mother, "as if deprived of her reason, uttered great cries."[188]

182 SHD, AG: Xw 49: Volontaires nationaux: Indre: letter of 17 March 1794.
183 Picard, ed., *Au service de la nation*, 27–8.
184 Bricard, *Journal du Cannonier Bricard*, 37.
185 Ibid., 39.
186 Ibid., 47.
187 Ibid., 177.
188 Ibid., 178.

Bricard's memoir is evidence that soldiers who fought in the revolutionary armies were not untouched by the revolution in sentiment that was transforming contemporary attitudes toward death. Witnessing so much death, however, tended to harden hearts rather than soften them. The surgeon Pierre-François Percy described how he ceased to hear the groans and cries of men upon whom he operated, noting that soldiers also acquired such insensitivity: "this apathy is a boon to the soldier, to which men could not be brought by all the philosophy in the world."[189] Philippe-René Girault experienced combat for the first time at the Battle of Valmy. "That is where I first saw dead and wounded," he wrote. "I felt at first an unpleasant sensation; but I soon saw such a large number that I became used to it and my sensibility was armoured for a very long time."[190] All the same, there were sights that were too much for even a hardened veteran like Girault. During the Austrian campaign of 1809 he came across a pile of charred corpses near the village of Ebersburg. "Never had I seen anything as terrifying as those grilled corpses lacking any human resemblance. Near the edge of the village, there was a pile that blocked the entrance to a street: it was a heap of arms and legs, of shapeless semi-carbonized bodies. At this sight, my heart stopped, my legs failed me and I could neither advance nor retreat, remaining immobile in contemplation of this sad spectacle in spite of myself. There were many officers and generals who had also been drawn there through curiosity. Like me they were floored. Tears rolled from every eye and nobody said a word [...] I had seen many battlefields, but I had never felt so much emotion."[191] Girault's horrified description shows the reality of the soldier's death that idealized representations were calculated to mask. As the revolutionary wars gave way to those of Napoleon, and as mass killing reached new levels of violence and horror, soldiers and civilians, artists, and publicists would all have to find ways of coming to terms with that reality.

189 Percy, *Journal des campagnes*, 31.
190 Girault, *Mes campagnes*, 17.
191 Ibid., 158.

4

Dying for the Emperor: The Napoleonic Wars

THE DEATH OF MARSHAL LANNES

On 22 May 1809, Marshal Jean Lannes, Duke of Montebello, was fatally wounded by a cannonball at the Battle of Aspern-Essling. The incident was recorded in a bulletin of Napoleon's Grande Armée, which stated prematurely that "an amputation has taken place and his [Lannes's] life is out of danger."[1] The bulletin, acknowledging that French losses had been "considerable," went on to describe the "most affecting" farewell between the marshal and Napoleon. The emperor, moved to tears, turned to those around him, saying, "On this day only a wound to my heart such as this could cause me to attend to other cares than those of my army." Lannes embraced Napoleon from his stretcher. "Within an hour," he said, "you will have lost a man who dies with the glory and the conviction of having always been your best friend."[2] This exchange of words and affection, celebrating Napoleon's humanity and the marshal's loyalty, became an integral part of the Napoleonic myth. At the official funeral held in Paris a year later, Napoleon's words as recorded in the army bulletin were inscribed on the face of a pyramid that surmounted Lannes's coffin.[3] The battlefield exchange between emperor and marshal was also the

---

1 Garnier, ed., *Les bulletins de la Grande Armée*, 446.
2 Ibid., 447.
3 The funeral, held on 6 July 1810, the anniversary of the Battle of Wagram, was a solemn public occasion. The funeral mass was celebrated in the church at the Invalides. Lannes's remains were then escorted to the Church of Sainte Geneviève for interment. During the revolution, this church had been repurposed as a Pantheon honouring the memory of great men. It was returned to its original function as a church under Napoleon, who nonetheless contributed to its complement of illustrious remains by adding those of imperial heroes such as Lannes. On Lannes's funeral, see *Journal de Paris*, 6 and 7 July 1810.

4.1. Albert-Paul Bourgeois, *Marshal Jean Lannes mortally wounded near Essling on 22 May 1809*. 1810.

inspiration for a painting displayed at the biennial Salon of 1810, by Albert-Paul Bourgeois as well as for numerous popular prints, including some in the naive style of the *images d'Épinal* that could be cheaply mass-produced and were a significant feature of popular culture up until the First World War. In Bourgeois's painting, the viewer is spared the sight of Lannes's gruesome injuries as well as of any battlefield violence. A sheet, only slightly tinged with blood, covers Lannes's lower body, including his amputated left leg. The fighting is evoked only by the distant flames of burning buildings, flickering against a darkening sky. Even the instruments of the attending surgeon are obscured from view. The physical realities of battlefield violence are not permitted to intrude upon the elevated sentiments expressed by the two men. As the dying general clasps his emperor's hand to his heart and Napoleon tenderly returns his gaze, a captivated circle of officer-witnesses models for viewers an attitude of reverential admiration (fig. 4.1).

The painting by Bourgeois, just as it hides from view the marshal's wounds, likewise fails to reveal how he finally died. Detailed information about both is provided in the memoirs of the chief surgeon to Napoleon's armies, Dominique-Jean Larrey. Confessing that treating Lannes,who was a personal friend, "was one of the most difficult circumstances of my life," Larrey described in clinical detail the effects of the cannonball, which had shattered the marshal's left knee before gouging the muscle of his right thigh.[4] Larrey recorded the debates that ensued between himself and fellow surgeons at the field surgery as they considered whether to amputate. Having removed the marshal's left leg in a procedure lasting two minutes, during which the patient "gave very few signs of pain," there was hope he might recover. However, in the following days, as he visited Lannes in the home of a local brewer where he was cared for in the village of Kaiser-Ebersdorf, on the south side of the river Danube, Larrey recorded that "I found the Duke extremely weak, deeply sad and with a deathly pallor. His ideas were incoherent and his voice halting; he complained of a heaviness of the head; he was unsettled, felt oppressed, and moaned frequently; he could not bear the weight of his bedcovers, although they were very light."[5] A week after the battle, Lannes was afflicted by a series of attacks involving high fever and delirium. Napoleon visited him once more. Finally, "the marshal went into a complete delirium which was of short duration, and he died several hours later in a state that was calm enough. It was," concluded Larrey, "at the end of the ninth day after the accident and the battle."[6]

Larrey's was not the only memoir to tell the story of the death of Marshal Lannes. Marcellin de Marbot, Jean-Marie-René Savary, Jean-Michel Chevalier and Louis-François Lejeune all recounted the tearful encounter between Napoleon and Lannes.[7] According to Marbot, Lannes was still "immersed in dark thoughts" inspired by the death of his old mentor, General Pouzet, who had just been struck in the head by a stray bullet and fallen dead at his feet, when he received his own mortal wound. Marbot described the emperor's tearful embrace with Lannes at the field surgery where the marshal's leg had just been amputated: "The emperor, kneeling beside the stretcher, wept as he embraced the marshal, whose blood soon stained his white cashmere vest." Marbot remained with Lannes throughout his evacuation to the island of Lobau and then to Kaiser-Ebersdorf, where

4 Larrey, *Mémoires*, vol. 3, 278.
5 Ibid., 282.
6 Ibid., 284.
7 Many of these memoirs are cited in the account of Lannes's death provided in Martin, *Napoleonic Friendship*, 41. See also Chevalier, *Souvenirs des guerres napoléoniennes*, 108.

after days of delirious suffering the marshal died in his arms. Marbot confessed that he, too, "was overcome by sorrow."[8] General Pelet affirmed that the entire army was "deeply moved" by the battlefield embrace of Napoleon and Lannes: "In any circumstance, this spectacle would have been harrowing; we were all the more affected, at the end of a battle that cost the army so many brave men."[9] Jean-Michel Chevalier wrote: "What a scene it was of two illustrious warriors giving each other the kiss of farewell. Not one of us could hold back his tears, only sobs could be heard, tears flowed from every eye ... so died, on the field of honour, the French Bayard, the bravest of the brave, Marshal Lannes, Duke of Montebello."[10] Much later, in 1830, Napoleon's valet, Constant, published a memoir that not only recounted this battlefield embrace, but also added a deathbed speech. With his last words to Napoleon, Lannes reaffirmed his devotion to the emperor – "I die for you" – but also offered some "last reproaches of friendship," warning Napoleon against his "insatiable ambition" and calling upon him to put an end to the war.[11] This version of Lannes's death has been treated with skepticism by memoirists and biographers alike.[12]

These evocations of the death of Marshal Lannes at the Battle of Aspern-Essling marked an important stage in the evolution of both the realities and representations of the soldier's death. They occurred at a moment when the scale and intensity of warfare rose to new and unprecedented levels, bringing with them a significant escalation in military mortality. Tributes such as that to Marshal Lannes provided an oblique justification as well as consolation for the deaths of so many soldiers by focusing on the person of Napoleon. In images such as that of Bourgeois the dying soldier's consolation is no longer the satisfaction that he has helped to save liberty or even to defend the homeland. Rather, it is the emperor's gratitude and care that are the reward for his loyalty and sacrifice. This propaganda helped to create powerful myths. In the short term, the myth of the caring emperor sought to compensate French soldiers and their relatives for their terrible losses. Subsequently, the myth of the suffering and devoted *grognards* of the imperial army helped to lay the foundation for an enduring cult of military glory.

8 Marbot, *Mémoires*, vol. 2, 201–3, 212.
9 Pelet, *Mémoires sur la guerre de 1809*, vol. 3, 335.
10 Chevalier, *Souvenirs des guerres napoléoniennes*, 108.
11 Wairy, *Mémoires de Constant*, vol. 4, 148.
12 Martin, *Napoleonic Friendship*, 43.

NAPOLEONIC BATTLES:
AN "INFERNAL SCENE"[13]

Images such as those inspired by the death of Marshal Lannes, which exalted both the soldier's sacrifice and its recognition by the emperor, were more necessary than ever by 1809, at least from the government's point of view, as the scale of warfare increased and the numbers of soldiers dying reached new heights. There was a sharp escalation in the intensity of warfare, beginning in 1809, which can be measured both in the size of armies and in the numbers of casualties. Prior to that year, none of the battles fought by Napoleon's armies had involved more than 100,000 men. Between 1809 and 1812, however, there were seven battles in which the size of the French armies exceeded that figure. At Wagram (1809) 160,000 French soldiers were present; at Borodino (1812), 124,000; at Leipzig (1813), 175,000.[14] Furthermore, there was coincidentally a steep rise in the numbers of men who were killed or wounded in battle. According to Gaston Bodart, French battlefield losses (killed and wounded) during the revolutionary wars had rarely exceeded 10 per cent of the total number of men engaged and peaked at 17.5 per cent at Arcola (1796). During the Napoleonic wars, it was not uncommon for the casualty rate to exceed 30 per cent. At Eylau (1807) the loss was 31 per cent; at Borodino (1812), 34 per cent; at Essling (1809), 35 per cent. The culmination of this escalating trend came in 1815, at Waterloo, where French casualties are estimated to have reached a horrifying 42 per cent.[15] The increase in battlefield death was paralleled by a rise in overall military mortality. Approximately 900,000 French soldiers died in the Napoleonic wars (1803–15), roughly twice as many as in the wars of the French Revolution (1792–1801). Of the generation of Frenchmen born between 1790 and 1795 and who reached maturity between 1810 and 1815, one in five would die serving in Napoleon's armies.[16]

13   "Tableau infernal." Le Roy, "Souvenirs," 106.

14   Bodart, *Losses of Life*, 106 and 118.

15   Ibid., 119. John Gill, in his authoritative work on the Battle of Aspern-Essling, provides a figure of 19,980 French casualties, "or approximately one-quarter of the men who fought on the left bank of the Danube." Gill, *1809: Thunder on the Danube*, vol. 2, 194.

16   Houdaille, "Pertes de l'armée de terre," 50. Houdaille calculates the loss of life during the revolutionary wars at 458,000. Jacques Houdaille, "Les armées de la Révolution," 845. Despite the steep rise in battlefield deaths, only one in ten soldiers who died during the Napoleonic wars did so because of enemy action, a lower proportion than during the revolutionary wars. See Houdaille, "Pertes de l'armée de terre," 35.

Napoleon himself bore considerable responsibility for the rising incidence of battlefield mortality. The unlimited nature of Napoleon's war
aims, as well as the primacy he gave to achieving them through the defeat
of the principal enemy army in a decisive battle, resulted in battles becoming bigger, more frequent, and more fiercely contested. As Napoleon raised
the stakes for which these battles were fought, the resistance of his foes
grew commensurately.[17] For the dynastic powers of Europe, the political
transformations wrought by Napoleon's victories became an existential
crisis that necessitated a military and ideological mobilization emulating
that of France. French tactics, honed under the revolution and perfected
by Napoleon, also accelerated the pace of operations and intensified the
shock of war. Involving the rapid concentration of force and resolute
offensive action, with infantry operating both in line and in column, those
tactics were as expensive in lives as they were effective.[18] Finally, the
concentration of field guns in massed batteries and in ever larger numbers
also increased the destructiveness of battles. The number of guns accompanying Napoleon's armies rose from two guns for every thousand men
in 1800 to three in 1809 and five in 1812.[19] The response of his opponents
was proportionate. On the Marchfeld at the Battle of Aspern-Essling on
22 May 1809, the Austrian army had 292 guns while the French, hampered
by the uncertainty of their lines of communication across the Danube,
deployed 154.[20] At Borodino, in 1812, where it is estimated that 71,000 men
were killed or wounded on both sides, the French had 587 guns and the
Russians 640.[21]

The Battle of Aspern-Essling was a prime example of the heightened
destructiveness of Napoleonic warfare: four thousand Frenchmen died in
the battle and another fifteen thousand were wounded, the majority, as
archaeological evidence shows, from the effects of cannon or musket balls.[22]
Marcellin Marbot provided a vivid account of the battle's ferocity. "On every

17 On Napoleonic strategy, see Paret, "Napoleon and the Revolution in War." On
Napoleon's relation to the logic of total war, see Bell, *The First Total War*, 232–41.

18 On Napoleonic tactics, see Muir, *Tactics and Experience*.

19 Lemaire, *Les blessés* 27.

20 Gill, 1809: *Thunder on the Danube*, vol. 2, 335; 339.

21 Smith, *The Greenhill Napoleonic Wars Data Book*, 391–2.

22 Parker, *Three Napoleonic Battles*, 98. A study of thirty skeletons excavated from the
battlefield of Aspern-Essling shows evidence of ballistic or blunt force trauma in twenty-one
skeletons, totalling twenty cases of ballistic and eleven cases of blunt force trauma. No
evidence was found of sharp force trauma. While this does not rule out the likelihood that
some wounds were caused by edged weapons – such wounds would not necessarily result in
skeletal damage – it does indicate that most deadly wounds were caused by firearms of one
sort or another. See Binder and Quade, "Death on a Napoleonic Battlefield," 66–77.

part of our line the carnage was terrible," he wrote. In the village of Essling the fighting was so intense, he said, that soldiers fought from behind heaps of bodies, amid burning houses.[23] General Pelet wrote that the struggle for Aspern was "the fiercest positional fight of which military exploits make mention: Aspern is crushed beneath a hail of enemy cannon fire, set on fire by shells, congested by the heaped bodies of both sides. Throughout the evening, we fight without cease, within and without; we contest in turn the church, the belfry, every street, every wall. Everything becomes a weapon: we entrench behind carts, harrows, ploughs. The action is so furious in the different streets of the village that the victor in one is then attacked from behind."[24] Compounding the suffering of French soldiers as they engaged in this grim close-quarters combat were the effects of the enemy artillery fire. As the Austrian forces commanded by the Archduke Charles turned from defence to attack, they brought at least a hundred guns – perhaps as many as 190 – to bear on the French centre. Captain Coignet recounted his experience of the Austrian bombardment, saying that round shot cut down three men at a time and "shells blew bearskin headpieces twenty feet in the air."[25] Senior officers were as vulnerable to the Austrian guns as the men they commanded. Delivering a message from Marshal Lannes to General Saint-Hilaire, whose division bore the brunt of the fighting in the centre, Marbot arrived at the latter's headquarters as it fell under a hail of enemy grape shot. "Many officers were killed," he wrote. General Saint-Hilaire lost a foot and subsequently died under the surgeon's knife. A fellow aide-de-camp of Marbot's, the "unhappy d'Albuquerque" was struck by a bullet that lifted him over his horse's head and threw him, lifeless, at the feet of Marshal Lannes. "That's the end of the story for that poor lad! But it is, at least, a glorious death!," Lannes is supposed to have remarked. Marbot himself was hit in the thigh but remained beside Lannes, who took personal command of Saint-Hilaire's division until he, too, became a victim of the Austrian guns.[26]

Statistics tell us that the prospect of dying of wounds received in combat during the Napoleonic wars was greater for officers like Marbot than for ordinary soldiers.[27] The vulnerability of officers affected even the highest

23   Marbot, *Mémoires*, vol. 2, 197–8.
24   Pelet, *Mémoires*, vol. 3, 301.
25   Coignet, *Les cahiers du Capitaine Coignet*, 161.
26   Ibid., 196–7.
27   Of the officers serving in Napoleon's armies, 11.5 per cent died in combat, 6 per cent from illness. For common soldiers, the proportions were reversed: 5.6 per cent died in battle, 15.6 per cent from illness. Delmas, ed., *Histoire militaire de la France*, vol. 2, *De 1715 à 1871*, 328–9. See also the studies of mortality in the Napoleonic armies of Jacques Houdaille: Houdaille, "Pertes de l'armée de terre," 27–50; Houdaille, "Les officiers du

ranks: nineteen of the twenty-one marshals who held active commands were wounded, many of them on multiple occasions. Besides Lannes, two others were killed: Marshal Bessières, struck in the chest by a cannonball at Rippach in 1813, and Poniatowski, wounded by a lance and two gunshots at Leipzig in 1813 and then drowned attempting to cross the Elster on horseback.[28] At Aspern-Essling, 216 French officers were killed and 756 wounded. Among the casualties were twenty-four generals, four of whom, including Lannes, were killed.[29] Major Claude Leroy eloquently described the apparently indiscriminate slaughter of a Napoleonic battlefield: "I will only uncover for you a little corner of the infernal scene that a battlefield abandoned by two armies represents, a field where tempest and lightning exploded, only a moment ago, now mute and silent like the death which inhabits it. Youth, beauty, valour, courage cannot move this pitiless monster. It strikes down everything in its rapid progress, officers and men."[30]

Although no respecter of rank, death on the battlefield nonetheless affected the different arms unequally. The highest rate of casualties, by far, was sustained by the infantry. In the Army of Egypt, 76 per cent of soldiers who were killed in battle or who subsequently died of wounds were from the infantry, 9 per cent from the cavalry, and 5 per cent from the artillery.[31]

Premier Empire," 1229–35. Among general officers, the numbers dying in battle exceeded 10 per cent. Georges Six calculates that of the 2,234 generals who served during the revolution and the empire, 230 died on the battlefield or from their wounds. See Six, *Les généraux de la Révolution et de l'Empire*, 284. Bernard Quintin indicates that of 1,190 generals serving from 1804 to 1815, 152 (12.76 per cent) died or were mortally wounded in combat. The figures he provides for colonels are 198 killed or mortally wounded out of 1,574 (13 per cent). Of other officers who served during the empire, 10,086 were killed, wounded, or disappeared, representing 11–12 per cent of those who served. See Quintin, "Premières réflexions sur les pertes," 72.

28 Lemaire, *Les blessés*, 84.
29 Smith, Greenhill *Napoleonic Wars Data Book*, 308–9.
30 Le Roy, "Souvenirs," 106.
31 This calculation is based on a table provided by Desgenettes, *Histoire médicale de l'Armée d'Orient*, 172–3. The table indicates a total of 4,413 combat-related deaths, including 3,348 infantry, 380 cavalry, and 235 artillery. Overall, counting deaths from all causes, including disease, 74 per cent of the soldiers who died in the Egyptian campaign were from the infantry, 7 per cent from the cavalry, and 8 per cent from the artillery. This table indicates that, most unusually, more soldiers died of wounds (50 per cent) than of disease (46 per cent). Medical historian Martin Howard attributes this to the "heroic" efforts by Desgenettes and his fellow medical officers to prevent and control the spread of disease. Howard, *Napoleon's Doctors*, 78. A recent analysis of the Egyptian campaign, however, reverses the balance, indicating that more soldiers died of disease (53 per cent) than of wounds (47 per cent). See Bernède and Chaduc, eds, *La campagne d'Égypte*, 13.

Of the 1,537 officers and men who were killed or fatally wounded at Austerlitz (1805), 79 per cent were infantry, 18.8 per cent cavalry, and 1.6 per cent artillery.[32] At the Battle of Eylau (1807) similar proportions pertained: 84.87 per cent of the 2,202 French fatalities were infantry, 12.83 per cent were cavalry, and 1.69 per cent belonged to the artillery.[33] These figures reflect not only the predominance of infantry on the battle-field, but also the vulnerability of dense formations of men, especially in column or square, fighting in close proximity to one another.

Among those who died in battle, the most fortunate were those who died instantly, or at least very quickly, usually as a result of wounds to the head or to the body's vital organs caused by the various types of projectile fired by contemporary firearms: round shot of various calibres, lead musket balls, or shrapnel from exploding shells. Many soldiers' letters and memoirs recount incidents when missiles narrowly missed the writer but abruptly ended the lives of comrades who were close by. In a letter written to his father two months after he was wounded in the Battle of Goetz, in June 1809, Sergeant Humblot stated that he had experienced no fewer than four such close calls. "Dear father I have been wounded in the arm but lightly. In all my campaigns I have been knocked over four times by [cannon] balls, the first time at Sicile [Sacile] the ball cut through the shako on my head; the second time the ball killed three men and myself [sic] in single file: the ball killed the first two and cut the head off the third and together with the head it knocked me flat covered with shit and brains; the two other times I was believed to be dead."[34] Sergeant Faucheur's account of his experience at the Battle of Leipzig is similar. His captain, he wrote, "behind whom I found myself, had just given the order to wait for his command to fire on the cavalry, when a shell arrived, taking off the back of his head and covering me with blood."[35] The projectile then passed a few centimetres from the sergeant's face before taking off the leg of a drummer. Fighting in Italy in 1809, Jérôme-Étienne Besse was also spattered with body parts as a shell killed two of his comrades and took off an officer's leg. Afterwards, he recalled, his companions used their knives to scrape the gore from his uniform.[36] At the Battle of Borodino, Alfred-Auguste Ernouf and the men of his regiment were ordered to lie down in the shelter of a redoubt to minimize casualties, while their officers "waited for death

32 Quintin and Quintin, *Austerlitz*, 259.
33 Quintin and Quintin, *La tragédie d'Eylau*, 435.
34 Humblot, "Une lettre d'un sergent," 152.
35 Jourquin, ed., *Souvenirs de campagne du Sergent Faucheur*, 229.
36 Jérôme-Étienne Besse, "Mémoires," 315.

standing up." This did not prevent Ernouf from being covered in the blood and brains of a grenadier whose head was taken off by a cannonball when he chose the wrong moment to stand up. Ernouf wrote that the bloodstains remained on his uniform for the rest of the campaign, "constantly before my eyes, like a *memento mori*."[37]

Far more fatal wounds were caused by firepower than by steel. Nevertheless, the latter was not inconsequential. Cavalry, although typically armed with pistols or carbines, relied heavily upon sword, sabre, and lance. The weight and function of swords varied, with a penetrating thrust from the sabre of a French *cuirassier* generally considered more deadly than a slash from a British light-cavalry sabre or even a heavy-cavalry broadsword. A British officer serving in Spain commented on "the comparatively harmless effect of sabre encounters, when contrasted with the more deadly working of musketry or thrusts from the straight sword of the French dragoon."[38] It was not uncommon for soldiers to survive multiple wounds from sword cuts. Historian Jean-François Lemaire cites the example of Brigadier-General Bachelet-Dainville, who received seven sabre cuts at the Battle of Jena (1806) and ten wounds from sword and lance at the Battle of Heilsberg (1807) before being killed outright by a musket ball at the Battle of Leipzig (1813). In Lemaire's words, "Where seventeen sword cuts failed, a single bullet was enough."[39] Vincent Bertrand was a French light infantryman who experienced the full range of harm cavalry might inflict on an isolated foot soldier. Attempting to surrender to three enemy cavalrymen in 1813, Bertrand was wounded by a pistol shot from the first, two lance strikes from the second, and three sabre cuts from the third![40] Generally, casualties in cavalry melees were light, and cavalry could do little harm to infantry formed into defensive squares, but they were often deadly in pursuit of enemy cavalry that had taken flight or of infantry that had lost formation. At the Battle of Pultusk (1806), surgeon Jean-Baptiste d'Héralde found himself among large numbers of wounded men from the eighty-eighth regiment of line infantry as they came under attack from Russian dragoons. "The Russians advanced, trampled us under the hooves of their horses, sabring as they passed all those who came within reach. They did not take prisoners; they sabred our unfortunate wounded while

---

37 Ernouf, *Souvenirs d'un officier polonais*, 278.
38 Leith Hay, *Narrative of the Peninsular War*, 243. Cited in Muir, *Tactics and Experience of Battle*, 109.
39 Lemaire, *Les blessés*, 43.
40 Bertrand, *Mémoires du Capitaine Bertrand*, 157–9.

shouting to them in good French: 'Now cry *vive l'Empereur!*'"[41] Eventually, said d'Héralde, the Russian cavalry were driven off by the four or five officers and seventy or eighty men who, rallying around their eagle, were all that by then remained of the thousand-man battalion. These survivors likewise gave no quarter to the Russian wounded.

AFTER BATTLE

Most wounds were not immediately fatal. The wounded with the best chance of survival were those who were still capable of walking and therefore of assisting their own removal from the battlefield. Indeed, the medical services were usually swamped by the "walking wounded" and therefore prevented from giving assistance to the more seriously wounded whose evacuation was often accomplished only with great difficulty or not at all. Soldiers with leg wounds were sometimes left to lie exposed and helpless on the battlefield for days or even weeks. Many soldiers recalled their anguish at having to abandon the wounded. Sergeant Bourgogne described the fate of soldiers wounded in the legs after an engagement during the retreat from Russia: "We saw many dragging themselves along painfully on their knees, reddening the snow with their blood; they lifted their hands to the sky while uttering heart-wrenching cries, begging us for help; but what could we do?"[42] If they did not die of shock, exposure, thirst, or starvation, the helpless wounded were sometimes dispatched or simply stripped of their clothes and possessions by scavengers. This was the fate of Marcellin Marbot following the Battle of Eylau, in which as many as 25,000 French soldiers became casualties.[43] Lying wounded and senseless among the dead, Marbot was stripped naked (except for his hat and one boot) by a pillaging soldier and only saved from death because his *valet de chambre* recognized Marbot's effects in the soldier's possession and went in search of his body on the battlefield, fortuitously finding him alive.[44] For others, by the time help arrived, it was too late. A *cuirassier* belatedly offered help by French postal workers scouring the battlefield five days after the Battle of Wagram opened his cloak to show a leg wound infested with maggots. "If I had been carried to the ambulance the day after the battle, they could have cut my leg off," he said. "You see now it is too late. It is no longer worth the trouble, but do me the pleasure of killing or carrying off that

41   Héralde, *Mémoires d'un chirugien de la Grande Armée*, 108.
42   Bourgogne, *Mémoires*, 120.
43   Howard, *Napoleon's Doctors*, 113.
44   Marbot, *Mémoires*, vol. 1, 354.

Kaiserlicke who is whining over there so that he can let me die in peace."[45] At Wagram, many of the wounded perished after the battle from the fires that swept through the fields of hay, which led soldiers to say, according to Marbot, "that the hay fires had killed nearly as many men as the [gun]fire of battle."[46] Lieutenant Chevalier wrote that by the position of their charred remains the wounded who had perished in the flames appeared still to beg for help from their comrades: "How terrible were their sufferings and how cruel their deaths!"[47]

The quality of care available for the wounded soldiers who were evacuated from the battlefield left much to be desired. The French army's *service de santé* was relatively well provided for compared with the medical services of other armies, and it was directed by dedicated and, at times, innovative physicians and surgeons. Notable among them – and the only ones whose names are inscribed on the Arc de Triomphe – were: René-Nicolas Desgenettes, who took charge of the medical services during the Egyptian campaign; Pierre-François Percy, whose ideas for an autonomous battlefield surgical service were ahead of their time; and Dominique-Jean Larrey, the chief surgeon of the Imperial Guard who performed prodigies as a battlefield surgeon.[48] Both Percy and Larrey had experimented during the revolution with the idea of an "ambulance": in Percy's conception, this was to be a vehicle (Percy called it a *wurst*) for conveying surgeons and their instruments to where they were needed; in Larrey's it involved the deployment of a fleet of light yet sturdy carriages for the evacuation of the wounded.[49] Despite the talents of these leading lights, and the dedication of many other *officiers de santé* who sacrificed themselves for the sake of their patients, not all medical personnel were equally competent or dedicated. Many were young medical students with minimal training who opted for a position as a surgeon with the army as the only way to avoid conscription as a soldier.[50] Furthermore, although the numbers of medical officers expanded from 1,085 in 1802 to 5,112 in 1812, they were woefully few in relation to the many thousands of sick and wounded who required their services.[51] The field surgeries where major operations were performed, often in poor light and exposed to the elements, were as infernal a scene as the battlefield itself. Lieutenant Tascher, a hussar wounded at the Battle

45   Lemaire, *Les blessés*, 240. *Kaiserlicke* was a French expression for an Austrian soldier.

46   Marbot, *Mémoires*, vol. 2, 267.

47   Chevalier, *Souvenirs des guerres napoléoniennes*, 125.

48   On these individuals and on the *service de santé* see the excellent study by Howard, *Napoleon's Doctors*, especially 51–74.

49   Ibid., 75–95.

50   Ibid., 25.

51   Ibid., 251.

of Jena, provided an unforgettable description: "What a frightful spectacle a field hospital represents at the time of a battle. There are 3,600 wounded here and there is a lack of surgeons, of bandages, of all that is necessary! The town is in flames on one side, given over to pillage on the other; blood is running in the streets, I don't believe there is anything more horrible to be seen than the great church: the dying are piled there upon the dead; heaps of arms and legs are beside the surgical chair. What a sight for one who awaits his turn."[52] Such spectacles became even worse in later battles, as ambulances were overwhelmed by vastly greater numbers of wounded. Larrey's performance of two hundred amputations after the Battle of Borodino was a remarkable feat of endurance, but it addressed the needs of only a tiny fraction of the 21,500 wounded French soldiers.[53] As many as ten thousand of these men eventually collected at the Abbey of Koloskoi to the southwest of Borodino. Captain Charles François judged that within eight to ten days three quarters of them were dead from lack of food and medical attention. François himself was placed in a room with twenty-seven other officers from his own regiment, five of whom had suffered amputations. They were, he said, "lacking absolutely everything." Seven of his companions died during the first night alone.[54]

Theoretically, in caring for the wounded, priority was given to the treatment of the most seriously wounded, regardless of nationality or rank. In practice, enemy wounded were often neglected by both sides and senior officers were more promptly treated than the men they commanded. Jean-Baptiste d'Héralde expressed his outrage at English surgeons in Spain who he claimed denied treatment to a Polish lancer in a military hospital for twenty-four days, leaving him to lie in his own excrement while his broken tibia became maggot-infested and gangrenous.[55] Generals often received the attentions of several surgeons at once while badly wounded men from the ranks were fortunate to receive any care at all. At Aspern-Essling, when the stricken Marshal Lannes was brought to the advanced ambulance on the left bank of the Danube, a conference ensued between Larrey and two other surgeons as they debated whether to amputate. Later, once Larrey's opinion had prevailed and the amputation had been performed, Lannes was sent to the island of Lobau, where his aide-de-camp, Marbot, attended to him. Marbot gathered soldiers' greatcoats to provide a mattress and he helped to alleviate the marshal's thirst by using one of his shirts to

52 Cited in Héralde, *Mémoires d'un chirugien*, 23.
53 Ibid., 133.
54 Ibid., 134; Jourquin, *Journal du Capitaine François*, 666–7.
55 Héralde, *Mémoires d'un chirugien*, 164–5.

filter the muddy river water.[56] Once communication had been reopened between the island of Lobau and the right bank, Lannes was quickly transported to the house in Kaiser-Ebersdorf where he eventually died. Here again his treatment was discussed by a team of doctors, including Dr Franck, a notable Viennese physician brought out for the express purpose of a consultation. Eighteen-year-old Louis-Jacques Romand, an ordinary soldier of two months' service struck by a musket ball that penetrated his left side on the same day as Lannes was wounded, had much greater difficulty obtaining assistance. Unable to walk, he had to beg passing soldiers to carry him to the field surgery on their rifles. "Once there," he recalled, "they deposited me at the foot of an oak and left me to my unhappy fate, not wanting, despite my entreaties, to carry me any farther." A friend who had accompanied Romand nevertheless went in search of a surgeon, who performed the necessary bullet extraction. "The sharp pains which this cruel operation caused me did not elicit from me a single cry," wrote Romand. "I simply passed out for a few moments. When I opened my eyes to the light, I was so weak, so overcome, that shortly after I fell into a state near enough to death."[57]

Rescued from this "place of horror" by survivors from his regiment, Romand was carried (again, on a couple of rifles improvised to make a stretcher) to a mill where he was placed with other wounded men. Here, he spent "the cruelest night of my life," prevented by his own wounds and the cries of other men from sleeping a wink. Rejoining his comrades, Romand lay on the sand for two days while he waited for the bridges to be repaired that would allow his transfer to Vienna. During this time he was "without assistance and so to speak deprived of the first necessities of life, since all we had to eat was a little horsemeat." Even the restoration of the bridges did not bring immediate relief, since the wounded who could walk rushed ahead, causing a traffic jam that delayed Romand's evacuation for another day and another night. Finally, he was placed on a cart to take him the five miles to hospital in Vienna. In his memoir Romand chose not to dwell on his sufferings during this "short but cruel journey […] I could, using words, only give a faint idea of them anyway."[58] All the same, Romand was luckier than many. One observer estimated that of the wounded who awaited their removal from the Island of Lobau, over half died from their privations.[59]

56 Marbot, *Mémoires*, vol. 2, 202–4.
57 Romand, *Mémoires de ma vie militaire*, 14.
58 Ibid., 14–15.
59 Chevalier, *Souvenirs des guerres napoléoniennes*, 110.

Romand's account shows the great difficulty ordinary soldiers had in obtaining even minimal treatment from the overwhelmed medical services after a major battle. Many thousands of soldiers during the Napoleonic wars must have spent their final moments in just the state of "frightful solitude" he described. The young soldier adopted a more cheerful tone in recounting his experiences once he had arrived at hospital in Vienna, where he remained for two months. He declared himself satisfied both with his medical care and with the bonus of sixty francs distributed by Napoleon to all soldiers who had been wounded.[60] Even when it was available, however, the medical care provided was a mixed blessing. As was the case with Marshal Lannes, many wounded men suffered lingering deaths, days or even weeks or months after receiving their wounds, despite the best efforts of the surgeons who attended them. Surgeons operating in appalling conditions and without anaesthetic understood the need to operate as quickly and as simply as possible. They achieved considerable dexterity in the brutal skill of amputating shattered limbs. According to historian Martin Howard, survival rates for their patients were between 60 and 80 per cent, comparable to those of twentieth-century battlefield surgery.[61] Larrey insisted that promptly performed amputations on the field of battle at Essling and at Wagram had saved the lives "of a great number of wounded who were [otherwise] condemned to a certain death."[62]

At times, amputations were performed simply to ease the suffering of men whose lives were beyond saving. There were occasions, however, when the doctors' ministrations appear only to have added to the torments endured by the dying. It is clear from Larrey's descriptions of some of his surgical operations that they were excruciating.[63] Particularly painful was his favoured remedy for tetanus. Larrey believed tetanus, which we now know is caused by a bacterium from the soil infecting wounds, was caused by a variety of other conditions, including damp, as well as changes in temperature. In Egypt, where he had first encountered the disease, Larrey experimented with cauterization as a remedy, applying red hot irons to various parts of the body, including the soles of the feet. He continued to use

60 Ibid., 15–16.

61 Howard, *Napoleon's Doctors*, 196. The more detailed records of later wars cast doubt upon such claims. During the Franco-Prussian War 80 per cent of amputations resulted in the death of the patient. Dr Chenu, the head of the army's medical services in that war, noted the tendency of field hospitals to make premature claims for the success of operations. See Chenu, *Rapport*, vol. 1, 494.

62 Larrey, *Mémoires*, vol. 3, 353.

63 Harold Parker provides a useful summary of some of the individual cases treated by Larrey and his colleagues at the hospital of Reveneck, following the Battle of Aspern-Essling. Parker, *Three Napoleonic Battles*, 82–98.

the same method to treat soldiers after the Battle of Aspern-Essling, insisting that this treatment, "justly recommended by the doctors of antiquity, produced marvellous results."[64] In his memoirs, Larrey gave details of several cases where he believed he had successfully applied this treatment, including that of Grenadier François Demaré, who had suffered a severe shoulder wound and was in the final stages of tetanus, limbs rigid and unable to swallow, despite the extraction of his front incisors to facilitate the introduction of a feeding tube. Although Demaré could not bear to have his wound touched, Larrey heated four red-hot irons and applied them directly to the wound. "This application was extremely painful," conceded Larrey. "However I had the courage to continue my operation until all the points of the wound were deeply and completely burned." Soon after, the patient experienced a general relaxation and in sixty days was fit enough to return to France. "This cure is one of the most remarkable of military surgery," concluded Larrey.[65] While Larrey was convinced of their efficacy, it is doubtful whether his cauterizations contributed anything positive to the patients' chances of survival. Soldiers like François Demaré survived despite their doctors as much as because of them. Other treatments, including the widely employed emetics, purgatives, and bleedings applied to all sorts of fevers and infections, also did more harm than good.

Understandably, it was not uncommon for seriously wounded men to refuse operations, which many must have feared more than death itself. In his account of the Egyptian campaign, Larrey referred to several generals who refused operations. Describing his success in treating wounds to the lower abdomen, Larrey stated that "General Bon was the only one who, afflicted with a wound of this type, died of it, because he did not want his wounds debrided, nor a catheter introduced into the bladder. The flow of urine soon gave rise to gangrene, which was favoured in its progress by the patient's corpulence."[66] General Lanusse, struck in the knee by a small calibre ball at the second Battle of Aboukir, was informed that he required amputation of the limb to save his life: "He refused it," recalled Larrey, "not wanting to survive, he told me, this unhappy day." Nevertheless, eight hours later, Larrey did indeed perform the operation, which took three minutes. Its purpose, however, was no longer to save the general's life but simply to ease his suffering as he died. General Baudot, likewise, refused amputation of his leg, "and, after several days of horrible torments, he died of gangrene."[67]

64 Larrey, *Mémoires*, vol. 3, 296.
65 Ibid., 301–2. See also Parker, *Three Napoleonic Battles*, 90–3.
66 Larrey, *Mémoires*, vol. 2, 165.
67 Ibid., vol. 2, 260–1.

WARS WITHOUT PITY

Although the battlefields of the Napoleonic wars – and the field hospitals adjoining them – were fearsome places, in certain theatres the French soldier had more to fear away from the battlefield. In Egypt, Calabria, and Spain, he was confronted by the terrors of "*la petite guerre*" – guerrilla warfare – which despite its name involved extremes of violence and cruelty that exceeded even those of the conventional battlefield. This was a form of warfare in which the enemy compensated for his weakness in conventional arms by concentrating his attacks on vulnerable French outposts or convoys, on isolated soldiers and stragglers. The latter could expect little mercy and in return their comrades gave little back, exacting a vengeance that was as cruel as it was indiscriminate. Civilians were the ultimate victims of this violence, which erased any distinction between combatants and non-combatants.[68]

In Egypt, French soldiers recognized the similarity between this unconventional warfare and the war many of them had experienced earlier in the Vendée. "We have the enemy everywhere," wrote Captain Rozis, "in front, behind and on the sides: just like the Vendée!"[69] They were shocked by the tortures and mutilations inflicted upon their victims by their Arab and Mameluke enemies. Captain François was unusually frank in his description of these atrocities and in describing the response of the French. "I said that Bonaparte had sent General Leclerc to Belbeis with employees, engineers, sappers, and bakers; some of them were captured and the peasants and Arabs after sodomizing them, cut off from some of them their noses, ears, arms, legs, etc., even their genitals. Those who were still alive after these operations were forced to heat the ovens they had set up and were placed in them by these cannibals. When we arrived, I saw these unhappy victims roasting in an oven. Our vengeance was confined to burning the villages where over eighty employees, butchers, sappers, masons, etc., had been sacrificed. One can judge by such horrors, with what barbarous characters we were dealing."[70] Later, taken prisoner himself, François became even more closely acquainted with the practices of the enemy that he and his comrades regarded as evidence of their barbarism.

68 On the course of these guerrilla wars and their totality see Bell, *The First Total War*, 263–301.

69 Rozis to his friend Grivet, 9 September 1798, in *Correspondance intime de l'armée d'Egypte interceptée par la croisière anglaise*, ed. Lorédan Larchey (Paris: René Pincebourde, 1866), 131. Cited in Boudon, *La campagne d'Egypte*, 173.

70 Jourquin, ed., *Journal du Capitaine François*, 227.

His captor forced him to march for two days bearing around his neck the heads of two French soldiers which had been strung together on a rope.[71]

In Spain, as Goya's incomparable images of the "Disasters of War" illustrate, French soldiers who fell into enemy hands were often subjected to extreme cruelty. Ferdinand Chantraine wrote to his parents from Seville in 1810 that during a march from Segovia to Madrid, "we saw along the road nine massacred Frenchmen, one of whom had his private parts cut off and placed in his mouth, another the eyes torn from his head, five fingers severed from his left hand and holding his private parts in his right hand."[72] Particularly vulnerable were aides-de-camp who were required to convey orders and other communications between armies. Marbot recalled coming across the body of one such officer who had fallen into the hands of partisans. He had been nailed upside down by the hands and feet to a barn door and roasted over a fire. "Happily for him," wrote Marbot, "his torments were over; he was dead!"[73] Over seven years, from 1807 to 1814, 250,000 French soldiers became casualties in the Peninsular War, an average loss of a hundred soldiers a day.[74]

The type of torture described by Marbot, combining elements of crucifixion and auto-da-fé, may well have been conditioned by the popular religiosity that underpinned the guerrilla war in Spain, reflecting the Spanish perception of the French as godless heretics. Similarly, the dolorist Catholicism that characterized popular religiosity in southern Italy also determined the atrocities committed on the bodies of French soldiers in Calabria. In 1806, General Lamarque discovered the bodies of eight men who had been crucified by rebels who had taken up the cause of the Bourbons against the French occupiers.[75] The fear of being roasted alive haunted the imaginations of French soldiers. "If every day we burn a few of their villages, unable to burn ours, it is us that they burn, when they are able to attack us," wrote Jean-Michel Chevalier.[76] Other atrocities commonly inflicted by partisans in Calabria – mutilating the victims' faces, cutting their throats, extracting their eyes, eviscerating them or severing their sexual organs – arose both from the distinctive features of local religious belief and also from more profound urges to dehumanize, humiliate, wreak

71　Ibid., 434.

72　Cited in Fairon and Heuse, eds, *Lettres de Grognards*, 182.

73　Marbot, *Mémoires*, 68.

74　Howard, *Napoleon's Doctors*, 115. On soldiers' perceptions of the war in Spain, see Montroussier-Favre, "Remembering the Other," 59–76.

75　Cadet, *Honneur et violences de guerre*, 315.

76　Chevalier, *Souvenirs des guerres napoléoniennes*, 79.

vengeance upon, and efface the identities of the victims.[77] Captured by partisans, Chevalier was forced to watch while a fellow prisoner had his eyes torn out and was then flayed alive. Only the timely arrival of a detachment of French infantry saved him from the same fate.[78] The infliction of such tortures represented a radicalization of violence fully reciprocated by the French army. "They were repaid in kind," recalled Léon-Micher Routier. "The fury of our soldiers knew no limits; all were massacred, without distinction of sex or age."[79] In Spain, too, the French were similarly pitiless, slaughtering an estimated 50,000 people, both soldiers and civilians, when they took Saragossa in February 1810.[80]

Atrocities such as those committed in Calabria and Spain were more easily inflicted because of the perceived alterity of the victims, much as they were facilitated in the civil war in the Vendée, or in colonial contexts, such as Egypt or Saint-Domingue. Philippe Beaudoin, serving in Saint-Domingue, wrote in his *carnet d'étapes* in September 1802 that a French soldier captured by the rebels had been found with his eyes and fingernails torn out and that many others had been castrated by enemy women. "So you see that it is hardly an agreeable war to fight," he concluded. "As soon as they fall into our power, we also shoot them right away."[81] The French did far worse than simply shooting their prisoners. General Rochambeau, who replaced General Leclerc as the commander of the French army in Saint-Domingue in November 1802, had some of them torn apart by dogs in an arena.[82] Under Rochambeau, as Matthieu Brévet notes, "executions took on a systematic, even genocidal, character."[83] Rochambeau was far from alone among the French officers in Saint-Domingue in his penchant for cruelty. Some of the most shocking atrocities took place while Leclerc was still in command, including the mass drowning by sailors of a thousand mulatto soldiers in French service to pre-empt their possible defection when Cap Français appeared about to fall to rebel forces in October 1802. That Leclerc was prepared to endorse similar actions is demonstrated by

77   Cadet, *Honneur et violences de guerre*, 304–9.
78   Chevalier, *Souvenirs des guerres napoléoniennes*, 83–4.
79   Routier, *Récits d'un soldat*, 68.
80   Bell, *The First Total War*, 284.
81   Beaudoin, *Carnet d'étapes*, 50.
82   The dogs, imported from Cuba to help hunt down rebels, had to be destroyed after they attacked wounded French soldiers during an expedition. Brévet, "Les expéditions coloniales," 57–8. Donatien-Marie-Joseph de Vimeur, vicomte de Rochambeau, was the son of Jean-Baptiste-Donatien de Vimeur, comte de Rochambeau, who fought and was wounded at Clostercamp, in 1760. Victor-Emmanuel Leclerc was Napoleon's brother-in-law, having married Pauline Bonaparte in 1797. He died of yellow fever on 2 November 1802.
83   Ibid., 99.

a letter of 7 October 1802 in which he rather implausibly reported that 170 out of 173 soldiers in the Eleventh Colonial Demi-Brigade had "strangled themselves" while aboard naval transport vessels.[84] It is important to note that these victims of French cruelty were, unlike those in Egypt, Calabria, or Spain, themselves soldiers serving in the French army at the moment they were done to death.

WORSE WAYS TO DIE

Most soldiers who died in Napoleon's armies did not die at the enemy's hands, whether on or off the battlefield. The majority succumbed to illness because of the extremely unhealthy circumstances of life on campaign. Unwashed, ill clad, poorly nourished, forced for months at a time to sleep in the open air or on filthy straw, soldiers were vulnerable to a wide range of debilitating and, to varying degrees, life-threatening illnesses. Pulmonary and intestinal diseases, including pneumonia and dysentery, were endemic, as was scabies. Particularly fearsome in their effects were epidemic diseases such as typhus or yellow fever, although it is possible that some of the fatalities attributed to these contagions were in fact caused by other, more "ordinary" illnesses. Yellow fever, transmitted through the bite of a mosquito, is usually held to have been the principal agent that destroyed the expedition sent to Saint Domingue in 1802. Of the 60,000 men ultimately sent to the Caribbean by Napoleon, it is estimated that only about 3,000 survived to return home.[85] Nevertheless, recent research suggests many of those who died may have become ill before they had even arrived in Saint Domingue or encountered a mosquito infected with yellow fever. Citing the example of the soldiers conveyed to Saint Domingue on board the *Théobaldis*, Matthieu Brévet indicates that of the 333 men who embarked for the expedition, 35 (17 per cent) died during the voyage and 133 (41 per cent) were hospitalized immediately upon arrival in Saint Domingue. This left only 165 (42 per cent) fit for active service. Brévet suggests that a possible cause of so many shipboard illnesses was leptospirosis, a disease transmitted through contact with the urine of an infected animal, especially rodents. The ubiquitous rats inhabiting naval vessels may have to share at least some of the responsibility for the miserable fate of the Saint-Domingue expedition.[86] Typhus was another epidemic disease, spread by rubbing the feces of infected lice into sores or scratches, that was greatly feared. It rampaged through the wounded soldiers of the Guard

84 Cited in ibid., 104.
85 Brévet, "Les expéditions coloniales," 21.
86 Ibid., 179.

and their comrades who gathered at Brunn after Austerlitz, adding as many as twelve thousand men who "were carried off obscurely by typhus" to the two thousand dead and six thousand "glorious" wounded from the battle itself.[87] It also contributed significantly to the disintegration of the French armies in Russia in 1812 and in Germany in 1813.[88] Finally, a disease that famously afflicted the Army of Egypt during the campaign of 1798–1801 was the bubonic plague. An official report attributed 1,689 of a total 8,915 deaths suffered by that army to "pestilential fever," which it attributed primarily to the bubonic plague.[89] The death toll from "ordinary illnesses," including dysentery, was even higher, however: 2,468. A final example of how a medley of ailments could erode the strength of an army is provided by the French army serving in Calabria. Between February 1806 and December 1807 that force lost eight thousand men – 44 per cent of its original strength – to all sorts of afflictions, including typhus, typhoid fever, malaria, consumption, and dysentery.[90] Jean-Michel Chevalier described a hospital in Cosanza in August 1806, filled with sick soldiers, but "without straw and without covers, lacking even water to drink, deprived of everything and without help of any kind. The first day, at least three hundred died, the second day almost as many, and the other days, sixty, fifty, forty."[91]

Soldiers who claimed to face the perils of shot and shell with equanimity confessed that the prospect of succumbing to a deadly illness filled them with dread. Captain Marbot, stricken by typhus at Ciudad Rodrigo in Spain in 1811 and who had seen his father succumb to the same disease at Genoa eleven years earlier, wrote, "Death on the battlefield seemed sweet compared to that which awaited me, and I was sorry not to have fallen there like a *soldier!*" To die in bed, of fever, while others fought nearby, he said, "seemed to me something horrible and almost shameful!"[92] In Egypt, Captain François, describing the impact of the outbreak of bubonic plague in the French army following the capture of Jaffa in 1798, said, "this terrible

---

87 Soubiran, *Napoléon et un million de morts*, 103. The words are from a fictional letter in which Soubiran writes as a soldier of the Imperial Guard, reproaching Napoleon for not giving the *service de santé* the resources to prevent the spread of the disease. Soubiran's implication is clear that the deaths were unnecessary.

88 Talty, *The Illustrious Dead*. Talty provides a vivid narrative of the Russian campaign, but may overstate the case that typhus was the principal cause of the army's destruction in Russia. For the scientific evidence, see Raoult et al., "Evidence for Louse-Transmitted Diseases," 112–20. See also Lobell, "Digging Napoleon's Dead," 40–3.

89 Desgenettes, *Histoire médicale de l'Armée d'Orient*, 172–3.

90 Nicolas Cadet, *Honneur et violences de guerre*, 231–3.

91 Chevalier, *Souvenirs des guerres napoléoniennes*, 85.

92 Marbot, *Mémoires*, vol. 2, 353.

scourge struck terror in the most courageous men."[93] Morale only improved, he said, once soldiers had followed his lead in adopting an attitude of detached fatalism, refusing either to fear the disease or to take precautions against it.[94] In other cases, discipline collapsed in the wake of epidemic disease. When the army in southern Spain was stricken by yellow fever in 1812, according to surgeon Jean-Baptiste d'Héralde, "stupor and indiscipline reigned within the army [...] At all times it was necessary, in order to defend one's lodging and provisions, to have one's sword in hand."[95] The temptation in such circumstances was to adopt a *carpe diem* philosophy, living immoderately in the expectation that time would be short. This outlook manifested itself at its most extreme in the Caribbean, where generals like Rochambeau held feasts and dances even as their armies succumbed to hunger and yellow fever. According to a Polish officer, soldiers serving in Saint-Domingue "gave themselves up to a raging debauchery, wallowing in stupor and fornication [...] The military hierarchy collapsed, order disappeared."[96]

Epidemic disease did not kill indiscriminately. As was the case when they were wounded, officers had a greater chance than the men they commanded of receiving the medical attention that would assist their survival. Ironically, given the paucity of resources provided by the French army's medical services, this often meant steering clear of the military hospitals. This is illustrated by the experience of Lieutenant Martin, who was stricken first by dysentery and then by typhus in the aftermath of the French defeat at Leipzig in 1813. Unable because of his weakness to keep up with his regiment, Martin recognized that he must rejoin it at all costs. "The regiment was my family; to leave it was to fall into isolation, and into all the miseries that a campaign holds for a sick soldier separated from his unit."[97] Setting out on foot to rejoin his comrades, Martin reached a point where he could go on no longer. "Finally, at the end of my strength," he later wrote, "I lay down beside a ditch to die. I was not the only one reduced to this extremity: many soldiers were lying down like me, and not all of them got up again."[98] Martin owed his survival in the first place to a passing miller, who took pity on him and conveyed him on his cart to Coblenz. Here, he might still have met his end in a completely overwhelmed and understaffed military hospital where ordinary soldiers were sent to die,

93   Jourquin, ed., *Journal du Capitaine François*, 275–6.
94   Ibid.
95   Héralde, *Mémoires d'un chirugien*, 183.
96   Cited in Brévet, "Les expéditions coloniales," 193.
97   Jourquin, ed., *Souvenirs de guerre du Lieutenant Martin*, 226.
98   Ibid., 227.

had it not been for a chance encounter with a fellow officer from his regiment and for his own status as an officer, which between them gained him admittance to a relatively well-provided civic hospital. In the hospital, he was nursed through the delirium of typhus. Martin reflected upon the advantages of rank: "Alas! Where on earth is equality to be found? Not even in the cemetery, whatever one says, at least above ground; why hope for it in a municipality?"[99]

The worse the sufferings endured in camp, on the march or in hospital, the less terrible the battlefield was perceived to be. François Guélat recalled a confrontation between the men of his battalion and Napoleon himself, which took place on the island of Lobau in June 1809, shortly after the Battle of Aspern-Essling. Guélat was "stupefied," he said, by the audacity of his comrades, who had been denied supplies for eight days and "were dropping from starvation." Hurling invectives at Napoleon, they demanded, "Lead us against the enemy at least [...] It would be better for us to die arms in hand than here of starvation."[100] Colonel Girard, writing while serving in Poland under the empire, expressed similar sentiments. Soldiers were far less afraid, he said, of the dangers of the battlefield than of losing their way and dying on Poland's muddy roads: "'To die in battle, that is nothing,' we said. 'But to die drowning in mud and without glory!'"[101] Such attitudes were far from irrational. The miseries of life while on campaign and the ever-present danger of an agonizing death away from the battlefield caused by famine or disease made the prospect of death in battle less awful than it might otherwise have been.

Inevitably, the best illustrations of this perspective are provided by the retreat from Russia in 1812. Captain François provided a vivid account of the suffering of the French soldiers during the retreat from Moscow. "On all sides were heard the cries and groans of those who, fallen, fought against the most frightful agony and died a thousand times while waiting for death."[102] For Jakob Walter, as he prepared to attempt the dangerous passage of the bridge over the Berezina in 1812, the alternatives were stark. "Only 'Straight ahead and in the middle!' must be the resolution," he said of his attempt to make the crossing. "'Here in the water is your grave; beyond the bridge is the continuation of a wretched life. The decision will be made on the bridge!'"[103] It seems a fair assumption that many soldiers

99 Ibid., 229.
100 Surrateau, "Une visite impromptue de Napoléon," 558.
101 Girard, *Souvenirs militaires*, 114.
102 Jourquin, ed., *Journal du Capitaine François*, 690.
103 Walter, *The Diary of a Napoleonic Foot Soldier*, 86.

felt this way before going into action. Death in battle – or, as in Walter's case, attempting a dangerous river crossing – was easier to contemplate when its alternative was simply "the continuation of a wretched life."

Many soldiers were ultimately vanquished by their own despair. Marbot described the fate of a regiment of Bavarian soldiers during the Russian campaign. These men, he wrote, "were very brave before the enemy; but once the danger was past, they would fall back into complete apathy. Nostalgia, or homesickness, took hold of them." The Bavarians admitted themselves to hospital, said Marbot, looking for "the room where one dies."[104] Even before the end of summer, when the weather was still mild, the regiment had begun to melt away.

Some men were desperate enough to take their own lives. Although Napoleonic propaganda continued the revolutionary tradition of representing suicide as an act of heroic resistance, it was more commonly one of hopeless capitulation. Captain Coignet noted the misery of the army's advance into Poland in the winter of 1806–07: "Discouragement began to make itself felt in the ranks of the old soldiers; there were some who, beside themselves with suffering, committed suicide. We lost sixty of them in the two-day journey to Pultusk, a miserable village covered in straw."[105] Captain Marbot, during the pursuit of Sir John Moore's army in Spain in 1808, witnessed three grenadiers who, "finding themselves incapable of continuing this arduous march, and not wishing to stay behind for fear of being tortured and massacred by peasants, blew their brains out with their own rifles!"[106] Marbot later observed how during the retreat from Russia even brave men were sometimes driven to this extremity: "Many soldiers of all ranks blew their brains out to put an end to their misery!"[107] In the Caribbean, where thirty-four (40.4 per cent) out of eighty-four general officers died on campaign, but only three are known to have died violent deaths, General Ferrand was celebrated for having "preferred a glorious death to a shameful flight" and taken his own life at the Battle of Ceybo in 1808.[108] As Matthieu Brévet points out, a print representing this event was false in almost every respect (fig. 4.2). Ferrand did not kill himself in the heat of battle, fighting Black insurgents, but in the aftermath of a defeat by Spanish forces, when he had already left the battlefield. Finally, Ferrand was represented with a full head of hair, although he was

104 Marbot, *Mémoires*, vol. 3, 160.
105 Larchey, ed., *Les cahiers du Capitaine Coignet*, 127.
106 Marbot, *Mémoires*, vol. 2, 92.
107 Ibid., vol. 3, 220.
108 L'Héritier, ed., *Fastes de la gloire*, no. 37.

FASTES DE LA GLOIRE.

FERRAND, Général de Division.

« Abandonné de ses meilleures troupes, le désespoir s'empare de son âme; alors il se brule la cervelle d'un coup de pistolet.»

4.2. *Fastes de la gloire.* "Ferrand, Divisional General. Abandoned by his best soldiers, his spirit succumbs to despair, and so he blows his brains out with a pistol shot."

in fact bald![109] More importantly, images such as this distorted the reality of military suicide in Saint-Domingue, which was more likely to be a gesture of hopeless despair than of heroic resistance. Matthieu Brévet cites the example of the Polish battalion commander Jasinski, who, prior to putting a bullet into his brain, penned a despairing letter to General Fressinet that also implied a loss of faith in the cause for which he was supposedly fighting: "Seeing myself encircled by over three thousand

109 Brévet, "Les expéditions coloniales," 114. Of the others who died violent deaths, one, Lavalette du Verdier, drowned; only one of 84 general officers, therefore, the vicomte de Noailles, who was killed in a naval engagement on 1 January 1804, died in combat. Similarly, among battalion and squadron commanders, although twenty-five (28.7 per cent) of eighty-seven died on campaign, only three are known to have died in combat. Ibid., 117.

Blacks, I can see no hope of holding on with such a weak detachment and rather than fall into the hands of a savage people fighting for its freedom, I prefer to take my own life."[110]

INDIFFERENCE
AND SENTIMENTALITY

Given the suffering they experienced themselves as well as that which they witnessed all around them, it is hardly surprising that many soldiers developed an attitude of numbed indifference. Sentiment was reserved for close friends and relatives. Albert Rocca described the attitudes of soldiers serving in Spain: "The habit of danger caused death to be seen as one of the most ordinary circumstances of life: One pitied wounded comrades; but as soon as they ceased to live, one felt an indifference toward them that went so far as irony. When soldiers recognized in passing one of their companions laid out on the ground, they said: 'He doesn't need anything now, he won't mistreat his horse anymore, he'll be able to get drunk' or other words of this kind which reflected in those who said them a stoic disdain for existence; it was the only funeral oration for our warriors who fell in battle."[111] One might even envy the dead. Sergeant Bourgogne described the death of a friend who was struck in the chest by a four-pounder cannon shot during the retreat from Russia. "When I saw him dead," he wrote, "I could not help myself from saying, loudly enough, 'Poor Marcellin! You are most fortunate!'"[112] Bourgogne admitted that during the retreat "we had become pitiless; we had become unfeeling towards ourselves, even more so towards others."[113] Jakob Walter also confessed to his indifference during the retreat from Moscow, "I myself could look cold-bloodedly into the lamenting faces of the wounded, the freezing, and the burned [...] and think of other things."[114] For Captain François, indifference to the suffering of others during the retreat was a condition of survival. "Anyone who allowed himself to be affected by the deplorable scenes of which he was the witness condemned himself to death; but those who closed their hearts to any sentiment of pity found the strength to resist so many evils."[115]

Comradeship eroded under the extreme conditions of the retreat from Moscow. Sergeant Bourgogne remembered with shame his selfish hoarding

110 Cited in Brévet, "Les expéditions coloniales," 191.
111 Rocca, *Oeuvres*, 107
112 Bourgogne, *Mémoires du Sergent Bourgogne*, 211.
113 Ibid., 225.
114 Walter, *The Diary of a Napoleonic Foot Soldier*, 66.
115 Jourquin, ed., *Journal du Capitaine François*, 690.

of a handful of potatoes which he jealously concealed from his comrades, eating them surreptitiously during the night. "On my part, it was an act of selfishness for which I have never forgiven myself," he wrote.[116] Bourgogne witnessed a far more extreme breakdown of solidarity, however, when hundreds of soldiers were burned to death in a post-house that caught fire after they had refused to allow others to use its roof for firewood. Other soldiers who witnessed this "truly hellish scene," wrote Bourgogne, were devoid of all human sympathy. Some, he said, used the heat from the fire to cook horsemeat, while others risked their lives, not to save the victims of the fire, but to steal from them. He described soldiers warming their hands from the fire, "as if they did not know that several hundred of their comrades, perhaps relatives, were warming them with their corpses."[117]

Despite this evident breakdown of comradeship, there were still notable acts of generosity and self-sacrifice during the retreat. Bourgogne cites the example of five or six hundred soldiers from the regiment of the Prince of Hesse-Cassel who pressed around their prince to keep him warm with their body heat during a night of exceptional cold. By the next morning, three quarters of them were dead.[118] In general, however, as Jakob Walter wrote, "only mutual support still procured true friendship." Walter, who was from Wurtemberg, and one of the many non-French soldiers serving in Napoleon's army, reserved his own kindnesses for soldiers from his homeland. Even this parochial solidarity was not always a match for the suspicions engendered by privation. One countryman with whom Walter shared his food accused him of stealing bread and became transformed into "a shameful caricature of a human being. Here I saw truly how low reason had sunk with us: our brains were frozen, and there was no feeling left."[119]

Although strained to the breaking point by conditions during the retreat from Moscow, the ties of friendship mattered to Napoleonic soldiers. Close friendships were formed by soldiers on campaign which they often came to depend upon, not only to learn the soldier's trade, but also for the mutual aid on which their survival often depended.[120] There were instances when the death of a close friend inspired intense outpourings of sorrow. René-Nicolas Desgenettes, head of the *service de santé* during the Egyptian campaign, noted the case of an officer who was deeply affected by the death of a young engineer during the siege of Acre in 1799. To Desgenettes, this was "a remarkable example of temporary insanity, produced by an excess

116 Bourgogne, *Mémoires*, 72.
117 Ibid., 77–8.
118 Ibid., 82.
119 Walter, *The Diary of a Napoleonic Foot Soldier*, 76.
120 On this theme, see Martin, *Napoleonic Friendship*, 68–100.

of sensibility." The officer had the misfortune to learn of his friend's death by stumbling upon his body as it was about to be buried under the arcades of an aqueduct: "A stupor took hold of him; soon he came to, and violently resisted those who sought to take him away from such a painful scene; he madly threw himself on the hastily covered grave of his friend, wanting to be buried with him; then came a subsidence, and he lost consciousness; advantage was taken of this to pick him up and carry him to the camp ... there, he awoke and abandoned himself again to tears and moaning ... Who did he not blame for the loss of his friend? He went as far as imprecations of fury ... finally, the repose which calms a part of human woes came to restore his reason without for all that extinguishing his sorrow."[121] Desgenettes's professional interest in what he clearly considered with clinical detachment as an extraordinary case of mental breakdown stands out in a report otherwise preoccupied with factors affecting the physical health of the Army of Egypt. Although Desgenettes clearly regarded the officer's grief as exceptional, his account is evidence nonetheless that soldiers were sometimes deeply distressed by the deaths of their comrades. For the most part, however, soldiers contained that distress within the formulas allowed by the values of masculine military honour. Vincent Bertrand, for example, described his search for a friend on the battlefield of Eylau:

We spent the night, wandering among the corpses, looking for our missing friends. I wanted to find a childhood friend whom I knew had been hit when the Russian fusillade had broken our square. A movement to the right of my regiment, as night was falling, at first misdirected my search, and it was upon returning to the front of the Eylau church, where for long hours our ranks had been decimated by the Russian cannonballs, that I found my poor friend, face down, horribly mutilated, but still holding his musket, brave in death, facing the enemy. I took his icy hand and held it in mine, but, hearing the beat to arms, I gave him, my heart full, a final goodbye, and returned to our bivouac. The next day, 9 February, we spent the day on the battlefield. We could thus rescue a few more wounded and we buried, to the extent possible, the dead. My friend was not forgotten and was buried with his musket still in hand.[122]

Bertrand's grief at his friend's death was clearly heartfelt. He expressed that grief, however, by doing honour to his friend's remains (assuring a proper burial) and to his memory (insisting that he had died "*en brave*").

121 Desgenettes, *Histoire médicale de l'Armée d'Orient*, 94.
122 Bertrand, *Mémoires du Capitaine Bertrand*, 29–32.

He also – at least according to his own testimony – kept the expression of his grief within the limits imposed by duty, returning to camp at the sound of the drums. Bertrand lost another close friend two years later, at the Battle of Wagram. The mention of this in his memoirs was no less heartfelt for all its brevity: "Among the dead whom I mourned with deep regret, was my bedfellow Lacour, a valorous soldier and a good fellow, to whom I was attached from the bottom of my heart."[123]

BLURRING THE LINE BETWEEN LIFE AND DEATH

The contrasting attitudes of indifference and sentimentality with respect to the deaths of comrades were also apparent more generally in the attitudes of soldiers toward the dead. At a time when new legislation in France was introduced to regulate the burial of the dead in individualized graves in suburban cemeteries, thereby ensuring a strict separation of the living and the dead as well as the permanent memorialization of individual lives, the experience of mass battlefield death worked in exactly the opposite direction.[124] While the bodies of senior officers like Lannes were recuperated from the battlefield, embalmed, and repatriated for burial, this was not the case for most soldiers who died in the Napoleonic wars. Occasionally, soldiers might honour their comrades with individualized graves and funeral rites. Jean-Baptiste d'Héralde recalled a lieutenant of light artillery who had shown conspicuous bravery at the Battle of Albuera, in Spain, whose men buried him beside the guns he had defended, firing two shots over his grave. Most of the battle's victims, however, as d'Héralde went on to explain, were incinerated and their remains subsequently buried in mass graves. "Large graves dug by the English were filled with the heads of the corpses they had burned. Two of those great graves had not been covered over. We could judge their depth from the amount of soil around them. We saw half-burned heads, heaped one upon the others. There were more than 1,200 in each grave. It was horrifying. Effectively, it was the English practice, after a battle, to burn all the dead; arms, legs, and trunks were consumed, but the heads would not burn. They dug large graves

---

123 Ibid., 60–2. Bedfellowship was one of four types of friendship pertaining among the ranks in Napoleon's armies analyzed by Brian Martin. Martin distinguishes between "the nighttime *camarade de lit* (bedfellow), the trusted *intime ami* (buddy), the comforting *pays* (hometown friend), and the admired *mentor* (mentor)." Martin, *Napoleonic Friendship*, 71.

124 The most significant legislation was the Decree on Graves of 12 June 1804. On the importance of this law in relation to the emergence of a new culture of death and burial in post-revolutionary France, see Legacey, *Making Space for the Dead*, 68–70.

where they threw them with the remaining bones that escaped combustion."[125] D'Héralde's appalled fascination for this "field of horror" is revealed by his confession that he visited it "many times" in the company of General Girard and once more together with his brother and the latter's comrades from the Army of Portugal.[126] His horror is indicative of the disjuncture between the practical necessities of disposing of large numbers of dead through incineration and burial in mass graves and the new conventions prescribing the respectful burial of the dead in individualized graves that were becoming normative in post-revolutionary France.

The experience of mass killing in the revolutionary and Napoleonic wars had the effect of temporarily reversing the trend toward the separation of the living from the dead. Soldiers' initial feelings of revulsion at the sight of dead bodies gave way to a callously utilitarian attitude. Not only were the dead pillaged of their valuables and stripped of their boots and clothes; they also served as ramparts, cushions, and pillows.[127] Captain François recounted that at the siege of Acre, in 1799, the Turkish gunfire prevented the French from burying or burning the bodies of "our unhappy brothers in arms who rotted in the ditches [...] It was necessary to spend twenty-four hours among these putrefying corpses that served us as retrenchments," he wrote. "The least putrefied were used as seats."[128] Jakob Walter described how, during the retreat from Moscow, people often froze because they were denied access to the warmth of campfires: "so they died away from the fire, and very often they were even converted into cushions in order that the living would not have to sit in the snow."[129] Walter himself discovered, after finding a warm spot on the ground to sleep one night that he had in fact slept on top of a dead man "whose unfrozen belly had served as my good bed."[130]

During the retreat from Moscow, the line between the living and the dead became increasingly indistinct. Jakob Walter described how, in bivouac, "soldiers who looked like specters [*sic*]," identified as hopeless cases by "the color [*sic*] of their faces, their husky breathing, and their dull muttering," were condemned by those who were only marginally more alive: "No one allowed these shades of death to drag themselves to the fire."[131] Captain François used similar language to describe officers and

125 Héralde, *Mémoires d'un chirugien*, 162.
126 Ibid.
127 Thoral, *From Valmy to Waterloo*, 31–2.
128 Jourquin, ed., *Journal du Capitaine François*, 310.
129 Walter, *The Diary of a Napoleonic Foot Soldier*, 72.
130 Ibid., 71.
131 Ibid., 72.

men huddling around campfires during the retreat: "there were those who, almost dead from fatigue, remained standing, like spectres, all night, around the bonfires that we lit when we could."[132] The struggle of the survivors to resist the dead and dying is also apparent in Captain François's description of his crossing of the Berezina: "My courage did not abandon me and by battling my way through the dead and dying, I succeeded in crossing the bridge and rejoining my division, my wounds reopened and bleeding."[133] François's words to a companion with whom he was tearfully reunited after the crossing are revealing of his sentiment to have had one foot in the grave: "All right, my good man, I must die no more."[134]

The urge to survive clearly inspired resistance to the wartime familiarity with death. In some soldiers that resistance expressed itself as horror or revulsion. Sergeant Bourgogne experienced a panic attack when he fell onto three bodies that lay beside an abandoned wagon carrying wounded men. "I was used to sleeping, for the last month, among like company," he recalled, "and I don't know if it was because I was alone, but something more terrible than fear took hold of me." Paralyzed by terror, Bourgogne eventually recovered his feet and his wits, fear giving way to anger. "I looked at the heavens, cursing, as if I defied them. I took my musket, struck it against the wagon, I may even have struck the poor devils who were under my feet."[135]

Sergeant Bourgogne's terror and subsequent defiance were instinctive reactions to being brought shockingly and literally face to face with death. Jacques-François Martin noted that other soldiers who, like Sergeant Bourgogne, generally viewed the dead and wounded with indifference, also had their limits, objecting to their comrades who "to avoid the wet earth, seated themselves on the dead." Those comrades, he said, "were forced to give way to that instinctive sentiment which does honour to humankind: *Respect to the dead!*"[136] In this case, the reaction against excessive familiarity with the dead was social rather than personal. All the same, the memories of Bourgogne and Martin reveal that the wartime transgression of the conventional boundaries between the living and the dead did not take place without some unease.

132 Jourquin, ed., *Journal du Capitaine François*, 682.
133 Ibid., 694.
134 Ibid., 696.
135 Bourgogne, *Mémoires du Sergent Bourgogne*, 142–3.
136 Jourquin, ed., *Souvenirs de guerre du Lieutenant Martin*, 188–9.

DYING FOR THE EMPEROR

Soldiers were of course not the only ones who had to come to terms with mass death during the Napoleonic wars. This was a challenge that confronted the whole of French society. The Napoleonic regime was itself compelled to develop strategies for representing so many deaths in a way that would enable it to hold onto the allegiance of an increasingly war-weary population. Of course, one possible strategy was simply denial, a refusal to admit the true extent of the losses. This was certainly an approach that was taken at times, particularly in the official bulletins reporting on the battles of the Grande Armée. The Battle of Eylau in February 1807, in which the French and Russian armies fought one another to a bloody stalemate in Poland, was the first great military setback suffered by Napoleon after the Egyptian campaign. The bulletin reporting on the battle numbered the French dead and wounded at 1,900 and 5,700 respectively.[137] In subsequent correspondence with his officials and with Josephine, Napoleon insisted that these figures were exaggerated, revising the figure of French dead downwards to 1,500. In fact, the most complete recent compilation estimates the true figure for French dead to be more than twice the official estimate, between 4,000 and 4,200.[138] Another strategy was to admit the scale of the disaster but to deny responsibility. This was the approach famously adopted in the notorious bulletin of December 1812, reporting on the disastrous retreat from Moscow, which blamed the army's destruction on the sudden onset of the Russian winter: "That army, so fine on the sixth, was quite different from the fourteenth."[139] Those responsible for Napoleon's propaganda recognized, however, that refusing to acknowledge the full extent of military losses and the suffering of the soldiers was not an effective way to prevent public alienation. As art historian David O'Brien has shown, Napoleonic propaganda was at its most effective when it produced works that "offered limited acknowledgments of military setbacks and their tremendous costs in terms of lives and human suffering."[140] The most important painting commissioned by Vivant Denon, Napoleon's director of artistic propaganda, Antoine-Jean Gros's *Napoleon on the Battlefield at Eylau*, made no attempt to hide the

---

137 Pascal, ed., *Les bulletins de la Grande Armée*, vol. 4, 104. The bulletin estimated that there were 7,000 Russian dead.

138 Quintin and Quintin, *La tragédie d'Eylau*, 463–4. See also O'Brien, *After the Revolution*, 158.

139 Pascal, *Bulletins de la Grande Armée*, vol. 5, 330.

140 O'Brien, *After the Revolution*, 155.

4.3. Antoine-Jean Gros, *Napoleon on the Battlefield at Eylau.* 1808.

horrors of the battlefield (fig. 4.3). True, it did displace most of those
horrors onto the bodies of Russian soldiers (only one dead Frenchman
is depicted), but the representation in its foreground of larger-than-life
piles of frozen corpses and of terrified wounded and dying men left little
to the imagination of a public avid for realistic representations of war.[141]
Most importantly, the representation by Gros of Napoleon in the middle
of this painting extending a hand in a Christ-like gesture of benediction
presented the emperor as a caring, compassionate leader who was not
only aware of but also able to heal the wounds of war. It was by appropriat-
ing concern for the suffering of war through representations such as this

141 By graphically depicting the horrors of war, Gros rebelled against much contemporary art criticism, which, as Katie Hornstein has shown, was uneasy about the depiction
of violence in battle paintings. Hornstein demonstrates that the ambivalence of the elite
artistic establishment concerning war art provided officer artists like Louis-Guislan Bacler
d'Albe and Louis-François Lejeune as well as historical panoramists such as Pierre Prévost
with an opportunity to satisfy an insatiable public demand for realistic depictions of war.
Panoramas represented contemporary battles in 360-degree paintings that were viewed
from the interior of a rotunda. Physical props added to the illusion of reality. Hornstein,
Picturing War in France, 22–41.

that Napoleon's government sought to pre-empt critics who might oppose it on humanitarian grounds.[142]

It is in this context that Albert-Paul Bourgeois's painting of the death of Lannes should be understood. Like Gros's *Eylau*, the painting acknowledged both the suffering of war and the compassion of Napoleon. Other Napoleonic paintings depicting fallen soldiers were far less effective in showing Napoleon as a caring leader. François-Henri Mulard's painting of *The Retaking of Dego and the Death of General Causse*, exhibited at the salon of 1812 and purchased by the emperor, depicted Napoleon in full imperial pomp even though it represented an event from the Italian campaign in 1796. The focus of the painting was on the triumphant figure of Napoleon on horseback, rather than on the dying general, depicted off to one side. As Yveline Cantarel-Besson writes, "Far from evoking the exemplary virtue of a hero's death, the painting expresses the joy and pride of a victory in which the dying man is invited to share."[143] The painting exemplifies the weaknesses of much imperial propaganda, representing hubris at a time when humility might have been more suitable for engaging a public burdened for too long by the high price of war. Jean Broc's painting of *The Death of General Desaix*, exhibited at the salon of 1806 and also purchased for the state, depicted Napoleon and Desaix in the centre of the painting, the former standing, the latter's body lying on the ground (fig. 4.4). Both are shown surrounded by grieving soldiers. The painting's purpose was above all to celebrate Napoleon, as the critic Chaussard confirmed. Dismissing Desaix with a few words – "born, to recall amidst the corruption of modern times, all the loyalty, all the simplicity of ancient knights" – he waxed eloquently on Napoleon: "At the centre of the painting, the vanquishing hero who contemplates avenging this illustrious victim and of covering his tomb with laurels [preserves] a calm and generous attitude appropriate to a general-in-chief, that is to say to the man who looks down upon the fates."[144]

Although Napoleonic propaganda continued to celebrate the heroic deaths of soldiers in a way that echoed the tradition of virtuous self-sacrifice promoted by the revolution, it moved steadily away from that tradition, shifting the focus inexorably from commemorating patriotic deaths on behalf of the nation to celebrating glorious deaths in the service of Napoleon.[145] This evolution was apparent in the bulletins of the Grand

142 O'Brien, *After the Revolution*, 154–76.

143 Cantarel-Besson, "Les morts exemplaires," 102.

144 Chaussard, *Le Pausanias français*, Salon de 1806 (Paris, 1808), 264–6. Cited in Bertaud, *Quand les enfants parlaient*, 335.

145 On this theme, see Hughes, *Forging Napoleon's Grande Armée*, 85–9.

4.4. Jean Broc, *The Death of General Desaix at the Battle of Marengo, 14 June 1800.* 1806.

Army, which, in reporting the words of dying soldiers, increasingly emphasized their personal devotion to Napoleon. After Austerlitz, General Valhubert was represented as a paragon of military honour, showing his obedience to orders by turning away four grenadiers who rushed to his aid when he lost his leg to a cannonball: "Remember the order of the day, he said in a voice of thunder, and hold your positions! If you return victorious, I can be picked up after the battle; if you are defeated, I no longer want to live."[146] His very last words, addressed in a letter to Napoleon written an hour before his death and reported in the thirty-third bulletin, insisted upon the glory to be won by dying for the emperor. "I would have liked to do more for you," wrote Valhubert. "I am not sorry to die, because I took part in a victory which assures you a happy reign. When you think of the brave men who were devoted to you, think of my memory."[147]

146 Pascal, ed., *Bulletins de la Grande Armée*, vol. 3, 228.

147 Ibid., 216–17. Jean-Baptiste d'Héralde was a surgeon sent by Marshal Suchet to attend to General Valhubert. D'Héralde's memoir confirmed Valhubert's rejection of assistance from the grenadiers. Nevertheless, the general was hardly left to languish on the battlefield, as was undoubtedly the lot of many ordinary soldiers who were wounded. D'Héralde and

The sixty-third bulletin of the Grande Armée reporting the death of Captain Auzouy, who was carried mortally wounded from the battlefield of Eylau in 1807, conflated service to Napoleon with loyalty to France. "Tell the emperor that I have only one regret," the dying officer was reported to have said, "which is that in a few moments I will no longer be able to do anything for his service, and for the glory of our fine France ... to her my last breath."[148] Auzouy, in his final phrase, seemed to place France above Napoleon in his priorities. There was no mention of France at all, however, in the last words reportedly uttered to Napoleon by General Duroc when he was mortally wounded by a cannonball at the Battle of Bautzen in May 1813. "My whole life," Duroc is supposed to have said as the emperor pressed the general's hand to his lips, "has been consecrated to your service, and I only regret its loss for the use it might still have been to you!"[149] As was the case for the heroes of the revolution, whether the fine words attributed to these dying soldiers were really spoken is to be doubted. General Desaix, killed at Marengo by a bullet that literally blew his heart to bits, could not possibly have uttered the phrase later attributed to him by General Berthier: "Go tell the First Consul that I die with the regret of not having done enough to live in posterity."[150] General Duroc, according to later testimony by Napoleon himself, spent his last moments, "when his bowels were falling out before my eyes," begging for the emperor to put him out of his misery.[151] Embellished or not, gestures of devotion to the emperor by wounded and dying soldiers became a staple of Napoleonic propaganda, represented in print and in iconography.[152] François Gérard's painting of the Battle of Austerlitz received favourable comment for its depiction of a fallen *cuirassier* clutching his breast as he turned his dying gaze upon the emperor. Marbot, who claimed to have been present, insisted upon the artist's accuracy in portraying the scene, including "that brave horseman who, without complaint despite having his body shot through

---

two of the general's aides-de-camp bore him to a place of safety and then supervised his removal to Brunn, carried on a stretcher by Austrian and Russian prisoners. General Valhubert died at Brunn six days after receiving his wound. D'Héralde said of him, "This general was violent but uncommonly brave and honest. He loved the soldiers and constantly concerned himself with their needs. He was greatly mourned by his brigade." Héralde, *Mémoires d'un chirugien*, 89–94.

148 Garnier, ed., *Bulletins de la Grande Armée*, 330–1.

149 Pascal, *Bulletins de la Grande Armée*, vol. 6, 76–7.

150 Cited in Gainot, "Les mots et les cendres," 127–38.

151 Napoleon's response, according to Lord Ebrington, was "I am sorry for you my friend, but there is nothing to be done, it is necessary to suffer until the end." Fortescue, *Memorandum of Two Conversations*, 18–19.

152 Prendergast, *Napoleon and History Painting*, 200–1.

by a bullet, had the courage to approach the emperor and dropped dead in presenting the standard he had just captured."[153] Gérard's painting was a celebration of imperial glory, representing the moment of Napoleon's triumph at Austerlitz. The dying *cuirassier*, content to give his life to share in that triumph, modelled the glorious death on behalf of the emperor that, in Napoleonic propaganda, came ultimately to displace the revolutionary model of patriotic martyrdom that had been promoted with such zeal under the Jacobin republic.

In the construction of monuments to soldiers who had died Napoleon also departed from revolutionary precedents, moving inexorably away from the patriotic commemoration of the revolution towards "autocelebration."[154] Many of Napoleon's monumental projects for Paris honoured his companions in arms as a means to elevate the prestige of the army, attach its soldiers and leaders to his person, and to celebrate his own glory. Those monuments were triumphal rather than funerary, celebrating glorious conquests and feats of arms rather than patriotic self-sacrifice. As historian Annie Jourdan has written, "Napoleon had little inclination to weep for the dead."[155] This evolution of Napoleon's priorities can be traced in the tortuous history of the projects for a monument for the Place des Victoires. An original decree of 18 Fructidor Year VIII (5 September 1800) called for the construction of a monument honouring Generals Desaix and Kléber, who had both been killed on the same day (14 June 1800), one by a bullet at the Battle of Marengo, the other by an assassin's blade in Alexandria, Egypt. Eventually, perhaps because Napoleon regarded Desaix more favourably than he did Kléber, the decision was taken to honour only the former. The commission was given to the sculptor Dejoux. A letter from the Minister of the Interior to Dejoux conveyed Napoleon's insistence that Desaix not be represented in the act of dying: "The First Consul desires, Citizen, that General Desaix be represented living and that his standing figure be represented in bronze. I ask you to suspend until further instruction the work which was to represent the general dying."[156] Not until Napoleon had personally approved a scale model of Desaix represented "in the moment he took possession of Upper Egypt, placing his hand upon an obelisk," was Dejoux able to proceed with his work.[157] Inaugurated on 15 August 1810 (Napoleon's birthday), the statue was viewed with general disapproval, both because of its nudity and because of its unbalanced proportions. The

153 Marbot, *Mémoires*, vol. 1, 261.
154 See Jourdan, *Napoléon*, 194–8.
155 Ibid., 199.
156 Biver, *Le Paris de Napoléon*, 156.
157 Ibid., 156.

emperor's Director of Museums, Vivant Denon, who began to consider ideas for a replacement, eventually suggested removing the statue altogether. In a letter to the Minister of the Interior, he questioned the very idea of placing a general's statue in one of the capital's public places: "Is it appropriate for a statue of a general to occupy a public place in the capital? Should this honour not be reserved for the Sovereign and for the trophies consecrating his victories and his power?"[158] Denon suggested that Desaix be honoured instead by an equestrian statue on the Pont de Jena. Desaix's unloved bronze statue remained for a while on the Place des Victoires, eventually masked from the public's prudish eye by scaffolding, before eventually it was quietly put into storage.

The same shift in priorities, from commemorating republican sacrifice to celebrating imperial triumph, was apparent in other monumental projects. The project for a national column as well as departmental columns honouring those who had died "for the defence of the homeland and for liberty," was first approved in 1800.[159] From the first it departed in a small but significant way from revolutionary tradition by stating that the names included on the columns would not belong exclusively to those who had died, but also to those who had been decorated by the award of weapons of honour.[160] The national column was projected for the Place de la Concorde, the Parisian departmental column for the Place Vendôme. A competition was held, four hundred designs submitted for adjudication, and a full-size model, designed by Moreau, erected on the Place de la Concorde. The model, featuring a statue of Minerva, did not meet with either official or public approval and neither of these projects progressed. In 1803, forgetting its function of commemorating those who had died for the homeland, Napoleon proposed a column for the Place Vendôme that would be topped by a statue of Charlemagne and ornamented by figures representing the existing 108 French departments. This idea, too,

---

158 Ibid., 160.

159 Jourdan, *Napoléon*, 203.

160 Arms of honour, which rewarded the valorous deeds of soldiers, were institutionalized by the Consulate by a law of 4 Nivôse Year Eight (25 December 1799). See Bertaud, *Quand les enfants parlaient*, 175. Similarly, Napoleon's project for completing the Madeleine as a Temple of Glory honouring soldiers of the Grande Armée envisaged the incorporation of gold tablets bearing the names of those who had died as well as of marble tablets with the names of soldiers who had been present at Ulm, Austerlitz, and Jena. Bas-reliefs would represent regimental colonels and corps commanders. Marshals were to be represented by statues. Again, the emphasis was placed on celebrating all who had shared in Napoleon's victories rather than on commemorating the dead. The same celebratory function was served by Napoleon's famous *Arc de Triomphe du Carroussel*, completed in 1808 and bearing bas-reliefs representing events from the 1805 campaign. See Biver, *Le Paris de Napoléon*, 235 and 178.

was abandoned when, following the victory at Austerlitz, the suggestion was made to celebrate the victory by raising a column, using the bronze of captured enemy guns, topped by a statue of Napoleon himself. The Vendôme Column, designed by Lepère and Gondoin and bearing eighty bas-reliefs representing the feats of French soldiers – especially of leaders like Ney, Murat, and Lannes – from the Austerlitz campaign, was inaugurated on 15 August 1810. The finished monument, celebrating Napoleon's victory, was far removed in spirit from the object of honouring the dead that had been conceived ten years before. As Annie Jourdan has insisted, the column embodied in the symbolic landscape of the French capital a major departure from the egalitarian, libertarian, and civic values of the French Revolution.[161]

Under Napoleon's empire the revolutionary cult of patriotic martyrs was co-opted by the cult of imperial glory. The military heroes of the empire did not cease to sacrifice themselves for the nation, but devotion to France was now indistinguishable from loyalty to the emperor. Furthermore, loyalty to the emperor was inextricably bound up with the military code of honour that was at the heart of Napoleon's regime. A hybrid of old-regime and revolutionary values, the Napoleonic code of honour emphasized self-control, determination, and fearlessness in the face of death, respect for the rules of war, the enemy, and non-combatants, fidelity to one's word, comrades, and superiors. It also insisted upon service to the emperor and to the greater good of the French people. Finally, it encouraged martial exploits by promising "honours," in the form of promotions, decorations, and pensions, to those who performed them. The words Honour and Homeland were constantly evoked by Napoleon in addresses to his army. The slogan "Emperor, Honour, Homeland" tellingly came to replace that of "Liberty, Equality, Fraternity" on the flags of the Grande Armée. This revised conception of honour became the essence of Napoleonic military culture and a principal source of motivation for the *grognards* of Napoleon's armies.[162] In 1802 Napoleon institutionalized it by creating the Legion of Honour, a system of pensions and decorations.[163] All members of the Legion, nine-tenths of whom were ultimately soldiers, received a cross that bore the words "Napoleon, Emperor of the French people" on one side, "Honour and Homeland" on the other.[164] Patriotism, honour, and loyalty

161 Jourdan, *Napoléon*, 203–7. See also Biver, *Le Paris de Napoléon*, 162–75.

162 On the evolution and importance of the Napoleonic concept of honour, see Hughes, *Forging Napoleon's Grande Armée*, 51–78.

163 See Bertaud, *Quand les enfants parlaient*, 165–202, especially 173–5. See also Cadet, *Honneur et violences de guerre*, 284–8.

164 Hughes, *Forging Napoleon's Grande Armée*, 62.

to Napoleon were therefore deemed to be mutually reinforcing. Under Napoleon, the Legion of Honour was supposed to provide the necessary rewards to encourage and provide compensation for the self-sacrificing virtues of patriotism.[165]

Tributes to the military heroes of the empire were public affirmations of this Napoleonic honour code. The official funeral ceremonies held to honour Marshal Lannes in 1810 were at once a reminder of honourable feats of arms, of martial solidarity, as well as of the army's loyalty to Napoleon and to France. The dates chosen for the funeral were themselves reminders of imperial triumphs: the procession of the marshal's remains from Strasbourg to Paris began on 22 May, the anniversary of Aspern-Essling, and their final transfer from the Invalides to the Pantheon occurred on 6 July, the anniversary of Wagram. After Lannes had spent four days lying in state under the dome of the Invalides, a funeral mass was celebrated in the Invalides church. The coffin, bearing Lannes's marshal's baton and his decorations, was then solemnly paraded across the city, escorted by four imperial marshals, their aides-de-camp, and by army units representing all branches of the service. The funeral chariot was surmounted by a pyramid bearing inscriptions and ornamented by allegorical statues representing Lannes's virtues: Strength, Justice, Prudence, and Temperance. Upon reaching the Pantheon, the coffin was received by a priest and solemnly transferred to its resting place by grenadiers who had fought in the same battles as the marshal. Notwithstanding the presence of clergy and civilian ministers, Lannes's funeral was profoundly military in character. In the words of historian Jean-Paul Bertaud, it was "an affair of warriors."[166]

LOYAL UNTO DEATH

The testimony of soldiers indicates that to a remarkable extent they internalized the values embodied in Napoleonic propaganda, confirming their willingness to die for the emperor. Even in dire circumstances, most soldiers did not hold Napoleon responsible for their suffering. Indeed, on occasion they expressed sympathy for the pain he suffered on their behalf. Captain Coignet, for example, described Napoleon after the death of General Duroc, at the Battle of Bautzen: "Napoleon entered the Guard's square, and spent the rest of the evening there, seated on a stool outside his tent, his hands joined, head bowed. We all surrounded him without moving; he kept the most doleful silence. 'Poor man!' said the old grenadiers. 'He has

---

165 Ibid., 67.
166 Bertaud, *Quand les enfants parlaient,* 342. See also Anon., *Honneurs funèbres rendus au duc de Montebello.*

lost his children.'"[167] Likewise, Vincent Bertrand refuted as an "infamous
lie" the idea that the remnants of the army in Russia resented Napoleon
leaving them to suffer and die while he returned to France: "The emperor
remained for us, I will not say a God, because we acknowledge only one,
but *our emperor*, neither more nor less."[168] Lieutenant Jean-Michel Chevalier,
remembering how he and his comrades rushed to offer Napoleon their
greatcoats when he called for one during the Battle of Aspern-Essling, said
of their devotion, "There was not one of us who was not willing to be hacked
to bits for him." Napoleon's ability to win the affection of his soldiers was
such, wrote Chevalier, "that he was loved like a father."[169] Even those soldiers
who endured terrible hardships as prisoners of war on the island of Cabrera
refused to hold Napoleon rather than their Spanish captors responsible.
"Do you mean [...] that in spite of all the evil he has done to all of us, you
still love him?" asked the prefect sent to supervise their repatriation at the
end of the wars. "Yes, we will always love him," they replied.[170]

All the same, there were some who, upon reflection, came to doubt
whether, in fighting for Napoleon, they were also fighting for France. Jean
Noël was a gunner who did not begin editing his memoir until 1850
(it was finally published by his grandson in 1895). While insisting that the
French army continued to fight with undiminished courage and loyalty,
Noël represented the invasion of Spain in 1808 as a decisive turning point
when for the first time, "we were being forced to fight for the ambition
and arrogance of one family, and not for the advancement of France or
for our own glory."[171] Noël mournfully reflected that "I still loved my career
as a soldier, but I should have been happier fighting for our national independence, rather than taking part in wars of conquest."[172] Lieutenant
Martin, who was far from immune to the charisma of Napoleon, likewise
reflected wistfully upon the difference between the motives of the imperial
and revolutionary armies: "The independence of the homeland, freedom,
the rights of man, were more elevated motives than the love of glory and
of conquests, and related more easily to a feeling of humanity and even of
sympathy for the sufferings of the peasant."[173] While reaffirming their

167 Larchey, ed., *Les cahiers du Capitaine Coignet*, 229.
168 Bertrand, *Mémoires*, 117–19.
169 Chevalier, *Souvenirs des guerres napoléoniennes*, 105.
170 Wagré, *Mémoire des captifs*, 116. Cited in Smith, *Prisoners of Cabrera*, 168. Smith
estimates that between 3,500 and 5,000, or up to 40 per cent of the total of around
11,800 French prisoners who were deposited by their Spanish captors on this barren island
in the Mediterranean died there. Ibid., 166–7.
171 Noël, *With Napoleon's Guns*, 79.
172 Ibid., 77.
173 Jourquin, ed., *Souvenirs de guerre du Lieutenant Martin*, 115.

pride in their service as well as their patriotism, soldiers like Noël and Martin picked apart the knot that in Napoleonic propaganda bound patriotism together with loyalty to the emperor. Their memoirs called into question the claim of that propaganda that in dying for Napoleon soldiers of the Grande Armée were also dying for France.

MOURNING THE DEAD

For civilians, too, it became increasingly difficult to accept the official representations of the war as the death toll mounted. The disfigured bodies of the wounded veterans who became a growing presence in French villages and towns provided a shocking everyday contradiction to the sanitized and aestheticized images of war disseminated by the regime.[174] Resistance to conscription, which persisted despite the growing numbers and effectiveness of the mobile columns that scoured the countryside in search of *insoumis*, was a reflection of public awareness of the poor prospects offered by service in Napoleon's armies.[175] For soldiers, that service entailed a desperate longing for news from home as well as an equally desperate need for resources to supplement their meagre (and often unpaid) wages.[176] The sorrow of enforced separation and the anxiety at the absence of news cut both ways, however, as the family members of soldiers themselves waited for news from the armies, often in vain. Sometimes, when news did arrive, it was in the form of a letter of condolence, written by a soldier's comrade and describing, more or less truthfully, the circumstances of his death.

Some family correspondence allows us to catch a glimpse of what the death of a soldier in Napoleon's armies meant to family members in France. The surviving letters that passed between Madelon Thiesset of Saint Quentin and her son, Louis Quentin Vatin, a cobbler in Pézenas, bear witness to a family whose lives were severely disrupted by war. Three of Louis's brothers, Augustin, Joseph, and Sevère, had joined the armies of the Republic by January 1793. Another brother, Pierre, and a sister, Louison, emigrated at about the same time. Letters from Madelon to Louis revealed her frustration at the lack of news concerning their fates. "I have no further news of your brothers Joseph, Sevère and Pierre or of your sister Louison," began one letter. "This causes me great anxiety[;] it is my greatest trouble[;]

174 Bertaud, *Quand les enfants parlaient*, 352.
175 Davenson, *Le départ du conscrit*. Cited in ibid., 286.
176 On the importance of correspondence in sustaining the link between soldiers and their families, see Forrest, *Napoleon's Men*, 161–70.

otherwise I am well."[177] Another reported that both Joseph and Sévère had been killed by rebels in the Vendée, although this later turned out not to be true.[178] Soon, however, there were real deaths to report. The first was that of Joseph, who had returned to Saint Quentin after serving at the siege of Mainz and then joining the supply services of the army in Strasbourg. Madelon's letter to Louis expresses a mother's grief. "It is with sorrow that I write to tell you of the death of your brother Joseph, which causes me great sadness," she wrote. "You don't need me to tell you the pain I felt at that moment." [179] Five years later, Louis's sister, Célestine, wrote to him again with news that a second brother, Augustin, had also died. Augustin, who had spent two years as a British prisoner-of-war before returning to France and rejoining his unit, suffered a fate much like that of Joseph. He had only shortly obtained a discharge from the army (for which Célestine claimed responsibility) and had rejoined his family when he was stricken by a "flux of the chest" and died after a short illness.[180] Augustin was predeceased by his mother, who according to Célestine, died and was buried on 13 November 1801.[181] This time, Célestine wrote of her own grief at the death of her brother: "I won't describe again the pain it caused me and which I still feel; my health was badly affected and I visibly lost weight."[182] What became of Sévère, the third brother who had joined the army, is uncertain. Célestine wrote to Louis in 1803, however, to say that she was almost certain that he had died, although she had not received any official notification.[183] The uncertainties and anxieties of war were far from over for Célestine, since her son was also conscripted and saw service in Spain. At the conclusion of hostilities in 1814, he came home only to return to the colours shortly thereafter, for fear of being taken for a deserter. On 15 June 1815, Célestine wrote that she had not heard from him for eight months, "and that causes me much disquiet."[184] For Célestine, who had first-hand experience of the hardships of war as a result of the enemy invasion and occupation of 1814, there was at least a happy ending as both her son and her nephew (Pierre and Louison's son, who had also served in Spain) returned to Saint Quentin before the end of 1816, where Célestine promptly helped them to find wives and to settle back into

177 [A]rchives [D]épartementales de l'Hérault, 1 J 1704 Famille Vatin, de Pézenas. 1766–1858. Letter of 16 Frimaire Year Three [6 December 1794].

178 Ibid. Letter of 4 August 1793.

179 Ibid. Letter of 26 Brumaire Year Four [17 November 1795].

180 Ibid. Letter of 7 Prairial Year Nine [26 May 1801].

181 Ibid. Letter of 13 Brumaire, Year Nine [3 November 1801].

182 Ibid. Letter of 1 Thermidor Year Nine [19 July 1801].

183 Ibid. Letter of 3 December 1803.

184 Ibid. Letter of 15 June 1815.

civilian life.[185] The correspondence of this one family, which lost three brothers directly or indirectly to the war in very ordinary ways, provides just a glimpse of the emotional suffering of the relatives, particularly mothers and sisters, they left behind.

Some grieving relatives sought ways to memorialize the husbands, sons, and brothers who failed to return home from the wars.[186] In Paris, the establishment of the Père Lachaise cemetery in 1804 provided a place for bereaved relatives to commemorate those who had been killed. The cemetery became the focal point for the new culture of death that emerged in the first third of the nineteenth century, a site that not only bridged the separation between the living and the dead but also provided a bucolic setting in which the rhythms of nature provided consolation to those who came to perform public or private acts of commemoration.[187] In its appropriation of nature and in its provision of individualized graves, even to its humblest inhabitants, Père Lachaise became one of the models for the military cemeteries that began to develop later in the nineteenth century and that proliferated after the First World War.[188] One of the most remarked upon tombs in Père Lachaise was that erected by the mother of Antoine de Guillaume Lagrange, a dragoon who was killed in Poland in 1807. As historian Erin-Marie Legacey explains, the lengthy epitaph that covered the monument "stands as an excellent example of an early nineteenth-century attestation of grief."[189] After describing the young soldier's many virtues and providing an idealized narrative of his death, the epitaph directly evoked the undying grief of his mother: "Oh my dear and beloved son! My best friend! The most precious thing in the world to me [...] Only death itself will bring my suffering to an end." What is most remarkable is the description provided of the young man's death: "When it was asked who would lead the charge he immediately volunteered [...] he threw himself forward and a bullet instantly pierced his heart! His final words on the

185 Ibid. Letter of 25 December 1816.
186 Hantraye, "Les sépultures de guerre," 10. Hantraye notes that under the Restoration, memorialization was sporadic and localized, depending upon private initiatives, usually undertaken by women, or by former combatants. Memorials were not welcome in public space. A monument erected at Sceaux by Claire Lenoir-Laroche in memory of her husband, an imperial count, was closed in 1820.
187 Legacey, *Making Space for the Dead*, 71–98. See also Etlin, *The Architecture of Death*.
188 Though those too poor to lease a private concession in perpetuity lay in a communal grave, their burial sites were nonetheless identifiable and could be marked. On the history of military cemeteries and their importance to the "cult of the fallen," see Mosse, *Fallen Soldiers*, 34–50.
189 Legacey, *Making Space for the Dead*, 88.

battlefield were: My mother! My poor mother!"[190] Leaving aside the implausibility, already noted, of a man whose heart has been pierced by a bullet saying anything at all, it is important that in this representation of the soldier's death his last utterance was not a gesture of loyalty to the emperor or of devotion to the homeland, but a statement of love and compassion for his mother. In fact, the epitaph's words may well have been a closer reflection of reality than officially sanctioned representations. There is evidence from soldiers' testimony that the last thoughts of dying soldiers were indeed for their loved ones at home. Sergeant Bourgogne recalled the despairing words of a fever-stricken officer during the retreat from Russia, who expected to die as a Russian prisoner-of-war. "My poor mother," he said, "What will she say when she finds out?"[191] Placed in the context of the propaganda that represented expiring soldiers expressing their willingness to die for Napoleon, epitaphs such as the one inscribed upon the monument to Antoine de Guillaume Lagrange in Père Lachaise cemetery expressed a very different message, evoking the soldier's sorrow at the enduring pain his death would cause to grieving relatives. The legacy of the soldier's death was no longer immortal glory but instead never-ending sorrow. The emperor whose monumental projects for the city of Paris were unfailingly triumphalist had unwittingly provided, in the cemetery of Père Lachaise, a site where relatives of the million French soldiers who had died in his armies might come to remember them and to grieve their loss.

REMEMBERING

Although the imperial adventure came to a final ignominious end with the defeat at Waterloo and the restoration of the Bourbon monarchy under Louis XVIII, the soldiers who had fought in Napoleon's armies were not forgotten. Wounded and discharged soldiers returned to their villages where they were instrumental in propagating a potent legend of the Grande Armée and its exploits.[192] In this, they were assisted by a proliferation of visual images, available in greater number and more cheaply than ever before because of the new technique of lithography. Collections like *Les fastes de la gloire*, which included fifty military prints engraved by Godefroy and was published in 1829, explicitly presented the heroism of Napoleonic soldiers as a model for future generations: "The children of those who accomplished such great things, and triumphed throughout Europe, must

---

190 Cited in ibid., 89.

191 Bourgogne, *Mémoires du Sergent Bourgogne*, 225.

192 Dwyer, *Napoleon: Passion, Death and Resurrection*, 169–92; Lucas-Dubreton, *Le culte de Napoléon*; Alexander, *Bonapartism and the Revolutionary Tradition*.

FASTES DE LA GLOIRE.

MAREY, Soldat.

« Que fais-tu là dit un officier prussien à l'intrépide Marey". J'apprends à mourir. Rends tes armes. Marey
enfonce sa baïonnette dans la poitrine, et dit: tu peux les prendre maintenant, je ne te les rends pas. »

4.5. *Fastes de la gloire.* "Soldier Marey. 'What are you doing there? said a Prussian officer to the intrepid Marey. I am learning to die. Surrender your weapons. Marey plunged his bayonet into his breast, and said, Now you can take them, I am not surrendering them to you.'"

have the actions of their fathers in view [...] They must be told: This is what those who came before you have done; be always worthy of them."[193] The lithographs depicted scenes of heroism from both the revolutionary and Napoleonic wars, mixing stories of prominent generals with those of ordinary soldiers. Print twenty-one, for example, illustrated the "almost supernatural intrepidity" of soldiers in the army of General Marceau by depicting a heroic double suicide (fig. 4.5). The print shows an ordinary soldier, Marey, holding a bayonet to his own breast as he supports the body of a French officer who has chosen to remove the bandages staunching his wounds rather than to allow himself to be taken alive. Asked what he is doing by a Prussian officer, Marey responds, "I am learning to die." Called upon to surrender his arms, Marey drives the bayonet home, saying, "Now

193 L'Héritier, *Fastes de la gloire*, Preface, unpaginated.

you may take them, I am not giving them to you."[194] Images like this affirmed the identity of the French soldier as one who always chose death before dishonour. The lithographs of Denis-Auguste-Marie Raffet, many of which illustrated the popular *Histoire de Napoléon* by Jacques de Norvins, also idealized the imperial *grognard* as an indomitable figure, enduring any hardship for the sake of his loyalty to flag and emperor.[195] In a print inspired by a poem by Christian von Zedlitz, Raffet depicted soldiers of the Grande Armée rising from their graves in answer to the drummer's call to arms for a ghostly night-time review (fig. 4.6). Images such as this nourished the militaristic nationalism that was at the heart of popular nostalgia for Napoleon, implying that the spirits of Napoleon and his soldiers lived on and that past glories might be revived.[196]

Popular songs and plays performed on the stages of the boulevard theatres were also important vectors for disseminating the Napoleonic legend. The veteran of Napoleon's wars was a figure frequently evoked in the songs of Pierre-Jean Béranger. In *Le vieux drapeau* (1820), a veteran lovingly preserves the tricoloured flag under which he had served, dreaming of some future day when he might dust it off and raise it aloft once more.[197] *Le vieux sergent* (1823) tells the story of a disabled old soldier who, while looking after his grandsons, is reminded by the spectacle of passing troops of his military service, recalling fondly a time when barefoot and hungry peasants had flocked to defend the republic and grateful nations had garlanded the brows of their liberators. "Happy the one who died in those festivals!" declares the Old Sergeant, referring to the battles in which he had fought. He ends each verse of the song with the refrain, addressed to his grandsons, "May God give you a fine death, my children!"[198] On the stage, where as many as six hundred plays celebrated the cult of Napoleon over the course of the nineteenth century, re-enactments of battles were especially popular. The Cirque-Olympique frequently staged such performances, employing large numbers of extras as soldiers in addition to horses to heighten the illusion of reality. The imperial *grognard*, ever willing to sacrifice himself for Napoleon, was a stock character in these Napoleonic plays.[199]

194 Ibid., no 21.

195 Norvins, *Histoire de Napoléon*. See Giacomelli, *Raffet*, 285–8; Buchinger, "*La pierre et l'empereur*," 326–7.

196 On the history of this poem, *Die Nächtliche Heerschau* and Raffet's interpretations of it, see Buchinger, "*La pierre et l'empereur*," 328–30.

197 Béranger, *Oeuvres complètes*, vol. 2, 260–3.

198 Ibid., vol. 3, 61.

199 Dwyer, *Napoleon: Passion, Death and Resurrection*, 180. See also Lecomte, *Napoléon et l'empire*; Bertaud, "Le théâtre et la guerre," 177–89; Samuels, *The Spectacular Past*, 116–26.

4.6. Auguste Raffet, *The Awakening.* 1843.

Throughout the nineteenth century, the unqualified readiness of Napoleon's soldiers to lay down their lives was constantly reaffirmed through images, words, songs, and theatrical spectacles. At the turn of the twentieth century, it was a play celebrating the Napoleonic cult, Edmond Rostand's *L'Aiglon,* that captivated Parisian audiences. Rostand's play focused upon a conspiracy to bring about the escape from Austrian captivity and return to France of Napoleon's son, the Duke of Reichstadt (played by Sarah Bernhardt). The escape attempt, arranged by a *grognard* named Flambeau, is foiled, and Flambeau, choosing suicide rather than capture, dies in the duke's arms. At this moment, in a scene reminiscent of Raffet's ghostly resurrection of the army of the dead, the French soldiers who died at Wagram arise from the grave, showing their wounds to the Duke and crying, "*Vive l'Empereur!*" This fantastic scene, evoking both Glory and Sacrifice, culminates with the duke offering his own life, as Napoleon's son, in expiation: "A son who offers himself in exchange, alas! for so many sons."[200] In the aftermath of national humiliation in the Franco-Prussian War and amid the uncertainty and divisions of the Dreyfus Affair, Rostand invited the French people to unite behind the figure of Napoleon and to emulate the spirit of self-sacrifice of the soldiers of the Grande Armée.[201]

The idealized soldiers of the imperial *épopée* celebrated by writers, artists, musicians, and playwrights set a standard against which the real soldiers of later nineteenth-century wars were measured. As France became engaged in a lengthy war of conquest in Algeria under Louis-Philippe in the 1830s and 1840s, official propaganda celebrated the roles of Louis-Philippe's five sons, most conspicuously in the massive paintings commissioned from Horace Vernet for the African galleries in the palace at Versailles.[202] Popular imagery, meanwhile, focused on the hardships and sacrifices of the ordinary soldier, likening them to those of imperial *grognards*. According to these representations, as Jennifer Sessions has shown, it was by emulating the "patriotic masculinity" of Napoleon's men that the soldiers of the *Armée d'Afrique* would revive the military glory of the empire and restore the virility of the French nation.[203]

There were limits to this identification between the soldiers of the Grande Armée and those of the Algerian conquest, as Sessions also shows. The vicious war of conquest in Algeria, characterized by punitive raids on Arab villages and the employment of extreme violence against civilians, was a poor fit with the mythic memory of the Napoleonic wars as essentially defensive and honourable. The heroic reputations of the soldiers of the *bataillons d'Afrique* did not live up to scrutiny, with the result that initiatives to memorialize their exploits remained stillborn.[204] Still, throughout the nineteenth century, publicists continued to view the exploits of French soldiers in the light of the legend of the Grande Armée. A collection of heroic anecdotes published in praise of the French and allied armies fighting in the Crimean War, for example, proclaimed that the French soldiers who fought in the Crimea were comparable to those who had fought in earlier battles, especially those of the Napoleonic wars.[205] Its author, Eugène Pick, dedicated the volume to his father, a soldier of

200 Rostand, *L'Aiglon*, 160.
201 For an insightful analysis of this play and its significance in the revival of the Napoleonic cult in fin-de-siècle France, see Datta, *Heroes and Legends*, 108–41.
202 Sessions, *By Sword and Plow*, 67–124.
203 Ibid., 137–42.
204 Ibid., 153–73.
205 Pick, *Les fastes de la guerre d'Orient*, vi.

Napoleon's Grande Armée, "who will see with pleasure that the sons know
how to beat the Russians today, just as well as their fathers, under
Napoleon I."[206] Of the military virtues exalted by Pick, the one to which
he gave pride of place was willingness to die for the homeland. The first
of his anecdotes is a florid military parable entitled "how courage comes,"
which tells the story of two soldiers, Jules and Alexandre, who participate
in the attack on the Malakoff redoubt in the climactic battle for Sebastopol.
The younger of the two soldiers, Alexandre, his fear swept away by patriotic
ardour, rescues the French flag on the city's ramparts and then dies wrapped
in its folds, having given instructions to Jules to send pieces of the flag to
their mothers.[207]

Pick's accounts of French soldiers dying in heroic hand-to-hand combat
on the ramparts of Sebastopol were as unrepresentative of reality as those
celebrating their heroism in the conquest of Algeria. Of the 95,615 French
soldiers who died in the Crimea, only 10,240 died on the battlefield.
Another 10,000 died of wounds while 75,000 – nearly four-fifths of the
total – died of disease, especially typhus.[208] Furthermore, while Pick focused
on the actions of individual soldiers in close-quarters combat with the
enemy, warfare in the Crimea was increasingly a long-distance affair, determined by superior firepower. The battle for Sebastopol lasted for a year
and was dominated by long-range artillery, prefiguring the attritional
warfare of the First World War. This was a type of warfare in which the
actions of individual soldiers were dwarfed by the machinery of industrialized warfare. Already, artists were beginning to devise new representational
strategies that reflected the new conditions.[209] Images of military heroism
like those presented by Eugène Pick were increasingly anachronistic, but
they offered a comforting illusion of French martial superiority by insisting
upon continuity with the past. Those images insisted that France was secure
because the soldiers of today were animated by the same spirit – the same
masculine ardour, the same honourable devotion to duty, the same willingness to die – as those who had fought at Valmy and at Waterloo.

206 Ibid.
207 Ibid., 353–6.
208 Delmas, ed., *Histoire militaire de la France*, vol. 2: *De 1715 à 1871*, 514.
209 Théophile Gautier, "Le siège de Sébastopol, tableaux de M. Durand-Berger," in
L'Artiste, no. 1 (26 April, 1857): 61. Cited in Hornstein, *Picturing War in France*, 151.

4.7. Édouard Detaille, *The Dream*. 1888.

CONCLUSION

As the popularity of Rostand's *L'Aiglon* testified, the Napoleonic myth of
Glory and Sacrifice remained very much alive in French culture at the end
of the nineteenth century. In celebrating that myth, however, publicists
represented it as a culmination rather than as a unique episode. Late
nineteenth-century representations were eclectic in their appeals to
the past, as likely to reference the heroic deaths of Bayard or d'Assas as
those of Bara or Latour d'Auvergne.[210] In this respect, Napoleonic propaganda was very similar. A play performed in 1807, *L'hôpital militaire ou la
garnison malade*, stated that the ideal warrior combined the greatness of
spirit of Charlemagne, the goodness of Henri IV, the bravery of d'Assas,

210 Datta, *Heroes and Legends*, 142–78.

and the modesty of Turenne. But in its summary of the military virtues the play gave pride of place to the soldier's willingness to die:

– What must a soldier love?
– A glorious death.
– What must he fear?
– A useless death.
– What must he hope for?
– Nothing.[211]

Over the course of the nineteenth century warfare became ever more deadly, but this ideal of a glorious death survived even the bloodbaths of Solferino and Sedan. Although in looking back there were some who came to question Napoleon's readiness to sacrifice French lives, there were very few who were prepared to go so far as to suggest that the sacrifice of those lives had not brought glory to France. As the nineteenth century gave way to the twentieth the view that the soldier's death was the gateway to personal and national redemption possessed even greater currency than it had enjoyed at the height of the empire. Maurice Barrès was one of the most ardent advocates at the turn of the century of both the Napoleonic myth and the cult of the dead. Not only did he see Napoleon as the embodiment of the masculine virtues required to regenerate France but he believed the dead might still be called upon in the nation's hour of need.[212] Édouard Detaille gave memorable artistic expression to this idea in his 1888 painting, *The Dream*, in which dead soldiers of the revolutionary and Napoleonic wars march in a ghostly parade above a regiment of sleeping soldiers (fig. 4.7). In the imagination of French Glory, the dead lived on to serve later generations as both inspiration and reproach.

211 B. de Rougemont, *L'hôpital militaire ou la garnison malade* (Paris: Mme Cavanagh, 1807). Cited in Bertaud, "Le théâtre et la guerre," 185.

212 On the development of both Catholic and Republican ideas concerning the cult of the dead after 1870, see Varley, *Under the Shadow of Defeat*, 56–76; on Barrès and the Napoleonic myth, see Datta, *Heroes and Legends*, 125–7.

5

Dying for Lost Causes: The Franco-Prussian War and the Paris Commune

THE DEATH OF HENRI REGNAULT

Henri Regnault was killed by a Prussian bullet that struck him in the temple as the last major engagement of the siege of Paris, the Battle of Buzenval, was sputterring to a close on 19 January 1871. Regnault was a twenty-seven-year-old artist serving in the sixty-ninth battalion and the sixteenth *régiment de marche* of the Parisian National Guard. By all accounts, he was an enthusiastic soldier, though an inexperienced one. He had rushed home from Tangiers upon the outbreak of the Franco-Prussian War and promptly volunteered for military service, though first his father and then his fiancée tried to talk him out of it. During the early days of the siege his desire for action prompted a brief stint in a company of irregulars, known as *francs-tireurs*. Since then, he had endured the full rigours of serving in the front lines, "sleeping in the snow on the frozen ground or swimming in the melt-off, sometimes going without bread the next day, marching all day pack on back, getting a taste of all the pleasures of the military life." All the same, his enthusiasm appears to have been undiminished: "In spite of all that we don't complain. We have got used to it and ask as reward only for good news from the provinces, and the joy of taking part in the final battle to deliver Paris."[1] Shortly before Buzenval, Regnault declined promotion to the rank of officer on the grounds that he would rather be a good soldier than a mediocre officer.[2] On the morning of the battle he was apparently still in good spirits; a friend from another regiment recalled chatting "cheerfully" with him on the slopes of Mont Valérien as

---

1 Duparc, *Correspondance de Henri Regnault*, 396.
2 Ibid., 399.

they prepared to go into action. Ominously, however, as the same friend took his leave, he pointed to the park wall of Buzenval, which appeared like "an immense grey snake" in the early morning light, as "a bad spot."[3] It was precisely here, where the fighting was heaviest, that Regnault's battalion was engaged and where, at the end of the day, he was killed.

In retrospect, the failure of the French attack at Buzenval came to appear foreordained. Georges Clairin, who fought alongside Regnault, recalled that General Trochu, the military governor of Paris and head of the Government of National Defence, had no expectation of success. He had planned the operation simply to demonstrate to the National Guard its own incapability and thereby to silence its demands for action.[4] General Auguste-Alexandre Ducrot, who commanded the right column of the French attack, was highly critical in his memoirs of Trochu's plan, writing that the large size of the attacking force – 100,000 men, including 42,000 national guardsmen – was detrimental to the attack, rather than an advantage. With only two bridges across the Seine over which to deploy and a hilly, wooded terrain between them and the enemy, the attackers were hampered by bottlenecks in front and behind.[5] Furthermore, the Prussians had prepared a defence in depth. "How do you expect to get at sharpshooters sheltered by a wall, fortified as solidly as the rampart of a redoubt?" asked Louis Jezierski, who witnessed the battle. "It was clear that our entire infantry could get itself shot down in front of that obstacle without breaking through it."[6] Although some positions were taken, especially on the left of the French line, at Montretout, repeated efforts throughout the day to overcome the main German positions resulted only in heavy casualties.[7] Finally, the French commander, General Trochu, gave the order to withdraw. It was as his comrades were beginning to retreat that Regnault insisted upon returning to the firing line. Accounts vary concerning the precise words he used and to whom they were addressed, but in the later recollection of Georges Clairin, Regnault simply stated, "I still have a few cartridges; I'm going to go fire them."[8] He then returned to the battle, leaving his friends to curse him for his stubborn

3 Frantz Jourdain, "Henri Regnault," in *La Vie Moderne*, 21 February 1885.
4 Beaunier, *Souvenirs d'un peintre*, 183.
5 Ducrot, *La défense de Paris*, vol. 4, 78.
6 Jezierski, *Combats et batailles*, 427.
7 General Ducrot calculated that the French army sustained 4,070 casualties, the German armies only 715. Ducrot, *La défense de Paris*, 188–91.
8 Beaunier, *Souvenirs d'un peintre*, 191.

determination "to be sure to have killed his Prussian"[9] and to agonize at
the prospect that they would never see him alive again.[10]

That agony was particularly acute for Clairin, Regnault's closest friend,
who vividly recalled it thirty-five years later. Returning to the battlefield
during the night, Clairin searched with diminishing hope for his friend:
first among the wounded who were enduring surgery in a field hospital,
then among the dead who lay on the battlefield. Overcome by horror,
exhaustion, and hunger, Clairin lay insensible on the ground until dawn.
He resumed his search of the battlefield several days later, by which time
the dead had been arrayed in orderly lines, awaiting their return to Paris
in butchers' carts. Regnault was not among them. Fearful of never finding
his friend's body, Clairin received word that it had been identified at the
cemetery of Père Lachaise. There, as women wept over the bodies of
the dead, he found Regnault's corpse lying naked in a wooden coffin, what
remained of his soldier's uniform to one side. According to Clairin's
account, it was at precisely this moment that Regnault's fiancée, Geneviève
Bréton, approached, prompting Clairin to protect his friend's dignity by
hurriedly covering his nakedness with the lid of the coffin. He then turned
to the task of preserving Regnault's memory, washing his face and, with
the assistance of sculptor Louis-Ernest Barrias, taking a plaster cast of his
face for a death mask.[11]

The death of Henri Regnault was also felt intensely by his fiancée. Writing
in her diary on 19 January, in the knowledge that Henri was fighting at
Buzenval, she declared that her passion for France must be very great for
her "not to curse the hours of distress that it has cost me this last while."
Praying to God for Henri's deliverance, she nonetheless imagined him
lying dead or wounded on the battlefield while she sat impotently waiting
for news: "perhaps he is stretched out on the wet earth, perhaps his adored
eyes will open no more to the sun he loved so much, perhaps he is wounded,
bloody?"[12] On the twentieth, Geneviève wrote more hopefully that she had
received word that Henri had been seen fighting in the late afternoon and
that presumably he was safe. Her next entry, over two weeks later, on
7 February, was filled with the despair of loss. Envisaging a retreat from
the world to spare her family from witnessing her endless suffering, she
saw herself as "a sort of living tomb, in which lies the memory of my love."

---

9 Frantz Jourdain, "Henri Regnault," in *La Vie Moderne*, 21 February 1885.

10 For a profound analysis of the contradictions in the texts relating the death of
Henri Regnault and for the responses to his death, see Gottlieb, *The Deaths of Henri Regnault*,
127–69.

11 Beaunier, *Souvenirs d'un peintre*, 195–6.

12 Bréton, *Journal, 1867–1871*, 208.

A little later, she imagined her wedding as a spectral marriage with death: "it is a skeleton that holds you in its fleshless arms, it is emptiness for which your ardent lips seek." Having pledged her life, her love, and her youth to her beloved, she wrote, "now all is finished."[13]

It was not just those closest to him who were affected by the death of Henri Regnault. *Le Monde Illustré* noted that at a time when "the devastated homeland no longer has time to mourn its sons, when individual losses pass unnoticed amidst the general catastrophe," the death of Regnault "moved and softened every heart."[14] This was particularly true of the artistic community, whose responses to Regnault's death, as Marc Gottlieb has shown, made the commemoration of that death different from those of other soldiers who were killed in the Franco-Prussian War. Many of the famous artists, poets, and musicians of the day attended his funeral at the Church of Saint-Augustin on 27 January. Camille Saint-Saëns played the organ, performing a march, which he later dedicated to Regnault. Leading poets hastened to put pen to paper and verses in his honour were declaimed from the stage of the Comédie-Française.[15] Despite the uniqueness of these early tributes, however, the commemoration of Regnault's death was part and parcel of a broader impulse to commemorate the dead of the Franco-Prussian War: *all* the dead, rather than just those distinguished by rank or by some extraordinary accomplishment. In this respect, it is noteworthy that at the same time as Georges Clairin was taking a plaster cast of Regnault's features for posterity, a photographer was busy taking photographs of other, unidentified, bodies at Père Lachaise, to enable families to reclaim the remains of their loved ones.[16] The monument erected in honour of Henri Regnault in a courtyard of the École des Beaux-Arts in 1876 was certainly a more expensive and elaborate structure than most of those raised in memory of the soldiers who died in 1870–71, but it belonged to a wider movement to provide respectful resting places for the dead and monuments to keep their memories alive (fig. 5.1). Significantly the Beaux-Arts memorial bore the names of nine other students from the school who died during the war, including four who had also died in the battle of 19 January.[17]

The monuments constructed to the memory of Henri Regnault in the decades following his death became the sites of a patriotic cult. This cult was fostered especially by La Ligue des Patriotes, the nationalist

13 Ibid., 213–16.
14 *Le Monde Illustré*, 4 February 1871.
15 Gottlieb, *The Deaths of Henri Regnault*, 162–9.
16 Ibid., 151–2. See also Brown, *Mass Violence*, 203.
17 *Le Petit Moniteur Universel*, 13 August 1876.

5.1. Monument to Henri Regnault, École des Beaux-Arts. 1876.

organization founded in 1882 by war veteran Paul Déroulède. Déroulède and his followers honoured Regnault and the other war dead by placing wreaths on the monument at the École des Beaux-Arts, on one occasion protesting to the Minister of War when the wreath was prematurely removed.[18] When the bust atop another monument to Regnault in the park at Buzenval mysteriously disappeared, the Ligue des Patriotes raised money for its replacement and then held an impressive ceremony to re-dedicate the monument.[19] In 1891, Octave Mirbeau wrote: "Henri Regnault has become one of numerous symbols of the homeland, his cult is obligatory and national, like taxes and military service."[20] In this respect, representations of Regnault's death were emblematic of how the events of "The Terrible Year" of 1870–71, including both the Franco-Prussian War and the Paris Commune, came to be remembered – and forgotten – in the culture of the Third Republic. Henri Regnault's willingness to sacrifice himself in a losing cause was represented as exemplary by publicists who sought to transform a military catastrophe into a moral triumph. That his death served no other purpose than to resist to his last cartridge connected Regnault to other military heroes of the Franco-Prussian War, especially to the marines whose defence of Bazeilles was immortalized by Alphonse de Neuville in *The Last Cartridge* (1873). Whether or not the wounded soldier on Barrias's monumental statue, *The Defence of Paris* (1879), was intended to be Regnault is a moot point, but it is surely no accident that the soldier is represented in the act of reaching into his ammunition pouch for one more cartridge (fig. 5.2).[21] Similarly, a famous vignette from Alphonse de Neuville's and Édouard Detaille's panorama of the Battle of Champigny, entitled "The bottom of the ammunition pouch" represented a soldier, at the end of his physical strength, passing his final cartridge to a comrade to continue the fight.

In the aftermath of the Paris Commune, Henri Regnault also became the acceptable face of the Parisian National Guard. This force of "improvised soldiers," to borrow the words of Georges Clairin,[22] fought alongside soldiers of the regular army during the first siege of Paris, but against them during the second siege, in defence of the Commune. The choice of remembering Regnault's death at Buzenval, fighting against the foreign enemy, was as significant as the choice to forget the deaths of thousands

18 *Le Petit Courier*, 27 February 1891.
19 *Le Drapeau*, 1 February 1913.
20 Octave Mirbeau, "Les beautés du patriotisme," *La Révolte*, 20 June 1891.
21 See Gottlieb, *The Deaths of Henri Regnault*, 186–7.
22 Beaunier, *Souvenirs d'un peintre*, 172.

5.2. Louis-Ernest Barrias, *The Defence of Paris.* (1878–83).

of other national guards, many of whom were killed by firing squads composed of other Frenchmen in the context of a bitter civil war. The memory of the Commune could not, however, be suppressed. Those who had died defending it in the civil war were memorialized in a language strikingly similar to that used to commemorate the soldiers who had died fighting the foreign enemy: a language that meant very different things to different people but that insisted upon the ideas of resistance and sacrifice, upon moral victory in spite of military defeat, and upon the promise of an ultimate redemption.

1870–71: MANY WAYS TO DIE

The Franco-Prussian War was fought in two stages. The first stage, lasting only six weeks, was marked by a sequence of bloody battles along the Rhine, beginning at Wissembourg, Froeschwiller, and Spicheren (4–6 August), continuing at Mars-la-Tour, Rezonville, and Saint-Privat, near Metz (14–18 August), and concluding at Sedan (1 September). Although the French armies achieved some tactical successes and on occasion inflicted heavy casualties on their enemies, these battles were a strategic disaster, ending with the Army of Lorraine trapped in the fortress of Metz and the Army of Châlons defeated and forced to surrender at Sedan. They were also a political disaster for Napoleon III, leading to the end of the Second Empire and to the proclamation of the Third Republic on 4 September. The war then entered its second phase with a Government of National Defence organizing new armies in the provinces, while the Prussian army laid siege to Paris. Despite the initial success of the Army of the Loire in recapturing Orléans, neither it nor the newly constituted Armies of the North and of the East were able to compel the Prussians to break their siege of Paris. Nor were they able to prevent a second French army, under the command of Marshal Bazaine, from surrendering at Metz at the end of October. The Army of the Loire was driven back from Orléans on 4 December and its remnants, reconstituted as the Second Army of the Loire, defeated at Le Mans on 12 January 1871. The Army of the North was defeated at Saint-Quentin on 18 January. The Army of the East, suffering terribly from the winter conditions as well as from supply problems after a failed offensive launched from Besançon, went miserably into Swiss internment on 30 January. Efforts by the capital's defenders to break the German siege also failed, as their offensives were driven back at Champigny and Le Bourget in December and again at Buzenval on 19 January. The war ended with acceptance of an armistice by the Government of National Defence on 28 January, followed by a peace treaty signed at Frankfurt on 10 May.

Despite its relative brevity, the war was extremely violent, with high casualties on both sides. Perhaps 139,000 French soldiers died, while 143,000 were wounded and 370,000 taken prisoner. German losses were approximately 50,000 killed or missing and 90,000 wounded.[23] Jean-François Lecaillon estimates that eight thousand French soldiers died each day during the battles of Rezonville and Saint-Privat; at Sedan, the mortality rate was seven thousand men a day.[24] The first phase of the war was bloodier than the second. Eighteen per cent of French soldiers who fought at the Battle of Sedan – nearly one in five – were killed or wounded. At the Battle of Wörth, 29 per cent, or nearly one in three, were casualties! In none of the major battles during the second phase of the war did French casualties exceed 10 per cent.[25] In large part it was the increased firepower of nineteenth-century armies that was responsible for such high casualties. Both armies were equipped with breech-loading rifles, the Prussian Dreyse needle-gun, and the French Chassepot, which possessed enhanced accuracy, range, and rates of fire in comparison to the muzzle-loading muskets of the Napoleonic wars. The Chassepot could fire eight to fifteen shots a minute to a range of 1,500 yards. A new weapon, the *mitrailleuse,* had also entered French service: a multi-barrelled precursor of the machine gun, it fired up to two hundred bullets in a minute. A young artillerist wrote with bloodthirsty relish to his mother of the destructive power of this weapon, asking her to imagine its operator transformed into a "tiger eager for blood," feasting on "the carnage and death that he spews out."[26] Finally, the artillery of both armies was rifled and fired explosive shells rather than solid shot. Although the Chassepot was superior to the needle-gun, when it came to artillery the Prussian breech-loading steel cannon had the advantage in range, rate of fire, and explosive charge over the French muzzle-loading bronze guns.[27] "A hail of projectiles poured death into our ranks," recalled one French cavalry officer of the effects of the Prussian guns at the Battle of Sedan.[28] "The shells fell on us so close together that the ground, like the crust of a volcano, trembled and exploded under our feet," remembered another who fought at the Battle of Loigny. "Earth, stones, shards of metal, everything was flying, screaming past us, as if carried away by a fantastic hurricane."[29] All told, the new weapons extended the

23 Drévillon and Wieviorka, eds, *Histoire militaire de la France*, vol. 2, 48; Chesnais, *Les morts violentes*, 175; Audoin-Rouzeau, 1870, 315.
24 Lecaillon, *Les Français et la guerre de 1870*, 104–5.
25 Bodart, *Losses of Life*, 146.
26 Chantron, *Souvenirs et impressions*, 32.
27 Wawro, *The Franco-Prussian War*, 52–64.
28 Chalert, *Impressions d'un soldat*, 23.
29 Maricourt, *Casquettes blanches*, 141.

battlefield and made it a more dangerous place. Although both armies had sought to adjust their tactics to the changes in technology, the battles of 1870 nonetheless witnessed massed infantry attacks and cavalry charges that would not have been amiss on Napoleonic battlefields. The war's heavy loss of life resulted in part from this combination of new technologies and partially reformed tactics.

On the battlefields of 1870, death came suddenly and from afar, delivered by an unseen enemy. "Every time a little white cloud appeared on the horizon," wrote Léon de Maricourt, "each of us could say to himself: the shell that is bound to kill me is on its way! And we could not help ourselves from finding this modern war sad and stupid, this war in which we kill without seeing one another."[30] Alexandre Chalert, a cavalry lieutenant whose regiment took heavy casualties at Sedan without ever getting to grips with the enemy, wrote of his respect for the French gunners who "got themselves killed to the last man by an enemy [who was] as invisible to them as to us."[31] Melchior de Vogüé, an infantry soldier at Sedan, recalled receiving an order to advance into a thicket while firing: "On whom? I never knew. The invisible adversary sent back the bullets with interest; little oak branches, chopped up, rained on our heads."[32] Another veteran of Sedan, Charles Habeneck, recognized that this new kind of war in which "one so rarely saw the enemy from whom one received so many shells and bullets," called for a new kind of conduct and a new kind of courage to replace traditional French élan: "what is needed above all, is not to lose one's cool, to make use of every protection. No swaggering."[33]

Not losing one's cool meant witnessing without flinching, amid the din of battle, the terrible effects of artillery and rifle fire on human and horse flesh. As his cavalry regiment prepared to charge at the Battle of Reichshoffen, recalled Georges de Moussac, a single shell took off the head of his colonel, severed the wrist of a squadron commander, and killed three other men as well as their horses. It was a myth, added de Moussac, that the colonel's horse had carried its rider's headless body into the enemy ranks.[34] De Moussac was also at Sedan, where he admired the self-possession of his commandant, who calmly lit a new cigarette when the one he was smoking was whipped away by a projectile. A few minutes later, however, he saw a *maréchal de logis* knocked to the ground together with his horse,

30 Ibid., 110.
31 Chalert, *Impressions d'un soldat*, 29.
32 Vogüé, *Devant le siècle*, 255.
33 Habeneck, *Les régiments-martyrs*, 69.
34 Moussac, *Dans la mêlée*, 19. Presumably de Moussac was referring to the death of Colonel de Lacarre, later a favourite subject for the painters of cavalry charges.

"both of them terribly mutilated, him lying under his horse which had its belly opened and burning."[35] A captain who commanded a company of Algerian *tirailleurs* at Sedan remembered opening his eyes after experiencing a massive explosion. "I am covered in mud; my blue tunic is stained with blood and bits of brains. I steal a glance to one side; my native lieutenant, Salem Ben Guibi, a civilized and intelligent negro, decorated in Mexico, is sprawled in a cross over my two sergeants [who were] killed by the same blast, all of them with their uniforms in shreds, bodies mutilated, and bleeding from many wounds. In front of them, the *tirailleur* at my side has lost his skull from the nose up; his brains splattered all over us."[36] As such horrific scenes multiplied, Narcy and his fellow officers struggled to maintain the resolve of their men, who became increasingly agitated. Some soldiers, however, insisted that they quickly became inured to such horrors. Alphonse Chantron admitted to his mother that the sight of the battlefield was "horrible: arms and legs cut off, hideous wounds, mutilated or chopped up bodies." All the same, he wrote, "Such is the frenzy, that one pays no attention to it; the victory one seeks prevents one's mind from dwelling on it; a man falls, stays down, without his cries stopping his comrades."[37] A volunteer who fought at Sedan agreed that little thought was spared for those who fell in battle: "there is no time for feeling, and danger makes one hard." He concluded by quoting a comrade: "On the battlefield, man is an ephemeral insect. He is forgotten as soon as he is gone."[38]

That the battlefield to which soldiers of all arms sought to adapt themselves was dominated by firepower is evident from the records of the field hospitals that took care of the wounded. Field hospital Number Five established itself at Ramaurie, approximately three kilometres from Sedan, where it cared for one German and 135 French wounded between 3 and 19 September 1870. All the French soldiers were wounded by firearms. A high proportion (48 per cent) of the wounds treated were to the extremities (fifty to the legs and feet; fifteen to arms and hands). Smaller numbers of wounds were to the head (thirteen, or 10 per cent) or to the chest and abdomen (sixteen, or 12 per cent); these had a very high rate of mortality (fourteen of twenty-five died). The evidence suggests that soldiers with leg or arm wounds had a much better chance of making it to an ambulance and of ultimately surviving than those whose wounds were to the head or trunk. This is not to say that wounds to legs and arms were not often fatal.

35 Ibid., 60.
36 L. de Narcy, *Journal d'un officier de Turcos* (Paris: Ollendorf, 1902). Cited in Lecaillon, *Été 1870*, 211.
37 Chantron, *Souvenirs et impressions*, 41.
38 Soret, *Notes d'un volontaire*, 57.

Wounds to the thigh, especially, often resulted in death, sometimes after the experience of agonizing amputations. Of twenty-two soldiers treated for thigh wounds at Ramaurie, six died. Of nine whose leg wounds resulted in amputation, eight died and one was listed as in "serious condition" at the time of writing.[39] Although the results of field hospital Number Five's surgeries were not as dire at five other locations where it was stationed during the war, the figures still make for grim reading. Overall, the hospital performed sixty-eight major operations, which resulted in thirty-eight deaths.[40]

The cases of individual soldiers make for harder reading still. The soldiers operated on by field hospital Number Five at Loury in early December included one identified only as Michel, whose leg, fractured by a bullet, was amputated on 3 December and who died of a "purulent infection" on 30 December. The next record is that of Lauferron, of the First Zouaves, whose left foot had been shattered by a shell. Wounded on 3 December, Lauferron died of tetanus on 17 December after having his leg amputated. The subsequent record is that of Étienne Pouchin, of the Second Artillery Regiment. Pouchin was struck by a shell fragment that caused a complex fracture to his right leg. His leg was amputated on 10 December and Pouchin died on the night of the operation.[41] It is difficult not to sympathize with a soldier who stated, after receiving and observing treatment in an ambulance attached to the Army of the Loire, "I ask myself, after a long experience of the ambulance, whether the surgeons do far more harm than good to the wounded."[42] His skepticism would seem to be justified by the report of the head of the army's medical service, which shows that eight of ten soldiers who endured major amputations died after surgery.[43]

Not all wounds were caused by firearms. Although field hospital Number Five had occasion to treat only one bayonet wound, which was superficial and quickly healed, it did experience an occasion when it had to deal with a significant number of wounds caused by edged weapons. This was following a cavalry combat at Artenay on 10 October. Of seventy-two French soldiers treated by the hospital who were injured by edged weapons, thirty-one had head wounds, mostly caused by German cavalry sabres. Most of

39 Peltier, *L'Ambulance no. 5*, 37–9.
40 Ibid., 78.
41 Ibid., 63.
42 Maricourt, *Casquettes blanches*, 209.
43 A total of 12,241 major amputations were performed by the medical service during the war, resulting in 9,838 deaths, a mortality rate of 80.3 per cent. Chenu, *Rapport*, vol. 1, 494.

these soldiers (twenty-eight) recovered. Relatively few soldiers arrived at the hospital with penetrating wounds to the abdomen or chest caused by cavalry lances, but they were generally much less fortunate. Five men out of eight who were injured in this way died of their wounds. Presumably, most victims of lance wounds died on the battlefield, without ever making it as far as an ambulance.[44] Although increasingly rare, full-scale cavalry encounters could still be lethal.

Some of the killing took place away from the battlefield. Although most of the violence of the Franco-Prussian War involved encounters between conventional armies, the existence of several hundred independent companies of *francs-tireurs* or "free shooters" raised the prospect of an unconventional "people's war" that would extend and deepen the conflict. The fears of the Prussian army in this respect were manifest in a policy that denied the legitimacy of irregular combatants and promised reprisals for civilians who gave them assistance. *Francs-tireurs* who were captured were summarily executed. In the Department of the Marne, for example, four men who belonged to a band of *francs-tireurs* were shot at Châlons-sur-Marne on 22 January 1871, while at Reims a local priest, the Abbé Miroy, was also executed on suspicion of possessing arms.[45] Hostages were taken to encourage the docility of local populations. Civilians became pawns in a vicious war of terror and counterterror. Captain Grange, the leader of a band of *francs-tireurs* in the Marne department, was frank about his use of exemplary executions to discourage local farmers and tradesmen from trading with the enemy. He acknowledged, though, that the Prussians used the same methods to deter men from joining his company. According to Grange, when three of his men were captured after an ambush, they were shot and their bodies dragged through the streets of Dormans, to be exposed to the townspeople on market day. "The bodies of the victims were laid on the ground, in the snow and mud, and in front of everyone," recalled Grange: "the Prussians spat in the faces of the dead when they didn't kick them. Such methods do not deserve comment."[46]

On one occasion at least, regular soldiers from the French armies were victims of the Prussian soldiers' fears of *francs-tireurs*. Forty-nine soldiers from a captured battalion of *gardes mobiles*[47] from the Marne were killed when their Prussian escorts were panicked by the sound of a rifle shot and,

44   Peltier, *L'Ambulance no. 5*, 49.
45   Tison, *Comment sortir de la guerre*, 38.
46   Germain and de Buxeuil, *Aventures des franc-tireurs*, 40.
47   At the end of the Second Empire *gardes mobiles* were reservists who, though they avoided full-time service in the annual call-up of conscripts, were subjected to fourteen non-consecutive days of military training each year.

believing themselves to be under attack, turned against their prisoners.[48] That the sparks of guerrilla warfare did not develop into a widespread conflagration was a consequence of the Government of National Defence's preference for folding free corps into regular formations as well as of the hostility aroused by the *francs-tireurs* among local populations fearful of reprisals. Nevertheless, the exploits of *francs-tireurs* were celebrated, as in a poem by Théodore de Bainville praising their role in the defence of Châteaudun. "They had the manly virtue," went one bloodthirsty stanza, "To kill before dying."[49]

The high mortality of the French army is only partially explained by violent confrontations with the enemy. Although precise figures are lacking, it is possible that as many French soldiers died from illness or from the hardships of campaign as died from wounds inflicted by the enemy.[50] Jean-Charles Chenu, compiling his report on the French medical services after the war, did not attempt to determine the proportion of French soldiers who had died of illness, but he acknowledged that it was much higher than that of the German armies. He also considered it remarkable that the number of German soldiers who died of illness was, "contrary to what is generally seen to happen in war," lower than the number killed in battle.[51] The difference between the two armies Chenu attributed to the superior clothing and footwear enjoyed by German soldiers, as well as to their relatively efficient commissariat, which kept them adequately nourished. Less generously, he also claimed that the German armies had been ruthless – and in violation of the Geneva Convention – in requisitioning medical facilities meant for the care of French soldiers. During the campaign of 1870–71, French soldiers were afflicted by various illnesses, including pneumonia, dysentery, typhus, and scurvy. Most deadly, however, were typhoid fever and smallpox. Deaths from these diseases steadily escalated in the unhygienic environment of camps and garrisons during the autumn and winter. At Langres, in the Department of Haute-Marne, fifty-seven

48 Germain and de Buxeuil, *Aventures des franc-tireurs*, 28. See also Meignan, *Les victimes*. The unfortunate *moblots* from the Marne did not have much of a war. They were sent into action with little training, vintage rifles, and very few cartridges. Those who survived the massacre at Passavant, in the Argonne, spent the rest of the war at a camp in Glogau, Silesia.

49 Cited by Milza, "*L'année terrible*," 191.

50 On the difficulty of arriving at a definitive calculation, see Chesnais, *Les morts violentes*, 175–7, and Bodart, *Losses of Life*, 149–51. Bodart estimates that 60,000 French soldiers were killed in action or died of wounds, while 61,000 died of illness.

51 Chenu, *Rapport*, vol. 1, lxxiii–lxxx. Chenu calculated that 24,009 German soldiers were killed in action, 28,596 died of their wounds, and 12,174 died of illness. The total deaths of the French armies, including those from both combat and illness, he calculated as 136,540.

soldiers died of illness in September and October, 285 in January and February. Over half of the six hundred men from the Langres garrison who died between 1 September 1870 and 31 March 1871 were struck down by smallpox; one-fifth by typhoid. Only eighteen men died of wounds.[52] The proportion of combat fatalities was much higher at Belfort, which became famous for its resistance during a lengthy siege under the leadership of Colonel Denfert-Rochereau, All the same, out of a total of 2,350 French soldiers who died during the siege, 555, or nearly a quarter, died from illness, mostly smallpox and typhoid.[53]

The suffering of the new armies raised by the Government of National Defence was particularly severe. An example is provided by the Army of Brittany, formed under the leadership of Émile de Kératry in the hope that sixty thousand Breton conscripts could be transformed into soldiers who would fight alongside the Army of the Loire. This hope foundered at the Camp of Conlie, six kilometres to the west of Le Mans. Although 49,000 men were at Conlie by mid-December, shivering in their tents and wallowing up to their knees in mud, the Ministry of War's promises to provide them with modern rifles remained unfulfilled. By late November, there were already many cases of smallpox, typhus, and dysentery. Kératry resigned in frustration on 27 November and his successor, General Marivauld, bluntly informed the government on the day he took over that the demoralized men "of whom scarcely half are armed, with rifles of eleven different models," should be sent home.[54] Only somewhat reluctantly, the government gave way. "The sight of these men is distressing," wrote a Rennes newspaper upon seeing the returned soldiers encamped on the city streets: "Clothes in tatters, covered in mud, faces pale, sickly, that is the appearance of these young men whom we saw pass by a month and a half ago spruced up and well dressed, asking only to be trained to march against the enemy."[55] A monument in the cemetery at Conlie lists the names of 131 men who did not survive the miseries of the camp.[56]

The Army of the Loire experienced many of the same problems of administration and supply. Challans de Belval, a regimental surgeon attached to a battalion of *chasseurs* serving with the Army of the Loire, provided a vivid account of the disastrous consequences of a chaotic transport and supply situation. After fighting in the Battle of Coulmiers (9 November 1870), and going without food for twenty-four hours, his

52   Chenu, *Rapport*, vol. 1, 500–9.
53   Ibid., vol. 1, 60.
54   La Borderie, *Rapport*, 63.
55   *Avenir de Rennes*, 20 December 1870. Cited in ibid., 77.
56   Guivarc'h, *1870–1871*, 183.

exhausted battalion was finally able to make camp. Instead of receiving food, however, the men were provided with a more than ample supply of brandy, "that is to say the liquid that is most deadly to men exhausted from cold, fatigue and hunger."[57] Many men were so inebriated when the unit moved off at six o'clock the next morning that they had to be left behind. The battalion had lost six men killed in the Battle of Coulmiers, said Challans, but over sixty to drink-related illness. Caring for the wounded was complicated by the difficulty involved in removing them from the battlefield in winter conditions as well as by the lack of qualified medical personnel. "It is sad indeed," wrote Challans later, "to have to say that after the Battle of Loigny, nearly three thousand French wounded were for eight days cared for by only three regimental doctors assisted by a few students." Among the wounded was General de Sonis, who had to wait, covered with snow, until the day after the battle to be removed from the battlefield and to have his leg amputated. De Sonis survived, but Challans was convinced that the delay in transporting the wounded, as well as the insalubrious conditions of the "miserable barns" where they were eventually treated, were responsible for many deaths.[58]

Among these provincial armies, the circumstances of the Army of the East during its failed campaign to relieve Belfort and to sever the Prussian army's lines of communication were most pitiable of all. The rail service struggled to redeploy General Bourbaki's two army corps from the Loire to Burgundy, the cold and hungry troops spending up to a week in cattle cars to reach their destination. Once there, the soldiers' struggle to survive in freezing winter conditions, without pay or provisions, steadily sapped their ability to fight. In mid-January, they fought a three-day battle along the Lisaine River, spending the nights miserably huddled around campfires they were forbidden to light. Historian Michael Howard describes the retreat of this army after the Battle of Héricourt, leading to its internment in Switzerland, as "one of the greatest disasters that has ever overtaken a European army."[59] Many of the vermin-ridden soldiers who struggled across the Jura mountains with only weevil-infested biscuit to eat and melted snow to drink succumbed to dysentery. The exhausted survivors were aptly described by a Swiss onlooker as "an army of beggars."[60]

57 Belval, *Carnet de campagne*, 148.
58 Ibid., 195 and 197.
59 Howard, *The Franco-Prussian War*, 426.
60 Cited in Audoin-Rouzeau, *1870*, 250. There were 90,000 men interned in Switzerland. Bourbaki had begun the campaign in the east with approximately 140,000 men. See Rousset, *Histoire générale de la guerre*, vol. 6, 9.

THE FIRST SIEGE OF PARIS:
EVERYONE A SOLDIER?

Although it was far from obvious to everyone at the time, the defeat of the
provincial armies during the second phase of the war effectively sealed
the fate of Paris. The armed forces defending the French capital were
insufficient on their own to break the Prussian siege. Unless one of the
provincial armies came to its assistance, the French capital would eventually
be compelled to capitulate for want of provisions. In appearance, Paris had
plenty of soldiers – as many as 450,000 – to confront the 250,000 Prussian
troops that eventually surrounded the city. The quality of these forces,
however, was very uneven. The best of them were 15,000 *marins fusiliers*,[61]
supplied by the navy. Two army corps that had managed to extricate themselves from the Army of Châlons provided another 85–90,000 men of
variable quality and experience. Additionally, there were 105,000 *gardes
mobiles*, most of them provincial. These were reservists with little or no
training, hastily mobilized during the crisis of August 1870. Parisians were
struck by their regional costumes and accents, especially those from Brittany,
many of whom spoke little or no French. Finally, there was the Parisian
National Guard. Traditionally a volunteer militia for local defence, this
force had been restricted to 36,000 men under the Second Empire, but it
expanded rapidly after the early defeats in the summer of 1870. It nearly
doubled in size (to 70,000 men) after General Trochu's appointment as
military governor of Paris on 18 August, and doubled again following a
decree of Léon Gambetta, the Minister of the Interior in the Government
of National Defence, on 6 September. Most important of all, however, was
the government's decision on 12 September to pay1.5 francs (or thirty
sous) a day to guardsmen without independent means, with an additional
seventy-five centimes for married men, plus twenty-five centimes for each
of their children. By the end of September, as workers from the suburbs
flooded into the city and the middle classes began to make their exit, the
National Guard had absorbed 300,000 men. Its effectiveness as an institution for the provision of public assistance did not, however, translate into
military effectiveness. Most guardsmen were attached to democratic
traditions whereby officers were elected and decisions consultative. They
therefore resisted attempts to militarize the National Guard by subjecting
it to control by the army or to impose military discipline.[62] At the end of
September, when volunteers for an offensive against the Prussians were

61 Naval riflemen.
62 Clifford, "Aux armes citoyens!," 33–4.

called for, only seven thousand men came forward. A decree of 8 November required each of the 190 battalions of the National Guard to supply four companies for front-line service. Despite this effort to find and employ battle-worthy soldiers from the National Guard, during the critical battles of December and January General Trochu reckoned he had only 150,000 troops that could be used for offensive operations.[63]

This is not to deny that the city's defenders were animated, at least in the beginning, by a genuine patriotic enthusiasm. Count Irisson d'Hérisson, an officer on the staff of General Trochu, confessed that on one day at least, "one would have had to be made of bronze not to be stirred and to hope." That day was 13 September, when he witnessed the massed ranks of regulars, *mobiles*, and national guardsmen in a military parade, "the finest review I saw in my life."[64] Parisian men proudly wore their military kepis and sported their rifles, even if these were for the most part antiquated rifles of an older model rather than modern Chassepots. "At first glance, what was striking in Paris under siege," recalled Count d'Hérisson, "was the number of uniforms." There was hardly a member of the government, he said, who did not wear at least a kepi. The streets, boulevards, and squares teemed with people wearing clothes that resembled, at least by their buttons and their cut, military uniform. "Thus, everybody was a soldier," he said, before qualifying his statement: "As for being a good soldier, that is another matter."[65]

Assessments by contemporaries of the abilities and potential of the National Guard during the first siege of Paris were highly partisan. Professional soldiers like d'Hérisson, who had made their careers in the army of the Second Empire, possessed little sympathy for the radicalism of the National Guard battalions from the working-class arrondissements of Paris and even less respect for their abilities as soldiers. The professionals' scorn in this respect may have been all the greater because they themselves had been found wanting in the battles to defend the frontier. Count d'Hérisson contrasted the military virtues of General Trochu, whom he judged to be a "soldier in every sense of the word, a soldier uniquely occupied by his flag, a soldier disdainful of all politics," with their absence in the National Guard. The latter, he said, showed little enthusiasm for fighting the Prussians and "only behaved somewhat appropriately from a military point of view when facing the French army."[66]

63 Dupuy, *La Garde nationale*, 496–502; Audoin-Rouzeau, *1870*, 183; Milza, "*L'année terrible*," 143–4.

64 Irisson, *Journal*, 153–4.

65 Ibid., 251–2.

66 Ibid., 195 and 252.

Equally disparaging was General Ducrot, who commanded several sorties by the Paris garrison prior to Buzenval, most notably the Champigny-Villiers offensive (30 November–3 December). Ducrot's disdain for the National Guard was such that he declined to make use of it in the Champigny affair, relying on the regular army units and the *gardes mobiles*, while the National Guard battalions were kept in reserve. Ducrot placed the lion's share of the blame for the failure of the Buzenval attack on the Government of National Defence for its insistence upon mounting the operation without giving the high command sufficient time to prepare. He nonetheless had little good to say about the part played in the battle by the National Guard. Certain individuals had fought heroically, he admitted, citing the example of the Marquis de Coriolis, "who, in spite of his sixty years, had taken up pack and rifle and come to seek death amidst the enemy," as well as that of Henri Regnault. "But if some notable individuals knew how to do their duty, knew how to get themselves killed," he continued, "the mass, in no way prepared by discipline to endure the long and nerve-wracking trials of the battlefield, found itself at the end of the day of the nineteenth completely overcome, discouraged, and absolutely powerless."[67] During the battle, Ducrot said, National Guard units had distinguished themselves by firing on other French soldiers (including their own commander-in-chief) whom they mistook for the enemy, by disobeying orders to attack, by seeking excuses to leave the field of battle such as taking care of the wounded, and by generally spreading discouragement and confusion. Ducrot repeatedly contrasted the shortcomings of the national guardsmen with the heroism of the line army and of the *gardes mobiles*. During an attack on one German position, for example, he claimed that national guardsmen, "crazed, terrified, ran to left and right, fired in every direction, and caused numerous victims in our own ranks." At the same moment, "the heroic Colonel de Monbrison [*sic*]" fell dead a few paces in front of a German NCO, while "the intrepid Fressinet, who seemed to be looking for death," carried on fighting after his horse was killed under him. Ducrot did credit a National Guard officer, Colonel de Rochebrune, with having fallen "equally in the first line" in the same action; he added a footnote, however, that the colonel had most probably been killed by friendly fire from his own men, since a spent bullet found later in his clothing was of a type fired by the inferior rifles issued to the National Guard.[68] Count d'Hérisson's account of Buzenval presented similar contrasts. In one anecdote he described a National Guard unit refusing three times to obey the order to attack a breach in one of the walls at Buzenval. He then related

67 Ducrot, *La défense de Paris*, vol. 4, 145.
68 Ibid., 126. Montbrison and Fressinet commanded battalions of *mobiles* from the Loiret.

how a sergeant of the line army, offered the choice of losing his sergeant's stripes or leading the way into the breach, went clear-eyed to a certain death.[69] For professionals like Ducrot and d'Hérisson, what defined a true soldier was his willingness to die, and it was precisely the lack of this quality in "the mass" of the National Guard that separated it from the regular army and even the *gardes mobiles*. In other words, in the eyes of the officers of the line army, the national guardsmen were not soldiers at all.

The National Guard also had its defenders. Among the most partisan was Arthur Arnould, who insisted not only that the officers of the line army had deliberately prepared the defeat of the National Guard at Buzenval, but that their nefarious intentions had been foiled by the latter's patriotism and heroism. "The National Guard demonstrated a magnificent spirit there; without guns, badly commanded, or deliberately misled, they captured all the enemy positions and even won the admiration of those soldiers who had been turned against them for many months."[70] For other advocates of the National Guard, claiming the Battle of Buzenval as a victory was a bit of a stretch. All the same, like Arnould they affirmed that the National Guard possessed a spirit that was lacking in the regular army. Charles Habeneck stated that the army of Paris, like the one defeated at Sedan, was a victim of its generals. "The great misfortune of this high command was to be too military to believe in the possibility of making use of the National Guard," he wrote, "and not military enough to organize it, to make serious soldiers out of it."[71] To Habeneck, however, the spirit of republicanism more than compensated in the National Guard battalions for a lack of military professionalism. Those battalions were "a great school of democracy," bringing together diverse classes and conditions. "We defy any soldier to have succeeded in bringing about such order and discipline, in a few hours, with ordinary soldiers."[72] Finally, insisted Habeneck, these republican citizen-soldiers did indeed know how to die, even when they knew beforehand that they were dying in a lost cause. "The National Guard did its duty on that day," he said of the Battle of Buzenval, "going to die knowing that it would lead to nothing." He then listed the casualties of his own regiment, the eighteenth. Out of a total of 1,600 men, 270 were killed or wounded: "it was just about decimated."[73]

69 Irisson, *Journal*, 314.
70 Arnould, *Histoire populaire*, 43.
71 Habeneck, *Les régiments-martyrs*, 129.
72 Ibid., 145 and 158.
73 Ibid., 193. Habeneck's count of the overall casualties of the eighteenth regiment are essentially borne out by Ducrot's figures, which total 269 officers and men killed and wounded. Ducrot, *La défense de Paris*, vol. 4, 189.

According to some observers, the disdain of the line army and especially of its officers prompted the National Guard to greater efforts. Louis Jezierski took a rosy view of the relationship between army and National Guard, emphasizing that the guardsmen were keen to prove themselves: "and above all to bring honour to their young flags in the eyes of the troops."[74] More specifically, the aspiration to give the lie to the army's criticisms may have had a part to play in the death of Henri Regnault. According to Georges Clairin, Regnault and his comrades were accosted by a general during a lull in the fighting at Buzenval. The general upbraided them for their inactivity, referring to the guardsmen as "thirty sous," an appellation which implied that their principal motive for taking up arms was to draw their daily wage. It may be that it was in response to the general's harsh words and to defend the honour of the National Guard that Henri Regnault went to his death.[75]

CIVIL WAR

It was just a few days after the Battle of Buzenval, on 22 January, that the first blood was shed in fighting between national guardsmen and government troops. Anger among the radical battalions of National Guard that the Government of National Defence was about to seek an armistice prompted an attempted insurrection. This was not the first such attempt. On 31 October 1871, national guardsmen under the leadership of Gustave Flourens had invaded the Parisian seat of the Government of National Defence, the Hôtel de Ville, with the purpose of creating a Committee of Public Safety to give a new stimulus to the war effort. That demonstration had ended in compromise and confusion, but it had at least ended peacefully. On 22 January, however, the authorities were better prepared, and Breton *gardes mobiles* fired on the demonstrators. In the exchange of shots that followed, five people were killed. Relations did not improve after the armistice, as national elections on 8 February revealed the political gulf between radical/republican Paris and the conservative/monarchist provinces. The new government of Adolphe Thiers did little to endear itself to Parisians, ending the moratorium on payments and rents that had saved many from destitution during the siege and establishing the new seat of government at Versailles, symbolically "de-capitalizing" Paris. Meanwhile, the balance of military strength shifted in favour of the National Guard. By the terms of the armistice, the garrison of Paris was reduced to

74 Jezierski, *Combats et batailles*, 425.
75 See Beaunier, *Souvenirs d'un peintre*; *Les Annales Politiques et Littéraires*, 26 January 1913.

12,000 men, which compared unfavourably to the several hundred thousand national guardsmen who were allowed to retain their weapons. During the month of February, the National Guard began to organize itself as a federation and on 15 March it elected a Central Committee to provide coordination and leadership. It also became radicalized as conservative contingents melted away, many of their middle-class members also joining the exodus from Paris. Finally, a bungled attempt by the government on 18 March to take control of the cannon that had been gathered on the heights of Montmartre and Belleville prompted the withdrawal of government forces from Paris and the beginning of civil war. The 18 March uprising, which led ten days later to the proclamation of the Paris Commune, was also marked by the spilling of blood, most notoriously that of two unpopular generals, Claude Martin Lecomte and Jacques Léonard Clément-Thomas. The generals were executed after Lecomte's men had mutinied rather than obey his orders to fire on the crowd defending the Montmartre cannon.

Once government forces pulled out of Paris, both sides began marshalling their forces. At Versailles, Marshal MacMahon and a group of conservative senior generals imposed strict discipline on a steadily growing force that brought together *gardes mobiles* from the provincial armies of the Government of National Defence and soldiers from the defeated line army, recently returned from captivity in Germany. In Paris, the Military Delegates of the Commune, first Gustave Cluseret and then Louis Rossel, attempted, with the same lack of success as the government-appointed commanders who had preceded them (including Clément-Thomas), to impose a measure of military discipline on the National Guard. Unwilling to compromise their democratic principles for military contingencies, the *fédérés* were citizens first and soldiers second.[76] The first skirmishes took place on the western outskirts of Paris on 1 April, with more significant encounters occurring on 3 and 4 April, as the Commune organized a sortie by four columns of troops. This was beaten back with heavy casualties, among them two of the more capable Communard commanders, Gustave Flourens and Émile Duval. The execution of five captives by order of General Gallifet on 1 April, followed by the summary killing of Flourens and Duval, among others, on 4 April, made clear from the very beginning that the *fédérés* of the Commune could expect little mercy from the Versailles army.[77]

After the initial clashes, the siege operations of the Versailles army were, as Robert Tombs has shown, deliberately cautious. The generals were determined not to risk a repeat of 18 March by placing their men in

76 Clifford, "Aux armes citoyens!," 193–297.
77 Tombs, *The War against Paris*, 78–9; 88.

situations that might ask too much of their loyalties or morale.[78] Attacks on the defences surrounding the city were prepared by intense artillery fire. Gradually, those defences began to crumble, Communard casualties to mount. The capture of Fort Issy on 8 May after a two-week siege and the loss of five hundred men prompted a crisis in the Commune's military leadership, as the aging revolutionary Charles Delescluze replaced Louis Rossel as War Delegate. Fort Vanves fell on 13 May. Finally, as the Communard forces began to melt away, intelligence that two bastions were undefended gave Versailles troops access to the city itself. On 21 May, they poured through the breached defences and commenced the task of reducing the barricades erected along the city streets. Thus began the final paroxysm of violence that crushed the Paris Commune, known ever since as the "Bloody Week."

The number of people killed during the repression of the Bloody Week remains controversial. Estimates have varied wildly between ten thousand and fifty thousand, with most authorities settling on a middle figure of twenty thousand. The most rigorous investigation of this question, by Robert Tombs, substantially diminished the number of people killed to a range between 5,700 and 7,400.[79] Tombs's analysis relied substantially on the records of Parisian cemeteries, discounting evidence of bodies buried or otherwise disposed of in the Bois de Boulogne and in the quarries of Belleville. Howard Brown has revised Tombs's estimate upwards by taking this evidence into account, arriving at an estimate of around 8,500 people killed.[80] Other historians point out that there may be additional burial sites that have never been discovered. John Merriman concludes on this basis that the number of people who were killed during the Bloody Week will never be known.[81]

Although the lower estimates proposed by Tombs and Brown reduce the scale of the violence during the Bloody Week from an apocalyptic to a more human level, this does little to diminish its extreme nature. The Versailles forces were pitiless toward the *fédérés* both during the fighting and, especially, in its aftermath. When a *fédéré* position to the south of Paris, the Moulin Saquet, was taken by Versailles troops on 3 May, some of the 300 *fédérés* dead were mutilated, their death certificates providing evidence for multiple bayonet and stab wounds.[82] A great many of those who died, however, did not die in the heat of battle. Rather, they were killed after

78   Ibid., 124–5.
79   Tombs, "How Bloody Was the *semaine sanglante*," 695.
80   Brown, *Mass Violence*, 195–6.
81   Merriman, *Massacre*, 254.
82   Tombs, *The War against Paris*, 120.

they had been captured, either with or without the benefit of a hasty trial by one of about twenty improvised courts martial.[83] At the Parc Monceau, the Lobau barracks, the Jardin de Luxembourg, and many other sites, prisoners were shot in batches. Individuals were executed after only the most cursory efforts to determine who they were and whether they were guilty of the crime of fighting for the Commune. To be caught bearing arms was sufficient to ensure summary execution, but in the absence of a weapon the presence of a bruise on the shoulder indicating the effect of a rifle's recoil was also enough to condemn its owner. Also damning was any element of apparel that derived from the uniform of the National Guard. A *fédéré* captured by the Versaillais was as likely to be executed for wearing a uniform as a *franc-tireur* captured by the Prussians for not wearing one. "We were pitiless" wrote a staff officer of the Second Division's operations in the vicinity of the Pantheon. "Anybody found in the quarter wearing National Guard uniform was put to death. Around the Pantheon, many bodies; bodies everywhere in the neighbouring streets … it was horrible!"[84] Charles Sutter-Laumann later recalled how his fate hung in the balance as he sought to convince the Versaillais officer to whom he had surrendered that the guardsman's uniform he was wearing was not a sign he had fought for the Commune. Having won over his captor, Sutter-Laumann was advised to get rid of any vestiges of uniform, "buttons, stripes, piping." The neighbourhood women then worked desperately to unstitch the military insignia from the uniforms of their menfolk. "Soon, there was not a single National Guard," he wrote. "A complete transformation had occurred. Everybody wore civilian clothing."[85]

Sutter-Laumann was saved by the combination of a silver tongue, a respectable demeanour, and the moderation of his captor. Others were not so lucky. Specific anecdotes are impossible to verify, and inevitably the most lurid of them were recounted in polemical works by former Communards. "The examples of atrocities accompanying the re-establishment of order in Paris offer an abundant crop," wrote Jules Bergeret. "We are embarrassed for choice."[86] There is much testimony, however, including that of impartial bystanders and of the perpetrators themselves, indicating that individuals were killed on the least suspicion of having acted in support of the

83 Robert Tombs indicates that anywhere between 21 and 41 per cent of the victims were executed following a court martial by one of about twenty impromptu courts martial that were established during the Bloody Week. Tombs, "How Bloody was the *semaine sanglante*," 695.

84 SHD AG 1k 262: Journal de marche d'un officier de l'Etat Major de la Division Susbielle, 42.

85 Sutter-Laumann, *Histoire d'un Trente Sous*, 318–19.

86 *Le 18 Mars, Journal Hebdomadaire*, no. 2, 42–3.

Commune. Wounded men in hospital were condemned by the evidence
of their wounds, the medical staff by the fact of having ministered to them.
There were several hospital massacres. At a field hospital in the Place Saint-
Sulpice a doctor who vainly protested against the killing of the men in his
care was swiftly put up against a wall and shot.[87] In the faubourg Saint-
Antoine, a woman was reportedly shot with a six-month-old baby in her
arms for having been overheard to say that "these brigands from Versailles
have killed my husband."[88] Some of the accounts of the killings indicate a
more calculated cruelty. A man who begged leave to say goodbye to his wife
and children before he was taken off for execution was rewarded by an
order, promptly obeyed, to shoot the entire family.[89]

As the previous examples show, women and children were among those
killed. The evidence for the legendary defence to the last woman of a
barricade in the Place Blanche by a legion of Amazons is lacking, but
women were certainly active in both the construction and defence of barricades during the final week of the Commune. They were also victims of
the repression, sometimes subjected to acts of special cruelty. "Legend is
already mingled with history," reflected Augustine Blanchecotte upon
hearing the story of a beautiful young woman who was captured clutching
a red flag to her breast bearing the words "Do not touch." The woman was
reportedly shot along with her forty-two companions.[90] Another anecdote
recounted the killing of a young woman in National Guard uniform who
was denied the mercy of a *coup de grâce* as she lay dying. An officer was said
to have fired a shot at her and then to have told the soldiers who were
about to finish her off, "Leave her to croak now like the cow she is."[91] Jules
Bergeret narrated a similar incident in his account of the Versaillais terror.
"On rue Port-Mahon, a convoy of prisoners was passing by. A young
woman from it collapsed, overcome by fatigue. A soldier opened her belly
with his bayonet and carried on his way with the column: a little later,
another soldier from the escort picked up the dying woman on the end
of his weapon and threw her into the porch of a store, shouting 'Go snuff
it further away, carrion!'"[92] According to Bergeret, citing the example of
a female medical worker shot at the Châtelet for wearing a red belt, some

87 Lissagaray, *Les huit journées de mai*, 122. Frerejean and Hoër, *Le siège et la Commune*, 246.
88 Ibid., 237..
89 Ibid., 245–6.
90 Blanchecotte, *Tablettes d'une femme*, 283–4.
91 Faix, *Histoire de la guerre civile de 1871*, 527. Cited in Dalotel, "La barricade des
femmes," 355.
92 *Le 18 Mars, Journal Hebdomadaire*, no. 3, 84.

women were killed simply for bearing the symbols of an allegiance to the Commune.[93]

Explanations for the savagery of the repression point to various factors: the wounded masculinity of the Versailles army's officers, who were bent on avenging their defeat in the war with Prussia; the social antagonisms pitting worker against bourgeois and town against country; the psychological conditioning of the Versailles troops through the dissemination of propaganda; the resentment of the latter at Paris and its National Guard for prolonging the war with Prussia and delaying their return home; the effects of the terrors generated by the intimacy of urban warfare. At various moments, it is likely that all these elements had a part to play. The memoirs of the Versailles generals are filled with disdain for their opponents. To General Vinoy, who had been in command of the Paris garrison on 18 March and was commander-in-chief of the Versailles army during the opening battles at the beginning of April (and later of the Reserve Army), those who fought for the Commune were neither soldiers nor Frenchmen, but "revolutionaries from every country, habitual rioters and professional insurgents ready to enrol under the flag of universal revolt."[94] Such opponents were criminals rather than legitimate enemies and did not deserve the protection owed the latter by the laws of war. When Émile Duval, one of the Communard generals, was captured and brought to him on 4 April, Vinoy peremptorily ordered the immediate execution of this "so-called general."[95] During the Bloody Week, generals sanctioned the violence. When three men accused of helping to start the fires that engulfed the city were brought before General Susbielle as he dined in a restaurant, the general ordered their immediate execution, adding the detail that signs identifying them as incendiaries should be pinned to their backs before they were taken away. They were shot in front of the Luxembourg Palace, to the applause of a substantial crowd. The following day, General Susbielle's dinner was again interrupted, this time to decide the fate of Jean-Baptiste Millière, one of the leading Communards. As Millière was also about to be executed in the same place as the three incendiaries, Captain Garcin, an

93 Ibid., 89.
94 Vinoy, *L'armistice et la Commune*, 253.
95 Ibid., 270. Interestingly, although Vinoy says of Duval that he was an "improvised general thanks to the revolt" and "one of the first to give his blood for it," he makes no mention of his own responsibility for ordering Duval's summary execution. Ibid., 193. According to a staff officer of the Second Division, Vinoy ordered Duval's immediate execution, to which the Communard general responded, "You are right, General, for if I held you I would do the same!" Duval then stepped to one side and awaited execution. Two of his aides-de-camp, upon their insistence, were shot alongside him. SHD AG 1K 262: Journal de marche d'un officier de l'Etat Major de la Division Susbielle, 2.

aide-de-camp of General Cissey, intervened. The captain declared that orders had been received from the commander-in-chief for Millière to be executed, on his knees, in the square in front of the Pantheon, on the grounds that this was where Millière himself had ordered the execution of twelve *fédérés* who had refused to fight for the Commune.[96] Interventions of this nature indicate not only that senior officers involved themselves directly in the killing but that they did so in a vindictive spirit.[97]

When the fighting was at its height, circumstances figured heavily in the violence. Victor de Compiègne, a Versailles soldier, vividly described "that horrible war that is called street warfare, where everyone fights for himself, man to man":

Where it is necessary to fight foot by foot, house by house, to jump into basements pistol in hand or to climb by some narrow stairway into the attics. Where the enemy shoots from behind and does not even wear a uniform. Two or three rifle shots are fired with almost perfect accuracy from a house and each one of them makes a victim of one of your comrades. Enraged, you break down the door, you bound into the house: the crime must be punished, the criminal shot immediately; but there are ten men there, all swear that they are innocent! So every soldier has to become the supreme judge, to see whether the rifle has recently been fired, if the hands are black with powder, if the shirt and the trousers of the civilian cover the uniform of the National Guard! No one will hold him to account for the right of life and death he will exercise amid women and children who cling to each other, pleading. Throughout the house, one hears only groans, shouts, and the explosion of firearms. On the street corner, one sees bodies stretched out or men who are about to die by firing squad.[98]

Victor de Compiègne's description of the war in the streets is revealing of the Versailles soldiers' state of mind, in which fear was compounded by rage at an enemy who killed one's friends and was, furthermore, not even a legitimate foe. According to some accounts, these circumstances generated a murderous frenzy in the Versailles soldiers. The corporal who

96 SHD AG 1K 262: Journal de marche d'un officier de l'Etat Major de la Division Susbielle, 49–50.

97 Robert Tombs shows that it was General Cissey, rather than Marshal MacMahon, who ordered the killing of Millière. Tombs, *The War against Paris*, 184–5. The details of Millière's execution were reported with bloodthirsty relish by the pro-Versailles newspapers. See *La Cloche*, 29 May 1871.

98 De Compiègne, "Souvenirs d'un Versaillais," 177–8.

arrested Millière and who later insisted on being part of the latter's firing squad was, according to a staff officer, in "an indescribable frenzy stemming from the fight he had been compelled to endure."[99] The same officer also recalled a horrified colleague who pleaded for the relief of his battalion. "Not only are the men exhausted," said the latter, "but they are like madmen. They have committed such a massacre in the quarter, that they see red. We are positively immersed in blood! Over 3,000 corpses of national guardsmen lie in the rue de Grenelle alone! It is horrible!" The staff officer marvelled that this was the same battalion which, on 18 March, had failed to prevent the surrender of General Lecomte and other officers to the insurgents.[100]

Much of the killing was done in cold blood, however, and the readiness of soldiers to participate in the mass killing of unarmed men, women, and children cannot be explained exclusively as an emotional response to the terrors of street warfare. The staff officer who recounted the eagerness of Millière's captor to be involved in the latter's execution claimed with respect to the killings he witnessed earlier at the War Ministry, "From the first instant the soldiers showed not the least repugnance at becoming members of the firing squad."[101] This apparent willingness of soldiers in the Versailles army to participate in mass executions is indeed remarkable, not just in view of the soldiers' earlier reluctance to fire on the crowds that resisted them on 18 March, but also in view of the evident repugnance of most soldiers for judicial executions during the earlier war with Prussia. Military executions were not unusual during the Franco-Prussian War. Soldiers often referred to them in their writings, usually with distaste. Camille Angevin described to his father the "horrible scene" as he and his comrades were compelled to serve as "sad spectators" at the execution for desertion of a soldier from their battalion in the Army of the North. "May God grant," wrote Angevin, "that this is the first and last time that such a thing should happen before our eyes."[102] There is evidence that some of the Versaillais soldiers felt similar sentiments of repugnance during the Bloody Week. In his posthumously published papers, Louis Rossel wrote: "A sort of reaction against summary executions took place in the attitude of the troops," some of whom he said absented themselves from sites of execution.[103] The cavalry officer Georges de Moussac later recalled the difficulty one of his comrades

99 SHD AG 1K 262: Journal de marche d'un officier de l'État Major de la Division Susbielle, 50.
100 Ibid., 37.
101 Ibid., 31.
102 SHD AG 1KT 842: Fonds Angevin. Letter of 22 January 1871.
103 Rossel, *Papiers posthumes*, 191.

had in carrying out "the sad mission" of giving the *coup de grâce* to victims
of executions.[104] De Moussac himself later witnessed the execution of
several Communards after they had been tried at Versailles, among them
Louis Rossel himself, who was executed at Satory in November. Although
noting that Rossel exchanged salutes with the men of his former regiment
as he went to his death, de Moussac does not appear to have experienced
any unease at the executions. "They were all very guilty with respect to
France!" was his judgment.[105] Overall, while soldiers' attitudes undoubtedly
varied, they appear to have been less troubled by the judicial executions
of the Bloody Week than by those of the war with Prussia.

This shift in the sentiments of soldiers is surely explained by the perceived
"otherness" of the victims who were executed during the Bloody Week. In
the weeks leading up to the assault on Paris, newspapers sympathetic to the
government were distributed to the Versailles army, which relentlessly
represented the Communards as foreigners and criminals.[106] One of those
newspapers, *Le Gaulois*, published unflattering biographies of the
Communard generals: Jaroslaw Dombrowski was "that frenzied conspirator," Gustave Cluseret, the "American general" who "only remembered he
was French to give himself the rights to be a revolutionary and civil war
leader."[107] More broadly, *Le Gaulois* condemned the Commune for
"barbarism" in expelling nuns from their convents and for "actions of the
most ignoble and the most cowardly ferocity" in its conduct of the war.[108]
The newspaper generally distinguished between the rank-and-file *fédérés*
and their leaders, claiming that the majority of *fédérés* were compelled to
fight against their will and insisting that these ordinary combatants could
expect generous treatment from the Versaillais.[109] The leaders, however,
were promised no such consideration. As the Bloody Week began, the
newspaper published an editorial which argued that the death penalty was
essential to punish the leaders of the rebellion, who had deliberately
"fanned to the limit the flames of civil war" to satisfy their ambitions.[110]
Representations of the *fédérés* also became more negative and less forgiving.
On 24 May, *Le Gaulois* wrote contemptuously of the columns of prisoners
escorted to Versailles, contrasting the few "true soldiers" in their ranks with
the "bizarre ones who wear uniforms stolen from the shops." Some of them,

104 Moussac, *Dans la mêlée*, 194.
105 Ibid., 201.
106 On the influence of the press on the Versailles army, see Tombs, *The War against Paris*, 109–23.
107 *Le Gaulois*, 25 April 1871.
108 Ibid., 13 May 1871.
109 Ibid., 7 May 1871.
110 Ibid., 21 May 1871.

it claimed, were "the dregs of the prisons" who had been unleashed like "animals from the Jardin des Plantes."[111] Metaphors comparing the Communards to wild animals or to savages from the colonies were to become a commonplace of anti-Communard propaganda.[112]

The rhetoric that first prepared and then accompanied the repression, which constantly insisted that the enemy were not truly soldiers, citizens of France, or even human, served to distance the men who did the killing from their victims, diminishing the sympathy and respect they might have felt had they perceived them to be French citizens and soldiers like themselves. Although the testimony of ordinary soldiers in the Versailles army is lacking, the officers who commanded them frequently echoed the dehumanizing imagery of the press. To Albert Hans, a *sous-lieutenant* of artillery in the Versailles army, the *fédérés* were "types of degenerates and intriguers, the poisonous mushrooms that emerge spontaneously from the soil in every revolution, the common scum that swells up and spreads over the paving stones, types that I had already seen elsewhere in the Orient, alongside the Pashas, and in Mexico, at the headquarters of the revolutionary leaders."[113] It seems very likely that the exposure of the troops to images that emphasized the "otherness" of the enemy – not soldiers, not French, not European, not human – made it easier to obey the orders of their officers to kill without mercy.

Confronted by an enemy bent upon their annihilation and that denied their existence as soldiers, citizens, and human beings, the Communards were finally left with only one way to resist: by dying well. This was the ultimate answer to those who insisted they were not real soldiers. If it was dying bravely that defined a soldier, then the men, women, and children who fought for the Commune would show that they were indeed soldiers. In his account of the Bloody Week, Lissagaray insisted that when confronted by death, "the conduct of the *fédérés* was everywhere admirable. None asked for mercy." Many, he said, folded their arms in front of the firing squad and gave the order to fire. As an example of fearlessness, Lissagaray told the story of a ten-year-old boy who was to be executed for having helped to defend a barricade in the rue du Temple. The youngster simply requested three minutes' grace before his execution so that he could give his watch to his mother. Accorded this reprieve, the boy made no effort to escape his fate, instead announcing his return and taking his place in front of the "stupefied" soldiers of the firing squad.[114] Lissagaray also cited at length

111 Ibid., 24 May 1871.
112 Merriman, *Massacre*, 205.
113 Hans, *Souvenirs d'un volontaire*, 4.
114 Lissagaray, *Les huits journées de mai*, 160.

an article by a Belgian journalist, which quoted the testimony of Versailles soldiers. "One of them said to me: 'We killed forty of this rabble at Passy. They all died like soldiers. Some folded their arms and held their heads high. The others opened their tunics and shouted to us: Fire! We do not fear death.'"[115] Lissagaray wrote *Les huits journées de mai* as a memorial to the courage of the Communards, and the book is filled with accounts of heroic deaths. As Lissagaray's evidence indicates, those who had no love for the Commune or for its defenders also acknowledged that courage. General Susbielle, recounting the execution of General Duval, who was shot by order of General Vinoy on 4 April, wrote that Duval had gone to his death "with a courage worthy of a better fate." Susbielle also commented on the bravery of two aides-de-camp who insisted upon sharing Duval's fate. "In any other circumstance this spirit of loyalty would have provoked cries of 'Mercy!'" he wrote, before adding that the memory of "the crime of 18 March" was too fresh and so "the voice of clemency kept silent."[116] Another anti-Communard witness to Communard courage was Augustine Blanchecotte, who wrote a vivid account of the defence to the last man by a detachment of *fédérés* of a barricade near the Pantheon. "When one sees so many ignorant people die so heroically for a bad cause," she wrote, "one is overcome by an irresistible desire to die as valiantly for a worthy cause."[117] In the battle's aftermath, Blanchecotte was affected by the sight of the body of a young gunner, one of three that lay in the street. "When someone shouted to him: 'Surrender!' he opened his jacket, uncovered his breast and was struck in the heart. Arms open, head high, body straight, he still has a proud appearance; his heart is no more than a large puddle of blood: he has poured out his whole youth!"[118] Geneviève Bréton, the bereaved fiancée of Henri Regnault, also paid tribute to the *fédérés* whose failings as soldiers were so often to be contrasted with her fiancé's heroism. Having overcome her grief and served as a nurse in a field hospital during the second siege of Paris, she admitted that the Versailles soldiers had fought bravely: "But as for the others, [they fought] like lions; you had to see them crossing the street on all fours, firing and leaving themselves exposed and counting their lives as valueless. The courage of error is as absolute as the courage of truth, one must admire it with the same impartiality."[119]

115 Ibid., 162.
116 SHD AG 1K 262: Souvenirs du Général Baron Bernard de Susbielle, 202. The crime to which Susbielle referred was the execution on 18 March of Generals Clément-Thomas and Lecomte.
117 Blanchecotte, *Tablettes d'une femme*, 276.
118 Ibid., 280–1.
119 Bréton, *Journal 1867–1871*, 240.

Once again, we are presented with impartial testimony that the supporters of the Commune "died like soldiers."

For the Communards shouting their defiance at their executioners, death was a performance that gave them the last word in the contest with Versailles. It affirmed their dignity as human beings and their courage as soldiers. It sanctified the cause for which they had fought, giving a sacred aura and an epic quality to the ten-week history of the Commune. Lissagaray wrote that he would never forget the death of Charles Delescluze, the Commune's third and last Military Delegate. On the evening of 25 May, having written a letter of farewell to his sister, Delescluze advanced alone, cane in hand, to the barricade at the top of the Boulevard Voltaire. Climbing the barricade, he was immediately shot down, falling onto the Place du Château d'Eau. "Delescluze walked to the barricade as the last Montagnards went to the scaffold," wrote Lissagaray. "The long day of his life had exhausted his strength; he had one last breath, he gave it. The Versaillais have concealed his body. But his memory will remain, buried in the heart of the people, as long as France is the holy land of the revolution."[120] By dying like soldiers the *fédérés* and those who perished with them on the barricades and before the firing squads became martyrs of the revolution. "The Mount of Martyrs has none more glorious," wrote Lissagaray of Eugène Varlin after describing the latter's brutal killing on the heights of Montmartre.[121] "He died gloriously for the world's salvation," went the words of a song honouring Louis Rossel, "As Christ died by the hands of the executioners."[122] The deaths of the Communards, celebrated in literary and in oral culture, transformed the defeat of the Paris Commune into a potent myth and a sacred inspiration for generations of socialists and revolutionaries in France and beyond.

REPRESENTATIONS

The last thing the Thiers government wanted was for the dead of the Commune to become the objects of a revolutionary cult. The disposal by the Versailles army of its victims' bodies in mass graves or through incineration made it difficult for relatives to recover the remains of their loved ones or for individual graves to become sites for politically charged pilgrimages

---

120 Lissagaray, *Les huit journées de mai*, 117–18. The Montagnards/"Mountaineers' were so named because they occupied the high seats in the National Convention of 1793–95. Their leaders were the radical revolutionaries who governed France during the Terror of 1793–94 and who went to the guillotine during the Thermidorian reaction.

121 Lissagaray, *Histoire de la Commune*, 379.

122 Brécy, *Florilège de la chanson révolutionnaire*, 104.

and demonstrations. The authorities' deliberate lack of regard for the physical remains of the dead Communards contrasted with the Commune's own efforts not only to identify those remains but also to honour them through public funerals.[123] It also contrasted with the unprecedented efforts made by the government in the aftermath of *l'année terrible* to provide respectful resting places for the soldiers who had died in the war with Prussia as well as to keep their memory alive through the commissioning of monuments and other commemorative works of art. Officially, the civil war was to be erased from memory, representations of it in both word and image banned by strict censorship.[124] At the same time, the memory of the war with the foreign enemy was to be kept very much alive, with the war dead at the centre of a patriotic cult aimed at resurrecting national pride from the ashes of defeat.

As Karine Varley has demonstrated, the cult of the war dead after 1870–71 was the product of a reconfiguration of nationalism which itself stemmed from changes in warfare and society that had been under way since the French Revolutionary Wars. As warfare became an affair of peoples rather than just their rulers, and as citizens became soldiers, the lives of the latter became more valuable. The increased lethality of warfare, however, meant that they also became more expendable. To resolve this paradox, the soldier's sacrifice on the battlefield was given ever greater significance as the fulfillment of both personal and national destinies. The cult of the war dead was also stimulated by contemporary attitudes toward death, which addressed the intolerable separation of the living from the dead by keeping the dead close, both physically and figuratively. In an age of declining religiosity and declining belief in the afterlife, the transfer of sacrality from Church to nation sanctified and provided a consolatory justification for the soldier's death. Finally, new developments in the reporting of war news, including eyewitness accounts from civilian journalists and vivid images produced by the technique of lithography, enhanced the public's awareness of the soldiers' suffering as well as their willingness to pay tribute to it after the war was over.[125]

The most significant manifestation of this heightened awareness of the war dead after 1871 was an unprecedented commitment by the state to look after the tombs of all soldiers, regardless of rank or nationality. No longer would the common soldier lie forgotten in an unmarked grave. This obligation was laid out in the Treaty of Frankfurt of 1871 and legally enshrined for the French state by a law of 4 April 1873, which provided

123 Brown, *Mass Violence*, 196–205.
124 Wilson, *Paris and the Commune*, 36–7; Tillier, *La Commune de Paris*, 247–51.
125 Varley, "Death and Sacrifice," 30–7; Varley, *Under the Shadow of Defeat*, 57–8.

for the burial of over 75,000 bodies in twenty-five ossuaries at a cost of over two million francs.[126] The construction of state-sponsored mausoleums encouraged local initiatives to build war memorials. There were already at least 457 of these by 1878 and many more were built in the following decades, serving as important sites for commemorative ceremonies.[127] The preoccupation with the war dead began, however, while the war was still under way. Indeed, the high visibility of the dead in wartime representations underpinned public awareness of the war's violence and of soldiers' suffering.

The dead figured prominently in French newspapers reporting on the conflict. Insofar as contemporary journalism broke new ground during the war, it was more through the images it presented of the dead than through its representations of combat, which largely remained true to established convention. The illustrated weekly *La Guerre Illustrée* gave little sense of the carnage in most of its reports of the battles of the summer of 1870. In reporting on the Battle of Forbach, the newspaper placed the emphasis first upon the thrill of battle as the outcome hung in the balance, then upon the heroism of the French soldiers fighting against impossible odds. The destruction of lives came almost as an afterthought. "Ground was won and lost, foot by foot. First our men fell back, then they regained the advantage. What a heroic struggle! By six o'clock, they had retaken their position. One against ten! A desperately murderous battle on both sides."[128] A similar emphasis characterized the newspaper's reporting of the French cavalry charges at the Battle of Reichshoffen. "In spite of the batteries, in spite of the machine guns, in spite of the jumble of men and horses who fell," went the report, "the French *cuirassiers* reached the Prussian regiments, breaking them, crushing them, pressing onward." "How many of those heroic soldiers returned?" the paper queried rhetorically. "One dares not ask!"[129] The newspaper's correspondent even managed to be reasonably upbeat after providing graphic descriptions of the wounded returning to Metz from the Battle of Gravelotte: "All of that is without a doubt hideous," he wrote. "One's heart rebels; but there is a heroic and grandiose aspect which overcomes you."[130] It was only with his visit to the battlefield at Gravelotte and his encounter with the dead that the correspondent appears to have been truly overcome by the horror of war. "At the end of an hour of this hideous spectacle, I left," he wrote.

126 Ibid., 59–61.
127 Ibid., 104.
128 *La Guerre Illustrée*, 13 August 1870.
129 Ibid., 17 August 1870.
130 Ibid., 27 August 1870.

"I could stay no longer. It seemed to me that I too must fall into that reddish mud and that my place was marked out amid those bodies crushed by artillery pieces."[131]

Jules Claretie was another war correspondent who was profoundly troubled by a visit to a battlefield, and by his encounter with the dead. It was necessary to see such sights, he wrote in the weekly *L'Illustration* after visiting the battlefield at Sedan, to understand "the frightful meaning of the word 'war.'" Like the writer for *La Guerre Illustrée*, Claretie was disturbed by the lifelike appearance of the dead: "One might take them, immobile as they are, for wax figures, and the feeling one has is at once painful, poignant and fantastic." He was also horrified by the mutilated bodies, ending his description of them by cursing "those who undertake these adventures and who, *lightheartedly*, order these massacres!"[132] *L'Illustration* and *La Guerre Illustrée* both carried many of the same illustrations. Prominent among them were images of the dead drawn by Auguste Lançon. These presented a striking contrast with conventional images of battlefield heroism. Théodore Gautier commented on the significance of Lançon's drawings as an objective portrayal of the reality of war. "There is no question here of official battles, with staff officers flitting around the victor and a few tasteful dead bodies to please the Academy in the foreground [...] They are rapid sketches, drawn from life in a traveller's notebook, by a brave artist, attached to an ambulance. Not one object that has not been seen, no line that is not sincere. No arrangement. No composition. It is truth in its unexpected horror, in its sinister strangeness. Such things cannot be invented. The darkest imagination would not go so far."[133] Gautier considered Lançon's drawing of "a corner of the battlefield of Bazeilles – the effect of a cannon shot" to be one of his most significant works. The image depicted the bodies of seven soldiers who had been killed by a single cannonball, lying in a freshly ploughed field (fig. 5.3). The awkward poses of the bodies, as disarrayed as the accoutrements surrounding them, was to Gautier a truthful representation of sudden death on the modern battlefield. Nothing, he said, could be "more sinister and more tragic than these bodies lying in the furrow like ears of cut wheat." The drawing, he said, "developed and painted in its bitter truth, would make a fine painting, terrible in its newness." Gautier was also impressed by Lançon's drawing of a mass grave containing both French and German dead. "Mr Lançon has made a drawing of one of these still gaping ditches that turns one's blood to ice," he wrote, despairingly. "Alas!

131 Ibid.
132 *L'Illustration*, 10 September 1870.
133 Ibid., 19 November 1870.

5.3. Auguste Lançon. *Bazeille behind the Park above the Balan Road,
1 September 1870.*

this ferocity, this madness, these monstrous wounds, these torrents of
blood, all that to end up asleep in the same furrow!"[134]

It was Lançon's depictions of the dead following the Battle of Champigny
(30 November – 3 December 1870) that had the greatest impact (fig. 5.4).
Both *La Guerre Illustrée* and *L'Illustration* devoted two-page spreads to his
drawing of the Brothers of the Christian Doctrine burying the dead. A
witness who wrote for *L'Illustration*, De la Grangerie, commented on
Lançon's drawing: "We will see whether the engraver's chisel has properly
conveyed the artist's impressions. For my part, I don't know whether I will
dare to turn the page. Those stiff torsos, those twisted limbs, those grimac-
ing mouths, those faces where the frost has left its red marks, those eyebrows
snowy with frost, those shapeless wrecks from the battle, crushed, burned,
eviscerated, this horrible bed where the lime will shortly be spread, the
whole of this monstrous tableau will remain forever in my memory."[135]
At the same time as he paid tribute to the veracity of Lançon's drawing,

134 Ibid.
135 Ibid., 17 December 1870.

5.4. Auguste Lançon. *Beside the Villiers Road, 8 December 1870.*

De la Grangerie supplemented that image with gruesome detail. By describing his own feelings, he also prompted an emotional response from readers. Although De la Grangerie quoted an observer who said Lançon's drawing was "in itself a sufficient protest against the horrors of war,"[136] the combination of image and text made an even more powerful statement.

136 Ibid.

Auguste Lançon was not the only French artist who saw the war at first hand or who aspired to a realistic representation of the soldier's death. Jean-François Lecaillon identifies over sixty artists who served in some military capacity during the war.[137] A good number of them, most notably Alphonse de Neuville and Édouard Detaille, achieved a more realistic representation of the soldier's experience than that of previous generations of military painters. Both artists went to great lengths to ensure the historical accuracy of their paintings. They visited the sites of the battles of Champigny and Rezonville before preparing their panoramas of those battles, and Neuville supposedly peppered a Parisian apartment with gunshots in his quest for authenticity in representing the "house of the last cartridge" defended by the marines at Bazeilles.[138] Detaille, the more obsessive of the two concerning historical detail, said of the panoramas, "I wanted to show a battlefield in its reality, without conventional poses, without excessive composition, and without any of those childish implausibilities that the public accepts with too much good faith."[139] Neither artist shied away from depicting the agony of the dying and the crumpled bodies of the dead (fig. 5.5). Jules Claretie, commenting on Detaille's *En retraite*,[140] a painting shown at the official Salon of 1873, wrote: "I have often wondered why painters of battles did not represent the dead as they are, with their angular and bizarre positions, their gestures like broken automatons. Mr Detaille shows us bodies but this time in all their horror. The arms are stiff, the lips uncover, in a sinister rictus, the long teeth of death."[141] Detaille recognized, however, that the quest for realism could go only so far. "An impression that one will never be able to convey," he wrote to a friend, "is that of disfigured corpses, of wounded without legs or arms, of that sort of museum of anatomy. Never could one permit oneself, I believe, to present that to the public."[142] Detaille quickly discovered the risk of offending public (and official) taste, as his painting of *Un coup de mitrailleuse*,[143] depicting a row of dead Saxon soldiers who had been cut down by machine-gun fire, was rejected by the Salon of 1872. Similarly, Lançon's *Morts en ligne!* received adverse criticism when it was shown at the Salon of 1874. Émile Bergerat wrote that it was "a horrible thing to see and unworthy of description,"[144] while Marius Chaumelin

---

137 Lecaillon, *Les peintres français*, 25–9.
138 Robichon, *Alphonse de Neuville*, 69–70.
139 In *Gazette des beaux-arts*, 1897/2. Cited in Robichon, *Édouard Detaille*, 40.
140 "In Retreat."
141 Claretie, *L'art et les artistes*, 157. Cited in Robichon, *La peinture militaire*, 90.
142 Claretie, *L'Art et les artistes*, 61. Cited in Robichon, *La peinture militaire*, 90.
143 "A machine gun strike."
144 *Journal Officiel de la République Française*, 19 May 1874.

5.5. Édouard Detaille and Alphonse de Neuville. *Infantry in a Sunken Road.* Fragment from the panorama of Champigny. 1882.

declared that Lançon's "livid, blackened, semi-putrified corpses could inspire nothing else in us but disgust, even though they are French soldiers 'killed in line!'"[145]

The realistic depiction of the war did not imply a detached or objective representation. Preferring a more intimate, anecdotal style of representation to that of earlier battle painters, the new generation of military artists led by Detaille and Neuville chose to represent episodes from the Franco-Prussian War that celebrated the resistance and sacrifice of French soldiers. By narrowing the focus to very localized events, it was possible to look away from the historical realities that French political and military leaders had been found wanting during the war and that the resistance of the French people to foreign invasion had been anything but consistent. Focusing on the courage of small groups of soldiers fighting to the limit of their abilities created the hopeful impression of a united people whose spirit was unbroken and whose honour had been preserved. By far the most significant of the episodes to be celebrated in this way was the defence of Bazeilles, on

145   *Le Bien Public,* 21 June 1874.

the outskirts of Sedan, by four regiments of marines (1 September 1870) against a Bavarian army of forty thousand men. The village of three hundred houses was destroyed by fire during the battle and thirty-nine civilians lost their lives, circumstances that fuelled accusations of German war crimes. In his famous painting of this event, *La dernière cartouche*,[146] Alphonse de Neuville focused not on the martyrdom of the town and its inhabitants, but on the resistance of the French marines. The artist condensed the battle to the final moment in the defence of a single house by a company under the command of Captain Lambert, who is represented directing a soldier as he fires the last remaining cartridge. Observing the scene from across a room full of wounded men and the debris of battle, a young *chasseur* stands, hands in pockets since he no longer has the means to fight, waiting stoically for death. While realistically evoking the soldiers' effort and exhaustion, Neuville took some poetic licence, most notably including a "turco"[147] and red-trousered soldiers from the regular army to reinforce the impression of a nation united in resistance (fig. 0.1).[148]

Choosing which events and individuals to commemorate and how to represent them was complicated by the political and religious divisions of France under the Third Republic, both at the national and local level. An event that focused the religious patriotism of Catholics was the Battle of Loigny (2 December 1870), which was celebrated for the sacrifice of the papal zouaves who, having returned to France from Rome upon the advent of the Third Republic, had fought and died under the banner of the Sacred Heart of Jesus. A memorial chapel was built at Loigny over an ossuary containing the bones of the dead. Paintings by Lionel Royer decorating the chapel combined realism and mysticism. One depicted the volunteers of the West receiving the eucharist on the morning of the battle while another showed its aftermath, with the wounded and frost-covered body of the zouaves' commander, General de Sonis, lying among the dead (fig. 5.6). In both paintings the soldiers were attended by a female allegory of Faith.[149]

Also combining realism and allegory, though in a more secular vein, was Ernest Meissonier's *Siège de Paris*, a painting begun in 1871 but only completed in 1884 (fig. 5.7). The theme of sacrifice was represented by the bodies of the "illustrious dead." In the foreground, Colonel Dampierre, killed at Bagneux in October 1870, is identifiable by his red sash. Beside him, crushed under a wounded horse, lies Captain Néverlée, a staff officer

146 "The Last Cartridge."

147 An Algerian *tirailleur*.

148 See Varley, *Under the Shadow of Defeat*, 152–74; Robichon, *Alphonse de Neuville*, 69–83; Milner, *Art, War and Revolution*, 55–7.

149 Varley, *Under the Shadow of Defeat*, 69; Tison, "Lionel Royer," 93.

5.6. Lionel Royer, *The Evening of 2 December 1870 on the Battlefield at Loigny.*
The Death of General de Sonis. 1910. Despite the painting's title, de Sonis survived
the battle and the subsequent amputation of his leg.

5.7. Ernest Meissonier, *The Siege of Paris (1870–71)*. 1884.

killed at the Battle of Champigny. Further back is the figure of General Renaudot. The suffering of civilians was also evoked, however; a national guardsman is overcome by grief as his wife holds up their dead infant, a victim of the famine. Meissonier, who was personally deeply affected by the death of Henri Regnault, placed him kneeling in the centre of the painting. Wearing his brown National Guard's uniform, Regnault expires beside a stalwart female allegory of the city of Paris, her head covered by a lionskin, her golden dress by a black veil of mourning. Meissonier said of his painting that it was an "heroic symphony of France": "It is honour, it is resistance!"[150]

Although Meissonier himself belonged to an older generation of artists, his painting of the siege of Paris marked a transition in the artistic representation of the Franco-Prussian War. The painting included historic figures like Henri Regnault, but the latter were extracted from their historical circumstances and placed in an allegorical and symbolic setting. By 1885, the postwar generation of artists led by Detaille and Neuville began to give

150 Gréard, *Meissonier*, 242–3; Cited in Milner, *Art, War and Revolution*, 211–12.

way to a new generation that continued to depict the war, but with less concern for specific events or individuals. The scenes they represented were generic in nature, more concerned with providing inspirational models for the future than with paying homage to the past.[151] Jules Monge's *Le clairon de Turcos blessé* (1884),[152] does not identify its subject by name; nor does it indicate where or when the battle in which he was wounded took place. Monge's work was also representative of a tendency, during a period of heightened nationalism, for representations of the war to become radicalized. The artist's 1894 painting, *Le dernier du bataillon*, clearly inspired by his earlier effort of 1884, shows the last remaining soldier from a battalion of "turcos" using his own blood to write a tribute to his comrades. François Robichon describes this painting as "the height of exaggeration and of evident bad taste."[153] Paintings of cavalry charges from this period were particularly prone to excess, as artists outdid one another to magnify their speed and fury. The culmination of this trend came with Pierre Victor Robiquet's *En folie!* (1911),[154] depicting the decapitation of Colonel de Lacarre as he led the Third Cuirassiers into action at the Battle of Elsasshausen. Perhaps the most striking representation of the soldier's death from this period, however, was Jean Joseph Weerts's *Pour l'humanité, pour la patrie* (1895).[155] Depicting a fallen *cuirassier*, arms outstretched and wrapped in a tricolour flag, beneath a crucified Christ, the image was a direct affirmation of the soldier's death as sacrifice; it sanctified the nation and represented death in battle as a sacred duty. The work of a convinced republican, the painting might be seen as confirmation that the Gallican Church, which had often contested with republicans the commemoration of 1870, had rallied to the republic. Weerts's association of religious and republican symbols in patriotic imagery set a precedent that was to be renewed during the First World War (fig. 5.8).[156]

These later artworks, focused heavily on the heroism of French soldiers, shunned the grim images of dead and dying soldiers produced closer in time to the war with Prussia. It was left to writers to take up the torch of realism laid down by Auguste Lançon. In *La débâcle* (1892), Émile Zola acknowledged the heroism of the soldiers defending Bazeilles, but he also described the military incompetence that abandoned them there in the first place. He pulled no punches in describing the suffering of soldiers,

151 Lecaillon, *Les peintres français*, 80.
152 "The wounded Turco trumpeter."
153 Robichon, *La peinture militaire*, 130.
154 "Madness!"
155 "For humanity, for the homeland."
156 Ibid., 134. See also Robichon, "La peinture du sacrifice," 179.

5.8. Jean Joseph Weerts, *For Humanity, for the Homeland*. 1895.

providing a gruesomely vivid picture of how they died on the battlefield
and in the field hospitals at Sedan. In *Les soirées de Médan* (1880), Zola and
five other collaborators exposed the human folly and frailty that attended
the war, its absurdity as well as its tragedy. *L'affaire du Grand 7*,[157] by Léon
Hennequin, tells the story of soldiers from a garrison who, enraged by the
death of one of their comrades, take their revenge not on the Prussian
enemy they have never encountered, but on the prostitutes in the local
brothel. An officer who is killed as he tries to stop the massacre deplores
the stupidity of his own death with his final words: "Pigs!! … Oh! the pigs! …
To die like this!"[158] The war's irrationality was also the theme of Henry
Céard's *La saignée*,[159] which cast a jaundiced eye on the sortie that led
to the "bloodletting" of Buzenval as the product of the commanding
general's dysfunctional relationship with his mistress. The French soldiers
of *Les soirées de Médan* are anything but heroic. In Joris-Karl Huysman's
Sac au dos[160] young conscripts are represented refusing to fight at the Battle
of Froeschwiller: "Let them go and get killed, they said, pointing to the
officers, that's their job! I've got children, the state won't look after them
if I'm killed!"[161]

Hennequin's story of how French soldiers whipped themselves up into
a frenzy and then embarked upon a massacre of prostitutes only seems
far-fetched if one can forget about the Bloody Week of the Paris Commune.
Many artists and writers strove to do just that. The Impressionists turned
away from the themes of war and revolution, filling their paintings of Paris
with scenes of sunlight and peace. But there were some who sought to
remember not only the reality of the massacres but also the courage of
the Communards. Ernest Pichio's 1875 painting of the executions in the
cemetery of Père Lachaise, entitled *Le triomphe de l'ordre*,[162] was condemned
by the conservative press for representing the "people of riot and crime"
as "martyrs and heroes."[163] Undeterred, two years later Pichio painted
La veuve du fusillé,[164] depicting a woman in mourning pointing out to her
children the words inscribed on a wall: "May 1871 / To the martyrs / without
names / who died for liberty."[165] Around the turn of the century, Maximilien
Luce also produced several paintings and lithographs that commemorated

157 "The Affair of the Big 7."
158 Hennique, *L'affaire du grand 7*, in *Les soirées de Médan*, 254.
159 "The Bloodletting."
160 "Pack on Back."
161 Huysmans, *Sac au dos*, in *Les soirées de Médan*, 156.
162 "The Triumph of Order."
163 *La Patrie*, 5 April 1875. Cited in Tillier, *La Commune de Paris*, 259.
164 "The Widow of the Executed."
165 Tillier, *La Commune de Paris*, 261.

5.9. Alfred Roll. *Paris Commune. Execution of a Trumpeter.* 1871.

the sacrifice of well-known Communards like Eugène Varlin as well as of the anonymous men and women who died on the barricades.[166]

Most striking among these images of Communard heroism was Alfred Roll's 1871 painting of the execution of a trumpeter. Wearing the uniform

---

166 Ibid., 474–8.

of the National Guard and boldly standing with legs astride and hands on hips, the trumpeter fixes his executioners with a defiant glare (fig. 5.9). In poetry, Victor Hugo also paid tribute to youthful heroism, recounting the story of the ten-year-old who put his killers to shame by returning to accept his execution after giving his watch to his mother.[167] Hugo's poem, by comparing the youth to the revolutionary child hero Viala, placed him in the same tradition as that celebrated by mainstream republicans. Jean-Joseph Weerts, for example, painted a well-known tribute to Bara, the youth hero most often associated with Viala, in 1883. At a time when the memory of civil war was over-written by a preponderance of imagery depicting a nation united in resistance to the foreign enemy, there were at least some who recognized that the Communards had demonstrated the same qualities of determination and self-sacrifice. All the same, it is doubtful many of the Communards would have appreciated the parallel. For the Communards and their heirs who, beginning in the 1880s, participated in annual May Day pilgrimages to the wall of the *fédérés*, one legacy of the Bloody Week was an abiding hatred for the army and a fervent anti-militarism.[168]

CONCLUSION

There was no consensus in France about how to remember the wars of 1870–71. This became very apparent in the early 1880s, when Paris was beset by what one writer referred to as an "epidemic" of panoramas.[169] Panoramas were the "virtual reality" experience of the nineteenth century, giving viewers who entered them the illusion of being present at an event that was represented on giant canvases surrounding them on all sides. In 1883 alone, Parisians were spoiled for choice by panoramas depicting scenes from the "Terrible Year." Not only could they see Detaille and Neuville's panorama of Champigny, but there were also those by Poilpot and Jacob of Buzenval and Reichshoffen and two more by Charles Castellani, of the siege of Belfort and the "final day" of the Commune of Paris. Opinion was divided about the merits of these representations. "Do you think visitors leave impressed and proud to have seen our soldiers falling under Prussian bullets and retreating before the victorious and arrogant enemy?"

167 Victor Hugo, "Juin, 1871." Cited in Frerejean and Hoër, *Le siège et la Commune*, 304–5.

168 In 1907, when the municipality of Paris proposed placing a monument by Paul Moreau-Vauthier, *Aux victimes des révolutions*, which honoured both Versaillais and *fédérés*, at the site of the wall of the *fédérés*, partisans of the Commune objected. Eventually, the sculpture was placed on an outside wall of the cemetery, where it remains. See Tillier, *La Commune de Paris*, 428–9.

169 *L'Opinion*, 31 August 1883.

asked *Le Patriote*. "Don't be misled!"[170] *Le XIXe Siècle* agreed. For too long, it claimed, viewers' eyes had been saddened by "painful images" of the war of 1870.[171] Opposing this view, however, was *La République Française*, which claimed that "renewing one's sorrows in this way brings about bitter pleasure together with a severe lesson." The newspaper considered it a sign of a people's virility to be able to look its defeats in the face. Besides, it noted, those defeats "did have some glory."[172]

For nationalists, the commemoration of 1870–71 was all about finding glory in defeat and consequently a basis for hope in the future. Indeed, as the representation of the war as a willing sacrifice took shape, it came to seem that the more hopeless the cause and the more futile the sacrifice, the greater was the glory.[173] One of the most powerful statements of this theme was the sculpture *Gloria Victis!* (Glory to the Victims), exhibited at the Salon of 1874 by Antonin Mercié. Directly inspired by the death of Henri Regnault and praised by Jules Claretie as "purely and absolutely beautiful," this sculpture idealized the soldier's death by detaching it entirely from its contemporary setting.[174] Mercié, studying in Rome after winning the prestigious Prix de Rome in 1868, took his inspiration from antiquity. The sculpture's dying warrior, his nakedness and failing strength put in relief by the flowing gown and powerful stride of the winged female allegory upon whom he subsides, conforms to the ancient ideal of a beautiful death: the death of a young man, in the prime of life, sword in hand (fig. 5.10).[175]

The nationalist movement exalted various exemplars of patriotic sacrifice after 1871. The death of Roland at Roncesvalles figured prominently as did the martyrdom of Joan of Arc.[176] Paul Déroulède, the leader of the Ligue des Patriotes, himself evoked a pantheon of heroes, from Prometheus to Napoleon, even as he acknowledged Mercié's unique ability to make manifest in stone and bronze the organization's ideals.[177] For Déroulède, the achievement of *revanche*, the reversal of the verdict of the war of 1870–71, would only be achieved by remembering and emulating the sacrifice of the soldiers who had given their lives in that conflict. His own

170 *Le Patriote*, 9 September 1883.
171 *Le XIXe Siècle*, 7 September 1883.
172 *La République Française*, 30 November 1881.
173 See Lecaillon, *Le souvenir de 1870*, 115.
174 Claretie, *L'art et les artistes*, 274.
175 Vernant, "La mort héroïque."
176 Schivelbusch, *The Culture of Defeat*, 128–47.
177 Both men spoke at the unveiling of the bust of Henri Regnault at Buzenval on 26 January 1871. Déroulède praised Mercié's monumental sculpture *Quand-même!*, which honoured the defenders of Belfort and which represented a dying soldier in modern uniform. See *Le Petit Caporal*, 27 January 1913.

5.10. Antonin Mercié, *Gloria Victis!* 1874.

model of the soldier's death, provided in his *Nouveaux chants du soldat*, was not that of a young, beautiful, ancient warrior, but of a grizzled sergeant from the Army of Africa, a veteran of Balaclava and Palestro. The song entitled "The Sergeant" is an intergenerational dialogue between the eponymous hero and a green recruit whom he prepares for combat. Dying at the end of a battle lost, the sergeant asks only that the young man carry his medal into battle on some future, "less disastrous" occasion.[178] If the young man of the future is unwilling to give his life for his country, wrote

178 Déroulède, *Nouveaux chants du soldat*, 92.

Déroulède in his final "soldier's song," his mother will have failed: "If he doesn't know how to die," he says to a putative mother, "you didn't know how to create."[179]

The Commune, too, had poets who sought to keep alive the memory of the dead and who dreamed of *revanche*. The *revanche* they imagined, however, was not against the foreign enemy, but against the French army that had crushed the Commune and was now exalted by nationalists as the instrument of *revanche* against Germany. Many of the *fédérés* who had given their support to the Commune did so out of a sense of outraged patriotism and from disgust at the *capitulards* who were ready to surrender to the Prussians. The trauma of the repression to which they were subjected in May 1871, magnified by the abrupt disappearance of the funeral rituals by which the living had come to manage their separation from the dead, reoriented their priorities. Remembering and avenging the dead from the civil war henceforth took precedence over any such obligation in relation to the foreign war. [180] Eugène Pottier, author of the *Internationale*, was pre-eminent among the poets of the Commune. The bitterness and anger of Pottier's verses are unrelieved by consolatory tales of glory. Like nationalist writers, however, Pottier also spoke of sacrifice and rebirth. In "Le monument des fédérés" he wrote of building a barricade in honour of the *fédérés* at the site of "the abbatoir, the charnel house," where "the butchers piled up [...] all our anonymous dead." Expressing outrage that the dead of the Commune should lie unnamed and unmarked, the song concluded, "On each paving stone, people, your chisel engraves / The date of a murder or the name of a martyr! [...] Let it be the call for revenge / The monument of the *fédérés*."[181] Like the nationalists who promised those who had died fighting for a losing cause a share in *revanche* when the time came, so did Pottier. "Vanquished of May, let your deaths be fruitful!" he declared in "Le rêve du forgeron,"[182] calling upon them to rise from the grave to carry the red flag to the united peoples of the world.[183] The few monuments eventually raised to the dead of the Commune did not match the hundreds built to preserve the memory of the soldiers who died in the Franco-Prussian War, but, as Pottier's verses illustrate, there were other ways, even for the losers of a civil war, to remember the dead.

179 Ibid., 96.
180 On this shift of perspective, see Lecaillon, *Le souvenir de 1870*, 61. Howard Brown makes a compelling argument for the traumatizing effect of the impossibility of providing funerals for thousands of dead in the aftermath of the Bloody Week. Brown, *Mass Violence*, 205–9.
181 Pottier, *Chants révolutionnaires*, 138–9.
182 "The Blacksmith's Dream."
183 Ibid., 143.

6

Dying for France:
The First World War

THE DEATH OF EUGÈNE-EMMANUEL LEMERCIER

We do not know exactly when or how Eugène-Emmanuel Lemercier died. All we know for certain is that the recently promoted sergeant of the 106th infantry regiment was "*porté disparu*" – listed as missing – at Les Éparges on 6 April 1915 and finally declared to have been killed in action by the Tribunal of the Seine on 28 December 1920.[1] The official record provides little information. The unit war diary indicates that on 5 April, the 106th regiment launched an attack on the crest of Les Éparges that was part of a broader offensive to drive the Germans off the heights of the Meuse to the southeast of Verdun. The attack began in the late afternoon but made painful progress, hampered by the steady rain, which turned the "clayey" soil to mud, as well as by heavy bombardment from enemy artillery. Many shells, both French and German, failed to explode. On 6 April, the Germans counterattacked. Using grenades, they drove the men of the 106th from their trenches. The latter put up a "desperate resistance" even though their rifles were clogged with mud and refused to fire. Ordered to retake the position they had lost, the 106th returned to the attack, reoccupying their position, "despite violent barrages of heavy artillery." The war diary concludes its entry for 6 April by stating that Lieutenant-Colonel Barjonet

1   Government of France, Ministère de la Défense, Base des Morts Pour la France de la Première Guerre Mondiale: Lemercier, Eugène Emmanuel, accessed 24 March, 2016, http://www.memoiredeshommes.sga.defense.gouv.fr/fr/arkotheque/client/mdh/base_morts_pour_la_france_premiere_guerre/resus_rech.php.

had received a light leg wound but was continuing in command and that one German officer and fifteen soldiers had been captured.[2]

Despite the paucity of these details, they do help us to imagine the circumstances in which Lemercier was killed. They tell us of the mud, the rain, the omnipresent shelling, and the intensity of the fighting as French and Germans contested the heights of Les Éparges. Other documents are more helpful. Lemercier's letters, addressed to his mother in the months preceding his death, provide further insights into the fighting. He described his participation in five days' intense fighting that followed an earlier French offensive, beginning on 17 February:

Our losses are frightful; those of the enemy, even worse. You cannot know, beloved Mother, what man is capable of doing to man. For the past five days my shoes have been slimy with human brains, I have trampled torsos, and encountered entrails. The men eat what little they have side by side with corpses. The regiment was heroic: we have no officers left. They all died like brave men. Two good friends, one a charming model for one of my last portraits, were killed. That was one of my frightful encounters of the evening. A white and magnificent dead body in the moonlight; I rested beside him. The beauty of things awakened in me [...]

Finally, after five days of horror which cost us twelve hundred men, we have been withdrawn from this abominable place.[3]

Besides providing a vivid depiction of the fighting in which he participated, Lemercier's letters are also revealing of his state of mind. As the encounter with his friend's body suggests, Lemercier was acutely aware of his own mortality. His letters to his mother are a brave attempt to prepare them both for the likelihood of his own death: "Let us be brave," he wrote on 23 February, "me among all these youthful dead, you, in anticipation. But God is over us."[4] At times Lemercier, a painter before the war, expressed acceptance that he might not live to fulfill his destiny as an artist. Should he fall, he wrote, another would pick up the torch.[5] On other occasions, his spirit rebelled. "Why am I sacrificed like this," he asked, "when so many

2   SHD, AG: Armée de Terre: 26 N 677/4: *Journal Militaire Officiel*, 106th regiment, 1er avril – 20 juin 1915 [1 April–20 June 1915], accessed 24 March, 2016, http://www.memoiredeshommes.sga.defense.gouv.fr/fr/arkotheque/inventaires/ead_ir_consult.php?&ref=SHDGR__GR_26_N_II.

3   Lemercier, *Lettres d'un soldat*, 143–4.

4   Ibid., 144.

5   Ibid., 124.

less worthy are kept safe? I had nonetheless something good to do on earth."[6] Overall, Lemercier sought comfort in the beauties of nature, perceptible even on the battlefield, and in his belief that the violence and death of even "this infamous war"[7] were part of a greater natural order. Surrounded by material destruction, Lemercier put his faith in a transcendent ideal: "Now I feel what life is. It is the instrument that clears the way of the soul toward the absolute."[8]

Lemercier was remarkable in his capacity to raise his eyes from the mud and blood of the battlefield to contemplate the divine. His intense spiritualism – and perhaps his sensitivity to his mother's feelings – prevented him from dwelling too long on the horrors he confronted. A more comprehensive vision of the same battlefield – and one that captures both the appalling scale of the loss of life as well as the terrifying vulnerability of flesh and blood to the engines of destruction – is provided by another soldier in Lemercier's regiment, Maurice Genevoix. Genevoix's memoir, published in 1923, entitled simply *Les Éparges*, evokes the names and personalities of the comrades with whom he fought. It is also a searing account of their suffering – and Genevoix's own – as those comrades went to their deaths. Although they died in many ways, Genevoix makes it clear from the very beginning that the principal agent of their destruction was artillery fire. Shells, both French and German, rained death down on the men of the 106th regiment. In January 1915, a time of relative calm, daily bombardments took a steady toll of lives, such as that of Fauvette, killed by a shell that exploded directly beneath his chair as he sat waiting to be shaved while his comrade Lardin, brush and razor in hand, was untouched.[9] The fighting intensified, however, when the French offensive began on 17 February, and the attacking infantry came under heavy and continuous bombardment. "The shells fall; everything is reduced to that, and it never stops. There are moments when one can hardly conceive of this continuing reality, this unbelievable persistence of the din, this perpetual quaking of the soil under such multiple blows, and that odour of the air, suffocating, corrosive, and those bursts of smoke always breaking out and dispersing."[10] Those shells, "which bury and un-bury, and which thunder and yelp with these strange stridencies, ignobly sniggering and gay,"[11] also kill. Genevoix's account of the five days' fighting that followed the French attack is a litany

6 Ibid., 146.
7 Ibid., 145.
8 Ibid., 139.
9 Genevoix, *Ceux de 14*, 536.
10 Ibid., 597.
11 Ibid., 603.

of men dying: suddenly, slowly; in ones and twos and threes and sometimes en masse; Mémasse, Libron, and Grondin decapitated; Perrinet cut in half; Legallais with a gaping hole in his back; Chabeau and Biloray delirious with pain; Laviolette stoic in resignation; Sicot weeping with sorrow. He describes the horror of sitting in a trench as the shells fell, a comrade beside him trembling uncontrollably with fear, and his own inexplicable survival as those around him were slaughtered by a direct hit from a 210 cm shell. "I felt it at once on my neck, struck by a formidable club, and in front of me, a red and angry furnace. That is how a shell kills you. I will not move my hands to push them into my open chest; if I could bring them close to me, I would bury my two hands in the warmth of my naked viscera, if I were standing before myself, I would see my pale trachea, my lungs and my heart through my staved-in ribs. Not a movement, for pity's sake! Eyes closed, like Laviolette, and dying alone?"[12] Yet Genevoix, saved by his very proximity to the blast, did not die. "I am alive, absurdly. This no longer surprises me. Everything is absurd."[13] Genevoix would live to mourn his comrades, the incongruity of his own survival heightened by the shock of the death of his close friend, Lieutenant Porchon, whose chest was indeed caved in by a 77-cm shell as he sought aid for a minor wound at a first aid post. Porchon's death, wrote Genevoix, caused him to feel a "contraction of the soul," arousing in him "a disgusted indifference towards everything I saw, the ignominy of the mud and the misery of the corpses, the sad day on the ridge, the fierceness of the shelling [...] What sense? None of this makes any sense. On the crest of Les Éparges, the whole world dances through time a sort of demented farce, revolves around me in a hideous jiggle incomprehensible and grotesque."[14]

When it was finally withdrawn from the front line, after five days' fighting, the seventh battalion had been reduced from 220 men to eighty. Genevoix's incomprehension remained: "Why? Why my trench filled with dead; all those dead torn to pieces, eviscerated, crushed, fallen one beside the other without having fired a cartridge?"[15]

In the days that followed, Genevoix visited the graves of some of his recently killed comrades in a nearby village. Some were there, but not all. Others remained on the battlefield, sometimes identifiable, but many of them quite literally blown to pieces. Fighting in the crater of one of the mines that was exploded under the German lines on 17 February, Genevoix noted that his hand came across something "elastic and cold, a bit sticky."

12 Ibid., 608.
13 Ibid.
14 Ibid., 607–8.
15 Ibid., 620.

Realizing that it was a morsel of human flesh, he looked around him for others: "there are many, far more than I would have imagined."[16] Afterwards, he wrote, "For four days I have been spattered by earth, blood, brains. I have been slapped across the face by lumps of entrails and on the hand by a tongue, from which hung the back of the throat."[17] Each of these "little sticky things that one could gather up by reaching out a hand," he reflected, had once belonged to a living person, who possessed a name: "Desoignes? Duféal? or Moline?"[18] The earth itself, he concluded, was reduced to infertility by this mixing of its substance with human remains, "tainted by poisons, by dead flesh, incurable from our foul torture."[19]

Such was indeed the probable fate of Eugène-Emmanuel Lemercier's mortal remains, however he died: mingled with the soil of Les Éparges either to taint that soil irreparably, as Genevoix imagined or, as in his own imagination, to feed new life. He was just one of 252,900 French soldiers who "disappeared" without trace in the fighting of the First World War.[20]

HOW SOLDIERS DIED

It is appropriate to begin a consideration of the soldier's death in the First World War with the story of a soldier who died fighting at Les Éparges in 1915. The struggle for Les Éparges, as Genevoix's memoir makes clear, possessed all the essential features that became characteristic of the great battles of the Western Front: a muddy, devastated landscape, criss-crossed with trenches and barbed wire; persistent attacks in which the attacker exchanged heavy losses for little gain; and a battlefield dominated by machine guns and artillery: above all, artillery. Between February and April, the French army attacked eighteen times at Les Éparges, eventually capturing the heights, at the cost of twenty thousand men wounded or killed.[21] Later battles of the First World War would add many other ingredients to this mixture of elements, including tanks, poison gas, flamethrowers, and aircraft. Methods of using these weapons experienced major transformations during the conflict. Nevertheless, the basic features of the war were already apparent at Les Éparges. As Genevoix's memoir so powerfully illustrates, the war on the Western Front was an unequal struggle that

16 Ibid., 579.
17 Ibid., 625.
18 Ibid., 600.
19 Ibid., 605.
20 Prost, "Compter les vivants et les morts," 51.
21 Clayton, *Paths of Glory*, 63. The gains were offset by a German counter-offensive that captured ground immediately to the west of Les Éparges. See Greenhalgh, *The French Army*, 79.

pitted flesh and blood against steel and high explosive. In previous wars, two-thirds of battlefield casualties had been caused by bullets from hand-held firearms and one-third by artillery fire. During the First World War, those figures were reversed.[22] Although there were slight variations over the course of the war, with the proportion of bullet wounds rising during the mobile operations of 1918, official statistics released by the government in 1924 indicated that artillery shells accounted for 60.2 per cent of wounds, bullets for 33.9 per cent, grenades for 2.4 per cent, and edged weapons for 0.3 per cent.[23]

The statistical record reflected other significant changes in how soldiers died. Over four years of fighting, 1,357,800 men from France and its overseas territories (36,000 were from Algeria and a similar number from other regions of the French colonial empire) lost their lives, most of them on the Western Front. This was a figure similar to the total deaths suffered by the French armies over the entire course of the revolutionary and Napoleonic wars. In other words, it reflected a major escalation in the intensification of warfare by comparison with earlier conflicts. Furthermore, for the first time the vast majority of soldiers died of wounds sustained in battle, rather than of illness.[24] The death rate varied considerably from one service to another: 22.6 per cent for the infantry; 7.9 per cent for the cavalry; 6 per cent for the artillery; 6.4 per cent for the engineers; 3.4 per cent for support services.[25] These figures help to explain the resentment of the *poilus* serving in the front lines toward the *embusqués* – shirkers, including civilian and military personnel in less exposed positions – whose chances of surviving the war were so much better than their own. Although that resentment also extended to officers, particularly those of the staff and support services, many soldiers recognized that officers serving in the infantry paid a disproportionately high tax in blood: 28,870 of 100,600 officers serving in the infantry were killed, 80 per cent of all officers killed during the war.[26]

22 Hardier and Jagielski, *Combattre et mourir*, 42–3; Larcan and Ferrandis, *Le Service de Santé*, 323.

23 Prost, "Compter les vivants et les morts," 56–8. François Cochet indicates that in the Franco-Prussian war of 1870, 70 per cent of French soldiers were killed by bullets, 25 per cent by shells. In the figures he gives for the First World War the proportions were 70 per cent killed by shells, 20–30 per cent by bullets. Cochet, "Mourir au front," 36–7.

24 Antoine Prost calculates that deaths caused by illness numbered 146,629. Prost, "Compter les vivants et les morts," 53.

25 Clayton, *Paths of Glory*, 222–3.

26 Jauffret, "L'officier français," 244–5.

In short, although there were "a hundred thousand ways to die"[27] on
the Western Front, more soldiers died from artillery fire than from any
other single cause. This is not to say that they all died in similar circumstances or that they had similar deaths. Artillery came in a great variety of
shapes and sizes during the First World War, and it had many different
functions. Heavy shells filled with high explosive were designed to destroy
trench systems and penetrate underground shelters; lighter shells filled
with hundreds of shrapnel balls might be used to mow down attacking
infantry; gas shells could incapacitate enemy gunners in the preparation
of an attack; creeping or rolling barrages gave cover to attacking infantry;
trench mortars – known as *minenwerfer* or *crapouillots* – brought plunging
fire to bear from short ranges. Soldiers quickly learned to recognize the
different sounds made by different types of shell, when it was necessary to
dive for cover or to reach for a gas mask, as well as when such evasive action
was futile. There was a world of difference between the danger from artillery
on a quiet sector of the front where desultory exchanges of fire were part
of the daily ritual and the danger experienced on the battlefields of
Verdun or the Chemin des Dames, where shells fell so thick and fast that
soldiers could do no more than huddle in their trenches and wait for death.
Capable of inflicting the most terrible mutilations, this weapon did more
than any other to transform the perception of the soldier's death from one
of active heroism to passive victimhood.

What made artillery such a defining factor was its ability to bring death
literally out of the blue, making survival evidently no more than a matter
of chance. Soldiers' recollections abound with stories of men killed by
artillery fire as they were engaged in the most peaceful of occupations,
apparently oblivious to danger. Maurice Genevoix witnessed the effects of
a 77-cm shell falling in the midst of three soldiers as they sat under a tree,
quietly smoking their pipes and enjoying a game of cards. When the smoke
from the explosion had cleared, "we saw a mutilated torso, half a man
hanging in the lower branches of the tree, and in the grass, beside the
other half of this dead man – its two legs spread – a wounded man who
slowly contorted."[28] Recounting a similar incident, Émile Carlier described
how, in June 1915, he witnessed a barber shaving a soldier behind the lines
and idly thought about asking for a shave. Coming by an hour later, he
wrote, "I see all around, up in the trees, on the trunks, on the grass, what
looks like shreds of red wool. Men with shovels scrape up these remains,
gather them together and place them in a wheelbarrow." A chance shell
had blown to bits the barber and his client. Carlier could congratulate

27 Citation in Hardier and Jagielski, *Combattre et mourir*, 41.
28 Genevoix, *La mort de près*, in *Ceux de 14*, 1027.

himself on his good luck in declining to wait for a shave, but no doubt the incident only contributed to his sense that on the Western Front survival was a matter of chance and sooner or later his luck would run out.[29]

Major offensives, involving an exponential intensification of artillery fire on both sides, cruelly diminished the odds of survival. It is estimated that during the ten-month Battle of Verdun in 1916, both sides fired a total of around thirty-seven million shells.[30] Médecin-major Chabeaux of the seventy-ninth RI,[31] caring for the wounded at the Mort Homme, wrote on 9 April, "Around my aid post, I counted thirty-two large explosions in a minute, and that went on for hours. The losses are terrifying; in the Seventh Company, there are rows of dead piled two and three deep beside the C[ommand] P[ost]."[32] Carlier's description of his regiment's participation in the notorious Nivelle offensives in the region of the equally notorious Craonne plateau in April 1917, emphasized the terrible effects of the shelling: "The shrapnel explodes over our heads. The shells fall in front, behind, to right and left."[33] Soldiers were helpless, whether advancing in the open or cowering in dugouts, to defend themselves against the horrible wounds and sudden death inflicted by artillery fire. Shells that penetrated the interior of closed spaces, such as a dugout or a command post, caused horrific slaughter. "Literally, it was butchery," wrote Genevoix in describing one such occasion at Les Éparges.[34] Carlier described the effects of a 77-cm shell exploding inside a dugout occupied by over fifty men: "It was horrible! Twenty men were killed instantly, blown to bits. A bloody rain of human debris was projected, in all directions. Thirty grievously wounded men, of whom many would succumb shortly after."[35]

Machine guns and rifles were second only to artillery in their effectiveness as instruments of death. Firing bursts of two hundred bullets a minute to a range of two thousand yards, the MG 08 was the German variant of the Maxim machine gun invented by Sir Hiram Maxim in 1884. It took a heavy toll of lives as the French army painfully sought to learn the lessons of how to wage a modern, industrialized war. The vulnerability of infantry advancing in the open against dug-in infantry and machine guns was emphasized by Louis Barthas in his description of an attack involving his regiment in December 1914. Hardly had twenty men advanced into no

29 Carlier, *Mort? Pas encore!*, 27.
30 Turbergue, ed., *Les 300 jours de Verdun*, 205.
31 *Régiment d'infanterie.*
32 Ibid., 204.
33 Carlier, *Mort? Pas encore!*, 68.
34 Genevoix, *La mort de près* in *Ceux de 14*, 1028.
35 Carlier, *Mort! Pas encore!*, 78.

man's land, he said, "before one machine gun started clattering, then two, then three. Bullets started smacking the lip of the trench like hailstones, making us pull down our heads. In the squad that went ahead of us, one man was shot right through the shoulder, squirting so much blood that he was surely going to die without immediate attention. But no stretcher-bearers were in sight, and you couldn't stop your march forward to take care of even your own brother [...] Even the stupidest of us knew we were going to our deaths."[36] Like many other soldiers who experienced the early months of the war, Barthas was appalled at the disfiguring injuries caused by bullets and assumed the Germans were firing explosive ammunition. He described the death of the schoolteacher Izard – "I think that an explosive bullet has torn his guts to shreds" – and the horrific facial wounds sustained by another soldier.[37] In fact, such injuries were the effect of the high velocity of bullets fired at short range.

Major offensives against strong defensive positions often resulted in disastrous casualties for the attacker. The heaviest losses were sustained during the first six months of the war, during the phase of open warfare, before the rival armies went to ground, digging trenches for their own protection. The greatest loss suffered by any army on the Western Front occurred on 22 August 1914, during the battles of the frontiers, when 27,000 men from the French army died. By the end of November 1914, there were 454,000 dead.[38] In 1915, the bloodletting continued, with offensives at Vimy Ridge and in Champagne costing another 1.2 million casualties, 350,000 of them dead or missing. Elizabeth Greenhalgh describes the casualties of the Champagne offensive – 143,567 wounded; 62,505 dead or disappeared – as "horrendous."[39] As the French army improved its firepower and methods, offensives became less costly. Contrary to a widely held perception, 1916 and 1917 were relatively economical in lives, although these were the years of the war's longest battle, at Verdun (February to October 1916), and of the disappointing Nivelle offensives (April and May 1917), the evident futility of which resulted in widespread mutiny.[40] Only a very painful learning process and a massive increase in artillery support would enable the French army to take the offensive with

---

36 Barthas, *Poilu*, 40.
37 Ibid., 43–4.
38 Greenhalgh, *The French Army*, 59.
39 Ibid., 117.
40 The entire French army sustained losses of 391,000 dead and missing between February and November, 1915; 350,200 between February and December, 1916. In 1917, the year of least mortality, the number of dead and missing was 189,300. Doughty, *Pyrrhic Victory*, 309; Greenhalgh, *The French Army*, 250.

greater success in 1918, though the resumption of mobile operations brought with it another elevation in mortality.[41]

Like artillery, rifles and machine guns were a constant danger in the front lines even during relatively calm periods between major offensive operations. There were times and places where both sides found it convenient to suspend or attenuate hostilities. Henri Despeyrières recounted a story he had heard of German troops who ironically responded to gunshots from the French lines by waving a flag on the end of a rifle, "as if it were just target practice. If we spend the winter here together," he concluded hopefully, "I believe we will end up keeping ourselves warm together, 'Pruscos' and French."[42] More often than not, however, soldiers who were unwary enough not to keep their heads down as they went about their business were likely to attract a sniper's bullet. Gabriel Balique put down the first deaths he encountered at the front to carelessness. "Another *tirailleur* who has got himself shot down," he wrote, unsympathetically. "He was placing bags of cement on the parapet, certainly a useful activity, but for which he could have, and should have waited for darkness. A bag hastily wrapped around his head and he is dragged away, dressed like a ham, leaving behind him a red and black trail of blood."[43] Marc Bloch stated that the greatest danger for a troop establishing itself at the front was in the hours immediately following its arrival, before the men had become accustomed to the "extreme prudence" that was necessary. "The first morning, we were cruelly afflicted," he wrote. "We had two dead and one wounded, all three struck by bullets to the head." Bloch described the potentially explosive effect of bullets striking the human head: "So died L ... Half his face was hanging like a shutter with broken hinges and one could see the interior of the cranium, just about empty."[44] The fact that bullet wounds to the head were likely to be more or less instantly fatal helps to explain why the proportion of head wounds treated in hospital (15.5 per cent of all wounds) was relatively low.[45]

In comparison to firearms of one kind or another, other instruments of death caused relatively few casualties. Edged weapons caused wounds in only 6,460 recorded cases, flammable liquids in even fewer: 951.[46] Soldiers

---

41 On the three phases of mortality on the Western front, see Cochet, "Mourir au front," 28–9.

42 Lafon, ed., *C'est si triste*, 63.

43 Balique, *Saisons de guerre*, 38.

44 Bloch, *L'histoire, la guerre, la résistance*, 151.

45 By comparison, the percentage of wounds to the extremities was much higher: 31.6 per cent for the upper limbs and 35.7 per cent for the lower limbs. Larcan and Ferrandis, *Le Service de Santé*, 324.

46 Prost, "Compter les vivants et les morts," 47.

themselves mocked the bayonet as an instrument of warfare. Henri
Despeyrières claimed that one could write "a whole book" on the uses to
which a bayonet might be put: as a tent peg, chandelier, roasting spit, or
can opener. Only by accident, however, might it be used "to stick
'les Boches.'"[47] There were, however, still occasions when the *arme blanche*
had a place on the modern battlefield. Trench raids, often conducted for
intelligence purposes or simply to harass the enemy, privileged the use of
grenades, knives, and, in the words of Antoine Martin, "anything that comes
to hand. We knock them out with blows from cudgels, shovels, picks, and
sometimes, if one has a good knife, it is used to hack the skinniest ones."[48]
Many soldiers – as many perhaps as one in two – took care to furnish themselves with the psychological comfort of a trench knife. Official statistics
almost certainly underestimate the injuries inflicted by trench knives of
one sort or another, since the penetrating wounds they caused to the neck
or body often resulted in death before there was any chance of the victim
reaching a field hospital where wounds were not only treated but also
documented.[49]

It is worth pointing out that the degree of fear attached to specific
weapons was not necessarily a function of their lethality. Poison gas, a quintessentially modern weapon at the opposite extreme from the primitive,
hand-to-hand combat described by Martin, was a case in point. Although
its use became increasingly common in the final year of the war, gas in its
various forms wounded far more than it killed. Olivier Lepick estimates
that 130,000 French soldiers were affected by gas, of whom 6,100 died
(although the latter figure does not include those whose health was
permanently impaired and whose lives were abbreviated despite surviving
the war). Overall, the 17,000 deaths inflicted by gas on all armies on the
Western Front represented 0.5 per cent of the total.[50] The indiscriminate
nature of the weapon, however, the uncertainty as to whether one might
unknowingly have already inhaled a fatal dose, as well as the prospect of
an agonizing, lingering death, all served to heighten anxiety. According
to Tuffrau, soldiers had nicknamed gas shells, "which explode noiselessly,
have no odour, but which can be fatal," "*roulette* shells." On 5 March 1917,
he noted that there had been "many cases yesterday" because of soldiers

47 Lafon, ed., *C'est si triste*, 108.
48 Martin, *La chasse à l'homme*, 95–6.
49 On the ubiquity of trench knives see the revealing analysis provided by Audoin-
Rouzeau, *Les armes et la chair*, 57–97. François Cochet argues, on the other hand, that the
use of trench knives has been greatly exaggerated. In the trenches, he says, "the true queen
was certainly the grenade." Cochet, "Mourir au front," 37.
50 Lepick, *La grande guerre chimique*, 315–19.

failing to appreciate the danger. "One man refused to put on his mask, under the pretext that he could smell nothing. Suddenly, vertigo, froth, foam, blackened face. He goes stiff, he dies."[51] Many deaths caused by gas were far less kind. Victims of phosgene gas slowly drowned in the mucus produced by their own lungs, coughing up as much as two litres of bloody liquid every hour for up to forty-eight hours, until they no longer had the strength to do so. The effects of phosgene poisoning were often delayed. Fifty-nine men of the Thirteenth Dragoons died as a result of a phosgene attack on the night of 27 October 1915: twenty-eight on the day of the attack, twenty the following day, and eight the day after that. The fifty-ninth victim died on 10 November, fourteen days after the event.[52] The introduction of mustard gas – known to the French as "ypérite" after Ypres, the location where it was first used – in the summer of 1917 added a new dimension to gas warfare, which also became increasingly sophisticated through the development of new delivery systems as well as countermeasures: above all gas masks of one type or another. Although mustard gas incapacitated far more than it killed – only 2.4 per cent of those it afflicted died – this colourless, virtually odourless gas contaminated places and things for a long time after its use, lying in wait for the unwary in low-lying ground. It attacked the mucous membranes and damp patches of skin, raising enormous blisters and causing temporary blindness, which in some cases became permanent.[53]

Despite its relative infrequency, a death caused by gas was undoubtedly to be feared. Paul Voivenel, a specialist in treating gas cases, described the suffering of the patients he treated during Easter 1917 at his ambulance at Dieulouard in the Moselle valley. "Eyes convulsed, chests heaving," most of them he said "were purplish and their neck vessels seemed ready to burst. Their lucid minds witnessed the death of their bodies." The lucky ones, he said, became delirious.[54] The relative infrequency of such deaths did not make them any the less terrifying. Lucien Laby recorded in his notebooks his struggle to master the fear caused by his first experience of a gas alert: "I started to tremble: a nervous, idiotic trembling, which I fought

---

51 Tuffrau, *1914–1918*, 144.

52 Audoin-Rouzeau, *Les armes et la chair*, 122. These fifty-nine deaths as the result of a single day's action represented nearly half the total fatalities (127) sustained by the regiment throughout the war. As Audoin-Rouzeau demonstrates, for the Thirteenth Dragoons, the potency of gas as an agent of death was self-evident. The experience of the regiment, in which twelve of the fifty-nine dead were junior or non-commissioned officers, illustrates the significantly higher mortality of men serving in these ranks.

53 Ibid., 133.

54 Voivenel and Martin, *La guerre des gaz*, 92.

against with all my strength, but in vain."[55] A trench newspaper recounting a gas attack in March 1917 rated this as the worst experience the war had to offer: "We have seen everything: mines, shells, tear gas [...] the most frightful wounds and the most murderous avalanches of iron, but none of this is comparable to this fog [of gas] which, for hours as long as centuries, veiled from our eyes the brightness of the sun, the light of day, the white purity of the snow."[56]

Another omnipresent, invisible terror that plagued soldiers in the front lines was caused by underground mining. Roland Dorgelès provided an unforgettable description of the terrors generated in the minds of soldiers by the sound of the enemy digging in their vicinity. In *Les croix de bois*, he described a squad of men who, over three days in a strongpoint on the aptly named "Mount Calvary," were driven nearly mad as they listened to the regular sound of an enemy pickaxe, knowing that its cessation would be the prelude to their extinction. "In closing your eyes, you could imagine those ignoble photographs from the illustrated papers, those gaping craters with rubble, iron, and bits of men sticking out, half buried."[57]

As the example of gas victims cited above illustrates, dying did not end on the battlefield. It continued in the communication trenches as the wounded were laboriously moved to aid posts. And it continued in the aid posts. The notebooks of Lucien Laby, who served as a regimental doctor in the front lines, provide a graphic account of aid stations overflowing with terribly wounded men. His entry for 23 May 1916, during an offensive at Verdun, is not untypical:

The wounded accumulate, so difficult is it to evacuate them over the slopes during the artillery fire. One of my stretcher bearers, Sandrin, is blown to pieces: nothing is to be found but a red mud: he was just back from leave, the poor kid! – Another, a hairdresser, is gathered up in a tent canvas from which emerge his intestines which are hanging out: I will never forget his cries of pain and his look of damnation. There are thirty wounded outside my aid post, all lying down: those who can crawl have left on their own. The lightly wounded serve as stretcher bearers whose limitless devotion cannot compensate for their numerical insufficiency. German prisoners and even the wounded also carry the stretchers: one of them, his thorax penetrated

55 Laby, *Les carnets de l'aspirant Laby*, 141.
56 *Le Filon*, 20 March 1917. Cited in Audoin-Rouzeau, *Les armes et la chair*, 135.
57 Dorgelès, *Les croix de bois*, 148.

from one side to the other by a bayonet, is a great help for carrying the poor buggers who have been moaning here for two or three days and as many nights.[58]

Laby's notebooks unsparingly describe the terrible wounds men sustained, the courage with which they endured them, as well as the impossibility of giving effective care. "Quite simply, it is appalling. I do my best, but what powerlessness!"[59]

The soldiers' suffering continued in the automobiles that carried them onwards to mobile surgical units – *autochirs* – as well as in the trains and hospitals to the rear. Georges Duhamel served as a surgeon throughout the war and in this role was deeply implicated in the life-and-death struggles of the men who came into his care. While his writings bear witness to the remarkable efforts made after 1914 to make surgical intervention more rapid and effective, his soldier patients often presented such severe wounds that there was little he could do beyond offer a measure of comfort or relief from pain. At Verdun, he wrote, some men had thirty or forty wounds.[60] At Sapicourt, Artois, in 1915, after five men were brought in to his ambulance badly wounded by splinters from a 210 cm shell, Duhamel wrote to his wife, Blanche, "Most of the people who are brought to us are so gravely wounded that we are powerless."[61] Previously, he was greatly affected by the resigned courage of a mortally wounded territorial who, on the operating table, said simply, "Put me to sleep and for always – And tell my wife and four children that my last thought was for them." "We all had tears in our eyes," wrote Duhamel.[62] Other deaths witnessed by the surgeon, however, did not come so quickly or with such lucidity. In *La vie des martyrs*, first published in 1917, Duhamel recounted the death of Carré, who died after five months of agonizing surgeries, including the amputation of both legs, his wasted body tormented by abscesses and bedsores, his great courage likewise depleted.[63] He also told the story of Madelan, who spent his final days in an incoherent delirium, beyond all human communication: "He no longer needed us or anyone; he no longer ate, no longer drank, and fouled himself like an animal, demanding neither help nor care."[64] The soldier's death, as Duhamel saw it, was not heroic, at least

58 Laby, *Les carnets de l'aspirant Laby*, 177.
59 Ibid.
60 Duhamel, *Vie des martyrs*, 100–1.
61 Duhamel and Duhamel, *Correspondance de guerre*, vol. 1, 402.
62 Ibid., 386. See also Duhamel, *Vie des martyrs*, 36.
63 Ibid., 25–32.
64 Ibid., 153–4.

not in the conventional sense of the word. "I had never seen anything so ugly or so bestial," he wrote, in describing the death of Lieutenant Dauche, caused by an inoperable shrapnel wound to the head.[65] Nor was there anything ordinarily heroic about the death of Fumat, reflected Duhamel, as he carried the large Auvergnat's body to the hospital's funeral chapel. After all, he had not died in combat; he had been mortally wounded while preparing the fire for soup. He had uttered no heroic words. "You are not a hero, Fumat!" wrote Duhamel, "You are only a martyr."[66] The prevailing sentiment conveyed by all these dying men, said Duhamel, was sadness. In a letter to Blanche, he wrote, "Since I have seen men die in war, I have never seen one die joyously, as the newspapers say. They die sad and they accept death all the same. That to me is much greater."[67]

Duhamel conceived of *La vie des martyrs* as a work of conciliation, appealing at the book's end for unity.[68] Understandably, he did not dwell on the shortcomings of the medical services or on institutional or personal conflicts that adversely affected the care of the wounded. Nevertheless, his correspondence with Blanche and his later autobiography indicate that he was painfully aware that these problems could at times be a matter of life and death. At the beginning of the war, the established medical theory, enshrined in the surgical instructions issued by Inspector-General Delorme, was that surgical intervention should be deferred if possible until the wounded soldier had been moved by train to a hospital in the interior. Duhamel later commented acerbically on these instructions that they "seemed to envisage a clean, correct war, comprising a great majority of aseptic, more-or-less conventional wounds [...] But we were very soon in the presence of barbarous wounds, monstrous states of dilapidation, infections, gangrenes, complex fractures, gaping joints."[69] Without prompt surgical intervention, such wounds rapidly developed gas gangrene and became fatal. Under the pressure of circumstance, surgical practice underwent a swift reversal. Delorme himself recognized the need for change and, beginning in 1915, mobile field hospitals such as those in which Duhamel operated ensured prompt surgical treatment as close to the front as possible. Surgical techniques and methods of care underwent constant improvement. Duhamel himself wrote of the almost "religious excitement" inspired when his *autochir* attempted its first blood transfusion

65 Ibid., 240.
66 Ibid., 165.
67 Duhamel and Duhamel, *Correspondance de guerre*, vol. 1, 1071.
68 On this theme, see his letter to Blanche of 4 June 1916. Duhamel and Duhamel, *Correspondance de guerre*, vol. 1, 1071.
69 Duhamel, *La pesée des âmes*, 45.

in October 1917.[70] The French medical service developed into one that was at least the equal of those of its allies. In the meantime, men died.

The situation was worst at the beginning of the war, during the phase of mobile operations when casualties were at their peak and medical evacuations at their nadir. Albert Bessières, who served on medical trains, described the desperate plight of wounded men who spent days confined in goods wagons and cattle cars in the late summer heat while their wounds festered and their throats parched. At Saint-Florentin, well behind the front during the Battle of the Marne, Bessières witnessed trainloads of wounded begging to be released from their captivity or to receive water. Flouting his orders, Bessières helped a *chasseur* with a gangrenous thigh wound off the train, although all he could do for him was to splash a little iodine into the wound. The chasseur had already spent two days on the train without medical attention.[71] By the time such men reached a hospital they were often beyond saving. Lucia Tichadou was a nurse at Brienne-le-Château during the Battle of the Marne. The hospital amphitheatre became a charnel house, she wrote in her diary on 11 September, replenished with twenty new bodies as those who died were carted off under straw to be buried in mass graves: "there is no time to make coffins." In the wards, the wounded were accommodated on mattresses placed on the floor between beds: "Gas gangrene spreads, passing from bed to bed," she wrote: "Still, you can't refuse a bed in which to die to the poor devils who have only a few hours left to them. One face succeeds another in the beds, one hardly has time to get to know them. We undress, bandage, close the eyes, a cloth over the face, a melancholy package, and then clean sheets for another poor wretch. I had six deaths on the same night in my room."[72] The rushed notation of Tichadou's diary reflects the pressure under which she worked and the impossibility of providing even minimal care to the dying. She later wrote of her indignation at a doctor who accused her of disrupting service by doting excessively on the wounded. She responded that the men in her care were not just numbers, that she would help them to the limit of her time and strength, and "that I would replace as far as possible the absent family."[73] Her diary bears witness to the impossible position of nurses as they sought to preserve the conventions surrounding death and dying amid mass death on an unprecedented scale.[74]

70 Duhamel and Duhamel, *Correspondance de guerre*, vol. 2, 657.

71 Bessières, *Le train rouge*, 35.

72 Tichadou, *Infirmière en 1914*, 74–5.

73 Ibid., 81.

74 On this theme with respect to British nurses, see Kelly, "Can One Grow Used to Death?," 329–49.

In the early months of the war, not just gas gangrene, but also tetanus and typhoid fever caused soldiers to lose their lives. Until the arrival at Brienne of a Dr Dreyfus, who had experience from the Balkan wars, all the patients with gas gangrene died, according to Tichadou, regardless of amputations. Dr Dreyfus introduced a method of performing two amputations – one immediately and another several days later – which began to save lives, if not limbs.[75] Eventually, all soldiers would be inoculated against typhoid and every wounded soldier would, in principle at least, receive an anti-tetanus injection. In September 1914, however, the most distressing cases for Lucia Tichadou were men infected by tetanus. She wrote of the terrible double guilt she felt at the thought she might herself have been responsible for transmitting the tetanus bacillus that killed Julien Montagne, who died on 26 September, and at her inability even to care for him during his last hours. "I am afraid of those eyes that follow me, that expect help from me. I can no longer do anything, not even spoil him like the others; if I want to care for the others and avoid contagion, I must approach him as little as possible. The doctor forbids me to touch the bandages. He is bathed in blood and still he calls me, begs me to change him, sees himself neglected, despairs, asks me how much time he has before he will die."[76] Tichadou, who found she could assist at operations with perfect equanimity, could not face Julien Montagne as, on the eve of his death, he was removed to an isolation ward. "I hid myself in order not to have to give him explanations," she wrote on 27 September: "He died yesterday, neck stiff and crooked, mouth open; a failure."[77]

There were other failures, particularly but not only at the beginning of the war. Georges Duhamel, appalled by his field hospital's erratic and domineering head surgeon, Dr Marcille, wrote despairingly to Blanche in November 1914, saying that the wounded were dying "like flies. It is depressing, abominable, and often due, alas, to recklessness on the part of the surgeon."[78] Marcille's methods, he wrote, "have caused the deaths of a large number of soldiers."[79] Conflicts between surgeons, aggravated by the fact that military rank was often not commensurate with surgical expertise, sometimes had fatal consequences. Claudine Bourcier, who nursed at a hospital established in the Casino at Biarritz, attributed several cases of

75 Tichadou, *Infirmière en 1914*, 78.
76 Ibid., 86.
77 Ibid., 88.
78 Duhamel and Duhamel, *Correspondance de guerre*, vol. 1, 100. On this subject, see also Duhamel, *La pesée des âmes*, 53–69; and Larcan and Ferrandis, *Le Service de Santé*, 137–41.
79 Duhamel and Duhamel, *Correspondance de guerre*, vol. 1, 101.

serious neglect resulting in death to conflict between civil and military surgeons. She later recounted in shocking detail the botched, belated, and futile operation – the patient woke up in the middle owing to an ineffective anaesthetic – that failed to save the life of an adjutant whose chest wound had, over many weeks of inattention, been allowed to develop gangrene. Bourcier was powerless to save the adjutant's life, but she fought and won a determined battle with her head nurse to be allowed to comfort him as he died. Interestingly, according to her account, he preferred her presence to that of his own mother, who he feared would not allow him to die peacefully: "She will throw herself on my body and will afflict me by preventing me from departing the earth."[80] "The poor mother," concluded Bourcier, "always believed her son had received all necessary care."[81]

For all these individual tragedies and institutional shortcomings, wounded men who were admitted to hospital had a far greater chance of survival than in earlier wars. Of the 2,754,724 such men for whom complete records exist, 48,981 died. Many of those who survived were physically or mentally disabled: 93,586 were amputees.[82] All the same, the fact that relatively few soldiers died of illness or wounds (approximately 200,000 all told) while in the care of the *service sanitaire* bears witness to the enormous effort and achievement of the fifteen thousand doctors and 100,000 nurses who provided their care.

Not all men died because of enemy action, either on the battlefield or in hospital. Some died as the result of accidents, wrongly identified as enemy soldiers in the confusion of battle. Others took their own lives, victims of the misery, isolation, and fear that had become too great a burden to bear. Paul Tuffrau's account of one such death, that of a soldier from the 289th RI who used his own rifle to blow his brains out, makes it clear that soldiers who lacked strong emotional support at home were particularly vulnerable. The soldier left letters behind which, in the form of Tuffrau's paraphrase, indicated that "he did not wish to die like a soldier" because he did not want his wife, "who made him suffer so much," to be eligible for a widow's pension.[83]

There were less drastic ways for those who had reached the end of their rope to seek escape than by taking their own lives. Running away, refusing to obey orders, or causing self-inflicted wounds were all ways out for those who could take the strain no longer. These avenues of escape carried their own risk of death, however, since the army sought to maintain discipline

80 Bourcier, *Nos chers blessés*, 34.
81 Ibid., 35.
82 Prost, "Compter les vivants et les morts," 47.
83 Tuffrau, *1914–1918*, 128.

through exemplary executions. The French army carried out approximately 600 judicial executions during the war, 430 of them before the end of 1915.[84] There were, however, many more soldiers who were shot by their officers without benefit of trial. General Blanc, for example, in command of the seventy-third regiment of colonial *tirailleurs*, admitted that he used his revolver to shoot twelve men as they fled in the face of the enemy on 23 September 1914.[85] Another example of an extrajudicial execution was recounted in a letter by the soldier Waterlot, one of six men whom General Boutegourd, Commandant of the Fifty-First Division, had shot without trial and without explanation following a retreat on 6 September 1914. Waterlot, remarkably, survived the execution, since the firing squad missed him with its volley and the lieutenant called upon to administer the *coup de grâce* found the task too repugnant. Waterlot lay still for a couple of hours, during which time he discovered that one other victim had survived, albeit with a broken leg. He then crept away to rejoin his regiment.[86]

Even soldiers who had the benefit of trial by either a regular or a special council of war were often just as puzzled as Waterlot evidently was concerning the reasons for their execution. Corporal Floch was one of six men from the 298th regiment who were executed at Vingré on 4 December 1914 for abandoning their position on 27 November. Having been captured in a surprise trench raid by the Germans, two squads of the regiment had freed themselves and fled along a communication trench. Despite reoccupying their position, twenty-four men were eventually tried. In his final letter to his wife Lucie, Corporal Floch wrote:

Twenty-four of us were brought before the council of war yesterday evening. Six of them, including me, were condemned to death. I am no more guilty than the others, but an example is needed. My wallet and its contents will come to you. I say my goodbyes to you in haste, tears in my eyes, my soul in pain. I humbly beg of you, on my knees, pardon for all the pain I am going to cause you and the predicament in which I will place you [...] My little Lucie, once again, I'm sorry. I will say my confession, right away, and hope to see you in a better world. I am innocent of the crime of which I am accused of abandoning my post. If, instead of escaping the Germans, I had remained their prisoner, my life would have been saved. Such is fate. My last thought; yours to the end."[87]

84 Bach, *Fusillés pour l'exemple*, 589–90.
85 Ibid., 319, 390–1.
86 Ibid., 247–8.
87 Hardier and Jagielski, *Combattre et mourir*, 79–80.

As was generally the case until June 1915, the executions were conducted as a spectacle calculated to make the most of their exemplary effect. Corporal Floche and his comrades were escorted by a picket of fifty men to a crossroads between Vingré and Noyon. There, seven companies from three regiments witnessed the executions, which occurred "without incident." The troops then paraded before the bodies and returned to their barracks.[88]

"A FINE DEATH": PATRIOTIC AND RELIGIOUS REPRESENTATIONS

These descriptions of how French soldiers died in the First World War, whether on the battlefield, in hospital, or before a firing squad, were not how the soldier's death was supposed to be: not, at least, in the representations that prevailed in France before 1914. Nationalist writers like Maurice Barrès, Charles Péguy, and Ernest Psichari exalted the soldier's death in the service of the nation as a moment of physical and spiritual perfection. "One would have thought he was going to meet his fiancée [...] already transfigured by joy," wrote Psichari in describing the death of Viollet, a 28-year-old French officer shot down as he spurred his mount forward against North African tribesmen in 1909. To Psichari, the lieutenant's death was a moment of perfection: "It is the culmination of a fine life, entirely devoted to action and yearning for self-immolation, of a fine, straight life, without deviations, unadorned, where there is nothing superfluous and nothing to add."[89] It was only logical that when Psichari himself died in battle, on 27 August 1914, Maurice Barrès should exalt his death in similar terms, as a willing and glorious sacrifice. "Our children," he wrote in *L'Echo de France*, addressing himself to Psichari's father, "went to save France, and yours, among them, leaping into death, put himself in the first rank, adding further to the glory of your illustrious family."[90]

The image of the soldier willingly, even joyfully, sacrificing his life for the *patrie* remained a staple of the patriotic press after 1914. The mass-circulation weekly *L'Illustration* published a drawing by Lucien Jonas in December 1914, entitled *The Death of a Soldier*, which was also published as a postcard (fig. 6.1). A lengthy caption described the drawing. The French soldier has participated in an attack that has overrun a German battery, capturing the guns and killing the enemy gunners. Mortally wounded,

88 Ibid., 80.

89 Psichari, *Les voix qui crient*, 217–18. Cited in Dufour, "Le sacrifice du soldat dans la littérature," 186.

90 *Écho de Paris*, 13 November 1914.

D'après l'illustration.   L Jonas

LA MORT D'UN SOLDAT.
« …Rassemblant ses dernières forces il a pu s'adosser
à un caisson et prendre dans sa capote une feuille de papier
Il écrit sa dernière pensée : «Je souffre… je suis seul…
adieu, mère ; adieu, ma femme et mes enfants chéris… Vive la France!…»

6.1. Postcard. *The Death of a Soldier.* L. Jonas.

though apparently unblemished, he sits with his back against a gun carriage, penning a last message to his loved ones. His final words, after saying goodbye to mother, wife, and children, are "Vive la France!" At the "supreme moment" of death, said the caption, "our children and our brothers [...] do not measure the cost of their sacrifice. They have done their duty and this sentiment brings them back to the time of departure, to the farewells of mobilization. They find themselves within their family, beside the loved ones who constituted their lives' happiness. And the same words come to mind: 'Adieu! ... Vive la France!'"[91] In this representation, the soldier's death became a homecoming, bringing him back in his final moments to the bosom of family and homeland. Numerous postcards illustrated this theme, representing the fallen soldier, peaceful in death, receiving his mother's kiss or being elevated to his immortal reward by buxom allegorical figures. *L'Illustration* also published an article by Henri Lavedan in honour of All Saints' Day – the Day of the Dead – on 30 October 1915, which denied that French soldiers went to their deaths in fear or sorrow. Rather, he said, they went "smiling and serene [...] proud and happy, regretting nothing, repeating a hundred times their 'pleasure' at such a death and declaring themselves favoured by destiny's choice. Not a single one, however painful his final moments, ever uttered a cry of despair, a bitter word."[92]

These idealized representations of the soldier's death had remarkable staying power, despite the realities that belied them. Nor was it just the patriotic press with its *bourrage de crâne*[93] that perpetuated such images. Soldiers themselves, in paying tribute to their fallen comrades, resorted to the same patriotic discourse. Émile Carlier, as we have seen, wrote frankly of the horrors he witnessed. But he also wrote admiringly of the death of his friend, Captain Roger Billiet, whom he described as belonging to "the race of officers without fear and without reproach," determined to share the same dangers as his men. "He stood at the door of his command post, impressing all by his coolness and his courage. What was bound to happen happened. Struck full in the heart by a shell fragment, Roger Billiet died bravely as he had lived, faithful to the principles and teachings he had received from childhood and which are summed up in a single word: Duty!"[94] Just as soldiers eulogized their officers, so the latter paid tribute to their men. Abel Fleury commanded a unit reduced from forty-eight men to twenty-two in an attack in October 1914. Fleury stated his admiration for "the fine spirit of the soldier! Not one gave way, hesitated,

91 *L'Illustration*, 12 December 1914,
92 Henri Lavedan, "La journée des morts," *L'Illustration*, 30 October 1915.
93 A term for propaganda.
94 Carlier, *Mort! Pas encore!*, 42.

or trembled. A wounded corporal asks me to loosen his belt: 'Go on, go on,' he said, 'the others need you.' Then, with a little red froth on his lips, he expired."[95]

Some of these heroic descriptions appear ironic, so seemingly foolhardy or futile were the actions they described. Captain Paul Rimbault described the death of his comrade Lieutenant Quinquet thus: "He was a brave man, having, unhappily for him, poor eyesight [...] My brilliant comrade was sublime in the attack. Having lost his pince-nez, he fell, without knowing it, on a German machine gun. This unexpected sight interrupted neither his elan nor his cries of victory; but soon the infernal machine ripped him to pieces."[96] Similarly, Émile Carlier described the death of Sergeant Lamy at the Battle of the Somme as a mismatch between courageous but frail humanity and the remorseless power of the machinery of war. Unable to persuade his men to leave their trench under enemy fire, Lamy clambered alone onto the parapet to give them encouragement by demonstrating how little danger there was: "the poor kid was cut down instantly."[97] Nevertheless, neither Rimbault nor Carlier intended any mockery of their comrades' behaviour in these descriptions. Rather, they sought to pay tribute to a courage that defied insurmountable odds.

Trench newspapers, which were written by soldiers for other soldiers to read and were often a vehicle for irreverent humour, nonetheless frequently included tributes to the dead that were solemnly un-ironic affirmations of honour and duty: "Colonel Bessan had a death worthy of the valiant soldier he always was," stated a letter in the *Echo des Guitounes*. "He fell, struck full in the chest, at the moment when he raised himself to his full height on the parapet of the enemy trench they had just taken to cry his affection and gratitude to his brave Regiment. He died without suffering, in our midst. He rests now in a little cemetery, sheltered from the enemy's insults; because we wanted this brave man to have the burial he deserved."[98] Such was a "good death," as it was imagined by the *poilus* themselves: quick, relatively painless, in the face of the enemy, in full view of one's comrades, the body respectfully buried.

For Catholic writers like Psichari and Péguy, the death of the soldier was idealized as a Christ-like sacrifice, an act that purified both the martyred soldier and the nation for which he gave his life. "If we believe in the purity of the blood poured out at Calvary," wrote Psichari, "how could we not believe, by the same logic, in the virtue of the blood spilled for the

95 Ferry, *Carnets secrets*, 131.
96 Rimbault, *Journal de campagne*, 36–7.
97 Carlier, *Mort? Pas encore!*, 39.
98 *L'Écho des Guitounes*, 10 November 1915.

homeland?"[99] This ideal also survived into the war years and beyond. Reflected from the beginning of the war in the idea of the *union sacrée* which united Catholics and republicans against the common enemy, it was expressed in visual media, as in a postcard representing the figure of Christ appearing on the battlefield to take the hand of a dying soldier. The idea of the soldier's death as a Christ-like sacrifice was given particularly fervent expression in the writings of Catholic priests who served at the front in a variety of roles, most notably as chaplains and stretcher bearers. Soldiers paid tribute to the courage of chaplains who scorned their own safety to minister to the men in the front lines. A number of these soldier-priests wrote of their experiences in the war, commonly insisting upon the patriotic and religious devotion of the French soldier. Jean-Norton Cru's verdict on the two books written by Georges-Maurice Ardant under the pseudonym Jean Limosin was that "One encounters only the religion of the catechism and a limitless optimism. According to Limosin the soldiers are extraordinarily pious; he accumulates accounts of masses, religious gatherings, edifying deaths."[100] Edifying deaths were certainly the stock-in-trade of Chanoine Payen, who published his *journal de route* in 1924. After recounting in glowing terms the "miracle" of the Marne, Payen described a *tableau vivant* he encountered in a cemetery, where, at the foot of the cross, lay the body of a young soldier who, his arms crossed and his eyes raised to heaven, represented all those who had died "on the field of honour, all the humble redeemers of France, uniting his sacrifice to the sacrifice of the Redeemer of the world."[101] Payen insisted that religious faith was the most important force sustaining the soldier's courage and that the blessing of the chaplain allowed the wounded soldier to die in peace. "What the chaplain represents to the wounded soldiers," wrote Payen, "is the village steeple, the family. One of them said to me: 'I see in you my father, my mother, my brothers, my sisters.' Then his eyes fixed themselves on me, a smile crossed his trembling lips, he added, 'For all of them, please Padre, kiss me!'"[102] Albert Bessières, whose memoir, *Le train rouge*, provided an account of his service as chaplain on a medical train, also recounted "edifying deaths" which emphasized "that spirit of sacrifice, that taste for action, that patriotic faith" which he claimed animated French youth.[103]

---

99 Psichari, *Les voix qui crient*, 189.
100 Cru, *Témoins*, 178.
101 Payen, *L'âme du poilu*, vol. 1, 71.
102 Ibid., 162.
103 Ibid., 210. On the ubiquity and potency of Catholic ideas of sacrifice in French nationalism at the time of the First World War, see Strenski, *Contesting Sacrifice*, 52–79.

SOLDIERS' STORIES: HORROR, FUTILITY, SACRIFICE

Despite their perpetuation, even in the writings of soldiers themselves, conventional religious and patriotic images of the soldier's death came under increasing criticism. Although Émile Carlier provided heroic narratives describing the deaths of his officers, he was also critical of civilians for failing to appreciate the sufferings of the infantry. A letter to his aunt written during the Battle of the Somme spared her of any illusions: "And what a spectacle! What horrendous visions that will never be erased from my memory. One night driven by hunger, I approached what I thought was the pack of a dead man. Horror! It was the trunk of a man cut clean across the waist, the arms and head torn off."[104] Carlier's subsequent words indicate that he approached what he saw as his inevitable death with anything but joy. "Nearly all my friends have fallen. Deprived of the affection of my wife, my children, my family, I felt some moral comfort from being in the company of good comrades with whom I was happy to share a full and complete community of ideas. One by one I have seen them disappear. Every day I feel more and more alone. I had six cousins in our regiment. Five are dead and the sixth has been taken prisoner. After what I have seen, the dangers to which we have been exposed and which await us, the considerable losses we have suffered, I have abandoned all hope of ever seeing my family again."[105] In words like these, a new vision of the soldier's death was beginning to emerge: a vision that was filled with horror and despair.

As is already evident from the notebooks of Émile Carlier, there was considerable variety in the attitudes soldiers expressed toward death and the ways in which they represented it. Soldiers' representations varied depending upon when they wrote, to whom and for what purpose. Marc Bloch, in writing letters of condolence following the death of a corporal in his unit, wrote very different accounts of how he died to the corporal's sister and to one of his comrades who had also served at the front, taking care to spare the sister any potentially distressing details.[106] In his 1930 novel *La peur* Gabriel Chevalier transcribed a letter which he said was typical of those written by soldiers during the war, filled with comforting illusions for the home front: "there is nothing true therein, nothing profoundly true [...] For those back at home we produce correspondence full of convenient lies [...] We recount to them *their* war, the one that will give them satisfaction, and we keep ours secret [...] To all the concessions

104 Carlier, *Mort? Pas encore!*, 149.
105 Ibid.
106 Bloch, *L'histoire, la guerre, la résistance*, 244–5.

we have made to the war, we add that of our sincerity."[107] Soldiers' perceptions and representations, like those of Chevalier himself, changed over time. Even during the war, as Pierre Chaine wrote, soldiers' perceptions depended upon circumstance: "An anonymous stretcher covered with a sheet, if it is encountered when one is going up to the line in a bad area, strikes the imagination more than the human debris one tramples underfoot upon being relieved when each finds in his own existence sufficient reason for optimism."[108] Despite the enormous casualties of the first five months of the war, it was psychologically easier to believe that deaths were to some purpose during the German invasion, before the front had stabilized, than later, when casualties were lower but their necessity less apparent and the end of the war harder to imagine. Many soldiers, particularly when writing to female relatives, sought to offer reassurance by making light of or simply omitting the dangers they confronted or the deaths they witnessed. Marcellin Prosper Floirac, a forty-year-old peasant from Quércy who was killed on 16 February 1915, was one of these. In relating to his wife an engagement in December 1914 in which his battalion had lost eight of nine officers and 295 men, eighty-two of them killed, Floirac commented only on the intensity of the French bombardment and enjoined her to place her trust in God. He made no mention of the casualties.[109] Similarly, Henri Despeyrières, in describing for his parents his baptism of fire in August 1914, sought to put their minds at rest: "I can tell you that the German shells are not very terrible. They do little harm and many of them do not even explode."[110] Subsequently, he assured them that although his regiment had suffered heavy losses in an offensive, there had been relatively few deaths. "Don't be too worried about me," he wrote. "By keeping cool one usually keeps out of trouble. I am always calm under fire, while those who flee are hit most often."[111] Despeyrières's journal, which for the time being he kept to himself, indicates that his private thoughts were less sanguine. "It is so sad to die at the age of twenty!,"[112] he wrote on 4 August, adding that he belonged to a sacrificed generation.

107 Chevalier, *La peur*, 335–6. On the lack of transparency in soldiers' correspondence, see Lyons, "French Soldiers " 79–95; Horne, "Soldiers, Civilians and the Warfare of Attrition," 223–49; and Baconnier, Minet, and Soler, "Quarante millions de témoins," 141–69.

108 Chaine, *Les mémoires d'un rat*, 16–17.

109 Floirac, *Vie et mort d'un fantassin*, 72; SHD, AG: Armée de Terre: 26 N 714/6, 207e régiment d'infanterie: J.M.O. 20 December 1914, accessed 19 April 2016, http://www.memoiredeshommes.sga.defense.gouv.fr/fr/arkotheque/inventaires/ead_ir_consult.php?&ref=SHDGR__GR_26_N_II.

110 Lafon, ed., *C'est si triste*, 40.

111 Ibid., 44.

112 Ibid., 81.

Subsequent letters became increasingly grim and despairing, as the war developed into one of deadly attrition and as their author lost his reticence. Following a costly offensive in June 1915, when his regiment had failed to hold the enemy trenches they had briefly occupied, he wrote to his mother, saying that "it is revolting to see how uselessly they cause poor little soldiers to be killed."[113] Already, Despeyrières was of the opinion that the best thing France could do was to make peace at any cost. The soldier who had been so determined to do his duty in August 1914, wrote after returning from the front in May 1915: "like my pals, I marched under duress."[114]

The letters of Marcel Papillon were similarly forthright in their denunciation of the war. On 25 September 1914, he wrote to his parents saying his regiment had lost at least a third of its strength in the Battle of Limey-Lironville and "I really believed I would never see you again." The words he used to describe the battle were "carnage" and "hecatomb."[115] On 25 January 1915, his summary of an engagement at Bois-le-Prêtre in which repeated German counter-offensives had been driven back, ended with the words, "What is happening at the moment is not a war: it is an extermination of men."[116] By 13 April, he had reached the depths of despair. "We have had a terrible week," he wrote. "It is shameful, frightful; it is impossible to imagine such carnage. We will never get through this hell. The dead cover the ground. Germans and French are piled upon one another, in the mud [...] Let those who want the war come and fight it, I've had a bellyful and I'm not the only one."[117] By the spring of 1915, Marcel Papillon, like Henri Despeyrières, clearly perceived the soldier's death as a pointless slaughter. Many others, if they did not already do so, would come to share their view, expressing a rejection of the war that animated the mutinies of 1917.[118] Maurice Pensuet, responding in September 1916 to his father's hope that in a month's time the Germans would have been ejected from France, responded despairingly, "In 1920 perhaps and even then not for certain."[119]

Not all soldiers, by any means, consistently felt or expressed such disaffection. Censors' reports indicate that the soldiers' sense that there was an

113 Ibid., 237.
114 Ibid., 227.
115 Papillon et al., "*Si je reviens*," 39.
116 Ibid., 81.
117 Ibid., 124.
118 On the evolution of soldiers' attitudes, see Hardier and Jagielski, *Combattre et mourir*, 125–35. The 1917 mutinies remain controversial. André Loez makes a strong case that they represented, not just dissatisfaction with how the war was being conducted, but a rejection of the war itself. See Loez, *14–18, les refus de la guerre*; see also Rolland, *La grève des tranchées*.
119 Pensuet, *Écrit du front: Lettres*, 253.

intolerable imbalance between the sacrifices demanded and the results achieved culminated following the Nivelle offensives of April 1917.[120] Many soldiers, even as they acknowledged the appalling nature of the war and the colossal scale of the bloodletting, refused to abandon their faith, whether that faith lay in God, nation, duty, or something else. Paul Tuffrau, for example, recorded vivid impressions of the horrors of the battlefield – "It is the most awful spectacle of destruction I have seen" – but he also wrote in his notebook on 28 May 1915 that his experiences had made his love of the *patrie* stronger than ever: "We will love it [the homeland] because we are creating it," he wrote. "Because we are making it by our bereavements, our sacrifices. It is made from our flesh and blood."[121] Paul Rimbault, too, although he railed against the popular images of war "with which one amuses children and distorts their understanding" insisted that he did so only because "by castigating these false glories [...] implicitly, I raise an altar to modest duty."[122] Henri Barbusse, the most famous of French soldier-writers, may not have shared precisely the same values as Tuffrau or Rimbault, putting his faith in socialism and anti-militarism rather than in the nation, but he certainly shared the former's view that the soldier's death was a redemptive sacrifice. This is clearly symbolized by a muddied and bloodied soldier in the final pages of *Under Fire* as he concludes an indictment of military glory by staring "wide-eyed at the ground and all the blood he had given to heal the world."[123] Barbusse expressed the disdain of the front-line soldier for shirkers and civilians in the rear, their heads stuffed with stories about "magnificent charges" and "soldiers who die with a smile on their lips."[124] Instead, he insisted, soldiers went into battle with their faces "tense, pale, profound," only too conscious of their vulnerability to machine gun bullets and artillery shells, of the value of the lives they were called upon to sacrifice: "They are not careless of their own lives [...] They are not the sort of heroes that people think they are, but their sacrifice has greater value than those who have not seen them will ever be able to understand."[125]

---

120 For analysis of soldiers' attitudes, as revealed by these sources, see Horne, "Soldiers, Civilians and the Warfare of Attrition," 240.

121 Tuffrau, *1914–1918*, 49, 74.

122 Rimbault, *Propos d'un Marmité*, 102.

123 Barbusse, *Under Fire*, 318. As Leonard Smith points out, Henri Barbusse's *Under Fire* "told a secular story of sin, damnation and redemption," in which the soldier's body paid the price for redeeming the world from the sins of militarism. Smith, *The Embattled Self*, 71. See also Smith, "Masculinity, Memory," 251–73.

124 Barbusse, *Under Fire*, 275.

125 Ibid., 227.

Although not himself a soldier, Georges Duhamel had a similar understanding of the soldier's sacrifice as Barbusse. The distinction made by
Duhamel between "hero" and "martyr" is crucial to his conception of the
soldier's death. At times, overcome by the "sad work, the continual company
of the dying and the mutilated,"[126] he gave way to despair. "This methodi-
cal and stupid destruction of fine young lives is something one cannot get
used to," he wrote to Blanche in August 1916: "Every day, there is another
arrival of fine young men more or less ruined, crushed, cut to pieces. One
ends up nauseated and depressed."[127] Nevertheless, this resolutely secular
man of science managed to retain a religious faith in the significance of
these deaths. Like Barbusse in *Under Fire*, Duhamel expressed his belief in
La vie des martyrs that despite its brutality and degradation the soldier's
death was still meaningful, his suffering itself a redemptive sacrifice. "Men
of France," he wrote, addressing himself to the wounded themselves, "your
naive greatness exculpates humanity for its greatest crime and raises it up
from its deepest degradation."[128]

One did not have to be a devout Christian, nor did one have to believe
in the piety of the French soldier or in the beauty of his death to associate
his suffering with that of Christ. Henry-Jacques was a soldier-poet whose
verses, published in the *Argonnaute*, a trench newspaper, often compared
the soldier's death to that of Christ. In one poem, entitled "Un Christ,"
passing soldiers address "a sort of prayer" to the figure of Christ on a roadside Calvary, saying:

> Your anguish is akin to ours,
> We die to save others.
> Today, we understand better
> Your three days of suffering.
> Ours has for three years
> Endured, and is not yet finished.[129]

In this representation, the soldier's suffering surpasses even that of Christ.
Like Duhamel and Barbusse, Henry-Jacques employed the same images of
sacrifice and martyrdom used in patriotic idealizations of the soldier's
death, at once echoing and repudiating those representations.

---

126 Duhamel and Duhamel, *Correspondance de Guerre*, vol. 1, 306.
127 Ibid., 374, 378.
128 Duhamel, *Vie des martyrs*, 175.
129 *L'Argonnaute*, no. 36, September 1917.

EXPERIENCING DEATH:
CHANGING ATTITUDES

On one level, soldiers' writings sought to communicate to their relatives or to posterity their evolving understanding of the meaning of the war and the value of their sacrifices. On another, more intimate, level those writings reveal, either consciously or unconsciously, how soldiers adapted psychologically in their encounters with death as they experienced it on the battlefields of the Western Front. Their descriptions of the dead, of how their comrades died, of the ways the dead were buried and commemorated, and how they prepared for their own deaths are all revealing of how deeply engrained cultural attitudes and practices were affected by the sudden irruption into French society of the mass death caused by industrialized warfare.

Many soldiers were deeply shocked by their encounters with the dead on the field of battle. Émile Carlier used the word "horror" to describe his feelings upon mistaking the remains of a human torso for a soldier's knapsack on the battlefield of the Somme. Charles Delvert used the same word in recounting an almost identical experience: "Horror! It is a human torso. One sees the whitening ribs and the viscera [...] One cannot bear to look upon this sight. I go away."[130] "Horror" was a word Carlier resorted to in describing other, similarly unpleasant, encounters. On 22 August 1916, the day following his arrival at the Somme front, he was laying a telephone cable along a collapsed trench. "A vile odour catches me by the throat. I am surrounded by clouds of fat flies. I feel stuck in my progress as if my feet were caught in the roots of trees. I see with horror that I am marching on human debris. Entrails have wrapped themselves around my shoe. Along the ground appear heads, stiffened arms, legs. I do not dare to look around me."[131] Paul Tuffrau, although he did not state his feelings, was clearly also deeply affected by his encounter with the dead on the battlefield of the Marne. "The battle was terrible. In a ditch, a zouave, his head shattered, plunges his bayonet into the side of a German. In the middle of the street, the corpse of an enormous Prussian officer, swollen by internal gases. And everywhere, everywhere, up to the stream that flows there, filled with equipment, bodies, bodies [...] Always that frightful odour of the charnel house."[132] The static nature of the fighting after the front had stabilized contributed to the combatants' sense that they were fighting in a charnel house. The fighting simply added new bodies to old, to be tossed

130 Delvert, *Carnets d'un fantassin*, 242.
131 Carlier, *Mort? Pas encore!*, 34.
132 Tuffrau, *1914–1918*, 34.

and turned in the mud under continuous bombardment. The battlefield at Verdun represented an extreme that soldiers struggled to describe. Gabriel Balique resorted to the language of the Old Testament to describe the "Babel of decomposing corpses" that he was compelled to traverse near Fort Souville.[133] "The most vivid imagination cannot conceive of such a hell," said L.L. Combes, writing to Marcel Papillon of the human remains he had encountered on the slopes of the "immortal Calvary" of the appropriately named Mort Homme at Verdun.[134]

What the ubiquity of these putrefying human remains did, of course, was to serve as a constant reminder to the living of their own mortality. As Albert Huet bluntly wrote with respect to the battlefield of the Champagne in 1918, "The endlessly turned over earth exposes sometimes a skull or a tibia. It means that shortly it will perhaps be my turn."[135] In attacking Mont Cuvelier later in the year, Huet stated, "that's three days now that we have been trampling on many dead and wounded [...] soon I will perhaps be like them."[136]

Soldiers did what they could to prepare for their own deaths. Many became fatalistic about their chances. "The war?" one soldier was recorded as saying. "It will go on until I am killed. The rest hardly matters to me."[137] Marcel Papillon wrote frankly to his parents in April 1915 after witnessing the destruction of his comrades' companies: "The butchery is beginning again, more intensely than ever. It is not possible that one can come through such a massacre again."[138] Commonly, soldiers prepared letters which they secreted on their persons or gave to comrades for delivery to relatives in the event of their deaths. Marc Bloch wrote a goodbye letter to accompany his last will and testament that began, "When you read this letter, I will have ceased to live," and ended with an affirmation that he "died certain of victory and happy – yes, truly happy, I say it in all the sincerity of my soul – to pour out my blood this way."[139] Gabriel Balique began his own farewell letter before embarking on a trench raid with the plea, "Especially do not weep if I do not return and if God summons me, because I will have had the finest death that one can wish for." He also took care to guard against any possible reproach by insisting that he had not volunteered for the

133 Balique, *Saisons de guerre*, 98.
134 Papillon et al., "*Si je reviens*," 297.
135 University of Florida's Digital Collection: Albert Huet, *World War I Diary*, accessed 20 April 2016, https://helenehuet.org/albert-huet-wwis-diary/.
136 Ibid., 20.
137 Tuffrau, *1914–1918*, 73.
138 Papillon et al., "*Si je reviens*," 120.
139 Bloch, *L'histoire, la guerre, la résistance*, 108.

mission he was about to undertake.[140] A somewhat unusual preparation, but one that is very revealing, is recounted in the notebooks of Paul Tuffrau. One of the men serving in the section he commanded, by the name of Hanot, presented him with a daisy, saying that he had sworn "a great oath" upon it and that Tuffrau was to send it to his wife. Hanot explained that he had vowed, in the event that Tuffrau should fall in battle, to kiss him on behalf of his wife: "And that, you know, nothing and nobody will stop me from doing, not even if they fire a pistol shot at me."[141] Tuffrau was moved nearly to tears by this gesture, which in its naiveté exposed what was more or less clearly perceived by all to be a fundamental problem of the soldier's death: that it occurred in the absence of family. Like so many other rituals that came to surround the soldier's death on the Western Front, Hanot's promise was calculated to compensate for that absence.

The notion that the ties binding the living and the dead were first and foremost familial ones is revealed by the evidence that some soldiers were far more affected by the deaths of loved ones at home than by those of comrades at the front. Antoine Martin was a Savoyard peasant who did his best, despite the heavy losses sustained by his unit in the opening engagements of the war, to reassure his wife of his good health and his good cheer. "It was on the day of my twenty-ninth birthday that I received the baptism of fire from the German cannon," he wrote. "That day my battalion had heavy losses. As for me, I am still in good health, without the tiniest scratch."[142] Yet the news of the death of the couple's fifteen-month-old child, Laurence, caused him almost unbearable suffering. "Despair came over me and I almost wished I were dead," he wrote.[143] A devout Catholic, Martin understood his son's death as a sacrifice required by God, taken in his place. He ended his letter with a heartfelt prayer that on All Saints' Day – the Day of the Dead – all the saints in heaven would pray to God "that this effusion of blood may cease."[144] Making sense of the war through his intense faith in intercessory powers, Martin understood death in sacrificial terms, but above all as a family affair. In his letters and notebooks, filled with his encounters with battlefield death, it was only the death of his son that elicited such an outpouring of feeling.

Henri Despeyrières expressed very similar sentiments. "I am now well used to death and I have seen so many departures that sometimes I remain almost indifferent," he wrote, but he was moved to tears by the news that

---

140 Balique, *Saisons de guerre*, 89.
141 Tuffrau, *1914–1918*, 60–1.
142 Martin, *La chasse à l'homme*, 25.
143 Ibid., 40.
144 Ibid.

his grandmother was dying: "feeling is awakened when I think of a being who loves me, whom you hold close[,] who is far from you and who goes away."[145] Also like Antoine Martin, Despeyrières was inspired by All Saints' Day to think of his departed relative – asking his parents to lay a wreath on his grandmother's grave on his behalf – and also of the unvisited graves of his comrades: "They are far and wide in the countryside. Nobody will have visited them; they already know oblivion even if they have not yet found peace."[146]

But the shared perils and hardships of the front created new bonds as powerful upon occasion as those that united families and that when ruptured by death caused similar emotional tribulations. Paul Tuffrau, recounting at length the death of Nérot, "my best soldier," in his notebook on 1 January 1915, acknowledged that "five months of suffering and dangers lived in common create powerful bonds."[147] Visiting the mortally wounded soldier in hospital, Tuffrau was unable to contain his tears as he promised to write to the dying man's family and gave him a farewell kiss. Later, he purchased a wreath, ordered a cross from a funerary shop, and attended Nérot's burial. At the cemetery, before the body was placed in the coffin, "I kissed him on the forehead, on behalf of his family."[148]

Different deaths were disturbing for different reasons. Especially agonizing or gruesome deaths were distressing to those who witnessed them, as is revealed in their descriptions. "The death of Jégoud was atrocious," wrote Charles Delvert, going on to describe the multiple wounds caused by a 130-cm Austrian shell, including one that opened Jégoud's body and broke his spine: "The terrible thing is that he still lived for four or five minutes."[149] Paul Tuffrau related the "terrifying details" of the death of Marmier, who in addition to suffering numerous mutilations from the explosion of a shell, was burned internally from inhaling phosphorous released by the explosion. None of Marmier's comrades could sleep that night, so affected were they by the sight of his suffering and the sound of his screams.[150]

The least that could be said of deaths like Jégoud's or Marmier's was that they were caused directly by enemy action. This could not be said of military executions, which denied to their victims the title of "*mort pour la France*" and the claim to have died on "the field of honour." Soldiers who were

145 Lafon, ed., *C'est si triste*, 50
146 Ibid., 73.
147 Tuffrau, *1914–1918*, 67.
148 Ibid., 65–7.
149 Delvert, *Carnets d'un fantassin*, 180.
150 Tuffrau, *1914–1918*, 149–50.

compelled to witness executions found them particularly repugnant. Those who described the execution of four corporals condemned for their role in the 1917 mutinies indicated that the experience occasioned them intense physical distress and caused several of their comrades to pass out, "one of whom had a nervous breakdown followed by a heart attack."[151] One explained that it was not the fact of the corporals' death that upset him, making him unable to eat for the entire day, but rather that of firing on "poor chums" he had served with for two years: "it is shameful."[152] Henri Despeyrières expressed similar disgust following an execution he had witnessed in 1915: "Such things do not cause fear, they do not intimidate, they do not make us think of the good we must do and of the crime that must be punished: they simply revolt."[153]

Another kind of death that inspired special repugnance was one that resulted in the soldier's complete physical annihilation on the battlefield. Although a soldier's instant obliteration in a shell burst at least spared his comrades the sights and sounds of his suffering, such a death was disturbing in a very different way. The elimination of any identifiable physical remains that might be recovered, buried, and eventually returned to the deceased's family removed an important marker of his very existence. In such cases there would not even be a lonely, unvisited grave. The words of Paul Mencier, who witnessed the destruction of a French artillery battery at the Battle of the Somme by a heavy shell, indicate how deeply affected he was by such an occurrence. "The shells arrive with the terrifying noise of an express, exploding with a great force and a terrible noise. The first four frame the battery which continues its fire but the fifth falls right on the first gun, blowing it to bits as well as the men who served it, who were never found, not even the tiniest bit. They were pulverized. It is a frightful vision[.] I will see it all my life."[154] It was not just shells that obliterated men. It was often not possible to recover the bodies of the dead or to treat them with the proper respect. Again, Paul Mencier's notebooks are revealing of soldiers' behaviours and attitudes in relation to the dead. In July 1918, as the army advanced, Mencier and his comrades encountered large numbers of enemy dead. Finding it repugnant to eat amid corpses and the clouds of flies these attracted, the French soldiers hastily buried a dozen bodies in a trench, topping the makeshift grave with a wooden cross. "I don't say they were properly buried because they lie however they fell," concluded Mencier: "Too bad, the living before the dead." He was, however, less

151 Rolland, *La grève des tranchées*, 180.
152 Ibid.
153 Lafon, ed., *C'est si triste*, 204.
154 Mencier, *Les cahiers de Paul Mencier*, 137.

forgiving of the stretcher bearers who failed to remove the corpses of enemy soldiers from the road, allowing the French columns to advance over them. "It feels bad to pass over human beings in that way; we were revolted by it," wrote Mencier. "Of all those bodies, nothing is left but a shapeless mess. They will be the vanished who will not even have a grave and yet they are men." Mencier and his comrades gave "those good-for-nothing stretcher bearers" a piece of their minds.[155] Mencier's unease at his complicity in obliterating the individual identities of the dead derived from the soldier's fear not just of death, but of complete annihilation: the annihilation of the common grave or that of "the vanished."

This resistance to the idea of total obliteration helps explain why soldiers were so determined to honour their comrades whenever possible by identifying their bodies, removing them from the battlefield, and according them a decent burial, hopefully as a prelude to returning them to their families. Soldiers were attentive to the care that was bestowed upon graves. Paul Tuffrau provided a careful description of a Moroccan soldier's grave, its plaque inscribed in pencil with a crescent and Arabic verses: "a sober tomb, very worthy of a soldier."[156] Gabriel Balique was less approving of his visit to a cemetery. "It is generally well done," he wrote, "except for the graves of three officers of the 283rd which are truly too bare: not to the honour of their comrades."[157] Marcel Papillon wrote to his parents of the painstaking care he took not only to provide a wreath for the grave of Raymond Simon, a soldier from his home town, but also to hire a photographer so that family members would have photographs of the grave.[158] Later, he would take as much care, aided by his sister Marthe, to ensure a wreath was placed on the grave of his brother Joseph, killed in a gas attack immediately upon arriving at the front in 1916. Marthe expressed her contentment at these arrangements: "He will appear less abandoned."[159] Soldiers were also conscious of the loneliness of these battlefield graves. Tuffrau, witnessing two women, dressed in black, visiting a soldier's grave at Villers-Châtel, saw the occasion as "horribly painful." The grave, indistinguishable from those surrounding it, he perceived to be "small and mean, and, alas! vulgar?" Perhaps it would have been better, he suggested, had the soldier's widow not visited at all.[160] The poet Henry-Jacques published a poem in May 1917 that was equally pessimistic. "A Dead Man"

155 Ibid., 201.
156 Tuffrau, *1914–1918*, 55.
157 Balique, *Saisons de guerre*, 155.
158 Papillon et al., "*Si je reviens*," 229–40, 251.
159 Ibid., 272.
160 Tuffrau, *1914–1918*, 93.

spoke to a nameless soldier buried under a wooden cross on the battlefield. "I have seen lots like you," says the speaker to the "Poor old chap whom nobody knows / Buried without name, like a dog."[161] Despite such reservations, far worse for the *poilus* was the idea that they might be prevented from honouring their dead as best they could. Gabriel Balique expressed his fury that on All Saints' Day, 1916, no leave had been granted to enable soldiers to visit the graves of their comrades. The cemeteries around Bois-le-Prêtre, he wrote, "stay deserted, populated only by the wandering spirits of the heroes cursing the leaders who impose ingratitude and oblivion." This, he concluded in outrage, was "to trample on hearts, scorn absolutely human nature, wound to an unsuspected degree ideas and beliefs."[162] Most soldiers saw the graves that proliferated on and around battlefields as temporary; eventually, they presumed, the bodies would be returned to their families. In describing the burial of fifteen soldiers in a common grave at Verdun, Abbé Thellier de Poncheville stated that each body had a bottle placed upon its breast with an identifying note within.[163] Marcel and Marthe Papillon were in agreement that the government had an obligation to bring the body of their brother Joseph home to them.[164] Gabriel Balique described the trouble that was taken to exhume the body of his brother, Francis, and to re-bury it in a suitable location, where the grave might be tenced and visited by family. Originally buried "without even a cover or a tent sheet!" the body was cleaned and reburied in a coffin. Balique recorded on 19 November that his parents had visited the grave at Château-Thierry: "They seem satisfied with the cemetery keeper and his wife who take good care of Francis's grave."[165]

As the war continued and as death became more commonplace, attitudes changed. "How indifferent one becomes," wrote Gabriel Balique after witnessing the burial of fellow lieutenant Vidal, killed by a mortar shell three days after getting married: "Each one says: what awaits us tomorrow? To each his turn, and nothing more … Even if we don't talk about it, this is a sentiment that we all feel more and more at the front."[166] "One becomes hard, indifferent, more or less passive, resigned to everything," said Paul Tuffrau.[167] Henri Despeyrières wrote to his parents that "We breathe, we eat, we live in the midst of death; we laugh and joke which is perhaps

161 *L'Argonnaute*, May 1917.
162 Balique, *Saisons de guerre*, 114.
163 Thellier de Poncheville, *Dix mois à Verdun*, 26.
164 Papillon et al., "*Si je reviens*," 255, 258.
165 Balique, *Saisons de guerre*, 183–6.
166 Ibid., 71.
167 Tuffrau, *1914–1918*, 86.

sadder. Ah! There are pictures the horror of which you will never understand." Despeyrières excused himself for writing about such things, saying,
"But then I am used to these horrors and this affects me less than it would
affect you."[168]

The bottom line was that the needs of the living took precedence over
those of the dead. Soldiers learned to leave their losses and their sorrows
behind. "We are used to this vision of death that is daily before our eyes,"
wrote Paul Mencier, "and [...] good humour recovers its rights, especially
when one sees civilians again and can no longer hear the guns." A clean
shirt, some wine, and a good night's sleep were enough, he said, to restore
men's spirits.[169] Gabriel Balique, returning to the rear after his regiment
had endured 70 per cent casualties at Verdun, stated that the natural
response of those who had survived was "a quest for enjoyment in all its
forms," including those "that would have seemed scandalous in ordinary
times." More serious reflection, he said, would have to wait until the end
of the war.[170] The Abbé Thellier de Poncheville aptly summarized this
outlook, saying, "One lives day to day, as if one had no past and no future."[171]

Soldiers even learned to laugh at death, albeit in a wry, self-mocking way.
Émile Carlier was greeted upon his arrival in the front lines for the first
time by a sign over the trench which read, "To die for the Homeland is a
very fine death. But there is nothing like living for it." "Evidently!" wrote
Carlier drily in his notebook.[172] Soldiers digging trenches joked that it was
better to dig holes in the ground for the living than for the dead.[173] Trench
newspapers were a significant vehicle for this type of humour. Under the
heading "Necrology," one such newspaper reported the deaths of
two battalion commanders in "particularly tragic circumstance."
One, Commander X, had "blown up in indignation." The other,
Commander Y, "had exploded with anger."[174] The same newspaper also
directed its mirth against mothers-in-law. "Don't you think it would be
possible, and even useful, to sacrifice a few thousand in the general interest?
The ugliest would be placed in our trenches, in the first line (it is certain
that most of them would resist all assaults), the others would be put in the
second line."[175] It was, of course, easier to mock the enemy dead than
French dead. A cartoon on the cover of *Le Front* made light of the soldier's

168 Lafon, ed., *C'est si triste*, 151.
169 Mencier, *Les cahiers de Paul Mencier*, 181.
170 Balique, *Saisons de guerre*, 102.
171 Thellier de Poncheville, *Dix mois à Verdun*, 244.
172 Carlier, *Mort? Pas encore!*, 11.
173 Hardier and Jagielski, *Combattre et mourir*, 159–60.
174 *Face aux Boches*, no. 1, August 1915.
175 Ibid., no. 3, October 1915.

distaste for bodies left to rot on the battlefield by depicting a German sentry who was not so much in an "advanced" position as in an "advanced" state of decomposition.[176] The conventions of reporting heroic French deaths were also mocked, however, as in the account entitled "Fallen in the Face of the Enemy," which described the death of Margot, who, "superbly indifferent, stood, heroically, at his observation post" until decapitated by an Austrian shell. A footnote reveals that Margot was a bird and company mascot. Another joke wryly acknowledged that many soldiers saw their only hope of survival in a "good wound," that would send them home alive, if not whole. Under the heading, "War Wounds through the Ages," the article claimed that one could be inoculated against wounds by the injection of a little steel or lead. "Oh! I know," it continued, "there are violent reactions [...] Not everybody tolerates equally this kind of treatment [...] But when the dose is well proportioned, when there is a good injection – what is called a good wound – the wounded person is immunized against bullets, shells, torpedoes, and gas for a time, sometimes for quite a while."[177]

Civilian attitudes also changed, in similar ways to those of the soldiers. Georges Duhamel, as a military surgeon, occupied a liminal space between front and rear, between soldiers and civilians. In *La vie des martyrs*, he noted that death had simply become too common to suspend, as it once did, daily life. His words unconsciously echoed those of Henri Despeyrières: "one eats and drinks beside the dead, one sleeps in the midst of the dying, one laughs and sings in the company of corpses." Death, said Duhamel, was like the monarch who allowed himself to be seen at his toilet: "still powerful, but familiar and a bit debased."[178] Duhamel's correspondence with his wife indicates that even he, an exceptionally compassionate doctor, was affected by this change. His letters from 1914 and 1915 make frequent reference to the efforts made at the ambulances to which he was attached to pay the necessary respects to the dead. On 7 December 1914, he described in detail the funeral held the previous day for two twenty-year-olds who had died within an hour of each other: "The little country priest went in front, with a kid in clogs as choirboy holding the cross. As officers we took the place of the family, behind the body; our men almost always come when they are free, plus a few women and the local mayor [...] I miss these indispensable ceremonies as infrequently as possible," he emphasized.[179] In July 1915, Duhamel sent a photograph "of our latest burial" to Blanche, pointing out to her the care taken to create a suitable

176 *Le Front,* no. 5, 1 September 1916.
177 *Horizon, Journal des Poilus,* August 1917.
178 Duhamel, *La vie des martyrs,* 173–4.
179 Ibid., 119–20.

resting place, "with fir trees at the entrance, crosses and easily read inscriptions." Since most of the men buried there were from Normandy, "we made a Norman portico with the inscription *pro patria* [...] There they are, over a hundred of them, all young: a cemetery of men, in the middle of the fields."[180]

Clearly it mattered a great deal to this busy surgeon to attend these "indispensable" tributes to the dead. Yet after September 1915 Georges's letters to Blanche cease to make any reference to soldiers' funerals or to his participation in them. This does not, of course, necessarily mean that he ceased to attend. Perhaps his attendance had itself become so commonplace that he no longer remarked upon it in his letters. Nevertheless, the lack of any such reference does seem to suggest a significant change. This may well have been connected to other changes in the life of the mobile field surgery that Georges also commented on in his letters to Blanche. On 15 September 1915, he explained that the methods of treatment had changed and patients were moved to the interior as soon as possible once they had been operated on. No longer would he care for the wounded as they recovered from surgery, sometimes over many weeks. While conceding the efficiency of the new system, Duhamel noted that he found the work less gratifying and somewhat unfeeling.[181] The sense of being on a surgical production line intensified in the spring of 1916, during the Battle of Verdun, when Duhamel's surgery was located at Glorieux, within range of the German guns. In the first two nights at Glorieux, he wrote, the unit performed 110 operations and innumerable dressings.[182] The following year, attached to a field hospital at Soissons, during the offensive on the Chemin des Dames, Duhamel was busier than ever. In a month, he told Blanche, with only three surgical teams, the field hospital had performed six hundred major operations.[183] To describe the work, Duhamel resorted to industrial metaphors; he referred to "this life of monotonous labour" and to himself as "a good worker in human flesh."[184] Inevitably, he feared he was losing touch with his patients. In his letters, there were fewer references to individual deaths. A sign of the times was Georges's response to Blanche's inquiry concerning the fate of the patient whom he had transfused in October 1917. "Sadly, he only survived for two days," he wrote. "He died during the offensive and it affected us less because we had lots of things to worry about and at

180 Ibid., 318.
181 Ibid., 434.
182 Ibid., 806–10.
183 Ibid., vol. 2, 379.
184 Ibid., 414.

that time, many others were dying."[185] Death and the ceremonies to honour the dead had simply become too mundane to mention.

Familiarity with death did nothing, however, to diminish the grief of those who were close to the one who died. Writing in 1949, Georges Duhamel recounted how, in his mind's eye, he had relived "thousands upon thousands of times," the death of his friend Henri Doucet, who had been killed by a bullet on his first day in the trenches. He imagined the young artist, unable to resist viewing the strange new landscape in which he found himself, heedlessly presenting himself as a target for enemy fire, suddenly choking on his blood and falling in the mud. And in words that might have served equally well as an epitaph for Eugène-Emmanuel Lemercier, he grieved that "the fine young man endowed with gifts and hope will not mature among us, will not continue the works full of grace and harmony we expected of him, that he would surely have given us for all to marvel at." He could not help himself, each and every day, said Duhamel, "through an exhausting effort of the spirit," from constantly reliving the death of his dear friend.[186] The letters of Blanche Duhamel also reveal how the death of the soldier was experienced by his loved ones far from the front. On 16 July 1916, Blanche informed Georges of the death of Olin, husband of Blanche's childhood friend, Sylvette Filacier. Olin's death was particularly distressing, wrote Blanche, because of its circumstances: the young man's last letters indicated that he had lost his courage and had taken to going alone into the woods to cry: "that poor big boy, so gentle, and who must have died so little convinced of the utility of his sacrifice. Oh! That's the worst of all."[187] Secondly, the way in which the news reached Sylvette, through a succession of letters from Olin's comrades and their family members, shrouded it in uncertainty, inflicting upon her a torment of alternating hope and despair. "It was so sad to see her beautiful little body contorting like that," wrote Blanche. "It was the third time she had received the blow and each time was, she said, harder than the last." Sylvette "suffered mortally," said Blanche, from the sense that what she feared the most in the world had come to pass and yet she continued to breathe, that she and her surroundings were unchanged by it.[188]

185 Ibid., 668.
186 Duhamel, *La pesée des âmes*, 76–7. On 14 April 1914, Duhamel wrote to his friend Charles Vildrac, saying that neither religious belief nor patriotism could console him for Doucet's death: "There is no consolation possible for us." Duhamel and Duhamel, *Correspondance de Guerre*, vol. 1, 162.
187 Ibid., 1093.
188 Ibid., 1098–9.

   Despite enduring grief, life went on. As an actress, Sylvette Filacier had little choice but to put a bright face on things, literally. Less than a year after Olin's death, on 2 April 1917, Blanche wrote to Georges that Sylvette had returned to Paris after a time working in sunnier climes. She was "all new, all different, all refreshed," having abandoned "that sad face and even her mourning clothes." Cinema and theatre directors would refuse to hire her otherwise, wrote Blanche, whose own practicality also got the better of her sorrow: "But she had to do it nonetheless since she has to live."[189]

REMEMBRANCE

On Sunday, 12 November 1916, Abbé Thellier de Poncheville celebrated mass four times for soldiers fighting in the last stages of the Battle of Verdun. The first was in the abandoned and dilapidated shower installation of a military camp; the second in the entrance to a military hospital, where the bread and wine symbolizing the sacrifice of Christ were placed on an altar covered with bandages that normally served to dress the wounds of French soldiers. The third took place in the ruins of a chapel at Béholle, already under reconstruction. The final service was conducted at the cemetery of La Chiffour, where the choir was placed in a half-dug trench, while the speakers stood on the pile of earth beside it, the better to project their voices. The Abbé was used to not only conducting multiple services, but also improvising them in the least propitious circumstances. Indeed, while accompanying a column of wounded who were blown up by a shell as they were making their way to the rear, Thellier had picked himself up in the midst of the chaos of wounded and dying men and shouted a blanket absolution at the top of his lungs.[190] As he began the service at La Chiffour, soldiers dressed in sky blue stood among the graves, in the spaces "where tomorrow their own tombs will open up."[191] As the service began, a fog swept in to obscure the sunshine of the morning. "Under this grey mist," recalled the priest, "the uniforms melt into a more homogeneous mass. Spirits fuse in the same way: ours, and those who have departed. We feel ourselves brought close to them, in the contemplation of their resting place which is designedly more intimate, as if to permit them better to converse with us." Abbé Thellier then enjoined those gathered around to listen to the voices of the dead, their "poor, dear travelling companions, so quickly fallen, so quickly buried, so quickly abandoned!" Those in the rear, he said,

189 Ibid., vol. 2, 247.
190 Thellier de Poncheville, *Dix mois à Verdun*, 141.
191 Ibid., 289.

with the important exception of their mothers, wives, and children, had already forgotten them. But "we who represent their military family [...] always ready to rejoin them in the same immolation, we cannot rid ourselves of our dead with such haste. They are too close to us." Thellier reminded his listeners that, as they marched over the dead bodies on the battlefield and fought to survive in their trenches and dugouts, they already had one foot in the grave: "our lives are half buried like theirs. We are closer to them than to the living at the rear." Furthermore, since their bodies would remain at the front until the peace, the dead "are immobilized at their posts, still holding by our sides the line where all together we must stop the enemy." Their companions in arms had a duty to carry on the fight, conscious that they were observed and judged by the dead. Beyond that, however, they had a duty once victory was achieved to guard the memory of those who had died: "We will not let them die a second time, in the indifference of their homeland." The dead would live on in those who returned home from the war as a reminder to future generations of their sacrifice and the duty to serve the same cause, the good of the homeland.[192]

Abbé Thellier's evocation of the dead fighting beside and living within their surviving comrades was far from original. The story of Lieutenant Jacques Péricard rousing the dead to help defend their trenches in April 1915 had been made famous by Maurice Barrès.[193] There was much, however, in the Abbé's speech to appeal to the sensibilities of the *poilus* who heard him, whether they shared his Catholic faith or not. His ready identification with the resentment they felt for the rear and its lack of appreciation for their sacrifices undoubtedly struck an important chord. His insistence upon the ties of family and that in the absence of his real family it was up to the soldier's military family to take care of him, whether living or dead, was just as important. Above all, by emphasizing the duty of remembrance, Thellier addressed a fundamental concern for every man who served on the front lines: what trace of his existence would be left behind? Thellier, whose field burials had not always allowed for proper identification of men buried in mass graves, was as aware as his listeners that not all of them could expect their bodies to be found and returned to their loved ones. What Thellier offered was the reassurance that, even if they could not be reunited with their families, their comrades would honour their memory in the same way as they honoured that of those who had already died.

192 Ibid., 289–93.
193 See Smith, *The Embattled Self,* 72–5.

Thellier offered the hope of remembrance, but fear of oblivion was not so easily dispelled. Henri Barbusse evoked this fear in the final chapter of *Under Fire* when, in the midst of a discussion about the meaning of the war, a soldier states that "We are machines for forgetting."[194] For those who had been sacrificed in the cause of military glory, said another, nothing would remain: "They won't ever be able to gather up all their names, their poor little nothings of names."[195] Barbusse's novel ended on a message of hope, based on the dawning realization of the soldiers that their real enemy was not Germany but capitalism and nationalism. Céline's message in his 1932 novel *Voyage au bout de la nuit* was more brutal. Bardamu, an anti-heroic figure if ever there was one, states unequivocally that all wars are forgotten sooner or later and that it was utterly pointless to allow oneself to be killed in one. He therefore escapes the madness of such self-immolation by feigning insanity and having himself committed to a lunatic asylum. Céline articulated as fact the fear alluded to by Abbé Thellier, the fear of soldiers that they would suffer not just one, but two deaths.[196] Much that was written, said, and done surrounding the soldier's death during the war was calculated to allay that fear of oblivion. After the war, this fear only intensified for those who remained, contributing, as we shall see, to radically divergent representations of the soldier's death.

194 Barbusse, *Under Fire*, 305.
195 Ibid., 317.
196 Céline, *Voyage au bout de la nuit*.

7

Dying for France:
The First World War: Aftermath

INTRODUCTION

No war before or since cost France so many lives in such a short period as the First World War. Approximately 1.35 million Frenchmen were killed over four years of war.[1] If this is compared with the approximately 1.5 million who were killed during the twenty-three years of the revolutionary and Napoleonic wars, it becomes clear how great a shock the war was to the French population. During the revolutionary and Napoleonic wars, the annual rate of loss was approximately 2,329 deaths per year per million of population; during the First World War the rate was 8,438 per million: 3.6 times higher! Not until 1950 would these population losses be recovered.[2] Furthermore, the soldiers who died left behind them 680,000 widows and 762,000 orphans, ensuring that the war had a deep and lasting effect on families.[3] Finally, it is worth noting that the losses were not borne equally by all sectors of the population. It was the young who suffered most; the greatest losses were sustained by those who reached the age of twenty in 1914. Peasants, too, suffered more than townsmen. And although the vast majority of those who died were from the lower classes, the elites suffered disproportionately. Of 345 men mobilized from the École Normale Supérieure, 143 were killed.[4] The French experience therefore mirrored that of Britain, where an Oxford or Cambridge

---

1 Precise calculations are difficult to establish. See Prost, "Compter les vivants et les morts," 41–60; see also Greenhalgh, *The French Army*, 277; and Dupâquier, ed., *Histoire de la population française*, vol. 4: *De 1914 à nos jours*, 54.

2 Ibid., 78.

3 Ibid., 57.

4 Ibid., 54–5.

graduate was five times more likely to be killed than a young man from the working class.[5]

The huge scale of loss, as well as the vast disparity between the expectations and realities of modern warfare – which first became evident in soldiers' own letters and journals – ensured that the war had a profound impact on people's attitudes and sensibilities. This chapter will address this impact by considering changes in the representation of the soldier's death. During the war, as we have seen, soldiers themselves began to replace idealized with disillusioned representations of the soldier's death. This change was given a powerful impulsion by the development of wartime photography, which itself sounded the death knell for the traditional imagery of war, most significantly the popular *images d'Épinal*. The documentary authority of such images, as well as that of official war artists, was appropriated by the popular pocket Kodak camera. Only a handful of artists dared take the aesthetic, political, and reputational risks of depicting the most horrific features of mass killing. In literary culture, though, the disillusioned view of the soldier's death came to the fore during the interwar years. By asserting the futility of the soldier's "sacrifice," as well as by keeping alive memories of the soldier's role both as the perpetrator and as the victim of violence, some writers proposed narratives that were at odds with the more consolatory representations of the commemorative culture that emerged so powerfully in civic spaces during this period. The difficulty in reconciling these discordant representations of the soldier's death contributed to changing public attitudes toward death, mourning, and war itself.

A CULTURE OF COMMEMORATION

A culture of commemoration rapidly took shape in the years immediately following the armistice of 11 November 1918.[6] The essential ingredients of this culture, which focused its rituals and ceremonies upon local memorials to the war dead, were inherited from the traditions that were elaborated following the war of 1870, although its mood was very different. After 1918 there was no hint of the spirit of *revanchisme* that had characterized the ceremonies of the earlier period. Those who participated in the commemorations of the interwar years imagined they were bearing witness to the end of all wars, not preparing for another one. Also influential in the shaping of this postwar culture of commemoration were the festivals and remembrances that had taken place during the war itself: the

---

5   Gregory, *The Last Great War*, 290.
6   For a considered treatment of how this culture emerged, see Sherman, *The Construction of Memory*.

continuing 14 July celebrations; the *journées de guerre* that had mobilized society in the raising of funds to recognize particular aspects of the war effort – there were "days" honouring the *poilu*, the 75-mm field gun, French mothers, France's allies, and so on; and the festivals held in the vicinity of Meaux, beginning in September 1915, to commemorate the "miracle of the Marne" in 1914. It was from these antecedents that the commemorative culture of the interwar years drew inspiration.[7]

The cornerstones of that culture were, on a national level, the ceremonies surrounding the tomb of the Unknown Soldier, located beneath the Arc de Triomphe in Paris, and, provincially, those focused upon the monuments to the dead that were erected in each of France's 36,000 municipalities, most of them in the five years from 1918 to 1923. Key legislative acts provided the foundation for the creation of these monuments. A law of 25 October 1919 stated that the names of the war dead would be recorded on a book of remembrance to be kept in the Pantheon. Each municipality would also receive a "golden book," in which would be inscribed the names of its own citizens who had died in the war. A national war monument was to be built in Paris and public funds provided to assist in the construction of a local memorial in each municipality. Finally, the law prescribed that an annual ceremony would be held throughout France on 1 or 2 November – corresponding to All Saints' Day and All Souls' Day, in the religious calendar – "in memory of and to the glorification of the heroes who died for the homeland."[8] The plans thus defined were subsequently modified. Effectively taking the place of the national war memorial in Paris (though not in principle) was the tomb of the Unknown Soldier. The popularity of an empty tomb honouring the war dead that had been placed beneath the Arc de Triomphe for the victory parade of 19 July 1919 helped convince the Chamber of Deputies to approve the transfer of the remains of an Unknown Soldier – "symbolizing at the same time the victory that saved the world and the heroism of the citizen who died for his fatherland" – to the Pantheon.[9] Subsequently, the deputies agreed, despite grumbling from the Left, to change the Unknown Soldier's final resting place to the site of the Arc de Triomphe because the latter, celebrating the military achievements of Napoleon, was linked more closely to the idea of the French nation than the Pantheon, which was associated with the less inclusive idea of the Republic.[10] Finally, after an unsuccessful attempt to place the commemoration on the first Sunday after 11 November, a law

7 Dalisson, *11 Novembre*, 31–55.
8 *Journal officiel de la République française. Lois et décrets*, 26 October 1919.
9 Ben-Amos, *Funerals, Politics, and Memory*, 218.
10 Ibid., 220. *Journal officiel de la République française. Chambre des députés*, 8 November 1920.

was passed on 24 October 1922 which established that the "commemoration of victory and peace" would take place annually on 11 November itself, which would also be a public holiday.[11]

These laws, negotiated through the complex interaction of legislators, the public, and interest groups such as the emergent ex-servicemen's organizations, which were highly influential and had approximately three million members by the 1930s, served to define the basic features that characterized the "golden age" of commemoration during the 1920s and 1930s.[12] Those commemorations were contested, particularly as political tensions intensified in the 1930s. The pattern of commemoration developed as a compromise between the interests of the state, which sought to place the accent on the achievement of victory, and those of the veterans' organizations, which encouraged a more sorrowful spirit, focused upon mourning the dead and insisting upon the horrors of war. Subsequently, the contestation between communists, right-wing leagues, and pacifists was played out over the course of the 11 November commemorations, with rival groups sometimes organizing separate or parallel events. Despite this political dimension, the 11 November commemorations served a more primal need: for bereaved families to reincorporate their loved ones – if only symbolically – and to complete the painful task of mourning their loss.

As we have seen, one of the most difficult things for soldiers and families to come to terms with during the First World War was that the soldier's death, among all its other miseries, was likely to take place far from home. In comforting their dying comrades or in honouring their remains, soldiers consciously sought to fill in for the absent family members who would normally perform those duties. As for those relatives themselves, their most urgent need upon learning of their loss was to locate their loved one's remains, ensure they were respectfully treated and, for many, to bring them home for interment. The latter task was fraught with difficulty. The organizational and financial obstacles to finding, exhuming, and transporting hundreds of thousands of bodies were daunting. Some government ministers also felt that the dead should remain where they had fallen and that the former battlefields should become an immense graveyard, as was the case for the war dead of the British Commonwealth. The determination with which parents and wives set about overcoming both political opposition and practical challenges to the transfer of remains bears witness to how deeply felt was their need to reclaim the absent bodies of sons and husbands. By the beginning of 1921, the process of transporting the war

11 Dalisson, *11 Novembre*, 50. *Journal officiel de la République française. Lois et décrets*, 26 October 1922.

12 Dalisson, *11 Novembre*, 58–67.

dead to their hometowns, upon request from the families and at public expense, finally got under way.[13] Ultimately, over 250,000 bodies were transferred in this way, some 30 per cent of the 700,000 identified remains buried in battlefield graves.[14] For many families, of course, remains were never found or identified. For them, the monuments and rituals of 11 November offered at least symbolic restitution.

The reincorporation of the war dead was symbolized most powerfully through the funerary and commemorative rites associated with the Unknown Soldier. Chosen from among eight bodies exhumed from the battlefield of Verdun by a young volunteer soldier who had lost his father in the war, the symbolic figure was paraded with great solemnity through Paris on 11 November 1920, from Place Denfert-Rochereau, where a replica of the lion of Belfort recalled the war of 1870; then to the Pantheon, evocative of the Third Republic's founding the same year; and finally to the Arc de Triomphe, the starting point for the parade in July 1919 celebrating that Republic's victory. Blessed at the conclusion of the ceremony by the archbishop of Paris, the sanctified remains were finally entombed under the Arc de Triomphe on 28 January 1921, beneath a stone slab bearing the inscription, "Here lies a French soldier who died for the fatherland, 1914–1918."[15] As it was conveyed across the city, the body of the Unknown Soldier was accompanied by a mother, father, widow, and orphaned child, symbolic of the bereavement of the nation in general, but also of all the bereaved families of France. As General Weygand wrote in 1932, the anonymity of the Unknown Soldier qualified him to become "the son of all the mothers who have not found their sons."[16] By participating in solemn pilgrimages to the tomb in Paris, where from 1923 a daily ceremony was held to reignite the flame of memory, French families could remember and mourn those they had lost.

There were other sites where this could also be done. The major ossuaries in northeastern France, principally those at Douaumont, Notre-Dame de Lorette, Hartmannswillerkopf, and Dormans, where the remains of unidentified bodies were interred, became important commemorative sites. Built as repositories for the fragmentary remains of tens of thousands of bodies, the ossuaries were paid for in large part by private donations. A particularly effective means for raising funds was by giving relatives who

13 On the debate concerning the transfer of bodies, see Sherman, *The Construction of Memory*, 76–7.

14 Pau, *Le ballet des morts* 281. See also Audoin-Rouzeau and Becker, *14–18, Retrouver la guerre*, 246.

15 Ben-Amos, Funerals, *Politics and Memory*, 222–3.

16 Weygand, *Le 11 Novembre*, 131, cited in Trevisan, *Les fables du deuil*, 82.

were willing to pay for it the right to have their dead soldier's name inscribed on the ossuary's stonework. The ossuaries' monumental scale and design, their religious design and decoration, their location on the sacred ground of former battlefields, and their combination of both the remains and the names of the dead made them pre-eminent among the monuments to the dead outside Paris.[17] Like the tomb of the Unknown Soldier, they became important sites of pilgrimage.

It was, however, the thousands of municipal war memorials, each inscribed with the names of the dead from its locality, that were the most important means for the symbolic reincorporation of the dead. On these monuments, the names of the dead took the place of bodies. Through the presence of those names local monuments became substitute tombs that symbolically reaffirmed the individuality of those who had died and restored them to the heart of the communities from which they had been taken.[18] The monuments and the names inscribed upon them were central to the commemorative rituals of 11 November. Those rituals usually took the form of a procession from the local church, where mass was celebrated, to the war monument. Here, usually accompanied by a minute's silence and the laying of wreaths, the names of the dead were solemnly intoned – often by an orphaned child – with each name followed by the pronouncement of its essential quality: "died for France." Flags were dipped toward the monument, while bugles and sometimes choirs gave musical tribute. Finally, the participants moved on to the cemetery to pay their respects to those war dead whose bodies had in fact been brought home. The influence of the veterans' organizations ensured that most ceremonies were devoid of triumphalism or militarism: rather, they were sorrowful occasions for remembering the catastrophe of the war and the sacrifice of the dead.[19]

17 Sherman, *The Construction of Memory*, 81–93; Becker, *War and Faith*, 123–30. Becker also notes that the memorial chapel of the Battle of the Somme, at Rancourt, resembled the ossuaries in form and function, with the exception that it was not a site for the interment of human remains.

18 Sherman, *The Construction of Memory*, 100–1. Sherman states that these monuments required of their devotees "a delicate process of transference," whereby emotion was displaced "from the body of the deceased to the inscribed name," which he says was "clearly akin to Freud's notion of mourning." Ibid., 85–6. On the significance of naming the dead on First World War memorials, see Laqueur, *The Work of the Dead*, 447–88. Laqueur argues that in an age of mass literacy and mass communication it had become intolerable for the end of ordinary lives to go unacknowledged. The demand for the names of the dead to be inscribed on war memorials was imposed on governments from below.

19 Antoine Prost emphasizes that the initiative for the construction of the monuments came from local communities and developed from the "cult of the fallen" that had begun to develop even before the war had ended. He therefore denies any suggestion that the monuments were "nationalist" in inspiration. Prost, *Republican Identities in War and Peace*, 13.

The war memorials themselves constituted an important representation of the soldier's death. Most monuments were simple steles, sometimes topped by a symbol, such as the French cockerel or the *croix de guerre*, the medal that was introduced during the war to recognize acts of bravery or devotion to duty. Even the simplest monuments, however, were inscribed with the names of the dead as well as the cause for which they died: "died for the motherland," for example, or "for right and for liberty."[20] By affirming that the dead had lost their lives fighting for a worthy cause, such monuments justified their sacrifice and offered a measure of consolation to mourning relatives. More elaborate – and expensive – monuments often included statuary. The figures represented were sometimes grieving women and children, or female allegories representing France or Victory, but the most popular figure was that of the ordinary French infantryman, the *poilu.* Depending upon the other figures and symbols with which he was associated, as well as the attitude of his pose, the presence of the *poilu* served to characterize the monument in a number of different ways: a *poilu* triumphantly brandishing a laurel wreath celebrated victory; one who adopted a stalwart stance embodied defiance; yet another who fell clutching the flag represented sacrifice.[21] As Daniel Sherman has shown, the inspiration for these symbolic *poilus* was the popular imagery of the war – most notably the *affiche* or poster – which had presented the public with idealized representations of French soldiers. The monumental *poilus* were therefore highly unrealistic – "tidy and well scrubbed," in Sherman's words – and often engaged in actions, such as the frontal assault, that were relatively uncommon in the real war.[22] Sherman points out that although dying *poilus* featured on many monuments, this had not been the case in French wartime posters. Inspiration had, therefore, to come from elsewhere. Dying soldiers were common in other forms of popular imagery. *Imagerie d'Épinal* continued its established tradition of representing heroic deaths. Postcards, too, presented idealized – and sometimes highly sentimental – images of dying soldiers: soldiers lifted up to heaven on the wings of angels; clasping photographs of fiancées; receiving a mother's comfort; or giving a final thought to wife and child (fig. 7.1). Patriotism was mixed with sentiment, however, and there were therefore images of dead or dying soldiers receiving tribute from female allegories of France or clutching the flag to their chests. None of these images was realistic. The sculptors for the most part managed to avoid the sentimentality of the postcards; no doubt this had

20 Niess, "La mort du soldat," 326–7.
21 On the various types of monument, see Prost, *Republican Identities*, 14–27; Daniel Sherman, *The Construction of Memory*, 180–213.
22 Ibid., 188.

LA DERNIÈRE PENSÉE

394

7.1. Postcard. *The Last Thought.*

worn thin by the end of the war. All the same, as Alexandre Niess has shown in his study of 1,157 monuments with sculptures of dead or dying *poilus*, their representations were highly idealized. Often, the stricken soldier falls backward or slumps to the ground, clutching the flag or letting fall his rifle. A good example is the monument sculpted by Jules Dechin at Chaulnes, in the Department of the Somme (fig. 7.2).[23] A female allegory extends a victory wreath toward the stricken *poilu*, whose left hand clutches his chest as he subsides to the ground. There is no hint of the mutilating wounds of modern warfare, or of the mud and squalor of the trenches. Dead bodies were represented even more rarely than dying ones and were often obscured in some way: by a veil of bronze, for example, or by placing them on the backs of monuments.[24] Often, the *poilu* was represented

23 For other examples see Rive et al., eds, *Monuments de mémoire*, 159–66.

24 Niess, "La mort du soldat de la Grande Guerre," 332–3. In his survey of the war monuments of the Marne, Niess notes the strikingly different ways in which one sculptor, Marius Giot, represented the soldier's death in the monuments he designed at Broyes and Sézanne. In the Broyes monument a dead soldier, with his chest uncovered for the sacrifice and his eyes closed, stands on guard. At Sézanne, a prostrate soldier is represented in the act of dying, his arms spread and left hand opened upwards to symbolize the giving up of his soul. Niess, *Cimetières militaires*, 61–5.

7.2. Monument to the Dead, Chaulnes.

294 Dying for France

clutching his heart, a gesture that might be taken to indicate either a fatal bullet to the heart or, more symbolically, his sacrifice on behalf of the things he held closest to his heart. Equally ambiguous were the female allegories with which dying soldiers were often represented. Most commonly, these allegories represented Victory, but they might easily be perceived as angels. Niess suggests the ambiguity may even have been intended, to circumvent the prohibition on religious symbols in public spaces.[25]

Antoine Prost characterizes monuments representing dying soldiers as either "funerary-patriotic" or "purely funerary," according to whether or not they associated the dying soldier with words, symbols, or allegories representing his homeland.[26] No doubt, different representations conjured different emotions: patriotic ones pride; funerary ones sorrow. Many monuments, particularly those in more devout regions, such as Brittany, Alsace, or the Vendée, were religious in inspiration. To believers, these offered hope and consolation. As Annette Becker has argued, even though the initiative came from the municipalities rather than from churches, the design of monuments reflected "a clear intention to blend the cult of the war dead with an affirmation of religious faith."[27] One might say the same of the 11 November commemoration itself, since the decree establishing it specifically suspended the restrictions of the 1905 law on the separation of church and state in order to facilitate church participation in a civic ceremony. This trend was a continuation of the spirit of the *Union sacrée* that had brought Catholics together with republicans and socialists in defence of France in 1914. It was also a tacit acknowledgment that a great many French people were encouraged by their faith to adopt an intensely religious understanding of the war. Theirs was an understanding that, while perceiving the war to be a punishment for sins and likening the soldier's suffering to that of Christ, sought consolation in the power of intercessory prayer offered to Mary and the saints, as well as hope in the promise of the resurrection. For believers, the soldier's sacrifice was a patriotic martyrdom that redeemed the nation and prepared his own ascension into heaven. These beliefs were reflected in the iconography of war monuments, although explicitly religious symbols such as the cross could only be employed if the monument was located within a churchyard or cemetery. The hope of resurrection was an important theme on war monuments. In some cases this was represented symbolically, by the cross

25 Niess, "La représentation des corps," 186–90. Niess demonstrates that monuments representing a dead or dying soldier were much more common in communities where religious observance remained strong.
26 Prost, *Republican Identities*, 25.
27 Becker, *War and Faith*, 130.

or by stalks of wheat. In others, the allusion was made explicit by associating the *poilu* with Christ, or by having him take the Saviour's place in scenes inspired by the canon of Christian iconography: most notably in Pietàs, where Mary cradles the dead body of her Son.[28]

The culmination of this intensely Catholic form of commemoration was in the imagery of George Desvallières, which was given form in the frescoes and stained glass windows he painted for the ossuary at Douaumont (1927), the Saint-Privat Chapel in the Department of the Gard (1919–25), the church of Wittenheim in Alsace (1929–31), and the Chapel of Remembrance in the rue Saint-Yves in Paris (1931). Desvallières's work was focused upon the passion of Christ, as well as its imitation by the *poilu*. In *The Flag of the Sacred Heart* Christ clutches his heart, symbol of the love of humanity that inspired his sacrifice, against the white of the tricoloured flag. He stands atop a calvary of barbed wire and battlefield debris; a shattered tree stands in for the cross of crucifixion. Instead of the *poilu* taking the place of Christ, as he does in so many war monuments, in Desvallières's painting it is Christ who takes the place of the *poilu*; the latter is figured in the painting only by the beret, uniform, and rifle of Desvallières's own son, Daniel, who was killed at Reichackerkopf on 19 March 1915. Originally painted in 1918 for the church Notre-Dame de Verneuil-sur-Avre, *The Flag of the Sacred Heart* was reworked in the extraordinary frescoes of the chapel at Saint-Privat. In three vivid tableaux Desvallières not only approximated the sacrifice of the *poilu* to that of Christ, but he also gave that sacrifice and the apocalypse of the war a cosmic significance by locating his depiction of them to the left of God enthroned in heaven, opposite *The Great Sacrifice of Calvary* representing Christ's crucifixion and Old Testament scenes symbolizing humanity's fall from grace. Justified by virtue of their sacrifice and helped in their ascension into heaven by the nurses who accompanied them at their deaths, the soldiers have helped to redeem humanity itself. Commenting on the windows he designed for the ossuary at Douaumont, Desvallières wrote, "What I wanted above all in these windows, was to associate the little crosses of our battlefields with the great Cross of Our Lord, and since we are Christ's members, I wanted to show that during the war,

---

28 Becker points to one "astonishing" pietà, on the war monument in the Czech cemetery at La Targette in the Pas-de-Calais, where *both* Jesus and Mary are replaced by *poilus*. Annette Becker, *War and Faith*, 136–7. A more classical version is that at Belcaire, in the Department of the Aude. See *Les Monuments aux morts: France (Aude), Belcaire* 11340, accessed 28 February 2022, https://monumentsmorts.univ-lille.fr/monument/20946/belcaire-place/. For other Christian war monuments, see Rive et al., eds, *Monuments de mémoire*, 197–201.

we were the most agonizing and the most bloody members."[29] Although
some viewers of his work accused Desvallières of sadism because of
his depiction of tortured bodies, the artist also depicted those bodies –
including that of Daniel – ascending into heaven to receive their eternal
reward (fig. 7.3). Desvallières's millenarian fervour, his extraordinary mix
of the sacred and the profane, of battlefield realism and Christian eschatol-
ogy, gave his work an almost unbearable intensity. It was not as comfortably
consolatory, perhaps, as the stone Pietàs that graced many cemeteries and
public squares, but for those who could bear to look, it offered hope.[30]

George Desvallières was not the only artist who, during the interwar years,
represented the soldier's death as a Christ-like sacrifice. During the fifteen
years following the war, an estimated three thousand churches that had
been destroyed during the war were rebuilt.[31] In many of these, stained
glass windows and frescoes were commissioned to commemorate the war
by representing the soldier's sacrifice. Some of these were as dolorist in inspiration as the works of Desvallières. An example is the image of a crucified
poilu painted by Hector Jonas for Valenciennes Cathedral in 1920. For the
most part, however, such works placed the emphasis upon consolation and
redemption rather than suffering. The images of dead or dying *poilus* represented in church art were as sanitized as those sculpted for the *Monuments
aux Morts*. The dying soldiers on church windows who received Christ's
consolation or were raised up to heaven were depicted with whole bodies,
wearing uniforms unblemished by mud or blood. Isabelle Saint-Martin
describes the "attitude of tenderness" conveyed in a mosaic by Maurice
Denis in the cathedral at Quimper: "On a battlefield where the wooden
crosses, ornamented by tricolour cockades, echo the great eucharistic cross
shining in the sky, Christ, kneeling beside the soldier, takes him gently in
his arms; the harmony of gold, blue, and pink colours confers a great gentle-
ness upon this scene, where battle still resounds."[32] In some artworks, the
religious inspiration was less overt but no less meaningful. In 1939 Georges
Leroux, in his painting *Aux éparges*, transformed a humble night-time burial
into a sacred descent from the cross (fig. 7.4). Though lacking in the overtly

29 George Desvallières, "Les vitraux de l'ossuaire de Douaumont," in *Les Échos de
l'Industrie d'Art*, no. 26 (September 1927): 20–1. Cited in Saint-Martin, "Représenter la
mort," 203.

30 On *The Flag of the Sacred Heart* and the Chapel of Saint-Privat, see the beautifully
illustrated work by Ambroselli, *Georges Desvallières*, 138–45. See also Becker, *War and Faith*,
147–50.

31 J.-P. Blin, "Le vitrail commémoratif de la Grande Guerre," in *Chrétiens dans la
Première Guerre Mondial*, ed. N.-J. Chaline, 167–196 (Paris: Éditions du Cerf, 1993). Cited in
Saint-Martin, "Représenter la mort," 197.

32 Saint-Martin, "Représenter la mort," 203.

7.3. Georges Desvallières, *The Poilu's Ascension*.

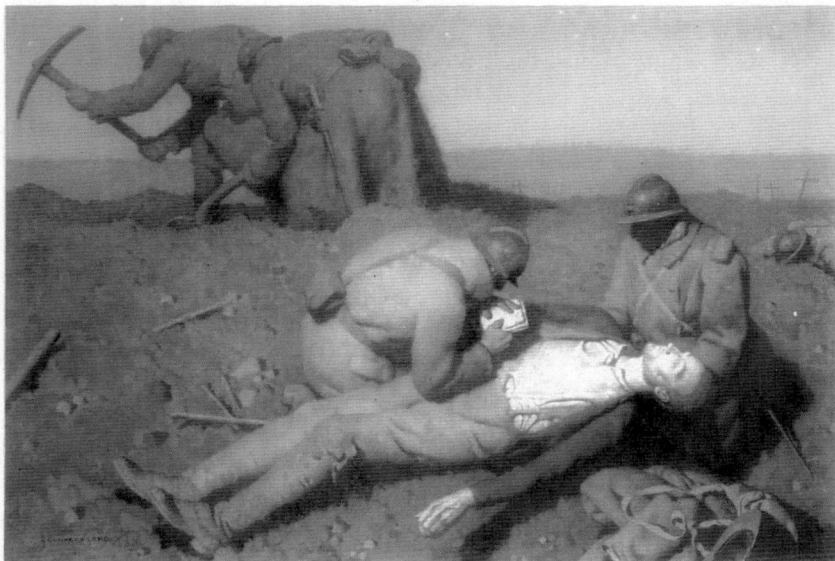

7.4. Georges Paul Leroux, *Night-Time Burial at Les Éparges, 1915.* 1939.

religious symbolism of church art, Leroux's painting conveyed the message
that the soldier's death served a redeeming purpose, both for the nation
and for the individual who sacrificed himself on its behalf.

IMAGES OF DEATH: OLD AND NEW

These consolatory images, although well suited to the culture of commemoration that emerged following the war, were at odds with the
representations of the soldier's death that acquired currency in other media.
In visual culture the emergence of photography and film was decisive in
undermining heroic representations of the soldier's death at the same time
as it subverted the authority of traditional media. Specifically, it heralded
the demise of the *images d'Épinal*, which had disseminated vast numbers
of military images since the seventeenth century. Although companies
continued to produce images in this style throughout the war,[33] their

33 For a good example of this imagery, see the images published by the Tolmer
Company in Paris under the title *La grande guerre*. These images can be seen in the online
gallery of the Fitzwilliam Museum. The Fitzwilliam Museum: La Grande Guerre Gallery
[2021], http://www.fitzmuseum.cam.ac.uk/gallery/lagrandeguerre/index.html.

stylized depiction of battlefield panoramas and heroic charges was singularly ill-adapted to the static, attritional warfare of the First World War. The number of such images, as Philippe Vatin has shown, steadily declined, from a high of ninety-eight in 1914 to a low of only twenty-two in 1918. Furthermore, companies like Tolmer found themselves cutting back on their print runs: evidence of declining demand for their product.[34]

Taking the place of the traditional popular imagery of war was the photograph, disseminated through the mass circulation daily and weekly papers, such as *Le Miroir* or *L'Illustration*. As Philippe Dagen has shown, *Le Miroir* had little reticence, despite official injunctions not to show images that might be disturbing to morale, about depicting the horrors of the battlefield, complete with dismembered and decaying bodies.[35] These images were readily available, since many soldiers, furnished with the relatively compact pocket Kodak camera, were quite willing to provide them. The *Miroir*, for example, announced in its issue of 9 April 1916 that it had awarded a prize of fifteen thousand francs to a *sous-lieutenant* who had photographed a line of advancing dragoons at the instant when two of them were killed by an exploding shell. The photograph, taken in September 1914, was first published in the paper's issue of 2 May 1915.[36] Certainly, the paper more commonly published photographs of the German dead, as in its issue of 9 May 1915, which reproduced a photograph of the body of a German officer hanging in the branches of a tree into which it had been blown (fig. 7.5). The photograph's caption, which referred to the corpse as a "sinister scarecrow," is revealing of the the newspaper's intent to present images of enemy dead in a degrading manner.[37] All the same, such images made abundantly clear the indignity of the soldier's death whatever his nationality. Similarly, the emphasis placed by the paper in its caption on the symbolic significance of a French bayonet in the foreground of a photograph depicting debris on the battlefield at Les Éparges hardly compensates for the macabre content of the photograph, in which the scattered bones might just as easily be French as German.[38] As the paper said in the caption to a photograph depicting a trench at Malancourt that was filled with bodies, "While photography is more or less powerless to convey a general sense of the battlefield, it provides gripping close-ups" (fig. 7.6).[39] The potency of such images lay in their capacity to represent,

34 Vatin, *Voir et montrer la guerre*, 115–16.
35 Dagen, *Le silence des peintres*, 190–2.
36 *Le Miroir*, 9 April 1916.
37 Ibid., 9 May 1915.
38 Ibid., 21 May 1916.
39 Ibid., 25 June 1916.

7.5. *On the Vauquois Lines: The Scarecrow.* Detail of a photograph from *Le Miroir*, 9 May 1915.

LE MIROIR · 11

DEVANT MALANCOURT PENDANT LA BATAILLE

— Une contre-attaque nous a ramenés dans cette tranchée pleine de cadavres —

Si la photographie est à peu près impuissante à rendre l'aspect général d'un champ de bataille, elle en donne le détail en des raccourcis saisissants. Celle-ci, en fut prise pendant l'une des phases les plus sanglantes de la bataille de Verdun, devant le fameux village de Malancourt, offre une vision nette d'une position de première ligne après un combat furieux. Sauf en cet endroit, la tranchée a été complètement nivelée par l'artillerie qui prépara notre contre-attaque. On juge ici de ses effets meurtriers.

7.6. *Before Malancourt during the Battle.* Photograph from *Le Miroir*, 25 June 1916.

with the accuracy and apparent impartiality of a machine, the reality of life and death on the front lines. Despite its determination to represent these images, through the accompanying captions, in a positive way, *Le Miroir*'s publication of them exposed the brutal face of modern combat to an audience avid for authentic images of the war. Similarly, although wartime audiences resorted to the cinema primarily as an escape from the war, the latter was also the venue for the dissemination of newsreels, which soundlessly displayed the human and material devastation of the war.[40]

The authority of the photograph and of film to bear witness to the reality of modern war undermined that of artistic representations in general, not only in the form of the intentionally naive *images d'Épinal*, but also in that of traditional battlefield painting, in the style of Édouard Detaille, as well as in the work of modernist artists, for whom the depiction of the soldier's death presented special difficulties. To be sure, traditional heroic representations did not disappear altogether. Painters of battle scenes continued to represent the soldier's death in idealized ways. Most of the 117 artists who participated in artistic missions to the front, however, deliberately avoided the subject of the soldier's death.[41] Georges Scott, one of the best known of those artists, whose work was frequently reproduced in the pages of *L'Illustration*, for the most part avoided representing dead or wounded French soldiers. When he did so, as in his painting of the wounded General Marchand, it was in an idealized way (fig. 7.7). The painting, which depicted the stricken general receiving the respectful salutes of French colonial troops and other wounded soldiers, underlined the brotherhood of arms uniting officers and men as well as soldiers from all parts of the French empire.[42] Another prolific war painter, François Flameng, did convey a more tragic vision of the war than Scott, but he too was cautious about representing dead or dying soldiers. Flameng's battlescapes frequently evoked the devastation caused by war. The bodies of dead soldiers figure in these paintings, but they are often virtually indiscernible and it is impossible to tell their nationality. Flameng's paintings simultaneously acknowledge and minimize the destruction of human life by placing it within the broader context of a devastated natural world. An example is his painting entitled

40 The production of newsreels about the war was initially in private hands. Brought under the supervision of the Ministry of War in 1915, it was eventually put in the charge of an Army Cinema Section in January 1917. French cinemas were required to show the weekly newsreel, the *War Annals*, produced by the army's official cinematographers. Pierre Sorlin writes, "Looking at the French newsreels today, we cannot avoid an impression of disaster, of the greatest calamity a country had ever experienced." Sorlin, "France: The Silent Memory," 123.

41 Vatin, *Voir et montrer la guerre*, 73.

42 *L'Illustration*, 13 November 1915.

7.7.　Georges Scott, *French Troops Salute the Wounded General Marchand, 1915.*

Craonne, 5 May 1917 (fig. 7.8). Although the painting shows French soldiers launching an attack, these living men are marginal figures, only just visible behind the crest of a hill. The viewer's eye is drawn instead to the three bodies – the blue-grey of their uniforms not clearly either French or German – that lie in the tangle of barbed wire stretching across the middle ground. The painting insists upon the desolation of the landscape rather than upon the accomplishment of a successful French attack. Images of the physical destruction caused by the German invasion of French territory were themselves a major feature of French propaganda during the war, so Flameng's paintings were patriotic at the same time as they were tragic.

For modernist painters, as Philippe Dagen has demonstrated, painting the subject of the soldier's death presented special difficulties.[43] On the one hand, the fracturing of time and space in modernist art seemed perfectly adapted to the representation of a war in which so much was happening at once. On the other, the intervention of the artist's vision and his drive to represent a reality beneath the surface appearance of things was at odds with the public demand for – and the promise of photography to provide – an impartial, authentic representation of the war's reality. Philippe Dagen argues that the taboo against depicting injured bodies was

43　Dagen, *Le silence des peintres.*

7.8. François Flameng, *Craonne, 5 May 1917.*

particularly problematic for modernist artists. He points to the paucity of
images representing death in the dozens of wartime drawings by Fernand
Léger, despite Léger's enthusiastic declarations that his cubist style was
ideally suited to capture the spirit of this modern war: "There is nothing
more cubist than a war such as this which more or less cleanly divides a
fellow into pieces for you and sends him to the four points of the compass."[44]
Léger's wartime oeuvre appears to reflect the artist's awareness that a
medium ideally suited to representing the dehumanization of warfare, as
human beings became cogs in the machinery of destruction, was less able
to do justice to the essential humanity of the dead. Only two of Léger's
drawings specifically depicted dead bodies, even though his duties as a
stretcher bearer brought him into constant contact with them and his
letters were filled with graphic descriptions of them. Revealingly, when
confronted by dismembered body parts on the battlefield, rather than
attempting to draw them, Léger expressed his need for a photograph to
capture that reality.[45] The work of another artist, André Mare, also seems
to reflect the limitations of cubism as a medium for representing the
soldier's death. Mare's depiction of soldiers tossed about by exploding
shells reveals a preoccupation with the formal interplay of geometric shapes

44 Cited in ibid., 174.
45 Ibid., 182–3.

rather than with the physical and emotional experience of war. The title of the work – *Billiards* – conveys the artist's detachment.[46]

Insofar as they were prepared to risk official disapproval or offending public taste by representing dead bodies, artists tended toward realism. The work of the English artist Christopher Nevinson exemplified this tendency. There is no evidence of his earlier attraction to cubo-futurism in his ironically titled *Paths of Glory*, which depicted the dead bodies of British soldiers lying in barbed wire.[47] In Germany, Otto Dix abandoned abstraction for a neo-realism – a "New Objectivity" – reflecting the influence of German Renaissance masters in completing his great works of the 1920s and '30s depicting the horrors of trench warfare.[48] In France, Luc-Albert Moreau has been identified with this tendency. Philippe Vatin perceives in Moreau's paintings of dead soldiers a realism reminiscent of Courbet.[49] Sylvie Dumaine makes a compelling case, however, that Moreau's painting was a pioneering form of French expressionism that packed a more powerful emotional punch than the more intellectual works of Félix Valloton and Otto Dix. In a memorable phrase, she writes, "the former painted with their heads and Moreau, with his guts."[50]

Typical of Moreau's work is a painting entitled *Unknown Soldier* (fig. 7.9).[51] The painting depicts a *poilu* lying on his back in his faded blue uniform beneath a leaden sky. The soldier's face is almost entirely hidden from view. Weighed down under its accoutrements, the body appears to subside into the undulating folds of the pulverized ground. There is no evidence of a wound or blood. Of the soldier's body only the blackening hands are visible. The painting's title and the absence of any distinctive facial features or wounds pertaining to its subject made it a suitable vehicle to bear the heavy symbolic meaning which, as we have seen, came to be attached to the idea of the Unknown Soldier. In the years following the war, Moreau returned constantly to the theme of the soldier's death. In this respect he differed from his friend and colleague Dunoyer de Segonzac who, despite sharing Moreau's grim view of the war, was more inclined to move on to other subjects once it was over. "Gravely wounded in 1918," wrote de Segonzac of Moreau, "he held onto a tragic obsession with Verdun, to which we owe the magnificent and painful *Suite de guerre* that remains the best

46 Vatin, *Voir et montrer la guerre*, 471.
47 Dagen, *Le silence des peintres*, 203–4.
48 Ibid., 212–27.
49 Ibid., 210.
50 Dumaine, "Luc-Albert Moreau," 397.
51 *Soldat Inconnu*.

7.9. Luc-Albert Moreau, *Unknown Soldier, Verdun 1914–1918*.

and true witness to the mute war of the infantry."[52] Louis Gillet said much the same thing. It was no accident, he wrote, that Moreau encountered the war writers Roland Dorgelès and Henri de Montherlant: "It was for them that he set himself to paint, to extract from his memory, as one frees oneself from an illness, the immense nightmare."[53] "The four years of war," said André Villeboeuf, "from which he suffered in his heart and his flesh, haunted him his whole life through. They gave birth to his great works."[54] In Moreau's paintings, men, the living scarcely distinguishable from the dead, seem to be pressed inexorably down into the ground. In *The Sinking Ones*, three soldiers are represented in the final moments before they are swallowed up by the mud (fig. 7.10). Sylvie Dumaine describes this scene as one of "the most unbearable" painted by Moreau.[55]

In Luc-Albert Moreau's works one rarely sees faces. In this sense his representation of the war diverges from the pattern discerned by Jay Winter,

---

52 Roger-Marx, ed., *Luc-Albert Moreau vu par ses amis*, 25. Dunoyer de Segonzac, like Moreau, produced illustrations for important works of war literature, most notably those by Roland Dorgelès. Kyriazi, *André Dunoyer de Segonzac*, 64–9.

53 Ibid., 26.

54 Ibid., 82.

55 Dumaine, "Luc-Albert Moreau," 382.

7.10. Luc-Albert Moreau, *The Sinking Ones.*

who argues that the predominant representation of war's terror at the time of the First World War was the face of the front-line soldier. Subsequently, says Winter, as warfare became ever more dehumanized, artistic representations of war and terror "turned away" from depicting the human face.[56] Whether those of the living hidden by hunched shoulders, protecting helmets and gas masks, or those of the dead pressed unseeing into the soil, the faces of Moreau's soldiers are obscured more often than not. A striking exception to this is *The Death of Riquet*, in which the dying solider is not only named but depicted with his face fully visible and the specificity of his fatal head wound apparent (fig. 7.11). By insisting upon these details Moreau provided a powerful reminder of the individuality of the war's victims. His dead and dying soldiers are otherwise anonymous, Unknown Soldiers representing both the loss of individuality and the loneliness of a war in which their inevitable, collective fate is simply to be swallowed up by the battlefield. Moreau's work strove at once to represent the dehumanizing nature of modern warfare and to insist upon the individual humanity of each of its victims.[57]

Jean-Julien Lemordant was another artist who insisted upon the individuality of the soldier's death. Like Moreau, Lemordant was a soldier-artist who was severely wounded – indeed, partially blinded – during his service at the front.[58] His depiction of a *Solitary Death* puts the face of the dying man in stark relief, insisting above all upon the feature that is most identifiably individual in any human being. There is not even a helmet or uniform to give Lemordant's dying man a corporate identity. In this sense, he is even more solitary than Moreau's *Unknown Soldier*, his suffering and death unique to him alone. The same could be said of another drawing, entitled simply *Suffering*, which was described in a 1935 article as follows: "A head that falls over, which can no longer hold itself up, eyes that close, because everything dances before them, a mouth clenched to contain groaning,

56 Winter, *War beyond Words*, 31.

57 This is a point emphasized by Sylvie Dumaine. Dumaine, "Luc-Albert Moreau," 369.

58 When he lost his sight at Monchy-le-Preux in October 1914, it was the third time Lemordant had been wounded since the beginning of the war. He was finally rescued by German medical personnel after lying for three days on the battlefield. Lemordant spent eighteen months in German captivity before he was repatriated. Subsequently, exaggerated accounts circulated in the press concerning Lemordant's war service, the extent of his wounds, and the impairment of his vision, as well as his captivity and escape attempts in Germany. Lemordant himself muddied the waters by his own variable accounts of these experiences. He clearly "milked" his reputation as the "blind artist." Regardless of these controversies, the bullet that entered Lemordant's right eye and exited through his left temple caused the artist enduring difficulties with his health and vision: difficulties that were significantly relieved after an operation that followed a car accident in 1935. See Cariou, *Jean-Julien Lemordant*, 90–7, 129–30.

7.11. Luc-Albert Moreau, *The Death of Riquet.*

cheeks hollowed from fever, moist temples. Nothing but a face; the body can be guessed at, inert beneath the overcoat which covers it; one hears the shallow and rapid breath of this man who truly is nothing any longer except one thing: Suffering."[59] "These graphic descriptions of the moment when life passes into death," writes Philippe Vatin of Lemordant's portraits, "are, by their sincerity, their modesty, superior in dramatic intensity to paintings of corpses."[60]

The vogue for these artistic representations of the soldier's death developed only during the 1930s, when the threat of a new war made the lessons of the previous one seem especially pertinent. Lemordant's expressive works depicting suffering soldiers were produced between 1925 and 1935.[61] It was in 1937 that they were displayed by the Museum of the Great War, at Vincennes. "It is a nightmare vision," announced *Le Temps*. "The miseries of war which destroys objects as well as men, which mixes the latter, still living, with the earth, so that they are confounded with one another [...] Horror, pain to the utmost limits of feeling [...] What a teaching! What a lesson!"[62] The most important works by Moreau date from 1932–33 and his illustrations for Montherlant's *Chant funèbre pour les morts de Verdun* from 1936.[63] It was also in 1936 that René Marca published a series of forty lithographs entitled *The Nightmare of the War*. These focused upon the suffering of the *poilu* who, in the final print, is represented on the cross of crucifixion. In images such as "Terror" and "Under the Bombardment," Marca depicted the emotional dimension of that suffering, wherein the soldiers' fear is displayed in their contorted facial expressions and cringing bodies. In others, such as "the tragic trench" with its crude depiction of dismembered bodies, or "the common grave," which showed soldiers stacking the dead like so much firewood, he emphasized both the brutality and the banality of the soldier's death. Marca's images, like those of Moreau, harmonized with both the pacifist spirit of the veterans' movement, which reached its apogee in the early 1930s, and with the commemorative culture which that movement did so much to shape and foster. Ironically, however, it would not be until another war had already begun, in the spring of 1940, that one of the biggest displays of First World War artists would take place, at the Pavillon de Marsan in Paris, featuring over a hundred works by Dunoyer de Segonzac and Luc-Albert Moreau alone.[64] Nevertheless, despite

59 Lelièvre, "L'oeuvre de guerre de J.-J. Lemordant," 18.
60 Vatin, *Voir et montrer la guerre*, 461.
61 Cariou, *Jean-Julien Lemordant*, 130–1.
62 *Le Temps*, 16 June 1937.
63 "Funeral Song for the Dead of Verdun." Montherlant, *Chant funèbre*.
64 Vatin, *Voir et montrer la guerre*, 249.

this late proliferation, what demands explanation, in the words of Philippe Dagen, is the "silence of the painters" before the fact of the soldier's death.[65] Nor was it just the painters who were silent. For, as Joëlle Beurier has demonstrated, the representation of the dead, whether through photographs or through artists' depictions, experienced a steady decline in the mass circulation papers from the end of 1914. It was as if, once the heroic images of the soldier's death had been discredited by photographs depicting its stark reality, it could not be represented at all.[66] This repression is a theme to which we will return. In the meantime, it is sufficient to note that the artistic representations that emerged so painfully from the artists' studios in the 1930s had already become a dominant feature in the world of literature.

WAR BOOKS:
FROM SACRIFICE TO SLAUGHTER

The literary production of the First World War demonstrates that it was easier to write about death than to paint it. During the war, as the previous chapter has already shown, soldiers' confrontation with the realities of modern warfare led them progressively to reject pre-war representations of warfare as well as idealized representations of the soldier's death. Writers like Rimbault, Barbusse, and Duhamel dismissed as so much *bourrage de crâne* the idea that soldiers went joyously to their deaths. The disillusioned representations of war in the works of these and other writers helped to generate a major cultural shift in France whereby war, once perceived as an ultimate manifestation of national strength, courage, and honour, came to be perceived as a universal catastrophe.[67] Many war novels published after 1918, reflecting a pervasive current of disappointment with the postwar settlement, were even more despairing than those written during the war years; they depicted the soldier's death with the same grim horror as Barbusse and with the same sorrowfulness as Duhamel, but without the same faith in its purpose. For Roland Dorgelès, who wrote *Les croix de bois*[68] in 1919, the soldier's suffering was redeemed only by the camaraderie of the front, which united both living and dead through an indissoluble bond. In common with many others, Dorgelès emphasized the impersonal nature of modern combat, where soldiers died without ever seeing, let alone coming to grips with, the enemy. "It was a battle

65 Dagen, *Le silence des peintres*.
66 Beurier, "Voir ou ne pas voir la mort?," 63–8.
67 On this theme, see Prost, *Republican Identities*, 93–105.
68 "The Wooden Crosses."

without enemies, death without combat," was how the narrator of *Les croix de bois* described one battle. "Since we began fighting in the morning, we had not seen twenty Germans. The dead, nothing but the dead."[69] The novel insists upon the capriciousness and the banality of the soldier's death. Gilbert witnesses the death of a comrade. "Was he sad? Hardly [...] On this poor, empty wasteland, it was just one more body, another blue sleeper that would be buried after the attack, if possible."[70] The soldiers in Gilbert's squad die, one after the other, not heroically, with patriotic sentiments on their lips, but despairingly, clinging hopelessly to lives they have already lost. Berval dies in the arms of Gilbert, incoherently cursing and forgiving his unfaithful wife. Gilbert himself, whose wife Suzy has also taken up with another man, dies alone in a woods, his only comfort as he waits for stretcher bearers who never come the words of a nostalgic song about Montmartre he had once sung with his comrades. In this account, whether one is brave or a coward makes no difference. Broucke dies from a German bombardment because he has taken the place on sentry duty of Bouffioux. His last words to his comrade express disgust: "I dunno what you've got for guts, but it ain't much."[71] Bouffioux himself is killed shortly thereafter, at the beginning of the attack that results in the massacre of the remainder of the squad. Sulphart alone survives to experience a "hero's return," greeted by public indifference and the news that his wife has run off with a Belgian, taking the furniture with her.

Even more despairing was René Naegelen's *Les suppliciés*,[72] published in 1927, which tells the story of the disillusionment of Jacques Féroul. One after the other, Jacques's comrades are killed. Bourdon is among the first to die, struck full in the face by a shell burst. Jacques watches in terror as the wounded man, sightless and with a terrible wound where his face had been, staggers blindly into no man's land, where he collapses.[73] Even more gruesome are the deaths of two soldiers caught by an exploding shell as they shelter beside Jacques in a crater: one eviscerated, the other with his leg shattered, their bodies grotesquely entwined. "The disemboweled one, already dead, is losing his entrails, the other tries to shake himself free, rolls horrified eyes; he has a mangled left leg, a red stain which spreads on his greatcoat. He looks at Jacques, a mute question, a silent prayer, opens his fly, a last unconscious act which precedes the end, and dies

69 Dorgelès, *Les croix de bois*, 190.
70 Ibid., 187.
71 Ibid., 255.
72 "The Tortured Ones."
73 Naegelen, *Les suppliciés*, 122–3.

urinating on the gaping wound of his comrade."[74] Jacques also bears witness to the peculiar mix of callousness and compassion with which soldiers confronted the deaths of their companions. Courtois Léon has both legs horribly mutilated by a shell. Unable to remove him from the trenches, all his comrades can do is to make the dying soldier comfortable and keep him company during his last moments: "It is a sight they have witnessed many times, and they contemplate it without curiosity, nor with evident pain."[75] Those final moments over, the captain utters an epitaph that conveys how banal the soldier's death had become: "It's too bad, we won't find anybody else in the company as good at patching up shoes."[76] Jacques's closest friend, Georges Schmidt, is killed even as the war approaches its final months, mutilated by a shell blast and unrecognizable. By this time, Jacques has been robbed of all hope: "What has become of his youthful enthusiasm for the war for Justice and Civilization? Where is his ardour of September '15? His faith in war killing war? All gone! He no longer has even his stoic courage of April '17. He was still ready, then, to sacrifice his life, because he believed in Victory, in Peace dawning over fields of the dead [...] Now, he has nothing, nothing but the anguish of death one day laying him low, bloody, under the rain, the wind, bullets and shells, beneath the pitiless heavens and the indifferent Gods."[77] Here, through the disillusioned gaze of Jacques Féroul, we are confronted by a vision of the soldier's death that is utterly without hope or consolation.

This disenchanted view of the soldier's death was confirmed in the 1930s in novels by Jean Giono and Céline. In Giono's *Le grand troupeau*,[78] the parallels between men going to war and sheep going to slaughter are explicit: "to the abbatoir," comments one character as he witnesses troops preparing to mount an offensive.[79] Giono's attitude toward the war is revealed through the story of Olivier Chabrand, who ensures his own survival through a self-inflicted wound after witnessing the massacre of his comrades. Olivier's self-mutilation is approvingly likened to the action of a fox that has the courage to escape its trap by biting off its own foot.[80] The rejection of war at all costs was the lesson taught by Giono. This point of view was not dissimilar to that expressed in *Voyage au bout de la nuit*,[81]

74 Ibid., 134.
75 Ibid., 154.
76 Ibid., 165.
77 Ibid., 288.
78 The novel was translated into English under the title *To the Slaughterhouse*. Giono, *To the Slaughterhouse*.
79 Giono, *Le grand troupeau*, 242.
80 Ibid., 246.
81 "Journey to the end of the night."

the 1932 novel by Louis-Ferdinand Destouches, who wrote under the pen name of Céline. For Ferdinand Bardamu, Céline's anti-hero, the war was an "apocalyptic crusade," a "mass flight, toward murder in common, toward the fight,"[82] a fight which, like every war before it, was destined to be forgotten. The only certainty the war offered the soldier was the inevitability of death; the only uncertainties his exact manner of dying and whether death would be inflicted by his own side or by the enemy.[83] Bardamu's views were bitterly contemptuous of officers, whether they sacrificed their own lives or those of the men they commanded. He unsympathetically recounted the fate of his colonel, eviscerated by the same shell that decapitated a cavalry trooper reporting to him and with whom he died in a gory embrace. "They embraced each other for that moment and for all time but the trooper no longer had his head, nothing but an opening above the neck, with blood gurgling up like jam in a pot. The colonel's belly was opened up, his face twisted in pain."[84] "So much the worse for him!" Bardamu concluded. "If he had left at the time of the first shots, that would not have happened to him."[85] For Bardamu himself – and for Destouches/Céline, who avoided returning to the front after being wounded early in the war by feigning shell shock – the only rational response to the war was indeed to take flight: to preserve his own life at all costs, even if the only way to escape the madness of war was by pretending to be mad himself.

SHEEP OR WOLVES?

In considering the "soldier's tale" presented in *Voyage au bout de la nuit* Jay Winter has argued that the book's author, Destouches/Céline, was engaged in a process of "self-fashioning," which sought to reconcile his identity with his pre-war life and his wartime memories. The identity he thereby fashioned – that of a cowardly malingerer who launched vitriolic attacks on Jews and women under the cover of false claims of shell shock – was an extreme one that few veterans would have been eager to claim for themselves. Indeed, Winter presents the narrative of René Cassin as a more normative case. Cassin, severely wounded in October 1914, survived both his wounds and the incompetent care he received from the medical services to become a leader of the veterans' movement and of the campaign for human rights. Despite the trauma of his war experience, Cassin, says Winter,

82 Céline, *Voyage au bout de la nuit*, 19.
83 Ibid., 33.
84 Ibid., 23.
85 Ibid.

was able to assimilate it to his pre-war identity as a patriotic Frenchman and as a Jew. Although poles apart, the examples of Destouches/Céline and Cassin are useful in illuminating the challenge of integrating memory and identity that confronted all veterans of the Great War. Winter argues that between the unshaken identity of Cassin and the false one construed by Destouches/Céline were the more or less uncertain ones of shell-shocked soldiers who struggled in vain to bring memory and identity into line.[86] This was a challenge that many veterans wrestled with for the remainder of their lives. Some memories were particularly difficult to integrate. Understandably, in a war that had placed death "at the core of representations,"[87] the biggest challenge was to assimilate memories of violent death. And it was easier for most veterans to do this by representing themselves as death's victims rather than as its agents.

Antoine Prost convincingly argues in his study of the French veterans' movement after the First World War that the prevalence of images representing the sacrifice of French soldiers helped to occlude more troubling memories of those soldiers as the perpetrators of mass killing. The soldier's experience of death, says Prost, was not reduced to agonized victimhood, although that was the aspect that was easiest to discuss since it both evoked sympathy and conveyed the correct message about the horrors of war. Some French soldiers, notes Prost, were also executioners: "and that experience, though rejected, buried deep within consciences, smothered in silence, nonetheless marked the combatants."[88]

Given their reluctance to talk about it, there is an absence of direct testimony on the part of soldiers concerning their involvement in the act of killing. From what evidence there is, however, it is apparent that not all French soldiers were bothered by such involvement. Lucien Laby, although a medical doctor, wrote repeatedly in 1914 of his determination to remove the armband that identified him as a non-combatant, go up to the front and realize his childhood dream "to drop some Boches."[89] Finally, on 9 November 1914, he was able to record proudly in his notebook that he had achieved his goal in killing at least one German and that, having accomplished "my duty as a Frenchman," he could return to his role as a doctor.[90] Laby subsequently went so far as to express his approval of the slaughter of three German machine gunners whose carotid arteries had clearly been deliberately cut after their position had been overrun: "truly

86 Winter, *Remembering War*, 52–76.
87 Prost, *Republican Identities*, 98.
88 Prost, *Les anciens combattants*, vol. 3: *Mentalités et idéologies*, 14.
89 Laby, *Les carnets de l'aspirant Laby*, 72.
90 Ibid., 80.

it is fine work." His description of one of his men jubilantly standing on
the bodies to make them bleed and another smoking the dead men's
tobacco hints at the state of combat-generated exaltation that facilitated
such massacres.[91] Even soldiers who detested the war were capable of killing
in the heat of the moment or in exceptional circumstances. Marcel
Papillon's letters to his parents were anything but bloodthirsty, but even
he, outraged that "a Boche had the cheek to enter my cabin and to make
off with one of my shoes," expressed his satisfaction at firing three shots
into the backside of the disappearing German and of subsequently recovering his shoe, along with the intruder's abandoned rifle and haversack.[92]

Other soldiers were clearly unsettled by their involvement in killing.
Antoine Martin recounted to his wife in December 1914 an attack that
had caught the German defenders sleeping, leaving the enemy trenches
"filled with corpses": "we did them in at will."[93] The following month, he
felt compelled to write to reassure her that such experiences had not served
to brutalize him. "Yes, one is a bit crazy at the time, intoxicated by the
powder and by the racket [...] we are like beasts. But immediately after, it
is over, and one thinks no more of it, except to say what one did, and for
the bodies lying between the trenches."[94] Paul Tuffrau, after calling upon
the best shot in his company to shoot a German soldier who had unwittingly
left himself exposed while enjoying the morning air in the front lines,
expressed his revulsion at the killing: "These murders, where one man who
is protected kills another, revolt me." For Tuffrau, the cowardliness of the
act was compounded by the commonness of the executioner: "a big,
awkward peasant, rustic, appearance lumpish and simple."[95]

Both Martin and Tuffrau were troubled by their actions: Martin for what
they said about him as a loving husband and father; Tuffrau for what they
implied about his self-perception as an honourable and civilized officer.
As a particularly compelling example of the long-term difficulty soldiers
had in coming to terms with memories of their participation in acts
of violence, both Antoine Prost and Leonard Smith cite the case of
Maurice Genevoix. As we have seen, Genevoix provided an unforgettable
account of French soldiers suffering under German bombardment in his
narrative of the fighting at Les Éparges. In the same work he also described
the experience of hand-to-hand fighting in the struggle for possession of
a mine crater at the outset of the February 1915 offensive. On this occasion,

91 Ibid., 117.
92 Papillon et al., "*Si je reviens*," 174.
93 Martin, *La chasse à l'homme*, 56
94 Ibid., 77.
95 Tuffrau, *1914–1918*, 115.

Genevoix and two comrades shot and killed a German soldier who suddenly confronted them, waving a Mauser.[96] This killing troubled Genevoix far less than those he was responsible for in September 1914, when he found himself overrun by Germans during a night-time attack. Placing a German helmet on his head, Genevoix ran alongside the enemy soldiers toward his own lines, taking the opportunity to kill three of them with shots to the head. Although he recounted this incident in *Sous Verdun*, first published in 1916, he suppressed it in later editions and did not restore it until 1950, when a footnote was added confessing to a "lack of honesty in voluntarily omitting one of the episodes of the war that shook me most profoundly and which marked my memory with an indelible imprint."[97] Genevoix continued to struggle with his memories of this experience for the rest of his life. Clearly, he had great difficulty reconciling the memory of his action in killing three unsuspecting German soldiers from behind to his own sense of self: far more difficulty than in coming to terms with his later action when firing on a battle-crazed enemy who was doing his best to kill him.[98]

Even more difficult to acknowledge than the fact of killing was the idea that some soldiers had positively developed a taste for it. This notion, at odds with the pacifist sentiments of the French veterans' movement as well as the widespread aversion to war during the 1920s and 1930s, was given prominence in the extraordinary 1934 novel of Roger Vercel, *Capitaine Conan*.[99] The eponymous anti-hero of the novel, Captain Conan, the commander of a "free corps" of French soldiers whose specialty is the trench raid – he proudly claims responsibility for "fifty-two Fritzes rubbed out in eighteen raids"[100] – asserts that it was elite warriors like his who had won the war: "It is the knife that won the war, not the gun! A *poilu* who would hold fast against an armoured train will flee at the very thought of men who come with a dagger [...] There were perhaps three thousand of us, not more, who used them, on all fronts. It is those three thousand who are the real victors! The others only had to mop up behind![101] Conan also acknowledged, however, that his inevitable fate, as well as that of his comrades, was to be rejected once they were no longer useful. The same "swine" who had armed them with trench knives would cry: "Hide that! It

96 Genevoix, *Ceux de 14*, 583.

97 Ibid., 51. See also Frost, *Les anciens combattants*, vol. 3: *Mentalités et idéologies*, 15.

98 Smith aptly summarizes the significance of Genevoix's struggle to reconcile memory and identity. The various versions of the story, he writes, "really told a single tale – his attempt to master experience by creating an embattled self in various guises as humane narrator." Smith, *The Embattled Self*, 100.

99 "Captain Conan."

100 Vercel, *Capitaine Conan*, 16.

101 Ibid., 189.

is not a French weapon, the fine nickel-plated sword of our ancestors [...]
And then, hide your hands, too, your filthy hands that dabbled in blood
while we, we had gloves to point our range finders."[102] Conan's avowal
and Vercel's novel provide eloquent testimony to the difficulty of assimilat-
ing memories of wartime blood lust in the inter-war years. The contrast
between the acceptable image of the *poilu* nobly sacrificing his life for the
homeland and the unacceptable one of killers like Conan is emphasized
in the final scene of the novel, as the narrator goes in search of his former
comrade. He finally locates Conan, who is dying of cancer, in a cafe of an
obscure French village, close by the monument to the dead, where, "in real
bronze [...] a soldier dies standing up, without disturbing a fold of his
greatcoat, without letting go of the flag he clutches to his heart."[103] Some
memories of the war, Vercel implies, could be idealized and immortalized
in bronze; others were to be placed under a veil and quietly forgotten.

CHANGING ATTITUDES

Vercel's evocation of the war monument and its heroically dying *poilu* at
the conclusion of *Capitaine Conan* is a wry comment on the commemorative
culture that had developed after the war, which insisted upon the soldier
nobly and willingly sacrificing his life, not endeavouring, through fair
means and foul, to take the lives of others. Through its frank exposure of
this latter reality, Vercel's novel might be seen as anti-monumental in nature.
Indeed, Carine Trevisan sees many of the texts that emerged from the
experience and memory of the First World War as anti-monuments, resisting the closure offered by the civic culture of commemoration.[104] Trevisan's
study points to the insufficiency of the rituals of commemoration in assuag-
ing individual grief. Indeed, many of the texts to which she refers insist
upon the incommensurability of that grief, the impossibility that it could
ever be alleviated. In these writings grief was permanently etched on the
bodies of mothers and widows, made manifest in their sterility, and endured
as a curse by the next generation.[105] The war novels of the interwar years,
by insisting upon the individuality of the soldiers who died, the specificity
of their wounds, the extent and the pointlessness of their torture, refused

102 Ibid.
103 Ibid., 215.
104 Trevisan, *Les fables du deuil*, 73.
105 Ibid., 103–24.

the consolation of collective commemoration or of the official discourse of sacrifice. The wounds they exposed were ones that never healed.[106]

Collective commemoration of the war dead was a mass movement initiated from below that was hugely successful in creating symbols and rituals to heal the wounds of war and enable the comrades and relatives of those who had died to grieve their loss. For some, however, that loss was too great. The case studies of mourning presented by Stéphane Audoin-Rouzeau demonstrate that for many relatives of men killed in the First World War the tomb of the Unknown Soldier or a name inscribed upon a war memorial was cold comfort. Hence, the extraordinary efforts made by Jane Catulle-Mendès to recover the body of her son, Primice, killed on the Chemin des Dames in the spring of 1917. This took no fewer than three separate trips to the front, over six months, as well as some determined trading upon her status as wife of a famous poet, to accomplish. It was also accompanied by the dedication of a cult to her son by Jane, focused upon the tomb she prepared for him at Mormellon but incorporating "relics" that included his war letters, bloodstained personal effects from the front, locks of hair, milk teeth, and portraits. Jane pointedly stayed away from the official victory parade of 14 July 1919. Although professing not to believe in religion or an afterlife, she nonetheless sanctified the memory of her son, capitalizing "*Toi*" when she addressed herself to him in her writing and praying to him to accord his protection to another son, Robert.[107] More elaborate was the cult dedicated by his parents to Maurice Gallé, who was killed during the Battle of the Somme on 25 September 1916. Unable to exhume their son's body until 1920, Maurice's parents subsequently not only erected a massive stone calvary on the site where he died, at Bouchavesnes, but also transformed the family home at Creil into a shrine dedicated to his memory. Maurice was eulogized as a pious Christian who gave his life willingly for his fatherland. "Let us not weep for those who fall, for they are the happy ones," words from one of Maurice's letters from the front, were transcribed on a stone monument in the garden.[108] Letters,

---

106 In like manner, as Amy Lyford demonstrates, the Surrealists challenged the postwar tendency, encouraged by officialdom, to mask or minimize the wounds of war. "By focusing on dismemberment, surrealist artists and writers endowed the terrible experiences of the war with a physical and mental permanence." Lyford, *Surrealist Masculinities*, 68. Stephen Forcer also argues that the Surrealists' preoccupation with themes of altered states of consciousness, moral transgression, and the human drives of sex and aggression contained an acknowledgment that mass killing in war could be a pleasurable activity for some of its participants. In this sense, too, the Surrealists were more prepared than the rest of society to keep alive the darker memories of the war. See Forcer, "Beyond Mental," 85–107.

107 Audoin-Rouzeau, *Cinq deuils de guerre*, 203–51.

108 Ibid., 128.

portraits, and other relics recounted the story of the young hero's life and death in a series of "stations" within the house. These two examples point at once to the efficaciousness and the insufficiency of the culture of commemoration that emerged during and after the war. The parents of Maurice Gallé appear never to have questioned the consent of their son to the sacrifice demanded of him, nor the divine grace that was his reward. Jane Catulle-Mendès, however, was less willing to accept the sacrifice of her son for the sake of the homeland. "Nobody loves France more than me," she wrote. "But one loves nothing more than one's child."[109] Whatever the consolations of religion or patriotism, neither precluded enduring sorrow, a mourning that was, as Audoin-Rouzeau states with respect to Berthe Gallé, "infinite, interminable, unfinished."[110]

The micro-histories of mourning presented by Audoin-Rouzeau point to the difficulty – the impossibility, even – of the bereaved coming to terms with their loss and concluding the process of mourning. Several factors accentuated this difficulty. Relatives' awareness of the loneliness, agony, and degradation of the soldier's death was first among them. The absence of bodies, as we have seen, was another problem for which creative solutions – the tomb of the Unknown Soldier, the ossuaries, and communal war monuments – had to be found. Another obstacle was the expectation placed upon relatives to repress their suffering out of respect for the sacrifice of the dead. Sometimes this came from the dead themselves, as Maurice Gallé's injunction against tears illustrates. Germain Cuzacq, a peasant soldier from Gascony, wrote from Verdun to his wife Anna in June 1916, counselling her on how to cope with the news that his brother-in-law had been killed. "Share with them their sorrow," he advised her with respect to her relatives. But, he added, "In spite of everything, they must react by telling themselves that they are not the only families in mourning and that there will be many others before the intense battles of this sort are over."[111] Furthermore, the sanctification of the dead within the cult of patriotic sacrifice itself prevented the living from achieving the necessary separation from the dead, as the dead soldier risked becoming an object of perpetual veneration.[112]

109 Jane Catulle-Mendès, *La prière sur l'enfant mort* (Paris: A. Lemerre, 1921). Cited in ibid., 232.

110 Audoin-Rouzeau, *Cinq deuils de guerre*, 138.

111 Cuzacq must have been aware that he was also counselling his wife on how to deal with his own death, which occurred on 3 September 1916. Cuzacq, *Le soldat de Lagraulet*, 122–3.

112 Audoin-Rouzeau and Becker, *14–18, Retrouver la guerre*, 242–58.

The unprecedented scale of the losses sustained by French society in the war meant that it was not just individuals, but an entire society that was in mourning. The war's impact on collective mentalities, however, was far from straightforward. On the one hand, it brought to its apogee the cult of the dead which, since the Romantic era, had tended to dramatize death, emphasizing ostentatious expressions of grief and sorrow on the part of mourners, as well as elaborate funerals, while insisting upon individualized graves and monuments as sites of communion between the living and the spirits of the dead.[113] On the other hand, it demonstrated the incommensurability between such traditions and death on such a vast and terrible scale. In the words of David Cannadine, "What point was there in donning widow's weeds when the husband probably lay mutilated, unidentified and unburied on the fields of Flanders? What comfort could crepe or black-edged notepaper bring in the face of bereavement at once so harrowing, so unnatural and so widespread?"[114] "It is not worth the trouble to send me paper bordered in black," Germain Cuzacq instructed his wife in June 1916. The popular support for the construction of monuments to the dead, for the rituals of 11 November, and for pilgrimages to battlefield ossuaries and the tomb of the Unknown Soldier represented a highly creative effort to forge new and more efficacious traditions. But the commemorative culture's sanitized representation of the soldier's death was contradicted by the photographs in the newspapers and by the literary accounts that proliferated after the war. Even if they accepted that it was in the service of a glorious cause, the manner of the soldier's death which these media revealed could only be a source of distress for his relations. Far from the "fine" death of patriotic myth, it was not even a "good" death, in which the dying man and his family took charge of the occasion.[115] Rather, it was passive, lonely, and humiliating. Bereaved relatives therefore confronted a situation in which they were compelled to accept as a patriotic necessity a death that by its very nature was unacceptable. Joëlle Beurier argues that the only way to resolve such a contradiction was through a repression that stifled mourning and petrified grief. At the very moment,

113 Ariès, *The Hour of Our Death*, 409–556; Hutton, "Of Death and Destiny," 153. Thierry Hardier and Jean-François Jagielski write: "The return, as much on the field of battle as at the rear, of day-to-day death touching directly or indirectly the whole of the populations at war did not check the mental processes of respect for the individuality of deaths, of individual or collective mourning, of the cult of the dead of deep but resigned sorrow that had been born in the course of the decades preceding the conflict." Hardier and Jagielski, *Combattre et mourir*, 347.

114 Cannadine, *War and Death*, 218.

115 Ariès, *The Hour of Our Death*, 448; Ariès, *Essais sur l'histoire de la mort*, 63; Beurier, "Voir ou ne pas voir la mort," 67–8.

therefore, when mass death cut its deepest swaths through French society, the visible signs of mourning – mourning dress, in particular – became less apparent. Perhaps this was, as Beurier suggests, a first step toward the denial of death that became prevalent in Western societies by the second half of the twentieth century.[116]

At the very least, the war marked a turning point in terms of attitudes toward the deaths of young people. The Homeric ideal of the young warrior whose beauty was immortalized through death in battle was at last subjected to bitter attack.[117] To be sure, there is less evidence of intergenerational bitterness in the wartime writings of French soldiers than in those of their English counterparts. There is no French equivalent of Wilfred Owen's chilling "The Parable of the Old Man and the Young," which retells the biblical story of Abraham and Isaac with a savage twist in the tail, whereby Abraham chooses to kill his son "and half the seed of Europe, one by one."[118] Indeed, when Émile Carlier wrote a despairing letter to his aunt in September 1916 explaining what he perceived to be the inevitability of his own death, he wrote in a tone of sorrowful resignation rather than of bitterness: "Our generation must be sacrificed but our successors will see the victory."[119] Lucien Murat even saw it as his duty, as a twenty-one-year-old, to turn down a promotion, allowing an older man to take a safe office job, so that he could return to the front: "my place is opposite the Boches, as an example."[120] After the war, however, the idea of generational betrayal became a significant literary theme. "It was a war of the old," wrote Aragon, "for reasons which excited the old, which did not affect the young, and it was the young who fought it in their place."[121] Giono evoked this theme in several passages of *Le grand troupeau*, most notably in a scene where the shepherd Burle accuses the village elder Malan of

116 Beurier, "Voir ou ne pas voir la mort," 67–8. On the "denial of death," see Ariès, *The Hour of Our Death*, 559–601.

117 It did not vanish entirely, of course. There are echoes of it in the commemorative culture of the war, most obviously in the poem of Laurence Binyon, "For the Fallen," which is recited at British ceremonies of remembrance: "They shall grow / not old, as we / that are left grow / old: / Age shall not / weary them, nor / the years condemn." Laurence Binyon, "For the Fallen," in *Poetry of the First World War*, ed. Tim Kendall, 44.

118 Cited in Wohl, *The Generation of 1914*, 105. Wohl's chapter on "England: Lost Legions of Youth," demonstrates how potent the idea of a sacrificed generation was in Britain after the war.

119 Carlier, *Mort? Pas encore!*, 149.

120 Murat, *Carnets de guerre*, 131.

121 Aragon, *Pour expliquer ce que j'étais* (Paris: Gallimard, 1989), 35–6. Cited in Trevisan, *Les fables du deuil*, 30–1. Trevisan provides several further examples of how scenes in *Le grand troupeau*, *Les croix de bois*, and *Voyage au bout de la nuit* evoked the idea of the war as infanticide and of the homeland as a mother who, like Saturn, devoured her own children. Ibid., 31–5.

metaphorically trampling on his three sons with manure-covered boots: "you walk on their heads, on their mouths and on their eyes; you, yes, you Malan, even as you sit there, next to the fire, warming yourself, with your new pipe!"[122]

Giono's rejection of the idea of youthful sacrifice as a violation of the natural order of things reflected the terrible irony that the Great War's holocaust of youth occurred following a period when the chances of children surviving to outlive their parents had never been better.[123] The diminution of young people dying from other causes could only make the effects of war seem more aberrant. Henri de Montherlant, puzzling that "Death revolts us more, perhaps because life is less hard, perhaps because we are without religious hope," recognized the contemporary revulsion against war: 'To the question: 'is the good of war worth its evil?' without even knowing whether the good it sacrifices is recoverable, the present replies: no."[124]

This revulsion against war, in many ways a reflection of the changed representations and perceptions of the soldier's death, only intensified as the approach of a new war seemed to make a mockery of the sacrifices of the last. In the realm of film, it was in the 1930s that the most important French films representing the horrors of combat and the meaninglessness of the soldier's death were released. These were *Verdun, visions d'histoire*[125] (first released as a silent film in 1928, reissued with sound in 1931) and *Les croix de bois* (1932). Both films contained realistic scenes of the fighting, with *Les croix de bois* highlighting the emotional suffering of the *poilu*. Both films ended with a scene representing a field of crosses, evoking the tragic waste of the war. Although less focused on the fighting, Jean Renoir's *Grande illusion* (1937) and Abel Gance's remake of his 1918 film *J'accuse*[126] (1938) also expressed strongly pacifist sentiments. The shooting of the French aristocratic officer Boeldieu by his German counterpart, Raffenstein, at the climax of *Grande illusion*, suggested that the heroic death exalted by men of their pedigree had become as much an anachronism as the warrior class itself. *J'accuse* memorably recalled the dead – played by disfigured veterans of the war – from their sleep on the battlefield of Verdun as a

---

122 Giono, *Le grand troupeau*, 113. See Trevisan, *Les fables du deuil*, 31.

123 Between 1881 and 1911, mortality for infants aged one to five had declined by a massive 54 per cent. Dupâquier, ed., *Histoire de la population française*, vol. 3, 297.

124 Montherlant, *Chant funèbre*, 127, 132.

125 "Verdun: Visions of History."

126 "I Accuse."

ghostly warning for those who were ready once again to unleash the dogs of war.[127]

In the literary world, too, pacifism prevailed. Jules Romains published *Verdun*, the sixteenth volume of his epic serial *Les hommes de bonne volonté*[128] in 1938. Through the voice of Jerphanion, Romains mused on what kept men in the trenches before Verdun. It was the constraint of society, in the first instance, he said, that compelled men to fight. But beyond that, war was a social atavism in which primal urges of self-destruction and sexuality forged a complicit bond between executioners and victims: "'It's a business,' concluded Jerphanion, 'where there are many victims, but few innocent ones.'"[129] The point is driven home in the novel's concluding scene, which describes the death of Wazemmes, a dragoon whose political convictions were as fluid as his efforts to stay out of the front lines were unsuccessful. Having exchanged the royalism of the *marraine*[130] whom he had unsuccessfully courted for the republicanism of a typist he had just met, Wazemmes is called upon, on 9 April 1916, to lead an attack on a German trench by a battalion of green recruits. The youngsters are cut down by shellfire as they advance singing the Marseillaise. Wazemmes also dies: "He does not even have a second to tell himself that he has been wounded, that he is suffering horribly, and that it is over."[131] The final page of the novel provides an ironic comment on the gulf between the futility of Wazemmes's attack and the communiqué in which General Pétain described it as a heroic victory, concluding with the famous phrase, "*Courage ... on les aura!*"[132] The reader is reminded that it is only April, that the Battle of Verdun is far from over, and that a double chain of trucks ceaselessly traversing the *voie sacrée* from Bar-le-Duc continues to feed the war. In *Verdun* Romains had recast the soldier's death in a way that gave the lie to accounts of heroic sacrifice.

All the same, despite the pacifism expressed in literature, art, and film, as well as by the veterans' movement, remembrance of the soldier's death did not acquire, for most Frenchmen, the same taint of futility it acquired in British culture between the wars. The irony through which Britons came to perceive the war was largely alien to France. After all, French soldiers had, most of them, died on French soil and through their sacrifice they had finally succeeded in liberating that soil from the German invader.

127 On these French films, see the excellent analysis by Andrew Kelly, *Cinema and the Great War*, 101–27.

128 "The Men of Good Will."

129 Romains, *Les hommes de bonne volonté*, vol. 16: *Verdun*, 221.

130 Literally, "Godmother," a *marraine* was a woman who "adopted" a soldier, providing him with moral and material support by writing letters and sending small gifts to him.

131 Romains, *Les hommes de bonne volonté*, vol. 16: *Verdun*, 280.

132 "Have courage... We will get them!" Ibid., 281.

Whereas in Britain the high diction that had served to elevate and mask the experience of war was brought into disrepute by the war poets, in France even a word such as "Glory" remained an acceptable part of the lexicon.[133] Above all, the concept of sacrifice that was at the heart of the commemorative culture continued to dominate representations. The film version of *Les croix de bois* may have insisted upon the horrors of war, but it also deployed a wealth of Christian symbols to emphasize the sacrificial – and hence redemptive – quality of the soldier's death.[134] The commemorative culture in France was republican rather than patriotic, emphasizing the debt of the nation to its citizens rather than vice versa.[135] That culture therefore lacked the aggressive, nationalist tone that characterized its Germanic counterpart.[136] The idealization of the self-sacrifice of the war generation nonetheless imposed a burden upon subsequent generations not only of recognition but also of emulation. Roland Dorgelès, upon his "*Return to the Front*" in 1940, saw in the soldiers defending the Maginot line the reincarnation of the *poilus* of 1914–18, as well as of the same spirit of unity and self-sacrifice in defence of the nation that had characterized his own generation.[137] The experience of the First World War and the representations of the soldier's death to which it gave rise in film, photography, art, sculpture, and literature may have discredited the traditional idea of the "fine" military death, but it did little to diminish respect for the sacrifice of the common soldier and may indeed have increased it. As the French prepared to fight another war, that sacrifice remained a powerful inspiration.

133 This contrast between French and British remembrance of the war is made by Jay Winter. See Winter, "Cultural Divergences in Patterns of Remembering."

134 Martin Hurcombe demonstrates that this was an important means whereby Roland Dorgelès, who co-wrote the script for the film with two other writers, asserted the claim of the war generation to exercise moral and political leadership at a time when the veterans' movement was at the height of its influence. See Hurcombe, "The Haunting of Roland D," 141.

135 Prost, *Republican Identities*, 32.

136 George Mosse argues that while the cult of the fallen soldiers had similar traits throughout Europe, providing "a bridge from the horror to the glory of war and from the despair of the present to hope for the future," it was significantly more aggressive in Germany, where it was co-opted by the political Right: "in Germany there was a brutal edge to the cult [...] which was largely absent elsewhere." Mosse, *Fallen Soldiers*, 104–6.

137 Hurcombe, "The Haunting of Roland D," 142–6

8

Dying for la mère patrie*:*
Colonized Soldiers in the Second World War

INTRODUCTION

Captain Charles N'Tchoréré of the Fifty-Third RICMS[1] was summarily executed on 7 June 1940 by a German Panzer officer for insisting upon his rights as a French officer.[2] Captain N'Tchoréré, a native of Gabon who had served in the French army since joining as a volunteer in 1916, was one of very few non-European soldiers to obtain an officer's commission. He had served with distinction in Syria, where he was wounded in 1925; five years later he was awarded the Legion of Honour. On the day he was killed, Captain N'Tchoréré had finally been compelled to surrender after three days of heavy fighting during which he had led his company's stubborn resistance to the advance of General Rommel's Seventh Panzer Corps at Airaines, in the Somme. The Fifty-Third RICMS was virtually destroyed in the engagement, suffering 90 per cent casualties. German reports insisted upon the ferocity of the fighting, which resolved itself into desperate hand-to-hand combat. "The Blacks made use of every defensive possibility to the fullest," said a report in the *Pommerische Zeitung.* "Every house was defended. To break this resistance, it was necessary to activate the flamethrowers and, to overcome the last of the Senegalese, to kill them one by one."[3] In the aftermath of the fighting, the Germans separated the

1 Mixed Colonial Infantry Regiment of Tirailleurs Sénégalais. Mixed Colonial regiments were composed of both European and indigenous troops.

2 See Scheck, *Hitler's African Victims,* 27; Echenberg, *Colonial Conscripts,* 166–7; Fargettas, *Les tirailleurs sénégalais,* 143; Bigmann, *Charles N'Tchoréré face aux nazis,* 155. See also the details provided by the Ministère de Défense, Mémoire des hommes: Combattants africains de la seconde guerre mondiale, accessed 9 September, 2020, https://www.memoiredeshommes. sga.defense.gouv.fr/fr/_depot_mdh/_depot_front/articles/2430/n-tchorere-charles-_doc.pdf.

3 *Pommerische Zeitung,* 28 July 1940. Cited in Rives and Dietrich, *Héros méconnus,* 168.

surviving African soldiers they had captured from their white comrades, among whom were a number of officers. Captain N'Tchoréré refused an order to join the column of Black soldiers, protesting that he should be included in the group containing the officers. For this he was promptly taken aside and shot through the neck. He was not to know that a similar fate awaited the other African soldiers whom he had refused to join; they were shot the following day in the village of Lequesnoy-sur-Airaines, a few kilometres away.[4]

Although his remains were never found and despite the fact that little effort was made after the war to identify or punish the German officer responsible for his murder, Captain N'Tchoréré is one of the better known of the 1,500 to 3,000 African soldiers who were massacred by German soldiers after having been taken prisoner during the Battle of France.[5] In October 1940, he was awarded a citation that recognized him as a "company commander full of energy and bravery" who had "inflicted serious losses on the enemy" and also exhibited by his conduct under enemy fire an exemplary "defiance of danger."[6] In 1954, that citation was replaced by another, which added to the original wording: "Met a glorious death in the course of the action of 7 June 1940."[7] In 1965, a monument to N'Tchoréré's memory and to "all the combatants of Black Africa who shed their blood for France" was erected in the town of Airaines. This complemented another memorial, dedicated in 1953 to the "1200 Glorious Dead" of the Fifty-Third RICMS who had been killed in the fighting of 5–7 June 1940. "Passer-by," instructs an inscription on this memorial, "they fell united in brotherhood so that you could remain French."[8]

Charles N'Tchoréré was also memorialized in print. He was the subject of an adulatory biography penned in the 1960s by Louis Bigmann, a compatriot from Gabon who, like N'Tchoréré, also served in both the First and Second World Wars. In Bigmann's imagination, N'Tchoréré's was "an exemplary death." Although acknowledging that it had occurred "treacherously [...] disdaining all the laws of war, disdaining military honour and simple humanity," Bigmann made scant reference to the actual circumstances of N'tchoréré's post-combat killing, preferring instead to emphasize his heroism in the battle that had preceded it. "The captain accomplishes marvels. His men see him as he has always been, fearless

---

4 Scheck, *Hitler's African Victims*, 27. Scheck indicates the number of victims of this shooting is unknown: "perhaps fifty."

5 This is the best estimate of Raffael Scheck. See Scheck, *Hitler's African Victims*, 165.

6 Cited in ibid.

7 Ibid.

8 Rives and Dietrich, *Héros méconnus*, 169; Echenberg, *Colonial Conscripts*, 167–8.

despite the devilish cadence of automatic weapons, the deafening roar of the artillery. Decisive, phlegmatic, he is in the thick of the action, guiding one and another, encouraging the effort of all, ceaselessly presenting an example of the warrior virtues, so natural and so dear to Senegalese troops that they are galvanized by them in the depths even of the most intense conflagrations."[9] In Bigmann's account, N'Tchoréré became a French hero as well as an African one. These twin allegiances were reflected in the correspondence quoted by Bigmann between Charles and his son, Jean-Baptiste, who was fatally wounded on the same day as his father, also fighting in the Somme, near Remiencourt. To the son's expression of loyalty to France – "It is not her alone whom we serve but the whole of humanity" – the father replied, "Love humanity because that is all that counts, independently of issues of colour and suchlike! Be worthy of yourself, worthy of me, worthy of your country and of Africa, worthy finally of your name as a patriotic fighter."[10]

The death of Charles N'Tchoréré exposes several important aspects of France's experience of the Second World War. Firstly, it is a reminder that in this war as in others, the immediate aftermath of combat was often fatal to surrendering troops as they were killed by their captors in either hot blood or cold. Secondly, it points to the character of the Second World War as a genocidal and racial war, in which race was a crucial factor affecting one's chances of survival, both during combat and afterwards. Thirdly, the prominent role played by colonial regiments like the Fifty-Third RICMS is indicative of the importance of the French overseas empire in the events of 1939–45. Although the extent of its dependence varied, France relied heavily upon troops from its overseas colonies for its home defence in 1939–40, for its subsequent renaissance as a partner of the Allied war effort, and for its eventual liberation from Axis occupation. Many soldiers who died for France were not French; often, they died without ever setting foot on French soil. The sacrifice of colonized soldiers, when it has been acknowledged, has commonly been viewed through the lens of a paternalist and assimilationist colonial ideology; colonial soldiers willingly sacrificed their lives because of their child-like devotion to their French officers and their admiration for a *patrie* that offered the benefits of civilization as well as liberty, equality, and fraternity to all peoples. Careful consideration of the experience of those soldiers, however, reveals a more complex story. Their enthusiasm and motivation for fighting varied according to specific circumstances. Many were also increasingly disgruntled by the unequal treatment they received from the French state and its army. This malaise finally manifested

9 Bigmann, *Charles N'Tchoréré*, 125, 137, and 134.
10 Ibid., 123.

itself in a series of disturbances at the time of their demobilization, culminating in the Thiaroye mutiny of 1944, an event that has lately acquired notoriety as an occasion when French soldiers were killed "*par la France*" rather than "*pour la France.*" An enduring legacy of the war was the sense on the part of soldiers from France's overseas territories, both "native" and "European," that the *mère-patrie* had acquired through their sacrifice a debt in blood to be repaid. In sub-Saharan Africa and in Southeast Asia, this sentiment underpinned burgeoning nationalist movements for independence, although veteran colonized soldiers were themselves often ambivalent in their feelings toward such movements. In North Africa, especially Algeria, the story was especially complicated, as settlers of European descent took the view that any capitulation by France to independence movements would betray their own sacrifice on its behalf; meanwhile, many of the Muslim Algerians who fought with them to liberate France were driven to fight one another in Algeria's bitter war of independence. Exalted both in France as well as in their colonial and post-colonial homelands for valorous acts of self-sacrifice on the battlefield, colonized soldiers have sometimes been represented as unwitting victims – but also as agents – of French imperial domination. They were, ultimately, neither unquestioning nor undemanding in their loyalty to France. The sacrifice of colonized soldiers in French service during the Second World War, often far from willing, gave rise in post-colonial societies to an enduring sense of grievance.

FRENCH MEMORIES OF THE
SECOND WORLD WAR

The experience of colonized soldiers was in no way "typical" of the French experience of the Second World War. One would search in vain for such an experience. As Olivier Wieviorka has argued, French experience of the war was fractured and so, in its aftermath, was its memory. Colonized soldiers constituted one of many groups jostling for a share of the nation's recognition. Whereas national memory in the aftermath of the First World War had focused unequivocally on the front-line soldiers, whose collective sacrifice was symbolized by the tomb of the Unknown Soldier, French memories after the Second World War were divided. They encapsulated not only the relatively brief experience of conventional military conflict – limited in France to 1939–40 and after 6 June 1944 – but also the experiences of occupation by a foreign power and rule by a collaborationist state under the government of Marshal Pétain at Vichy.[11] In seeking a

---

11 Wieviorka, *La mémoire désunie*, 16.

focus for national memory after 1945, the figure of the soldier was no longer fit for purpose. The war had cost France roughly as many civilian lives as military ones and it had blurred the distinction between combatants and non-combatants.[12] Indeed, determining who had fought and died for France became a vexed question. Did it include the forty thousand soldiers from Alsace and Lorraine who had died wearing uniforms of field-grey, having been conscripted into the German *Wehrmacht?* What about those who had volunteered for German service? As for those soldiers who wore French uniforms, nearly two million spent the war in German prisoner-of-war camps, many without any experience of combat. Were they combatants? Did soldiers who had fought for Vichy against the Allies deserve the same recognition as those who had fought for the Free French? Similar questions were asked about civilians involved in the resistance. If blowing up railway lines made one a combatant, was that also the case for distributing clandestine newspapers? There were other groups who had claims to national recognition: civilians killed by Allied bombing; workers who had volunteered or been conscripted for war work in Germany; resisters and Jews who had perished in German concentration camps.[13]

Under the leadership of Charles de Gaulle, the provisional government did its best to overcome this diversity of experience and to lay the foundations for a unified national memory of the Second World War. This was a memory based on the myth of a general national resistance to the German occupation spearheaded by the Free French movement based in London. This myth, occluding the experiences of Vichy and collaboration, as well as the role of the Allies in liberating France, emphasized the military resistance and the role of the army. Commemorative ceremonies gave symbolic form to the myth. Of prime importance was the ceremony of 11 November 1945, which interred the remains of fourteen men and one woman who had died fighting for the liberation of France at Mont Valérien, the fort outside Paris where many resisters had been executed. The inclusion of fifteen individuals was an attempt by the ceremony's organizer, Henri Frenay, to capture the diversity of experience during the war, but also to create consensus by insisting upon the unity of purpose shared by all fifteen. In Frenay's own words, "In spite of the differences in place and

12   Jean Quellien estimates approximately 240,000 military deaths, including those of French soldiers fighting in the German army, and a maximum of 250,000 civilian deaths. Quellien, "Les pertes humaines," 262–5.

13   Ultimately, most prisoners of war were accorded the status of combatants by a law of 23 December 1949. Conscripts who had served in the German army were recognized by a law of 4 March 1958. Soldiers who had fought for Vichy were also ultimately assured their full benefits as former combatants. See Wieviorka, *La mémoire désunie*, 88–9.

circumstance in which they gave their lives, all, or nearly all, were volunteers and all died with the same determination and the same hope in their hearts. It is essential that the ceremonies of 11 November reinforce national unity by underlining, despite the diversity of their battles, the profound unity of our dead and thus of the homeland."[14]

The fifteen bodies interred at Mont Valérien did at least represent a variety of experiences. They included one prisoner of war, four resisters (one of whom was a woman), as well as colonized soldiers from Chad, Tunisia, Morocco, and Burkina Faso.[15] When it came to the broader distribution of honours, however, the Provisional Government was less inclusive. Of 1,038 individuals who were made Compagnons de l'Ordre de la Libération only six were women and only 15 per cent were born outside metropolitan France. Nearly three-quarters of them were soldiers – 587 of them officers – from the Free French Forces.[16] A Medal of the Resistance was instituted in 1943 and eventually awarded to 44,000 recipients,[17] but there was no medal specifically for prisoners of war, whose status as combatants was only grudgingly conceded in 1948. In the postwar rush to rename streets, squares, and metro stations, or to build monuments, it was uniquely the heroes of the internal or external Resistance who were celebrated. The collective unconscious, as Rémi Dalisson has argued, was entirely taken up by victorious *poilus* from the First World War and triumphant *résistants* from the Second; there was no room for the soldiers who had been defeated in 1940.[18]

The Gaullist myth of national resistance, somewhat in abeyance during de Gaulle's absence from power under the Fourth Republic, reached its apogee with the pantheonization of Jean Moulin on 18–19 December 1964.[19] Despite its success, however, that myth was never unchallenged. The French Communist Party, notably, celebrated its own role in the Resistance and honoured its own martyrs. Several of the latter were buried close to the wall of the *fédérés*, in the cemetery of Père Lachaise, sanctified by their association with the martyred revolutionaries of the Paris Commune.

14   Henri Frenay, *La nuit finira*, vol. 2: *Mémoires de résistance, 1943–1945* (Paris: Le Livre de Poche, 1975), 346. Cited in Wieviorka, *La mémoire désunie*, 346.

15   See the website for the Mont-Valérien memorial. Mont Valérien: Les dix-sept morts pour la France, accessed 22 January 2022, http://www.mont-valerien.fr/parcours-de-visite/le-memorial-de-la-france-combattante/les-dix-sept-morts-pour-la-france/.

16   L'Ordre de la Libération. Les femmes et les hommes compagnon de la libération, accessed 22 January 2022, https://www.ordredelaliberation.fr/fr/les-femmes-et-les-hommes-compagnon-de-la-liberation

17   Wieviorka, *La mémoire désunie*, 32.

18   Dalisson, *Les soldats de 1940*, 102–4.

19   Rousso, *The Vichy Syndrome*, 82–97.

Beginning in the 1970s, after de Gaulle had fallen from power, the Gaullist myth began to lose its hold. Both popular media and historical research stimulated greater awareness of the agency of the Vichy government and of French society in collaborating with the Nazis. Collective memories of the war began to shift away from the celebration of heroes and toward the recognition of victims, especially the Jews, a shift encouraged by high-profile trials such as that of Maurice Papon, a Vichy official who was convicted in 1998 of complicity in the deportation of Jews to Nazi death camps. By 2000, resistance organizations began to complain that memory of the Resistance was becoming obscured by that of the Holocaust.[20]

The memory of colonized troops and their experience of the Second World War has to a great extent been shaped by this broader pattern of remembrance. Lacking a powerful voice to assert their claims for public recognition or reward, the role of colonized soldiers was, to the extent that it was acknowledged at all in public discourse, made to conform to the Gaullist myth. Rallying promptly to the flag of Free France, soldiers from the colonies fought willingly and selflessly for the mother country. Over time, however, that representation has changed. Growing awareness of the cruelties they endured during the war and of the unequal treatment they received from the French army has made them victims as well as fighters. The easy assumption that colonized peoples owed a "blood debt" to their mother country has been transformed into a perception that the mother country owes them for the blood they spilled on its behalf.

COLONIZED SOLDIERS

France in the Second World War became, to a greater degree than at any other period of its history, dependent upon soldiers from its colonies. Although it is unclear how many reached Europe before the debacle of May–June, 1940, according to one estimate there were 10,000 Indochinese, 10,500 Madagascans, 68,500 Africans, and 340,000 North Africans among the 5,345,000 soldiers mobilized upon the outbreak of war in September 1939.[21] Perhaps 150,000 of these participated in the six-week Battle of France, in May–June 1940.[22] The defeat of 1940, together with the ensuing armistice and occupation, compelled those who were prepared to carry on fighting to rely almost entirely upon the resources of the empire.

20 Wieviorka, *La mémoire désunie*, 247.

21 Only 43,000 of these forces were in Europe in September 1939. Ageron, *Histoire de la France coloniale*, vol. 2, 312; Drévillon and Wieviorka, *Histoire militaire de la France*, vol. 2: *De 1870 à nos jours*, 363; Mabon, *Prisonniers de guerre "indigènes,"* 19.

22 Le Pichon, "Tirailleurs indigènes," 161.

The first substantial Free French units were raised in French Equatorial Africa following the declaration of those states for de Gaulle at the end of August 1940. It was these forces that won the first French victories over the Axis, at Kufra, in Libya (March 1941) and at Cub-Cub, in Eritrea (February 1941). Although officered by Frenchmen, these Free French forces consisted substantially of colonized soldiers. Of the 396 troops who participated in the siege of Kufra under the leadership of General Leclerc, 295 were Tirailleurs Sénégalais from Chad.[23] At Bir Hakeim, where 3,600 Free French forces under General Koenig established their military credentials by resisting the 37,000 men of General Rommel's Afrika Korps during a week-long siege (2–10 June 1942) before breaking out, those forces included units from every part of the empire: infantry battalions from French West Africa (FWA), French Equatorial Africa (FEA), French Polynesia, and North Africa; an artillery regiment from Madagascar; and a headquarters staff detachment from Indochina.[24] Later, following the Allied landings in Operation Torch and the abandonment of Vichy by France's remaining African colonies, much larger forces were raised. By November 1944, 176,500 "Europeans" from French North Africa had responded to the call to arms, as had an even larger number of "natives": 134,000 from Algeria, 26,000 from Tunisia, and 73,000 from Morocco.[25] Another 80,000 combatants came from sub-Saharan Africa.[26] A majority of the troops in the French armies that participated in the campaigns in Tunisia, Italy, and southern France between 1942 and 1944 came from France's overseas territories. Sixty per cent of the men in General de Lattre's First Army when it landed on the Mediterranean French coast in August 1944 were recruited from the indigenous populations of those territories.[27] Although the Gaullist myth of the Second World War elevated the armed metropolitan resistance fighter to iconic status as the vital agent of national liberation, it was arguably the relatively unsung colonized soldier who was a more essential figure. The "whitening" of de Lattre's army in the autumn of 1944, as African soldiers were replaced by resistance fighters from the Forces Françaises de l'Intérieur (FFI), began a process whereby colonized troops were removed not just from the army but also from their place in history and memory.

23 Ibid., 120; Deroo and Champeaux, "Panorama des troupes coloniales," 72–88.
24 Rives and Dietrich, *Héros méconnus*, 236. Adding to the multi-national flavour of this force was the Thirteenth regiment of the French Foreign Legion, with soldiers from many countries, including France, Belgium, Spain, Germany, and Austria. See Crémieux-Brilhac, *La France libre*, vol. 1, 457.
25 Miot, "L'armée de l'empire," 41; Le Gac, *Vaincre sans gloire*, 216.
26 Fargettas, *Les tirailleurs sénégalais*, 59.
27 Miot, "L'armée de l'empire," 41.

This dependence upon colonized soldiers was prefigured by the experience of France during the First World War, when over 600,000 were recruited for service in Europe, of whom approximately 100,000 were killed.[28] Although the recruitment of indigenous peoples for military purposes accompanied every phase of French imperialism, only in the first decade of the twentieth century was the idea seriously contemplated of depending upon them as an essential cornerstone of France's military strength. This was the grand idea laid out by General Charles Mangin in his 1910 book *La force noire*. Based on the racial stereotyping of the period and the dubious theory of "martial races," *La force noire* argued that Africa represented a reservoir of men whose aptitude for war was supposedly enhanced by their primitive state of physiological and social evolution, which were imagined to make them more amenable to military discipline and less susceptible to pain and harsh environments than more "advanced" peoples. Mangin believed that raising an army of African conscripts would enable France to overcome the challenge of its own demographic decline relative to Germany and provide an irresistible force on the battlefield. "In the battles to come," he concluded, "these primitives for whom life counts so little and whose young blood seethes as if ready to be spilled, will certainly measure up to the old 'French fury' and will revive it if need be."[29]

Mangin's advocacy for *la force noire*, though greeted skeptically by some, resulted during the First World War in the imposition of unprecedented levies of men in sub-Saharan Africa and ultimately won for Mangin the unflattering title of "the butcher of the Blacks." An estimated 200,000 soldiers from French West Africa and French Equatorial Africa were recruited for military service.[30] Some were volunteers, eager to serve *la mère patrie* because of their identification with French culture or from the hope of enhancing their status within colonial society. Blaise Diagne, the first Senegalese deputy to the French National Assembly, not only persuaded the Assembly to accord the benefits of full French citizenship to African soldiers from the "Four Communes" of Senegal, but in 1918 he was a very effective recruiting agent throughout French West Africa as France undertook a major new campaign to raise African soldiers. For the most part, however, the colonial authorities could recruit the desired numbers of men only by resorting to force, using methods that have been

28 Michel, *Les africains et la grande guerre*, 193; Deroo, "Mourir, l'appel à l'empire," 171.

29 Mangin, *La force noire*, 258. See Joly, "Le concept de 'race guerrière,'" 153–72.

30 All the same, France continued to rely most heavily on colonial troops from French North Africa. During the First World War, 175,000 Algerians, 40,000 Moroccans, and 80,000 Tunisians were mobilized. Deroo, "Mourir, l'appel à l'empire," 171.

compared to the "press" of the Napoleonic empire.[31] In February 1915, recruits in the town of Matam were escorted before the recruiting commission by distraught and weeping women who sang funeral songs each time one of their menfolk was selected for service.[32] That year witnessed widespread resistance to conscription, as five hundred villages rose in a rebellion that was pitilessly repressed by troops equipped with modern artillery and machine guns. French administrators commented admiringly on "the spirit of solidarity and sacrifice," on the discipline and the "acts of heroism" of the insurgents, who preferred to die in their burning villages rather than to surrender.[33]

For the indigenous recruits who, willingly or not, found themselves in the French army during the First World War, the price was high. Of 134,000 Tirailleurs Sénégalais who reached Europe, approximately 45,000, or one in three, did not return.[34] Combat losses were heavy, as these African soldiers participated in virtually every phase of the war, including the campaigns on the Gallipoli peninsula and in the Balkans. Commonly used as assault troops in offensive operations, during the final two and a half years of the war Tirailleurs Sénégalais were twice as likely to be killed as other soldiers in the French army.[35] They endured appalling losses in the notorious offensive on the Chemin des Dames in 1917. Between 16 and 18 April 1917, 7,415 Tirailleurs Sénégalais, 44–5 per cent of those deployed, became casualties in an attack orchestrated by General Mangin himself.[36] In a secret meeting of the Chamber of Deputies in June, Blaise Diagne condemned Mangin for treating Black soldiers as so much cannon fodder: "the pretence is kept up that human flesh can withstand artillery and bullets. Well, no! Not even that of negroes."[37] Combat was not all that African soldiers had to fear. A high proportion of those who died, perhaps a third of the total, succumbed to illness.[38] Their susceptibility to cold, damp conditions became apparent during 1914 and 1915, both in northern France and at Gallipoli. This ultimately led to a policy of "wintering," which involved removal to the south of France during the coldest months of the year. Even this policy was initially bungled, however, as a camp set up

31 Michel, *Les africains et la grande guerre*, 24.
32 Ibid., 35.
33 Cited in ibid., 59.
34 Most sources cite only combat losses (approximately 31,000), but a third of all deaths among the Tirailleurs Sénégalais were caused by illness. See ibid., 196, and Lunn, *L'odysée des combattants sénégalais*, 172.
35 Ibid., 176.
36 Ibid., 101.
37 Cited in Michel, "'Force noire' ou 'chair à canon,'" 248.
38 This proportion is suggested by Michel. See ibid., 251.

at Le Courneau near Bordeaux proved to be almost as deadly for African soldiers as the front lines. Housed in draughty Adrian huts, many of them came down with pulmonary illnesses. Between June 1916 and September 1917, when it was finally abandoned to soldiers arriving from the United States, 895 Tirailleurs died in the camp at Le Courneau.[39] Their deaths were a harbinger of those that were to come in the Frontstalags of the Second World War. Finally, in considering the mortality of African soldiers, the hazards of the voyage from overseas should not be forgotten. When the packet boat *Sequana* was sunk by a torpedo from UC-72 in the early hours of 8 June 1917, 198 of the four hundred Tirailleurs on board were drowned, effectively condemned by their inability to understand the instructions given in French for the vessel's evacuation. There were other Tirailleurs lost at sea, including those on board *l'Afrique*, a packet boat that foundered on 12 January 1920 as it was returning them to their homeland. Only fourteen of 192 Tirailleurs on board survived.[40]

These grim realities of colonized soldiers' experiences in the First World War had little effect on contemporary representations, which portrayed them either as savage and invincible on the battlefield or as unreliable and prone to panic, particularly in the absence of strong European leadership. Unit war diaries and military citations reflected both these contradictory discourses.[41] The image of the African soldier as a primitive and cruel warrior was deliberately fostered by French propaganda, which made much of the fondness of the Tirailleurs Sénégalais for hand-to-hand combat using the notorious *coupe-coupe*, a machete-like knife. This image was in turn magnified by German propaganda, which represented the very deployment of African troops in a war between Europeans as a war crime. In a pamphlet published in July 1915 in response to the Allied accusations of war crimes committed by the German army during the invasion of Belgium, the German foreign ministry accused African and Asian troops of "acts of cruelty which violate not only the recognized laws of war, but which also defy those of morality and humanity."[42] These mutually reinforcing images gave rise to their own reality, as the fears of German and African soldiers that they were each fighting an enemy who could be expected to show no mercy self-fulfilled in the form of grim, murderous encounters in the trenches. A rapidly escalating cycle of reprisals as atrocity was followed by

39 Mormone, Boyer, and Caule, *1914–1918*, 60.
40 Ibid., 46.
41 Cochet, "Stéréotypes contradictoires," 261–78.
42 Cited in Fargettas, *Les tirailleurs sénégalais*, 127.

counter-atrocity existed almost from the beginning of the war.[43] The German perception of African soldiers as barbarous savages, magnified many times over by the accusations of their sexual crimes against German women during the postwar occupations of the Rhineland and the Ruhr, impinged directly upon the fate of France's colonized troops in the Second World War, most importantly during the Battle of France in 1940.[44]

1940: FORGOTTEN VICTIMS

In the six-week Battle of France, beginning with the launching of the German invasion on 10 May 1940 and ending with the signature of the armistice at Compiègne on 22 June by the new government of Marshal Pétain, the French army suffered a comprehensive defeat. There were many victims of that defeat: an estimated 55–65,000 French and 30–50,000 German military personnel were killed, along with 21,000 French civilians.[45] Subsequently, 1,850,000 French soldiers became prisoners of war, the majority retaining that status until liberated by Allied armies in 1944 and 1945, though 30–40,000 died in captivity.[46] The reputation of the French army and of its soldiers were also victims of the defeat, as culprits were sought, principally among the civilian politicians of the now-defunct Third Republic, but also within the ranks of the army itself. Notoriously, General Maurice Gamelin, the commander-in-chief who was replaced during the battle, blamed the defeat on the lack of fighting spirit of the citizen-soldiers under his command. They were too soft, he claimed, lacked discipline, and were possessed by an "everyman-for-himself attitude."[47] Despite the subsequent efforts by the Vichy regime to restore the army's reputation so that it might serve as a bulwark of its conservative "national revolution," the damage was enduring. As the war shifted in favour of the Allies and as the Free French armies and the Resistance gained support, the campaign of 1939–40 became a bad memory most French citizens preferred not to dwell upon. Soldiers who survived the Battle of France and captivity as prisoners of war received little understanding upon their return home from a French public more inclined to celebrate the

---

43 A French writer, Alphonse Séché, claimed that Tirailleurs Sénégalais were inspired to fight with "a mystical rage" at the Battle of Dixmude in September 1914, after discovering a photograph on the body of a German soldier of one of their comrades who had been tortured to death. Michel, *Les africains et la grande guerre*, 83 and 237.

44 On realities and representations of the presence of French colonial soldiers in the occupation of Germany, see Le Naor, *La honte noire*, and Marks, "Black Watch on the Rhine."

45 Dalisson, *Les soldats de 1940*, 32.

46 Ibid., 32 and 36.

47 Cited in Alexander, "No taste for the fight?," 161.

victorious heroes of the Resistance and the Liberation than the defeated victims of 1940. The latter were also tainted because of their instrumentalization by Vichy propaganda and therefore inclined to keep their memories to themselves.[48] Among these forgotten soldiers of 1940 were thousands of colonized troops whose experiences had been especially bleak. A few like Charles N'Tchoréré became celebrated for acts of exemplary courage and sacrifice. Many more, however, were the unremembered victims of poorly documented massacres or of the privation and neglect they endured as prisoners of war.

In the immediate aftermath of defeat, the Vichy government and the French army defended the latter's reputation by insisting upon the overwhelming superiority in numbers – especially of weapons – enjoyed by the enemy. They could point to the high numbers of casualties – the figure of 100,000 French military dead was deemed authoritative until quite recently and is still cited by some writers – as evidence that the army had fought bravely: that the soldiers of 1940 had been as willing to die for *la patrie* as the *poilus* of the First World War.[49] Soldiers' memoirs lent their support to this perspective by emphasizing the hopeless odds they had confronted. In a memoir published in 1941, René Balbaud, an officer who was moved to Britain by way of Dunkirk, gave his view of German superiority: "we were literally crushed under the bombs, ground beneath the tanks, decimated by infantry fire."[50] Although such assumptions concerning the enemy's quantitative and qualitative superiority have been comprehensively disproved by historians, the claim that French soldiers had fought heroically in a hopeless cause provided the foundations for an enduring historical myth.

This more positive representation of the army's conduct gave symbolic significance to certain moments of the campaign: most notably the defence of the Loire crossings by the cadets from the Saumur cavalry college from 19–21 June when, although the battle was already lost, French soldiers died for the sake of honour alone. An article in the *Revue des Deux Mondes* published in 1941 described in glowing terms the willingness of the young cadets and their instructors to sacrifice their lives. "Lieutenant Roimarmier, rifle in hand, standing in front of his men, finds a glorious death. The officer-cadet Félix Pineau falls at the head of his patrol. While charging a machine rifle, the reserve officer-cadet Flandin, a young man

48 Dalisson, *Les soldats de 1940*, 99–115.

49 On the problem of calculating French losses in the Battle of France, see Arzalier, "La campagne de mai-juin 1940," 427–47; Bernard, "1000 victoires aériennes," 15–28.

50 Balbaud, *Cette drôle de guerre*, 94–6.

full of promise, is cut down by a shell; he dies after two long hours of agony, uttering these words: "My God, forgive me; help me ... *Papa, Maman* ... It is for France."[51] Such heroic anecdotes served a variety of interests, depending upon the moment of their composition. In the early days following the armistice they were useful to an army reeling from defeat and from the aspersions cast upon its spirit and conduct in the campaign of 1940. They then served the purposes of the Vichy state as it sought to make the army an agent of national revival. Finally, they were co-opted by De Gaulle and the Free French as evidence that the spirit of eternal France had endured despite the defeat as an inspiration to the Resistance. By 1960, when the French national monument to the Second World War was inaugurated at Mont Valérien, this mythic version of the 1940 campaign had become established in official commemorative culture. Symbolically overshadowed by tributes to the Resistance, only one of the sixteen sculptures erected at Mont Valérien to commemorate the events of the war refers to the Battle of France. Pierre Duroux's bas-relief *Saumur* represents a fallen soldier transfixed by a sword-cum-crucifix (fig. 8.1). "The soldier falls," reads an interpretive brochure, "but his sacrifice will not be in vain. From 19 to 21 June 1940, the cadets of the cavalry school, reinforced by the riflemen, the dragoons, the officer cadets of Saint-Maixent, fight a desperate battle against the Wehrmacht for the honour of the French army."[52]

Insofar as it received any attention, the experience of colonized soldiers who fought in the Battle of France was shaped to fit this mythic version of the battle as a tragedy partially redeemed by the heroic defence of French honour. This was the theme of Gabriel Bonnet's *Mémorial de l'empire: à la gloire des troupes coloniales*, published in 1941 with a preface by Marshal Philippe Pétain praising the Colonial Army – which was mainly recruited from French West Africa and French Equatorial Africa – as a "glorious symbol of French Unity."[53] Bonnet painted a picture of soldiers from the Colonial Army fighting heroically throughout the Battle of France until, "out of breath, practically without ammunition, without food, exhausted but not demoralized," they provided the "square of final resistance to fire the last cartridge, as did their glorious elders from the marine infantry at Bazeilles." The "fine instrument of war" that had been the Colonial

51 Chamard, "Les combats de Saumur," 221. See also Chamard, *Les combats de Saumur*, Macnab, *For Honour Alone*.

52 Anon., "Les seize hauts-reliefs du mémorial de la France combattante" (n.p., n.d.), unpaginated.

53 Bonnet, *Mémorial de l'empire*, unpaginated preface.

8.1. Pierre Duroux, *Saumur*. Sculpture for the national war memorial at Mont Valérien. 1960.

Army was broken by the campaign but its men could hold their heads high. Bonnet summed up his view of the campaign by paraphrasing the words of Francis I after the French defeat at Pavia in 1525: "All was lost, save honour." [54]

Bonnet reduced the Battle of France to a series of anecdotes illustrating the military virtues of the officers and men of the Colonial Army, most notably their devotion to duty and their willingness to die. Charles N'Tchorére was represented as "a magnificent example of courage, of sang-froid and of fearlessness" who worked tirelessly to inspire his men with his own "sense of honour, duty, and love of France, his adopted

54 Ibid., 29.

homeland." He was described as fighting "like a lion" during the battle for
Airaines, but in the account of his "glorious death," there was no mention
made of his brutal post-combat murder. "After a superb defence of several
days, during which he subjected the enemy to heavy losses, he braved death
rather than fall into the adversary's hands. His end was admirable."[55]
Bonnet's glossing over the crimes of the Wehrmacht was a function of
Vichy's policy of collaboration with the Third Reich. Nowhere in this
celebration of military sacrifice is there a mention of the massacres of
African soldiers during the campaign. The author's identification with
Vichy is apparent in his use of N'Tchoréré's story to make an appeal to
the "Children of the Empire." "Children of the Empire, you are that warm
and turbulent youth, full of life and enthusiasm, to whom the Marshal
also speaks. You are the future and the hope of our fine Black army of
tomorrow. Sow the generous ideas which must enrich the fields with future
harvests. Lift your hearts with a unanimous spirit and always remember
your rallying cry: 'For France, always present!'"[56] The story of N'Tchoréré's
death was therefore adapted to serve the design of Vichy to represent the
heroism of the French army in defeat as sowing the first seeds of a national
and imperial renaissance.

The idea that indigenous soldiers were ready at a moment's notice to
answer the call to arms was an essential theme of Bonnet's book. After
describing the death of a Madagascan who was killed alongside two Bretons
as all three operated a machine gun, Bonnet wrote: "May the invocation
of his sacrifice remind everyone that beyond the bright shores of the
Mediterranean simple men in the depths of the savannah still put their
faith in France, and that they love this France to the point where, one fine
day, they come from their distant lands of Asia, Africa, or Madagascar, very
simply and without fuss to have their good yellow or black faces drilled
for her."[57] Bonnet provided many illustrations of this naive imperial patriotism. One story was that of Sergeant Kotonou Nama Taraoré. After fifteen
years of service as a Tirailleur Sénégalais, Kotonou had retired to his village
to farm millet and engage in local politics. Upon the declaration of war
in 1939, however, "without losing a moment," he volunteered to rejoin
the army and insisted upon being sent to France. There, on 21 May, as a
sergeant in the Tenth Company of the Sixth RICMS, he participated in
a counterattack led by Lieutenant Ghesquières. "Right away they were upon
the enemy; the lieutenant brought down two of them one after the other
at point blank range. A German officer stood before Kotonou, who did

55 Ibid., 37–8.
56 Ibid., 39.
57 Ibid., 99–100.

not hesitate, spitting him on his bayonet ... But the other had time to fire a pistol shot which brought down brave Kotonou."[58] Bonnet concluded the anecdote in time-honoured fashion. Addressing himself to Kotonou he insisted that the latter's loss – he would never now become a village chieftain – was France's gain: "You are in the paradise of brave men, the leader of the forty-five Tirailleurs of the Tenth Company fallen on the field of honour [...] But, thanks to you, thanks to them, France will live!"[59]

The essential themes of Bonnet's tribute to the Colonial Army, emphasizing the naturally warlike qualities of indigenous soldiers, their fearlessness in the face of death, as well as their absolute loyalty to their European officers and to France, continued to dominate representations of colonized soldiers long after the Second World War. In *Héros méconnus 1914–1918, 1939–1945: Mémorial des combattants d'Afrique Noire et de Madagascar*, first published in 1990, the authors emphasized many of the same themes – and recounted many of the same anecdotes – as Bonnet. They too paid tribute to Kotonou's heroism, declaring, "Brave Kotonou Nama Taraoré, although nothing obliged you to leave your village, you came to defend France. Although we did not know you at the time, you were our Brother in Arms, and we salute your memory."[60] In their account of the efforts by the Sixth RICMS to resist the German advance through the Ardennes, the authors first gave homage to the regiment's French commander, emphasizing that he was constantly alongside his men on the firing line, "showing by his presence the paternal affection he had for his men."[61] They then provided anecdotes demonstrating the proficiency of the Tirailleurs Sénégalais in hand-to-hand combat as well as their loyalty to their officers and to France.[62]

Regardless of the patriotic veneer of works like the *Mémorial de l'empire* and *Héros méconnus*, there is no reason to doubt their insistence that the Battle of France was fiercely fought. The commander of the Sixth RICMS reported that between 16 and 28 May his regiment had lost 26 officers, 95 NCOS, and 598 other ranks,[63] while the German forces responsible for inflicting those casualties stated that "the enemy is fighting stubbornly, sometimes with cunning and, when he is surrounded, he defends to the last man. He almost never surrenders."[64] Bonnet echoed Mangin

58 Ibid., 114.
59 Ibid.
60 Rives and Dietrich, *Héros méconnus*, 159.
61 Ibid., 157.
62 Ibid., 159.
63 Ibid., 157.
64 Cited in Fargettas, *Les tirailleurs senegalais*, 141 and 335.

8.2. A Tirailleur Sénégalais serving with the 6th Army in 1940.

in linking the tenacity of African soldiers to the warlike attributes of the "martial races" from which they were recruited.[65] It seems more likely that African soldiers fought so stubbornly above all because they had little choice. In the last resort, white soldiers could leave the firing line either through desertion or surrender, but for Blacks those options presented far greater risks. Their lack of familiarity with the country where they were fighting as well as their skin colour made it difficult for them to run away or to blend into the civilian population. Nor could they expect any mercy from their captors if they surrendered. Indeed, it was not uncommon for their officers to motivate them by insisting upon the brutal treatment they

65 Bonnet, *Mémorial de l'empire*, 115.

could expect from the enemy. Amadée Fabre, commander of the Twenty-fourth RTS[66] fighting in the Oise, bolstered his men's fighting spirit by telling them that the Germans "took no Black prisoners and that, in any case, we were predestined to die."[67]

As had been the case during the First World War, the stubborn resistance of African soldiers served to intensify the hostility of their German enemies. Soldiers in the German army were psychologically conditioned by years of propaganda, beginning with the anticolonial wars of the nineteenth century and extending through the experiences of the First World War and the "Black Horror" of the Rhineland occupation, to perceive that resistance as a manifestation of the savage, unregulated methods of warfare employed by an uncivilized people. This conditioning was fertile ground for a further propaganda offensive begun at the end of May 1940 by Joseph Goebbels's propaganda ministry, which was itself a major factor impelling soldiers of the Wehrmacht to commit acts of violence against African soldiers far exceeding those of the previous war. Reports in the Nazi newspaper the *Völkischer Beobachter* represented African soldiers as blood-thirsty animals, savagely using their *coupe-coupes* to cut the throats of German soldiers.[68] It was in the wake of this propaganda campaign, during the second phase of the invasion that began with operations on the Somme on 5 June and ended with fighting in the vicinity of Lyons on 19–20 June that the vast majority of the massacres perpetrated against African prisoners of war took place.

Raffael Scheck's study of the German army's massacres of African troops shows that there were thirty-three separate occasions during May and June 1940 when African soldiers who had been wounded or taken prisoner were killed by their captors. In many cases, it is unclear how many soldiers were killed in combat and how many were killed after the fighting had ended, particularly since some German units seem to have made it a policy not to take prisoners. Most historians accept Scheck's estimate of the number killed in the massacres as between 1,500 and 3,000. All but two of these incidents, sometimes involving only one or a few victims but on occasion as many as a hundred, occurred after 5 June.[69] Witnesses to the massacres testified to the fury of the Germans both at the perceived

66   Régiment de Tirailleurs Sénégalais.

67   Cited in Scheck, *Hitler's African Victims*, 135.

68   A compelling case for the influence of Nazi propaganda is made by Raffael Scheck. See ibid., 101–17.

69   Ibid., 54–7. There are no reliable figures for total African losses in the Battle of France. Myron Echenberg provides an estimate of 10,000 men killed and 15–16,000 taken prisoner. Echenberg, *Colonial Conscripts*, 88. See also Lawler, *Ivoirien "Tirailleurs" of World War II*, 87–8.

illegitimacy of the French making use of "savages" in a war between civilized nations as well as at what they saw as the "treacherous" methods of warfare employed by African soldiers, including shooting from concealment and making use of their fearsome *coupe-coupes*. From their own statements, clearly many German soldiers regarded these "crimes" as sufficient justification for denying their captives the protections of the Geneva Conventions. Ironically, while the Germans honoured the fierce but futile resistance of the French defenders of Saumur, saluting the wounded cavalry cadets as "brave soldiers,"[70] they condemned that of the Twenty-Fifth Regiment of Tirailleurs Sénégalais at the Convent of Montluzin, near Lyons, which transpired at precisely the same moment of the campaign (19–20 June): "These fellows are not men, they are beasts. They showed it again today," a German officer was reported to have said of the latter.[71] Far from honouring the wounded at Montluzin, the furious Germans slaughtered the surviving African troops as well as some of their white officers under the eyes of the convent's nuns.[72]

The anger of the Germans expressed itself in violent and threatening demonstrations. A French officer serving with the Twenty-Fifth RTS who was taken prisoner at Lentilly, in the Rhône Department, witnessed the rage of an officer who plucked a *coupe-coupe* from a pile of surrendered weapons. Brandishing it in front of his men, the German gesticulated and shouted for a full five minutes before taking out his wrath on a fallen motorcycle, beating in its fuel tank, cutting its cables, and smashing its headlight before throwing the *coupe-coupe* back into its pile.[73] It did not take much for such violent demonstrations to escalate into deadly attacks on captive French troops, especially Blacks. In certain instances, the killings occurred in the heat of the moment and were carried out by troops enraged by unexpectedly heavy losses in the preceding battle. This appears to have been the case at Montluzin, where one hundred men of the *Grossdeutschland* and the ss *Totenkopf* divisions were killed in their assault on the monastery.[74] On other occasions, the violence came well after the fighting had ended and was more calculated. An attack by a prisoner on an ss officer at a prison camp at Clamecy resulted in a decision to shoot twenty prisoners in reprisal.

70 Chamard, *Les combats de Saumur,* 111.

71 Cited in Fargettas, *Les tirailleurs sénégalais,* 159. These words contrast with those reportedly spoken by a German officer to French civilians with respect to the cadets who defended the bridges at Saumur: "Be proud of them. They were heroes." Macnab, *For Honour Alone,* 146.

72 Fargettas, *Les tirailleurs sénégalais,* 147 and 153; Scheck, *Hitler's African Victims,* 38 and 140.

73 Fargettas, *Les tirailleurs sénégalais,* 159–60.

74 Scheck, *Hitler's African Victims,* 139–40.

When twenty others refused to dig graves for those who had been selected, they too were executed.[75]

One of the most notorious massacres occurred at Chasselay, near Lyons, on 20 June, when sixty or seventy captured Tirailleurs Sénégalais were ordered to run across a field and then fired on at point-blank range by the heavy machine guns of German tanks. Not all were killed in the first fusillade and the tanks crushed the dead and wounded under their tracks as they went in pursuit of the remainder. Meanwhile, French Captain Gouzy witnessed the Panzer grenadiers "calmly aiming their rifles to shoot our unhappy Tirailleurs like rabbits. At the end of an interminable quarter of an hour, not a living thing moved."[76] When the local pharmacist, Madame Morin, visited the site the following day, she encountered "an atrocious spectacle, a smell of butchery: a pile of corpses and all around some scattered bodies, mutilated." There were fifty-one dead and only two severely wounded survivors, one missing an arm and the other with both legs crushed. Madame Morin spoke to the latter: "He tells me he is twenty years old, that he is Catholic and asks me for news of his captain: 'Dead?' I tell him, 'No, wounded.' 'That good' and he smiles. He adds, 'You will come with me, you hospital?' 'No, but I will go to see you' and when I went there, he had died of gangrene."[77] Altogether, approximately a hundred Black soldiers were victims of massacres in the Lyon region. A handful of survivors, some of them wounded, found protection from courageous French civilians.[78]

The massacre at Chasselay was both an expression of and the logical end point of the dehumanization of African soldiers by the victorious German army. Julien Fargettas notes that the massacres often took on the form of a traditional "hunting scene." At Chasselay, the Tirailleurs were invited to flee and then shot down "like rabbits." On another occasion, at Mareuil-la-Motte, in the Oise Department, a French marine witnessed a similar scene as a German officer on horseback shot down one running Tirailleur after another with his revolver as if he were participating in a trap-shoot.[79] Hunting down and killing African soldiers like wild animals was a way of dehumanizing and asserting dominance over a feared enemy. This urge also manifested itself in the seizing of trophies, stealing items of the enemy's equipment – such as the dreaded *coupe-coupe* – or taking photographs of him, either alive or dead (fig. 8.3). The dehumanization of the enemy

75 Ibid., 36.
76 Fargettas, *Les tirailleurs sénégalais*, 149.
77 Ibid., 149.
78 Scheck, *Hitler's African Victims*, 40.
79 Fargettas, *Les tirailleurs sénégalais*, 154.

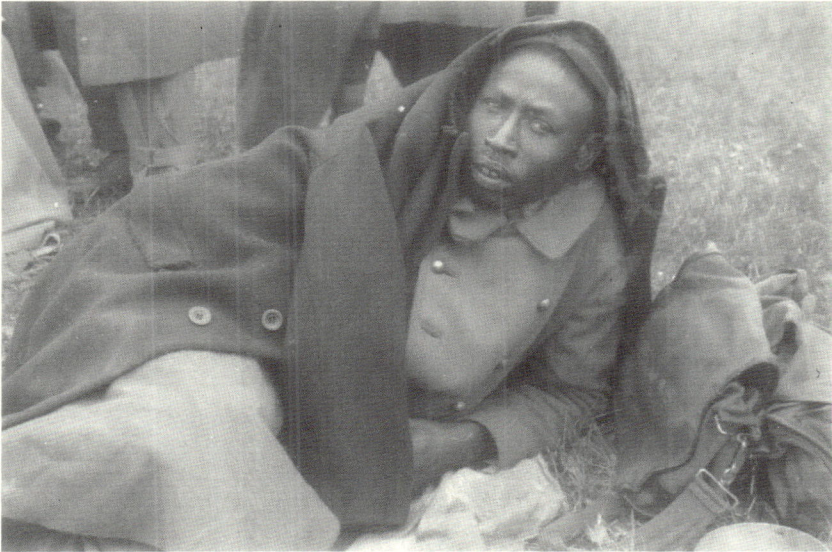

8.3. A Tirailleur Sénégalais in German captivity in 1940, waiting to be taken to Germany. The soldier in the photograph has borrowed a greatcoat to keep warm. In the first days after the defeat of 1940, many POWs were placed in compounds with no shelter. German soldiers took photographs of them as trophies.

extended beyond death itself. In the aftermath of the Battle of France, it was often impossible to identify the bodies of Black soldiers because German soldiers had deliberately removed their identity tags.[80] This erasure of their names and identities was evidently a way of denying them an essential human attribute. Furthermore, the German military authorities resisted efforts to provide respectful burials to the African soldiers who had been killed. One German memorandum insisted that since Black soldiers "fought like savages and maltreated and even killed a great many German prisoners who had the misfortune to fall into their hands [...] the Commander of the German Army does not wish and expressly forbids the embellishment of the graves of Black soldiers."[81]

This systematic dehumanization of African soldiers by the German army, which sought to erase every trace of their existence as human beings,

80 Ibid., 156–7.
81 Ibid., 158.

meant that the early efforts by French civilians to memorialize those soldiers were extremely significant. They were a way of re-establishing the
victims' identities as human beings. The first such initiative came at
Chasselay, where a cemetery for 188 Tirailleurs Sénégalais killed in battle
or subsequently massacred was inaugurated by a Muslim Imam on
8 November 1942, in the presence of officials of the Vichy regime. The
cemetery was built to resemble a West African village, or "Tata." The following
year, on 11 November 1943, the political orientation of a demonstration
honouring the victims of the massacres at Clamecy stood in stark contrast
to the one at Chasselay. In an act both of commemoration and of resistance,
local townspeople paid tribute to the forty-one soldiers who had been shot
on 18 June 1940 by placing upon their mass grave the colours of the flags
of the principal Allies and a floral cross of Lorraine. In 1948 a monument
was inaugurated at Clamecy in honour of forty-three soldiers (two others
who were killed at the camp in Clamecy in July 1940 were also included).
At the same time, their bodies were relocated to the municipal cemetery.
Finally, in 2012, the names of all forty-three, finally recovered after painstaking research, were inscribed on the monument. These were all important
steps in re-humanizing the African soldiers who were murdered in 1940.[82]

FRONTSTALAGS: LIFE – AND DEATH – IN CAPTIVITY

The armistice signed at Rethondes on 22 June 1940 did not end the suffering of colonized soldiers, although by making them prisoners of war it
changed its nature. Many continued to be victims of violent mistreatment
during the early days of their captivity, as they were force-marched to
prisoner-of-war (POW) camps in Germany. Edouard Kouka Ouédraogo
later recalled how he and other survivors of the massacres of Black soldiers
following the fighting on the Somme were compelled, among many other
cruelties, to run sixty or seventy kilometres a day by guards on bicycles who
simply shot those who fell behind. Forbidden to receive food or water from
civilians, thirst-crazed men who broke ranks to drink from a water fountain
were machine-gunned.[83] Only 40,000 colonized POWs who ended up in
captivity were taken to Germany. In July, Hitler decided that he did not
want "inferior" races contaminating German soil, and the process began
of sending nearly all colonized soldiers back to France. Most who were

82 Scheck, *Hitler's African Victims*, 162–3; Vigreux, "Le 11 Novembre 1943," 153–71.
83 Édouard Ouédraogo, "Composition française," in SHD, 5 h 16. This harrowing
account is reproduced in Onana, *La France et ses tirailleurs*, 131–7. See also Scheck, *French
Colonial Soldiers*, 32–4.

taken prisoner in the later stages of the campaign remained in France, where they were placed in extremely primitive provisional POW camps or Frontstalags that were often little more than patches of ground surrounded by barbed wire. Shelter, sanitation, and food were all inadequate, and the guards, who were in the first instance front-line troops, continued to mete out harsh treatment. It was "the regime of the rutabaga and the stick," recalled Léopold Sédar Senghor, imprisoned in a Frontstalag at Poitiers. Senghor wrote that the first camp commander, Captain Hahn, was "a very hard officer" who once ordered the guards to fire on a Senegalese POW who was caught stealing potatoes. The POW was killed.[84] Gradually, however, conditions improved. Most white soldiers were sent on to POW camps in Germany and the number of Frontstalags fell from fifty-eight in September 1940, to twenty in 1941, to eight in April 1942.[85] Both the administration and the amenities of the camps improved. At Poitiers, according to Senghor, the camp was transformed by a new commander, a Lieutenant Bayle. Washrooms and toilets with running water were built, stone pathways constructed between barracks, and a sports field provided. The POWs were better fed: "we have a greater variety of vegetables and of better quality," wrote Senghor.[86] For some at least of the approximately 90,000 colonized troops who, for a longer or shorter time, experienced life in the Frontstalags of occupied France, conditions were bearable.[87] For many, however, even as their general circumstances became less deprived and their treatment more humane, incarceration in the Frontstalags marked the beginning of a long, slow decline ending in illness and death. Although statistical evidence is lacking, the Frontstalags may have been as deadly for colonized soldiers as the battlefield.

The experience of colonized soldiers in the Frontstalags has been closely studied by Raffael Scheck, Sarah Ann Frank, and Armelle Mabon.[88] Although these POW camps were unusual in that they were located, from the prisoners' point of view, on "home" ground, where they benefited from a generally sympathetic local population, they were nonetheless places of hardship, where food shortages were frequent, rats and lice ubiquitous, violence

84 Senghor, "Senghor: le manuscrit inconnu," 25.

85 Recham, "Les indigènes nord-africains," 109–125.

86 Senghor, "Senghor: le manuscrit inconnu," 25.

87 On the sources relating to the calculation of the numbers of colonial pows, see Scheck, *French Colonial Soldiers*, 27–31. A report by Dr Marcel Bonnaud of 8 October 1941 stated that there were by then 68,550 men in the Frontstalags: 43,973 North Africans, 15,777 Senegalese, 3,888 Madagascans, and 2,471 Indochinese. Recham, "Les indigènes nord-africains," 114.

88 See Scheck, *French Colonial Soldiers*, 167–240; Frank, "Life in the Frontstalags"; Frank, *Hostages of Empire*; Mabon, *Prisonniers de guerre "indigènes,"* 46–67.

administered by guards or other inmates common, and epidemic disease
a constant threat. Most prisoners were required to work, which greatly
affected their circumstances (fig. 8.4). Small work commandos sometimes
gained access to extra food, particularly if they were engaged in farm work,
as well as opportunities for escape, but medical care was harder to come
by. The French Red Cross and other domestic and colonial organizations
provided food and cigarettes – and sometimes colonial delicacies such as
couscous and kola nuts – but some POW communities benefited more than
others. Generally, Moroccan POWs received more aid than Algerians or
Tunisians, who in turn received more than sub-Saharan Africans,
Madagascans, or Indochinese. These disparities contributed to tensions
between ethnicities, which sometimes erupted into violent disturbances.

Raffael Scheck and Sarah Ann Frank provide compelling evidence that
the Vichy authorities campaigned actively to ameliorate conditions in the
camps and to encourage the release of their inhabitants. Germany shame-
lessly offloaded its responsibilities to feed these POWs onto Vichy, which,
by encouraging their employment in agriculture and forestry, passed the
responsibility on to French farmers and businesses. Although there were
some misgivings, French civilians were generous in helping to provide
food.[89] Continuing a tradition from the First World War, many prisoners
received parcels of food and clothing from French *marraines de guerre.*[90]
"French women, by their disinterested generosity and their courage,
are France's best propagandists," wrote Senghor.[91] Conditions did improve,
at least until the later stages of the war, when the remaining prisoners were
removed to Germany in chaotic circumstances.[92] By July 1944, the numbers
in captivity had already fallen to thirty thousand, and perhaps half of
the remainder escaped during the liberation of France.[93] All the same, the
unsanitary conditions and the poor nutrition in the camps contributed to
the spread of epidemic disease, first dysentery and then tuberculosis,
and to a high rate of mortality. Most historians have followed the lead of
contemporary sources in assuming the peculiar susceptibility of Africans

89 Scheck, *French Colonial Soldiers,* 60–90; Frank, "Life in the Frontstalags."
90 "godmothers."
91 Senghor, "Senghor: le manuscrit inconnu," 26.
92 Sarah Ann Frank argues, however, that Vichy's interest in ameliorating the conditions of colonial POWs diminished after November 1942, when it simultaneously lost
control of its African colonies and, as French guards began to replace German ones in the
Frontstalags, gained greater access to prisoners. These changed circumstances meant that
Vichy was less concerned about the effects of German propaganda upon the loyalties
of colonial POWs and therefore less interested in their material well-being. Frank, "Life in
the Frontstalags."
93 Scheck, *French Colonial Soldiers,* 31.

8.4. Tirailleurs Sénégalais, prisoners of war, working on the landing ground for German Focke-Wulf Fw-189 reconnaissance aircraft at Bordeaux-Mérignac.

to tuberculosis. Hélène de Gobineau, whose role on a French commission inspecting conditions in the camps in northeastern France enabled her to befriend many African POWs, wrote that "tuberculosis kills them as quickly as it devours our newborns. They are not like us, demi-immunized by breathing the air of the metro[;] their organism does not know how to react against the sickness."[94] Raffael Scheck cites medical studies, however, which refute the idea that Africans are particularly susceptible to tuberculosis. Scheck argues that the high rate at which they fell ill to the infection in the Frontstalags is better explained in terms of immune systems weakened by privation and other illnesses than in terms of ethnicity.[95] It is important to note, however, that releasing the sick from captivity often did nothing to save them from tuberculosis. The "hecatomb" of deaths deplored by Gobineau[96] in the first years of captivity was simply displaced from the Frontstalags to hospitals, mostly in the southern zone. Thus, Sassi (or perhaps Sani) Bakary, a thirty-year-old private from Senegal, endured

94 Gobineau, *Noblesse d'Afrique*, 20.
95 Scheck, *French Colonial Soldiers*, 202.
96 Gobineau, *Noblesse d'Afrique*, 20.

a peripatetic existence following his release from a Frontstalag on 22 April 1943, moving from the military hospital of La Chappelle Saint-Mesmin (Loiret) to hospitals in Périgueux (Dordogne), Marseille (Bouches-du Rhône), and finally to Roanne (Loire), where he died on 1 March 1945, nearly two years after first falling ill to tuberculosis.[97]

Nineteen forty-one was the year of highest mortality. After that, as medical services were organized and as the camps released seriously ill prisoners for repatriation (in theory, at least), mortality declined. At Bayonne, there were fifty-one deaths in 1941, twenty-one in 1942, and thirteen in 1943.[98] Exactly how many colonized soldiers died from the hardships and illnesses they suffered in captivity is unknown. Julien Fargettas cites an official estimate from April 1945 that 2,600 had died in captivity before the liberation, but puts little faith in it.[99] Myron Echenberg asserted that half of the 15–16,000 West Africans who became POWs (approximately 7,500) did not survive, but Mabon considers this an overestimate, as does Raffael Scheck, who cites a much lower figure of five thousand deaths among all colonial POWs, a mortality rate of 5 or 6 per cent.[100] Sarah Ann Frank arrives at a slightly lower percentage than Scheck, of 3.4 per cent.[101] This problem is complicated by the evidence that conditions were often as dire for colonized soldiers who evaded capture or who were released from the Frontstalags. Many who were not already so ill that they went directly to hospital ended up in Groupements Militaires d'Indigènes Coloniaux Rapatriables (GMICR), which were established in February 1943 and which put colonized soldiers to work in circumstances that differed little from those they had experienced in the Frontstalags.[102] Soldiers freed from captivity had to endure the same hardships as did French civilians, without enjoying the same social networks and connections that would facilitate their survival. Any calculation of the overall mortality of colonized soldiers in France during the years of the German occupation would need to include the deaths that occurred outside the Frontstalags. Although statistical evidence is lacking, it does not seem implausible to suggest that the hardships of

97 Biographical details provided by the Ministère de Défense, Mémoire des hommes: Parcours individuels. Combattants africains de la seconde guerre mondiale, accessed 9 September 2020, https://www.memoiredeshommes.sga.defense.gouv.fr/fr/article.php?larub=286&titre=combattants-africains-de-la-seconde-guerre-mondiale.

98 Mabon, *Prisonniers de guerre "indigènes,"* 59.

99 Fargettas, *Les tirailleurs sénégalais*, 226.

100 Echenberg, Colonial Conscripts, 88; Mabon, *Prisonniers de guerre "indigènes,"* 59; Scheck, *French Colonial Soldiers*, 10; The source of Scheck's figure is Leleu, Passera, and Quellien, eds, *La France pendant la seconde guerre mondiale*, 114–17.

101 Frank, *Hostages of Empire*, 146.

102 Rives and Dietrich, *Héros méconnus*, 285.

captivity and occupation may have been as deadly to some contingents of colonized soldiers as the fighting in the Battle of France had been. Some nationalities appear to have adapted more successfully to camp life than others, keeping up their morale and acquiring positions of relative power. Senghor commented that "It is the Indochinese and the Madagascans who appear to react the least, and to adapt the worst. The Arabs and the Senegalese are most readily cheerful."[103]

Evidently, illness took a far greater toll of colonized soldiers' lives during the occupation than did acts of violence. A moving testimonial to the suffering of those soldiers – and to their dignity in the face of death – is the memoir written by Hélène de Gobineau, entitled *Noblesse d'Afrique*. In her introduction, the author described how sick soldiers were released from Frontstalags to the care of French hospitals only once there was little chance they might recover.

They came to us still smiling, happy with freedom. In three months, skeletal, they had finished spitting out their lungs.

There is Koalaba, the Peul, thin as a tree in winter, who refuses to die. He knows that death only takes us lying down, he stays sitting, night and day in his death bed, he does not want death to put his life to sleep. He keeps himself awake, telling himself stories of Podor.

There is Fatoum who, the morning of his last day, dressed himself smartly, to be photographed standing to attention before death.

There is Tairou who encloses in his suitcase everything we give him, because he knows that the suitcase will be able, after the war, to make the journey to Guinea to take his three sons the last gift from their father.[104]

Gobineau's stories of her hospital encounters with African soldiers personalize and individualize the experience of mass death. The chapter entitled "About the Death of Idrissa" is typical. It begins by describing the decline of Idrissa, a Sudanese Tirailleur dying of tuberculosis but preserving his "will to suffer while smiling" to the very end. It then tells how Fatokoma, Idrissa's closest friend and a devout Muslim, sought at once to manage his own grief, dignify his comrade's death, and express appreciation for the medical care he had received. At the story's end, after burying Idrissa's remains in a modest ceremony at Pantin, Fatokoma prepares to depart Paris by train. He leaves behind a suitcase of gifts for the doctor who had cared for Idrissa, with a note attached: "This suitcase for doctor. Idrissa my

103   Senghor, "Senghor: le manuscrit inconnu," 30.
104   Gobineau, *Noblesse d'Afrique*, 20.

brother is dead. God wanted it. It is not doctor's fault, he worked day and
night, all man can do he did. Suitcase is big thank-you for white doctor."[105]
By recounting in intimate detail the words and actions of dying soldiers,
each identified by name, and of their grieving comrades, Gobineau paid
tribute to their unique identities and personalities as human beings.

Recognizing that so many colonized soldiers died of illness during the
occupation should not lead us to assume they were simply passive victims.
Gobineau's memoir opens with the story of Mamadou Sarr, a Tirailleur
Sénégalais determined to avenge the comrades whose massacre he had
witnessed in 1940 but whose resistance ended tragically with his death in
another massacre at the time of the liberation.[106] Many soldiers who evaded
capture or who later regained their freedom became members or leaders
of resistance movements. The authors of *Héros méconnus* state that colonial
soldiers were involved in maquis or resistance groups in thirty-five departments and that they participated in a hundred significant engagements.[107]
Some died violent deaths because of this determination to keep fighting.
One of the better known of these soldiers was Addi-Bâ, a Guinean who
organized the escape of a group of Tirailleurs Sénégalais from the
Frontstalag at Neufchâteau. After helping to facilitate his comrades' safe
passage to Switzerland, Addi-Bâ remained in France, where he became
one of the leaders of a maquis group in the Vosges. Tracked down by the
Gestapo, Addi-Bâ was captured, subjected to torture, and then shot on
18 December 1943.[108] Over fifty Tirailleurs Sénégalais joined the maquis
fighting in the Vercors in 1944, and there were Madagascans, Senegalese,
and Indochinese who fought nearby with the maquis de l'Oisans. Eleven
of the 189 names on the monument commemorating the dead of this
group are Vietnamese.[109] A striking photograph shows the death of one
of these *maquisards*, a Tirailleur Indochinois named N'Guyen (fig. 8.5).
Artfully composed, the photograph shows the dying soldier surrounded
by his comrades, his head solemnly cradled by an African while his hand
is held by a Jewish chaplain. The scene is dominated by the figure of
the unit's commander, Captain André Lespiau Lanvin. Resembling
artists' representations of the descent from the cross by its focus upon the
deep respect shown the dying man by those surrounding him, the photograph insists upon the idea of sacrifice. Eight of the ten soldiers surrounding

---

105   Ibid., 107–22.
106   Ibid., 35–47.
107   Rives and Dietrich, *Héros méconnus*, 304.
108   Ibid., 289–91. See also a fictionalized account of Addi-Bâ's life: Monénembo, *The Black Terrorist*.
109   Rives and Dietrich, *Héros méconnus*, 304.

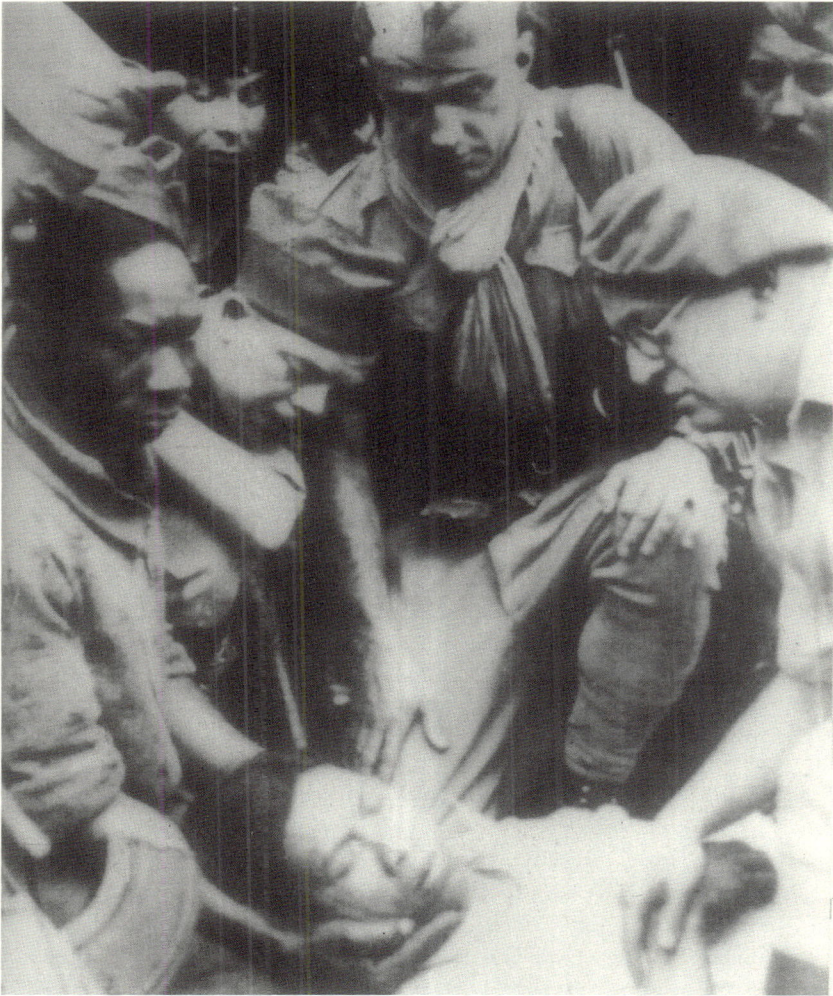

8.5. Photograph of the *maquis de l'Oisans*. Musée de la Résistance nationale, Champigny-sur-Marne.

N'Guyen have their eyes turned down toward the face of the dying soldier. Of the remaining two, the African appears lost in his own thoughts as he looks to one side, while the other, possibly a North African, fixes the camera with an unsmiling stare. as if to express disapproval for its intrusion into an intensely personal occasion. The photograph powerfully expresses the ideal of an interracial brotherhood of arms at the same time as it sanctifies the soldier's death.[110] Such iconic images of military resistance and sacrifice, through their prominence in patriotic histories such as *Héros méconnus*, served to reinforce the dominant French narrative of the Second World War as that of a nation united in resistance. This visibility itself helped to keep in the shadows the many French military personnel who became captives of the enemy in 1940 and who were destined to remain so until the end of the war. Like the system of honours established by French governments after the war, narratives and images that placed the emphasis upon acts of resistance, escape, and sacrifice provided the essential components for a positive national memory of the war, but they did so by excluding those groups that had not shared in those activities or experiences. Most soldiers of 1940, those who experienced defeat and then years of captivity either in France or Gernany, were condemned in the French national memory to oblivion or to obloquy.[111]

RENAISSANCE: AFRICAN ARMIES

While the colonized soldiers who remained in France after the defeat of 1940 languished in the Frontstalags, developments were taking place in the colonies themselves that would lead to a French military rebirth. Under the leadership of General Charles de Gaulle, various elements of the French metropolitan and colonial armies turned their backs on Vichy and its collaboration with the Axis, coming together to constitute the Free French forces. In turn, these forces were themselves fused, in the summer of 1943, with the Army of Africa in the army of the French Committee of National Liberation. This military revival was an unsteady and conflict-ridden process, with episodes of bitter fighting that pitted Frenchman against Frenchman – and Tirailleur Sénégalais against Tirailleur Sénégalais – which left behind a legacy of resentment and suspicion. In Gabon, the fratricidal conflict between Vichy and Free French forces resulted in the deaths of thirty-six French soldiers on both sides. In Syria, where 1,216 were killed, the only units that refused to fight one another were those belonging to the French Foreign Legion. "The Legion will not fight the Legion," declared Prince Amilakvari, the Georgian commander of the Legion's First Free French battalion.[112] In spite of these internecine conflicts, the accumulation of

---

110 Ibid.

111 Dalisson, *Les soldats de 1940*, 128. Dalisson demonstrates that postwar French governments only belatedly and reluctantly accorded honorific recognition to the soldiers of 1940, establishing restrictive definitions of "combatant" that not all soldiers could meet. Medals for escapers and resisters were approved before a medal for all combatants.

112 Crémieux-Brilhac, *La France libre*, vol. 1, 167, 196–7.

military accomplishments by the Free French forces gave growing credibility
to de Gaulle's claims to his own legitimacy as the leader of the French
people and to France's place as one of the four great powers leading the
fight against the Axis. This military rebirth began in French Equatorial
Africa, the principal states of which rallied to de Gaulle in "three glorious
days" from 26 to 28 August 1940. It also depended very heavily on
indigenous troops from these colonies. Later, the successful Allied
invasions of Algeria and Morocco brought the Army of Africa, two-thirds
of which consisted of indigenous troops, within the Free French camp.[113]
The first significant action in which Free French forces fought successfully as an independent force against those of the Axis occurred in the
context of General Leclerc's[114] famous expedition that culminated in
the capture of Kufra from the Italians on 1 March 1941. The surrender
of the fort was given added symbolic significance by the "Kufra oath" sworn
by Leclerc and his men that they would continue their march until the
French flag was raised over the cathedral at Strasbourg.[115] As Eric Jennings
has shown, Leclerc was disparaging in his assessments of the quality of
African soldiers. Nor did he have any qualms about agreeing to terms
of surrender with the Italian garrison that required the French force
occupying the fort to be composed exclusively of Europeans, effectively
acquiescing to the Italians' implication that African soldiers were not
honourable foes. Yet three-quarters of Leclerc's military personnel for this
expedition were Africans, and he depended even more heavily upon them
when he set out on the Fezzan expedition in December 1942.[116] Jennings
estimates that overall 27,000 indigenous soldiers from French Equatorial
Africa served in the Free French forces between 1940 and 1944, representing between a third and a half of the total of approximately 70,000 men
and women who joined the Free French forces before the summer
of 1943.[117] Patriotic French historiography has celebrated the enthusiasm
with which these colonized subjects rallied to the cause of Free France.
The evidence, however, is that many answered the call to arms reluctantly,
or even under duress.

113 Recham, *Les musulmans algériens*, 236.
114 Leclerc was the "nom de guerre" of Philippe de Hauteclocque.
115 Notin, *1061 compagnons*, 268; Crémieux-Brilhac, *La France libre*, vol. 1, 617.
116 Jennings, *Free French Africa*, 120–1; Crémieux-Brilhac, *La France libre*, vol. 1, 624.
General Koenig, the French commander at Bir Hakeim, was also negative in his judgment
of indigenous troops, insisting that one-third of a battalion needed to be Europeans for it to
be capable of meeting the demands of modern warfare. Fargettas, *Les tirailleurs sénégalais*,
196–7.
117 Jennings, *Free French Africa*, 141. See also Crémieux-Brilhac, *La France libre*,
vol. 1, 698.

Establishing the attitudes and motivation of the African soldiers who fought in the Free French armies is extremely difficult, given that many of those soldiers were illiterate and very few wrote accounts of their experiences. Those who did so generally belonged to an educated elite that was imbued with the assimilationist values of the colonizing power. Taught to view France as their *mère-patrie* and the source of inestimable benefits to its colonized subjects, these soldiers wrote with pride of their service and of the patriotic idealism that inspired it. In this respect, they were in the tradition of Bakary Diallo, whose memoir of his service as a Tirailleur Sénégalais in the First World War was published in 1926. Describing his arrival in France following the outbreak of war in 1914, Diallo wrote unreservedly of his "fidelity and devotion" to "the nation whom God has made the faith of humanity."[118] It might be assumed that this overblown patriotism was specific to the mood of enthusiasm that was a real, if exaggerated, phenomenon at the beginning of the First World War. It is striking, however, that Louis Bigmann, whose biography of Charles N'Tchoréré is in many respects also an autobiography, devoted a chapter of his book to the story of how the two friends, along with seven other companions, enlisted for military service in 1916. Educated together at the Montfort School, this group of young men belonged to a nationalist youth organization, L'Aurore Gabonaise,[119] which saw no contradiction between their loyalties to Gabon and to France: "So, for us, France and Gabon were simply one and the same thing, although with different geographical features. Anything was excusable if it was meant to serve them."[120]

In Bigmann's narrative, there was a fundamental continuity linking the patriotic sentiments of 1916 to those of 1939. The devotion of Tirailleurs like himself and Charles N'Tchoréré to France and to Africa was as absolute as it was unchanging. Bigmann cites a speech supposedly given by N'Tchoréré in September 1939 in his capacity as commander of the school for *enfants de troupe*[121] in Senegal. Its sentiments are every bit as exalted as those of Bakary Diallo in 1914. "We must keep our gaze fixed resolutely on the flag because it is the symbol of the homeland," N'Tchoréré began. "The true soldier," he continued, must "be ready, if necessary for the supreme sacrifice," happy to die "having never, at any moment, betrayed

118 Diallo, *Force-bonté*, 117–18.
119 "Gabonese Dawn."
120 Bigmann, *Charles N'Tchoréré*, 93.
121 "Troop children." A school for the children of servicemen and their wives. Charles N'Tchoréré was appointed head of the school in 1927 after he had been seriously wounded while serving in Syria, remaining in this post until 1939.

the honour of our flag."[122] The speech, which Bigmann says was recounted to him by one of N'Tchórére's pupils while they were both POWs in France during the war, is replete with the patriotic vocabulary of the Third Republic, including *flag, honour, sacrifice.* Despite Bigmann's insistence upon N'Tchórére's commitment to Africa, the most striking feature of the speech is the absence of any referent that might be identified as specifically African. Equally telling is the anecdote with which Bigmann prefaces his biography, describing the sinking of the SS *Falaba*. According to Bigmann, the *Falaba* was torpedoed in 1915 while carrying eight hundred Tirailleurs Sénégalais from Senegal to Le Havre. As the ship went down, he wrote, "As imperturbable as if on parade, without hesitation, the eight hundred Senegalese of the unit, bayonets fixed, stand stiffly, impeccably to attention, and sink with the ship, heads held high, shoulder to shoulder."[123] Given that the sinking of the *Falaba* occurred on 28 March 1915, en route from Liverpool to West Africa, with the loss of 104 lives, Bigmann's story bears little relation to historical fact. Concocted to illustrate "the bravery and the sense of honour of Africans,"[124] its significance lies, once again, in its lack of any African referent. Indeed, it is a story with more than an echo of that of the sinking of *Le Vengeur* in 1794, famously mythologized by the revolutionary leader Bertrand Barère. In Barère's account, the crew of *Le Vengeur* refused to surrender to their English foes, preferring to go to a watery grave proclaiming their loyalty to the Republic.[125] Louis Bigmann and Charles N'Tchórére (at least in Bigmann's rendering of him), like Bakary Diallo before them, articulated a discourse of patriotism and sacrifice that was essentially French. It is little wonder that as Charles N'Tchórére prepared to lead his men into action for the last time on 7 June 1940, he is supposed to have turned to a young lieutenant and gestured toward his company, saying, "the square at Waterloo, don't you think?"[126] Educated at the Montfort school in Gabon by the Catholic brothers of the Order of Saint Gabriel and later at the training school for officers at Fréjus in Provence, Charles N'Tchórére modelled himself not on the warriors of Africa but on the soldiers of Napoleon's Imperial Guard.

It was not just volunteers from the educated elite of African society, such as Charles N'Tchórére and Louis Bigmann, who expressed their loyalty to

122 Bigmann, *Charles N'Tchórére*, 93.

123 Ibid., 24.

124 Ibid., 23.

125 Barère, *Rapport fait au nom du Comité de Salut publique, sur l'héroïsme des républicains montant le vaisseau le Vengeur; Le Moniteur Universel*, 10 July 1794. See also Roquincourt, "Le mythe du Vengeur," 481–2; Schneider, "Le mythe du vaisseau *Le Vengeur*," 71–121.

126 Rives and Dietrich, *Héros méconnus*, 169.

France. Raphaël Onana came from a humble agricultural village in Cameroon. Having left home as an adolescent to live in the home of his uncle, a soldier with a somewhat peripatetic existence, Onana's education was patchy and he had only a partial mastery of French when he joined the Cameroon militia in 1939. He admitted in a memoir written long after the war that his motivation in joining the army was to escape the boredom and hardship of life as a peasant farmer. He was also attracted by the uniform and the prospect of having a weapon "more powerful than the rifles that certain native chiefs possessed."[127] All the same, Onana claimed to have felt a strong attachment to France. His memoir opens with a vivid description of his feelings as he lay severely wounded in the sand at Bir Hakeim in June 1942, his left leg shattered by a mine. Although consumed by pain and fear, recalled Onana, he took inspiration from de Gaulle's telegram to General Koenig on 9 June 1942, instructing the latter to tell his men that "all of France is watching you and that you are its pride."[128] Onana had heard de Gaulle's words on the morning of the day he was wounded. "So, in this very place where, presently, I am lying, I bask in a great pride, despite my crushed leg, which hurts more and more. I know that the whole of France, Free France, of course, is watching me and admires me; I know that the whole of France is proud of what I have done and of what my comrades continue to do. Beyond the enormous distance, beyond the shadows of the night, this France, whom I do not know and whom I love with all my heart, saw me fall; she commiserates with my pain. She knows that I fell for her, so that she could recover a bit of her lost dignity and honour. The whole of France is watching me."[129] Aware of the reputation of Axis soldiers for killing wounded soldiers who were dark skinned, Onana reflected that "if I should be finished off by the enemy, my only consolation would be the fact to have died for the free world and, especially, for France."[130] Considering himself "an armoured man"[131] who had been accorded supernatural protection against death by rituals performed by a witch doctor around the time of his birth, Onana survived both his wound and capture by the enemy. Taken to Italy, he had his left leg amputated and spent five months as a prisoner of war before he was repatriated after an exchange of prisoners in November 1942.

127 Onana, *Un homme blindé*, 146.
128 Cited in Crémieux-Brilhac, *La France libre*, vol. 1, 464.
129 Onana, *Un homme blindé*, 13.
130 Ibid., 12–13.
131 "Un homme blindé."

Fifty-three years later, he was still proud to assert that "It was out of love for France that I went to war [...] I am a happy man."[132]

While these very few written accounts by African soldiers express strong patriotic sentiments towards France, the oral testimony of many others tells a rather different story. Nancy Ellen Lawler interviewed 109 veterans from the Korhogo region of Ivory Coast for her book *Soldiers of Misfortune: Ivoirien "Tirailleurs" of World War II*. Most of these veterans expressed pride in their military performance. Those who had fought in the Battle of France looked back on it as evidence that African soldiers were superior to Europeans. "We were stronger than the whites," said one. "When the shooting came, the whites ran."[133] All the same, it is also clear from Lawler's evidence that it was not primarily for love of France that most of these men became soldiers. The methods used to recruit men for the army were little changed from those used in the First World War, although they no longer provoked widespread rebellion. The influence of tribal and village leaders, the enticement of a signing-on bonus, the attraction of a uniform, the prospect of emancipation from forced labour or of allowances for family members: all these factors, singly or in combination, encouraged the flow of recruits. The words of veterans make it clear that many had no choice. "I was forced to join," said Daouda Tuo-Donatoho concerning his recruitment in 1937. "At that time everything was forced – forced labor. I was drafted. I was the only one taken that year from the village ... The village chief chose me. I had to go."[134] "I was in uniform," recalled Tiorna Yeo of his own recruitment. "I was not happy, but I had to do it [...] The uniform was pretty, but we didn't know if we would come back."[135]

For all that a military uniform was attractive to some because of the status it conferred upon the bearer, to others it was a sign of subjection. When Joseph Issoufou Conombo and his fellow students from the School of Medicine in Dakar were called up for military service in 1939, they refused to accept the Tirailleur Sénégalais uniform, with its distinctive red chechia and belt. To these educated Africans, that uniform was the "clothing of slavery," which identified them as French "subjects" rather than citizens. The day following their protestation, the recalcitrant medical students were convoked by a group of officers, who gave them five minutes to take up the offending uniforms; otherwise they would be considered mutineers and face a firing squad without further ado![136] The new recruits hastened

132   Ibid., 252.
133   Lawler, *Soldiers of Misfortune*, 80.
134   Ibid., 48.
135   Ibid., 47.
136   Conombo, *Souvenirs de guerre*, 34–6.

to obey. The colonial army clearly had no qualms about resorting to coercion even in dealing with the elites of African society.

Once in uniform, many African soldiers had little idea of the cause for which they were fighting. In the civil war between Vichy and Free France, it was largely a matter of chance as to which side they were on. The testimony gathered by Lawler demonstrates that many Ivory Coast soldiers serving with the Vichy forces in Syria were stunned to find themselves suddenly fighting other Africans. "The Camerounians [*sic*] attacked us," recalled Namble Silué. "We were amazed because they weren't Germans. They were Black. Why were they attacking us? They had never told us we were fighting against the French."[137] It is hardly surprising that following their defeat only 1,500 of the 4,000 Tirailleurs Sénégalais in General Dentz's army chose to transfer their allegiance to the Free French Army; the majority preferred to return home. The testimony of one soldier who did switch sides indicates that he did not feel himself to be a free agent in this transition. "They captured us and took off our French uniforms," he said of the Free French forces in Syria. "They gave us English ones. We had an English rifle and cannon and American war vehicles. Then we all pushed the Germans back [...] [In Tunisia] de Gaulle made us move a lot [...] We attacked the Germans."[138] It is hard to escape the conclusion from such testimony that a great many African soldiers serving in the Second World War fought simply because they had to; they were at the mercy of forces that were beyond their power as individuals to resist. "I was not a volunteer – I was forced to go," were the blunt words of Nanga Soro, another Ivoirien Tirailleur who served in Tunisia. "There were no volunteers."[139]

In North Africa, too, where there was an impressive mobilization of both European and indigenous populations following Operation Torch, material considerations prevailed over ideological ones in compelling men to serve. Timour Ali Oubassou, who enlisted as a Moroccan *goumier* in 1943, was typical of many. "I wanted to have money and to escape misery and oppression," he recalled. "At the time I knew that the world had been at war and that we would be sent abroad where the war was more difficult. However, I didn't have any other choice."[140] The cause of liberating the mother country excited little enthusiasm among either Europeans or

137 Lawler, *Soldiers of Misfortune*, 143.
138 Ibid., 161.
139 Ibid., 162.
140 Interview with Timour Ali Oubassou conducted by Moshe Gershovich at Beni Mellal in January 1998. In Gershovich, "Stories on the Road," 51. Also cited in Le Gac, *Vaincre sans gloire*, 80.

Muslims in French North Africa. One sign of this was the relatively high number of deserters and *insoumis*. On 1 November 1944, there were 2,700 of these, plus another 15,200 cases under investigation, representing 1.5 per cent and 8.6 per cent respectively of all personnel from French North Africa on active service.[141] For many Europeans, their economic interests damaged by the severing after operation Torch of all ties with the homeland and bemused by the initial confusion surrounding the goals and allegiances of their new leaders in Algiers, the war was simply too far away. For Muslims, the call to arms raised more fundamental questions about whether the sacrifices demanded of them were commensurate with their inferior status within colonial society and within the army itself. In February 1943, Ferhat Abbas sent to the United Nations a "Manifesto of the Algerian People" demanding an amelioration of the status of Muslim subjects as a condition of their participation in the war. A later "addition to the Manifesto" added demands for independence as well as equal pay and equal opportunity for advancement within the army. The concessions that were forthcoming – the granting of equal pay to Muslim soldiers on 6 August 1943 and the abolition of the status of "subject" for Muslim Algerians on 7 March 1944 – were grudging and belated. In July 1944, a police commissar in Constantine warned his superior of "widespread propaganda" circulating within the Muslim community which sought to persuade them "that they are fighting for a country that is not theirs and that their sacrifice on the fields of battle where they represent the great majority, is useless since their independence is under discussion and far from being conceded."[142]

Despite the concern of officials at the lack of enthusiasm and the widespread absenteeism that greeted the initial call-up of annual classes of conscripts, there was no widespread resistance. Ultimately, 14.5 per cent of the European and 1.9 per cent of the indigenous populations of French North Africa responded to the call to arms after November 1942.[143] Enthusiastic or not, indigenous soldiers from throughout the empire were very conscious of the inequalities that set them apart from their white comrades in the French army. A report on the morale of the First Armoured Division of October 1943 commented that prior to the equalization of pay rates in August 1943, "the native did not understand that his contribution to the common task should be compensated less than that of a European."[144]

141 Ibid., 84–5.
142 Cited in ibid., 108
143 Ibid., 56 and 68.
144 Cited in Recham, *Les musulmans algériens*, 254.

The equalization of pay, however, only went so far to redress the unequal treatment of colonized troops. Indemnities paid to support the families of indigenous soldiers were a fraction of those paid to support those of Europeans. While a European with a wife and two children received an indemnity of 1,833 francs, an indigenous soldier in the same circumstances received only 450 francs. Reports on their morale emphasized that indigenous soldiers from North Africa were very much concerned about whether their families received the support to which they were entitled and whether it was sufficient to sustain them.[145] More mundane matters concerning the quality of food and clothing also impinged upon their awareness of their unequal status. A report from the First Armoured Division of December 1944 commented that "North African natives inspired more by a personal logic than by the spirit of the Coran do not understand why the necessities of war oblige them to eat pork but do not take them into account for the distributions of wine."[146]

For some colonized soldiers, like Joseph Conombo, what particularly rankled was the army's failure to insist they receive respectful treatment from white soldiers who were junior to them in rank. As an auxiliary doctor with the Tirailleurs Sénégalais, Conombo was outraged by the refusal of European soldiers in the mess of the infirmary where he worked to bring meals to Black doctors. One of those soldiers went so far as to slap a Black colleague of Conombo's. In seeking to have the insubordinate soldiers punished, Conombo came up against a brick wall. His European superiors were unwilling and the Black officers in the regiment unable to sanction the behaviour of the white soldiers. "They are WHITES and a NATIVE cannot punish!" raged Conombo. In despair, the Black doctors contemplated leaving the army: "the time has come to desert, we can no longer put up with this bad treatment, these humiliations."[147] They did not follow through with this intention, however, and according to Conombo the situation improved markedly as the hard work of training in the mountains of Morocco bred mutual respect between Europeans and Africans. "Comradeship, even the brotherhood of arms, effectively began to grow," he wrote. "The officers take greater care to improve the living conditions of their troops as well as their own comportment. We felt this as a true relief and, in three months, all resentment had dissipated."[148]

145 Ibid., 255.
146 Ibid., 257.
147 Conombo, *Souvenirs de guerre*, 49–50.
148 Ibid., 52.

COMBAT: BROTHERS IN ARMS?

Joseph Conombo's blithe assertion that the experience of serving together rapidly forged a brotherhood of arms between races may seem a bit too good to be true. All the same, many soldiers idealized in similar terms the bonds that developed between men of different origins as they shared the hardships, fears, and dangers of war. Jacques Augarde, in his history of the Moroccan Tabors, cited the evidence of Lieutenant Reveillaud, who attributed the high morale of the Tabors to "the fraternity uniting French and Moroccans, to the constant effort of the ones to bring themselves closer to the others, by respect for their customs, by a marked interest in their religion and by knowledge of their language."[149] Reveillaud pointed to the "monolithic unity" of a section led by Chief Adjutant Allard as a model of this fraternity. After two years of exemplary leadership by Allard, "his *goumiers* adored him, he could ask everything of them and obtain everything from them."[150] In combat, according to Reveillaud, this loyalty translated into a successful attack led by Allard, who was mortally wounded in the engagement. Pierre Lyautey, an officer who served with a Groupement de Tabors Marocains (GTM) in Italy wrote of the relationship between French officers and colonized soldiers: "Our men belong to our family. A Mokkadem,[151] a Mouan,[152] a *goumier* is attached to his officer who knows his relatives, his village and defends his interests."[153] Julie Le Gac, in her history of the French Expeditionary Corps (CEF) in Italy, cites the words of Daniel Rouillot on the camaraderie between French and colonized soldiers that developed under fire: "We went to the attack together, we died together."[154] Le Gac also quotes very similar words from the future president of an independent Algeria, Ahmed Ben Bella, who wrote in his memoirs of his experience fighting in Italy that "between the French and Moroccans there reigned, at the front, an admirable solidarity. All felt themselves to be equal before death. Enemy bullets did not discriminate, nor did friendship."[155]

Evidence of the strength of these interracial bonds of camaraderie is provided by the distress expressed by soldiers whose comrades were killed. A French officer recalled his horror when a Moroccan soldier under his

---

149 Jacques Augarde, *La longue route des Tabors*, 50.
150 Ibid. A *Goum* was a Moroccan company, a *goumier* a foot soldier.
151 Sergeant.
152 Corporal.
153 Lyautey, *La campagne d'Italie* 1944, 81.
154 Le Gac, *Vaincre sans gloire*, 367.
155 Ibid.

command was swept off a mountainside in Abruzzo by a gust of wind during a night-time descent:

All I see is a body which falls, without a cry, into the void. Lying on the mound of snow, I call Brahim by screaming his name, but I see and hear nothing. I understand. Brahim has fallen into the hole and disappeared into it for eternity. Anyone who tried a rescue (with what means?) would go to their death. I say a short prayer to God, "Allah irahamou!" May God have mercy on him! Turning our backs, the descent resumes, sadder than ever [...] I must energetically forbid seventeen *goumiers* suffering from frostbite from taking their shoes off and walking barefoot in the snow [...] One *goumier*, a youth, will die of cold and exhaustion two hours before our return to the base. We will not forget our dead.[156]

The officer's final sentence, uttering his commitment to the duty of memory, conveys the lasting impact upon him of these deaths of Moroccan soldiers.

There were limits, however, to this sympathy between soldiers of different ethnicities. Bernard Lasalle, who served in the First Army during the campaigns fought in Alsace and Germany, recalled the very different feelings aroused in him by the deaths of a Jewish *pied-noir*[157] from his section and that of a North African Tirailleur whom he did not know. The death of the former, horribly mutilated by an exploding shell, was remembered by Lasalle as "the worst memory I have of this war [...] It is one of those terrible images that will not be erased from my memory until my last breath." The death of the Tirailleur, Lasalle confessed apologetically, he found less shocking, both because it occurred in the dark, which obscured the man's wounds, and because "I did not have the same points in common nor the same friendly complicity with this North African Tirailleur as with my Jewish *pied-noir* pal whose death caused me much pain."[158]

Whatever its real limits may have been, General René Chambe, in his account of the French army's campaign in Italy, idealized the fraternity between French and colonized soldiers. In describing the successful attack on Castelforte on 12 May 1944 by the Fourth Regiment of Tirailleurs Marocains, Chambe praised the leadership of Sergeants Morrachini and Abd-el-Krim, "one French, the other native," who took the initiative in

156 Lanquetot, *Un hiver dans les Abruzzes*, 97.
157 *Pieds-noirs* – "black feet" – was a term used for European settlers in Algeria. It referred to the black leather shoes worn by the colonists.
158 Bouchet de Fareins, *De l'ain au Danube*, 79.

leading the assault, but who were both killed, the former, "by a bullet straight to the heart," the latter "cut down by a salvo of mortar projectiles." The two sergeants, wrote Chambe, "represented exactly" the leadership qualities of the cadres of the Army of Africa, just as the Tirailleurs under their command were a model of that army's devotion to duty and its observance of "the most strict, most absolute discipline."[159] The officers, too, Chambe was at pains to insist, were worthy of the men in whom they had nurtured these qualities. He concluded his account of the action by describing the heroic death of Lieutenant Chédeville, who, although seriously wounded, returned to the battlefield from a casualty clearing station to lead his men in a final attack. Retaking a height that had been lost to the enemy, Chédeville was killed by a bullet to the head. Chambe was didactic in affirming the meaning of such devotion to duty, which united soldiers both vertically and horizontally, across differences of rank and race. "A country which still sees its soil give rise to men like Chédeville, like Désormeau, like Morrachini and so many others, a country which, by humane policies, succeeds in arousing upon the territories of its empire so much devotion, like that of Sergeant Abd-el-Krim, of Tirailleurs Mohamed, Boudjema, Kélifa, Amor Ben Messaoud, that country, if it knows how to use such resources, if it knows how to show itself to be worthy of such great spiritual riches, if it is able to eliminate from the direction of its affairs the fomenters of disorder and indiscipline and confide its destiny to true leaders, that country may hope for everything from the future."[160] General Chambe's eulogy to the Army of Africa, and to the brotherhood of arms uniting French and Muslim soldiers, resonated most powerfully among European settlers in North Africa. To the *pied-noir* community in Algeria, the sacrifice of Algerian Muslims for the liberation of France was evidence of their affection for their colonizers. In the years after 1945, that sacrifice was to provide an emotive weapon in the colonists' struggle against the movement for Algerian independence.[161]

In the meantime, the ethos of the African army so admired by General Chambe was itself partly responsible for the heavy loss of French and colonized soldiers' lives, most notably in the Italian campaign of 1943–44. The reputation of the Army of Africa as a refuge for the traditional virtues of the warrior and an outlet for the adventurous urges of French youth helped to foster an atavistic military culture that insisted primarily upon the physical and moral qualities of its soldiers. The focus of training was on toughening up recruits so that the battlefield held no surprises. To this

159 Chambe, *L'épopée française d'Italie*, 169–71.
160 Ibid., 173.
161 Le Gac, *Vaincre sans gloire*, 496.

end, combat training made use of live ammunition and was often lethal to
its participants. In the seven months between the end of the Tunisian
campaign and the beginning of its involvement in the Italian campaign,
the army suffered 438 accidental deaths (31 per cent of the total
of 1,858, the majority of which were a result of illness), eighty of them as
a result of a grenade or mine explosion.[162] The purpose of instruction,
according to General Guillaume, was to encourage "the burning will to
vanquish and as corollary the acceptance of sacrifice."[163] This emphasis
on the fighting spirit of the army, which was only increased by awareness
of its perceived shortcomings in this respect during the *drôle de guerre*[164] of
1939–40, inevitably led to the neglect of the sophisticated material, logistical, and administrative demands of modern military operations. These
shortcomings were accentuated by the impatience of the army's leaders to
redeem its reputation on the battlefield at the earliest possible opportunity.
Launching men into battle with inadequate preparation, experience, equipment, food, and medical care was a recipe for a high butcher's bill.

Arriving in Italy in November 1943, the CEF under General Alphonse
Juin began its first offensive in the mountains of Abruzzo on 15 December.
To the consternation of its American allies, the CEF was lacking in the barest
essentials necessary to wage mountain warfare in winter. The troops were
not equipped with warm winter clothing, let alone waterproof boots, snow-
shoes, or sunglasses. There were also deficiencies of signals equipment,
artillery, and medical services. In all these areas, the CEF was compelled to
fall back on the Americans. French soldiers were fed American K-rations –
supplemented unreliably by the French commissariat with foodstuffs
suited to the diets of either French or Muslims – and many were also treated
for their wounds and illnesses in American hospitals. French infantry
attacked with artillery support provided by American guns. French doctors
depended upon the Americans to supply them with penicillin. The rubber-
soled American shoes with which most French soldiers were equipped,
however, were "very hard and very painful" as well as lacking in traction
on rocky ground; soldiers quickly learned that their best hope of keeping
their feet healthy was to obtain leather-soled German boots from an enemy
corpse or prisoner.[165] The padded jackets worn by German soldiers also
recommended themselves, although one French lieutenant discarded his
when he was nearly shot by one of his own men who misidentified him as

162 Ibid., 207–8.
163 Ibid., 208.
164 Phony war.
165 Pierre Lyautey, *La campagne d'Italie*, 31 and 63; Lanquetot, *Un hiver dans les Abruzzes*, 65.

an enemy. "I stripped off the German jacket," he recalled, "and, in my American uniform, rediscovered the cold."[166] Pierre Lyautey idealized the "demodernization" of warfare in Italy, where mules replaced trucks as the essential means of military transport. "We have left the civilization of the automobile and we have, in our kingdom of the Aurunci mountains, our legs and those of our horses," he wrote. "The knights of the round table in their *djellabas*[167] are the Templars of the Liberation."[168] In describing the preparations made by General Guillaume to launch the decisive attack on Mount Ausonia in May 1944, Lyautey summed up the general outlook of the CEF: "No munitions. No supply. Forward, all the same, forward."[169] Notwithstanding Lyautey's approval for his superiors' contempt for the material constraints of warfare, the inattention of the French high command to supply and to auxiliary services adversely affected the health and morale of the army and contributed to its relatively high number of casualties.[170]

Although deficient in equipment and supplies, the CEF nonetheless more than vindicated the expectations of its high command with respect to its fighting spirit. Most importantly, under the leadership of General Juin it asserted a significant place for itself as Allied strategy evolved, winning the respect of the British and Americans for its military achievements. Thrown impetuously into battle in Abruzzo in mid-December, the Second Division of Moroccan Infantry (DIM) overcame initial failure, stiff German resistance, and awful winter conditions to drive the enemy off the mountain heights where it had established the defences of the Winter Line. The following month, the Third Division of Algerian Infantry (DIA) launched a successful attack on the Belvedere, to the north of Monte Cassino, and, supported by the Second DIM, fought hard to hold onto it in the face of fierce enemy counterattacks. An undated summary of the battle for the Belvedere in the French military archives gives a sense of the battle's intensity: "In total, Hill 700 was taken four times, Hill 771 was taken three times, Hill 915 was taken two times and counter-attacked without success by the enemy four times, Hill 862 was taken two times and counter-attacked by the enemy twelve times."[171] With the Allied armies prevented from advancing along the Liri valley by the German defences along the Gustav Line and on Monte Cassino, it was General Juin and the CEF who found the key to unlock those

166 Ibid., 86.

167 Loose-fitting outer robe worn by Moroccan troops.

168 Lyautey, *La campagne d'Italie*, 42. On the concept of the "demodernization" of warfare during the Second World War, see Bartov, *Hitler's Army*, 12–28.

169 Lyautey, *La campagne d'Italie*, 68.

170 On these logistical and medical deficiencies, see Le Gac, *Vaincre sans gloire*, 242–5.

171 Cited in ibid., 263. See also Juin, *La campagne d'Italie*, 78–9; Cadeau and Cadeau, "Retrouver son rang," 21–27.

8.6. Moroccan "Goumiers" preparing to fire a mortar on the Italian front (April 1944).

defences, by means of an assault over the Aurunci mountains. This began on 11 May 1944 and culminated in the capture of the peak of Itri-Rocade (18 May), which opened the way for American General Mark Clark's Fifth US Army to advance on Rome. Clark expressed his appreciation to Juin on 13 May: "The French army has preserved as sacred its finest warrior traditions. It is an honour to have your troops in the formation of the Fifth Army."[172]

A high price was paid in lives for these accomplishments. In the first month of operations in Italy, the CEF lost 13.9 per cent of its strength, which compared with losses of 5 per cent for the Americans and 3.5 per cent for the British over two months.[173] Between 1 April and 4 June 1944, French losses (killed, wounded, and missing) were 13.3 per cent of all effectives, considerably higher than those of the British (4.8 per cent), Americans (7.8 per cent), and Poles (8.5 per cent).[174] Overall, the CEF, which averaged a strength of 75,000 effectives, lost 6,577 men killed and 23,506 wounded over 222 days, a daily rate of loss of 1.8 per 1,000 combatants.

172 Cited in Martel, ed., *Histoire militaire de la France*, vol. 4: *De 1940 à nos jours*, 201.
173 Le Gac, *Vaincre sans gloire*, 249 and 524.
174 Ibid., 528.

By comparison, during the campaign to liberate France the French First Army suffered losses of 13,874 killed and 42,256 wounded from an average strength of 220,000 men, a daily rate of loss of 0.96 per 1,000. In other words, the Italian campaign was twice as murderous for the French forces engaged in it as was the First Army's campaign for the liberation of France.[175] For officers, the Italian campaign was particularly deadly: 212 officers were killed, representing 11.01 per cent of the total. This was twice the percentage of fatalities for regular soldiers in the CEF (5.24 per cent) and, once again, significantly higher than the proportion of officer fatalities in the First Army (7.55 per cent). The proportion of killed to wounded was also much higher for officers: one to 1.73 rather than one to 3.57 for ordinary soldiers.[176]

It was not just officers, the vast majority of whom were French, who suffered a disproportionately high rate of loss. Overall, the infantry sustained much heavier casualties than any other branch of the service. A report drawn up by the Army's First Bureau on 14 March 1944 calculated that the Second DIM had lost seventy-eight men per day over seventy-five days of combat, while the Third DIA had lost 103 per day over forty-five days of combat: the percentage of losses for the Second DIM was 92.8 per cent; for the Third DIA it was 89.5 per cent. Meanwhile, for the artillery, losses after a month of combat amounted to 75 men, 1.5 per cent of 5,500 men.[177] The crucial point here is that in the CEF colonized soldiers were for the most part employed as infantry. Three-quarters of a battalion of Tirailleurs consisted of indigenous troops. As John Ellis has demonstrated in his study of the British and American armies, "In World War II as in most others it was 'the poor bloody infantry' that did most of the fighting and most of the dying."[178] In the American army in Italy, although infantry riflemen made up only 11 per cent of a division's total personnel, they accounted for 38 per cent of its casualties.[179] In the CEF, it was primarily indigenous North African soldiers who served in this unenviable role. By the army's own calculation, indigenous soldiers represented 52.4 per cent of personnel in the Second DIM and the Third DIA and accounted for 66.2 per cent of all deaths.[180] Historian Belkacem Recham judges that it would be "too pretentious and totally hazardous" to provide a figure for the number of

175 Forissier, "Le corps expéditionnaire français," 641.
176 Ibid., 644–5.
177 Recham, *Les musulmans algériens*, 244.
178 Ellis, *On the Front Lines*, 164.
179 Ibid.
180 Le Gac, *Vaincre sans gloire*, 282.

North African casualties during the Italian campaign.[181] All the same, after carefully perusing the available evidence, he concludes that a plausible estimate of the proportion of the French army's losses sustained by indigenous troops, in the majority North African, between the beginning of the Tunisian campaign in December 1942 and the German surrender in May 1945 would be in the region of 50 per cent.[182]

For the soldiers whose destinies are so bleakly represented in these statistics, death came in many ways. As was the case in the First World War, the greatest number of wounds were caused by shell or grenade fragments. In Italy, where the attritional deadlock came closer than elsewhere to resembling the conditions on the Western Front in the First World War, the proportion of wounds caused by shells or grenades was 64.6 per cent, slightly higher than the wartime average of 59.5 per cent. The proportion caused by bullets came a distant second: 25.9 per cent in Italy, 26.3 per cent for the war in its entirety. Mines and booby traps accounted for 7.5 per cent of wounds in Italy, 9.7 per cent overall. Edged weapons barely register in statistical terms, accounting for 0 per cent of wounds in Italy, 0.5 per cent in all theatres.[183] This might be accounted for either in terms of the irrelevance of "cold steel" on the modern battlefield or in terms of the relatively greater lethality of these weapons in hand-to-hand combat; since stab wounds were often fatal they rarely figure in records based on soldiers who survived at least long enough to reach a hospital. The latter explanation is, as we have seen, that provided by Stéphane Audoin-Rouzeau with respect to the First World War. During the Second World War, colonized soldiers retained their fearsome reputation as specialists in the use of knives. According to Julien Fargettas, that reputation was deserved, noting that when their *coupe-coupes* did not suffice, the Tirailleurs Sénégalais were as adept with axe and grenade, as they proved when they participated in the attack by the Twenty-Fourth Bataillon de Marche (BM) on Hill 541 in Italy on 13 May 1944; they left the hillside "piled with German corpses."[184] The Tirailleurs Marocains had a similarly fearsome reputation.

The penchant of colonized soldiers for using knives was relevant to their own fates chiefly insofar as it was used by their enemies as justification for a refusal to accord them the same rights and protections guaranteed to legitimate combatants by the Geneva conventions. We have already seen

181 Recham, *Les musulmans algériens*, 244.

182 Ibid., 245.

183 The statistics on the causes of wounds are provided by Forissier, "Le corps expéditionnaire français," 646.

184 "Edged weapons." Fargettas, *Les tirailleurs sénégalais*, 203.

the consequences of this in the context of the Battle of France. That it remained a factor in subsequent campaigns is apparent from the memoir of Raphaël Onana. As he lay wounded in the sand at Bir Hakeim, Onana had little reason to expect humane treatment if he were discovered by Italian or German troops. He remembered the fate of the soldiers of the Third Indian Brigade, who instead of being taken into captivity after being overrun by Rommel's troops, were simply disarmed and left to die in the desert. Onana recalled that the few who managed to reach Bir Hakeim were "wandering ghosts, half mad, whose eyes protruded from their sockets."[185] He wrote that awareness of their likely fate if captured was a powerful motivator for France's African soldiers. "What did we have to lose, opposed to the terrible Germans, of whom we had been told that they were inhumane and of whom the human wrecks of Indians had brought us, in a compelling way, the proof of their cruelty, barbarism, and racism? We had nothing whatsoever to lose. To die instantly of a bullet which cuts you down, by chance, in full combat, seemed to us to be a fate clearly more enviable than to be captured, tortured, and put to death in conditions of maximum horror and shame. That is why, at Bir Hakeim, we gave the best of ourselves, from the first attack by the Germans and Italians."[186] As we have seen, Onana's expectations of inhumane treatment by the enemy were not fulfilled. Bir Hakeim was a disaster for the 3,700 Free French soldiers who fought in it. During the siege and the subsequent break-out, 171 were killed and 130 wounded. An uncertain number – either 763 or 814 – went missing. Between 600 and 650 of the latter were taken prisoner, of whom 154 would later perish at sea when the ship taking them to Italy was sunk. As for the remaining 160 "missing," they died individually or in small groups in the desert, either in unrecorded skirmishes or of thirst. The bodies of ninety-five of them were recovered five months later and buried alongside those of their comrades at Bir Hakeim. However, while many of Onana's African comrades did indeed suffer the same fate as that of the Indian soldiers which he described, they at least do not appear to have done so because of deliberate mistreatment by their Axis captors.[187] The extent to which fear of inhumane treatment by the enemy motivated colonized soldiers during the subsequent campaigns in Italy and for the liberation of France is uncertain, but one can assume that the psychological conditioning of soldiers on both sides of the lines continued to exert its influence.

185 Onana, *Un homme blindé*, 240.
186 Ibid., 241.
187 Crémieux-Brilhac, *La France libre*, vol. 1, 461; see also Broche, *La cathédrale des sables*, 373–8.

The commanders of the CEF represented the heavy losses sustained by their men as evidence of the readiness of the latter to sacrifice themselves. General Juin, in his later account of the attack on the Belvedere, paid tribute to the Fourth Regiment of Tirailleurs Tunisiens, the performance of which, he asserted, gave the lie to an adage of the Army of Africa that "Tunisians were women, Algerians men, and Moroccans lions"[188] when it came to war. "We saw return, our hearts overflowing at once with pity and pride, haggard, hairy, in greatcoats tattered and soaked by mud and blood, the glorious survivors of this regiment which had just had, over eight days of uninterrupted combat on an impossible terrain where the enemy could strike from all sides, fifteen officers killed including the colonel, 264 tirailleurs and NCOs killed, nearly eight hundred wounded and over four hundred missing including six officers. It had lost nearly two-thirds of the effectives engaged. All the company commanders had been killed or wounded."[189] Juin paid special tribute to Captain Tixier, one of the company commanders, who had been blinded and "frightfully mutilated" when he lost the top half of his face to a shell fragment while leading his men in the final attack on Hill 771. "The idol of his men," according to Juin, Tixier died in hospital in Naples "after atrocious suffering endured with incomparable courage." Juin wrote that the doctor and nurse whom he found weeping at Tixier's bedside described him as "a gallant man and a true knight."[190] In his account of the "martyrology" of the Fourth Tunisian Regiment, Juin did not neglect "properly Tunisian heroes," such as lieutenants El Hadi and Bou Akaz, both killed in leading assaults on the hills surrounding the Belvedere. In Juin's account, El Hadi continued to command his company after losing his forearm to a shell fragment, leading his men in an attack on Hill 470. Mortally wounded by a burst of machine-gun fire, El Hadi ordered a flare to be fired to announce the hill's capture, shouted "Vive la France!" and died.[191] To Juin, the emergence of indigenous officers like El Hadi who were animated by the same spirit of sacrifice as

188 Juin, *La campagne d'Italie*, 32.

189 Ibid., 77.

190 Ibid. René Chambe used similar language in describing the death of Captain Tixier. According to Chambe's account, Tixier had torn the badges of rank from his uniform as he lay among the wounded, to ensure that even more severely wounded men would be attended to first. "In truth," concluded Chambe, "it was truly a lord, a knight, that was driven on that February morning to the cemetery of Naples and who will keep guard there, with his cross of opened arms, as witness to French greatness." Chambe, *Le bataillon du Belvédère*, 240.

191 Juin, *La campagne d'Italie*, 67–8; see also Chambe, *Le bataillon du Belvédère*, 60–5.

their French counterparts was evidence of the "veritable miracle of the French presence in the ranks of the Army of Africa."[192]

Juin's approving reference to the language of chivalry in describing Captain Tixier was consistent with his representation of the CEF throughout its engagement in Italy. At the beginning of the campaign, his Order Number One of 25 November 1943 reminded his soldiers that they would be fighting on battlefields where "very pure heroes of our race" had fallen and evoked the names of Gaston de Foix, Bayard, and Desaix. The CEF would be taking the same path, he said, though in the opposite direction, as that taken many times before by French armies, whether they followed the symbols of the monarchy, the empire, or the republic. "The time has come," he declared, "for you to show the faith that inspires you and to testify to your military valour and to your spirit of sacrifice." Juin enjoined his soldiers to live up to the army's traditions of "honour and discipline" by manifesting with respect to the Italian population "an attitude of reserve and propriety," explicitly warning them against "indecent familiarity [...] excessive pride or brutalities that harm our cause."[193] At the very end of the campaign, when the CEF occupied the town of Siena, Juin was again mindful of France's military traditions: "I thought of that other French leader, Blaise Monluc, who long ago had covered himself with glory for having sustained a prolonged siege" in that city.[194] The conduct of the CEF did not match its leader's expectations. Far from exemplifying the traditions and ideals evoked by General Juin, its behaviour once the deadlock was broken was more reminiscent of the medieval tradition of the *chevauchée*, as soldiers compensated the frustrations and losses they had endured by subjecting the civilian population to a campaign of rape and pillage. The Italian Ministry of War claimed in 1945 that soldiers from the CEF were responsible for 1,041 of 1,119 acts of sexual violence committed by Allied soldiers against Italian civilians. All but six of these attacks were attributed to soldiers of colour.[195] Historian Julie Le Gac estimates that 3,000 to 5,000 Italian women and children were raped by soldiers of the CEF. Of the relatively few soldiers who were inculpated for sexual crimes (156 in total), most were colonized soldiers from North Africa (56 per cent were born in Morocco, 33 per cent in Algeria, and 2 per cent in Tunisia).[196] Although this behaviour was condemned by the French high command, many French officers viewed it with indulgence; the *razzia* with its promise of

192 Juin, *La campagne d'Italie*, 78 and 80.
193 Lanquetot, *Un hiver dans les Abruzzes*, 201.
194 Juin, *La campagne d'Italie*, 161.
195 Le Gac, *Vaincre sans gloire*, 445.
196 Ibid., 443–7.

booty and sexual conquest was perceived to be essential to the traditions of Moroccan warriors. Pierre Lyautey was critical of the harsh penalties imposed on soldiers who were caught sending pillaged objects home through the mail. "After so many exploits, our men deserved to send to their families in the villages of the Atlas a sheet, a tablecloth, a covering. This sweet compensation was denied to them. Not one of us will take anything home from Italy. Bonaparte was more generous with the soldiers of Lodi and Arcola. And yet our men will have charged twenty times as at Arcola."[197] Lyautey, while insisting that sexual crimes committed by soldiers of the CEF were strictly punished, also implied that sexual conquest was an inevitable consequence of military triumph, something that just happened without specific human agency or volition: "The men are drunk from attacking and the women are intoxicated by the conquering manner of the victors. Well then, bodies unite with one another under the starlight."[198] Only one soldier from the CEF inculpated for rape was sentenced to death and executed following trial by a French military court, but twenty-eight others were summarily executed after they were caught *in flagrante delicto.*[199] Solange Cuvillier, a female ambulance driver serving with the CEF, recalled that at Spigno, "we could hear women's screams above the sounds of the war which plunged us into despair." Called upon to relocate a young female victim in a straitjacket, Cuvillier remembered this episode as "the only shameful moment of my war."[200]

Just as their conduct toward Italian civilians failed to match their generals' expectations, colonized soldiers' attitudes toward life and death on the front lines were often a far cry from the models of patriotic self-sacrifice exalted by those same generals. A disillusioned view of the war, from the perspective of a junior officer commanding a section of Tirailleurs Marocains, is provided in the autobiographical novel by Jean Durkheim, *Tirailleur couscous.* Durkheim prefaces his book with the words, "This is a true story," explaining that it was lived by the shock troops of the Moroccan formations that were "bled white" in the campaigns fought in Tunisia, Italy, France, and Germany from 1942 to 1945. The book is dedicated to Durkheim's comrades who had died along this "bloody road that ended in Victory."[201] Lieutenant Murjean, the main protagonist, is much less interested in achieving a glorious death than he is in finding ways to stay alive from day to day. Murjean knows that the odds against him surviving for

197 Lyautey, *La campagne d'Italie*, 85.
198 Ibid., 85.
199 Le Gac, *Vaincre sans gloire*, 432 and 461.
200 Cuvillier, *Tribulations d'une femme*, 46.
201 Durkheim, *Tirailleur couscous*, 7–8.

long are stacked against him: "a shock fusilier who speaks of the after-war is a utopian."[202] Murjean and his comrades also know that their commanders have little interest in their well-being; in fact, they are quite willing to sacrifice them for meaningless objectives. In a chapter entitled "The Patrol of the Stiffs,"[203] which takes place in Italy in May 1944, Murjean is assigned to take a patrol into no man's land for no better reason than to improve the unit's loss statistics by recovering the bodies of the dead. Reducing the number of soldiers listed as "missing" and thereby increasing the number of those listed as "killed" was expected to add to the number of citations awarded to the unit: the calculation was that every *croix de bois*[204] was worth two *croix de guerre*.

The "Patrol of the Stiffs" provides a brutally unsentimental picture of life and death on the front lines. During his mission, Murjean encounters a German patrol entrusted with an identical objective. Several days of fraternization ensue, as the two patrols collaborate in the search for corpses, exchange rations, play cards together, and generally take a break from the war. They discover that they have much in common and little interest in destroying one another. The German lieutenant generously rubs salve into Murjean's feet, which are tortured from wearing his American boots. This peaceful interlude comes to an end with a French attack in which Murjean engages in a desperate effort, which he knows is likely to be futile, to save one of his men, who is seriously wounded and incapable of moving. The wounded man is Kaddour ben Embarek, better known as "Dix-huit-douze" from the final digits of his matriculation number, a twenty-two-year-old from a nomadic tribe in the Atlas mountains who had been "volunteered" for military service by his village chieftain simply because the latter did not like him. Aware that Kaddour is dying, Murjean seeks to shield the young man from the knowledge of his impending death. To this end, he refuses Kaddour's request that he take possession of his valuables – his bracelet, watch, wallet, and pen – so that they might be returned to his family. Murjean's reflections show a genuine sympathy for his comrade but also an awareness of the pitiless treatment of the dead, even by their own side: "The stretcher bearers, unfailingly and pitilessly, plunder the dead and leave them nothing but their clothes."[205]

The callous attitude of the stretcher bearers toward the dead also characterizes relations among the living. As the section prepares to go into battle, Murjean himself exhibits a brutal pragmatism in negotiating with

202 Ibid., 153.
203 Ibid., 89–193.
204 "Wooden cross."
205 Durkheim, *Tirailleur couscous*, 144.

his sergeant the selection of a point man. Aware that this was a uniquely dangerous assignment, Sergeant Ahmed ben Moktar had chosen "Dix-sept-zéro-huit," because of personal animosity, and thereby "practically condemned to death [...] a robust, durable Tirailleur capable of carrying heavy loads of munitions and always equipped with an oil can."[206] Unwilling to accept his sergeant's choice but equally unwilling to undermine his authority, Murjean proposes an alternative. "Trente-quatorze" is a newcomer recently transferred from a company of muleteers for what were presumed to be disciplinary reasons: "Thus, the solution imposed itself: 'No-one knows this "Trente-quatorze." He has a nasty look about him ... What the fuck if he dies!'"[207] Inevitably, "Trente-quatorze" is "killed instantly, at point blank range. Point man against blockhouse, the winner is known in advance. The noble uncertainty of sport is absent from the debate."[208] After the death of "Trente-quatorze" Murjean pre-emptively puts forward another replacement point man, Lahcen-le-boujadi, "a blockhead and a moron." From that moment on, no one in the section, Lahcen included, is under any illusions: "the future of Lahcen-le-boujadi no longer has any prospect in the long run."[209]

Condemned to a ruthless pragmatism in their relations with one another by their circumstances, the soldiers of *Tirailleur couscous* are also under no illusions that they will be remembered, even by their comrades. The final irony of "The Patrol of the Stiffs" is that Murjean comes across the body of the German lieutenant, Hartschmidt, who had earlier cared for his feet and realizes that both Hartschmidt and Kaddour had probably died at the hands of the enemy soldiers with whom they had so recently fraternized. As the patrol moves on, Murjean realizes that he can no longer remember all the faces of the comrades with whom he had fought in Tunisia and who had since been killed: when he thinks of one comrade he sees the face of another. Perhaps Kaddour and Hartschmidt will one day also become fused in his memory.

Murjean does survive the war, but in the final chapter of *Tirailleur couscous*, he reflects on the arbitrary whims of fate that caused him to live while others died and recognizes that he will forever be haunted by the war: "The war, it is never over for the survivors. It sticks, it sticks eternally to the skin of the shock troops of the front lines, it sticks to them like an insane tunic of Nessus."[210] The death of the soldier in *Tirailleur couscous*

206 Ibid., 131.
207 Ibid., 132.
208 Ibid., 148–9.
209 Ibid., 150.
210 Ibid., 237.

is not a purposeful sacrifice willed by its victim but the outcome of a perverse twist of fate over which he has no control. The soldier's only protection is a cynical pragmatism that is the very antithesis of patriotic idealism. This is the "truth" told by Jean Durkheim's novel about the experience of metropolitan and colonized soldiers serving in the French army during the Second World War. The disillusioned soldiers of *Tirailleur couscous* are not heroes who cry "Vive la France!" as they die scaling the summits of Italian mountains. Rather, they are the counterparts of the war-weary *poilus* of *Les croix de bois* and *Les suppliciés*, coerced by the war rather than consenting to it.

DISCONTENT: THIAROYE

Colonized soldiers fighting in the French army during the Second World War did not expect to receive nothing in return. As Gregory Mann has demonstrated in his study of West African veterans, the imposition of compulsory military service on the peoples of FWA, beginning with the establishment of the first regiment of Tirailleurs Sénégalais in 1857, bound the colonizing power and its subjects in a web of mutual obligations that was shaped both by the words and ideas of French civilian administrators and army officers, as well as by those of indigenous soldiers and veterans.[211] At a minimum, a Tirailleur might expect to be given a uniform and food in return for his service, but his expectations might also extend to many other tangible and intangible benefits: monetary reward, a pension, respect, a reserved position in the civil service, exemption from taxes or the legal obligations of the *indigénat*,[212] even French citizenship. Over time, the balance of mutual obligation shifted. The belief that Africans had a debt to be paid in their own blood for the benefits of French civilization was turned on its head; rather, France was perceived to owe something in return for the African blood spilled in its defence.[213] When the French state failed to fulfill its obligations and the expectations of soldiers or veterans went unsatisfied, which was often the case, the latter did not remain silent. At times, their discontent manifested itself in protest, disobedience, and violence, most notoriously in the "mutiny" at the Thiaroye camp on the outskirts of Dakar, on 1 December 1944.

211   Mann, *Native Sons*, 4.

212   This was the legal code applied to French subjects. In FWA it imposed labour obligations on indigenous peoples and gave colonial administrators the right to impose punishments arbitrarily without trial. See ibid., 70–1.

213   Ibid., 187–9.

Protests and disturbances involving colonized soldiers erupted on frequent occasions during the war, but it was upon the conclusion of their military service and during repatriation to their homes in Africa that they were most likely to feel the incommensurability of the sacrifices they had made and the compensations they were likely to receive from the French state. The demobilizations that followed the end of the First World War in 1918 and the fall of France in 1940 both resulted in considerable turmoil in West Africa, as bands of poorly provided-for former soldiers threatened the property and security of civilian populations as well as the authority of local leaders. The attitudes of returning soldiers were summed up in the words of one First World War veteran who stole a bull, claiming that "having risked his life for France, he was certainly owed a bull."[214] Although some veterans of that war were able to translate their military service into relative success in civilian life, often as translators or as rural policemen, many more were unable even to establish a claim to the veterans' pensions and disability benefits to which they were theoretically entitled. In 1945, the distrust of thousands of African soldiers awaiting demobilization and repatriation as the Second World War approached its end was intensified by awareness of how poorly earlier generations had been treated. Not that these later combatants did not have enough discontents of their own. Some units of Tirailleurs Sénégalais were kept in action until the very end of the war, fighting costly battles to eliminate stubborn pockets of German resistance on France's Atlantic coast.[215] The majority, however, including the 20,000 African troops who fought in General de Lattre's First Army during the invasion of Provence, were withdrawn from active service in the autumn of 1944 in a process of *blanchissement*, or "whitening" (fig. 8.7).[216] Although justified by the tradition of "wintering" African troops, the policy was motivated by the concern of Charles de Gaulle to associate more closely internal resistance movements, the Forces Françaises de l'Intérieur (FFI), with the Free French armies and thereby to limit their autonomy. African soldiers were unhappy to be unceremoniously discarded on the eve of victory, compelled to give up their arms and sometimes even their uniforms to newcomers from the FFI whom they considered their inferior as soldiers. Ditiemba Silué recalled that although he and his comrades were happy to escape the cold, "Some

214 Ibid., 77.
215 Jennings, *Free French Africa*, 168–71.
216 As Eric Jennings points out, the French Army had already undergone an earlier "whitening" in 1943, when General Leclerc insisted upon the replacement of Black African soldiers by European and indigenous North African soldiers as his famous "L force" became the Second Armoured Division. Ibid., 163–4.

8.7. "Whitening" the army: FFI (Forces françaises de l'intérieur) exchange their civilian clothes for the uniforms of the Tirailleurs Sénégalais they are about to relieve (October 1944).

were furious when we left [...] because we had started the war and it was almost over now and we were being replaced by French troops who had been afraid. We wanted the Africans to win the war."[217] These rejected liberators, their ranks swollen by the remaining POWs freed from the Frontstalags and unable to return home because of a lack of shipping, were left in a state of limbo in military camps in the south of France. Still subject to military discipline but deprived of many of the necessities – heat, light, food, even shelter – that might have helped to make life bearable, they inevitably chafed at the restrictions on their freedom of movement and reacted angrily to racial insults and unfair treatment.

These discontents erupted in at least fifteen violent incidents in 1944 and 1945, mostly in the south of France, but also wherever the unhappy soldiers were sent on the unsteady path to repatriation. In late October

217 Lawler, *Soldiers of Misfortune*, 179.

and November 1944, there was trouble at Monshire Camp, near Liverpool, where four hundred Tirailleurs Sénégalais were dispatched en route for West Africa. Denied the right to eat in the British sergeants' mess, African NCOS responded by forcing their way in.[218] The following month, escalating confrontations at Versailles between police and mostly North African soldiers culminated in an attack by the latter on a police station during which shots were fired and eighteen policemen were taken hostage. A police lieutenant who was severely beaten narrowly escaped with his life.[219] A sequence of violent disturbances around Fréjus and St Raphaël turned deadly on 19 August 1945, when a clash between French military police and a group of Tirailleurs Sénégalais resulted in a French officer shooting an African soldier. Seeking revenge, four hundred of the latter's comrades subsequently fell upon another unlucky military patrol, stabbing one *gendarme* to death and wounding two others.[220]

The most notorious of these disturbances occurred at Thiaroye, a barracks outside Dakar, on 1 December 1944. The violence at Thiaroye was precipitated by the return on the *Circassia* of 1,280 former POWs from the Frontstalags. The grievances of these men were magnified by their concerns that many of them had not received the back pay and demobilization bonuses to which they were entitled, nor the sums earned while compelled to work as POWs. They also objected to having any French francs they had received converted into half as many West African francs. When the commander of the garrison, General Dagnan, gave orders on 27 November for five hundred men to prepare to depart for Bamako, the new arrivals flatly refused to leave until they had been properly paid. The general, believing that he had himself nearly been taken prisoner, decided on a show of strength. On 1 December 1944, he arrived at the camp with several companies of infantry and armoured vehicles, including a light American M-3 tank. After a lengthy confrontation, the order was finally given to fire. The volleys of infantry and machine-gun fire were reportedly brief, but deadly. According to the official report, twenty-four of the "mutineers" were killed on the day and eleven others later died of their wounds. Thirty-five others were also wounded.[221] As Julien Fargettas has argued, the tragedy at Thiaroye was the consequence of a failure by the French civil and military authorities in West Africa to appreciate that the returning soldiers were

218 Echenberg, *Colonial Conscripts*, 100.
219 Fargettas, *Les tirailleurs sénégalais*, 274.
220 Ibid., 275–6.
221 Armelle Mabon casts doubt on the veracity of these figures, suggesting that the real number of deaths may have been as high as several hundred. Mabon, *Prisonniers de guerre "indigènes,"* 204–7.

intent not upon overturning the colonial system, but simply on receiving treatment that recognized them as the equals of the Europeans alongside whom they had fought. Fargettas cites a military report of April 1945 as evidence of the state of mind of the demobilized soldiers: "The native soldiers complain of not enjoying the same rights as metropolitan soldiers, while like them they defend the same homeland."[222] What these colonized soldiers were insisting upon, in other words, was that a Black life was worth as much as a white one. Sadly, the men who died at Thiaroye for the sake of that principle would not even have the right to the words "*mort pour la France*" written on their death certificates.

CONCLUSION: FROM "*MORTS POUR LA FRANCE*" TO "*MORTS PAR LA FRANCE*"

Thiaroye marked neither the beginning nor the end of veterans' struggles for fair treatment by the French state. This struggle focused for many years on the issue of pensions, especially on the right of soldiers from the colonies to be paid at the same rate as those from the metropole. The veterans' case was presented in the National Assembly in 1947 by Jules Ninine in a language that insisted upon the equality of sacrifice: "If the 'blood tax' should be the same for everyone, it is beyond dispute that the 'blood price' should also be the same for everyone [...] without distinction of race or color, legal status or religious belief."[223] By the 1950s, the French government had largely conceded the point and enormous progress was made in providing pensions and other benefits to West African veterans. In 1960, however, an obscure clause in a budgetary law "crystallized" the pensions of veterans from newly independent colonies; that is, it froze their pensions at the amounts set at the time of independence. This ensured steadily declining incomes for veterans for the next forty years, until a decision by the Council of State in 2001 recognized the legitimacy of a claim by Second World War veteran Amadou Diop to the same pension as a French national, with arears to be paid dating back to the moment of "crystallization."[224] All the same, it was not until November 2006 that legislation approved by the French National assembly established that all colonial troops had a right to the same *retraite du combattant* as French veterans,[225] and only in

---

222 Fargettas, *Les tirailleurs senegalais*, 293. On Thiaroye, see also Fargettas, "La révolte des tirailleurs sénégalais ce Tiaroye," 117–30; Mabon, *Prisonniers de guerre "indigènes,"* 193–214; Scheck, "Les prémices de Thiaroye," 73–90.

223 Cited in Mann, *Native Sons*, 123.

224 For discussion of the implications of this decision, see Mann, *Native Sons*, 184–6.

225 See *Le Monde*, 15 November 2006.

2010 did another constitutional ruling eliminate inequalities between Europeans and non-Europeans for the *pension de retraite* based on rank and length of service.[226]

While not a turning point in the ongoing struggle of colonized soldiers for equality, Thiaroye did mark a significant new departure in terms of how they and their sacrifices were represented. As texts and images representing the massacre at Thiaroye have proliferated so has a post-colonial representation of the Tirailleur Sénégalais.[227] This representation is not without ambiguities. In the series of poems entitled *Hosties noires*, Léopold Sédar Senghor deplored France for betraying its ideals through its conduct as a colonial power and for conscripting Africans as agents of their own oppression:

> Yes Lord, forgive France who hates her occupiers and yet
> lays so heavy an occupation upon me
> Who opens the triumphal way to heroes and treats the
> Senegalese as mercenaries, makes them the Black watch-
> dogs of Empire.[228]

Yet in his poem "Tyaroye," while asking reproachfully "is it thus true that France is no longer France?," Senghor represented the massacre in positive terms as a foundational sacrifice, the blood of the victims the source of a new hope. Addressing himself to these "martyrs," Senghor wrote:

> No, you have not died for nothing. You are the
> Witnesses of immortal Africa
> You are the witnesses of a new world which will be tomorrow.[229]

The tone of other, later, representations of Thiaroye was often angrier and less hopeful than Senghor's poem. These works, expressed through media intended to reach a wide public, insisted that the soldiers who died at Thiaroye were killed "*par la France*" rather than "*pour la France*." Most important in this respect was the feature film produced in 1988 by Sembène

226 See *Le Monde*, 13 July 2010. *A carte du combatant* was required to obtain the *retraite du combatant*. Nominally, any soldier who spent ninety days in a combat zone qualified for a *carte du combatant*.
227 See Fargettas, "La révolte des tirailleurs sénégalais de Tiaroye," 127–8.
228 Senghor, *Prose and Poetry*, 136.
229 Senghor, *Oeuvre Poétique*, 95.

Ousmane, *Camp de Thiaroye*, which provided an emotive and spectacular reconstruction of the massacre. Ousmane's film represented the massacre as a deliberate and vengeful act of betrayal on the part of General Dagnan. Having given his word to the mutinous Tirailleurs that they would be paid at the rate they demanded, the general sends in the tanks in the dead of night. Without warning, three tanks begin shelling the barracks in which the unsuspecting soldiers are sleeping. Their machine guns then open up on the half-naked and defenceless men as they attempt to flee. A short animated film produced by Rachid Bouchareb in 2004 was also effective in presenting a simple but compelling version of the event. This told the story of one African soldier's experience in the war: his enlistment, his action in saving the life of a French officer in 1940, his imprisonment in Germany, his return to Senegal, and finally his death at Thiaroye. The short film evokes anger at the ingratitude of the French and sorrow for the loss endured by the wife and daughter of the Senegalese soldier. Anger at injustice is also the theme of a graphic novel by Patrice Perna and Nicolas Otero, entitled *Morts par la France: Thiaroye 1944*. This work graphically represents the events leading up to Thiaroye, but it also focuses upon the heroic struggle of historian Armelle Mabon against what is represented as a concerted effort by French academic, military, and political authorities to cover up the massacre. In this interpretation, official denial is represented as a perpetuation of the original crime.[230] Recent generations of Africans, for whom the evils of colonialism have eclipsed those of Nazism, are less inclined to be forgiving of France than Senghor was.

Moving beyond the massacre at Thiaroye, African writers and film producers have asserted their own voices in imagining the deaths of colonized soldiers. Two years after the success of *L'ami y'a bon*, Rachid Bouchareb returned to the screen with *Indigènes*, a film that focused on the role of North African soldiers in the liberation of Provence and Alsace. Although beholden to Hollywood formulas, *Indigènes* went beyond those conventions in its emphasis upon the army's unequal treatment of colonized soldiers as well as upon the enduring debt incurred to them by French society for their sacrifice. All but one of the four "natives" who are the subjects of the film die in combat. The sequence of deaths culminates with that of Saïd, obliterated by a German shell as he heroically attempts to save the life of the *pied-noir* sergeant, Martinez, with whom he has developed an intense love–hate relationship. The relationship between Saïd and Martinez represents the complicated human relations engendered by the French presence in North Africa. Bouchareb's film generated a significant public

---

230 Perna and Otero, *Morts par la France*.

and critical response, prompting the government of Jacques Chirac to take action in "decrystallizing" veterans' pensions.

Less conventionally heroic and redemptive than films like *Indigènes* are some literary works that also represent the experiences and deaths of colonized soldiers. *Morts pour la France*, a novel published by Doumbi-Fakoly in 1982, presents a grim picture of the experiences of Tirailleurs Sénégalais during the war, including the massacres of 1940, tortures, and medical experimentation in Nazi concentration camps, as well as the massacre at Thiaroye. The novel has the merit of giving voice to soldiers themselves, who express their feelings, often in Tirailleur French, as they endure their suffering. Its narrative offers little hope. One of its most memorable characters is a shell-shocked veteran of the First World War known as Dieudonné Verdun. He sees the latest generation of Tirailleurs off to war in 1939, warning them of the hell of mechanized warfare that awaits them, and he welcomes the survivors back in 1944. Having waited in vain for the return of his own First World War comrade, the despairing veteran ends his own life by throwing himself into the sea.[231]

Another novelist who imagines the war from the point of view of the African combatant is Patrice Nganang. In *La saison de prunes*, Nganang considers the motivations and perceptions of diverse Europeans and Africans involved in the Kufra and Fezzan expeditions of 1941 and 1942. The ripe plums evoked by the novel's title are themselves a metaphor for the lives of the young Tirailleurs whose stories it tells, several of whom die violent deaths. The author insists upon the gulf of communication and understanding between African soldiers and their European officers. As Colonel Leclerc marvels at the courage of Tirailleur Bilong, wounded twenty times in a hopeless attack on the aerodrome at Murzuk, he does not perceive how his false promises of promotion have played upon the youth's masculine pride and sexual longing. In the final analysis, Nganang casts doubt on the veracity of all accounts of soldiers' deaths. In a chapter entitled "Two Versions by Tirailleurs, Plus One"[232] the death of Tirailleur Philothée is narrated from the perspective of a "true-true" Senegalese, from that of a Cameronian, and finally from that of a Frenchman. In the first, Philothée expires in the arms of his comrade Hegba, who then dies in a hail of Italian bullets. In the second, Philothée confesses to Hegba that he had killed the latter's mother and intentionally triggered the Italian mine that had cut him in two. Hegba then bayonets Philothée and shoots himself. Finally, there is a version from a Frenchman, Fouret, who insists that the deaths were nobody's fault, since he and his comrades had provided

231 Doumbi-Fakoly, *Morts pour la France*.
232 Nganang, *La saison des prunes*, 404.

perfect covering fire and it was an excess of emotion that had prompted Hegba to rush to his friend's assistance: "C'est la guerre."[233] The more or less fantastic nature of these stories, drawing on African traditions of storytelling, challenge the notion that any version of the soldier's death is "true." They are a reminder of the many lenses through which any soldier's death might be perceived and that any version – "*pour la France*" or "*par la France*" – tells only a small part of the story.

Colonized soldiers were not alone in feeling forgotten and betrayed by metropolitan France in the aftermath of the Second World War. North African soldiers of European descent also felt excluded from national recognition. They resented the occlusion of their contribution to the liberation of France by a national memory that focused primarily on the metropolitan Resistance. It was Charles de Gaulle who, through influential speeches, three volumes of memoirs, and the orchestration of seminal commemorative occasions, did most to define this official memory. The consecration on 18 June 1960 by de Gaulle of Mont Valérien as the national memorial to *la France combattante*,[234] did much to raise the importance of the Resistance in national consciousness. Even more important was the pantheonization of the resistance martyr Jean Moulin on 18–19 December 1964, in a ceremony which by its martial aspect and the prominent part played by de Gaulle simultaneously insisted upon the military character of the Resistance and upon de Gaulle as the incarnation of national identity.[235] Since the war, 2,130 French streets have been renamed in Moulin's honour.[236] This inscription in the French landscape of a consensual myth of a nation united in resistance intentionally overlooked the politically divisive realities of internecine conflict and collaboration with the foreign enemy. It also downplayed the contributions of colonized soldiers from all parts of the French overseas empire. Marcel Crivello, a French Algerian who published his memoir of the war in 1996, bemoaned the failure of France to recognize the heavy losses suffered by the Army of Africa. Citing the example of the Seventh Regiment of Tirailleurs Algériens, which he claimed had suffered 5,584 casualties – twice its normal strength in effectives – during the campaigns for Tunisia, Corsica, and Italy, Crivello acknowledged the bitterness of North African soldiers at the silence that greeted their

233 Ibid., 409.

234 Fighting France.

235 On de Gaulle's role in creating a national myth of resistance and on the importance of the pantheonization of Jean Moulin, see Rousso, *The Vichy Syndrome*, 82–97. On the Gaullist representation of the Resistance as above all a military, masculine, and essentially French movement, see Gildea, *Fighters in the Shadows*, 1–19.

236 Quellien, "La mémoire de la Résistance," 282–3.

sacrifices, "While the French Resistance is glorified, notwithstanding its insignificance in relation to the population of the Metropole [...] Few young and not so young people in France know of the long road of LIBERATION that led the troops from AFRICA to the DANUBE. These military exploits are ignored and hardly cited in school history books."[237] The bitterness expressed by Crivello on behalf of his comrades, like that of indigenous writers, artists, and politicians who have evoked the experiences of colonized soldiers, bears witness to what has been aptly described as a "disunited memory" of the war.[238] Ironically, the feelings by both indigenous peoples and by European colonists that there was a blood debt owed to them by the mother country was an important factor once the war was over in setting these erstwhile allies against one another as well as against the homeland they had helped to liberate. Blood debts are sacred and brook little by way of compromise.

237 Crivello, *Souvenirs de là-bas*, 58.
238 Wieviorka, *La mémoire désunie*.

9

Dying for l'Algérie française:
The Algerian War

THE DEATH OF CLOVIS CRESTE

Sergeant Clovis Creste died as a result of an ambush by insurgent forces as he and a handful of men under his command were, on the morning of 26 October 1958, gathering wood in the vicinity of their base in the Algerian village of Tacheta-Zouggara, Whether he died in the first burst of gunfire heard by one of his men shortly after 10:00 o'clock that morning, or whether he was taken prisoner and killed later is uncertain. Not until 8:50 a.m. the following day did searchers find his body, in a location which they had already explored. The medical examiner determined that Sergeant Creste had received sixteen wounds, including one to the heart, from 9-mm bullets, most probably fired from a sub-machine gun model MAT 49. He was judged to have died instantly.[1]

As is made clear in the moving memoir written many years later by his daughter, who was six years old at the time of her father's death, Clovis Creste died because of his love for his young family. In October 1958, although only thirty years old, he had been in the army, in one way or another, since June 1944. He had fought in the liberation of France, in Indochina, as well as in Algeria, and had postings in Senegal and Morocco. Awarded eight citations and described in a report from 1957 as "a courageous non-commissioned officer. Capable of maximum efficacy in a shock troop, commando, etc.,"[2] Sergeant Creste nonetheless applied for an SAS (Section Administrative Spéciale) posting that year, for the simple reason that SAS officers were permitted to have their families join them. On 20 April 1957, Clovis wrote to his wife Francine: "I find the days very long

---

1 Erlingsen, *Soldats perdus*, 671–8.
2 Ibid., 604.

and I would give ten years of my life to be close to you and our Hélène. Both of you, who are my reason for living."[3] Although he looked forward to ending his fifteen years' military service in 1959 and taking up farming in his native Lot-et-Garonne, by choosing the SAS he would be able to get on with family life without delay. For Clovis Creste, however, choosing the SAS was fatal. Living close to the Muslim population and assigned the task of helping to win that population's allegiance by bettering their lives, the functions of SAS officers and NCOs were partly military, partly administrative. Dedicated to providing for the education, health, and welfare of local people, SAS personnel were very much on the front lines in the struggle with the Algerian independence movement, led by the Front de Libération Nationale (FLN), for the hearts and minds of Algeria's indigenous populations. They were vulnerable to the efforts by the FLN to intimidate those populations or to suborn the contracted Algerian soldiers – *moghazni* – upon whom they depended for security.[4] Clovis Creste arrived at his new posting at an uncertain time, when the FLN was increasing its activity and his detachment, SAS Carnot, was suffering a lack of stable leadership. Although Francine and Hélène had joined him in Algeria as soon as he received his first SAS posting, in 1957, their dreams of a happy future together were cruelly dashed by the spray of bullets that killed him on 26–7 October 1958.

In so many respects, the death of Clovis Creste was unremarkable: a life snuffed out without witnesses and without glory, on a humble mission to collect wood. Only the diligent research of Clovis's daughter, over thirty years after his death, allows us to see, through scraps of evidence painstakingly assembled, a very remarkable life, lived against the odds. Clovis had survived many hardships, from the intense poverty and abandonment of his childhood, through the rigours of resistance in the *maquis* and in the Free French army during the Second World War to the dangers of the wars in Indochina and Algeria, before his luck finally ran out with less than a year to go to complete his fifteen years of military service. Only this background, and the personal testimony of Hélène herself, enable us to feel the tragedy of Clovis Creste's death and the vast emptiness it left in the lives of those who were closest to him. Yet the very obscurity of that death, brought about by unseen assailants in mysterious circumstances, tells us something important about the type of war France was fighting in

3 Ibid., 600.

4 At the end of 1958, there were 679 SAS sections with 964 officers, 679 NCOs, and 16,000 *moghazni*. Ibid., 671. Between 1956 and 1962, seventy-three SAS officers and thirty-three NCOs were killed by the FLN, as well as 612 moghazni. Rotman and Tavernier, *La guerre sans nom*, 195–6.

Algeria: a war fought against a shadowy enemy in which pitched battles were rare, sudden ambushes all too common: where both sides stepped outside the normal limits of conventional warfare, resorting to the assassin's bullet and the terrorist's bomb on one side, to *la gégène*[5] and *la corvée de bois*[6] on the other.

Clovis Creste was one of 23,196 French soldiers to die in the Algerian war between 1954 and 1962.[7] Sometimes referred to as a "war without name" since the French government refused to acknowledge it as such until 1999, the Algerian war was the most bitter and divisive of France's wars of decolonization. It followed hard on the heels of another of those wars, that fought in Indochina from 1945 to 1954 and was in many ways shaped by the experience of that conflict. Both wars followed a pattern that would eventually be defined as "asymmetric warfare," in which a modern, well-equipped, conventional army supported by all the resources of a powerful state confronted an apparently much weaker opponent: an opponent with few weapons or material resources, but animated by a strong, ideologically charged sense of injustice. Both ended in defeat for France. In Indochina, military defeat in a poorly judged but fiercely contested trial of strength with Ho Chi Minh's Vietminh forces at Dien Bien Phu resulted in French withdrawal in 1954. In Algeria there were no battles on the scale of Dien Bien Phu, and the French methods of counter-revolutionary warfare were effective in suppressing – though not eliminating – the FLN insurgency. Those methods were politically counterproductive, however, sapping French support both at home and abroad, leading ultimately to a political and diplomatic defeat, rather than a military one, as France conceded Algeria's independence by the Evian Accords of March 1962. Both wars were characterized by a comparable asymmetry in casualties, as the French army inflicted losses upon the enemy that were many times greater than those it suffered in return. In both cases, also, more civilians were killed than soldiers. In Indochina, 92,000 soldiers belonging to the *Union française* were killed, 20,000 of them from metropolitan France. The numbers of Vietnamese soldiers and civilians estimated to have been killed were between 300,000 and 500,000. In Algeria, approximately 23,000 French

---

5   A euphemism for torture, *la gégène* referred to the portable generator carried by soldiers to power radios, which could also be used, through connecting electrodes, as an instrument of torture.

6   A euphemism for clandestine execution: literally "work in the woods." It is ironic, given the meaning attached to this expression, that it was going on a real *corvée de bois* that resulted in Sergeant Creste's death.

7   This is the figure provided by the Minister of Defence in 1986. See *Journal officiel de la République française*, Débats parlementaires. Assemblée nationale. Question écrites et réponses des ministres, 4 August 1986, 2469; See also Ageron, "Les pertes humaines," 170.

soldiers were killed. Their FLN opponents suffered from 153,000 to 155,000 military deaths. Somewhere between 200,000 and 250,000 Algerian civilians also lost their lives.[8] Up to half a million individuals died in each of these wars, but only a small proportion – roughly equal in both conflicts – were from the French hexagon. The annual death rate of soldiers from the metropole over seventeen years of war was approximately 2,500.

Despite these similarities between the two conflicts, the Algerian war was far more unsettling to French society than the war in Indochina. The soldiers who died at Dien Bien Phu were celebrated for their sacrifice fighting against insurmountable odds, in the established tradition of heroic defeats like those at Camerone, Bazeilles, and Saumur. In Algeria not only were there no such epic battles but there was also a fundamental contradiction between the imperative to recognize the soldiers who were killed and the French government's denial that the war was anything more than a police operation to preserve order in a region that was, unlike other French overseas territories, an integral part of France itself. Unease at the army's conduct in Algeria, which to some began to seem disconcertingly like that of the German army during its recent occupation of France, encouraged public indifference, even hostility, toward those who served. In Algeria, unlike Indochina, many French soldiers were conscripts; understandably, they resented risking their lives in a war for which there was diminishing support at home. Although they were much less likely to be killed than soldiers from the generations that had fought the First and Second World Wars, they were also much less accepting of such a fate. In the First World War, one soldier died for every six who were mobilized; in the Algerian war, the proportion was one for every sixty-one.[9] On average, the First World War *poilu* was ten times more likely to be killed than an *appelé* in the Algerian war. This decline in military mortality was, however, matched by a growing refusal, manifested above all by the conscripts themselves, to accept those deaths that did occur. Historian Jean-Charles Jauffret writes that "It was a fundamental difference between the national service soldiers at war in Algeria and their predecessors from other wartime generations that they never got used to witnessing the deaths of their

---

8 For the comparison of the human losses in the two conflicts, see Journoud, "Les guerres coloniales," 482–3. The French army deaths in Indochina included those of 11,000 foreign *légionnaires*, 15,000 Africans and North-Africans, as well as 46,000 Vietnamese. On the debate surrounding civilian casualties in the Algerian war, see Stora, *La gangrène et l'oubli*, 180–4.

9 This calculation is based on the official figures, which indicate that in the First World War 8,410,000 men were mobilized, of whom 1,383,000 were dead or missing; in the Algerian war, 1,419,125 men were mobilized and 23,196 killed.

comrades."[10] Looking back, we can see this repugnance as evidence of a long-term evolution of social attitudes toward a rejection of the necessity of the soldier's death. In the context of a "war without name" where their sacrifices seemed unappreciated both by the people at home and by those whom they had supposedly been sent to protect, many soldiers began to question whether there was any point to their deaths or to their military service. Such doubts intensified when it became apparent that France would capitulate to the demands for Algerian independence. One conscript confessed that he hated de Gaulle for guiding French policy in that direction. "I cannot understand this waste and these deaths for nothing," he wrote.[11] In these circumstances, it was the military professionals who shored up the ideal of the soldier's death as a heroic sacrifice. Their alienation from the values of French society was dramatically exposed, however, by the failed military putsch of April 1961. At odds with civil society as well as with national political leadership, the soldiers who led and supported the putsch justified their disobedience by reference to their dead comrades and to a time-hallowed code of professional honour that transcended patriotism itself.

"A SAVAGE WAR OF PEACE"

The title of Alistair Horne's classic work on the Algerian war, *A Savage War of Peace*, aptly identifies two salient features of the war: its reputation for an unusual degree of savagery in the way it was fought; and the official denial, sustained by the French government until 1999, that it was a war at all.[12] It was the disjuncture between an official discourse that referred to the role of the army as "pacification" or "the maintenance of order" and the reality of a merciless and unscrupulous fight to the death that dominated many French soldiers' experiences and perceptions of the war. It was quickly apparent to most of the nearly 1.5 million young Frenchmen who eventually served in Algeria that the conflict they were called upon to fight was, in scale and intensity, a war. For the government to acknowledge as much, however, would undermine its position that Algeria was an integral part of France; the French people, it insisted, could hardly be at war against themselves. When the war began, with a series of armed attacks on about thirty administrative and military targets throughout Algeria by the Armée de Libération Nationale (ALN)[13] on and around 1 November 1954, the

10 Jauffret, "The War Culture of French Combatants," 110.
11 Martel, *La section*, 107.
12 Horne, *A Savage War of Peace*.
13 The military wing of the FLN.

independence movement possessed a paltry force of no more than seven hundred militants, armed with only four hundred firearms.[14] It steadily grew in numbers, however, raising funds to buy arms from Algerians working in France and training soldiers in camps provided by the newly independent neighbouring states of Tunisia and Morocco. By the end of 1958, at its highest point, the ALN had at least 60,000 men under arms in Algeria itself, and another 10,000 outside.[15] The numbers of French combatants also underwent rapid growth. From only 49,000 men in the summer of 1954, they reached a strength of 83,000 by February 1955,[16] and, following the recall of 60,000 men who had recently completed their military service, 188,000 in January 1956.[17] The recourse to conscription and the extension of the standard period of compulsory military service from eighteen months to twenty-seven facilitated another doubling of the army's size in 1956, which reached 400,000 men by the end of the year and 450,000 by December 1957.[18] Additional manpower was provided by Français de Souche Nord-Africaine[19] (FSNA), native Algerian troops, some of whom were integrated in regular army units but who for the most part served under French officers in separate units, known as *maghzen* and *harkas*.[20] There were 118,000 FSNA, both regular and auxiliary, serving with the French army by the end of the war.[21] The army acquired weapons at the same time as it acquired men, most notably an array of light machine guns, mortars, and portable firearms (such as the ubiquitous machine pistol MAT 49, mentioned above in relation to the death of Clovis Creste), as well as light tanks and armoured vehicles. Air power was also an essential element, including light aircraft (the Harker T-6) for reconnaissance and support of ground forces, as well as American "flying banana" helicopters that were used not only for the rapid deployment of the famous parachute battalions that were the principal means for hunting down ALN detachments but also for the removal of the wounded. In 1959 alone, French

14 Ageron, "Aux origines de la Toussaint 1954," 28.
15 Pervillé, "L'armee française au combat," 47.
16 Stora, *Histoire de la guerre d'Algérie*, 13–14.
17 Jauffret, "L'armée française au combat," 43.
18 Pervillé, "L'armée française au combat," 46. Of the French soldiers who served in Algeria between 1954 and 1962, 1,179,523 were *appelés*/conscripts. Jean-Charles Jauffret, "Pour une typologie des hommes," 387. The total number of those who served in all branches of the French army in Algeria was 1,419,125. See *Journal officiel de la République française*, Débats parlementaires. Assemblée nationale. Questions écrites et réponses des ministres, 4 August 1986, 2469.
19 "French of North African origin."
20 Soldiers serving in these units were known as *moghazni* and *harkis*.
21 Ageron, "Les supplétifs algériens," 11; Guy Pervillé, "L'armée française au combat," 51.

military helicopters deployed 170,000 commandos and completed 7,500 medical evacuations.[22]

The war went through a succession of phases that corresponded to changing means and objectives. A significant escalation occurred on 20 August 1955, as an FLN-led uprising of peasants in the region of Philippeville resulted in a brutal massacre of 123 civilians followed by an even more vicious repression in which as many as 12,000 Algerians may have been killed.[23] It was immediately following the events at Philippeville that the first class of recently liberated conscripts was recalled for service in Algeria. Initially, the French army deployed heavily armed forces appropriate for conventional operations but unsuitable for engaging lightly armed and highly mobile guerrillas. The army, however, soon fell under the sway of officers who had experienced defeat in Indochina and who were determined to redeem that defeat by demonstrating in Algeria that they had learned its lessons. Colonels Paul Ducourneau, Roger Trinquier, and Marcel Bigeard were military leaders who scorned conventional tactics and discipline and who resorted to the same improvised methods of warfare employed by the guerrillas they sought to destroy. Under the leadership of commanders-in-chief Raoul Salan (November 1956 – December 1957) and Maurice Challe (December 1957 – March 1960), these colonels led the way in taking the war to the FLN, whether that involved penetrating the cells of urban guerillas who planted bombs in cafes and casinos during the Battle of Algiers or rooting out detachments of ALN fighters from their mountain fastnesses in Kabylia and the Aurès. In September 1957, work was completed on the construction of an electrified fence – named the Morice Line in honour of the French minister of defence – along the frontier with Tunisia that was calculated to deny ALN forces operating in Algeria access to external reinforcements and support. This led, during the winter of 1957–58 to some of the largest battles of the war, culminating in the Battle of Souk-Ahras at the end of April 1958, a significant defeat for the ALN in which it lost over six hundred of eight hundred fighters. French military success reached its zenith in the second half of 1959, as General Challe concentrated his forces in a General Reserve that was employed in major offensives such as Operations Sparks (*Étincelles*) and Binoculars (*Jumelles*), aimed at destroying the ALN forces in the Hodna Massif and Kabylia. By the end of the year the ALN had lost 26,000 men

---

22 Villatoux, "Pilotes d'hélicoptères," 456. For a survey of the system of combined arms developed by the French army in Algeria, see Jauffret, *Soldats en Algérie*, 135–62.

23 Stora, *Histoire de la guerre d'Algérie*, 17–18.

killed and over 10,000 taken prisoner; its remaining companies were reduced to an increasingly desperate struggle simply to survive.[24]

While their military successes convinced many French generals and officers that victory was within their grasp, they came at considerable political cost. The destruction of the FLN networks in the Battle of Algiers was accomplished only through mass arrests and the systematic torture of suspects, several thousand of whom "disappeared." The struggle for the Morice Line led, on 8 February 1958, to the violation of the Tunisian frontier and the bombing by French aircraft of the village of Sakiet, resulting in eighty deaths, including those of many women and children. The military offensives of the Challe Plan were accompanied by the intensification of a policy of *regroupement*, which displaced two million Algerian civilians from their homes and enclosed them in camps, where many suffered deprivation and misery. Such contraventions of human rights and international law unsettled the army's morale, divided opinion in France, and won growing international support for the cause of Algerian independence in forums such as the United Nations. Although it was pressure from the generals in Algiers that helped to bring about the return to power of Charles de Gaulle in May 1958, the new president was increasingly committed to seeking a negotiated end to the war, even if that involved facing down the opposition of a jaded military leadership. As for the contingent of French conscripts serving their time in Algeria, the advent of *Charlot-la-Quille* aroused hopes they would soon be going home.[25] A political turning point was reached when de Gaulle made his speech of 16 September 1959, which held out the promise of self-determination to Algeria. Negotiations with the FLN would not begin until 1960, however, and in the meantime the war continued, complicated after February 1961 by the Organisation Armée Secrète (OAS), which brought its own campaign of terror to bear against perceived opponents of *l'Algérie française*. The OAS was led by General Salan, who also instigated a failed putsch attempt in April 1961, shattering the

---

24 Jauffret, *Soldats en Algérie*, 120.

25 "Charlie La Quille." La Quille – literally, "Skittle" – was the symbol of the conscript's liberation from military service. Soldiers counted the days remaining until they received their "skittle." One explanation for the origin of this symbol is that it was the name of a boat sent in 1939 to collect convicts who had served their time in the penal colony of Cayenne. See Jauffret, *Soldats en Algérie*, 228. Prior to that, however, popular imagery depicting soldiers returning home from their military service showed them with a metal cylinder containing their discharge papers. The metal cylinder was their "skittle." Conscripts and convicts alike carved wooden skittles as symbols of their anticipated release from servitude. See Hopkin, *Soldier and Peasant*, 209. *Charlot* is a diminutive form of the name Charles, but it also has a more sinister meaning as a word for an executioner, a reference to Charles Sanson, the name of several members of the Sanson dynasty of Parisian executioners.

unity and morale of the army he had once commanded. The final, unhappy stages of the war included bloody confrontations between the OAS and the army at Bab-el-Oued and a massacre in the rue d'Isly in Algiers, as panicked *tirailleurs algériens*, provoked by the OAS, fired into a crowd of *pied-noir* demonstrators.

All these circumstances impinged upon the French soldier's experience of the war. That experience varied enormously according to time and place, as well as to the nature and function of each soldier's posting. For many, service in Algeria meant above all the tedium and discomfort of serving in one of the five thousand military posts through which the army sought to impose its presence throughout Algeria. For others, it meant arduous marches in the outback and fierce firefights as they hunted down ALN formations. Yet others patrolled the Morice Line or experienced life in garrisons in cities such as Algiers and Oran. There was a fundamental divide between the experience of the large numbers of sector troops policing the outback and the minority of soldiers, far better provided for in equipment, officers, and training, who constituted the General Reserve.[26] The latter, concentrated for coordinated attacks on the ALN, included the parachute battalions of various formations, among them the Foreign Legion. Although many of these formations incorporated conscripts, they were dominated by professional, career soldiers who saw themselves as a warrior elite in comparison with the reluctant conscripts who made up the rest of the army. Parachute drops were rare in an operational context, but it was the "paras" who, led by colonels like Ducourneau and Bigeard, became the shock troops of the French army in the Algerian war.[27]

Whether professionals motivated by *esprit de corps* or conscripts doggedly keeping their heads down and counting the days until they could return home, French soldiers of whatever stripe acknowledged that they were engaged in a conflict that often contravened the usual rules of war. As Albert Camus wrote in 1956, this was a war in which "everyone appeals to the other's crime as the authority to go even further."[28] The respect for the laws of war, such as those defined by the Geneva Convention of 1949, was undermined from the beginning by the French civil government's abdication of political authority to the army, by the latter's adherence to the notion of "collective responsibility" that sanctioned reprisals for acts of terrorism or sabotage, and by the refusal to acknowledge the status of

26 According to one calculation, in 1958 the General Reserve consisted of 30,000 men, representing 6 per cent of the army's total of around 500,000 men. Jauffret, *Soldats en Algérie*, 85.

27 For consideration of this "two speed army," see ibid., 81–90.

28 Cited in ibid., 249.

enemy fighters as legitimate combatants. Furthermore, the doctrine of revolutionary war itself embodied a lack of respect for the conventional rules of war.[29] Racist assumptions about the enemy combined with experience of the war on the ground to encourage extremes of violence. The letters and memoirs of most French soldiers betray their conviction that they were fighting barbaric enemies who inflicted cruel and humiliating tortures upon their victims. This belief, as a letter written by Jean-Pierre Villaret to his family in April 1957 illustrates, was informed by racist stereotypes and used to justify the mistreatment of Algerian captives. "Don't concern yourselves about the 'cruelties' we make these guys submit to," he wrote. "Alas, we are dealing with a stubborn race [...] and only blows make them understand."[30] Villaret's perception of the war as one fought without mercy on either side – "no quarter [is given] and so much the worse for anyone who falls alive into the hands of his adversaries"[31] – was widely shared by other French soldiers. Even if they had not seen with their own eyes the mutilated bodies of comrades whose throats had been cut or whose sexual organs had been cut off and stuffed in their mouths, they had certainly heard about them. According to one writer, accounts of such atrocities were a preoccupation of recruits even as they prepared to embark for Algeria.[32] Once in combat, it was generally understood that a soldier's last bullet was for himself. Villaret declared that "for my part, I have decided that if one day I must fall into their hands, I would blow my head off first."[33]

French soldiers justified their own savagery by reference to that of the enemy: the expectation that the enemy would show no mercy justified giving none in return. That savagery was, however, as visceral as it was calculated. Georges Mattei, who deserted the French army to become a supporter of the FLN, described in an autobiographical novel how the discovery of the bodies of five soldiers, two of which had been mutilated, aroused a savage lust for vengeance among the men of his company that was assuaged only by the beating and torture of prisoners. The novel describes the fate of one of these victims:

They doused him in water. His wrists were tied together, they wrapped them in wet rags to which they attached the electrodes. The two wires were linked to the dynamo of a field telephone, behind, [where] a soldier sitting astride turned the crank while frequently changing the rhythm. Experience had

29 Ibid., 256–65.
30 Villaret and Courilleau, *Lettres de deux appelés*, 77–8.
31 Ibid.
32 Delpard, *20 ans pendant la guerre d'Algérie*, 20.
33 Villaret and Courilleau, *Lettres de deux appelés*, 107.

taught him that by varying the movement he could change the intensity of the current and thus the electric shocks were more intense and more difficult to bear.

The man screams and contorts himself, he trembles, convulses with the jerks of an amusing puppet [...] The soldiers busied themselves around the victim with the gestures of busy craftsmen, moving the electrodes to place them precisely on the temples, under the tongue, on the prick, in the [ear] canal, on the balls.[34]

The following day, Mattei's narrator wakes to see "strange fruit hanging from the trees. The bodies of the tortured were swinging, heads down, before the eyes of the villagers."[35] The tortured men are killed as they hang there by the volley of a soldier's machine pistol. Mattei summed up the ruthless logic of the war as he saw it: "Here, to give death or to receive it is to have your balls cut off."[36]

The cruelty of the soldiers in Mattei's novel is animated by a mixture of instinctive rage and deliberate calculation. Renaud de Bary, who participated in a remarkably similar torture session in January 1962, combining beatings, electricity, and water, recalled how the experience of tripping over the severed head of the soldier he was supposed to replace on guard duty caused him to lose all control:

I lost my head, my feet still stained with the blood of the severed head I had bumped into in going on guard, I set to hitting the hardest. The blood which had been spilled caused me to lose all reason and I really think that I was the one who shouted the loudest and all the resentment of our intolerable life returned. Someone had to get hold of me, I was unable to stop. And then, I collapsed, vomiting again and again, unable to stop. I left the ruins of the village and collapsed on the ground, semi-unconscious. I hardly saw the transfer at arm's length of the human wrecks to a military truck.[37]

By his own account, de Bary's uncontrolled violence stemmed from a combination of the release of months of pent-up tension living in a military outpost and the shock of the encounter with his comrade's severed head: "How can I forget that hurriedly chopped off head, dripping with already congealing blood, that huddled body, those eyes still open and glassy, that

34 Mattei, *La guerre des Gusses*, 37.
35 Ibid., 39.
36 Ibid., 32.
37 Bary, *La 4ᵉ batterie*, 91–2.

blood which soaked my boots and my cries for help? And he was one of my closest companions."[38]

The perceived savagery of the enemy, as well as the urge to avenge comrades who had been killed, greatly diminished any inhibitions French soldiers had about killing. The killing of prisoners, either in the immediate aftermath of combat or after they had been tortured, was often recorded in French war diaries with the dubious explanation, "shot while trying to escape." One soldier, his Christian values sorely tested by his comrades' conduct, recorded his anguish and sense of isolation at being unable to prevent this maltreatment of prisoners. "One cannot go a hundred metres without encountering a hanged [body] or a corpse," he wrote. "I am alone in refusing to accept these executions of prisoners."[39] Other soldiers also expressed their shock or unease at the army's lack of concern at the wanton destruction of Algerian lives. Jean-Pierre Martel confessed himself to be "sad and ill at ease" following his first encounter with the enemy, during which he had, as section leader, taken the decision to finish off a severely wounded enemy soldier whom his captain had refused to remove by helicopter. Writing to his father about the incident, Martel was disappointed to receive only patriotic platitudes in response: "Unused as I was to confiding such personal matters to him," Martel wrote many years later, "his response deprived me, forever, of any inclination to do so again."[40] Antoine Prost, who served in the Algerian war before achieving a distinguished career as a leading historian of twentieth-century France, was also disturbed by his new comrades' casual disdain for human, particularly Algerian, life. Prost recorded in his *carnet de route* a conversation with a fellow officer soon after his arrival in Algeria in February 1960:

I explain to him everything that seems to me unacceptable, in particular ... indifference to death and the execution of prisoners. Some shocking replies: "To me a *fellagha*, that's an outlaw, it is no longer a man, it is like a viper, a scorpion; if I encounter one, I crush it." Or with respect to innocents who are killed in a bunch: "If, among fifty guys I have killed, there are only two who could have planted a bomb in Algiers, I figure that I have won." How terribly life and death are devalued here. They are no longer things of importance.[41]

38 Ibid., 92.
39 In "'Les jeunes soldats devant les tortures,' Numéro saisi de *France-Observateur*, Extrait du 2 mai 1957." Archives de la Contemporaine, 4/DELTA/08801 carton 1955–1961, no. 136.
40 Martel, *La section*, 59.
41 Prost, *Carnets d'Algérie*, 39.

Engaged on an operation two months later, Prost passed three French soldiers from another company squabbling over the possessions of a severely wounded enemy soldier. He recorded in his journal that as he moved on, "three detonations tell me that he has been finished off. It seems that he was grievously wounded in any case, but one of ours would have been evacuated in the same conditions." Prost's grim reflection on the incident was, "If a wounded [man] is not finished off, it is in order to torture him before he is killed."[42]

The perception of the enemy as implacably cruel did not necessarily preclude respect for him. Pierre Leulliette, a parachutist, admitted to feeling indifference after a firefight in which enemy soldiers had been killed by French ground support aircraft – "We have lost all emotion. The death of these people, no bigger from afar than grains of wheat, does not affect us." – but also shame and pity: "These dead fill me with shame; I know however that, had they captured me alive in their woods, they would not have hesitated, to make me speak, to torment my body until I screamed to death [...] Shame and pity, however, because if they were sometimes cowardly and beasts of prey, they were also men of great courage."[43] Enemy soldiers rarely surrendered, wrote Leulliette, since they were in little doubt of the treatment they could expect. Most of them, he said, "die bravely, in place, as men, that is to say standing up," and would rather blow themselves up with a hand grenade than be taken alive: "Everybody here respects their courage," he concluded.[44]

HOW SOLDIERS DIED: AMBUSHES AND ACCIDENTS

By comparison with earlier wars, relatively few French soldiers died in the Algerian war. "We were not a new *génération du feu*,"[45] wrote Pierre Montagnon, who commanded the Second Parachute Regiment of the Foreign Legion. Comparing the casualties of the Algerian war with those of the First World War, Montagnon commented that an estimated 23,000 deaths in the entire Algerian conflict was equivalent to the mortality of only twenty-three days of the First World War, when an average of 1,000 *poilus* died every day.[46] The official total of French military deaths

42 Ibid., 98–9.
43 Leulliette, *Saint Michel et le dragon*, 137.
44 Ibid., 143.
45 "Front generation."
46 Montagnon, *L'honneur, pas les honneurs*, vol. 1, 271.

announced in 1986 was 23,196, of whom 15,583 died in combat.[47] The
estimated number of ALN combatants who died, between 153,000 and
155,000, was roughly ten times as many, a measure of the French army's
vastly greater resources in men and modern weapons technology.[48] Another
pertinent comparison can be made to the war by which Algeria was
conquered in the nineteenth century. Historian Jacques Frémeaux calculates that 150,000 French soldiers lost their lives in Algeria between 1830
and 1871, 50,000 of them during the eight years of most intense fighting
from 1840 to 1847. Comparing the eight-year periods 1840–47 and
1954–62, absolute losses during the first were more than double those of
the second. The comparison is far more shocking, however, if we consider
these losses as proportions of the total numbers of men engaged. Frémeaux
calculates that the French war dead from 1840–47 represented 16.6 per cent
of the 300,000 who served; those from 1954–62 only 1.25 per cent of an
estimated total of two million.[49] Clearly, a French soldier fighting in the
Algerian war of decolonization was more than ten times less likely to die
than his counterpart fighting in the war of conquest. On the other hand,
if he did become one of the unfortunate 1.25 per cent, he was much more
likely to die a violent death. Frémeaux calculates that 80 per cent of deaths
during the war of conquest were caused by disease, the effects of which
were accentuated by harsh conditions of service. Only officers, who were
relatively well fed and well cared for, were more likely to die of wounds
sustained in combat than of disease.[50] In 1954–62, an army inoculated
against smallpox, tetanus, and diphtheria suffered only 5 per cent of its
fatalities because of illness.[51] Relieved by the advances of medical science
and modern logistics from the fears of sickness and starvation, it was above
all the threat of a violent death at the hands of Algerian nationalists that
preyed upon the minds of French soldiers.

The French army that fought in the Algerian war of 1954–62 evidently
did a lot more killing than it did dying. Although much less likely to lose
their lives than soldiers who fought in earlier wars, French soldiers in the

47 *Journal officiel de la République française*, Débats parlementaires. Assemblée nationale.
Question écrites et réponses des ministres, 4 August 1986, 2469.

48 Ageron, "Les pertes humaines," 170–2.

49 Frémeaux, *La France et l'Algérie*, 255–6. The figure of two million, often cited as the
number of French service personnel in the Algerian war, exceeds the total of 1,419,125
provided by the Ministry of Defence in 1986. See *Journal official de la République française*,
Débats parlementaires. Assemblée nationale. Questions écrites et réponses des ministres,
4 August 1986, 2469.

50 Jacques Frémeaux, *La France et l'Algérie*, 256–8.

51 Ibid. A total of 1,144 French military deaths were attributed to illness. See Ageron,
"Les pertes humaines," 170.

Algerian war were nonetheless highly sensitized to their vulnerability to sudden ambushes that would result not just in death but also in torture and emasculation. In Algeria, it was particularly apt that the French expression for "massacred" – *égorgé* – was literally the same as that for having one's throat cut. The army's macabre expression for this commonplace and fatal mutilation was the "Kabylia smile."[52] A conscript recalled his horror at coming across the bodies of two comrades by the side of the road, "lying in their blood, half decapitated. They had their throats completely cut and only the skin at the back of the neck kept the heads attached to the victims' bodies." The two men had simply left their post for a walk: "That was the war in Algeria!" recalled the conscript. "There was no front, no armed battle of army against army, but numerous underhand terrorist acts, like this one."[53] As the classic tactic of guerrilla warfare, ambushes were indeed a common occurrence. They ranged from small-scale attacks on one or two soldiers who had let their guard down, as in the previous example, to well-organized attacks on motorized convoys or on company-sized formations operating in the mountainous terrain of Kabylia or the Aurès. In Algeria, ambushes were inextricably associated with ideas of massacre and emasculation. Some French soldiers developed a lasting terror of knife attacks. "I have always been afraid of steel weapons," recalled Fernand Fournier fifty years after his service in Algeria. "I had no fear of bullets, or of mines, although God knows how much we were exposed to them. But I had a horror of the dagger which 'turned my guts to water.'"[54] Another soldier recalled the constant tension caused by the fear of ambush at the post where he was stationed. The enemy was "nowhere and everywhere," he said, waiting for an opportune moment to strike. On one occasion, it was the absence of an escort that cost the life of the company quartermaster, who drove off on his daily mail run and was never seen again. On another, a *harki* sergeant who had served in Indochina was gunned down in broad daylight as he strolled through a village market.[55] Yet another soldier recalled how seven men belonging to his company had been killed when they set their weapons aside to go for a swim in a nearby river.[56] Constant vigilance imposed a strain from which soldiers periodically sought release, sometimes with fatal consequences. One conscript described the pattern of life during his service in Algeria: "The weeks pass by, following a quasi-mechanical rhythm, [comprising] boredom, confinement and gasps of

52 Rotman and Tavernier, *La guerre sans nom*, 247.
53 Fournier, *Paroles d'appelés*, 56–67.
54 Ibid., 38.
55 Ibid., 40–2.
56 Ibid., 83.

oxygen in town, themselves interspersed by attacks." The deaths of comrades who fell victim to terrorist attacks in Algiers, he said, "were like road accidents. In this *ubu*-like universe, one could die for a piece of Roquefort one wanted to eat in a restaurant [...] one should not have stepped inside, but one went there to escape the confinement."[57]

The tactic of the surprise attack or ambush was a classic strategy of weakness. It was the only possible strategy for the ALN, which was sorely disadvantaged in numbers and in weapons, allowing it to make the most of its meagre assets, especially familiarity with the terrain. Effectively, this strategy involved retiring in the face of superior force and going to ground, reserving offensives for those rare moments when the French army let down its guard or by some error of judgment allowed formations to become isolated and vulnerable. Given its classic definition in the writings of Sun Tzu and updated for modern nationalists by Mao Zedong, this method of revolutionary warfare was one with which the French army had become only too well acquainted in Indochina. Far less numerous than the Vietminh, the ALN departed from this system only at its peril, as was the case during the 1958 battles to contest the impermeability of the Morice Line. Otherwise, the war developed a pattern defined by French army *ratissages*[58] aimed at flushing out and destroying ALN *katibas*,[59] as well as by the occasional ripostes of the latter, resulting in *accrochages*[60] and *embuscades*,[61] which were generally brief in duration but also fierce in intensity. The firefights that concluded these operations were unequal contests in which the ALN found itself up against a highly sophisticated combined arms team that included mechanized formations and artillery, as well as air support. The primitively armed *djoundi*[62] who went to ground in a rocky grotto in Kabylia could expect to be blasted out of it by a variety of weapons, including field mortars and heavy artillery, as well as aerial bombs. Perhaps most terrifying of all, he might well be incinerated by napalm, a weapon also extensively deployed by French aviation. It is not surprising that Pierre Montagnon judged that "Save for an error in execution, a rebel group located is a rebel group destroyed. Despite his courage, the *djoundi* has only two choices: surrender or sell his life dearly[,] if he is confronted by *paras* or legionnaires."[63] What does seem remarkable, however, is that

---

57 Maury, *L'empreinte de la guerre*, 170.
58 "Combing."
59 A *katiba* was a company-sized formation of 100 men.
60 "Engagement."
61 "Ambush."
62 "Fighter."
63 Montagnon, *L'honneur, pas les honneurs*, vol. 1, 105.

Montagnon attributed this unequal situation entirely to the disparity in leadership and training between the two sides, rather than to the disparities in numbers and in the weapons at their disposal. Just as courageous as the enemy, he wrote, the French *paras* and foreign legionnaires were "superbly prepared for war and well officered."[64]

French soldiers who were at the sharp end of the Algerian war were even less likely than their senior officers to recall the generally unequal nature of the contest; what understandably dominated their memories were those occasions when the tables were turned against them. For the most part, survivors of ambushes recalled only the sudden terror at finding themselves under attack as well as the arbitrariness with which matters of life and death were decided. A conscript from the class of 1956 provided a vivid recollection of the experience of an ambush in response to an inquiry concerning his worst memory of the war:

I was at the head of the convoy charged with opening a road through a valley, when I fell into a terrible ambush[.] We were encircled, the rebels ten yards away. I was on a scout vehicle, happily, otherwise I would have been cut to pieces. An enormous rock had crashed at my feet deep inside the scout vehicle, as well as a grenade. I was hit by shrapnel, and by a bullet which went through my left hand [...] Another nicked my left cheek and ear; another bullet struck my right thorax [...] all in the space of twenty minutes. I saw death, more frightful and sad than one can say[.] I do not seek to understand why I am still alive[;] for me that is a miracle. A sergeant who was beside me and who saved my life was hit by a bullet that pierced his right shoulder, both lungs and his spinal column; he is now in the Invalides, in Paris, paralyzed for life; another sergeant who was behind me had his throat cut by a machine gun burst. He died beside me, in the helicopter. All three of us were from the same contingent, with twenty-three months of service.[65]

The soldier's brief account, filled with survivor's guilt, powerfully conveys the suddenness and intensity of such ambushes, as well as the vulnerability and impotence of those on the receiving end. The French army may have enjoyed a huge superiority in men and weapons, but that was not how it felt to those who were on the receiving end of an ALN ambush.

The most notorious ambush, involving twenty-two soldiers from the Ninth Colonial Infantry Regiment, near Palestro on 18 May 1956, was of

64 Ibid.
65 Grall, *La génération du Djebel*, 30–1.

newly arrived conscripts led by an over-zealous officer, Hervé Artur. Possibly
going farther than his orders required, Lieutenant Artur led his men into
terrain in the foothills of Kabylia that was ideal for guerrilla warfare and
which the regional FLN military commander, Ali Khodja, used to his advantage. Surprise was complete, and the resistance of Artur's men under a
withering fire from single-shot and semi-automatic weapons short-lived.
Within a quarter of an hour, sixteen of them, including Artur, lay dead. Of
the remaining six, four were wounded and either died or were finished off
by their captors as the latter withdrew into the hills; the bodies of two were
later found lying by the roadside, but those of the other two were never
recovered. One of the two unwounded Frenchmen taken prisoner was
accidentally killed in the ensuing operation to rescue them, leaving the
other, Pierre Dumas, as the sole survivor. [66]

Although the French army generally kept a tight rein on the press and
declined to advertise its setbacks, the Palestro massacre was given wide
publicity. The military reports were vague, but the press implied that the
bodies of the French dead had generally been subjected to mutilation:
"horribly massacred," said *L'Express*; "savagely mutilated," wrote *Le Monde*.[67]
Accounts of barbarous cruelty inflicted upon the victims of the Palestro
massacre were, as Raphaëlle Branche shows, "opportunistically exploited"
by the French government and its supporters in the press to represent the
war it was fighting in Algeria to the French people as a necessary defence
of civilization from criminal rebels who sought to undermine peace and
stability by perpetrating cowardly and bloodthirsty attacks.[68] The idealism
of Hervé Artur and the innocence of his men were both emphasized, as
were their civilian backgrounds. Labelling the ambush a "massacre" and
insisting upon the civilian identities of both perpetrators and victims denied
its military character and associated it with earlier massacres of civilians,
the Palestro massacre of 1871 and the Philippeville massacres of 1955.[69]
Emphasizing the atavistic cruelty of the enemy justified the emergency
measures taken by the government as well as its decision to deploy conscripts
in Algeria. It also conditioned the punitive violence of the several thousand
French soldiers who, on 19 May, descended upon the village of Djerrah,
near where the bodies of the French soldiers were discovered. That

66 A meticulous analysis of the ambush at Palestro and of narratives that emerged
from that event is provided in Branche, *L'embuscade de Palestro*.
67 *L'Express*, 25 May 1956; *Le Monde*, 21 May 1956.
68 Branche, *L'embuscade de Palestro*, 84.
69 Ibid., 79, 179–80.

afternoon, forty-four Algerians in the vicinity of the village were summarily executed and the village itself razed to the ground.[70]

Ambushes prepared by one side or the other often led to very sudden and close encounters between French soldiers and their enemies. Pierre Leulliette reflected that the ideal of modern war was "the great anonymous, remorseless massacre." But, he declared, "We are not yet there: one sees very well who one kills, and that they are men, like us."[71] Often, combat amounted to short bursts of fire as adversaries surprised one another at close quarters. Jean-Pierre Martel recounted how he fired instinctively at an enemy whom he came across at a distance of only nine metres: "I have just killed a man without even realizing that I was firing. My map has fallen at my feet, my machine pistol hangs alongside my body in its usual place. I am trembling like a leaf [...] I have saved my life, a feeling which drugs me and which I will experience upon every contact with death."[72] The deadly intimacy of such encounters was intensified by the character of the war as a civil war, with Muslim Algerians engaged on both sides of the conflict. Jean-Jacques Servan-Schreiber provided a vivid account of an ambush at Sakamody in which a unit of Algerian auxiliaries was wiped out by enemy forces armed with machine guns provided by deserters from the same unit. To Servan-Schreiber, the tragedy of the Algerian war was symbolized by the fates of the idealistic SAS officer, Marcus, who commanded the unit, and of his second-in-command, Houach Bousquine. The latter, "son of a penniless family of the Philippeville casbah [...] cut off from his two brothers who had gone over to the *maquis*, sometimes racked by doubts, but at bottom certain he was serving a just cause in an honest experiment," was left bleeding to death in a ditch while his comrades' bodies were stripped and mutilated.[73] More personal was the bitter recollection of another soldier who recalled as his worst memory of the war the occasion when soldiers from an Algerian *harka* went over to the enemy, massacring their European comrades beforehand: "That night I lost all my friends, and especially my best friend, who had never left me since our enlistment (fourteen months together) [...] Of all my conscript comrades, only two of us survived. For that night and the traitors I hold a feeling of horror and disgust."[74]

70 Ibid., 181.
71 Leulliette, *Saint Michel et le dragon*, 240.
72 Martel, *La section*, 60.
73 Servan-Schreiber, *Lieutenant in Algeria*, 69 and 64.
74 Grall, *La génération du Djebel*, 103.

Not all French soldiers who died in Algeria did so because of enemy action. "As paradoxical as it seems," writes Maurice Mateos-Ruiz, "the greatest risk run by a conscript in Algeria was to be the victim of an accident!"; 7,678 deaths, roughly one-third of all French fatalities, were caused accidentally, principally by the mishandling of firearms or by road accidents.[75] A conscript stationed 15 kilometres from the town of Bougie recalled that soldiers from his post were permitted to drive into town and that on one occasion five soldiers were killed when the vehicle carrying them overturned. "Unhappily," he concluded, "accidents relating to traffic and to the maintenance of weapons were not uncommon."[76] Antoine Prost affirmed in his journal that "an accident is more to be feared than a fight." On one occasion, he recorded one death and seventeen wounded as the result of an overturned truck; on another, one dead and eleven wounded following the accidental explosion of a rifle grenade as the soldier carrying it jumped down from a truck.[77] Accidents caused by friendly fire, often a consequence of poor communication between different units operating in the same region, particularly at night, also caused unnecessary casualties. Pierre Leulliette recounted the story of a panicky young soldier who while on guard duty accidentally shot and killed his own sergeant. Although mortified by his fatal error, "the murderer," wrote Leulliette, was not subjected to any punishment. Reflecting on the banality of the incident, Leulliette confessed that "I still think a bit about the dead sergeant. But I know that in a few days I will have definitively forgotten him."[78] In the realm of fiction, Claude Klotz, author of the novel *Les appelés*, testified to the reality of friendly-fire fatalities by having four fictional conscript-friends, inadequately trained and led, kill one another in the course of a night-time operation.[79] Further evidence is provided by the diary entry of conscript Marc Secail of 30 July 1959: "Two fatal firearms incidents both consequent upon non-observation of the rules concerning the relief of armed sentries in insecure zones have in less than three weeks caused the deaths of two young conscripts."[80]

75 Mateos-Ruiz, *L'Algérie des appelés*, 76.
76 Fournier, *Paroles d'appelés*, 63.
77 Prost, *Carnets d'Algérie*, 102 and 132.
78 Leulliette, *Saint Michel et le dragon*, 329.
79 Klotz, *Les appelés*; Mateos-Ruiz, *L'Algérie des appelés*, 77.
80 Archives de la Contemporaine, F/Delta/Reso831/Documents relatifs à la guerre d'Algérie. Marc Secail, *Livre de bord, guerre d'Algérie*, 38.

IDEALIZING THE SOLDIER'S DEATH

The high proportion of accidental deaths suffered by the French army in Algeria was an obstacle to the idealization of those deaths. Nor did it help that the French enjoyed such immense advantages in numbers and resources or that their casualties were so much lower than those of their enemy. The French knew from long experience that heroic defeat was more glorious than overwhelming domination. For many of the young French soldiers who had been raised on the myths of their own country's resistance during the Second World War, their role in Algeria was uncomfortably close to that of the Nazi occupiers. From this perspective, the ALN resembled the *maquisards* who had resisted the German occupation. Alain Boeuf, a soldier from the Vercors region, famed for its place in the history of the French resistance, stated that when he discussed the war with other conscripts, "the image that came to me spontaneously was that we were the ones who in Algeria were the troops of occupation and that the resisters were on the other side."[81] Even those who felt such parallels were a distortion of the truth were unsettled by them. "When you have seen in Algeria how easily men can become helpless playthings of the set-up into which they are thrown," wrote Jean-Jacques Servan-Schreiber, "you don't feel you have the right to condemn the men of the *Wehrmacht* any longer."[82] While some soldiers felt pride in their service, others sensed that they were fighting on the wrong side of history. "My worst memory," wrote one, was "the moment of truth when the idealistic little French boy scout realized that the army to which I belonged was nothing but an army of occupation and acted like one."[83] These soldiers remembered the war only as an intensely painful episode in their lives. A conscript from the class of 1952 recalled for service in Algeria wrote that he could think of no "best memory" from the five months he had spent there and that he remained haunted by the violence and torture he had witnessed: "Those five months were interminable, and some youths spent twenty-four or twenty-seven months there!"[84]

Such alienation did not afflict the senior officers responsible for prosecuting the war in Algeria. Those officers went to considerable lengths to represent the war as one that, despite its brutalities, was honourable and even glorious. For them, to die in combat was the natural destiny of the

81 Rotman and Tavernier, *La guerre sans nom*, 174.
82 Servan-Schreiber, *Lieutenant in Algeria*, 200.
83 Grall, *La génération du Djebel*, 80.
84 Ibid., 50.

soldier, and it was his willingness to accept that fate which set the true warrior apart from ordinary men. It was Colonel Marcel Bigeard, commander of the Third Colonial Parachute Regiment (RPC), who did most to promote the idealization and aestheticization of the soldier's death during the war in Algeria. A veteran of the liberation of France, of the war in Indochina, and of Dien Bien Phu, Bigeard modelled a brand of military masculinity which the Third RPC, clad in its signature leopard camouflage battle dress and peaked *casquettes à la Bigeard*, modelled in turn for the rest of the French army. Bigeard was, like Jean Lartéguy's fictional Colonel Raspéguy for whom he was the inspiration, a man for whom other men were willing to die. He also knew how to valorize his soldiers' deaths. Referring to the death in an ambush of a trainee officer named Guy Cadot, on 9 November 1955, Bigeard declared that "The greatness of Cadot must lift us up, enable us to endure and to hope!" In his Christmas message to his men, Bigeard declared that their suffering would have its reward: "Lost in the mountains, in the cold, in the rain, you are unconsciously accomplishing great things […] This trial added to others, will make you strong, healthy, as resilient as leather, as hard as steel."[85] Bigeard idealized the war as one fought without hatred by men devoted to high principles: "This war is ungrateful, but capital for our country; it must be fought and fought well, at our level, in the hope that our motherland will become again what she once was. Our enemy certainly has a great ideal; he must be fought without weakness and without hate."[86] In aestheticizing the war in general, and the soldier's death in particular, Bigeard had an able collaborator in Sergeant Marc Flament. Also a veteran of the war in Indochina, Flament was new to photography when he was posted to Algeria in 1955, but an experienced artist and caricaturist. Flament saw his photographic work as in the tradition of the great figures of French military art: "I will witness epic battles, and, like the Army painters with their 'battle scenes' I will bear witness in images through my photos: like Alphonse de Neuville, Detaille, Flameng, Simond, Georges Scott, or Jonas, I will sublimate the soldiers' heroic legend by seeking beyond their brutal and mundane reality artistic images, true syntheses and complete spectacles of a war as yet unknown. For me, arriving at Sidi-Ferrruch, the 'Bigeard circus' that I will photograph will never be anything but the face of this war – but it will be adorned by the stunning colours that in earlier times illuminated our epics."[87] Flament's application of the principles of artistic composition to military photography

85 Cited in Flament, *Les beaux-arts de la guerre*, 188.

86 Ibid., 189–90.

87 Ibid., 201. On Marc Flament, see also Bastien Chastagner and Damien Vitry, "La guerre d'Algérie vue par trois photographes amateurs," accessed 2 March 2022, https://

9.1. Photograph by Marc Flament. *Twilight of the Gods.* Soldiers carrying the body of a dead comrade in the Algerian war. 1957.

transformed the soldiers whose deaths he recorded into religious martyrs. Instinctively, he composed his photographs according to the formulas used by the Italian Renaissance masters of religious painting. As Flament later explained, in composing his portrait of Lieutenant Roher, who was killed in the Sahara, he used the same symmetries as those in a Renaissance painting of the martyrdom of Saint Sebastien.[88] Another photograph echoed Titian's painting of Christ being placed in his tomb. It showed a

imagesdefense.gouv.fr/media//pdf/dossiers_thema/dossier-la-guerre-d-Algerie-vue-par-trois-photographes-amateurs.pdf; and Chominot and Stora, *Regards sur l'Algérie,* 29–61.
  88 Flament, *Les beaux-arts de la guerre,* 264.

9.2. Photograph by Marc Flament. *The Death of Sergeant Sentenac,*
22 November 1957.

dead paratrooper who was half-dragged, half-carried toward an evacuation
helicopter, a limp hand catching the light as it trailed in the sand.[89]
Christian iconography was not Flament's only inspiration, however, as is
revealed in his description of a photograph he took as a dead soldier was
carried away on a stretcher by four parachutists during an operation in
May 1957: "The image composes itself all alone in my viewfinder, vibrant
with serenity, and the corpse which moves away seems to be carried toward
that resting place reserved for dead battle heroes, toward some Valhalla!
The scene is surreal. Sublime emotion, it is the Twilight of the Gods! The

89 Ibid., 275.

9.3. Photograph by Marc Flament. *The Death of Sergeant Sentenac,* 22 November 1957.

right arm of the corporal has slipped out of the stretcher as if in an appeal. Where are the Valkyries? The knight's sword placed on the body is a machine pistol. One after the other, I take many shots against the light."[90] In this way, Flament recomposed the soldier's death as a pagan apotheosis, a rite of passage uniting the dying man with the warriors and gods of Norse mythology. He entitled the photograph *The Twilight of the Gods* (fig. 9.1).

Flament's most famous photographs of a dying soldier were those taken on 21 November 1957 of Staff Sergeant René Sentenac, a survivor of Dien Bien Phu as well as of an epic escape from a Vietnamese prison camp, who

90 Ibid., 226.

was killed by gunfire during an operation in the Sahara. On this occasion, as Flament recalled, the dying man, covered by his tent and head raised on an elbow, was aware of the photographer's presence: "Very quickly, I capture his rictus of pain. We look at one another. As if to apologize for it, I say to him: 'Back in Algiers, I will give you plenty of photos; you will see.' He gives a resigned nod of the head and begins to take shuddering breaths. The flies, now, are upon him" (fig. 9.2).[91] Finally, as he prepared to leave, Flament took a last shot, "a very wide field half into the light," as Sentenac, now still, lay with his head propped on a knapsack (fig. 9.3). The image would be widely distributed, featuring in the army's official newspaper *Le Bled* and in the weekly news magazine *Paris-Match* as well as on the wall of Bigeard's command post. The handsome features of Sentenac appear composed in the photograph, as if, having accomplished his ulti- mate destiny as a soldier, he is finally at peace. The photograph would appear at the very end of *Aucune bête au monde*, a pictorial tribute to the "paras" co-authored by Bigeard and Flament and dedicated to Sentenac. In his dedication, Bigeard wrote, "Of us all, he was the luckiest, because he achieved his death after having led the tormented life he had chosen." And he reinforced this message that Sentenac's death in combat was one the sergeant would have chosen for himself in the caption he wrote to accompany Flament's final photograph. "He had to make one last effort to die. He well knew that he had won, and that is why his peaceful face seemed to us so beautiful. What he was looking for on the other side of the crest was not a handful of Bedouins and their rifles, but that impossible thing that had haunted him for so long and which is to be found only in sacrifice and death. It alone allows one to merge oneself with that which is most great, most inaccessible. It was his way, Sentenac's, to understand God. And that, no beast could do."[92] Although the title of *Aucune bête au monde* referred to a quotation from Antoine de Saint-Exupéry,[93] the book's idealization of the soldier's death as an apotheosis, achieved as the culmi- nation of a personal struggle against man and nature in the unforgiving purity of the desert, echoed the ideas of Ernst Psichari from before the First World War. Bigeard's words and Flament's photographs proclaimed that the soldier's death was meaningful in and of itself, regardless of the

91   Ibid., 262.

92   Bigeard and Flament, *Aucune bête au monde*, unpaginated. On the death of Sentenac, see also Patrick-Charles Renaud, *Se battre en Algérie*, 155–6.

93   Bigeard's title is a reference to the words spoken by the pilot Henri Guillaumet to Antoine de Saint-Exupéry following his struggle to survive after crashing his aircraft in the Andes: "What I have done, I swear, no beast could ever have done." Saint-Exupéry commented on this sentence that it was "the noblest that I know." Saint-Exupéry, *Terre des hommes*, 46.

outcome of the battle and of the cause for which he fought. In Bigeard's conception, which ignored the vast disparity in resources between the French army and its nationalist opponents, the war was one between equals in which both sides respected their enemy's prowess, courage, and sacrifice.[94] On campaign, he wrote, soldiers' thoughts turned equally "to our comrades killed in full fury or crushed in their foxholes, and to the others whom they had killed, whom we had killed and who might also have become our comrades."[95] In this conception soldiers of both sides were united by their recognition that death in combat was the supreme moment that gave meaning to the soldier's life. All the same, such expressions of respect for the enemy did not stop French soldiers from displaying the bodies of their enemies in a manner that was the very opposite of the way their own dead were sanctified. These displays were calculated to demonstrate power over the enemy and to terrorize the civilian population (fig. 9.4).

Bigeard's personal reputation and his knack for publicity did much to found the myth of the paratrooper, which came to dominate French representations and perceptions of the war in Algeria. There were two sides to this myth: the paratrooper as angel, embodying a heroic ideal of military masculinity and serving as a defender of civilization; and the paratrooper as demon, betraying the civilized values he was supposed to be defending by resorting to torture, reprisals, and summary executions.[96] Although they constituted only 3–5 per cent of the French forces in Algeria, the "paras" enjoyed an outsized reputation. In Indochina, their heroism in the defence of Dien Bien Phu enabled France to glean some consolation from an otherwise humiliating defeat. Their distinctive uniforms – leopard camouflage battle dress and green, red, and blue berets for the Foreign Legion, Colonial and Metropolitan regiments, respectively – and the swagger with which they wore them set the paratroops apart from the rest of the army, as did their role as "intervention" forces, employed specifically as elite combat units. In the words of historian Frank Talbott, "It was they, roaming the length and breadth of Algeria, often carried to the assault in helicopters, who fulfilled the romantic image of war as an enterprise of danger, of continuous movement and action."[97] Jean-Pierre Martel, a conscript whose regiment played a supporting role for a unit of the Foreign Legion, wrote enviously of the legionnaires: "When we met them in the

94 Frank Talbott commented insightfully on the photographs in this collection, writing that "they were a far cry from the usual realities of the Algerian war." See Talbott, "The Myth and Reality," 75.

95 Bigeard and Flament, *Aucune bête au monde*, unpaginated.

96 Dine, *Images of the Algerian War*, 28.

97 Talbott, "The Myth and Reality," 71.

9.4. Bodies of Algerian combatants after an operation in the Dahra region, 1961. The bodies have been placed in the precinct of a military post and the female population of the village has been assembled by the soldiers "to be witnesses to the human cost of this operation." The purpose of such degrading spectacles was to terrorize the civilian population.

field, they were magnificent with their warriors' appearance. Beside them, we looked like a band of tattered down-and-outs."[98] Politicians, to their own eventual detriment, could not resist the paratroop charisma and unashamedly promoted them as a symbol of their commitment to preserve *l'Algérie française* by giving them a prominent place in public events such as the Bastille Day parades on the Champs-Elysées. This strategy badly

98   Martel, *La section*, 61.

backfired when the paratroop regiments came to believe that their loyalty to *l'Algérie française* superseded their loyalty to the government itself. They would play a prominent part in the events of May 1958, which ended the Fourth Republic and returned Charles de Gaulle to power, as well as in the failed coup attempt of April 1961.

An essential ingredient of the myth of the paratrooper was the cult of death. Bigeard affirmed this by inscribing on the barrack walls of his unit the slogan, "Paratrooper, you are made to die!"[99] Even more than the other traits that he supposedly embodied – athleticism, sexual prowess, comrade-ship – it was his willingness to die that set the paratrooper apart from lesser, especially civilian, men. In this conception, death became the ultimate destiny of the soldier, rewarding his quest for the Absolute and preserving his moral purity from the pettiness and corruptions of civilian life. The romantic ideal of the paratrooper was brought most vividly to life in the best-selling novels of Jean Lartéguy, *The Centurions* (1960) and *The Praetorians* (1961).[100] These novels retraced the lives of a fictional Band of Brothers from the battlefields and prison camps of Indochina – where they learned through Vietminh example the methods of revolutionary war – through their disenchanted return to France and their subsequent escape to a new war in Algeria. Through the words of Colonel Raspéguy (loosely modelled on Colonel Bigeard), Lartéguy defined the paratroop unit as "a sort of close communion in hardship, danger, and death."[101] Raspéguy's men are not conventional heroes, but warriors who will do whatever it takes to win. They meet atrocity with counter-atrocity. When two of their number are discovered with their throats cut and their sexual organs in their mouths, they respond by cutting the throats of twenty-seven Muslims. They resort unhesitatingly to torture and to summary executions. All the same, at the conclusion of *The Praetorians*, when it becomes apparent that the paratroopers' plans for a coup in Algiers have been foiled, their intelligence officer, the enigmatic Boisfeuras, chooses a hero's death in combat as the ultimate expression of his disdain not only for the politicians and generals who had frustrated the paratroopers' designs but also for the comrades who were less ready than him to carry their rebellion to its logical end. "I took you for men," he says to them, "and you're nothing but good soldiers."[102]

99 Perrault, *Les parachutistes*, 164.
100 For a literary assessment of Jean Lartéguy see O'Connell, "Jean Lartéguy," 1087–97.
101 Lartéguy, *The Centurions*, 295.
102 Lartéguy, *The Praetorians*, 235.

Lartéguy clearly had Sentenac's death in mind as he wrote the passage describing the death of Boisfeuras, which, like Sentenac's, takes place in the sands of the Sahara. Like Sentenac, Boisfeuras props his head on his hand in his dying agony. Philippe Esclavier, the comrade who tells Boisfeuras's story, says, "His photograph, the one of him dying, is now hung up in most of the paratroop officers' messes. Boisfeuras has become a sort of symbol."[103] Lartéguy's account of Boisfeuras's death, however, also provided a wry commentary on the idealization of Sentenac. The final words attributed to Boisfeuras by the photographer who witnessed his final moments are a denial of purposeful existence – "Life, what an idiotic dream" – rather than the heroic declaration recorded on the official citation, which echoed the motto of the paratroops: "Victory is his who dares the most."[104] Skeptical of the official citation, the father of the dead hero refuses even to inscribe the words "He died for France" on Boisfeuras's tombstone. It is left to Esclavier, the officer who in *The Centurions* articulates the paratroopers' perception of themselves as latter-day Roman warriors heroically defending the frontiers of civilization, to sum up the lesson of Boisfeuras's death: "For us, the captains in these wars which we could only lose, the hated defenders of a bourgeois order that indulges in the luxury of a clean conscience while obliging us to protect its privileges, there was nothing left but to die or disappear, for we had ceased being useful and were becoming dangerous."[105]

Evidently, many paratroopers internalized the values embodied in the heroic myth of the paratrooper. Jean-Pierre Villaret, a paratrooper in a regiment of Hussars, returned from leave in September 1957 to discover that a close friend had been killed. In a letter to his family, Villaret accorded his comrade a hero's death: "he fell facing the enemy, as a true Hussar."[106] All the same, reflecting that his friend's mother, who had already lost her husband in the Second World War, would have an unbearable burden of grief now that she had also lost her only son, Villaret wrote that he was torn between pity and anger: "I would like to be able to do something for that poor woman and also to massacre hundreds of Arabs."[107] Otherwise, Villaret shared the alienation from civil society – and especially civilian politicians – that characterized the paratrooper mentality. Witnessing the "comedy" of Parisian politics, he wrote, caused him to question what he was doing in

103 Ibid., 301.
104 These dying words – "Qui ose gagne" – were attributed to Sentenac by Marcel Bigeard. See Bigeard, *Pour une parcelle de gloire*, 338.
105 Ibid., 313–14.
106 Villaret and Courilleau, *Lettres de deux appelés*, 152.
107 Ibid., 151.

Algeria: "What! Get oneself killed here, but for whom? For what?" Patriotism, for Villaret, was not enough: "Don't talk to me of idealism and of mother country, at least not in its symbolic form; don't speak to me of sacrifices [...] because there are too many of them."[108]

ATTITUDES OF SOLDIERS AND CIVILIANS

The bitterness expressed by many soldiers concerning the sacrifices they were called upon to make was accentuated by their sense that those sacrifices were only dimly appreciated by people at home. Pierre Leulliette's perception was that the public's general attitude was one of indifference – "let those who are sent to die, die ... and be silent!"[109] – but that it viewed the deaths of regular soldiers differently from those of conscripts. "What a business it is, a death in a regiment of conscripts! Announcement, communiqué, letters to relatives, etc. [...] Is it not the case that mayors even use the bodies returned from Algeria to organize, upon the coffins' return, painful demonstrations?"[110] On the other hand, claimed Leulliette, the deaths of regular soldiers were treated as an occupational hazard. "They didn't have to enlist" expressed the public attitude.[111] Reminding his readers that only about fifty thousand troops were truly "operational," Leulliette commented ironically that a German-born foreign legionnaire was far more likely to be called upon to die for France than a French conscript. Most French soldiers, he wrote disparagingly, "wait for the end guarding some farm surrounded by grapes."[112]

Leulliette's jaundiced assessment of conscripts who served in Algeria is only partially borne out by the testimony of the latter. Marc Secail – who despite his own anti-militarism expressed a rather grudging admiration for the foreign legionnaires he encountered – commented in a postscript to the diary he kept in Algeria that while small minorities of conscripts like himself either actively supported or opposed the war, the majority simply sought to keep their heads down and wait for *la quille*, which signified their return to civilian life: "those conscripts did not feel themselves to be concerned by this war, some went so far as to balk at or to refuse to participate in patrols in the month before *la quille*."[113] Maurice Mateos-Ruiz,

108 Ibid., 157–8.
109 Leulliette, *Saint Michel et le dragon*, 148.
110 Ibid., 117.
111 Ibid.
112 Ibid.
113 Archives de la Contemporaine, F/Delta/Reso831/Documents relatifs à la guerre d'Algérie. Marc Secail, *Livre de bord, guerre d'Algérie*, 109.

however, described a process he referred to as *engrenage*, whereby conscripts became caught up in the machinery of war. Their participation in operations alongside regular forces helped to prompt this process, which was powerfully accelerated by the desire to avenge the deaths of comrades. "After the deaths of their friends," wrote Mateos-Ruiz, "this war which concerned them only a little, becomes a truly personal and passionate affair for each one. The brave little conscripts of the beginning have become enraged and dangerous wolves."[114] The testimony of individual soldiers bears witness to this change of heart. "Surprised to find myself bellicose," wrote one after two of his friends were killed in an ambush. "I remark a clear change in myself, I have, since the engagement, a clear tendency to lose detachment."[115] Jean-Pierre Martel, who came to regard his section as "an ephemeral and protective family like none I have ever again encountered,"[116] wrote of his emotional response to witnessing death in combat. Following an ambush in which nine French soldiers had been killed and three wounded, Martel had tried desperately to save one whose femoral artery had been severed: "His blood spurts between our fingers with incredible strength. He dies very quickly while calling for his mother [...] I feel the unworthy rush of adrenaline and joy: 'I am alive, me.' This is transformed into aggression, but I don't have time to listen to all this tumult: we must get out of here."[117] Martel's anger was still intense days later as he stood stiffly to attention at the funeral ceremony for the nine soldiers who had been killed: "I was not sad, I was angry and cold."[118] By this time, though, his anger was directed less toward the enemy than toward the officers whom he held responsible for leading inexperienced soldiers into an ambush. Far from sharing Secail's indifference to the war, Martel was personally committed to the cause of *l'Algérie française* and saw domestic opposition to the war as a betrayal of his comrades who had died for that cause.[119]

The journal of Antoine Prost does not indicate as intense an emotional response to combat and to the deaths of his comrades as the memoir of Martel. Nevertheless, it does demonstrate an evolution in his attitude from a very reluctant beginning – "I don't want to kill, nor to be killed stupidly for nothing" – to a more engaged middle – "I don't wish for a glorious combat, principally because of the risks, and also because of what I think.

114 Mateos-Ruiz, *L'Algérie des appelés*, 76.
115 Maury, *L'empreinte de la guerre*, 176.
116 Martel, *La section*, 10.
117 Ibid., 131.
118 Ibid., 136.
119 Ibid., 166.

But what can one do, when one is there, except what is necessary to preserve one's self-respect and one's authority over the troops[?]" – and to a final preference for action rather than idleness: "Personally, I feel a certain nostalgia for operations: the early morning departures on the Bou Saada road in the cabin of my Ford, the assembled battalion, the bivouacs. This feeling of being caught up in a great machine – security – with at the same time the most total uncertainty about tomorrow, the next hour, and the possibility of combat always present, at once anticipated and feared."[120] Clearly, the attitudes of soldiers were as complex and multi-faceted as the war of which they were a part.

Nor were civilian attitudes toward the war any less complex than those of soldiers. The indifference to the war that many soldiers discerned on the part of civilians was real. It was hard to take much interest in a war that seemed interminable and inconclusive, particularly when there was so much with which to be preoccupied at home. The Algerian war occurred in the middle of the *Trente glorieuses*, the thirty years that followed the end of the Second World War, when France was in full transformation. The economy was booming, peasants were changing into businessmen and citizens into consumers. A new generation preoccupied with air travel and automobiles, rock music and television, had little interest in the French empire or in the values that had sustained it.[121] All the same, whatever they may have felt about the war or about Algeria, relatives of individual soldiers often cared a great deal about their fates. In his collection of testimony from conscripts who served in Algeria, Fernand Fournier included a text written by the sister of Louis Viard, an eighteen-year-old conscript who was one of fourteen soldiers who died when the convoy transporting them was ambushed on the coastal road N 17, between Ténes and Le Guelta on 12 November 1956. Louis Viard's sister recalled the grief she and her mother experienced when the mayor of Sainte-Suzanne-sur-Vire came to inform them of his death. "We were so overcome that we could not hold back our sobs. The pain was so intense that we could not speak, we were no longer ourselves. The priest tried to console us by saying that he died as a Christian, that a mass had been celebrated on his behalf. The policemen spoke of a death with honour, of duty accomplished, of dying for France. The mayor emphasized that he had not suffered, and that sadly thirteen other soldiers had suffered the same fate. We remained

120 Prost, *Carnets d'Algérie*, 63, 95, and 175.

121 On metropolitan indifference to the war and on the importance of these social and cultural changes, see Stora, *La gangrène et l'oubli*, 115–17, 211–14.

inconsolable, supporting one another in our terrible pain."[122] Only the
return of Louis's remains and their incorporation within the family tomb
in July 1957 provided any consolation to his mother and sister. "That
moment," his sister recalled over forty years later, "still moves me as if it
had happened yesterday."[123] The words of Hélène Erlingsen, daughter of
Clovis Creste, the soldier with the account of whose death this chapter
began, also bear witness to the enduring grief of family members. The most
painful moment of her years-long quest to learn about her father's fate
came in 2003, as she consulted a much-redacted report on his death in
the offices of the police services at the Charenton fort, on the outskirts of
Paris. Overcome by emotion, she was incapable of taking notes. Her request
for a photocopy denied, and unable to hold her tears in check, she returned
to her home in Toulouse, for the time being empty-handed. "To confront
the death of one's father, even fifty years later," she wrote, "is an ordeal."[124]
Such testimony is a reminder of the enduring suffering occasioned by the
tragedy of individual deaths. For France, the Algerian war has been difficult
to remember; for Louis Viard's sister and Clovis Creste's daughter, it was
impossible to forget.

FORGOTTEN SOLDIERS: *HARKIS*

Individual memories of the Algerian war, whether those of combatants or
of their civilian relatives, have until recently remained essentially private,
lacking any consolation that might have been provided by public commemoration. The Fifth Republic, embarrassed by its origins in a crisis
generated by the Algerian war and haunted by that war's legacies of defeat,
division, and internecine violence, consigned its memory to public oblivion.
Public commemoration and collective memory were dominated instead
by the heroic and unifying myth of French resistance during the Second
World War.[125] Only grudgingly was official recognition accorded to the
Algerian war. In December 1974, the National Assembly did at least
grant those who fought in it the official status of combatants that would
allow them to draw pensions commensurate with those of soldiers who
fought in other wars. Not until June 1999, however, did it concede the
legitimacy of referring to the conflict as a war and only in 2002 was an
official memorial established in Paris to those who had died. Even that

122 Fournier, *Paroles d'appelés*, 110.
123 Ibid.
124 Erlingsen, *Soldats perdus*, 673.
125 Stora, *La gangrène et l'oubli*, 220–2.

belated memorial, on the Quai Branly, which scrolls through a digital roll call of the dead (22,959 names), leaves empty spaces in the national memory.[126] It includes the names of 3,010 Algerian auxiliaries who were killed prior to 18 March 1962, but not those of untold thousands more who were vengefully slaughtered in the months that followed. Estimates vary between 10,000 and 150,000, with the scholarly consensus settling on 60–80,000.[127] Assuming the accuracy of that consensus, then the number of Algerian Muslims in French service killed in the war's aftermath was at least three times that of their European counterparts killed over its entire course. These soldiers, as well as many of their family members, including women and children, were subjected to acts of extreme cruelty as local leaders exacted a ritualistic vengeance for decades of colonialism. Khélifa Haroud, a *harki* who spent five months in military camps run by the ALN, recalled the fate of his fellow prisoners: "Sometimes, they chose a number of them and gave them pick-axes. They had to dig a hole where they were buried up to the shoulders[;] then they amused themselves by jumping from head to head as in hopscotch; or else, instead of burying the men, they filled the hole with straw and set fire to it. It was as horrible as the cries one heard at night because they were strangling one or they cut his throat, bleeding him to death."[128]

After several months of imprisonment, Khélifa Haroud weighed only forty kilos and was described by his wife as a "living dead man."[129] She had her own suffering to bear; her infant daughter died of starvation because she was afraid to go out to find food and other villagers were afraid to be seen giving help.

Despite the scale and horror of this tragedy, the *harkis* have nevertheless been condemned to a "triple silence" by the Algerian and French postwar states as well as by veterans themselves.[130] To the French army, as well, the memory of the *harkis* was a source of shame, given its failure either to honour guarantees against their abandonment or to protect them from their fate. In the aftermath of the war, it seemed that only diehard

126 For a thorough survey of the problem of the history of the war's memorialization which considers provincial as well as Parisian memorials, see Aldrich, *Vestiges of the Colonial Empire*, 136–56

127 Faivre "Introduction historique," in *Harkis: Soldats abandonnés*, 15–35. See also Faivre, *Les combattants musulmans*, 152–61.

128 Jordi, 'Khélifa Haroud: harki," 366.

129 Ibid.

130 Evans, "The Harkis," 128–9. Evans notes that although the *harkis* were denied the right in 1999 to lay a wreath honouring their dead at the Arc de Triomphe, two years later the date of 25 September was established as "France's first national Harki remembrance day." Ibid., 133

supporters of *l'Algérie française*, such as the officers who had participated in the putsch attempt of April 1961 and the OAS, wished to remember the *harkis*: to these individuals, the abandonment of "the most faithful children of France" was an indelible stain on the honour of the French army.[131]

CONCLUSION: A GENERATION SACRIFICED?

In purely numerical terms, although their war dead did not equal the 1.5 million "martyrs" later claimed by the Algerian state, Muslim Algerians, on whichever side they fought, collectively suffered a far greater loss of life than did Europeans serving in the French army. Nor, as has been noted, did France's losses in Algeria come close to matching those of its earlier wars. Despite this relatively low rate of military mortality, Raphaël Delpard nonetheless subtitled his book on French conscripts in the Algerian war "Sacrificed Generations."[132] Given that the concept of a generation sacrificed has commonly been applied, concerning France at least, to wars in which the loss of life was far greater than in the Algerian war, especially the First World War, it is worth considering why exactly Delpard employed this term.[133] He clearly did not intend to restrict its meaning to those soldiers who were killed in the war. Rather, he considered all French soldiers who had served in Algeria, whether they survived the war or not, to have been sacrificed.[134] They were, he wrote, sent to fight a war for which they were psychologically and militarily unprepared, against a people for whom they felt no animosity. Those who returned home, filled with shame and horror by their experience of this "dirty war," were rendered mute by society's indifference. "Before the indifference that he perceives, the conscript clams up, [and] turns inward upon his traumatized memory. He melts into the crowd, his forever-lost youth his only baggage." For some,

131 Ageron, "Les supplétifs algériens," 20. See also Ageron, "Le 'Drame des harkis,'" 3–15; Hélie de Saint-Marc, who participated in the failed coup of April 1961, compared the abandonment of the *harkis* to the notorious "Vel d'hiv" roundup of Jews during the Second World War as "one of the most shameful pages of French history." Saint-Marc, *Mémoires*, 290.
132 Delpard, *20 ans pendant la guerre d'Algérie*.
133 See, for example, on the First World War, Horne, *Death of a Generation*. On the Second World War, see Dalisson, *Les soldats de 1940*.
134 Delpard is not alone in making the exaggerated claim that three million Frenchmen served in Algeria. Delpard, *20 ans pendant la guerre d'Algérie*, 9. Jean-Charles Jauffret provides a more precise figure for the number of conscripts: 1,179,523. Jauffret, "Pour une typologie des hommes," 387. The total number of service personnel who served in Algeria, according to the Ministry of Defence, was 1,419,125. See *Journal officiel de la République française*, Débats parlementaires. Assemblée nationale. Question écrites et réponses des ministres, 4 August 1986, 2469.

denial of their war experience led to a sort of self-annihilation: "They think they are dead somewhere in Algeria."[135] For these survivors, life after Algeria was a sort of living death.

Although unashamedly partisan in its insistence that the war should never have been fought and one-dimensional in its insistence that conscripts universally rejected the war, Delpard's book makes an important point. Many soldiers who survived the war were angry at what they perceived to be the wasted sacrifice of their young lives. Some did not consider themselves to be much better off than their comrades who had been killed. A central paradox of the Algerian war in comparison with earlier wars was the unwillingness of conscript soldiers to accept a loss of life that was a fraction of that suffered with far greater resignation by those of earlier generations. Clearly, to many young soldiers, by comparison with their fathers' or their grandfathers' wars, their own was perceived to serve a less worthy cause, to employ less reputable means, and to promise less substantial results or rewards. While some professional soldiers in Algeria could confront death with equanimity as an occupational hazard or even as the fulfillment of a personal quest, men of the "contingent," conscripted for service whether they liked it or not, were more inclined to view the deaths of their comrades as a senseless waste, serving no useful purpose. The anger that many expressed in relation to those deaths may be best understood as the manifestation of a broader rage against the war and its waste of lives. Perhaps the most eloquent expression of this rage was provided by Daniel Anselme, a writer who never served in Algeria but whose 1957 novel *On Leave* powerfully conveyed the sense of those who had that they were a sacrificed generation. Jean Valette, one of three soldiers whose leave in Paris is the subject of the novel, is uncommonly precise in articulating the view that the survivors of their service in Algeria will be just as destroyed by it as those who are killed. "We're losing our youth and we'll lose the rest of our lives if it goes on much longer. I don't mean those who are already staying for good and the heaps of guys who'll end up that way soon. Listen hard: I'm speaking for all of us who will come back [...] What will they have got out of it if things go on at this rate [...] Maybe a motor scooter from the bonus, if they save it up. But what else? What will they get out of it apart from a motor scooter? What will they bring back in their heads? In their hearts? All our youth, all our lives are being wasted away."[136] The image of sacrificed youth is given symbolic expression later in the novel when one of the soldiers' uniforms tumbles out of its suitcase to lie "like a

135 Delpard, *20 ans pendant la guerre d'Algérie*, 300–1.
136 Anselme, *On Leave*, 116.

cardboard cutout of human remains on the carpet." Laughing hysterically, one of the three friends declares, "That's our youth on the floor! Best years of our lives!"[137]

Like the vast majority of the over one million young men who were conscripted for service in Algeria, the three friends of Anselme's novel do not shirk their service. Their bitterness at society's indifference toward them, however, knows no bounds. Anselme's picture of a Paris "ashamed of its badly dressed soldiers," yet consuming "whole cohorts of them, painting itself with their blood, morning, noon, and night, like a tart using lipstick," of a public indifferent to men in uniform but impassioned by the automobiles on the Champs-Elysées, evokes the moral confusion of a society in full transformation, selfishly discovering the joys of consumerism while heedlessly dispatching its youth to deal with unwanted legacies from the colonial past. *On Leave* powerfully conveys the anger of the last generation of French conscripts to be sent to war and their resentment at being called upon to fulfill the time-honoured rites of service and sacrifice for an indifferent homeland in a war without name.

137 Ibid., 140–1.

Conclusion

"Attack! Assault, assault!" The negotiator heard the desperate shouts on his telephone at 2:16 p.m., followed by the sounds of a struggle, accompanied by cries and groans. Unsure of what was happening, the negotiator spoke into the telephone: "Arnaud … Radouane … What's happening?" There was no reply. Then came two shots in quick succession, followed by a third. Finally, eight to twelve minutes after the initial appeal was heard, the security forces launched their attack. They were too late. By the time the Groupe d'Intervention de la Gendarmerie Nationale (GIGN)[1] reached him and killed his assailant, Colonel Arnaud Beltrame had already been shot three times and received several knife cuts to his throat. The wounds to his throat were fatal. Transported to the hospital at Carcassonne, Colonel Beltrame died on the morning of 24 March 2018. His wife Marielle and Father Jean-Baptiste, the Catholic priest who was to have performed a religious marriage ceremony for the couple in a few weeks' time, were at his side.[2]

Colonel Arnaud Beltrame of the Gendarmerie Nationale[3] died at the hand of Radouane Lakdim, a self-proclaimed holy warrior of the Islamic State organization (ISIS), after volunteering himself in exchange for a civilian hostage, a thirty-nine-year-old female employee of the Super U supermarket in Trèbes, in the Aude Department. On the morning of

---

1   "Intervention Group of the *Gendarmerie Nationale*."

2   For accounts of the events of 23 March 2018, see Carichon, *Arnaud Beltrame*, 169–84; Duplessy and Leprince, *Arnaud Beltrame*, 15–42; Alexis Feertchak, "Attentat de Trèbes: Le récit, minute par minute, du sacrifice d'Arnaud Beltrame," in *Le Figaro*, 22 June 2018; Soren Seelow and Julia Pascal, "'Taisez-vous c'est moi qui négocie': récit de l'attentat de Trèbes vu de l'intérieur," in *Le Monde*, 22 July 2018.

3   This is essentially a military formation with several branches entrusted with preserving domestic security. General Marc-Watin Augouard wrote in a report of 2008, "The military character of the gendarmerie is not just a strong element of its identity; it conditions its existence." Cited in Carichon, *Arnaud Beltrame*, 96.

23 March, Lakdim had already shot two men as they sat in their car in Carcassonne, seriously wounded a CRS officer as he returned to his barracks after a run, and, having driven to Trèbes, killed a butcher with a shot to the head as he stood behind his counter at the Super U. After taking his hostage, Lakdim demanded in exchange for her freedom the release of Salah Abdeslam, the surviving terrorist captured following the attack on the Bataclan nightclub in Paris on 13 November 2015. Advancing toward the agitated hostage taker alongside the officer commanding the Peloton de Surveillance et d'Intervention de la Gendarmerie (PSIG), Colonel Beltrame brushed past the officer, tersely insisting that the latter withdraw: "Shut up, it's me who negotiates. Get out of the supermarket." Ignoring his subordinate's pleas to find cover, Beltrame stood with his hands raised and spoke to the terrorist. "Let her go and take me in her place," he said, indicating the shop clerk.[4] Surrendering his pistol, the colonel disappeared into the store with the attacker, who shortly released his original hostage. A two-and-a-half-hour stand-off ensued, which ended only at 2:13 p.m. when the negotiator spoke briefly with the two men, first with Beltrame and then with Lakdim. It was at this moment that Beltrame, clearly counting on both Lakdim's distraction and on the prompt intervention of the GIGN, made his ultimately fatal attempt to overpower his captor.

The death of Colonel Arnaud Beltrame because of his deliberate choice to protect a civilian's life at the risk of his own had a profound impact on the French public. Newspapers and politicians hastened to pay tribute to Beltrame. Some people laid flowers on his grave in the village of Ferrals-les-Corbières, others placed them at the gates of their local gendarmerie. Municipalities renamed parks, squares, and streets in his honour. On 28 March 2018, Colonel Beltrame was also given a national funeral in which his flag-draped coffin was paraded through the streets of Paris, from the Pantheon to Notre Dame Cathedral and then to the courtyard of the Invalides. President Emmanuel Macron spoke at length during the ceremony, emphasizing not only that Colonel Beltrame had died "in the service of France," but that he embodied a quintessentially "French spirit of resistance [...] This inflexible determination in the face of barbaric nihilism awoke at once in our memories the great figures of Jean Moulin, of Pierre Brossolette,[5] of the Martyrs of the Vercors,[6] and the fighters of the

4 Ibid.

5 Jean Moulin and Pierre Brossolette were major resistance leaders who were tortured and killed by the Gestapo. The reputation of Moulin, pantheonized by de Gaulle in 1964, came to eclipse that of Brossolette, who did not receive the same honour until 2015.

6 Fighters of the maquis who mounted an uprising in support of the Normandy landings in 1944 that was ruthlessly suppressed by German forces.

maquis. Suddenly there arose darkly in the spirit of all French people, the chivalrous shades of the knights of Reims and Patay,[7] of the anonymous heroes of Verdun and of the Just [Among the Nations], of the companions of Joan and those of Kieffer[8] – finally, of all those women and men who, one day, had decided that France, French liberty, French fraternity would survive only at the cost of their lives, and that this was worth the price."[9] By evoking Joan of Arc and the knights of the Hundred Years War, the soldiers of Verdun, as well as the civil and military leaders of Free France and the Resistance, together with their anonymous followers, Macron proposed that there was a fundamental continuity in French history: that many generations of French men and women had been fighting and dying for the same idea of France, one that was inseparable from the abstractions of liberty and fraternity. Macron's speech implied that the sacrifice of each generation was imbued with something of the spirit of all those who had come before. Arnaud Beltrame's action on 23 March 2018 therefore embodied not just the spirit of resistance of the Second World War, but also the patriotic idealism of the First World War, as well as the religious and chivalrous values of the Hundred Years War.

President Macron was deliberately eclectic in his evocation of the pantheon of French heroes in his tribute to Arnaud Beltrame. Other commentators were more exclusive. Catholics took possession of Beltrame as a Christian hero whose action in exchanging his life for another was inexplicable without reference to his Christian faith. Insisting upon the idea of sacrifice, some compared Colonel Beltrame to Maximilien Kolbe, the Polish priest who had offered his life in exchange for that of another inmate of Auschwitz in 1941.[10] Jean-Baptiste, the priest from whom Beltrame received the last rites, declared his belief "that only a Christian faith inspired by charity could have demanded of him this superhuman sacrifice."[11] These assertions provoked the ire of the Left.[12] Laurent Joffrin reminded the

7 The site of a key victory for French forces over those of the English in 1429, during the Hundred Years War.

8 Philippe Kieffer was a naval officer who commanded French commandos during the Second World War, fighting at Dieppe, Normandy, and in the liberation of France.

9 Emmanuel Macron, "Homage national au Colonel Arnaud Beltrame," 28 March 2018, https://www.elysee.fr/emmanuel-macron/2018/03/28/hommage-national-au-colonel-arnaud-beltrame

10 Arnaud Beltrame's own mother expressed her repugnance at the idea that he intentionally sacrificed his life when he offered himself in exchange for the female hostage. "My son did not sacrifice himself," she wrote, insisting that he had every intention of overcoming the terrorist in the supermarket at Trèbes. Beltrame, *C'était mon fils*, 91.

11 Cited in Ghislain de Montalembert, "Arnaud Beltrame, un officier, un héros, un chrétien," in *Le Figaro*, 30 March 2018.

12 For analysis of these debates, see Duplessy and Leprince, *Arnaud Beltrame*, 101–27.

readers of *La Libération* that Arnaud Beltrame had been decorated for
bravery in Iraq long before he had discovered his Christian faith. "To speak
only of his Christian faith is to imply that his act of heroism is its direct
consequence," wrote Joffrin, "which nobody can support absolutely.
And behind this implication, there is another: only the Catholic identity
gives a meaning to the existence of citizens otherwise disorientated by an
epoch without ideals and without common values, undermined by individualism and mercantile consumerism." Protesting what he saw as the
exclusivist ideology of the Right – "Always Catholic and French!" – Joffrin
preferred to see Beltrame as embodying the republican virtues of fraternity
and humanity. "The itinerary of the procession that will follow the coffin
of Arnaud Beltrame translates this spirit of fraternal unanimity: it will arrive
at the Invalides, holy of holies of the military spirit. But it leaves from the
Pantheon, temple of republicanism."[13]

The death of Arnaud Beltrame, together with its political and cultural
aftershocks, is evidence that the theme of the soldier's death still has profound resonance for French society. His death and its many representations
are evidence that the soldier's death is infinitely malleable and, ultimately,
unknowable. In the flood of tributes and commentaries that followed his
killing, Arnaud Beltrame was represented in the guise of Christian saint,
chivalric knight, courageous patriot, brave *résistant*, devoted gendarme,
and antique hero. Yet nobody besides Arnaud Beltrame can know for
certain what he thought, felt, or intended during the final hours of his life.
Some reasonable deductions can be made by gathering evidence from his
personal history and the testimony of those who knew him, as well as by
considering the culture and values of the institutions that shaped his identity
and outlook. In all probability, the influences and motives that prompted
Colonel Beltrame to act as he did were as multiple and complex as that
action was itself singular and straightforward. The same might be said of
the other deaths considered in this study. The idea of dying for France,
encapsulated in the expression *mourir pour la patrie*, is a simple concept
behind which lies a much more complicated history.

Although the chapter heading for each of the periods or conflicts considered in this study implies a singular motive for which soldiers were
prepared to die, the reality is that soldiers fighting in any war at any time
die for many reasons, some of which they may be aware of and capable of
articulating and others that may be obscure to them or upon which they
remain silent. We began by considering the importance of honour, a value
of supreme importance to the Renaissance nobility that conditioned the

13 Laurent Joffrin, "Arnaud Beltrame: un héros pour mémoires," in *La Libération*,
27 March 2018.

behaviour of the knightly class during its long twilight. Although their personal honour took precedence over all other loyalties for warriors like La Trémoille, Bayard, or Monluc, honour was a commodious principle that ideally incorporated service to God, king, and country but which at times justified rebellion against royal authority as well as service in the employ of a foreign sovereign. Only very slowly, as the concept and powers of an impersonal state developed, did other allegiances, to king and country, and then to the nation, begin to overtake honour as reasons for which soldiers were called upon to sacrifice their lives. All the same, honour has enjoyed remarkable longevity as a fundamental motivation for warriors. It survived and prospered even as warfare became democratized. While the eighteenth and nineteenth centuries raised the nation to a pinnacle as the supreme cause for which they were called upon to sacrifice their lives, soldiers have often found honour to be a more immediate and compelling companion. While defence of their newly won freedoms inspired the soldiers in the armies of the French Revolution, by the time those armies embarked upon the conquest of Europe under Napoleon honour had returned to the fore. When French liberty was no longer threatened, soldiers continued to fight and die for their own reputations, for those of their regiments, and for the honours that tokened the respect of their emperor. Subsequently, honour has been an important referent for battles fought in a losing cause, justifying famous "last stands" at Camerone (1863), Bazeilles (1870), Saumur (1940), and Dien Bien Phu (1954). Honour also rushes in to fill the void in situations where the way of patriotism does not appear clear or where soldiers find political leadership or civilian support wanting. The soldiers who opposed the policy of Charles de Gaulle's government during the Algerian war and who supported the OAS usually did so by insisting that their honour took precedence over other considerations. Their self-justifications echoed, sometimes consciously, those of the seventeenth-century *frondeur* nobility.

As the continued relevance of honour as a source of motivation indicates, soldiers' motives for fighting have often had little to do with patriotism. Men who had little reason to feel loyal to the French nation preferred to face death rather than endure the shame of failing what they perceived as an essential test of manhood, or of losing the respect of their comrades. Failure for a soldier to demonstrate the required qualities of courage in the face of the enemy might have far-reaching consequences. If he survived, it might permanently impinge upon his prospects for marriage, employment, or social advancement. If he were killed, it might deny his relatives a pension or taint their own reputations. Furthermore, the soldier's willingness to sacrifice himself was influenced by his perception of his unit as a surrogate family whose members depended upon one another for their survival.[14] This awareness explains the desperation of Lieutenant Martin to rejoin his regiment when he became ill with typhus during the campaign of 1813, as it does the paternal affection of Jean-Pierre Martel toward the men he commanded in Algeria in the 1950s. Loyalty to the company or regiment works perfectly well as a substitute for patriotism, as is exemplified by the twin mottos of the French Foreign Legion: "*Honneur et Fidélité*" and "*Legio Patria Nostra.*"[15]

Like honour itself, the ideal of an honourable death in battle as a suitable end for a warrior is one that has proved remarkably durable. Representations of the deaths of Charles de la Trémoille at Marignano (1515), the Chevalier d'Assas at Clostercamp (1760), General Desaix at Marengo (1800), Ernst Psichari in Champagne (1914), and Sergeant Sentenac in the Sahara (1951) all conformed to a template that was established by the writers of the ancient world. Since the time of Homer, publicists have celebrated the death of the hero in the face of the enemy, ideally in the moment of victory, killed instantly from a blow struck by a worthy opponent and happy to sacrifice his young, beautiful life.[16] Writers from the Renaissance to the French Revolution were raised on the Greek and Roman classics, and it was from these that they derived their models of a fine death. Those models have, remarkably, survived the declining prestige of the classics and even the discredit brought upon them by the hyperbole of over-blown patriotic propaganda. Soldiers themselves internalized the values of that propaganda. Napoleonic *grognards*, First World War *poilus*, *appelés* of the Algerian war, even some Tirailleurs Sénégalais, resorted to a variant of this model in imagining ideal deaths for their comrades or themselves. To be sure, many of them showed their awareness that few soldiers experienced such fine deaths and that idealized representations of those deaths were often simply implausible. The instinctive resort to this model, however, is revealing of its enduring capacity to lend dignity to the dead and consolation to the living.

In fact, soldiers' deaths have rarely conformed to the ideal. The Renaissance panegyrists who celebrated the deaths of Bayard and Louis de la Trémoille were already trying to put a square peg in a round hole, exalting the nobility of combat as a face-to-face contest between equals even as it became an arbitrary slaughter in which firearms killed at a distance. The absolute numbers as well as the proportion of combat deaths has since escalated at rates commensurate with the growing firepower of

14   On expressions of this perception in popular culture, see Hopkin, *Soldier and Peasant*, 165.

15   "Honour and Loyalty"; "The Legion Is Our Homeland."

16   Vernant, "La belle mort d'Achille," 501–10; Vernant, "La mort héroïque," 69–86.

armies. This culminated during the First World War, when approximately two-thirds of all casualties were caused by artillery fire and 86 per cent of all deaths were a consequence of wounds received in combat.[17] The experience of the First World War, when eight million Frenchmen were mobilized and one in six of them died, was exceptional. Prior to that conflict, most soldiers did not die in battle. The Napoleonic wars are famous for their battles, yet fewer than one soldier in ten died on the battlefield.[18] Disease was more deadly than enemy action. In the Crimean War (1854–56), 20,000 men died in battle or from wounds sustained in combat; 75,000, nearly four times as many, died of disease, principally cholera.[19] The French intervention in Mexico (1861–67) is remembered by the French army chiefly because of the Battle of Camerone (1863), in which a company of sixty-five men from the Foreign Legion fought until forty-nine were dead or mortally wounded, twelve had been captured, and only three remained to surrender. Yet when the Legion departed Mexico in 1867, it had lost nineteen officers and 328 men in combat, twelve officers, and 1,589 men to disease.[20] Even in the Franco-Prussian war (1870–71), despite the terrible effects of the enemy's enhanced firepower at battles like Sedan or Saint-Privât, the number of French soldiers who died from smallpox, typhus, or some other disease was roughly equal to the number who were killed in battle or who died later of their wounds.[21] Difficult as it might be for us to understand, the hardships of life on campaign which made soldiers so vulnerable to disease also made them long for battle. To the soldiers who angrily confronted Napoleon on the island of Lobau after the Battle of Aspern-Essling, it was preferable to chance their luck on the battlefield, to make a bid for glory or at least a quick death, rather than face the torture of dying slowly from hunger or illness.

Even when they did result from combat, soldiers' deaths in modern war were for the most part anything but beautiful. Renaissance warriors expressed their repugnance at the effects of firearms, Napoleon's *grognards* their horror at being splattered by the brains of their comrades or at the

17 Chesnais, *Les morts violentes*, 179.

18 Jacques Houdaille estimates that 4.6 per cent of French soldiers serving in the armies of Napoleon died in battle. Houdaille, "Pertes de l'armée de terre," 35.

19 Ibid., 170.

20 Gouttman, *La guerre du Mexique*, 270–81. Estimates of casualties for the French army as a whole in Mexico are of similar proportions: approximately three times as many deaths from disease as from enemy fire. Gouttman estimates that 6,500 French soldiers died in Mexico, 1,500 in combat, 5,000 from disease, principally yellow fever. Ibid., 507.

21 Gaston Bodart estimated that the number of men killed or mortally wounded was 60,000 while the number who died of illness was 61,000. Bodart, *Losses of Life*, 151. See also Chesnais, *Les morts violentes*, 175.

sight of heaps of charred corpses. During the First World War, the surgeon Georges Duhamel acknowledged the ugliness of the soldier's death even as he sought desperately for ways to affirm its nobility. Death in war was banal as well as ugly, inspiring numbed indifference as often as horror. The ubiquity of death in wartime temporarily blurred the separation between the living and the dead at the same time as it diminished respect for the dead. Napoleon's men used the dead for cushions; those of the First World War made ramparts of their bodies. The enormous number of soldiers who died in the First World War, and the many terrible ways in which they died, undermined heroic representations of the soldier's death. The publication of photographs of battlefields strewn with human remains and of dismembered corpses discredited the heroic and sanitized representations of the hitherto ubiquitous *imagerie d'Épinal*. Although visual artists hesitated to reproduce images of the wounded body, there were some, like Luc-Albert Moreau, who contrived to do so in ways that communicated the suffering and despair of the soldier's death. Writers, too, in the aftermath of war, disseminated a disenchanted representation of the soldier's death as pointless misery, devoid of any notion of redemptive sacrifice. Without ever describing scenes of battle or of soldiers dying, Jean Giono encapsulated this viewpoint through his allegory of the slaughterhouse. These literary and artistic works stood as an enduring reproach to the consolatory images of the prevailing culture of commemoration.

The imperative to memorialize the dead through civic ritual and the construction of monuments existed even at the time of Francis I, but it did not concern most people until warfare became democratized at the time of the revolutionary and Napoleonic wars. During its most democratic phase, the revolution honoured the deaths of ordinary soldiers in tributes identifying them as martyrs of liberty. This democratic impulse did not endure. Under the Directory, it was the deaths of generals like Hoche and Marceau that were recognized, while Napoleon shifted the emphasis from honouring the dead to celebrating victory. Most soldiers who died in these wars were still buried in unmarked mass graves. The Franco-Prussian War marked a new determination to provide dignified resting places for all the war dead, resulting in the construction of ossuaries as well as many funerary and commemorative monuments.[22] This commemorative impulse culminated following the First World War, when the convention was established that every soldier who died should be buried in an individual grave unless his body could not be identified, in which case his name should be inscribed on a stone monument.[23] The naming of the dead was, as Thomas Laqueur

22 Varley, *Under the Shadow of Defeat*, 56–76, 104–12.
23 Capdevila and Voldman, *War Dead*, 46–8.

emphasized, central to the commemorative culture to emerge from the First World War and to an emotional economy – an age of "necronominalism" – which insisted upon recognition for the passing of ordinary lives.[24]

The commemorative culture that emerged from the First World War was conditioned by the absence of so many bodies. It was therefore focused upon symbolic sites of memory: battlefield ossuaries where the unidentified remains of the dead were collected, communal monuments on which their names were inscribed, above all the tomb of the Unknown Soldier beneath the Arc de Triomphe, which every bereaved family could imagine as the final resting place of the soldier for whom they grieved. The ceremonies that honoured the dead at these sites of memory adapted the nineteenth-century cult of the dead to the needs of a society in which nearly every family or commune had lost someone to the violence of war. The First World War marked both the culmination and the beginning of the end for the traditional cult of the dead. Soldiers' comrades as well as their female relatives struggled to uphold the established conventions of death at the same time as these came to seem increasingly impractical, inappropriate, or emotionally unsatisfying. The stylistic changes to widows' mourning clothes were a tacit recognition that, especially in wartime, women whose husbands had been killed still had lives to live.

There was no experience of military death on a comparable scale to that of the First World War in France's subsequent twentieth-century wars. In the Second World War, the number of soldiers who died was somewhere between 150,000 and 195,000.[25] This number was not only seven to nine times fewer than the number who were killed during the First World War, but it was also much more unequally distributed than during the previous conflict. It included 32,500 of the 130,000 men from Alsace-Lorraine who were compelled to serve in the German army.[26] Remarkably, after the defeat of 1940, more Frenchmen died fighting on the eastern front for Germany than died fighting in the west alongside the Allies.[27] Otherwise, the high proportion of colonized troops recruited after 1940 meant that families in Senegal and Morocco were more likely to be bereaved than those in metropolitan France. Furthermore, during the Second World War, soldiers' deaths were roughly matched by those of civilians. All these factors impinged

---

24 Laqueur, *The Work of the Dead*, 366.

25 The lower estimate is that of Pieter Lagrou; the higher is provided by Jean Quellien, who notes the importance of taking into account those soldiers – 36 per cent of the total – who died of accidents or illness. See Lagrou, "Les guerres, les morts," 320; Jean Quellien, "Les pertes humaines," 262–3.

26 Ibid., 262.

27 Lagrou, "Les guerres, les morts," 317.

upon the culture of commemoration after 1945. For the most part, new war memorials were not built; rather, the tradition began of adding to existing monuments plaques bearing the names of those who had died in the latest war. Otherwise, in the aftermath of the Second World War, the sacrifice of the soldier was partially eclipsed by that of the *résistant,* as the rulers of the Fourth and Fifth Republics forged a national identity based on the myth of universal resistance. The opposition cultivated its own version of the myth, communists identifying themselves as the "party of 75,000 *fusillés,*" on the basis of a vastly inflated estimate of those who were shot by the Germans.[28] A cornerstone of the "resistancialist myth" was the pantheonization of Jean Moulin in 1964.[29] The soldiers who had died fighting in the Second World War were honoured on 11 November 1945, when nine of them – including six from the colonies – were among the fifteen French citizens interred in the national war memorial at Mont Valérien. The military dead who were honoured still outnumbered the civilians. All the same, the location of this new site of memory, at a fort where resisters had been executed, placed them in the shadow of the Resistance.[30]

Since 1945, the number of French soldiers killed in war has continued its downward trend: 40,000 in Indochina, 24,000 in Algeria, 678 in External Operations (since 1963).[31] The shift in military mortality since the First World War was summed up by former chief-of-staff of the French Army Elrick Irastorza in an interview given in 2014. Twelve years of war in Afghanistan, he said, was equivalent in the number of deaths to twenty minutes in the First World War.[32] As the soldier's death has become less common, it has also become less acceptable. This represents a sea change in culture and mentalities that requires explanation, one that has been to a large extent occluded by an official discourse which denies that anything much has altered. According to that discourse, as we have seen, there has been a fundamental continuity extending over hundreds of years in the readiness of citizens to sacrifice their lives for France. Yet that readiness has in fact varied greatly according to time and place. Even during the First World War, when the sacrificial impulse achieved its broadest acceptance, there were limits – much debated by historians – to the consent of

28 Rousso, *The Vichy Syndrome,* 19.
29 Ibid., 82–97.
30 See reports in *Le Monde,* 12 and 13 November 1945.
31 Figures calculated with the assistance of the *Mémoire des hommes* database.
32 Maxime Tellier, "101 ans après la grande guerre," in *France Culture,* 11 November 2019, https://www.franceculture.fr/histoire/101-ans-apres-la-grande-guerre-la-mort-du-soldat-est-devenue-intolerable.

soldiers and citizens. During the revolutionary and Napoleonic wars, when universal conscription was first introduced, there was widespread resistance in some regions. The revolt in the Vendée broke out in 1793 when the National Convention attempted to raise men for the republican armies. In the nineteenth century, although generalized military service made the annual recruitment of conscripts a standard rite of passage for French youths, individual attitudes were often ambiguous. Recruits who drew an unlucky number at the recruitment lottery sometimes pinned a black ribbon to their hats as a symbol of mourning.[33] The war in the Vendée is also an example of how wars have often divided the French people against one another, rather than uniting them. The fact that French soldiers and their colonized subjects fought and died on both sides during the Second World War and the wars of decolonization has made especially problematic the representation and remembrance of those wars.

The divided loyalties and ambiguous moralities of both the Second World War and the wars of decolonization were important factors in affecting public attitudes toward the soldier's death. The Algerian war was the last fought by a mass army of conscripts. The disillusionment of many *appelés* in Algeria stemmed from their perception that the war they were fighting was not, like the First and Second World Wars, an existential struggle engaging the whole of French society. They were acutely aware of the disengagement of friends and family at home. Since the end of the war in Algeria, as European unification has pushed armed conflict to the continent's periphery, France's military interventions have been on a small scale and in complex political and military settings, most notably in Central Africa, Lebanon, the Balkans, and Afghanistan. Unlike the "total" wars of the past, these interventions are marginal to the concerns of most French people, whose attention is drawn to them above all when there are French casualties. The avoidance of casualties has consequently loomed large as a significant strategic calculation.

The public antipathy toward the soldier's death has also been encouraged by broader cultural change, especially changes in Western society's relationship with death. The decline in observance of the nineteenth-century conventions surrounding death accelerated after the First World War as society ceased to come to a halt to pay its respects to the dead. Life became healthier and death less familiar. Death was marginalized and medicalized, the dying quietly dispatched to hospital while around them normal life carried on uninterrupted. Mortality itself declined as vaccinations and antibiotics were deployed against infectious illnesses.

33 Hopkin, *Soldier and Peasant*, 150.

Life expectancy rose from fifty-two years in 1920 to seventy-six in 1990, the most spectacular gains coming in the twenty years from 1938 to 1958, when eleven years were added to the average life span. At the beginning of the twentieth century, one infant in seven died before its first birthday; by the 1980s, it was one in a hundred.[34] The reduction in infant mortality exposed the unnaturalness of youthful death caused by the violence of war. The rise of individualism also made the idea that was essential to the generations of the First and Second World Wars – the soldier's willing sacrifice for the sake of the *patrie* – increasingly alien to the generations that followed.

The professional nature of the modern French army and the formal ending of compulsory military service in 2001 have also served to distance the French public from the army and its values. Christophe Barthélemy sees a fundamental conflict between military and civilian values in contemporary France. "What is sacred for the soldiers is no longer so for the core of contemporary society. For the former, the mission is sacred and their lives may have to be 'sacrificed' for it [...] Inversely, for most French and Europeans today, it is human life, the fight against pain, youth, the 'normal' course of life from childhood to retirement that have become sacred."[35] Whereas death in combat is full of meaning for soldiers as the ultimate expression of their commitment to the profession of arms, to civilians it is a failure and a tragedy.

Barthélemy argues that solemn state funerals for French soldiers killed in action undermine public support for military operations by focusing on the emotion of compassion for the "victims." He proposes as an antidote for public incomprehension greater transparency about the risks of the military profession as well as more recognition for the heroism of its practitioners. Yet the vision of war and of the soldier's death that prevails in contemporary France is anything but heroic. The novels dealing with France's wars that have won the Goncourt prize in recent years all belong to the literature of disenchantment. Patrick Rambaud's *La bataille* (1997) represents in brutal detail the Battle of Aspern-Essling, graphically describing the death of Marshal Lannes as well as those of fictional soldiers. Alexis Jenni's *L'art français de la guerre* (2011) portrays the French as the perpetrators of a distinctively nasty "art of war" both in the colonies and at home. Pierre Lemaître's *Au revoir là-haut* (2013) focuses on the suffering and alienation of a *gueule cassée*[36] after the First World War, but also casts

---

34 Dupâquier, ed., *Histoire de la population française*, vol. 4, 234.

35 Barthélemy, *La 'judiciarisation' des opérations militaires*, 226.

36 "Smashed face." This was the expression used for soldiers with severe facial mutilations.

a critical eye on the postwar commemorative culture. The experience of the First World War remains an essential referent for this disenchanted, tragic representation of war and of the soldier's death. Films like *Un long dimanche de fiançailles*[37] (2004) and *La vie et rien d'autre*[38] (1989) reflect poignantly on the deaths of soldiers in that war as well as on the implications for those, especially women, who were left behind to pick up the pieces of their lives. The graphic novels of Jacques Tardi dealing with the experience of the First World War are unsparing in their representation of the violence done to soldiers' minds and bodies. These and other cultural artifacts reflect the enduring significance of the First World War as a turning point in the representation of the soldier's death.

Official tributes confirm this tragic view of war even as they resist it. Most tributes emphasize the value of lives lost, regardless of their numbers. The dedication on 11 November 2019 of a new national memorial to soldiers who had died in "external operations" (OPEX) since 1963 identified them as belonging to a fourth "front generation," or *génération du feu*, after those of the First and Second World Wars and of the wars of decolonization.[39] The intergenerational comparison, which President Macron also insisted upon in his speech at the monument's inauguration, affirmed that soldiers of all four generations had died in the same cause – "pour la France."[40] This comparison glossed over the disparity between the numbers of soldiers who died from each generation, avoiding the fact that a century ago France consented to a level of sacrifice that would be unthinkable today. The memorial sculpted by Stéphane Vigny represents a funeral cortège of six soldiers from different branches of the armed forces, "one woman and five men, representative of the French army in its diversity." The bronze figures shoulder an invisible coffin. The absence of a figurative representation of the dead soldier invites viewers to fill the void with their own memories of the dead (fig. 10.1). In the words of the sculptor, "The whole of the community participates in the grieving by helping to fill this absence."[41] The monument powerfully evokes the loss of war. The dead soldier, said Emmanuel Macron, is represented here as "the absent, the eternal, the irreplaceable. The emptiness he leaves, the lack he creates, is the heaviest of burdens. The six shoulders of our soldiers hardly suffice to

37 "A Very Long Engagement."

38 "Life and Nothing But."

39 Nathalie Guibert, '11 Novembre: les soldats morts en opérations extérieures entrent dans la mémoire collective," in *Le Monde*, 11 November 2019.

40 "For France." Speech of Emmanuel Macron, 11 November 2019, https://www.youtube.com/watch?v=WVuA5B_ZMMU.

41 Cited on the memorial garden's interpretive panel.

10.1. Monument to those who died in external operations. Sculptor:
Stéphane Vigny.

support it."[42] President Macron also acknowledged in his speech the "operational, human, familial consequences" of his decisions concerning military
interventions, that he was keenly aware of "the tragic part" of those decisions.[43] While one French general, François Lecointre, commented upon
the need "to reintroduce a vision of the tragic in our post-'sixty-eight-ish
society" and thereby to "revirilize" society, it is difficult to see how a monument evoking so poignantly the burden of loss is likely to fulfill those
hopes.[44] The reflection it offers on the soldier's death as essentially tragic
indicates how greatly society's attitudes have changed toward the ideal
for which so many generations have spilled so much blood: the ideal of
dying for France.

42 Speech of Emmanuel Macron, 11 November 2019, https://www.youtube.com/
watch?v=WVuA5B_ZMMU.

43 Ibid. See also Nathalie Guibert, "11 Novembre: les soldats morts en opérations
extérieures entrent dans la mémoire collective," in *Le Monde*, 11 November 2019.

44 Cited in ibid.

Bibliography

ARCHIVAL SOURCES

Archives de la Contemporaine

4/DELTA/08801 carton 1955-1961, no. 136. France. Algérie (Guerre d'Algérie).
Appels et tracts.
F/Delta/Reso831/Documents relatifs à la guerre d'Algérie. Marc Secail, *Livre de Bord, Guerre d'Algérie*.

Archives départementales de l'Hérault

1 J 1704. Famille Vatin, de Pézenas, 1766-1858. Accessed 27 February 2022,
https://archives-pierresvives.herault.fr/archive/resultats/tresors/vignettes/
FRAD034_00000016g/n:31?RECH_S=1+J+1704&RECH_TYPE=
exact&type=tresors.

Archives nationales

AA 62, pl. 1550, no. 47. Mémoire adressé par le prêtre assermenté Bricoteaux
ci-devant dominicain, à l'Assemblée nationale, pour célébrer le courage
du chasseur Lelarge lors de l'épisode de Clostercamp.

Service Historique de la Défense, Archives de Guerre

Armée de Terre: 26 N 714/6, *Journal Militaire Officiel*, 207ᵉ régiment d'infanterie,
20 December 1914. Accessed 24 March 2016, http://www.memoiredes
hommes.sga.defense.gouv.fr/fr/arkotheque/inventaires/ead_ir_consult.
php?&ref=SHDGR__GR_26_N_II.

Armée de Terre: B 5/7-12; B 5/7-13; B 5/7-73; B 5/8-17; B 5/8-20; B 5/8-27; B 5/8-2; B 5/8-39; B 5/8-56: Correspondance: Armée de l'Ouest. Accessed 24 March 2022, http://recherche-archives.vendee.fr/archives/fonds/ FRAD085_SHD_B.

Armée de Terre: 26 N 677/4: *Journal Militaire Officiel*, 106ᵉ régiment d'infanterie, 1 April – 20 June 1915. Accessed 24 March 2016, http://www.memoire deshommes.sga.defense.gouv.fr/fr/arkotheque/inventaires/ead_ir_consult. php?&ref=SHDGR__GR_26_N_II.

Armée de Terre: 1K 262: Souvenirs du Général Baron Bernard de Susbielle; Journal de marche d'un officier de l'Etat Major de la Division Susbielle.

Armée de Terre: 1Kt 842: Fonds Angevin.

Armée de Terre: Xw 30: Volontaires nationaux: Doubs, Drôme, Eure.

Armée de Terre: Xw 49: Volontaires nationaux: Indre.

Armée de Terre: AG Xw 66: Volontaires nationaux: Meuse.

Gouvernement de France, Ministère de la Défense, Base des Morts Pour la France de la Première Guerre Mondiale: Lemercier, Eugène Emmanuel. Accessed 24 March 2016, http://www.memoiredeshommes.sga.defense.gouv. fr/fr/arkotheque/client/mdh/base_morts_pour_la_france_premiere_ guerre/resus_rech.php.

University of Florida's Digital Collection: University of Florida Institutional Repository

World War I Diary of Albert Huet. Accessed 20 April 2016, https://helenehuet. org/albert-huet-wwis-diary/.

NEWSPAPERS

Le 18 Mars, Journal Hebdomadaire.
L'Ami Jacques, Argus du Département du Nord.
Annales Patriotiques et Littéraires de la France et Affaires Politiques de l'Europe.
L'Anti-fédéraliste.
L'Argonnaute.
Le Bien Public.
La Cloche.
Le Courrier de l'Armée d'Italie.
Le Courrier des Départemens.

Le Drapeau.
Echo de Paris.
L'Echo des Guitounes.
Face aux Boches: Bulletin Destiné à la Destruction du Cafard dans les Boyaux du Front.
Le Figaro.
Le Gaulois.
Gazette de France.
Gazette National, ou le Moniteur Universel.
La Guerre Illustré.

Horizon, *Journal des Poirus.*
L'Express.
Le Front.
L'Illustration.
Journal de Paris
Journal des Hommes Libres.
Journal Officiel de la République
    Française.
Le Messager du Soir.
Le Miroir.
Le Monde.
Le Monde Illustré.
L'Opinion.

Le Patriote.
Le Patriote Français.
Le Père Duchesne.
Le Petit Caporal.
Le Petit Courier.
Le Petit Journal.
Le Petit Moniteur Universel.
La République Française.
La Révolte.
Révolutions de Paris.
La Vie Moderne.
Le XIXe Siècle.

PRINTED WORKS

Ageron, Charles-Robert. "Aux Origines de la Toussaint 1954." In *La France en guerre d'Algérie: novembre 1954 – juillet 1962,* ed. Laurent Gervereau, Jean-Pierre Rioux, and Benjamin Stora, 20–9. Nanterre: Bibliothèque de documentation internationale contemporaine, 1992.

– "Le 'Drame des harkis': Mémoire ou histoire?" In *Vingtième Siècle. Revue d'Histoire,* no. 68 (October-December 2000): 3–15.

– ed. *Histoire de la France coloniale, 1914–1990.* Vol. 2. Paris: Armand Colin, 1990.

– "Les pertes humaines de la guerre d'Algérie." In *La France en guerre d'Algérie: novembre 1954–juillet 1962,* ed. Laurent Gervereau, Jean-Pierre Rioux, and Benjamin Stora, 170–5. Nanterre: Bibliothèque de documentation internationale contemporaine, 1992.

– "Les supplétifs algériens dans l'armée française pendant la guerre d'Algérie." *Vingtième Siècle. Revue d'Histoire,* no. 48 (October-December 1995): 3–20.

Agrippa d'Aubigné, Théodore. *Histoire universelle.* 10 vols. Paris: Librairie Renouard, 1886–1909.

Alberge, Claude. "Vie et mort des soldats de l'an II à l'Hôpital de l'Egalité de Pézenas." *Études sur Pézenas et Sa Région,* no. 2 (1971): 9–29.

Aldrich, Robert. *Vestiges of the Colonial Empire in France: Monuments, Museums and Colonial Memories.* Houndmills: Palgrave Macmillan, 2005.

Alexander, Martin S. "'No taste for the fight'? French Combat Performance in 1940 and the Politics of the Fall of France." In *Time to Kill: The Soldier's Experience of War in the West, 1939-1945,* ed. Paul Addison and Angus Calder, 161–76. London: Pimlico, 1997.

Alexander, R.S. *Bonapartism and the Revolutionary Tradition in France: The Fédérés of 1815.* Cambridge: Cambridge University Press, 1991.

Ambroselli, Catherine. *Georges Desvallières et la grande guerre*. Paris: Somogy, 2013.

Anonymous. *Archives parlementaires de 1787 à 1860: recueil complet des débats législa-*
tifs et politiques des chambres françaises, imprimé par ordre du Sénat et de la Chambre
des députés. Première série (1787–1799). 82 vols. Paris: Librairie Administrative
de P. Dupont, 1879–.

– "Le dernier combat de Marceau et les honneurs funèbres rendus à Marceau."
Carnet de la Sabretache: Revue d'Histoire Militaire Rétrospective (1899): 272–87.

– *Éloge funèbre du Général Joubert, Prononcé à Paris, le 15 Vendémiaire an 8, au Temple*
de la Jeunesse. Paris: Bertrand-Quinquet, n.d.

– *Éloge funèbre de Lazare Hoche, Prononcé dans le temple de Pithiviers, département*
du Loiret, le 30 vendémiaire, l'an VI. N.p.: Imprimerie J.F. Sobry, n.d.

– *Honneurs funèbres rendus au duc de Montebello, maréchal de l'Empire, présidés par*
SAS le Prince archichancelier de l'Empire, duc de Parme, dans l'église des Invalides, le
6 juillet 1810, anniversaire de la bataille de Wagram. Paris: Impr. Impériale, 1810.

– *Pompe funèbre du général Joubert, tué sur le champ de bataille.* Paris: Gauthier, n.d.

– *Précis historique sur le Régiment d'Auvergne, Depuis sa création jusqu'à présent,*
précédé d'une Épitre aux Manes du Brave Chevalier d'Assas. Clostercamp, 1783.

– *Procès-verbal de la Cérémonie funéraire en mémoire du Général Joubert.* N.p.:
Imprimerie de J. Gratiot et Compagnie, n.d.

– *Procès-verbal de la cérémonie funèbre qui a eu lieu sur la place de la Liberté, à Lyon,*
le 30 Vendémiaire an 6, en mémoire du Général Hoche. Lyons: Imprimerie de
Ballanche et Barret, Year Six [1797–98].

– *Recueil général des pièces, chansons et fêtes données à l'occasion de la prise du Port-*
Mahon. N.p., 1757.

– "Les seize hauts-reliefs du mémorial de la France combattante." N.p., n.d.

– *Vie politique et militaire de Latour-d'Auvergne, Descendant du Grand Turenne, Premier*
Grenadier des Armées françaises, tué à la bataille de Neubourg, le 9 Messidor an 8.
Paris, Year Eight [1799–1800].

Anselme, Daniel. *On Leave.* Translated by David Bellos. New York: Faber and
Faber, 2014.

Ariès, Philippe. *Essais sur l'histoire de la mort en Occident.* Paris: Éditions
du Seuil, 1975.

– *The Hour of Our Death.* Translated by Helen Weaver. New York: Alfred A.
Knopf, 1981.

Arnould, Arthur. *Histoire populaire et parlementaire de la Commune de Paris.* Lyons:
Éditions Jacques-Marie Laffont et Associés, 1981.

Arzalier, Jean-Jacques. "La campagne de mai-juin 1940. Les pertes?" In
La campagne de 1940: Actes du colloque: 16 au 18 novembre 2000, ed. Christine
Levisse Touzé, 427–47. Paris: Éditions Tallandier, 2001.

Aucourt, Claude Godard d'. *L'Académie militaire ou les héros subalternes.* N.p., 1745.

Audoin-Rouzeau, Stéphane. *1870: La France dans la guerre.* Paris: A. Colin, 1989.

– *Cinq deuils de guerre, 1914–1918.* Paris: Éditions Tallandier, 2013.

– *Les armes et la chair: trois objets de mort en 1914–1918.* Paris: A. Colin, 2009.

Audoin-Rouzeau, Stéphane, and Annette Becker. *14–18, Retrouver la guerre.* Paris: Gallimard, 2001.

Augarde, Jacques. *La longue route des Tabors.* Paris: Éditions France-Empire, 1983.

Auton, Jean d'. *Chroniques de Louis XII.* Edited by R. de Maulde la Clavière. 4 vols. Paris: Librairie Renouard, 1889–1895.

Babelon, Jean-Pierre, ed. *Chevalier d'Assas: Histoire et légende, exposition organisée par la direction générale des Archives de France.* Paris, 1960.

Bach, André. *Fusillés pour l'exemple 1914–1915.* Paris: Tallandier, 2003.

Bächtiger, Franz. "Marignano: Zum 'Schlachtfeld' von Urs Graf." *Zeitschrift fuer schweizerische Archaeologie und Kunstgeschichte* 31 (1974): 31–54.

Baconnier, Gérard, André Minet, and Louis Soler. "Quarante millions de témoins." In *Mémoire de la Grande Guerre: Témoins et témoignage,* ed. Gérard Cassini, 141–69. Nancy: Presses Universitaires de Nancy, 1989.

Balbaud, René. *Cette drôle de guerre.* London, New York, Toronto: Oxford University Press, 1941.

Balique, Gabriel. *Saisons de guerre: Notes d'un combattant de la Grande Guerre, août 1914 – décembre 1918.* Paris: L'Harmattan, 2012.

Bangerter, Olivier, *Novare 1513: Dernière victoire des fantassins suisses.* Paris: Economica, 2012.

Barbusse, Henri. *Under Fire.* Translated by Robin Buss. London: Penguin Books, 2003.

Barère, Bertrand. *Rapport fait au nom du Comité de Salut public, sur l'héroïsme des républicains montant le vaisseau le Vengeur.* N.p., Year Two [1794].

Barnaud, Nicolas. *Le secret des finances de France, descouvert, et départi en trois livres, par N. Froumenteau.* N.p., 1581.

Barthas, Louis. *Poilu: The World War I Notebooks of Corporal Louis Barthas, Barrelmaker, 1914–1918.* Translated by Edward M. Strauss. New Haven and London: Yale University Press, 2014.

Barthélemy, Christophe. *La "judiciarisation" des opérations militaires: Thémis et Athéna.* Paris: L'Harmattan, 2012.

Bartov, Omer. *Hitler's Army: Soldiers, Nazis, and War in the Third Reich.* Oxford: Oxford University Press, 1992.

Bary, Renaud de. *La 4ᵉ batterie: Journal intime d'un appelé en Algérie (1ᵉʳ mars 1961 – 5 janvier 1963).* Paris: L'Harmattan, 2014.

Beaudoin, Philippe. *Carnet d'étapes: souvenirs de guerre et de captivité lors de l'expédition de Saint-Domingue.* Paris: Librairie Historique F. Teissèdre, 2000.

Beaunier, André. *Les souvenirs d'un peintre.* Paris: Bibliothèque Charpentier, 1906.

Becker, Annette. *War and Faith: The Religious Imagination in France, 1914–1930.* Translated by Helen McPhail. Oxford and New York: Berg, 1998.

Bell, David A. *The Cult of the Nation in France: Inventing Nationalism, 1680–1800.* Cambridge, MA: Harvard University Press, 2003.

– *The First Total War: Napoleon's Europe and the Birth of Warfare as We Know It.* Boston and New York: Houghton Mifflin, 2007.

Bellay, Martin and Guillaume du. *Mémoires: collection complète des mémoires relatifs à l'histoire de France.* Vol. 17. Edited by M. Petitot. Paris: Foucault, Libraire, 1821.

Beltrame, Nicolle, with Arnaud Tousch. *C'était mon fils.* Paris: Albin Michel, 2019.

Belval, Challan de. *Carnet de campagne d'un aide-major, 15 juillet 1870 au 1er mars 1871.* Paris: Librairie Plon, 1902.

Ben-Amos, Avner. *Funerals, Politics, and Memory in Modern France, 1789–1996.* Oxford: Oxford University Press, 2005.

Benedict, Philip. *Graphic History: The "Wars, Massacres and Troubles" of Tortorel and Perrissin.* Geneva: Librairie Droz, 2007.

– *Rouen during the Wars of Religion.* Cambridge: Cambridge University Press, 1981.

Benedict, Philip, Lawrence M. Bryant, and Kristen B. Neuschel. "Graphic History: What Readers Knew and Were Taught in the *Quarante Tableaux* of Perrissin and Tortorel." *French Historical Studies* 28, no. 2 (Spring 2005): 175–229.

Benoist-Méchin, Jacques. *Ce qui demeure, lettres de soldats tombés au champ d'honneur 1914–1918.* Paris: Albin Michel, 1942.

Benoit, Christian, Gilles Boëtsch, Antoine Champeaux, and Éric Deroo, eds. *Le sacrifice du soldat: corps martyrisé, corps mythifié.* Paris: CNRS Éditions / ECPAD, 2009.

Bérenger, Laurent Pierre. *École historique et morale du soldat et de l'officier.* 3 vols. Paris: Nyon, 1788.

Béranger, Pierre-Jean. *Oeuvres complètes de Béranger.* 4 vols. Paris: Perrotin, Éditeur, 1834.

Berkovich, Ilya. *Motivation in War: The Experience of Common Soldiers in Old-Regime Europe.* Cambridge: Cambridge University Press, 2017.

Bernard, Vincent. "1000 victoires aériennes et 100,000 tués: les mythes héroïques du printemps 1940." In *Les mythes de la Seconde Guerre Mondiale,* vol. 2, ed. Jean Lopez and Olivier Wieviorka, 15–28. Paris: Éditions Perrin, 2017.

Bernède, Allain, and Gérard-Jean Chaduc, eds. *La campagne d'Égypte, 1798–1801: Mythes et réalités.* Paris: Musée de l'Armée, 1998.

Bernos, Charles-Étienne. "Souvenirs de campagne d'un soldat du régiment de Limousin (1741–1748)." *Carnet de la Sabretache: Revue d'Histoire Militaire Rétrospective* 10 (1902): 668–90, 737–62.

Bertaud, Jean-Paul. *La révolution armée.* Paris: Éditions Robert Lafont, 1979.

– "Le Théâtre et la guerre à l'époque de Napoléon." In *Armée, guerre et société à l'époque napoléonienne,* ed. Olivier Boudon, 177–88. Paris: Éditions SPM, 2004.

– "Military Virility." In *A History of Virility,* ed. Alain Corbin, Jean-Jacques Courtine, and Georges Vigarello; trans. Keith Cohen, 303–24. New York: Columbia University Press, 2016.

– *Quand les enfants parlaient de gloire: l'armée au coeur de la France de Napoléon.* Paris: Aubier, 2006.

– *Valmy: la démocratie en armes.* Paris: Gallimard, 1989.

– *La vie quotidienne des soldats de la Révolution, 1789–1799.* Paris: Hachette, 1985.

Bertaud, Jean-Paul, Daniel Reichel, and Jacques Bertrand. *Atlas de la Révolution française,* vol. 3: *L'armée et la guerre.* Paris: Éditions de l'École des Hautes Études en Sciences Sociales 1989.

Berton, Henri-Montan. *Le nouveau d'Assas, trait civique en un acte et en prose.* Paris: Des Lauriers, 1791.

Bertrand, Vincent. *Mémoires du Capitaine Bertrand.* N.p.: Friedland Books, 2017.

Besenval, Pierre Victor. *Mémoires de M. Le Baron de Besenval.* Vol. 1. Paris: Chez F. Buisson, 1805.

Besse, Jérôme-Étienne. "Mémoires du capitaine Jérôme-Étienne Besse, ancien soldat de la Grande-Armée." *Revue de l'Agenais* (1892): 255–62, 308–20.

Bessières, Albert. *Le train rouge: deux ans en train sanitaire.* Paris: Gabriel Beauchesne, 1917.

Beurier, Joëlle. "Voir ou ne pas voir la mort? Premières réflexions sur une approche de la mort dans la Grande Guerre." In *Voir ne pas voir la guerre: histoire des représentations photographiques de la guerre,* 63–8. Paris: Somogy, 2001.

Biard, Michel, and Claire Maingon. *La souffrance et la gloire: le culte du martyre de la Révolution à Verdun.* Paris: Vendémiaire, 2018.

Bigeard, Marcel, and Marc Flament. *Aucune bête au monde.* Paris: Éditions de la Pensée Moderne, 1959.

Bigeard, Marcel. *Pour une parcelle de gloire.* Paris: Plon, 1975.

Bigmann, Louis. *Charles N'Tchoréré face aux nazis.* Paris: Éditions Duboiris, 2010.

Bimberg, Edward L. *Mountain Warriors: Moroccan Goums in World War II.* Mechanicsburg: Stackpole Books, 1999.

Binder, Michaela, and Leslie Quade. "Death on a Napoleonic Battlefield – Peri-mortem Trauma in Soldiers from the Battle of Aspern 1809." *International Journal of Paleopathology* 22 (2018): 66–77.

Binyon, Laurence. "For the Fallen." In *Poetry of the First World War: An Anthology,* ed. Tim Kendall, 44. Oxford: Oxford University Press, 2013.

Biver, Marie-Louise. *Le Paris de Napoléon.* Paris: Librairie Plon, 1963.

Black, Jeremy. *European Warfare, 1494–1660.* London and New York: Routledge, 2002.

– *European Warfare, 1660–1815*. London: UCL Press, 1994.

Blanchecotte, Augustine. *Tablettes d'une femme pendant la Commune*. Paris: Didier et Cie., 1872.

Bloch, Marc. *L'histoire, la guerre, la résistance*. Paris: Gallimard, 2006.

Bodart, Gaston. *Losses of Life in Modern Wars: Austria-Hungary; France*. Oxford: Clarendon Press, 1916.

Bois, Jean-Pierre. *Fontenoy 1745: Louis XV, arbitre de l'Europe*. Paris: Economica, 1995.

Boltanski, Ariane. "'Dans cette bataille, tomba et fut écrasée la tête du serpent': Les usages idéologiques de la mort du prince de Condé dans le camp Catholique." In *La Bataille: Du fait d'armes au combat idéologique, XIe–XIXe siècle*, ed. Ariane Boltanski, Yann Lagadec, and Franck Mercier, 123–41. Rennes: Presses Universitaires de Rennes, 2015.

Bonnet, Gabriel. *Mémorial de l'empire: à la gloire des troupes coloniales*. Toulouse: Sequana, 1941.

Bouchet, Jean. *Le panégyrique du chevalier sans reproche, ou Mémoires de la Trémouille*. Paris: J.-L.-F. Foucault, Libraire, 1820.

Bouchet de Fareins, Serge. *De l'Ain au Danube: Témoignages de vétérans de la Première Armée Française (1944–1945)*. Paris: L'Harmattan, 2012.

Boudon, Jacques-Olivier. *La campagne d'Egypte*. Paris: Belin, 2018.

Bourcier, Claudine, *Nos chers blessés: Une infirmière dans la Grande Guerre*. Saint-Cyr-sur-Loire: Alan Sutton, 2002.

Bourdeille, Pierre de. *Oeuvres complètes de Pierre de Bourdeille, seigneur de Brantôme*. Edited by Ludovic Lalanne. 11 vols. Paris: Renouard, 1864–82.

Bourdon, Léonard. *Convention nationale. Recueil des actions héroïques et civiques des républicains français*. Paris: Imprimerie Nationale, Year Two [1793–94].

Bourgogne, Adrien-Jean-Baptiste-François. *Mémoires du Sergent Bourgogne (1812–1813)*. Edited by Paul Cottin and Maurice Henault. Paris: Librairie Hachette, 1910.

Bourquin, Laurent. "Les carrières militaires de la noblesse au XVIIe siècle: Représentations et engagements." In *La noblesse de la fin du XVIe siècle au début du XXe siècle: un modèle social?*, ed. Josette Pontet, Michel Figeac, and Marie Boisson, 271–88. Anglet: Atlantica, 2002.

Bouscayrol, René. *Cent lettres de soldats de l'an II*. Paris: Aux Amateurs de Livres, 1989.

Branche, Raphaëlle. *L'embuscade de Palestro: Algérie 1956*. Paris: Éditions La Découverte, 2018.

Brécy, Robert, *Florilège de la chanson révolutionnaire*. Paris: Les Éditions Ouvrières, 1990.

Bréton, Geneviève. *Journal, 1867–1871*. Paris: Éditions Ramsay, 1985.

Brévet, Matthieu. "Les expéditions coloniales vers Saint-Domingue et les Antilles (1802–1810)." Unpublished doctoral thesis. Université de Lyon II, 2007.

Bricard, Louis-Joseph. *Journal du Canonnier Bricard*. Paris: Librairie Ch. Delagrave, 1891.

Broche, François. *La cathédrale des sables: Bir Hakeim, 26 mai–11 juin 1942*. Paris: Belin, 2019.

Brockliss, Laurence, and Colin Jones. *The Medical World of Early Modern France*. Oxford: Clarendon Press, 1997.

Brown, Howard. *Mass Violence and the Self: From the French Wars of Religion to the Paris Commune*. Ithaca and London: Cornell University Press, 2018.

Buatois, Olivia. "Un général du Directoire: Joubert." Unpublished master's thesis, Université de Bourgogne, Dijon, 1990.

Buchinger, Kirstin. "'*La pierre et l'empereur*': Remembering the Revolutionary and Napoleonic Wars in French Lithography." In *War Memories: The Revolutionary and Napoleonic Wars in Modern European Culture*, ed. Alan Forrest, Étienne François, and Karen Hagemann, 317–39. Houndmills: Palgrave Macmillan, 2012–13.

Buton, Philippe, and Marc Michel, eds. *Combattants de l'empire: les troupes coloniales dans la Grande Guerre*. Paris: Vendémiaire, 2018.

Cadeau, Yvan, and Ivan Cadeau. "Retrouver son rang et gagner sa place. Le rôle du Belvédère dans l'Armée Française Renaissante." *Guerres Mondiales et Conflits Contemporains*, no. 259 (July–September 2015): 21–37.

Cadet, Nicolas. *Honneur et violences de guerre au temps de Napoléon: la campagne de Calabre*. Paris: Vendémiaire, 2015.

Calvet, Musée. *La mort de Bara: De l'événement au mythe: Autour du tableau de Jacques-Louis David*. Avignon: Musée Calvet, 1989.

Cannadine, David. "War and Death, Grief and Mourning in Modern Britain." In *Mirrors of Mortality: Studies in the Social History of Death*, ed. Joachim Whaley, 187–242. London: Europa Publications, 1981.

Cantarel-Besson, Yveline. "Les morts exemplaires dans la peinture militaire." *Revue de l'Institut Napoléonien*, no. 133 (1977): 97–105.

Capdevila, Luc, and Danièle Voldman. *War Dead: Western Societies and the Casualties of War*. Translated by Richard Veasey. Edinburgh: Edinburgh University Press, 2006.

Carichon, Christophe. *Arnaud Beltrame, gendarme de France*. Monaco: Éditions du Rocher, 2018.

Cariou, André. *Jean-Julien Lemordant*. Plomelin: Éditions Palantines, 2006.

Carlier, Émile. *Mort? Pas encore! Mes souvenirs, 1914–1918, Par un ancien soldat du 127ᵉ R.I.* Douai: Société Archéologique de Douai, 1993.

Carloix, François. *Mémoires de la vie de François de Scépeaux, sire de Vielleville et comte de Durestal, maréchal de France*. Paris: Ed. du commentaire analytique du Code civil, 1838.

Carroll, Stuart. *Blood and Violence in Early Modern France*. Oxford: Oxford University Press, 2006.

Céline, Louis-Ferdinand. *Voyage au bout de la nuit*. Paris: Folioplus Classiques, 2006.

Chaine, Pierre. *Les mémoires d'un rat*. Paris: Éditions Tallandier, 2008.

Chalert, Alexandre. *Impressions d'un soldat. La campagne de 1870 racontée par un lieutenant alsacien pendant sa captivité à Mersebourg*. Strasbourg: Treuttel and Wurtz, 1908.

Chamard, Elie. "Les combats de Saumur: Juin 1940." *Revue des Deux Mondes* 64, no. 2 (15 July 1941): 211–25.

– *Les combats de Saumur, Juin 1940*. Paris: Éditions Berger-Levrault, 1948.

Chambe, René. *Le bataillon du Belvédère*. Paris: Éditions J'ai Lu, 1965.

– *L'épopée française d'Italie*. Paris: Flammarion, 1952.

Champier, Symphorien. *Histoire des gestes du preux et vaillant Chevalier Bayard Dauphinois*. Lyon: Benoist Rigaud, 1580.

Chantron, Alphonse. *Souvenirs et impressions d'un jeune captif*. Lyon: Imprimerie Emmanuel Vitte, 1904.

Charron, Pierre. *De la sagesse, Trois livres*. Paris: Chez David Douceur, 1604.

Chenu, Jean-Charles. *Rapport au conseil de la Société française de secours aux blessés des armées de terre et de mer sur le service médico-chirugical des ambulances et des hôpitaux pendant la guerre de 1870–1871*. 2 vols. Paris: Librairie Militaire de J. Dumaine, 1874.

Chesnais, Jean-Claude, *Les morts violentes en France depuis 1826*. Paris: Presses Universitaires de France, 1976.

Chevalier, Gabriel. *La peur*. Paris: Le Dilettante, 2008.

Chevalier, Jean-Michel. *Souvenirs des guerres napoléoniennes*. Edited by Jean Mistler and Hélène Michaud. Paris: Hachette, 1970.

Chominot, Marie, and Benjamin Stora. *Regards sur l'Algérie: 1954–1962*. Paris: Éditions Gallimard / Ministère de la Défense, 2016.

Clairville, Charles. *Quatorze ans de la vie de Napoléon, ou Berlin, Potsdam, Paris, Waterloo et Sainte-Hélène*. Paris: Barbier, 1830.

Claretie, Jules. *L'art et les artistes français contemporains*. Paris: Charpentier, 1876.

Clarke, Joseph. *Commemorating the Dead in Revolutionary France: Revolution and Remembrance, 1789–1799*. Cambridge: Cambridge University Press, 2007.

– "'Valour Knows Neither Age nor Sex': The *Recueil des Actions Héroïques* and the Representation of Courage in Revolutionary France." *War in History* 20, no. 1 (January 2013): 50–75.

Clayton, Anthony. *Paths of Glory: The French Army 1914–1918*. London: Cassell, 2003.

Clifford, Dale Lothrop. "Aux armes citoyens! The National Guard in the Paris Commune of 1871." Unpublished PhD dissertation, University of Tennessee, 1975.

Cochet, François. "Mourir au front et à l'arrière-front." In *Le soldat et la mort dans la Grande Guerre*, edited by Isabelle Homer and Emmanuel Pénicault, 27–40. Rennes: Presses Universitaires de Rennes, 2016.

– "Stéréotypes contradictoires." In *Combattants de l'empire*, ed. Philippe Buton and Marc Michel, 261–78. Paris: Vendémiaire, 2018.

Collignon. "Ode funéraire sur la mort du Général Joubert." N.p.: Chez Gauthier, n.d.

Compiègne, Victor Du Pont de. "Souvenirs d'un Versaillais pendant le second siège de Paris." In *1871 – La Commune de Paris – Les Versaillais*, by Victor de Compiègne and Laurent Martin. Paris: Éditions Laville, 2012.

Conombo, Joseph Issoufou. *Souvenirs de guerre d'un "Tirailleur Sénégalais."* Paris: L'Harmattan, 1989.

Constant, Jean-Marie. *La noblesse française aux XVIᵉ et XVIIᵉ siècles*. Paris: Hachette, 1985.

Contamine, Philippe. "Mourir pour la patrie." In *Les lieux de mémoire* (1986). *II: La Nation*, vol. 3, ed. Pierre Nora, 11–44. Paris: Éditions Gallimard, 1986.

Cornet, Mathieu-Augustine. *Discours prononcé par Cornet, Président du Conseil des Anciens, à l'occasion de la mort du général Joubert*. Paris: Imprimerie Nationale, Year Seven [1798–99].

Cornette, Joël. *Le roi de guerre: Essai sur la souveraineté dans la France du Grand Siècle*. Paris: Éditions Payot et Rivages, 2010.

Corvisier, André. *L'Armée française de la fin du XVIIᵉ siècle au ministère de Choiseul: le soldat*. 2 vols. Paris: Presses Universitaires de France, 1964.

– "La mort du soldat depuis la fin du Moyen Age." In *Les hommes, la guerre et la mort*, by André Corvisier, 367–94. Paris: Economica, 1985.

– "Les 'héros subalternes' dans la littérature du milieu du XVIIIᵉ siècle et la réhabilitation du militaire." *Revue du Nord* 66, no. 261–2 (April-September 1984): 827–38.

– *Les hommes, la guerre et la mort*. Paris: Economica, 1985.

Courtilz de Sandras, Gatien. *La conduite de Mars*. Cologne: n.p., 1693.

– *Mémoires de Charles de Batz-Castelmore Comte d'Artagnan*. Paris: Chez Henri Jonquières, Éditeur, 1928.

Crémieux-Brilhac, Louis. *La France libre*. 2 vols. Paris: Éditions Gallimard, 2013.

Crivello, Marcel. *Souvenirs de là-bas et d'ailleurs*. Flayosc, Var: privately published, 1996.

Crouzet, Denis. *Les guerriers de dieu: la violence au temps des troubles de religion vers 1525 – vers 1610*. 2 vols. Paris: Champ Vallon, 1990.

– "Un chevalier entre les 'machoires de la mort': note à propos de Bayard et de la guerre au début du XVIᵉ siècle." In *La vie, la mort, la foi, le temps: mélanges offerts à Pierre Chaunu*, ed. Jean-Pierre Bardet and Madelein Foisil, 285–94. Paris: Presses Universitaires de France, 1993.

Cru, Jean-Norton. *Témoins: Essai d'analyse et de critique des souvenirs de combattants édités en français de 1915 à 1928*. Nancy: Presses Universitaires de Nancy, 1993.

Cuvillier, Solange. *Tribulations d'une femme dans l'armée française ou le patriotisme écorché*. Paris: Éditions Lettres du Monde, 1991.

Cuzacq, Germain. *Le soldat de Lagraulet: Lettres de Germain Cuzacq écrites du front entre août 1914 et septembre 1916 recueillies et commentées par Pierre et Germaine Leshauris*. Toulouse: Eché, 1984.

Dagen, Philippe. *Le silence des peintres: les artistes face à la Grande Guerre*. Paris: Hazan, 2012.

Dalisson, René. *11 Novembre: du souvenir à la mémoire*. Paris: Armand Colin, 2013.

– *Les soldats de 1940: une génération sacrifiée*. Paris: CNRS Éditions, 2020.

Dalotel, Alain. "La barricade des femmes." In *La Barricade*, ed. Alain Corbin and Jean-Marie Mayeur, 341–55. Paris: Publications de la Sorbonne, 1997.

Datta, Venita. *Heroes and Legends of Fin-de-Siècle France: Gender, Politics, and National Identity*. Cambridge: Cambridge University Press, 2011.

Dejaure, Jean-Elie Bédéno. *Le nouveau d'Assas, trait civique en un acte et en prose mêlé de chants*. Paris: Vente, 1790.

Delmas, Jean, ed. *Histoire militaire de la France*, vol. 2: *De 1715 à 1871*. Paris: Presses Universitaires de France, 1992.

Delpard, Raphaël. *20 ans pendant la guerre d'Algérie: Générations sacrifiées*. Neuilly-sur-Seine, Éditions Michel Lafon, 2001.

Delvert, Charles. *Carnets d'un fantassin (7 août 1914 – 16 août 1916)*. Clamecy: Éditions des Riaux, 2003.

Deroo, Eric, and Antoine Champeaux. "Mourir, l'appel à l'empire." In *Culture coloniale en France. De la Révolution française à nos jours*, ed. Pascal Blanchard, Sandrine Lemaire, and Nicolas Bancel, 163–72. Paris: CNRS Éditions/Autrement, 1994.

– "Panorama des troupes coloniales françaises dans les deux guerres mondiales." *Revue Historique des Armées*, no. 271 (July 2013): 72–88.

Déroulède, Paul. *Nouveaux chants du soldat*. Paris: Calmann Lévy, Éditeur, 1883.

Deruelle, Benjamin. *De papier, de fer et de sang: Chevaliers et chevalerie à l'épreuve de la modernité (ca 1460 – ca 1620)*. Paris: Publications de la Sorbonne, 2015.

– "'Faire bonne guerre': Idéal chevaleresque, comportements guerriers et régulation sociale dans la bataille de Dreux (1562)." In *La bataille: du fait* *d'armes au combat idéologique, XIe–XIXe siècle*, ed. Ariane Boltanski, Yann Lagadec, and Franck Mercier, 109–22. Rennes: Presses Universitaires de Rennes, 2015.

Desgenettes, René-Nicolas Dufriche. *Histoire médicale de l'Armée d'Orient.* Paris: Croullebois, 1802.

Diallo, Bakary. *Force-Bonté.* Paris: F. Rieder et Cie., Éditeurs, 1926.

Diderot, Denis et al., eds. *Encyclopédie ou dictionnaire raisonné des sciences, des arts et des métiers.* 39 vols. Geneva: chez Pellet imprimeur-libraire, 1777–79.

Diefendorf, Barbara B. *Beneath the Cross: Catholics and Huguenots in Sixteenth-Century Paris.* New York and Oxford: Oxford University Press, 1991.

Dine, Philip. *Images of the Algerian War: French Fiction and Film, 1954–1992.* Oxford: Clarendon Press, 1994.

Dodman, Thomas. *What Nostalgia Was: War, Empire, and the Time of a Deadly Emotion.* Chicago: University of Chicago Press, 2018.

Dorat-Cubières, M. *Les regrets d'un Français sur la mort de Latour-d'Auvergne-Cornet, premier grenadier de la République; Précédée d'un notice historique sur sa vie et ses exploits, ou Le modèle des guerriers; Poème adressée aux Armées françaises.* Paris: n.p., Year Eight [1799–1800].

Dorgelès, Roland. *Les croix de bois.* Paris: Albin Michel, 1931.

Douazac. *Dissertation sur la subordination, avec des réflexions sur l'exercice et sur l'art militaire.* Avignon, 1753.

Doughty, Robert A. *Pyrrhic Victory: French Strategy and Operations in the Great War.* Cambridge, MA: Belknap Press of Harvard University Press, 2008.

Doumbi-Fakoly. *Morts pour la France.* Paris: Éditions Karthala, 1982.

Drévillon, Hervé. *Batailles: scènes de guerre de la Table Ronde aux tranchées.* Paris: Éditions du Seuil, 2006.

– *L'impôt du sang: le métier des armes sous Louis XIV.* Paris: Tallandier, 2005.

– *L'individu et la guerre: du Chevalier Bayard au Soldat inconnu.* Paris: Éditions Belin, 2013.

Drévillon, Hervé, and Olivier Wieviorka, eds. *Histoire militaire de la France.* 2 vols. Paris: Perrin / Ministère des Armées, 2018.

Dubois, Alexis. *La mort du Chevalier d'Assas, ou la bataille de Clostercamp. Pièce patriotique, en trois actes et en prose.* Lyons: de l'Imprimerie de P. Bernard, 1791.

Ducrot, Auguste-Alexandre. *La défense de Paris (1870–1871).* 4 vols. Paris: E. Dentu, 1875–78.

Dufour, Frédérique. "Le sacrifice du soldat dans la littérature." In *Le sacrifice du soldat*, ed. Christian Benoit Gilles Boëtsch, Antoine Champeaux, and Éric Deroo, 183–7. Paris: ECPAD and CNRS Éditions, 2009.

Duhamel, Georges. *La pesée des âmes, 1914–1919.* Paris: Mercure de France, 1949.

– *Vie des martyrs et autres récits des temps de guerre.* Paris: Omnibus, 2005.

Duhamel, Blanche, and Georges Duhamel. *Correspondance de guerre, 1914–1919.* 2 vols. Paris: Honoré Champion Éditeur, 2007.

Dumaine, Sylvie. "Luc-Albert Moreau (1882–1948): Un peintre dans la Grande Guerre." Unpublished doctoral thesis, University of Lille, 2011.

Dupâquier, Jacques, Alfred Sauvy, and Emmanuel Le Roy Ladurie, eds. *Histoire de la population française.* 4 vols. Paris: Presses Universitaires de France, 1988–89.

Duparc, Arthur. *Correspondance de Henri Regnault.* Paris: Charpentier et Cie, 1872.

Duplessy, Jacques, and Benoît Leprince. *Arnaud Beltrame, le héros dont la France a besoin.* Paris: Éditions de l'Observatoire / Humensis, 2018.

Dupuy, Roger. *La Garde nationale.* Paris: Gallimard, 2010.

Durkheim, Jean. *Tirailleur couscous.* Paris: Éditions France-Empire, 1965.

Dwyer, Philip. *Napoleon: Passion, Death and Resurrection.* London: Bloomsbury Publishing, 2018.

– "Public Remembering, Private Reminiscing: French Military Memoirs and the Revolutionary and Napoleonic Wars." *French Historical Studies* 33, no. 2 (2010): 231–58.

– "War Stories: French Veteran Narratives and the 'Experience of War' in the Nineteenth Century." *European History Quarterly* 41, no. 4 (2011): 561–85.

Ellis, John. *On the Front Lines.* New York: Wiley, 1991.

Echenberg, Myron. *Colonial Conscripts: The Tirailleurs Sénégalais in French West Africa, 1857–1960.* Portsmouth, NH, and London: Heinemann and James Currey, 1991.

Erlingsen, Hélène. *Soldats perdus: de l'Indochine à l'Algérie, dans la tourmente des guerres coloniales.* Paris: Bayard, 2007.

Ernouf, Adolphe-Auguste. *Souvenirs d'un officier polonais: scènes de la vie militaire en Espagne et en Russie (1808–1812).* Paris: Charpentier, 1877.

Etlin, Richard. *The Architecture of Death: The Transformation of the Cemetery in Eighteenth-Century Paris.* Cambridge, MA: MIT Press, 1984.

Evans, Martin. "The *Harkis*: The Experience and Memory of France's Muslim Auxiliaries." In *The Algerian War and the French Army, 1954–1962: Experiences, Images, Testimonies,* ed. Martin S. Alexander, Martin Evans, and J.F.V. Keiger, 117–33. Houndmills: Palgrave Macmillan, 2002.

Fairon, Émile, and Henri Heuse, eds. *Lettres de grognards.* Liège: Imprimerie Bénard, S.A., 1936.

Faivre, Maurice. "Introduction historique." In *Harkis: soldats abandonnés,* ed. Fonds Pour la Mémoire des Harkis, 17–35. Paris: XO Éditions, 2012.

– *Les combattants musulmans de la Guerre d'Algérie: des soldats sacrifiés.* Paris: L'Harmattan, 1995.

Fargettas, Julien. "La révolte des tirailleurs sénégalais de Tiaroye, entre reconstructions mémorielles et histoire." *Vingtième Siècle. Revue d'Histoire,* no. 92 (October-Decenber 2006): 117–30.

– *Les Tirailleurs Sénégalais: les soldats noirs entre légendes et réalités 1939–1945.*
Paris: Éditions Tallandier, 2012.

Favre, Robert. *La mort dans la littérature et la pensée françaises au siècle des lumières.*
Lyons: Presses Universitaires de Lyon, 1978.

Ferry, Abel. *Carnets secrets 1914–1918: suivis de lettres et notes de guerre.* Paris:
Bernard Grasset, 2005.

Fiaux, Louis. *Histoire de la guerre civile de 1871.* Paris: G. Charpentier, 1879.

Flament, Marc. *Les beaux-arts de la guerre.* Paris: Éditions de la Pensée
Moderne, 1974.

Fléchier, Esprit. *Oraison funèbre de Turenne.* Paris: J. Delalain, 1851.

Florange, Robert III de la Marck, lord of. *Mémoires du Maréchal de Florange dit
le Jeune Adventureux.* Edited by Robert Goubaux and P.-André Lemoisne.
2 vols. Paris: Librairie Renouard, 1913–24.

Forcer, Stephen. "Beyond Mental: Avant-Garde Culture and War." In *Aftermath:
Legacies and Memories of War in Europe, 1918–1945–1989,* ed. Nicholas Martin,
Tim Haughton, and Pierre Purseigle, 85–107. Farnham, Surrey, and
Burlington. VT: Ashgate Publishing, 2014.

Forissier, Robert. "Le Corps expéditionnaire français dans la campagne d'Italie
et son service de santé (décembre 1943–juillet 1944)." *Médecine et Armées,*
no. 22–8 (1994): 635–72.

Forrest, Alan. *Napoleon's Men: The Soldiers of the Revolution and Empire.* London
and New York: Hambledon and London, 2002.

Fortescue, Hugh. *Memorandum of Two Conversations between the Emperor Napoleon
and Viscount Ebrington at Porto Ferrajo, on the 6th and 8th of December, 1814.*
London: James Ridgway, 1823.

Foucault, Michel. *Discipline and Punish: The Birth of the Prison.* Translated by
Alan Sheridan. New York: Vintage Books, 1979.

Fournier, Fernand. *Paroles d'appelés: leur version de la guerre d'Algérie.* Paris:
L'Harmattan, 2014.

Frank, Sarah Ann. *Hostages of Empire: Colonial Prisoners of War in Vichy France.*
Lincoln: University of Nebraska Press, 2021.

– "Life in the Frontstalags: Colonial Prisoners of War in Occupied France."
In *Incarceration and Regime Change: European Experiences in and around the Second
World War,* ed. Christian G. De Vito, Rolf Futselaar, and Helen Grevers, 53–79.
New York: Berghahn Books, 2016.

Franklin, Alfred. *Les grandes scènes historiques du XVIe siècle.* Paris: Fischbacher, 1886

Frémeaux, Jacques. *La France et l'Algérie en guerre 1830–1871, 1954–1962.* Paris:
Commission Française d'Histoire Militaire, Institut de Stratégie Comparée,
Economica, 2002.

Frerejean, Alain, and Claire L'Hoër. *Le siège et la Commune de Paris: Acteurs
et témoins racontent 1870–1871.* Paris: l'Archipel, 2020.

Gainot, Bernard. "Le dernier voyage: rites ambulatoires et rites conjuratoires dans les cérémonies funéraires en l'honneur des généraux révolutionnaires." In *La voix et le geste: une approche culturelle de la violence socio-politique*, ed. Philippe Bourdin and Mathias Bernard, 97–113. Clermont-Ferrand: Presses Universitaires Blaise-Pascal, 2005.

– "Les mots et les cendres: l'héroïsme au début du Consulat." *Annales Historiques de la Révolution Française*, no. 324 (April–June 2001): 127–38.

Garat, Dominique Joseph. *Éloge funèbre de Joubert, commandant en chef de l'armée d'Italie, prononcé au Champ-de-Mars le 30 fructidor an 7 par Garat.* N.p.: Imprimerie de J. Gratiot et Compagnie, n.d.

Gardenty. *La bataille de la Moskowa, ou l'Orpheline de la Bérésina. Pièce militaire, historique, en trois actes mêlés de couplets, et en deux tableaux. Dédiée à la Vieille et à la Jeune Armée.* Paris, 1840.

Garnier, Jacques, ed. *Les bulletins de la Grande Armée.* Paris: Éditions Soteca Napoléon 1er, 2013.

Genevoix, Maurice. *Ceux de 14.* Paris: Omnibus, 1998.

Germain, José, and René de Buxeuil. *Aventures des francs-tireurs de la Champagne, 1870–1871.* Soissons: Impr. du "Démocrate soissonais," 1909.

Germani, Ian. "Dying for Liberty in the French Revolutionary Wars." *French History and Civilization: Papers from the George Rudé Seminar* 9 (2020): 97–108.

– "'The Most Striking and the Most Terrible Examples': The Experience of Military Justice in the Armies of the French Revolution." In *Experiencing the French Revolution*, ed. David Andress, 113–33. Oxford: Voltaire Foundation, 2013.

– "The Soldier's Death: From Valmy to Verdun." *French History and Civilization: Papers from the George Rudé Seminar* 6 (2015): 133–48.

– "The Soldier's Death in French Culture: A Napoleonic Case Study." *Journal of War and Culture Studies* 9, no. 3 (August 2016): 1–15.

Germa-Romann, Hélène. *Du "Bel Mourir" au "Bien Mourir": le sentiment de la mort chez les gentilshommes français (1515–1643).* Geneva: Librairie Droz, 2001.

Gershovich, Moshe. "Stories on the Road from Fez to Marrakesh: Oral History on the Margins of National Identity." *Journal of African Studies* 8, no. 1 (2003): 43–58.

Gervereau, Laurent, Jean-Pierre Rioux, and Benjamin Stora, eds. *La France en guerre d'Algérie: novembre 1954 – juillet 1962.* Nanterre: Bibliothèque de documentation internationale contemporaine, 1992.

Giacomelli, H. *Raffet: son oeuvre lithographique et ses eaux-fortes.* Paris: Bureau de la Gazette des Beaux-Arts, 1862.

Gibelin, Antoine-Esprit. *Éloge funèbre de Dugommier, Général en chef de l'Armée des Pyrénées orientales.* Aix: Prosper Mouret, n.d.

Gildea, Robert. *Fighters in the Shadows: A New History of the French Resistance.*
Cambridge, MA: Belknap Press of Harvard University Press, 2015.

Gill, John H. *1809: Thunder on the Danube: Napoleon's Defeat of the Habsburgs*, vol. 2:
The Fall of Vienna and The Battle of Aspern. London: Frontline Books, 2008.

Giono, Jean. *Le grand troupeau.* Paris: Éditions Gallimard, 1931.

– *The Battle of Pavia, 24th February 1525.* Translated and edited by A.E. Murch.
London: Peter Owen, 1965.

– *To the Slaughterhouse: A Novel.* Translated by Norman Glass. London:
Owen, 1969.

Girard, Étienne François. *Souvenirs militaires du Colonel Girard.* Paris: Bernard
Giovanangeli Éditeur, 2010.

Girault, Philippe-René. *Mes campagnes sous la Révolution et l'empire.* Paris:
Le Sycomore, 1983.

Gobineau, Hélène de. *Noblesse d'Afrique.* Paris: Présence Africaine Éditions, 2014.

Gottlieb, Marc. *The Deaths of Henri Regnault.* Chicago and London: University
of Chicago Press, 2016.

Gouttman, Alain. *La guerre du Mexique, 1862–1867: le mirage américain de Napoléon
III.* Paris: Perrin, 2008.

Grall, Xavier. *La génération du Djebel.* Paris: Éditions du Cerf, 1962.

Grasset Saint-Sauveur, Jacques. *Les fastes du peuple français en tableaux raisonnés
de toutes les actions héroïques et civiques du soldat et du citoyen français.* Paris: Chez
Deroy, 1796.

Gréard, M.O. *Meissonier Ses souvenirs – ses entretiens. Précédés d'une étude sur sa vie
et son oeuvre.* Paris: Librairie Hachette, 1897.

Greenhalgh, Elizabeth. *The French Army and the First World War.* Cambridge:
Cambridge University Press, 2014.

Grégoire, Henri-B. *Rapport sur les moyens de rassembler les matériaux nécessaires
à former les Annales du Civisme, et sur la forme de cet ouvrage.* Paris: Imprimerie
nationale, n.d.

Gregory, Adrian. *The Last Great War: British Society and the First World War.*
Cambridge: Cambridge University Press, 2008.

Guinier, Arnaud. *L'honneur du soldat: éthique martiale et discipline guerrière dans
la France des lumières.* Paris: Champ Vallon, 2014.

Guiomar, Jean-Yves. *L'invention de la guerre totale.* Paris: Éditions du Félin, 2004.

Guivarc'h, Marcel. *1870–1871: Chirugie et médecine pendant la guerre et la Commune:
un tournant scientifique et humanitaire.* Paris: Éditions Louis Pariente, 2006.

Habeneck, Charles. *Les régiments-martyrs: Sedan-Paris.* Paris: Librairie
Pagnerre, 1871.

Hall, Bert S. *Weapons and Warfare in Renaissance Europe.* Baltimore: Johns Hopkins
University Press, 1997.

Hans, Albert. *Souvenirs d'un volontaire versaillais.* Paris: F. Dentu, Éditeur, 1873.

Hantraye, Jacques. "Les sépultures de guerre en France à la fin du Premier Empire." *Revue d'Histoire du XIXe Siècle* 30, no. 8 (2005), https://doi. org/10.4000/rh19.1007.

Harari, Yuval Noah. *The Ultimate Experience: Battlefield Revelations and the Making of Modern War Culture, 1450–2000.* Basingstoke: Palgrave Macmillan, 2008.

Hardier, Thierry, and Jean-François Jagielski. *Combattre et mourir pendant la Grande Guerre (1914–1925).* Paris: Imago, 2001.

Heller, Henry. *Iron and Blood: Civil Wars in Sixteenth-Century France.* Montreal and Kingston: McGill-Queen's University Press, 1991.

Héralde, Jean-Baptiste de. *Mémoires d'un chirugien de la Grande Armée.* Edited by Jean Chambenoit. Paris: Éditions Historiques Teissèdre, 2002.

Hopkin, David M. *Soldier and Peasant in French Popular Culture, 1766–1870.* Woodbridge: Boydell Press, 2013.

Horne, Alistair. *A Savage War of Peace: Algeria 1954–1962.* New York: New York Review Books, 2006.

– *Death of a Generation: From Neuve Chapelle to Verdun and the Somme.* London: Macdonald, 1970.

Horne, John. "Soldiers, Civilians and the Warfare of Attrition: Representations of Combat in France, 1914–1918." In *Authority, Identity and the Social History of the Great War,* ed. Frans Coetzee and Marilyn Shevin-Coetzee, 223–49. Providence and Oxford: Berghahn Books, 1995.

Hornstein, Katie. *Picturing War in France, 1792–1856.* New Haven and London: Yale University Press, 2017.

Houdaille, Jacques. "Les armées de la Révolution d'après les registres matricules." *Population* 38, no. 4/5 (1983): 842–9.

– "Les Officiers du Premier Empire (1803–1815)." *Population* 50, no. 4/5 (July-October 1995): 1229–35.

– "Pertes de l'armée de terre sous le premier Empire, d'après les registres marticules." *Population* 27, no. 1 (1972): 27–50.

Hould, Claudette, ed. *L'image de la Révolution Française.* Quebec: Musées du Québec, Les Publications du Québec, 1989.

Howard, Martin R. *Napoleon's Doctors: The Medical Services of the "Grande Armée."* Stroud: Spellmount, 2006.

Howard, Michael. *The Franco-Prussian War: The German Invasion of France, 1870–1871.* London and New York: Methuen, 1961.

Hughes, Michael J. *Forging Napoleon's Grande Armée: Motivation, Military Culture, and Masculinity in the French Army, 1800–1808.* New York and London: New York University Press, 2012.

Humblot. "Une lettre d'un sergent du Premier Empire." *Carnet de la Sabretache* 10 (1902): 150–3.

Hurcombe, Martin. "The Haunting of Roland D.: Roland Dorgelès, Remembering the Dead, and the Long Aftermath of the Great War (1919–1940)." In *Aftermath: Legacies and Memories of War in Europe, 1918–1945–1989*, ed. Nicholas Martin, Tim Haughton, and Pierre Purseigle, 129–47. Farnham, Surrey, and Burlington, VT: Ashgate, 2014.

Hutton, Patrick H. "Of Death and Destiny: The Ariès-Vovelle Debate about the History of Mourning." In *Symbolic Loss: The Ambiguity of Mourning and Memory at Century's End*, ed. Peter Homans, 147–70. Charlottesville and London: University Press of Virginia, 2000.

Irisson d'Hérisson, Maurice d'. *Journal d'un officier d'ordonnance: juillet 1870 – février 1871*. Paris: Paul Ollendorff, Éditeur, 1885.

Jacquart, Jean. *Bayard.* Paris: Fayard, 1987.

Jaeglé, Rachel. "Bara: un enfant de Palaiseau entré dans l'histoire." In *Héros et héroïnes de la Révolution française*, ed. Serge Bianchi, 333–42. Paris: Éditions du Comité des Travaux Historiques et Scientifiques, 2012.

Jauffret, Jean-Charles, "L'Armée française au combat de 1954 à l'envoi du contingent." In *La France en guerre d'Algérie: novembre 1954 – juillet 1962*, ed. Laurent Gervereau, Jean-Pierre Rioux, and Benjamin Stora, 40–5. Nanterre: Bibliothèque de Documentation Internationale Contemporaine, 1992.

– "L'officier français en 1914–1918: la guerre vécue." In *Mémoire de la Grande Guerre: Témoins et témoignage*, ed. Gérard Cassini, 229–47. Nancy: Presses Universitaires de Nancy, 1989.

– *Soldats en Algérie 1954–1962: Expériences contrastées des hommes du contingent.* Paris: Éditions Autrement, 2000.

– "The War Culture of French Combatants in the Algerian Conflict." In *The Algerian War and the French Army, 1954–62: Experiences, Images, Testimonies*, ed. Martin S. Alexander, Martin Evans, and J.F.V. Keiger, 101–16. Houndmills: Palgrave Macmillan, 2002.

Jauffret, Jean-Charles, and Charles-Robert Ageron, eds. *Des hommes et des femmes en guerre d'Algérie.* Paris: Éditions Autrement, 2003.

Jennings, Eric. *Free French Africa in World War II: The African Resistance.* Cambridge: Cambridge University Press, 2015.

Jezierski, Louis. *Combats et batailles du siège de Paris.* Paris: Garnier Frères, 1872.

Joliclerc, Étienne. *Joliclerc, volontaire aux armées de la révolution: ses lettres (1793–96).* Paris: Perrin et Cie., 1905.

Joly, Vincent, "Le concept de 'race guerrière.'" In *Le soldat et la mort dans la Grande Guerre*, ed. Isabelle Homer and Emmanuel Pénicault, 153–72. Rennes: Presses Universitaires de Rennes, 2016.

Jones, Colin. "The Military Revolution and the Professionalisation of the French Army under the Ancien Régime." In *The Military Revolution Debate: Readings on the Military Transformation of Early Modern Europe*, ed. Clifford J. Rogers, 149–68. Boulder, CO: Westview Press, 1995.

Jordi, Jean-Jacques. "Khélifa Haroud: Harki, 1957–1967." In *Des hommes et des femmes en guerre d'Algérie*, ed. Jean-Charles Jauffret, 360–71. Paris: Éditions Autrement, 2003.

Jourdan. *Discours de Jourdan (de la Haute-Vienne), sur la pétition de la mère du général Marceau*. Paris: Imprimerie nationale, Year Five [1796–1797].

Jourdan, Annie. *Les monuments de la Révolution française: une histoire de représentation*. Paris: Honoré Champion Éditeur, 1997.

– *Napoléon, héros, imperator, mécène*. Paris: Aubier, 1998.

Journoud, Pierre "Les guerres coloniales des 'soldats perdus' 1945–1962." In *Histoire militaire de la France*, vol. 2: *De 1870 à nos jours*, ed. Hervé Drévillon and Olivier Wieviorka, 479–585. Paris: Perrin, Ministère des Armées, 2018.

Jourquin, Jacques, ed. *Journal du Capitaine François dit le Dromadaire d'Égypte, 1792–1830*. Paris: Tallandier, 2003.

– ed. *Souvenirs de campagne du Sergent Faucheur, fourrier dans la Grande Armée*. Paris: Tallandier, 2004.

– ed. *Souvenirs de guerre du Lieutenant Martin, 1812–1815*. Paris: Tallandier, 2007.

Juin, Alphonse. *La campagne d'Italie*. Paris: Éditions Guy Victor, 1962.

Kalyvas, Stathis N. *The Logic of Violence in Civil War*. Cambridge: Cambridge University Press, 2006.

Keegan, John. *The Face of Battle*. New York: Viking Press, 1976.

Kelly, Alice. "'Can One Grow Used to Death?' – Deathbed Scenes in Great War Nurses' Narratives." In *The Great War: From Memory to History*, ed. Kellen Kurschinski, Steve Marti, Matt Symes, and Jonathan F. Vance, 329–49. Waterloo, ON: Wilfrid Laurier University Press, 2015.

Kelly, Andrew. *Cinema and the Great War*. London and New York: Routledge, 1997.

Kern, Stephen. *The Culture of Time and Space, 1880–1918*. Cambridge, MA: Harvard University Press, 1983.

Kersers, B. Buhot de, ed. *Correspondance de la Tour d'Auvergne (Corret)*. Bourges: Impr. Vve. Tardy-Pigelet et fils, 1908.

Klotz, Claude *Les appelés*. Paris: J.C. Lattès, 1982.

Kyriazi, Jean Melas, *André Dunoyer de Segonzac: sa vie, son oeuvre*. Lausanne: Harmonies et Couleurs, 1976.

La Borderie, Arthur Le Moyne de. *Rapport fait au nom de la commission d'enquête sur les actes du Gouvernement de la Défense nationale: le Camp de Conlie et l'Armée de Brétagne*. Versailles: Cerf et Fils, 1873.

Laby, Lucien. *Les carnets de l'aspirant Laby, médecin dans les tranchées, 28 juillet 1914 – 14 juillet 1919*. Edited by Sophie Delaporte. Paris: Bayard, 2013.

Lafon, Alexandre, ed. *C'est si triste de mourir à 20 ans: Lettres du soldat Henri Despeyrières 1914–1915*. Toulouse: Éditions Privat, 2007.

Lagadec, Yann, and Stéphane Perréon. *La bataille de Saint-Cast (Bretegne, 11 septembre 1785): entre histoire et mémoire*. Rennes: Presses Universitaires de Rennes, 2009.

Lagrou, "Les guerres, les morts et le deuil: bilan chiffré de la Seconde Guerre Mondiale." In *La violence de guerre 1914–1945*, ed. Stéphane Audoin-Rouzeau Annette Becker, Christian Ingrao, and Henry Rousso, 313–27. Paris: Éditions Complexe, 2002.

Lalanne, Ludovic, ed. *Journal d'un bourgeois de Paris sous le règne de François Premier (1515–1536)*. Paris: Renouard, 1854.

Lamoral Le Pippre de Noeufville, Simon. *Abrégé chronologique et historique de l'origine, du progrès, et de l'état actuel de la maison du roi*. 3 vols. Liège: Chez Everard Kints, 1734–35.

Langres, Lombard de. *Mémoires pour servir à l'histoire de la Révolution française*. Paris: Auguste Welen et Compagnie, 1823.

Lanquetot, André. *Un hiver dans les Abruzzes: Le 8ᵉ Régiment de Tirailleurs Marocains et le 3ᵉ Groupe du 63ᵉ Régiment d'Artillerie d'Afrique: Italie 1943–1944*. Vincennes: Service Historique de l'Armée de Terre, 1991.

Larcan, Alain, and Jean-Jacques Ferrandis. *Le Service de Santé aux armées pendant la Première Guerre Mondiale*. Paris: Éditions LBM, 2008.

Larchey, Lorédan, ed. *Journal de marche du Sergent Fricasse de la 127ᵉ demi-brigade*. Paris. L. Larchey, 1882.

– *Les cahiers du Capitaine Coignet*. Paris: Hachette, 1888.

Larrey, Dominique-Jean. *Mémoires de chirugie militaire et campagnes de D.J. Larrey*. 4 vols. Paris: J. Smith, 1812–17.

Lartéguy, Jean. *The Centurions*. Translated by Xan Fielding. New York: Penguin Books, 1961.

– *The Praetorians*. Translated by Xan Fielding. New York: Penguin Books, 1961.

Laqueur, Thomas. *The Work of the Dead: A Cultural History of Mortal Remains*. Princeton, NJ: Princeton University Press, 2015.

Lawler, Nancy Ellen. *Soldiers of Misfortune: Ivoirien "Tirailleurs" of World War II*. Athens: Ohio University Press, 1992.

Leboeuf, J.J. *La patrie reconnaissante, ou l'apothéose de Beaurepaire*. Paris: L'Imprimerie Civique, 1793.

Lebrun, François. *Les hommes et la mort en Anjou aux 17ᵉ et 18ᵉ siècles: Essai de démographie et de psychologie historiques*. Mouton, Paris, La Hague: Mouton et Cie., 1971.

Lecaillon, Jean-François. *Été 1870: la guerre racontée par les soldats.* Paris: Bernard Giovanangeli, Éditeur, 2002.

– *Les Français et la guerre de 1870.* Paris: L'Artilleur, 2020.

– *Les peintres français et la guerre de 1870.* Paris: Bernard Giovanangeli, Éditeur; Éditions des Paraiges, 2016.

– *Le souvenir de 1870.* Paris: Bernard Giovanangeli, Éditeur, 2011.

Lecomte, L.-H. *Napoléon et l'empire racontés par le théâtre, 1797–1899.* Paris: Librairie Jules Raux, 1900.

Le Fur, Didier. *Marignan, 13–14 septembre, 1515.* Paris: Perrin, 2004.

Le Gac, Julie. *Vaincre sans gloire: Le corps expéditionnaire français en Italie, (novembre 1942 – juillet 1944).* Paris: Les Belles Lettres / La Ministère de la Défense – DMPA, 2018.

Legacey, Erin Marie. *Making Space for the Dead: Catacombs, Cemeteries, and the Reimagining of Paris, 1780–1830.* Ithaca and London: Cornell University Press, 2019.

Leleu, Jean-Luc, Françoise Passera, and Jean Quellien, eds. *La France pendant la Seconde Guerre Mondiale.* Paris: Fayard, 2010.

Lelièvre, Pierre. "L'oeuvre de guerre de J.–J. Lemordant." *L'Art et Les Artistes* 30, no. 160 (1935): 1–29.

Lemaire, Jean-François. *Les blessés dans les armées napoléoniennes.* Paris: Lettrage, 1999.

Lemercier, Eugène-Emmanuel. *Lettres d'un soldat: août 1914 – avril 1915.* Paris: Bernard Giovanangeli, Éditeur, 2005.

Le Naor, Jean-Yves. *La honte noire: L'Allemagne et les troupes coloniales françaises.* Paris: Hachette, 2003.

Léonard. *Relation exacte et impartiale de ce qui s'est passé à Nancy, le 31 août et les jours précédens.* Nancy, n.p., 1790.

Le Pichon, Tanneguy. "Tirailleurs indigènes, soldats au service de la France." In *Le sacrifice du soldat,* ed. Christian Benoit, Gilles Boëtsch, Antoine Champeaux, and Éric Deroo, 158–67. Paris: ECPAD and CNRS Éditions, 2009.

Lepick, Olivier. *La grande guerre chimique: 1914–1918.* Paris: Presses Universitaires de France, 1998.

Le Roux, Nicolas. *Le crépuscule de la chevalerie: noblesse et guerre au siècle de la Renaissance.* Paris: Champ Vallon, 2015.

Le Roy, Claude-François-Madeleine. "Souvenirs de C.-F.-M Le Roy, Major d'Infanterie, vétéran des armées de la république et de l'empire (1767–1851)." *Mémoires de la Société Bourguignonne de Géographie et d'Histoire* 29 (1914): 1–317.

Lesur, Charles-Louis. *L'apothéose de Beaurepaire.* Paris: Chez la Citoyenne Toubonne, n.d.

Leulliette, Pierre. *Saint Michel et le dragon: souvenirs d'un parachutiste*. Paris: Éditions de Minuit, 1961.

L'Héritier, Louis-François, ed. *Fastes de la gloire. Collection de 50 gravures représentant des sujets militaires*. Paris: Raymond, Éditeur, 1829.

Lissagaray, Prosper-Olivier. *Histoire de la Commune de Paris de 1871*. Paris: Librairie du Travail, 1929.

– *Les huit journées de mai derrière les barricades*. Brussels: Bureau du Petit Journal, 1871.

Lobell, Jarrett A. "Digging Napoleon's Dead." *Archaeology* 55, no. 5 (September-October 2002): 40–3.

Loez, André. *14–18, les refus de la guerre: une histoire des mutins*. Paris: Gallimard, 2010.

Lucas-Dubreton, Jean. *Le culte de Napoléon, 1815–1848*. Paris: Albin Michel, 196c.

Lucenet, Monique. *Médecine, chirugie et armée en France au siècle des lumières*. Sceaux: I&D, 2006.

– "La mortalité dans l'infanterie française de 1716 à 1748 selon les contrôles de troupes." In *Le soldat, la stratégie, la mort: mélanges André Corvisier*, ed. Pierre Chaunu and André Corvisier, 397–407. Paris: Economica, 1989.

Lunn, Joe. *L'odysée des combattants sénégalais 1914–1918*. Paris: L'Harmattan, 2014.

Lyautey, Pierre. *La campagne d'Italie 1944: souvenirs d'un goumier*. Paris: Librairie Plon, 1946.

Lyford, Amy. *Surrealist Masculinities: Gender Anxiety and the Aesthetics of Post–World War I Reconstruction in France*. Berkeley, Los Angeles, London: University of California Press, 2007.

Lynn, John. *Battle: A History of Combat and Culture*. Boulder, CO: Westview Press, 2003.

– *Giant of the Grand Siècle: The French Army, 1610–1715*. Cambridge: Cambridge University Press, 1997.

Lyons, Martyn. "French Soldiers and Their Correspondence: Towards a History of Writing Practices in the First World War." *French History* 17, no. 1 (2003): 79–95.

Mabon, Armelle. *Prisonniers de guerre 'indigènes': visages oubliés de la France occupée*. Paris: La Découverte, 2019.

Macnab, Roy. *For Honour Alone: The Cadets of Saumur in the Defence of the Cavalry School, France, June 1940*. London: Robert Hale, 1988.

Mailles, Jacques de. *Très joyeuse, plaisante et récréative histoire du Gentil Seigneur de Bayart, composée par le loyal serviteur*. Edited by M.J. Roman. Paris: Librairie Renouart, 1878.

Mainz, Valerie. "Deflecting the Fire of Eighteenth-Century French Battle Painting." In *Battlefield Emotions 1500–1800: Practices, Experience, Imagination*, ed. Erika Kuijpers and Cornelis van der Haven, 229–47. London: Palgrave Macmillan, 2016.

Mallet, Michael, and Christine Shaw. *The Italian Wars, 1494–1559.* Edinburgh Gate: Pearson, 2012.

Mangin, Charles. *La force noire.* Paris: Hachette, 1910.

Mann, Gregory. *Native Sons: West African Veterans and France in the Twentieth Century.* Durham and London: Duke University Press, 2006.

Marbot, Marcellin. *Mémoires du Général Baron de Marbot.* 3 vols. Paris: Plon, Nourrit et Cie., 1891.

Marcellin Prosper Floirac. *Vie et mort d'un Fantassin Quercynois: Lettres de Marcelin Prosper Floirac à sa femme Joséphine (1914–1915).* Cahors: Archives Départementales du Lot, 2000.

Marchal, Caroline. *L'hommage politique aux soldats français morts en Afghanistan.* Paris: L'Harmattan, 2013.

Maricourt, Léon de. *Casquettes blanches et Croix rouge: souvenirs de 1870.* Paris: Librairie de Firmin-Didot et Cie, 1892.

Marks, Sally. "Black Watch on the Rhine: A Study in Propaganda, Prejudice and Prurience." *European Studies Review* 13 (1983): 297–334.

Martel, André, ed. *Histoire militaire de la France,* vol. 4: *De 1940 à nos jours.* Paris: Presses Universitaires de France, 1994.

Martel, Jean-Pierre. *La section: Journal d'un appelé en Algérie (1959–1961).* Paris: Éditions de Paris, 2009.

Martin, Antoine. *La chasse à l'homme: lettres de guerre et carnet journalier d'Antoine Martin (1914–1915).* St-Michel-de-Maurienne: Éditions 73 – La Croix-Blanche, 1989.

Martin, Brian Joseph. *Napoleonic Friendship: Military Fraternity, Intimacy, and Sexuality in Nineteenth-Century France.* Durham: University of New Hampshire Press, 2011.

Martin, Jean-Clément. *La guerre de Vendée 1793–1800.* Paris: Éditions du Seuil, 2014.

– *Violence et révolution: essai sur la naissance d'un mythe national.* Paris: Éditions du Seuil, 2006.

Martin, Ronald. "The Army of Louis XIV." In *The Reign of Louis XIV,* ed. Paul Sonnino, 111–26. New Jersey and London: Humanities Press International, 1990.

Masson, Rémi. *Les mousquetaires ou la violence d'état.* Paris: Vendémiaire, 2013.

Mateos-Ruiz, Maurice. *L'Algérie des appelés.* Biarritz: Atlantica, 1998.

Mattei, Georges M. *La guerre des gusses: Roman.* Évreux: Balland, 1982.

Maury, Eugène, ed. *Lettres de volontaires républicains (1791–1794).* Troyes: Imprimerie G. Arbouin, 1901.

Maury, Isabelle. *L'empreinte de la guerre: paroles d'appelés en Algérie*. Paris: J.C. Lattès, 2012.

Mauvillon, Eléazar de. *Le soldat parvenu, ou mémoires et aventures de M. de Verval, dit Bellerose*. La Haye Chez Pierre de Hondt, 1779.

Mazon, Albin, *Notes et documents historiques sur les Huguenots du Vivarais: Dernières guerres civiles du XVIe siècle jusqu'à la mort d'Henri III (1577 à 1589)*. Privas: Imprimerie centrale de l'Ardèche, 1903.

McManners, John. *Death and the Enlightenment: Changing Attitudes to Death among Christians and Unbelievers in Eighteenth-Century France*. Oxford: Clarendon Press, 1981.

Meignan. Guillaume. *Les victimes de la Basse et de Passavant*. Châlons: Impr. de T. Martin, 1871.

Mencier, Paul. *Les cahiers de Paul Mencier, 1914–1919*. Guilherand: La Plume du Temps, 2001.

Merchet, Jean-Dominique. *Mourir pour l'Afghanistan*. Paris: Éditions Jacob-Duvernet, 2008.

Merriman, John. *Massacre: The Life and Death of the Paris Commune*. New York: Basic Books, 2014.

Michel, Marc. "'Force noire' ou 'chair à canon': Diagne contre Mangin." In *Combattants de l'Empire*, ed. Philippe Buton and Marc Michel, 241–57. Paris: Vendémiaire, 2018.

– *Les Africains et la Grande Guerre: l'appel à l'Afrique*. Paris: Éditions Karthala, 2014.

Milner, John. *Art, War and Revolution in France 1870–1871: Myth, Reportage and Reality*. New Haven and London: Yale University Press, 2000.

Milza, Pierre. *"L'année terrible."* 2 vols. Paris: Perrin, 2009.

Miot, Claire. *La Première Armée française. De la Provence à l'Allemagne, 1944–1945*. Paris: Perrin, 2021.

– "L'armée de l'Empire ou l'armée de la Nation: front et arrières pendant la Seconde Campagne de France (1944–1945)." In *Guerres mondiales et conflits contemporains*, no. 259 (July-September 2015): 39–55.

Monénembo, Tierno. *The Black Terrorist*. Translated by C. Dickson. New York: Diasporic Africa Press, 2015.

Monluc, Blaise. *Commentaires et lettres de Blaise de Monluc, maréchal de France*. Edited by Alphonse de Ruble. 5 vols. Paris: Mme Ve Jules Renouard, 1864–72.

Monnier, Raymonde. "Le culte de Bara en l'an II." In *Joseph Bara (1779–1793) Pour le deuxième centenaire de sa naissance*, 37–53. Paris: Ville de Palaiseau/ Société des Études Robespierristes, 1981.

Montagnon, Pierre. *L'honneur, pas les honneurs: Mémoires*, vol. 1: *Avec le 2e REP en Algérie*. Paris: Bernard Giovanangeli, Éditeur, 2018.

Montherlant, Henri de. *Chant funèbre pour les morts de Verdun.* N.p., 1936.

Montroussier-Favre, Laurence. "Remembering the Other: The Peninsular War in the Autobiographical Accounts of British and French Soldiers." In *War Memories: The Revolutionary and Napoleonic Wars in Modern European Culture,* ed. Alan Forrest, Étienne François, and Karen Hagemann, 59–76. Houndmills: Palgrave Macmillan, 2012–13.

Moriceau, Jean-Marc. *La mémoire des croquants: chroniques de la France des campagnes, 1435–1652.* Paris: Tallandier, 2018.

Mormone, Jean-Michel, Patrick Boyer, and Jean-Pierre Caule, *1914–1918: le Bassin d'Arcachon.* Arcachon: Société Historique et Archéologique d'Arcachon et du Pays de Buch, 2008

Mosse, George L. *Fallen Soldiers: Reshaping the Memory of the World Wars.* New York and Oxford: Oxford University Press, 1990.

Moussac, Georges de. *Dans la mêlée: journal d'un cuirassier de 1870–1871.* Paris: Perrin et Cie, 1910.

Muchembled, Robert. *Une histoire de la violence: de la fin du Moyen Âge à nos jours.* Paris: Éditions du Seuil, 2008.

Muir, Rory. *Tactics and the Experience of Battle in the Age of Napoleon.* New Haven and London: Yale University Press, 1998.

Murat, Lucien. *Carnets de guerre et correspondances: 1914–1918.* Paris: L'Harmattan, 2012.

Naegelen, René. *Les suppliciés.* Paris: La Baudinière, 1927.

Nassiet, Michel. *La violence, une histoire sociale: France, XVI–XVIIIe siècles.* Paris: Champ Vallon, 2011.

Nebelthau, E. *Roger de la Fresnaye.* Paris: Paul de Montaignac, 1935.

Nganang, Patrice. *La saison des prunes.* Paris: Éditions Philippe Rey, 2013.

Niess, Alexandre. *Cimetières militaires et monuments aux morts de la Grande Guerre.* Langres: Éditions Dominique Guéniot, 2005.

– "La mort du soldat de la Grande Guerre: Représentations dans les monuments aux morts de la Marne." In *Des vivants et des morts: des constructions de la "bonne mort,"* ed. Simone Pennec, 323–36. Brest: Université de Bretagne Occidentale, 2004.

– "La représentation des corps sur les monuments aux morts." In *Le soldat et la mort dans la Grande Guerre,* ed. Isabelle Homer and Emmanuel Pénicaut, 177–93. Rennes: Presses Universitaires de Rennes, 2016.

Noël, Jean-Nicolas-Auguste. *With Napoleon's Guns: The Military Memoirs of an Officer of the First Empire.* Edited and translated by Rosemary Brindle. London: Greenhill Books, 2005.

Notin, Jean-Christophe. *1061 compagnons: histoire des compagnons de la libération.* Paris: Perrin, 2000.

Norvins, Jacques de. *Histoire de Napoléon*. Paris: Furne, 1839.

O'Brien, David. *After the Revolution: Antoine-Jean Gros, Painting and Propaganda under Napoleon*. University Park: Pennsylvania State University Press, 2006.

O'Connell, David. "Jean Lartéguy: A Popular Phenomenon." *French Review* 45, no. 6 (May 1972): 1087–97.

Oestreich, Gerhard. *Neostoicism and the Early Modern State*. Cambridge: Cambridge University Press, 1982.

Olander, William. "Pour transmettre à la postérité: French Painting and Revolution, 1774–1795." Unpublished doctoral thesis, New York University, 1983.

Onana, Charles. *La France et ses tirailleurs*. Paris: Éditions Duboiris, 2003.

Onana, Raphaël. *Un homme blindé à Bir-Hakeim*. Paris: L'Harmattan, 1996.

Palmer, R.R. "Frederick the Great, Guibert, Bülow: From Dynastic to National War." In *Makers of Modern Strategy: From Machiavelli to the Nuclear Age*, ed. Peter Paret, 91–119. Princeton: Princeton University Press, 1986.

Papillon, Marthe, Joseph Papillon, Lucien Papillon, and Marcel Papillon. *'Si je reviens comme je l'espère': lettres du front et de l'arrière, 1914–1918*. Paris: Bernard Grasset, 2003.

Paré, Ambroise. *Oeuvres complètes*. 3 vols. Edited by J.-F. Malgraine. Paris: J.B. Ballière, 1840–1841.

Paret, Peter. "Napoleon and the Revolution in War." In *Makers of Modern Strategy: From Machiavelli to the Nuclear Age*, ed. Peter Paret, 123–42. Princeton: Princeton University Press, 1986.

Parker, Harold T. *Three Napoleonic Battles*. 2nd ed. Durham, NC: Duke University Press, 1983.

Pascal, Adrien, ed. *Les bulletins de la Grande Armée*. 6 vols. Paris: Lesage, 1841–44.

Pau, Béatrix. *Le ballet des morts: état, armée, familles: s'occuper des corps de la Grande Guerre*. Paris: La Librairie Vuibert, 2016.

Payen, Joseph-Eugène. *L'âme du poilu: journal de route d'un aumônier militaire au 7ᵉ corps pendant la Grande Guerre, 1914–1918*. Besançon: Imprimerie Jacques et Demontrond, 1924.

Pelet, Jean-Jacques-Germain. *Mémoires sur la guerre de 1809 en Allemagne*. 3 vols. Paris: Roret, 1824–26

Pellabeuf, René. *Ma campagne d'Italie dans les tabors marocains (1943–1944)*. Aix-en-Provence: privately published, 1994.

Peltier, G. *L'ambulance no. 5*. Paris: Adrien Delahaye, 1871.

Pensuet, Maurice. *Écrit du front: lettres de Maurice Pensuet, 1915–1917*. Paris: Tallandier, 2010.

Perna, Patrice, and Nicolas Otero. *Morts par la France: Thiaroye 1944*. Paris: Les Arènes, 2018.

Perrault, Gilles. *Les parachutistes*. Paris: Éditions du Seuil, 1964.

Pervillé, Guy. "L'Armée française au combat de 1956 à 1962." In *La France en guerre d'Algérie: novembre 1954 – juillet 1962*, ed. Laurent Gervereau, Jean-Pierre Rioux, and Benjamin Stora, 46–53. Nanterre: Bibliothèque de Documentation Internationale Contemporaine, 1992.

Pétigny, Xavier de. *Beaurepaire et le premier bataillon des volontaires de Maine-et-Loire à Verdun, juin–septembre 1792*. Angers: G. Grassin, 1911.

Petitfils, Jean-Christian. *Le véritable d'Artagnan*. Paris: Tallandier, 1981.

Percy, Pierre-François. *Journal des campagnes du Baron Percy, chirurgien-en-chef de la Grande Armée*. Vol. 1. Paris: Tallandier, 1986.

Pichichero, Christy. *The Military Enlightenment: War and Culture in the French Empire from Louis XIV to Napoleon*. Ithaca and London: Cornell University Press, 2017.

– "Le Soldat Sensible: Military Psychology and Social Egalitarianism in the Enlightenment French Army." *French Historical Studies* 31, no. 4 (Fall 2008): 553–80.

Pick, Eugène. *Les fastes de la guerre d'Orient: histoire politique, militaire et maritime des campagnes de Crimée*. 2nd ed. Paris: Imprimerie Napoléonienne des Arts et de l'Industrie, 1856.

Pontis, Louis de. *Collection des mémoires relatifs à l'histoire de France*, vol. 31: *Mémoires du sieur de Pontis*. Edited by M. Petitot. Paris: Foucault, Libraire, 1824.

Porchnev, Boris. *Les soulèvements populaires en France au XVIIe siècle*. Paris: Flammarion, 1972.

Potel, Ken. *Les oubliés du 1er Empire*. Paris: Pleine Vie, 1999.

Potter, David. *Renaissance France at War: Armies, Culture and Society, c. 1480–1560*. Woodbridge, Suffolk: Boydell Press, 2008.

Pottier, Eugène. *Chants révolutionnaires*. Paris: Éditions Sociales Internationales, 1937.

Pouget, François-René Cailloux. *Souvenirs de guerre (1790–1831)*. Edited by Thierry Rouillard. Paris: La Vouivre, 1997.

Prendergast, Christopher. *Napoleon and History Painting: Antoine-Jean Gros's "La bataille d'Eylau."* Oxford: Clarendon Press, 1997.

Prost, Antoine. *Les anciens combattants et la Société Française 1914–1939*. 3 vols. Paris: Presses de la Fondation Nationale des Sciences Politiques, 1977.

– *Carnets d'Algérie*. Paris: Tallandier, 2005.

– "'Compter les vivants et les morts': l'évaluation des pertes françaises de 1914–1918." *Le Mouvement Social* 1, no. 222 (2008): 41–60.

– *Republican Identities in War and Peace: Representations of France in the Nineteenth and Twentieth Centuries*. Translated by Jay Winter with Helen McPhail. Oxford and New York: Berg, 2002.

Psichari, Ernest. *Les voix qui crient dans le désert: Souvenirs d'Afrique.* Paris: Louis Connard, Librairie-Éditeur, 1920.

Pujo, Bernard. *Vauban* Paris: Éditions Albin Michel, 1991.

Pupil, François. "Le dévouement du Chevalier Desilles et l'Affaire de Nancy en 1790: Essai de catalogue iconographique." *Le Pays Lorrain,* no. 1 (1976): 73–110.

Quarré d'Aligny, Pierre. *Mémoire des campagnes de M. le comte Quarré d'Aligny, sous le règne de Louis XIV, jusqu'à la paix de Riswich.* Beaune: Imprimerie Arthur Batault, 1886.

Quellien, Jean. "La mémoire de la Résistance au travers des noms de rues." In *La France pendant la Seconde Guerre Mondiale. Atlas historique,* ed. J.-L. Leleu, F. Passera, J. Quellien, and M. Daeffler, 282–3. Paris: Librairie Arthème Fayard and the Ministry of Defence, 2010.

– "Les pertes humaines." In *La France pendant la Seconde Guerre Mondiale. Atlas historique,* ed. J.-L. Leleu, F. Passera, J. Quellien, and M. Daeffler, 262–5. Paris: Librairie Arthème Fayard and the Ministry of Defence, 2010.

Quintin, Bernard. "Premières réflexions sur les pertes militaires pour fait de guerre." In *Armée, guerre et société à l'époque napoléonienne,* ed. Jacques-Olivier Boudon, 165–74. Paris: Éditions SPM, 2004.

Quintin, Danielle, and Bernard Quintin. *Austerlitz, 2 décembre 1805: dictionnaire biographique des soldats de Napoléon tombés au champ d'honneur.* Paris: Éditions Archives et Culture, 2004.

– *La tragédie d'Eylau, 7 et 8 février 1807: dictionnaire biographique des officiers, sous-officiers ou soldats tués ou blessés mortellement au combat.* Paris: Éditions Archives et Culture, 2007.

Ramsay, Andrew. *Histoire de Henri de la Tour d'Auvergne, Vicomte de Turenne, Maréchal-Général des Armées du Roi.* 2 vols. La Hague: Jean Neaulme, 1736.

Raoult, Didier, Olivier Dutour, Linda Houhamdi, Rimantas Jankauskas, Pierre-Édouard Fournier, Yann Ardagna, Michel Drancourt, et al. "Evidence for Louse-Transmitted Diseases in Soldiers of Napoleon's Grand Army in Vilnius." *Journal of Infectious Diseases* 193, no. 1 (2006): 112–20.

Recham, Belkacem. "Les indigènes nord-africains prisonniers de guerre (1940–1945)." *Guerres mondiales et conflits contemporains,* no. 223 (July 2006): 109–25.

– *Les musulmans algériens dans l'Armée Française (1919–1945).* Paris: L'Harmattan, 1996.

Redier, Antoine. *Gestes français.* Le Puy: Éditions Xavier Mappus, 1944.

Renaud, Patrick-Charles *Se battre en Algérie.* Paris: Grancher, 2008.

Renaudot, Théophraste. *Récit véritable de la vie et de la mort du Mareschal de Gassion.* Orléans: Chez Gilles Hotot et Gabriel Frémont, 1647.

Renoult, Adrien-Jacques. *Souvenirs du docteur Adrien-Jacques Renoult.* Paris: Impr. de C. Jouast, 1862.

Réunion des Musées Nationaux. *La Révoluton française et l'Europe 1789–1799,* vol. 3: *La Révolution créatrice.* Paris: Éditions de la Réunion des Musées Nationaux, 1989.

Reynier, Quentin. "Le héros militaire, la mort et l'honneur sous le Directoire: quelle menace pour la République?" In *Héros et héroïnes de la Révolution française,* ed. Serge Bianchi, 195–220. Paris: Éditions du Comité des travaux historiques et scientifiques, 2012.

Ribon, Pierre. *D'Artagnan en Ardèche: la révolte de Roure en 1670 d'après les archives authentiques et inédites du Roi Louis XIV.* Valence: Éditions de la Bouquinerie, 2001.

Rigal, J.L., ed. *Mémoires d'un Calviniste de Millau.* Rodez: Imprimerie Carrère, 1911.

Rimbault, Paul. *Journal de campagne d'un officier de ligne.* Paris: Librairie Militaire Berger-Levrault, 1916.

– *Propos d'un Marmité (1915–1917).* Paris: L. Fournier, 1920.

Rive, Philippe, Annette Becker, Olivier Pelletier, Dominique Renoux, and Christophe Thomas, eds. *Monuments de mémoire: les monuments aux morts de la Première Guerre Mondiale.* Paris: Mission Permanente aux Commémorations et à l'Information Historique, 1991.

Rives, Maurice, and Robert Dietrich. *Héros méconnus 1914–1918, 1939–1945: mémorial des combattants d'Afrique noire et de Madagascar.* Paris: Association Française Frères d'Armes, 2006.

Rivière. *Discours prononcé par le Cen. Rivière, Professeur à l'École centrale du Département du Lot, à la cérémonie funèbre du Général Hoche.* Cahors: Chez Richard, n.d.

Robichon, François. *Alphonse de Neuville, 1835–1885.* Paris: Éditions Nicolas Chaudin et Ministère de la Défense, 2010.

– *Édouard Detaille: Un siècle de gloire militaire.* Paris: Éditions du Toucan / L'Artilleur, 2020.

– "La peinture du sacrifice ou la mort du soldat de 1870 à 1918." In *Le sacrifice du soldat,* ed. Christian Benoit, Gilles Boëtsch, Antoine Champeaux, and Éric Deroo, 177–82. Paris: ECPAD and CNRS Éditions, 2009.

– *La peinture militaire française de 1871 à 1914.* Paris: Association des Amis d'Édouard Detaille, 1998.

Rocca, Albert Jean Michel. *Oeuvres: Le mal du pays (1817–1818, inédit).* Edited by Stéphanie Genand with Aline Hodroge. Paris: Honoré Champion Éditeur, 2017.

Rochambeau, Jean-Baptiste-Donatien de Vimeur. *Mémoires militaires, historiques et politiques de Rochambeau: ancien maréchal de France, et grand officier de la Légion d'honneur.* Vol. 1. Paris: Fain, 1809.

Roeck, Bernd, "The Atrocities of War in Early Modern Art." In *Power, Violence and Mass Death in Pre-Modern and Modern Times,* ed. Joseph Canning, Hartmut Lehmann, and Jay Winter, 129–40. Aldershot: Ashgate, 2004.

Roger-Marx, C., ed. *Luc-Albert Moreau vu par ses amis.* Paris, 1960.

Rolland, Denis. *La grève des tranchées.* Paris: Éditions Imago, 2005.

Rolland-Boulestreau, Anne. *Les colonnes infernales: violences et guerre civile en Vendée militaire (1794–1795).* Paris: Fayard, 2015.

Romains, Jules. *Les hommes de bonne volonté,* vol. 16: *Verdun.* Paris: Flammarion, 1938.

Romand, Louis-Jacques. *Mémoires de ma vie militaire, 1809–1815.* Besançon: Imprimerie Copie Service, 1981.

Roquincourt, Thierry. "Le mythe du Vengeur." In *Révolution et République. L'exception française,* ed. Michel Vovelle, 481–2. Paris: Kimé, 1994.

Rossel, Louis. *Papiers posthumes.* Edited by Jules Amigues. Paris: E. Lachaud, Éditeur, 1871.

Rossignol, Jean. *La vie véritable du Citoyen Rossignol, vainqueur de la Bastille et général en chef des armées de la république dans la guerre de la Vendée.* Paris: Librairie Plon, 1896.

Rostand, Edmond. *L'Aiglon: drame en six actes, en vers.* Paris: Librairie Charpentier et Fasquelle, 1900.

Rotman, Patrick, and Bertrand Tavernier. *La guerre sans nom: les appelés d'Algérie 1954–1962.* Paris: Éditions du Seuil, 1992.

Rousset, Léonce. *Histoire générale de la guerre franco-allemande (1870–71).* 7 vols. Paris: Librairie Illustrée, 1895–98.

Rousso, Henry. *The Vichy Syndrome: History and Memory in France since 1944.* Cambridge, MA, and London: Harvard University Press, 1991.

Routier, Léon-Michel. *Récits d'un soldat de la République et de l'Empire.* Paris: Éditions du Grenadier, 2001.

Rowlands, Guy. *The Dynastic State and the Army under Louis XIV: Royal Service and Private Interest, 1661–1701.* Cambridge: Cambridge University Press, 2002.

Saint-Blaise, Juliani de. *Journal du siège et de la prise de Maestricht.* Paris: Impr. de Nego, 1674.

Saint-Exupéry, Antoine. *Terre des hommes.* Paris: Éditions Gallimard, 1939.

Saint-Marc, Hélie de. *Mémoires: les champs de braises.* Paris: Éditions Perrin, 2002.

Saint-Martin, Isabelle. "Représenter la mort dans les vitraux commémoratifs: De l'imitatio Christi à la promesse de la vie éternelle." In *Le soldat et la mort dans la Grande Guerre*, ed. Isabelle Homer and Emmanuel Pénicault, 195–208. Rennes: Presses Universitaires de Rennes, 2016.

Samuels, Maurice. *The Spectacular Past: Popular History and the Novel in Nineteenth-Century France.* Ithaca and London: Cornell University Press, 2004.

Sandberg, Brian. "'His Courage Produced More Fear in His Enemies Than Shame in His Soldiers': Siege Combat and Emotional Display in the French Wars of Religion." In *Battlefield Emotions 1500–1800, Practices, Experience, Imagination*, ed. Erika Kuijpers and Cornelis van der Haven, 127–48. London: Palgrave Macmillan, 2016.

Saulnier, N.-F. Guillaume. *Le siège de Thionville.* Paris: Maradan, n.d.

Scheck, Raffael. *French Colonial Soldiers in German Captivity during World War II.* Cambridge: Cambridge University Press, 2014.

– *Hitler's African Victims: The German Army Massacres of Black French Soldiers in 1940.* Cambridge: Cambridge University Press, 2006.

– "Les prémices de Thiaroye: l'influence de la captivité allemande sur les soldats noirs français à la fin de la Seconde Guerre mondiale." *French Colonial History* 13 (2012): 73–90.

Schivelbusch, Wolfgang. *The Culture of Defeat: On National Trauma, Mourning, and Recovery.* Translated by Jefferson Chase. London: Granta Books, 2001.

Schmitt, Jacques. *La vie brève de Barthélemy Joubert, le grenadier bressan.* Bourg-en-Bresse: Musnier-Gilbert Éditions, 1999.

Schneider, Herbert. "Le mythe du vaisseau *Le Vengeur* de 1794 à 1951: Textes – Images – Musique." In *Acta Musicologica* 77, no. 1 (2005): 71–121.

Senghor, Léopold Sédar. "Senghor: le manuscrit inconnu." *Jeune Afrique* 51, no. 2637 (24 July 2011): 25–30.

– *Oeuvre poétique.* Paris: Éditions du Seuil, 1990.

– *Prose and Poetry.* Translated by John Reed and Clive Wake. London: Oxford University Press, 1965.

Sergent-Marceau, Emira. *Présentation au conseil des Cinq-Cents du portrait du général Marceau.* Paris: Imprimerie nationale, Year Six [1797–98].

Servan-Schreiber, Jean-Jacques. *Lieutenant in Algeria.* Translated by Ronald Matthews. New York: Alfred A. Knopf, 1957.

Sessions, Jennifer E. *By Sword and Plow: France and the Conquest of Algeria.* Ithaca and London: Cornell University Press, 2017.

Sévigné, Marie de Rabutin-Chantal, marquise de. *Lettres de Madame de Sévigné, de sa famille et de ses amis.* 17 vols. Paris: Hachette, 1862–68.

Sherman, Daniel J. *The Construction of Memory in Interwar France.* Chicago and London: University of Chicago Press, 1999.

Six, Georges. *Les généraux de la Révolution et de l'Empire.* Paris: Bordas, 1947.

Smith, Denis. *Prisoners of Cabrera: Napoleon's Forgotten Soldiers, 1809–1814.* Toronto: Macfarlane Walter and Ross, 2001.

Smith, Digby. *The Greenhill Napoleonic Wars Data Book.* London: Greenhill Books, 1998.

Smith, Leonard. *The Embattled Self: French Soldiers' Testimony of the Great War.* Ithaca and London: Cornell University Press, 2007.

– "Masculinity, Memory, and the French First World War Novel." In *Authority, Identity and the Social History of the Great War,* ed. Frans Coetzee and Marilyn Shelvin-Coetzee, 251–73. Providence and Oxford: Berghahn Books, 1995.

Soret, H. *Notes d'un volontaire au 50ᵉ de ligne.* Paris: Librairie de E. Dentu, 1872.

Sorlin, Pierre. "France: The Silent Memory." In *The First World War and Popular Cinema: 1914 to the Present,* ed. Michael Paris, 115–37. New Brunswick, NJ: Rutgers University Press, 2000.

Soubiran, André. *Napoléon et un million de morts.* Paris: Kent-Segep, 1969.

Starkey, Armstrong. *War in the Age of Enlightenment, 1700–1789.* Westport, CT, and London: Praeger, 2003.

Stephenson, Michael. *The Last Full Measure: How Soldiers Die in Battle.* New York: Broadway Paperbacks, 2012.

Stora, Benjamin. *Histoire de la Guerre d'Algérie 1954–1962.* Paris: Éditions la Découverte, 1993.

– *La gangrène et l'oubli: La mémoire de la guerre d'Algérie.* Paris: La Découverte, 1991.

Strenski, Ivan. *Contesting Sacrifice: Religion, Nationalism, and Social Thought in France.* Chicago and London: University of Chicago Press, 2002.

Surrateau, Jean René. "Une visite impromptue de Napoléon dans l'Île Lobau en juin 1809." In *Annales historiques de la Révolution française* 40, no. 194 (October–December 1968): 557.

Sutter-Laumann, Charles. *Histoire d'un Trente Sous.* Paris: Albert Savine, Éditeur, 1891.

Talbott, Frank. "The Myth and Reality of the Paratrooper in the Algerian War." *Armed Forces and Society* 3, no.1 (November 1976): 69–86.

Talty, Stephan. *The Illustrious Dead: The Terrifying Story of How Typhus Killed Napoleon's Greatest Army.* New York: Crown Publishers, 2009.

Taousson, J. "Palestro 1956: Le massacre des rappelés." *Historia Magazine,* no. 216 (21 February 1972): 713–19.

Thellier de Poncheville, Charles. *Dix mois à Verdun.* Paris: J. de Gigord, Éditeur, 1919.

Thibeaudeau, A.C. *Recueil des actions héroïques et civiques des républicains français.* Paris: Imprimerie Nationale, Year Two [1793–94].

Thomas, Antoine-Léonard. *Poésies diverses de M. Thomas.* Lyons: Chez les Frères Périsse, 1763.

Thoral, Marie-Cécile. *From Valmy to Waterloo: France at War, 1792–1815.* Houndmills: Palgrave Macmillan, 2011.

Thou, Jacques-Auguste de. *Histoire universelle.* 16 vols. London, n.p., 1734.

Tichadou, Lucia. *Infirmière en 1914: journal d'une volontaire, 31 juillet – 14 octobre 1914.* Marseille: Éditions Gaussen, 2014.

Tillier, Bertrand. *La Commune de Paris, Révolution sans images? Politique et représentations dans la France républicaine (1871–1914).* Paris: Champ Vallon, 2004.

Tison, Stéphane. *Comment sortir de la guerre? Deuil, mémoire et traumatisme (1870–1940).* Rennes: Presses Universitaires de Rennes, 2011.

– "Lionel Royer, un artiste vétéran de l'armée de la Loire: entre témoignage et reconstitution épique." In *1870, entre mémoires régionales et oubli national. Se souvenir de la guerre franco-prussienne,* ed. Pierre Allorant, Walter Badier, and Jean Garrigues, 89–103. Rennes: Presses Universitaires de Rennes, 2019.

Tombs, Robert. "How Bloody was *la Semaine sanglante* of 1871? A Revision." *Historical Journal* 55, no. 3 (2012): 679–704.

– *The War against Paris 1871.* Cambridge: Cambridge University Press, 1981.

Trevisan, Carine. *Les fables du deuil: la Grande Guerre: Mort et écriture.* Paris: Presses Universitaires de France, 2001.

Tuffrau, Paul. *1914–1918: Quatre années sur le front: carnets d'un combattant.* Paris: Éditions Imago, 1998.

Turbergue, Jean-Pierre, ed. *Les 300 jours de Verdun.* Paris: Éditions Italiques, 2006.

Varley, Karine. "Death and Sacrifice in the Franco-Prussian War." *History Today* 70, no. 8 (August 2020): 30–41.

– *Under the Shadow of Defeat: The War of 1870–71 in French Memory.* Houndmills: Palgrave Macmillan, 2008.

Vatin, Philippe. *Voir et montrer la guerre: images et discours d'artistes en France (1914–1918).* Paris: Les Presses du Réel, 2013.

Vercel, Roger. *Capitaine Conan.* Paris: Albin Michel, 1934.

Vernant, Jean-Pierre, "La 'belle mort' d'Achille." In *Entre mythe et politique,* by Jean-Pierre Vernant, 501–10. Paris: Éditions du Seuil, 1996.

– "La mort héroïque chez les Grecs." In *La traversée des frontières,* by Jean-Pierre Vernant, 69–86. Paris: Éditions du Seuil, 2004.

Vess, David M. *Medical Revolution in France, 1789–1796.* Gainesville: University Presses of Florida, 1975.

Vigreux, Jean. "Le 11 Novembre 1943 et la mémoire du massacre de Clamecy." In *Des soldats noirs face au Reich: les massacres racistes de 1940,* ed. Johan

Chapotot and Jean Vigreux, 153–70. Paris: Presses Universitaires de France, 2015.

Villatoux, Marie-Catherine. "Pilotes d'hélicoptères de l'armée de l'air en guerre d'Algérie." In *Des hommes et des femmes en guerre d'Algérie*, ed. Jean-Charles Jauffret and Charles-Robert Ageron, 443–56. Paris: Éditions Autrement, 2003.

Villaret, Jean-Pierre, and Michel Courilleau. *Lettres de deux appelés (1957–1958)*. La Roche-sur-Yon: Centre Vendéen de Recherches Historiques, 2008.

Vinoy, Joseph. *Campagne de 1870–1871. L'armistice et la Commune, opérations de l'armée de Paris et de l'armée de réserve*. Paris: Henri Plon, Imprimeur-Éditeur, 1872.

Virien, Commandant. "Souvenirs de ma vie militaire." *Carnet de la Sabretache: Revue d'histoire militaire rétrospective* (1905): 225–56.

Vogüé, E. Melchior de. *Devant le siècle*. Paris: Armand Colin et Cie., 1896.

Voivenel, Paul, and Paul Martin. *La guerre des gaz: Journal d'une Ambulance Z*. Paris: La Renaissance du Livre, 1919.

Voltaire. *Oeuvres complètes de Voltaire*. 52 vols. Paris: Garnier Frères, 1877–1885.

– *Siècle de Louis XIV*. 3 vols. Paris: n.p., 1820.

Vovelle, Michel. "L'enfance héroïque sous la Révolution française." In *La mort de Bara: autour du tableau de Jacques-Louis David*, 29–39. Avignon: Fondation du Muséum Calvet, 1989.

– *La mort et l'occident de 1300 à nos jours*. Paris: Gallimard, 1983.

– *Piété baroque et déchristianisation en Provence au XVIIIe siècle*. Paris: Éditions du Seuil, 1978.

Wagré, Louis-Joseph. *Mémoire des captifs de l'Île de Cabréra, et adieux à cette île où 16,000 français ont succombé sous le poids de la misère la plus affreuse*. Paris: Chez l'Auteur, 1835.

Wairy, Constant. *Mémoires de Constant, premier valet de l'empereur, sur la vie privée de Napoléon, sa famille et sa cour*. 4 vols. Paris: Ladvocat, 1830.

Walter, Jakob. *The Diary of a Napoleonic Foot Soldier*. New York: Penguin Books, 1993.

Wawro, *The Franco-Prussian War: The German Conquest of France in 1870–1871*. Cambridge: Cambridge University Press, 2003.

Weigley, Russell F. *The Age of Battles: The Quest for Decisive Warfare from Breitenfeld to Waterloo*. Bloomington and Indianapolis: Indiana University Press, 1991.

Weygand, Maxime. *Le 11 novembre*. Paris: Flammarion, 1932.

Wiewiorka, Olivier, *La mémoire désunie: le souvenir politique des années sombres, de la Libération à nos jours*. Paris: Éditions du Seuil, 2010.

Wile, Aaron. *Watteau's Soldiers: Scenes of Military Life in Eighteenth-Century France*. New York: Frick Collection, In association with D. Giles, Ltd, 2016.

Wilson, Colette E. *Paris and the Commune, 1871–1878: The Politics of Forgetting*. Manchester: Manchester University Press, 2007.

Winter, Jay. "Cultural Divergences in Patterns of Remembering the Great War in Britain and France." In *Britain and France in Two World Wars: Truth, Myth and Memory*, ed. Robert Tombs and Émile Chabal, 161–77. London, New Delhi, New York, Sydney: Bloomsbury, 2013.

– *Remembering War: The Great War between Memory and History in the Twentieth Century*. New Haven: Yale University Press, 2006.

– *Sites of Memory, Sites of Mourning: The Great War in European Cultural History*. Cambridge: Cambridge University Press, 1995.

– *War beyond Words: Languages of Remembrance from the Great War to the Present*. Cambridge: Cambridge University Press, 2017.

Wohl, Robert. *The Generation of 1914*. Cambridge, MA: Harvard University Press, 1979.

Wood, James B. "The Impact of the Wars of Religion: A View of France in 1581." *Sixteenth-Century Journal* 15, no. 2 (Summer 1984): 131–68.

– *The King's Army: Warfare, Soldiers, and Society during the Wars of Religion in France, 1562–1576*. Cambridge: Cambridge University Press, 1996.

Zemon Davis, Natalie. *Society and Culture in Early Modern France*. Stanford: Stanford University Press, 1975.

Zola, Émile, Guy de Maupassant, Joris-Karl Huysmans, Henry Céard, Léon Hennique, and Paul Alexis. *Les soirées de Médan*. Paris: Éditions Flammarion, 2015.

Index

Spéciale), 389–90, 390n4;
as "savage war of peace," 393;
soldiers' experiences, 397;
terrorization of civilians, 415,
416; torture, 391n5, 396,
398–9
Algiers, Battle of (1956–57), 395,
396, 404
Aligny, Count d', 71
All Saint's Day, 263, 273, 274,
277, 287
Alviano, Bartolomeo d', 33, 38
Amardel (captain), 118
ambulances, 83n95, 151
ambushes, 403–7. *See also* guerrilla
warfare
American Revolutionary War, 69
Amezay, Bastard of, 27, 28
Amilakvari, Prince, 356
amputation, 39, 135, 152, 154,
154n61, 155, 203, 203n43, 258
ancien régime. *See* old regime
Angers, 40–1
Angevin, Camille, 219
*Annales Patriotiques et Littéraires
de la France* (newspaper), 105
annihilation, physical, 275–6
Anseaume, Louis: *The Militiaman*, 72
Anselme, Daniel: *On Leave*, 425–6
Anti-fédéraliste (newspaper), 106–7
Aragon, Louis, 322
Arc de Triomphe, 151, 287, 289, 435
Arc de Triomphe du Carroussel,
177n160
Arcola, Battle of (1796), 144
Ardant, Georges-Maurice
(Jean Limosin), 265
Ariès, Philippe, 98–9
aristocracy: cavalry and, 24;
comparison to ordinary soldiers
in Italian wars, 33–4; on death
by disease, 38–9; fine death ideal,

24–5, 40, 41, 63; French Wars
of Religion casualties, 54; military
service in old regime, 40, 40n88,
80–1. *See also* fine death; honour
Armée de Libération Nationale
(ALN), 393–4, 393n13, 395–6,
397, 402, 404, 409. *See also*
Algerian war; Front de Libération
Nationale (FLN)
arms of honour, 177n160
Army of Africa, 356, 357, 367, 374,
387–8
Army of Brittany, 206
Army of Châlons, 199, 208
Army of Egypt, 147, 147n31, 160–1,
166–7. *See also* Egyptian campaign
Army of Lorraine, 199
Army of Portugal, 169
Army of the East, 199, 207, 207n60
Army of the Loire, 199, 203, 206–7
Army of the North, 199, 219
Army of the Pyrénées Orientales,
131–2
Arnould, Arthur, 211
arquebus, 24, 24nn18–19, 28, 29–30,
32, 33, 39
Ars, Louis d', 26
art: introduction, 11–12; cubism,
304–5; First World War, 261–3,
262, 295–8, *297*, *298*, 302–11, *303*,
304, *306*, *307*, *309*; Franco-
Prussian War, 4, 5, 226–34, *227*,
228, *230*, *232*, *233*, *235*, 238–9;
French revolutionary wars, 93–5,
94, *104*, *108*, *110*, 112–13, *113*,
114, *125*, *190*, 191; French Wars
of Religion, 55, 55–6, *57*;
Impressionism, 236; lithography,
12, 184, 224; Marignano battle, 21,
21, *22*; modernist, 303–5;
Napoleonic wars, *141*, 141–2, *164*,
171–3, *172*, 172n141, *174*, 184–6,